TOWN PLANNING

PRINCIPLES, PROCESS AND PRACTICE

TOWN PLANNING

Principles, Process and Practice

A. K. JAIN

Foreword by **VIJAY GARG**
President Council of Architecture

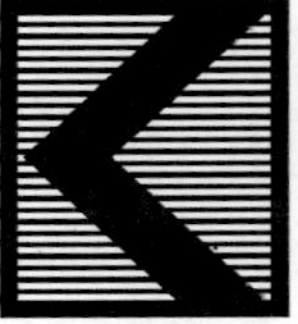

KHANNA BOOK PUBLISHING CO. (P) LTD.

Publisher of Science, Technology and Engineering Books

4C/4344, Ansari Road, Darya Ganj, New Delhi - 110002

Phone: 011-23244447-48, **Mobile:** +91-99109 09320

E-mail: contact@khannabooks.com

Website: www.khannabooks.com

Dear Readers,

To prevent the piracy, this book is secured with HIGH SECURITY HOLOGRAM on the front title cover. In case you don't find the hologram on the front cover title, please write us to at contact@khannabooks.com or whatsapp us at +91-99109 09320 and avail special gift voucher for yourself.

Specimen of Hologram on front Cover title:

Moreover, there is a SPECIAL DISCOUNT COUPON for you with EVERY HOLOGRAM.

How to avail this SPECIAL DISCOUNT:

Step 1: Scratch the hologram
Step 2: Under the scratch area, your "coupon code" is available
Step 3: Logon to www.khannabooks.com
Step 4: Use your "coupon code" in the shopping cart and get your copy at a special discount
Step 5: Enjoy your reading!

Price: ₹ 550.00

ISBN: 978-93-86173-40-9

Town Planning *by*
A.K. Jain

First Edition: 2019
Reprint: 2023, **2024**

To view complete list of books, Please scan the QR Code:

Published by:
Khanna Book Publishing Co. (P) Ltd.
CIN: U22110DL1998PTC095547

Visit us at: **www.khannabooks.com**
Write us at: **contact@khannabooks.com**

Printed in India.

वास्तुविद अधिनियम, 1972 के अंतर्गत भारत सरकार का एक स्वायत सांविधिक निकाय
(An Autonomous Statutory Body of Govt. of India, under the Architects Act, 1972)

Foreword

Future-Proofing our Towns
Understanding the basics & history to allow designing for Flexibility and Adaptive Reuse

We learn with time, buildings learn with time, most conspicuously cities learn with time, but often a city isn't allowed, it is so locked up in planning laws that paralyze its adaptability. - Stewart Brand

Accumulated in the piles of paper & records in the offices of the planning authorities and in the minds of decision makers, are bits of information in a form of official planning notes. A.K. Jain captures those small but important bits and offers it to the future generation in form of this book titled **"Town Planning: Principles, Processes and Practices".** This book captures the understanding and the rationale of those thoughts as they manifest themselves as solutions to urban challenges in different towns & cities.

It is important to pass these compiled bits of information in form of a book, from generation to generation, as these are part of our planning history and have shaped the towns we see it today. A.K. Jain understands the importance and fulfills his responsibilities to guide and educate the future generation in form of this book.

A.K. Jain believes that unless one learns the Planning Principles, the Processes and the Practices of the past, one cannot help our country achieve the objectives of the 74th constitutional amendment. He believes that, even though with the 74th Constitutional Amendment Act (1992), wherein the urban local bodies had been assigned greater role in urban planning and governance, yet there is no meaningful participation of people in their affairs. His book attempts to change that situation.

This book educates the untrained minds, to understand the current administrative system & the current policies, a system wherein there is only one channel of decisions & flow of instructions, that is from top to bottom. It's a situation wherein there is frequent supersession of local and municipal bodies that shows total disregard to the principle of people's representation.

He strongly believes that the planners, architects and engineers have a key role in urban transformation. He elaborates that, these set of trained minds need to master the planning thoughts and observe the society as it grows, and then advise the local decision makers to decide wisely. This would turn the system to "Bottom to Up" and ensure true grass root change. But this would require a more professional approach towards town planning and urban development. An approach that would be the key to providing any solution in the future.

India Habitat Centre, Core - 6A, 1st Floor, Lodhi Road, New Delhi - 110 003 India
Ph.: 91-11-24648415, 24654172-73, Fax : 91-11-24647746, Email : coa@ndf.vsnl.net.in, web : www.coa.gov.in

वास्तुविद अधिनियम, 1972 के अंतर्गत भारत सरकार का एक स्वायत सांविधिक निकाय
(An Autonomous Statutory Body of Govt. of India, under the Architects Act, 1972)

After we decided to to pursue Planned Development, we adopted the system of master plans to achieve growth. It was a big shift from the organic growth of the past. Today, after almost 6 decades, we have realized that our country needs something that works for us, so we brought back age old concepts of Mixed Landuse & Transit Oriented Development. Although only time will tell whether these would work or not, but they are part of present thoughts that will continue to shape our towns for years to come. This book discusses these ideas.

Even though we have defined Towns as places that have, Population exceeding 5,000 & at least 75% of males employed outside the agricultural sector & a minimum population density of 400 persons per sq km. Per this definition, the census 2011 identifies 7936 such settlements and in midst of this chaotic situation, we have 60% of our population living. Yet we do not have an model township that can be seen as an example.

A. K. Jain has a rich and diverse experience as a Commissioner Planning at DDA and understand how the decision makers think. He knows how the master plans were made in the past. He has seen the city evolve and has witnessed the response of the planners to changing needs and time.

He had experience of the decades, when the Master Plan was one of the most powerful planning idea that arose from the political ideology and commercial needs of those time. This new idea is currently debated in this skeptical age, where citizens have started seeing the master plans as straitjackets and oppressive. Where do we head from here, what should be our goals and ambitions for our towns and cities. He attempts to educated the young mind on such concepts and teaches them how to respond to new thoughts and needs.

So I am sure A.K. Jain will take the readers to a journey that will reveal to them the past, and educate them about the thoughts that have shaped our towns and cities, with an hope that the coming generation will be aware on how their predecessors decided and performed administrative regulation and planning to create an fair and inclusive settlement.

Vijay Garg
President Council of Architecture

India Habitat Centre, Core - 6A, 1st Floor, Lodhi Road, New Delhi - 110 003 India
Ph.: 91-11-24648415, 24654172-73, Fax : 91-11-24647746, Email : coa@ndf.vsnl.net.in, web : www.coa.gov.in

Preface

In India, 377 million people out of its total population of 1210 million, are living in 7936 cities and towns. Although the Indian cities generate 60% of GDP and 70% of jobs, most of them are unplanned with poor housing and basic infrastructure services. One out of every four persons in Indian cities lives below the poverty line and about two-thirds of urban poor are living in unplanned settlements and slums, lacking rudimentary services.

To make the cities more liveable and inclusive, the Government of India has embarked upon several programmes, such as Smart Cities Mission, the Atal Mission for Rejuvenation and Urban Transformation (AMRUT), Pradhan Mantri Awas Yojana and Historic City Development Augmentation Yojana (HRIDAY). The focus of these missions is on core infrastructure services like adequate and clean water supply, sanitation and solid waste management, efficient public transportation, affordable housing for the poor, power supply, IT connectivity, e-governance and citizen participation along with town planning, legal and municipal reforms.

The Sustainable Development Goals (SDGs) aim at making the cities and human settlements inclusive, safe, resilient and sustainable (Goal No. 11). Goal number 13 of SDGs calls for combating climate change and its impacts. These require a new paradigm of planning, which aligns with the socio-economic change, new policies and the SDGs. These involve legal, institutional and financial reforms and the mobilisation of public and private resources. Town planning provides an empirical understanding of the problems to work out the urban strategies.

The focus of city planning is to protect the rights of the poor, informal sector, women and vulnerable communities. This means humanising the city and imbibing it with inclusion, imaginaries and innovations. Town planning plays an important role in making the city safer, and enrich its cultural space and ecology. The city can be inclusive if it provide housing, water, sanitation, electricity and jobs to all. A city integrates environment, infrastructure services, education, healthcare facilities, gender safety and equity. The solutions have to emerge from the voices of people and engage with the local culture, climate and ecology.

In a rapidly changing scenario, it is necessary to develop alternative ways of land management, urban transport, infrastructure development, pollution prevention and governance. A low carbon city manifests a sustainable approach towards urban transport, ecology, water conservation, recycling, the recovery of the rivers and water bodies. This implies adopting the concepts of green, walkable city, non-polluting transport, use of solar energy, recycling, smart systems and Transit Oriented Development.

The book 'Town Planning- Principles, Process and Practice' in its 14 chapters captures various urban issues and explains how these integrate into a composite framework of urban planning. The book covers the syllabus of various universities.

This work has drawn on support of innumerable people and institutions, including the Delhi Development Authority, UN Habitat, Association for Settlements and Housing Activities (ASHA), CSE, CEEW, HUDCO, HSMI, INTACH and TCPO. I have benefitted from large number of books and papers by various authors and researchers as acknowledged in the bibliography given at the end of the book.

Special thanks to architect Vijay Garg, President Council of Architecture for his graceful and inspiring foreword. He has been a pioneer in guiding and regulating more than 450 Architecture Schools and professionals in India.

The manuscript would not have seen the light of the day without the dedication and enthusiasm of the Khanna Book Publishing Co., especially Mukul Seth, an energetic and humble youngman, who has done an excellent job in converting my unwieldy manuscript in this presentable book. He is doing a great service in the dissemination of knowledge.

A.K. Jain

Contents

CHAPTER

1

INTRODUCTION: TOWN PLANNING AND URBAN CHALLENGES

Town Planning is defined as the art and science of ordering the use of land, siting of buildings, infrastructure services, social amenities and communication routes so as to secure the maximum practicable degree of economy, convenience and beauty. It aims at guiding the physical growth of the city creating buildings and environment to meet the social, cultural, economic and recreational needs and to provide a healthy environment for people to live, work and play.

As such, town planning is a process concerned with the orderly development of human settlements and use of land, protection of the environment, public welfare and the design of the urban environment which includes air, water, infrastructure services, transportation and communication networks. Town and country planning covers regional planning, city planning, rural planning, environmental planning, community planning, area planning and urban design. Town planning involves knowledge management, abstraction, strategic management and implementation.

Urban planning is closely linked with the fields of architecture, landscape architecture, civil engineering, real estate, public administration, infrastructure services, traffic and transport planning.

Purpose and Evolution of Town Planning

There is evidence of town planning dating back to the Mesopotamian, Indus Valley, Minoan, and Egyptian civilizations in the third millennium BCE. Beginning in the 8th century BCE, Greek cities and cities also adopted orthogonal plans. These cities were developed for variety of purposes, suh as centres of rule, military defence and public convenience. However, many cities still grow organically and sometimes chaotically.

Urbanisation grew at a dramatic rate after the industrial revolution in the 19th century. As a result, urban life of the working poor and pollution became the matters of public concern. Around 1900, new urban planning models were developed to mitigate the consequences of the industrial age. Today the issues such as sustainability, air pollution, climate change, gender equity, safety, traffic congestion, livelihoods, creation of jobs, social housing, land values, legislation and zoning codes are in the frontline of town planning.

Urban Demography

In India, the total number of towns and cities have increased from 5161 in 2001 to 7935 in 2011. There are 475 Class I cities (each with a population above 1 lakh) and the number of million plus cities increased from 35 in 2001 to 53 in 2011. The 53 million plus cities together constitute 42.63 per cent of the total urban population, while the 475 Class I cities together constitute 70.20 per cent of the total urban population. As per Census 2011, there are 3 mega-cities, viz. Greater Mumbai (18.4 million), Delhi (16.8 million) and Kolkata (14.1 million) which have crossed the 10 million population mark, while five cities, viz. Chennai, Bengaluru, Hyderabad, Ahmedabad and Pune have each attained more than 5 million population. From 377 million urban population in 2011, it is projected that by the year 2031, 600 million people will live in urban areas and 78 cities in India will become metropolitan (million plus). Although the Indian cities generate 60% of GDP and 70% of jobs, the state of housing and basic infrastructure services remain awfully poor, impeding sustainability and economy.

Table 1.1: India's Urban Trajectory

Year	**2011**	**2031**
Population	1210 million	1440 million
Urban Population	377 million (31.16%)	600 million
Cities and Towns	7935	-
Million + Cities	53	78
Housing Shortage	18.78 million units	30 to 40 million units
Slum Population	65.49 million	100 million

Source: Census of India, 2011 & McKinsey Report, 2010.

The trends of urban population in 29 Indian states and seven UTs for the year 2011 indicate that among the UTs, high percentages were recorded in Delhi (97.50%), Chandigarh (97.25%), Lakshadweep (78.08%), Daman and Diu (75.16%) and Puducherry (68.31%). Among the States, the percentage share of urban population was high in Goa (62.17%), Mizoram (51.51%), Tamil Nadu (48.45%), Kerala (47.72%), Maharashtra (45.23%) and Gujarat (42.58%).

The States and UTs that have observed high decadal growth of urban population during 2001- 2011 are Daman and Diu (218.8%), Dadra and Nagar Haveli (218.2%), Sikkim (156.5%), Kerala (92.8%), Lakshadweep (86.6%), Tripura (76.2%) and Nagaland (66.6%). The States that have recorded significant growth of urban population during 2001-11 are Kerala and the four northeastern States of Sikkim, Tripura, Nagaland and Manipur.

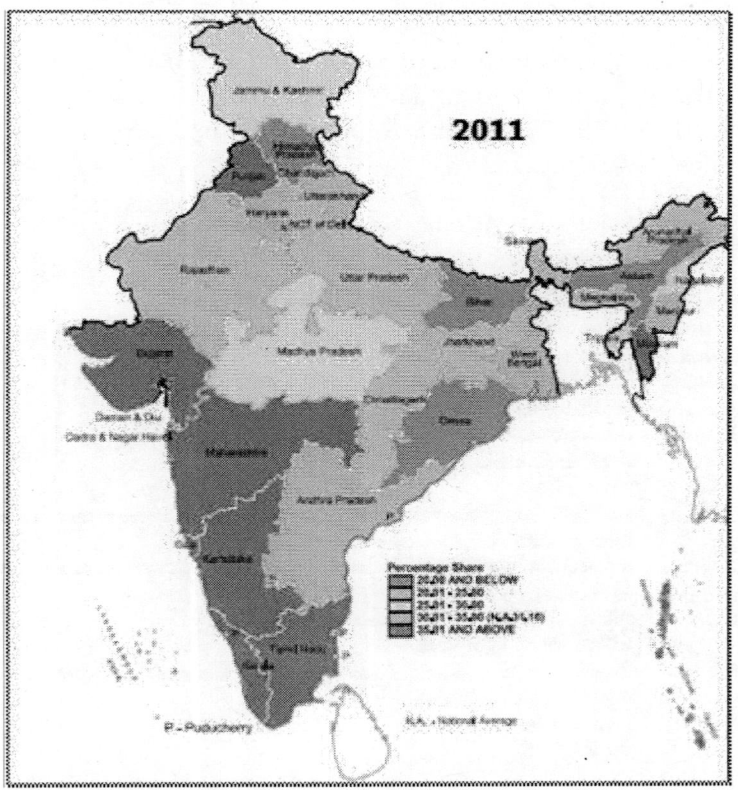

Figure 1.1: Percentage of Urban Population in Indian States and Union Territories (2011)

Source: Census of India (2011): Provisional Population Totals, Paper 2, Volume 1 of 2011, Rural – Urban Distribution, India, Series 1

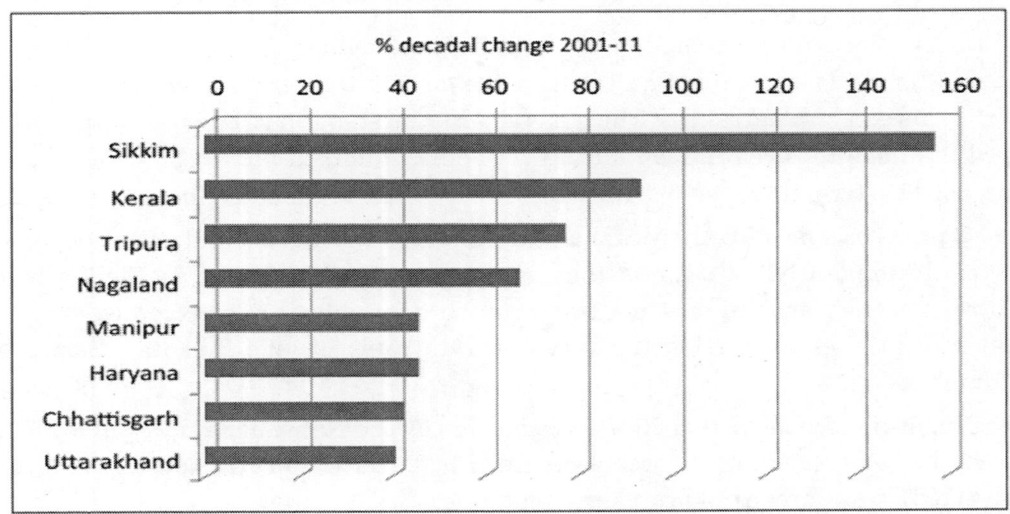

Figure 1.2: Indian States Experiencing High Growth of Urban Population, 2001-11

Source: Census of India (2011): Primary Census Abstract – Data Highlights, India, Series 1.

In terms of numbers, urban population in 2011 was above 20 million in Maharashtra (50.82 million), Uttar Pradesh (44.50 million), Tamil Nadu (34.92 million), West Bengal (29.09 million), Andhra Pradesh (28.22 million), Gujarat (25.75 million), Karnataka (23.63 million) and Madhya Pradesh (20.07 million).

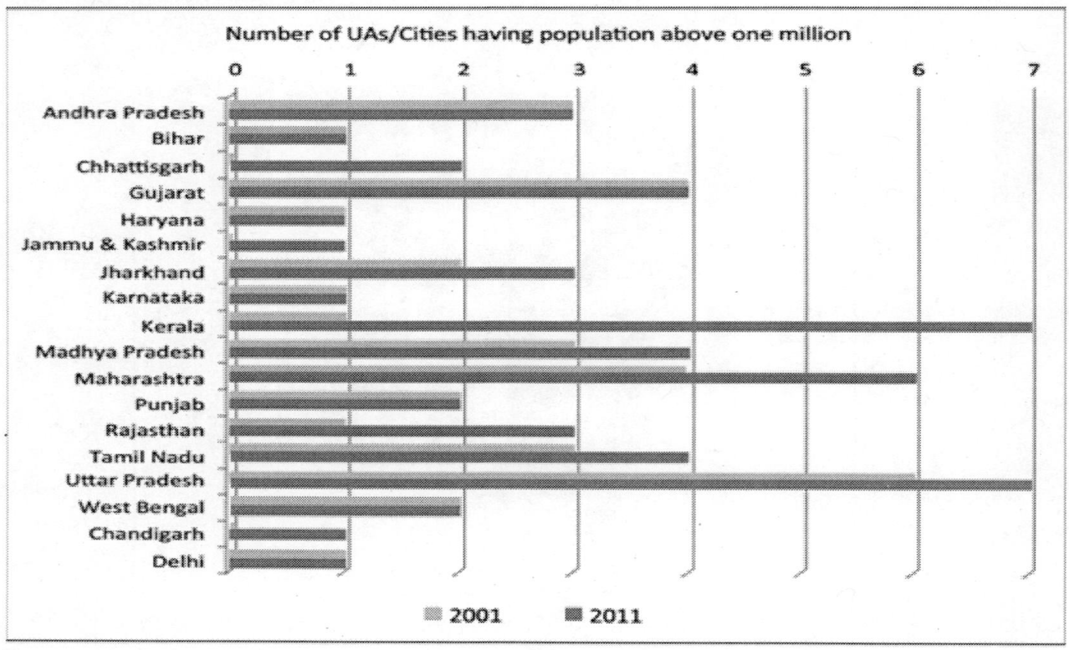

Figure 1.3: Number of Million Plus UAs/Cities

Source: Based on Census of India, 2001 & 2011.

The 53 UAs/cities with a population of more than one million are situated in 18 States/UTs (Figure 1.3). Kerala and Uttar Pradesh have the largest number (seven million plus UAs/cities each), followed by Maharashtra, which has six. Kerala stands out, because the population has jumped from one to seven million during 2001-11. No million plus UAs/ cities exists in any of the northeastern states or in Himachal Pradesh, Uttarakhand, Goa and Orissa.

Table 1.2 provides a list of UAs/cities that have recorded the highest and lowest population growth rates during 2001-11. It shows that as many as five UAs/cities in Kerala, one in Maharashtra (Vasai Virar) and one in Uttar Pradesh (Ghaziabad) have recorded very high growth rates. UAs/cities registering the lowest growth rates include Kolkata, Kanpur and Greater Mumbai.

Data on migration for the period 2007-08 conducted by the National Sample Survey Office, (which covered a total of 125,578 households, of which 79,091 were rural households and the remaining 46,487 were urban) indicates the following:

- Nearly 57% of urban migrant households migrated from rural areas.

- Rural to urban migration stream shared nearly 20% of the total internal migrants.
- Nearly 60% of male migrants and 59% of female migrants had migrated from rural areas.

Table 1.2: UAs/Cities Experiencing Highest and Lowest Population Growth, 2001-11

UAs/Cities	State	High Growth Rate 2001-11 (%)	UAs/ Cities	State	Low Growth Rate 2001-11 (%)
Malappuram UA	Kerala	896.80	Kolkata UA	West Bengal	6.87
Thrissur UA	Kerala	461.85	Kanpur UA	Uttar Pradesh	7.53
Vasai Virar City	Maharashtra	316.34	Greater Mumbai UA	Maharashtra	12.05
Kannur UA	Kerala	229.76	Dhanbad UA	Jharkhand	12.20
Kollam UA	Kerala	192.04	Durg-Bhilainagar UA	Chhattisgarh	14.68
Ghaziabad UA	Uttar Pradesh	143.58	Ludhiana City	Punjab	15.40
Kozhikode UA	Kerala	130.68	Jabalpur UA	Madhya Pradesh	15.44

Source: Census of India, 2011

Definition of Urban Area

In India, 'an urban area' is defined by the Office of the Registrar General and Census Commissioner in the following way:

All statutory places with an urban local government are called 'Statutory Towns.'

The Census of India may declare an area as urban or Census Town, if it satisfies the following three criteria simultaneously:

(a) A minimum population of 5,000;

(b) At least 75% of male working population engaged in non-agricultural pursuits; and

(c) A density of population of at least 400 per sq. km. (1,000 person per sq. mile).

'Cities' are urban areas with 1 lakh (0.1 million) and above population. Others are termed as 'towns'. 'Metropolitan cities' are defined as those cities with 10 lakh (1 million) and above population. 'Urban Agglomerations (UAs)' are defined as continuous urban spread constituting a town and its adjoining out growths (OGs), or two or more physically contiguous towns together and any adjoining urban outgrowth of such towns. An Urban Agglomeration must consist of at least a statutory town and its total population (i.e. all the constituents put together) should not be less than 20,000 as per the 2001 Census.

An 'out growth (OG)' is a viable unit such as a village or a hamlet or an enumeration block made up of such village or hamlet and clearly identifiable in terms of its boundaries and location. Some of the examples are railway colony, university campus, port area, military camps, etc. which have come up near or outside a statutory town or a village. While determining the outgrowth of a town, it has been ensured that it possesses the urban features in terms of infrastructure and amenities such as pucca roads, electricity, water, taps, drainage system, educational institutions, post offices, medical facilities, banks, etc. and is physically contiguous with the core town of the UA.

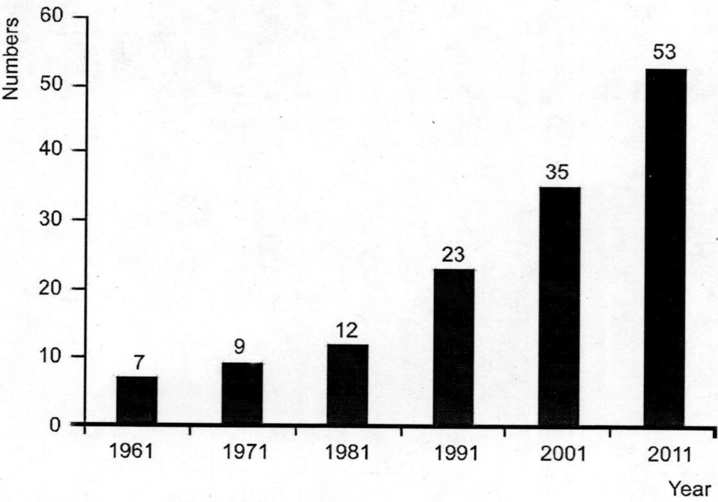

Figure 1.4: Number of Metropolitan Cities

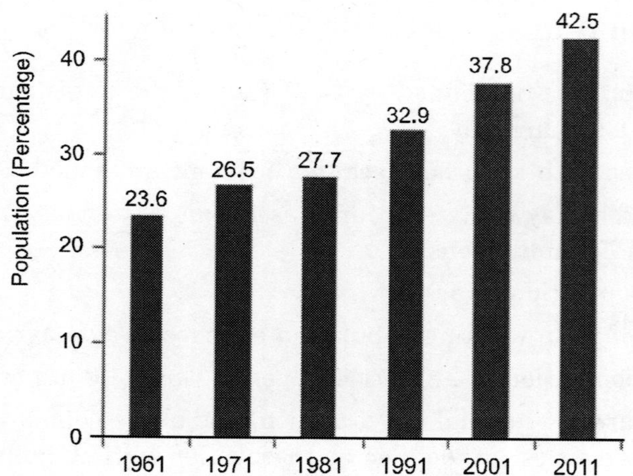

Figure 1.5: Percentage of Urban Population in Metropolitan Cities during 1961-2011

Source: NIUA & HUDCO/HSMI, Metropolitan Cities in India, Phase I, Report, 2012-13.

Mini-metros and Towns

Mini Metros: They include Hyderabad, Ahmedabad, Pune, Coimbatore, Chandigarh, they are growing fast, have more well-to-do homes than metros because of a higher density of professionals and skilled migrants.

Tier I Towns: 33 towns with population of over 10 lakh, including Jodhpur, Visakhapatnam, Indore, Bhopal, Jaipur, Lucknow, Kanpur, Allahabad, Surat, Baroda, Patna, etc.

Tier II Towns: 28 towns with population above six lakh but below 10 lakh, such as Mangalore, Thiruvananthapuram, Raipur, Jalandhar, Amritsar, Bhubaneswar, Mangalore, Nashik, Ranchi, Bhopal, Raipur, etc.

Tier III Towns: 152 towns, with population between two to six lakh, such as Siliguri, Shimoga, Agartala, Sonepat, Aizwal, Vellore, etc.

Tier IV Towns: 201 towns with one-to-two lakh populations, such as Shimla, Dibrugarh, Wardha, etc.

Peri-Urban Towns: Around 4,600 towns with population under 1 lakh, which surround big cities or are next to highways.

Table 1.3: Census 2011

Total Population	1210.2 million
Growth rate	17.64% (2001-11)
Literacy	74.04%
Population density	382 persons/sq. km
No. of Districts	640
No. of Sub-district	5924
Towns	7936
Municipal/Census Towns	3893
Urban Agglomerations	476
Villages	6,41,000
Urban population	377 million (31.16 percent)
Metropolitan cities (+million population)	47

Source: Census of India and other sources.

As per Census 2011:

- 377 million i.e. 31.2% of the total population of India lives in urban settlements.
- No. of cities/towns: 5161 in 2001; 7935 in 2011.
- More than 42% of urbanites live in 53 million plus metros
- Decadal growth of urban population is more than rural growth.

It is projected that more than 50% of the India's population will be urban by 2050.The normative basis of the Census of India for defining a town and a village, does consider the work pattern, level of infrastructure and services, housing stock and living conditions. Some alternative definitions argue for a more comprehensive approach. For example, Uchida and Nelson (2008), have proposed an agglomeration index, as the basis of urban definition which is based on three factors—population density, population of a large urban centre and travel time to that large urban centre. These factors are mapped in a composite manner, as given below:

1. Specify a threshold value to each of the three criteria: minimum population density, maximum travel time and minimum population size that define large cities.
2. Locate the center of defined large cities from the Global Rural-Urban Mapping Project (GRUMP) human settlements database.
3. Determine the border surrounding that large city center based on the maximum travel time. This boundary is computed from a cost-distance model that estimates travel time to the city over a cost surface. This surface has a spatial resolution of approximately 1 km. and is derived from GIS data on: (i) the transport network, (ii) off road surfaces derived from land cover data and (iii) slope and estimates of the average travel speeds for each permutation of these data.
4. Create (i) population and (ii) population density grids at 1 km. spatial resolution for the particular year. This is based on the average of two global gridded population data sources, GRUMP and LandScan.
5. Aggregate the population of all the grid cells that satisfy all three thresholds. The result is analogous to urban population. The proportion of this number to that country's total population is the agglomeration index.

It will be useful to conduct an exercise for India on the basis of agglomeration index, which may provide a more exact map of its urbanization.

Co-relation between Urbanisation and Incomes

The links between urbanization and per capita income have grown stronger in the Indian economy (the fitted line for the level of urbanization and PCGSDP for 2001 are upward sloping, with R2, or the explanatory power, being 0.549 and 0.614 respectively), indicating that cities hold the key to economic growth. Urbanization is gradually aligning itself with the economic growth processes in India, although the interlinkage effect are still quite low by international standards.

Table 1.4: Correlation between Urbanisation & Per Capita Income

State/Uts	Urbanisation level 2011 (%)	Urbanisation Rank 2011	PCGSDP 2009-10 (₹)	Rank-PCGSDP
Delhi	97.50	1	116886	2
Chandigarh	97.25	2	118136	1
Puducherry	68.31	3	88158	3
Mizoram	51.51	4	45982	17

Tamil Nadu	48.45	5	63547	9
Kerala	47.72	6	59179	12
Maharashtra	45.23	7	74027	6
Gujarat	42.58	8	63961	8
Karnataka	38.57	9	52097	13
Punjab	37.49	10	60746	10
A & N Islands	35.67	11	74340	5
Haryana	34.79	12	50365	16
Andhra Pradesh	33.49	13	51025	15
West Bengal	31.89	14	41219	20
Uttarakhand	30.55	15	59584	11
Manipur	30.21	16	27332	26
Nagaland	28.97	17	45353	18
Madhya Pradesh	27.63	18	27250	27
Jammu & Kashmir	27.21	19	30582	25
Tripura	26.18	20	35799	22
Sikkim	24.97	21	68731	7
Rajasthan	24.89	22	34042	23
Jharkhand	24.05	23	27132	29
Chhattisgarh	23.24	24	38059	21
Arunachal Pradesh	22.67	25	51405	14
Uttar Pradesh	22.28	26	23395	30
Meghalaya	20.08	27	43555	19
Odisha	16.68	28	33226	14

Source: NIUA & HUDCO/(HSMI) 2013, Metropolitan Cities in India, Phase I Report, 2012-13, New Delhi

The above Table reveals the following;

- Coefficient of Correlation between levels of Urbanisation & PCI among States=0.8
- Over 60% of GDP comes from urban areas
- Declining Rural holdings: 1971=>3 ha; 2010=>1 ha

- Miniscular holdings=> vulnerable farmer
- Facilitate migration to cities, make cities hub for economic growth
- Small cities are growing the fastest
- Almost 40% of towns are unplanned village like "Quasi Towns" which face haphazed growth without infrastructure services.

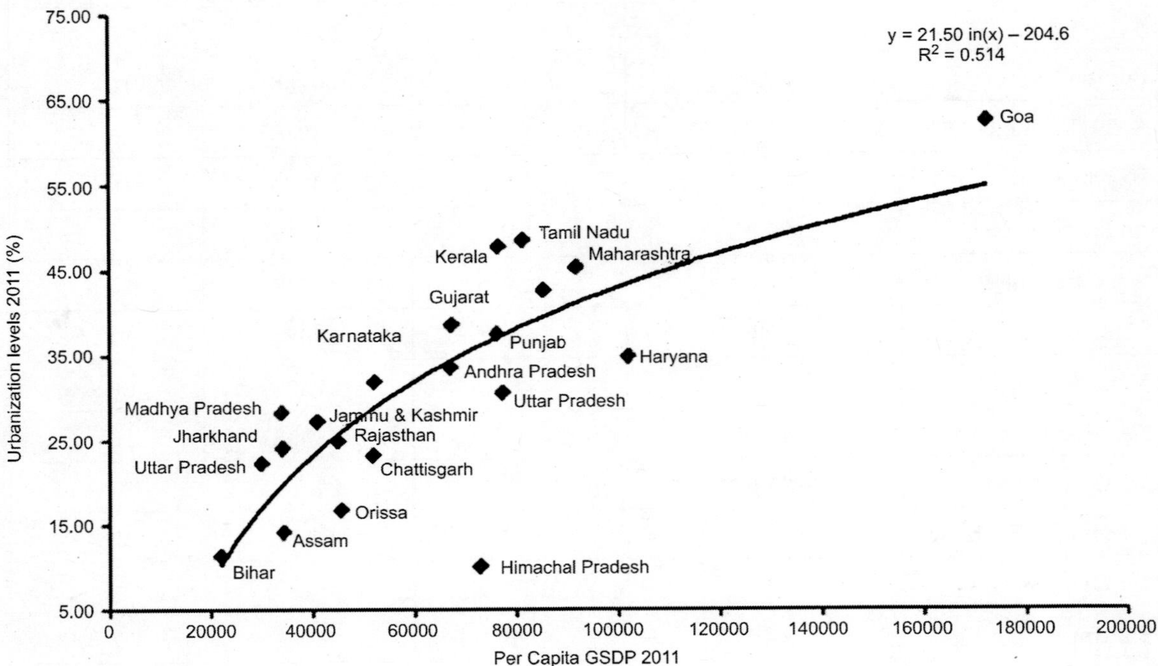

Figure 1.6: Inter-linkage effects of per capita income and urbanization levels across the States (2011)

Source: NIUA & HUDCO / (HSMI) 2013, Metropolitan Cities in India, Phase I Report, 2012-13, New Delhi

Urbanisation and Development Issues

According to the Census reports, 44% of the urban population growth in India between 2001 and 2011 was due to natural increase and 29.5% to the reclassification of rural settlements into census towns. Millions of people every year flock from villages to cities in hope of finding jobs and basic sustenance. However, many of them find the living conditions in urban areas bordering almost to inhuman levels. One out of every three persons in Indian cities lives below the poverty line and about one-fourth of India's urban poor are living in unplanned settlements and slums, lacking rudimentary services. They often have no hope from the government and have no idea of the 'development'.

Development means the building of societies in which people are able to enjoy security, good health, decent housing, clean water and modern water supplies. It depends upon people having the opportunity to earn a good living and knowing that they have some security in hard times.

On the contrary poverty means the people living without electricity, without transportation, without security of job, food and shelter, without right on the city, its services, justice and equity. Money and income are the easiest measures of growth, but poverty is far more complex issue. The World Bank in its ground breaking Report 'Voices of the Poor' highlights the multi-dimensional nature of poverty. *'Poverty is hunger, poverty is lack of shelter. Poverty is being sick and not being able to see a doctor. Poverty is not having access to school and not knowing how to read. Poverty is not having a job, is fear for the future, living one day at a time. Poverty is loosing a child to illness, brought about by unclean water. Poverty is powerlessness, lack of representation and freedom'.*

Many poor people live in places which are unfit for human habitation. Supply of drinking water and electricity is unreliable, level of cleanliness and the condition of drainage are abysmal. Informal sector activities are poorly regulated; air and surface water pollution is increasing; built and natural heritage is being lost; vital public transportation links are missing, traffic management is poor, educational and health institutions fail to meet growing demands; safety and security of citizens are major concerns; and socio-economic inequalities are widening.

In short, India is facing a state of unplanned urbanisation. As a result the urban population is growing, many cities lack clean sanitation facilities, water supply and solid waste management, and face the problems of environmental degradation.

Cities and towns are considered as engines of economic growth and social transformation. Recent policy initiatives to bring large number of people under the formal financial system or identification structures are articulating such intents. However, India's urban work force is becoming increasingly informal, with nearly half of the urban workforce being self-employed. The share of urban areas' contribution to India's GDP is set to reach 70% with a concurrent, constant rise in informal employment across all economic sectors. The low level of education and skills are the prime reasons for the vulnerability of the workforce. The manufacturing sector in India's economic structure has resulted in a rise of unskilled rural labourers joining the informal urban economy. Ambiguities in defining 'formal,' 'legitimate,' 'informal' and 'illegal' and their constant usages requires clarity. This has led to social exclusion, and has created 'divided cities'. Almost 40-50% of the people in large Indian metropolitan cities reside in slums with degrading living conditions. Access to affordable housing options in cities is still a dream. The skewed land and real estate market have added to the deprivations of the urban poor.

Ecology and Climate Change

India's urbanisation and economic development are changing the lifestyles of its people. Increasing production, mobility, consumption and living in comfort, are enhancing the carbon emissions and climate change. Models predict an average increase in temperature of 2.3 to 4.8°C in India for the benchmark doubling of carbon dioxide scenario. Although per capita carbon emissions in India are one of the lowest in the world, at 1.2 metric tonnes (mt) per year, it is predicted to become double within next 10 years. Already in the urban areas the people with cars and air conditioners emit 4.5mt of CO equivalent per year, while the low income people without car and air conditioners, emit an average of 1.1 m of CO_2/GH gases. As per UN Climate Change Panel, a benchmark of 3.0 mt per capita per year should be the upper limit. This implies that planned urbanisation is necessary for sustainable growth by increasing productivity and allowing innovation and new ideas, such as livelihood guarantee, walk to work, urban agriculture, zero polluting industry, smart sanitation and other urban services.

Urban Policies and Programmes

To make the cities more livable and inclusive, the Government of India in 2015 embarked on Smart Cities programme for 100 cities and the Atal Mission for Rejuvenation and Urban Transformation (AMRUT) for 500 cities. The focus is on core infrastructure services like adequate and clean water supply, sanitation and solid waste management, efficient urban mobility and public transportation, affordable housing for the poor, power supply, IT connectivity, e-governance and citizen participation along with municipal reforms and providing aid to the state governments and the ULBs.

With the commitment that by the time the nation completes 75 years of Independence, every family will have a pucca house with water connection, toilet facilities and 24x7 electricity supply. The Central Government has launched (2015) "Pradhan Mantri Awaas Yojana for Housing for All by 2022". The mission seeks to provide 20 million housing (revised to 12 million) and take up the Slum rehabilitation project. The program provides interest subsidy of 6.5 per cent on housing loans with tenure of up to 15 years for EWS and LIG, which works to nearly Rs 100,000 to Rs 230,000 per unit. It promotes slum free cities and mandates house in the name of women, or joint ownership.

For conservation of urban heritage and cultural resources, the Government of India (2015) has launched the Historic City Development Augmentation Yojana (HRIDAY), which initially covers 12 cities viz. Ajmer, Amrawati, Amritsar, Badami, Dwarka, Gaya, Kanchipuram, Mathura, Puri, Varanasi, Velankanni and Warangal.

Swachh Bharat Mission (SBM) is another major initiative of the Government of India, covering 4,041 statutory towns and 6 lakh villages, to clean the streets, roads and infrastructure of the country. SBM includes focus on provisioning of household toilets, community toilets, public toilets, solid waste management and bringing in behavioural change in people regarding healthy sanitation practices, which aim to make cities and villages clean and hygienic.

The restoration of rivers is a high priority on the agenda of the Government of India. Namani Gange Plan aims to integrate the efforts to clean the river Ganga, with an outlay of ₹ 200,000 million for the next five years. It focuses on pollution abatement, interception, diversion and treatment of waste water flowing in the open drain through bio-remediation, in-situ treatment, use of innovative technologies, sewage treatment plants (STPs), effluent treatment plants (ETPs) and rehabilitation and augmentation of existing STPs. Short term measures include-arresting the pollution at exit points on riverfront to prevent inflow of sewage, effluents and solid waste into the river.

All these missions focus on urban transformation of India. However, their success is largely contingent upon rigourous, sustained efforts of the urban local bodies and meticulous local planning, together with legal, institutional and financial reforms, which facilitate and mobilise public, private and peoples' resources.

Smart Cities Mission

Smart Cities Mission, launched by the Prime Minister on 25th June 2015, aims to drive economic growth and improve the quality of life of people by enabling local area development and harnessing technology, especially technology that leads to Smart outcomes.

The focus is on sustainable and inclusive development. The core infrastructure elements in a Smart City include the following:

(i) adequate water supply,

(ii) assured electricity supply,

(iii) sanitation, including solid waste management,

(iv) efficient urban mobility and public transport,

(v) affordable housing, especially for the poor,

(vi) IT connectivity and digitalization,

(vii) good governance, especially e-Governance and citizen participation,

(viii) sustainable environment,

(ix) safety and security of citizens, particularly women, children and the elderly, and

(x) health and education.

Some typical features of comprehensive development in Smart Cities are described below.

- Promoting mixed land use — planning for 'unplanned areas' containing a range of compatible activities and land uses close to one another in order to make land use more efficient. The States will enable some flexibility in land use and building bye-laws to adapt to change;
- Housing and inclusiveness — expand housing opportunities for all;
- Creating walkable localities — reduce congestion, air pollution and resource depletion, boost local economy, promote interactions and ensure security. The road network is created or refurbished not only for vehicles and public transport, but also for pedestrians and cyclists, and necessary administrative services are offered within walking or cycling distance;
- Preserving and developing open spaces — parks, playgrounds, and recreational spaces in order to enhance the quality of life of citizens, reduce the urban heat island effects and promote eco-balance;
- Promoting a variety of transport options — Transit Oriented Development (TOD), public transport and last mile para-transport connectivity;
- Making governance citizen-friendly and cost effective — increasingly rely on online services to bring about accountability and transparency, especially using mobiles to reduce cost of services and providing services without having to go to municipal

offices; form e-groups to listen to people and obtain feedback and use online monitoring of programs and activities with the aid of cyber tour of worksites;

- Giving an identity to the city — based on its main economic activity, such as local cuisine, health, education, arts and craft, culture, sports goods, furniture, hosiery, textile, dairy, etc;
- Applying Smart solutions to infrastructure and services in area-based development in order to make them better. For example, making Areas less vulnerable to disasters, using fewer resources, and providing cheaper services.

The strategic components of the Smart Cities Mission are city improvement (retrofitting), city renewal (redevelopment), city extension (Greenfield development) and a Pan-city initiative in which Smart Solutions are applied to identified parts of the city.

Retrofitting aims to transform the existing built-up areas and make them more efficient and liveable. Redevelopment aims the upgradation of the existing built-up environment, alongwith co-creation of a new layout with enhanced infrastructure, mixed land use and increased density. Redevelopment envisages a minimum area of 50 acres. Greenfield development (more than 250 acres) aims to address the needs of expanding population by Smart solutions using innovative planning, plan financing and plan implementation tools (e.g. land pooling/ land reconstitution) with provision of affordable housing, especially for the poor.

Pan-city development envisages application of Smart Solutions to the existing city-wide infrastructure, services and urban transport, including waste water recycling and smart metering. For, assured electricity supply, at least 10% of the energy requirement have to be from renewable sources. The smart cities is visualized to incorporate, rain water harvesting, IT connectivity and digitization, pedestrian friendly pathways, encouragement to non-motorised transport (e.g. walking and cycling), intelligent traffic management, non-vehicle streets/zones, smart parking, energy efficient street lighting, innovative use of open spaces, replacing overhead electric wiring with underground wiring, encroachment-free public areas, and ensuring safety of citizens especially children, women and elderly). In the case of redevelopment and greenfield Smart Cities, in addition to the essential features mentioned above, at least 80% buildings should be energy efficient and green. Of the total housing provided, there should be at least 15% in the affordable housing category.

The 100 Smart Cities have been distributed among the States and UTs on the basis of an equitable criteria, based on urban population of the State/UT and the number of statutory towns in the State/UT. The Ministry of Urban Development has already selected 98 cities and towns for development as smart cities based on the 'City Challenge' competition. Of these 24 cities are capital cities; 24 are business and industrial centres; 18 are of cultural and tourism importance; 5 are port cities and 3 are educational and healthcare hubs. In terms of population, 8 cities have population up to one lakh. These are – Panaji (Goa), Diu, Silvassa (Dadra & Nagar Haveli), Kavaratti (Lakshadweep), Dharmashala (Himachal Pradesh), New Town (West Bengal), Pasighat (Arunachal Pradesh) and Namchi (Sikkim). 35 cities have population between one and five lakh; 21 cities are in the population range of five to ten lakh; 25 have population of above 10 lakh and below 25 lakh; 5 in the range of 25 to 50 lakh and 4 cities (Chennai, Greater Hyderabad, Ahmedabad and Greater Mumbai) have population each above 50 lakh.

Smart Cities Mission envisages the integration with other missions, particularly the AMRUT and Swachh Bharat Mission. It aims to harness the public, private and community resources and Central Government grants and funding. Capacity building and implementation focus are necessary to achieve the results. Planning should be based on a comprehensive information system, digitized mapping and geo-portal. The planning of smart cities should relate with local culture and climate. It should be inclusive that provides jobs, livelihoods, local economic dynamism and a venue of cultural expression, learning and communication. Several smart city projects have been initiated in India, which include a network of smart cities on Delhi-Mumbai Industrial Corridor and GIFT Gandhinagar. Various State governments are preparing the blueprints for the smart cities, Amravati, the new Capital of Andhra Pradesh, being the latest.

Table 1.5: Smart Cities Shortlisted by the MOUD

No.	Name of State/UT	No. of cities shortlisted	Names of selected Cities	Population of Cities
1.	Andaman & Nicolbar Islands	1	1. Port Blair	1,40,572
2.	Andhra Pradesh	3	1. Vishakhapatnam 2. Tirupati 3. Kakinada	18,78,980 3,74,260 3,50,986
3.	Arunachal Pradesh	1	1. Pasighat	24,656
4.	Assam	1	1. Guwahati	9,62,334
5.	Bihar	3	1. Muzaffarpur 2. Bhagalpur 3. Biharsharif	3,93,724 4,10,210 2,96,889
6.	Chandigarh	1	1. Chandigarh	10,55,450
7.	Chhatisgarh	2	1. Raipur 2. Bilaspur	10,47,389 3,65,579
8.	Daman & Diu	1	1. Diu	23,991
9.	Dadra & Nagar Haveli	1	1. Silvassa	98,032
10.	Delhi	1	1. New Delhi Municipal Council	2,49,998
11.	Goa	1	1. Panaji	1,00,000
12.	Gujarat	6	1. Gandhinagar 2. Ahmedabad 3. Surat 4. Vadodara 5. Rajkot 6. Dahod	2,92,797 55,77,940 44,67,797 17,52,371 13,23,363 1,30,530

13.	Haryana	2	1. Karnal 2. Faridabad	3,02,140 14,14,050
14.	Himachal Pradesh	1	1. Dharamshala	22,580
15.	Jharkhand	1	1. Ranchi	10,73,427
16.	Karnataka	6	1. Mangaluru 2. Belagavi 3. Shivamogga 4. Hubali-Dharwad 5. Tumakuru 6. Davanegere	4,84,785 4,88,292 3,22,428 9,43,857 3,05,821 4,35,128
17.	Kerala	1	1. Kochi	6,01,574
18.	Lakshadweep	1	1. Kavaratti	11,210
19.	Madhya Pradesh	7	1. Bhopal 2. Indore 3. Jabalpur 4. Gwalior 5. Sagar 6. Satna 7. Ujjain	19,22,130 21,95,274 12,16,445 11,59,032 2,73,296 2,80,222 5,15,215
20.	Maharashtra	10	1. Navi Mumbai 2. Nashik 3. Thane 4. Greater Mumbai 5. Amravati 6. Solapur 7. Nagpur 8. Kalyan-Dombivali 9. Aurangabad 10. Pune	11,19,000 14,86,000 18,41,000 1,24,00,000 7,45,000 9,52,000 24,60,000 15,18,000 11,65,000 31,24,000
21.	Manipur	1	1. Imphal	2,68,243
22.	Meghalaya	1	1. Shillong	3,54,325
23.	Mizoram	1	1. Aizawl	2,91,000
24.	Nagaland	1	1. Kohima	1,07,000
25.	Odisha	2	1. Bhubaneshwar 2. Raurkela	8,40,834 3,10,976
26.	Puducherry	1	1. Oulgaret	3,00,104
27.	Punjab	3	1. Ludhiana 2. Jalandhar 3. Amritsar	16,18,879 8,68,181 11,55,664

28.	Rajasthan	4	1. Jaipur	30,73,350
			2. Udaipur	4,75,150
			3. Kota	10,01,365
			4. Ajmer	5,51,360
29.	Sikkim	1	1. Namchi	12,190
30.	Tamil Nadu	12	1. Tiruchirapalli	9,16,674
			2. Tirunelveli	4,74,838
			3. Dindigul	2,07,327
			4. Thanjavur	2,22,943
			5. Tiruppur	8,77,778
			6. Salem	8,31,038
			7. Vellore	5,04,079
			8. Coimbatore	16,01,438
			9. Madurai	15,61,129
			10. Erode	4,98,129
			11. Thoothukudi	3,70,896
			12. Chennai	67,27,000
31.	Telangana	2	1. Greater Hyderabad	67,31,790
			2. Greater Warangal	8,19,406
32.	Tripura	1	1. Agartala	4,00,004
33.	Uttar Pradesh	12	1. Moradabad	8,87,871
			2. Aligarh	8,74,408
			3. Saharanpur	7,05,478
			4. Bareilly	9,03,668
			5. Jhansi	5,05,693
			6. Kanpur	27,65,348
			7. Allahabad	11,12,544
			8. Lucknow	28,17,105
			9. Varanasi	11,98,491
			10. Ghaziabad	16,48,643
			11. Agra	15,85,704
			12. Rampur	3,25,313
34.	Uttarakhand	1	1. Dehradun	5,83,971
35.	West Bengal	4	1. New Town Kolkata	36,541
			2. Bidhannagar	6,33,704
			3. Durgapur	5,71,000
			4. Haldia	2,72,000

Note: The smart cities in Jammu & Kashmir and one in Uttar Pradesh are yet to be decided.
Source: MOUD, 2016.

Urbanisation and Land Policy

During the initial years after the Independence, the socialist policies for land acquisition and urban development such as the large scale land acquisition, development and disposal policy were adopted. Land Acquisition Act of 1894 had been applied for acquisition of land for planned development with government centric planning, land management and development, including infrastructure services, housing and construction.

The liberalization of the Indian economy (1992) gave a new direction to urban and infrastructure development and the private sector entered in a big way in real estate, housing and infrastructure projects including ports and airports, rail freight corridors and Special Economic Zones (SEZs). According to CAG report (2013), 45,635 Ha of land was notified for SEZs, of which 28,488 Ha has been utilized, while 17,147 Ha of land is still unused. The emergence of transport corridors with a substantial increase in industrial investment, services, flow of goods and people along them has been a significant feature of spatial change in recent years. The "Golden Quadrilateral" network of National Highways linking Delhi, Mumbai, Chennai and Kolkata, as well as North-South and East-West Corridors, promote this type of growth. One of the recent initiatives is 1,483 kilometre long Delhi-Mumbai Industrial Corridor (DMIC) and 1,279 kilometer long Delhi-Kolkata (Eastern) Rail Freight Corridor. A separate corridor for freight trains would enable the Railways to achieve higher speed, facilitate guaranteed transit time to the customer, reduce unit cost of transportation and provide a competitive edge over the other modes of transport.

The Right to Fair Compensation and Transparency in Land Acquisition, Rehabilitation and Resettlement Act, 2013 has replaced the Land Acquisition Act of 1894. It obliges the government and others to give rehabilitation package to displaced people, if they buy over 50 acres of land in urban areas and 100 acres in rural areas. Under the new Act land can be acquired by the government for its own use, or for the public purposes. Farmers will get four times the market price in the rural areas, while in the urban areas it will be double the market price.

The acquisition of land under new Land Acquisition Act is not only difficult, but also very expensive. There is no options but to adopt new ways of planning and development. The option should facilitate optimum use of land with rationalized FAR/FSI and densities. The brownfield development has to be taken up in a big way, rather than green development, and to ensure planned development of public services, urban transport, greens and social housing. Land Pooling, Town Planning Scheme, Transferable Development Rights and Accommodation Reservation can be the alternative methods of land assembly for planned development.

According to various studies, land pooling model provides a viable alternative to compulsory land acquisition for urban development. This needs a new capacity building in the agencies dealing with urban development, together with legal reforms and simplified procedures based on digitized revenue records. This also involves adopting scientific methods of valuation of land, and Circle Rates and re-engineering land development norms, specifications and practices.

Housing and Slums

India recorded a slum population of 65.49 million in 2011 according to the Registrar General and Census Commissioner. A decadal comparison shows that India's slum population increased by 25% during 2001-11. At the all-India level, about 5% of India's total population and 17% of India's total urban population lives in slums. Due to rising population, the slum households, numbering 13.92 million in 2011, have grown by 37% during 2001-11. The data further shows that during the 2001-11, while the share of slum population in India's total population increased, its share in India's total urban population has come down.

Table 1.6: Urban and Slum Population in India

Indicator	2001	2011
Total population of India (in billion)	1.02	1.21
Urban population of India (in million)	286.1	377.1
Urban to total population (%)	27.81	31.16
Decadal growth of urban population (%)	31.51	31.80
Number of statutory and census towns	5,161	7,933
Number of UAs/cities (population > 100,000)	384	475
Number of UAs/cities (population > 1 million)	35	53
Total slum population of India (in million)	52.37	65.49
Absolute change in slum population, 2001-11 (in million)	-	13.12
Decadal growth of slum population, 2001-11 (%)	-	25.1
Slum population to India's total population (%)	5.09	5.41
Slum population to India's total urban population (%)	18.3	17.4
Number of slum households in India (in million)	10.15	13.92
Absolute change in number of slum households, 2001-11 (in million)	-	3.77
Decadal growth of slum households, 2001-11 (%)	-	37.1
Number of Indian towns reporting slums	1,743	2,613

Source: Office of the Registrar General and Census Commissioner, India, 2011.

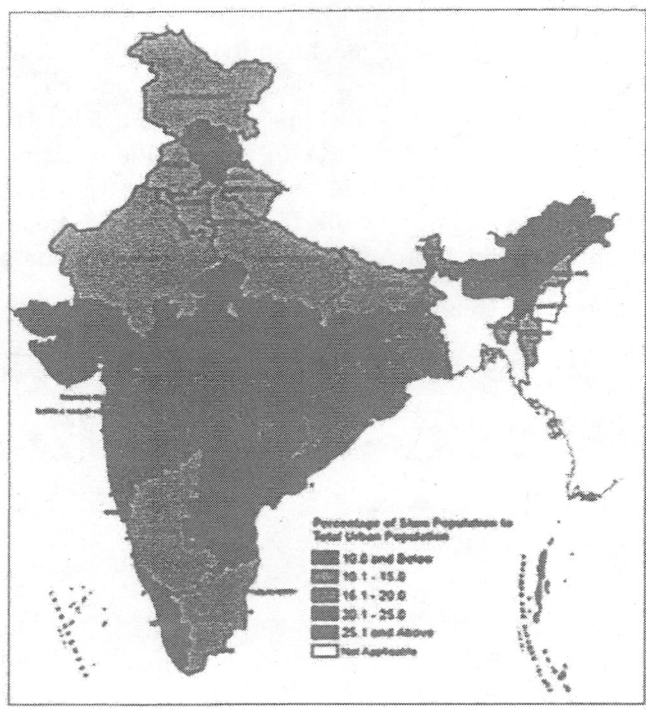

Figure 1.7: Share of Slum Population in Total Urban Population of State, 2011

Source: Office of the Registrar General and Census Commissioner, 2011

Table 1.7: Housing Stock in Slums and Amenities available to Slum Households, 2011

Housing Stock Indicators		Status (%)	Amenities Indicators		Status (%)
Households by type of occupied census house	- Permanent - Semi-permanent - Temporary	77.7 16.0 5.3	Households by main source of drinking water	- Tap water - Hand pump - Within premises - Outside premises	74.0 12.7 56.7 43.3
Households by ownership status	- Owned - Rented	70.2 26.3	Households by sanitation	- Latrine facilities (within premises) - Public latrine - Open - Bathing facility - Closed drainage - Open and no drainage	66.0 15.1 18.9 81.0 36.9 63.1
Households by number of dwelling rooms	- No exclusive room - 1 room - 2 rooms - 3 rooms - 4+ rooms	4.4 44.8 29.5 12.3 8.9	Households by main source of lighting	- Electricity - Kerosene - Any other - No lighting	90.5 8.2 0.7 0.5

Source: Office of the Registrar General and Census Commissioner, 2011

The housing conditions in the slums as indicated in Table 1.7 reveal the following:

- 43.3% of households do not have any main source of drinking water within premises, and according to the census office, the dwellers have to travel about 100 metres or more to collect drinking water.
- 34% of households do not have toilets within premises and people either use public latrines or defecate in the open.
- 19% of households have no bathing facility.
- 63.1% do not have closed drainage connectivity.
- 0.5% of households have no electricity.

The data indicates that slum dwellers are facing a number of problems, namely unsafe housing, fear of eviction/insecurity of tenure, high-density rooms, loss of time and income in obtaining drinking water, lack of toilet facilities within premises (implying lack of privacy, especially for women and girls), health and hygiene problems, and insufficient lighting in houses. India's urban housing shortage, estimated at 18.78 million, is confronted by the following major issues:

- Location vis-à-vis potential of jobs, economic growth, regional balance and housing demand.
- Policy Supports and Incentives for Affordable Housing
- Land availability, along with the basic services, amenities and work places.
- Housing Development, Building Technology and Resources.
- Financing: Housing Cost and access to finance

A more systematic, GIS based land inventory can release substantial public land for affordable housing redevelopment in existing urban areas. The financing of the social housing can be supplemented by mortgage gurantee fund, social housing fund, micro financing, land housing-infrastructure bundling, Mutual Fund, Provident, Insurance and Pension Funds, General Obligation Bonds, etc.

Optimizing the densities and FAR/FSI can be the effective tools to reduce the cost of social housing. An industrial approach can convert housing construction into housing production, saving both cost and time. Proven technologies and approaches and regulatory support can enable large-scale, low-cost housing production. Industrial approaches (using components manufactured off-site), standardization, and improved purchasing and other processes can reduce the time by one third.

Urban Governance

The process of urban development is intimately linked with the system of governance. It concerns the participation of civil society, the issues of transparency and ethics and a democratic decision making process. In this the urban local bodies play a key role.

Independent India inherited a colonial set up of urban local bodies, which continued in the post-independence era. The District Collector remains a strong link between the government and the people in the towns. Only one channel of decisions, orders and instructions flows, which is from top to bottom, having no meaningful participation of people in their affairs. Frequent supersession of local and municipal bodies shows total disregard to the principle of people's representation. During last decades the government initiated grass-root reforms in the management of local bodies. With the 74th Constitutional Amendment Act (1992) the urban local bodies have been assigned greater role in urban planning and governance. The responsibility for providing basic services and implementing development programs is mainly of the local government. India has the distinction of having the largest number of democratically elected local governments in the world-more than 250,000 rural and urban local bodies with almost 3 million elected representatives. However, in most of the States, as the governments are reluctant to part with their powers. Poor municipal capacity and finances are acting as barriers in the area of decentralization, and the strengthening of the local bodies.

India, with more than 1210 million people, 3.3 million sq. km of area, 29 States, 7 Union Territories and 671 districts, 8000 odd cities and towns and 6.41 lakh villages, needs to have a differential and effective governance structure which addresses the local issues in its ecological, social, cultural and economic contexts. Urban land, housing and planning are State subjects which are inextricably linked with the political and governance system.

Debriefing and Review

1. How would you define town planning? What is its purpose?
2. Briefly explain the process of town planning.
3. How town planning can help in inclusive development?
4. Write a note on India's urbanisation trends.
5. Explain the relationship between urbanisation and socio-economic growth.
6. How town planning can address the issues of ecology and climate change?
7. What are the current government programmes on urban development, housing and infrastructure services?
8. Explain the following:
   (a) Smart Cities Mission
   (b) AMRUT
   (c) HRIDAY
   (d) PMAY
9. Briefly explain the salient features of Land Aquisition, Rehabilitation and Resettlement Act, 2013 vis-a-vis urban development.
10. Explain the role of governance in planned development.

CHAPTER

2

Evolution of Town Planning

Culture is integral to human survival, and cities and buildings keep alive the memories of cotemporary culture. They are not just the material remains of cultural pattern but are the living things of the people, their economy, knowledge, arts, faith, morals and customs. They also provide lessons how the city builders and society addressed the issues of dichotomy between urban and rural and natural and built form in the pursuit of community development. The human settlements attempt to respond to the issues of climate change, security, safety, employment and poverty.

Man's yearning for change, life, liberty and pursuit of happiness are never ending. He constantly pursues social, cultural and economic development, better infrastructure services, technological innovations, better health and education. The human settlements manifest the cultural, political, social and economic development. The historic cities epitomise and express human culture and civilisation and reflect the contemporary idea of urban space.

Indus Valley (2300 to 1600 BC)

The earliest human settlements in Indian sub-continent were at Mohenjo-daro, along the Indus River that produced the Harappan culture which persisted from 2300 to 1600 B.C. At its zenith, around 1600 BC Mohenjo-daro was prosperous community who worked as farmers, craftspeople, herders, brick masons, and builders. They cultivated wheat, barley, dates, melons, legumes, and various other crops and husbanded animals, cattle, goats, sheep, pigs, and fowl. To the north of Mohenjo-daro, was situated a zone of high agricultural productivity and along the Ravi River, rested the town of Harappa, the most prominent of the northern Indus Valley settlements. The site, with its high ground and alluvium for cultivation, was ideal for the settlement, where Harappa came up. Due to its location on the Indus river, it was a gateway city to the Hindu Kush, Baluchistan and Afghanistan and several trade routes converged on the town. The Indus River afforded boating and communication with the plains. The city was laid with underground drainage and had courtyard houses, public squares, markets and granaries.

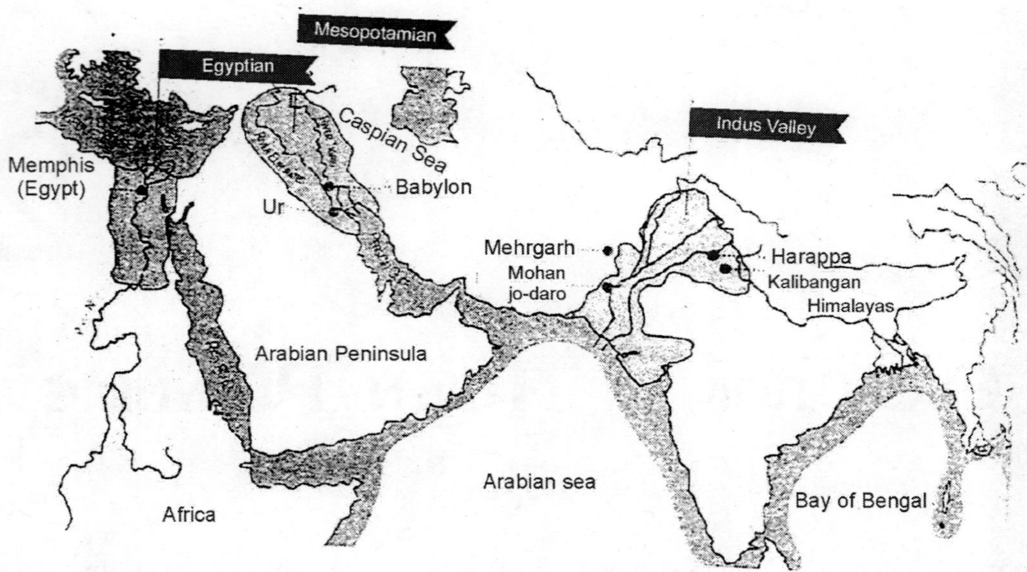

Fig. 2.1: The Indus Valley civilization flourished at the same time as the Akkadian civilization in Mesopotamia and evolved from the villages of predecessors, using the Mesopotamian model of irrigated agriculture, while controlling the formidable annual floods by an elaborate drainage system.

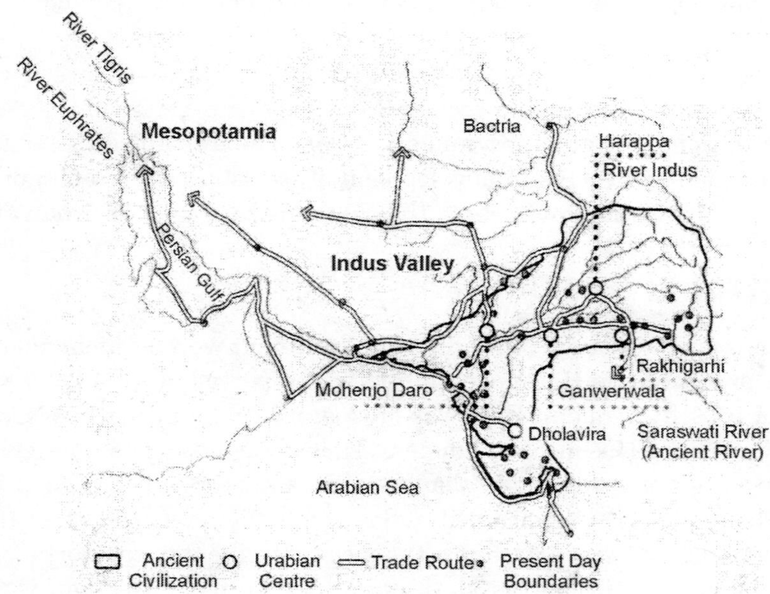

Fig. 2.2: The twin cities of Mohenjo-daro and Harappa were centres of civilisation. Both cities were a mile square with defensive outer walls. Cities were divided into lower dwellings and the citadel, alongwith civic amenities and services.

Fig. 2.3: Street with underground drainage in Mohen-jo-daro.

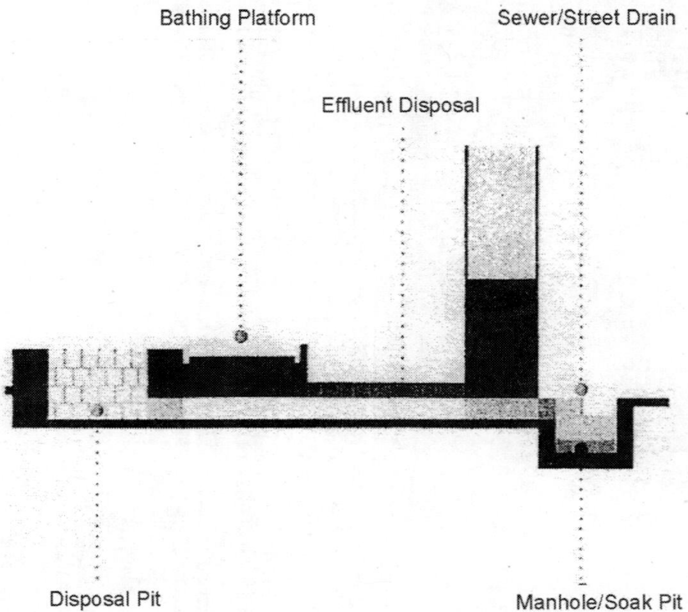

Fig. 2.4: Drainage and sewerage in Mohen-jo-daro.

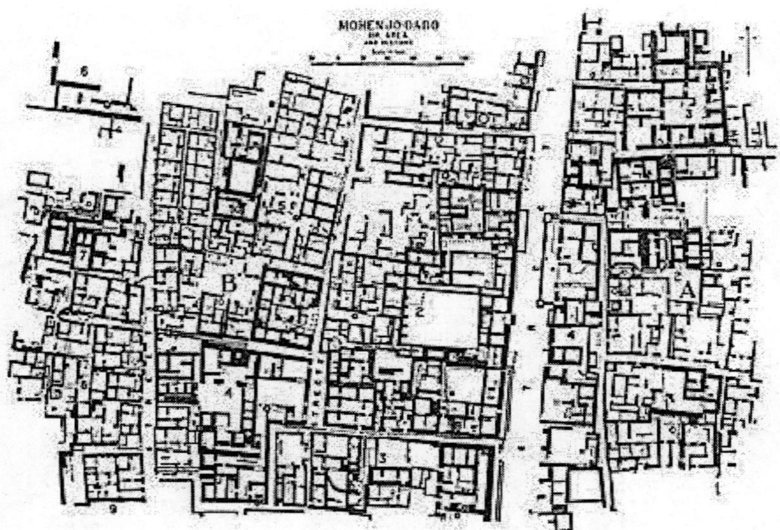

Fig. 2.5: Plan of Mohenjo-daro

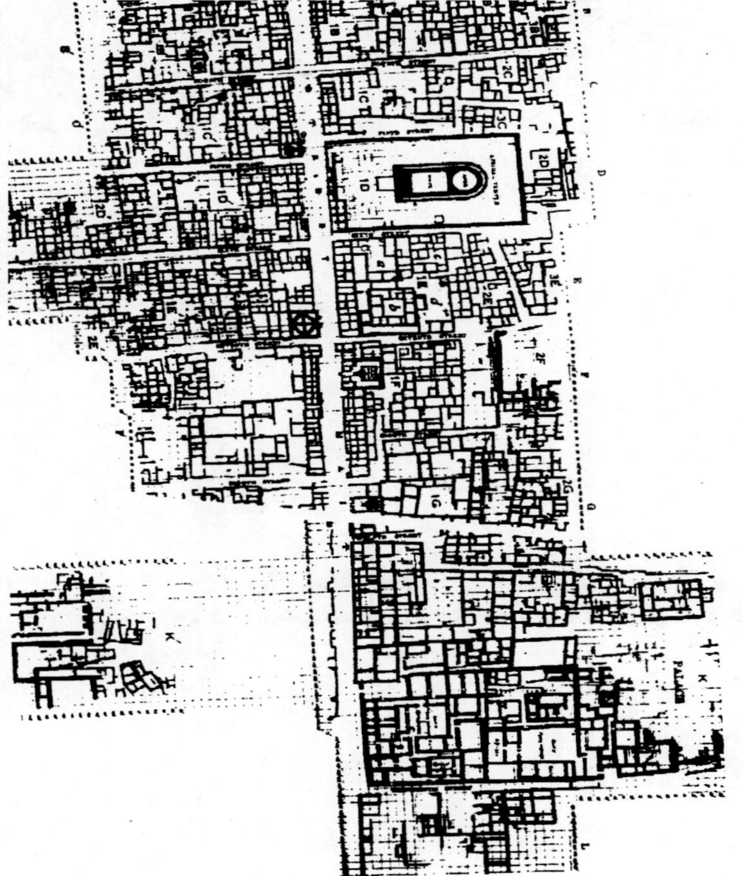

Fig. 2.6: Sirkap Town, Taxila

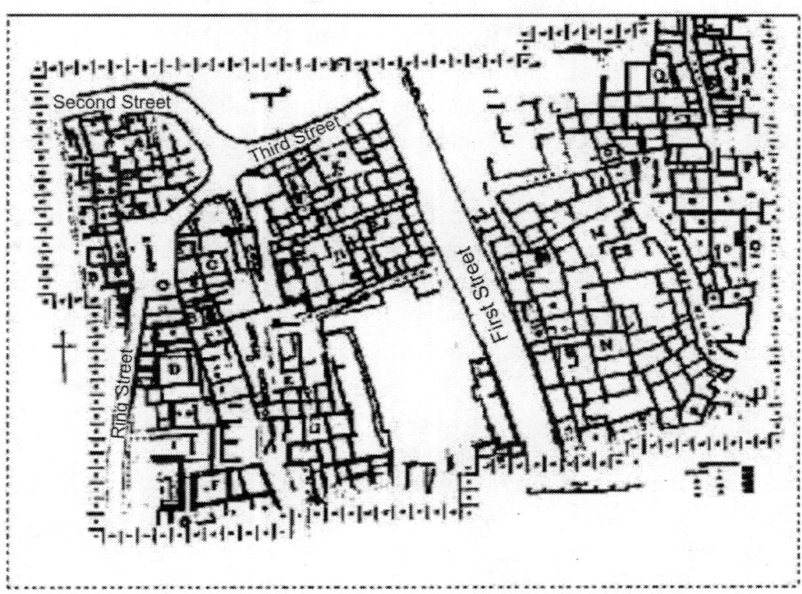

Fig. 2.7: Bhir Mound, Taxila (1000 BC)

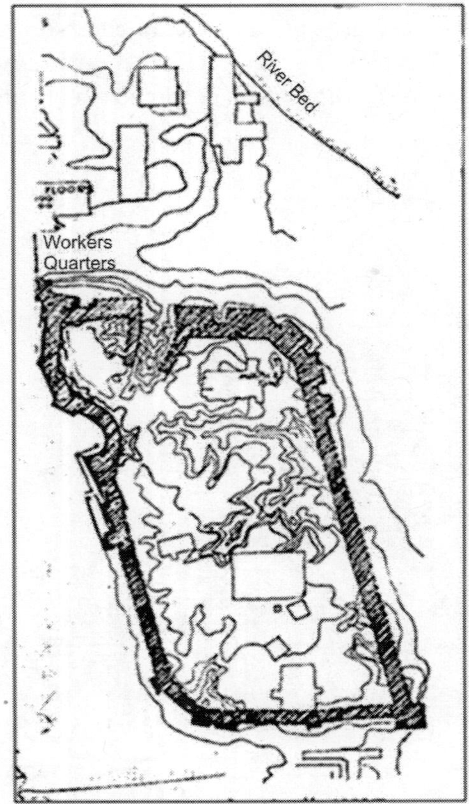

Fig. 2.8: Citadel at Harappa

The inhabitants used gravity flow to convey water from the river via stone channels to open fields below. The Harappan culture of the Indus Valley was a relatively short-lived experience, lasting about 500 years. Theories concerning the cause of the decline range from possibility of a large-scale geological cataclysm and tectonic disturbance, having altered the flow of the Lower Indus River.

The decline of the Harrapan culture in the second millennium B.C. shifted the focus to the Ganges River region following the incursions of Aryans from the north between 1500 and 1200 B.C. where large cities developed and metallurgy, agriculture, pottery, jewellery, spices, textiles and other trades propelled the economy. The Vedas chronicled the Aryan way of life. The link between nature and human remains outstanding characteristics of the vedic culture.

Egypt, Nile Valley (3000 BC and Later)

Egyptian pyramids, tombs and surrounding settlements are some of the earliest evidence of urbanisation in the Nile Valley. Ramses III, during his reign between 1182 and 1151 B C, engaged the slaves to build pyramids, cities and gardens. The Egyptian culture revolved around Pharaoh, the lord. The concept of life after death led to the construction of the pyramids. The settlements grew along the Nile river. The pomp and splendour of pharaoh led to development of advanced construction technologies of stone cutting and carving. At El Amarna along the Nile, larger private residences had come up as shown by paintings on the walls of tombs near Thebes. A typical mansion at El Amarna and other locations enclosed as large as three-quarters of an acre, their own gardens which also provided food.

Fig. 2.9: The Pyramids of Egypt epitomise the human strength and determination

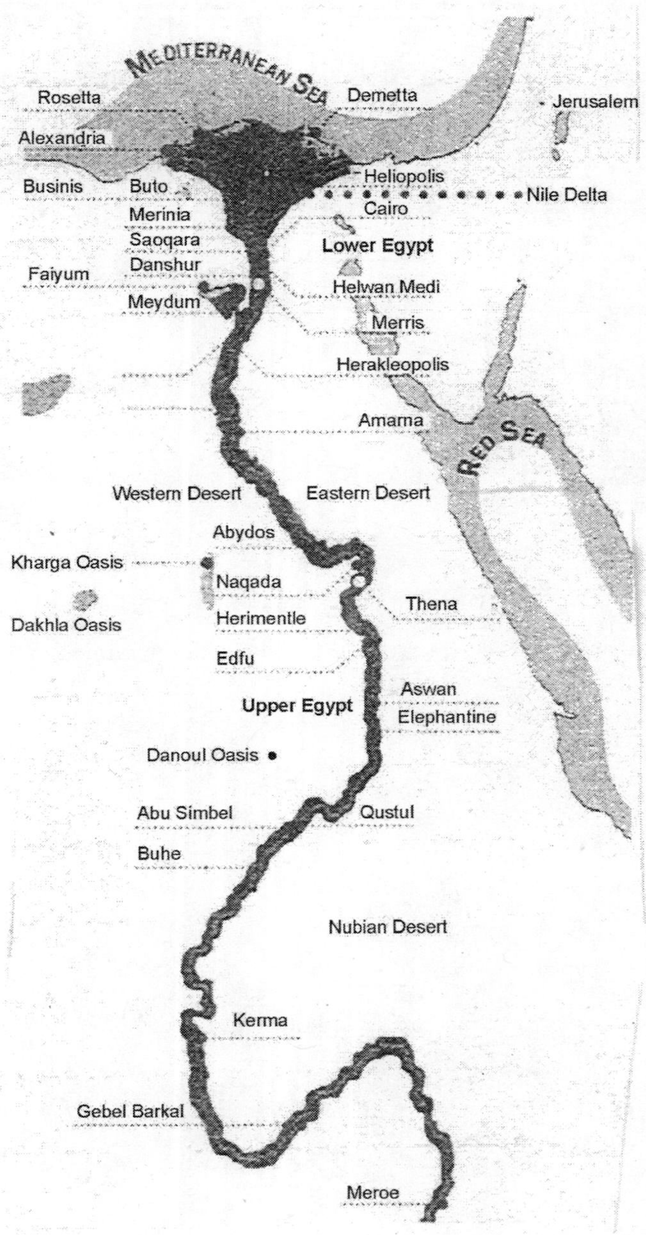

Fig. 2.10: The Nile Valley

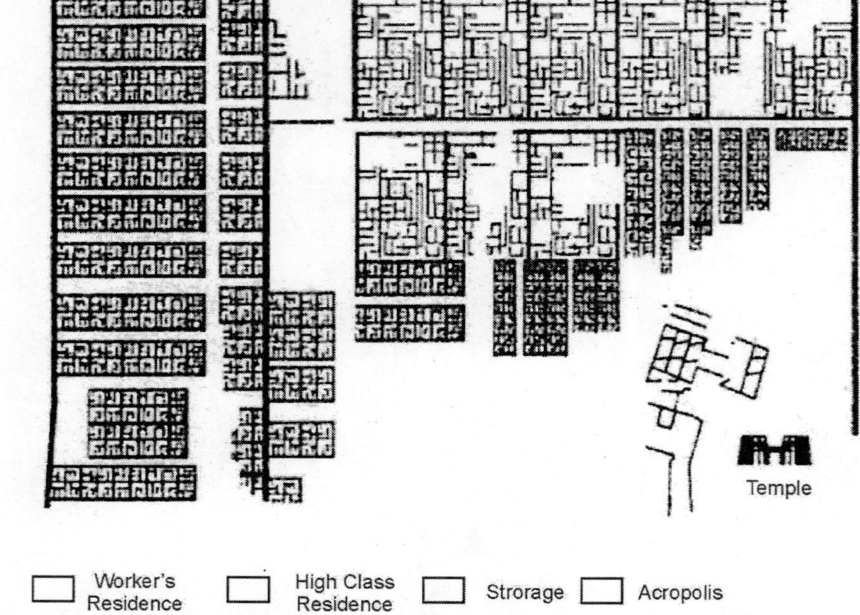

Fig. 2.11: Cities with workers quarters grew along the pyramids and River Nile

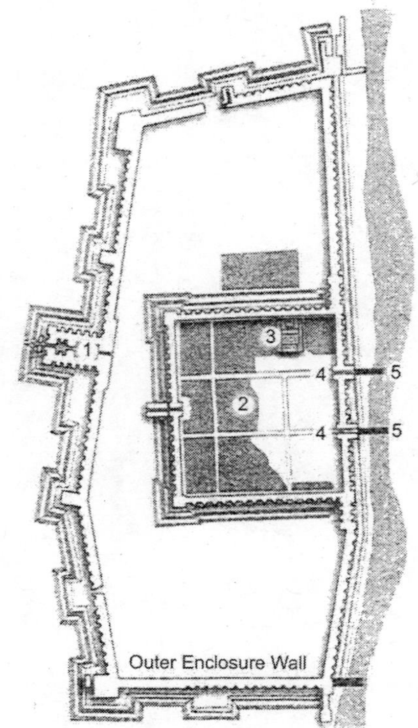

Fig. 2.12: Fortified cities were planned along the River Nile

The conversion of natural landscape to agricultural use was only a part of the change in the quality of human adaptation to the landscape. With more dependence on urban life, humans were relatively free from immediate dependence on the agriculture and maintained an interplay of social structure and division of labour, which epitomized a new relationship between humans and the urban space.

Mesopotamian Civilisation and Cities

Mesopotamia civilisation evolved mainly in the land between the river Tigris and Euphrates. The region witnessed the rise of several ancient civilizations like the Sumerian (5000 to 2330 BC), the Akkadian, Babylonian (2330 to 525 BC), Assyrian empire (1800 to 613 BC) and Persian (525 BC onwards).

The indigenous Sumerians and Akkadians (including Assyrians and Babylonians) dominated Mesopotamia from the beginning of written history (c. 3100 BC) to the fall of Babylon in 539 BC, when it was conquered by the Achaemenid Empire (the first Persian Empire). It fell to Alexander the Great in 332 BC and after his death, it became part of the Greek Seleucid Empire.

Mesopotamia is the site of the earliest developments of the Neolithic Revolution from around 10,000 BC. It has been identified as having inspired some of the most important developments in human history including the invention of the wheel, the planting of the first cereal crops and the development of cursive script, mathematics, astronomy and agriculture.

Asia Minor

Asia Minor, a peninsula also called Anatolia, comprises most of the Asian part of modern Turkey and the Armenian highland. Many great historical people, like the Hitties. Lydian Greeks, Persians, Armenians, Romans, Goths, Minoans, Byzantines and Turks, have lived in or occupied Asia Minor. Troy is one of many famous cities that were in Asia Minor long ago. The earliest settlement was Catal Huyuk near present Konya which dated back to 9000 BC. Akkadian Dynasty (2334-2083 BC) where it is known as "The Land of the Hatti" was inhabited by the Hittites covered most of Asia Minor and rivaled Egypt as a rival Middle Eastern power. It was destroyed by the invaders towards the end of the 12th century BC. Anatolia came to power in the 9th century BC. Hittites culture survived by Carchemish, Mild and other small states in eastern Asia Minor until about 700 BC.

Hittites Civilisation (1680-1180 BC)

The Hittite kingdom, which at its height controlled central Anatolia, north-western Syria down to Ugarit, and Mesopotamia down to Babylon, lasted from roughly 1680 BC to about 1180 BC. After 1180 BC, the Hittite polity disintegrated into several independent city-states, some of which survived till around 700 BC.

Assyrian Civilisation (1800 BC- 613 BC)

Assyrian originated in the upper Tigris river valley in the Armenian mountains, and established a thriving metropolis.

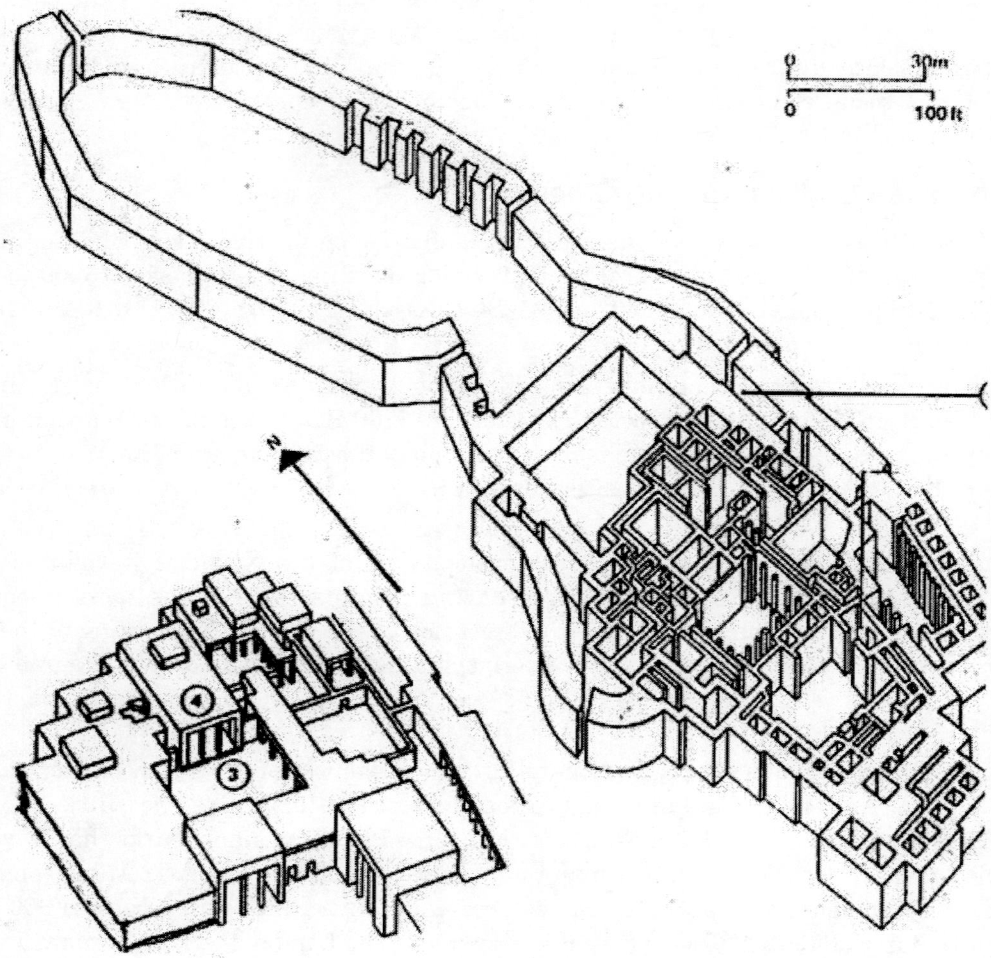

Fig. 2.13: Citadel of Tiryns (1330 BC)

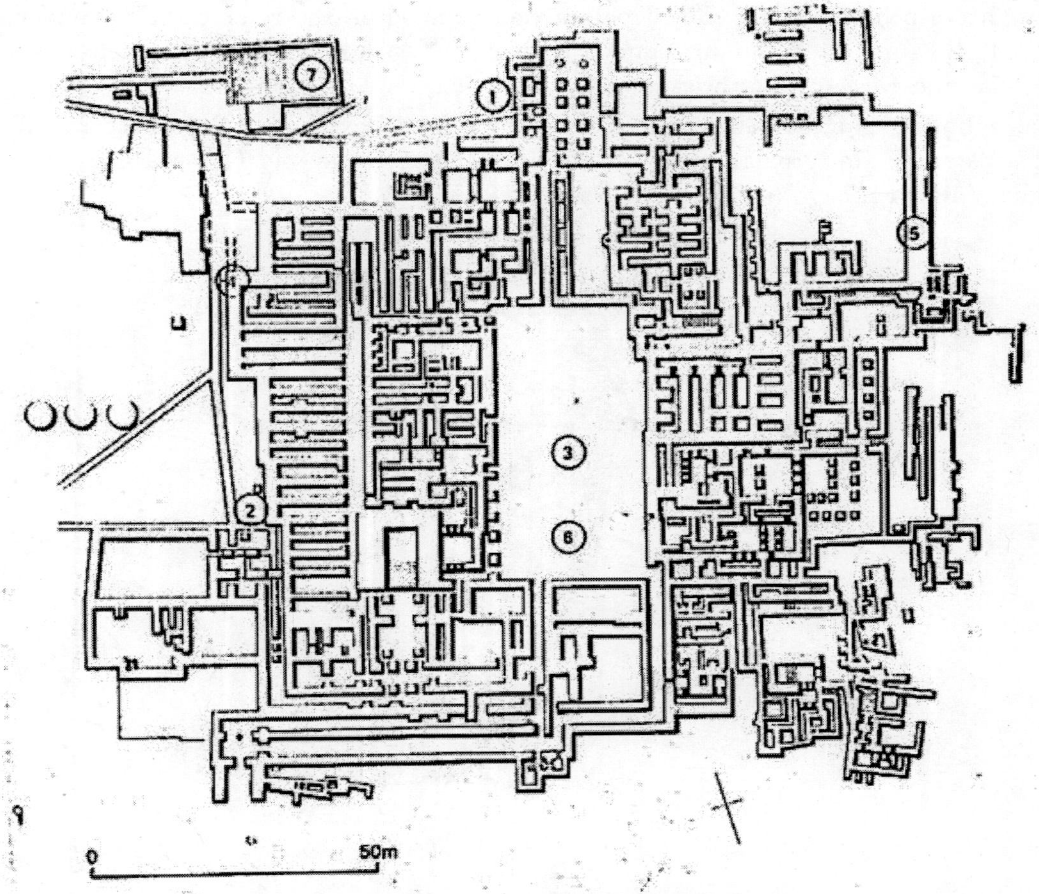

Fig. 2.14: Knosses, Crete (1550 BC)

Sumerian Civilization

Sumerian cities were protective, compact, horizontal and adapted well to climate. The market was near the center. River was an important element of the city and developed for transportation as transport was mainly by water. Some examples of Sumerian cities are given below:

Ur-Babylon	2000BC (2000 people)
Khafage	2700 BC (12000 people)
Eshnunna	2300 BC (5000 people)

The Sumerian cities had roads developed parallel to riverbank and across them. Stepped pyramids or Ziggurats and gardens were the highlights of the city.

Ur-Babylon by Herodotus lies in a great plain. It had a grid iron pattern of 120 feet square. The houses had 3 to 4 storeys. There was a great wall around the city. Roads were all straight with bronze gates. Royal palace was planned on the river bank surrounded by great wall, Ziggurat, (temple) surrounded by wall of two furlongs length, which was eight storey high and was made of bricks.

Nebuchadnezzar (605-562) who reigned for 43 years , extended political control all over the Mesopotamia. He reconstructed Babylon in elaborate style and restored many temples throughout Babylon.

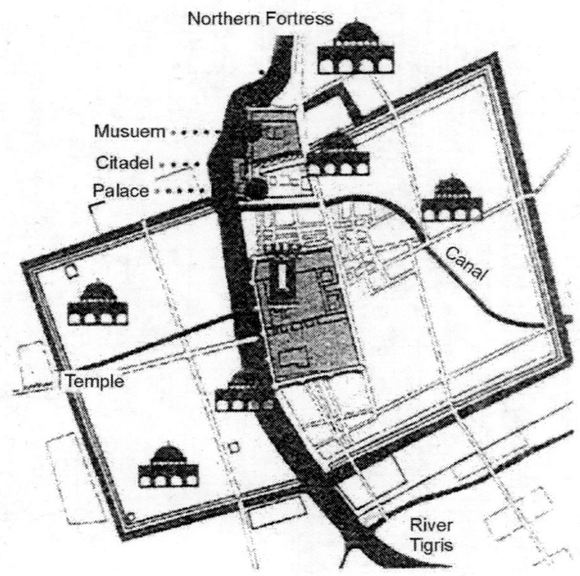

Fig. 2.15: Plan of Babylon Fortified City

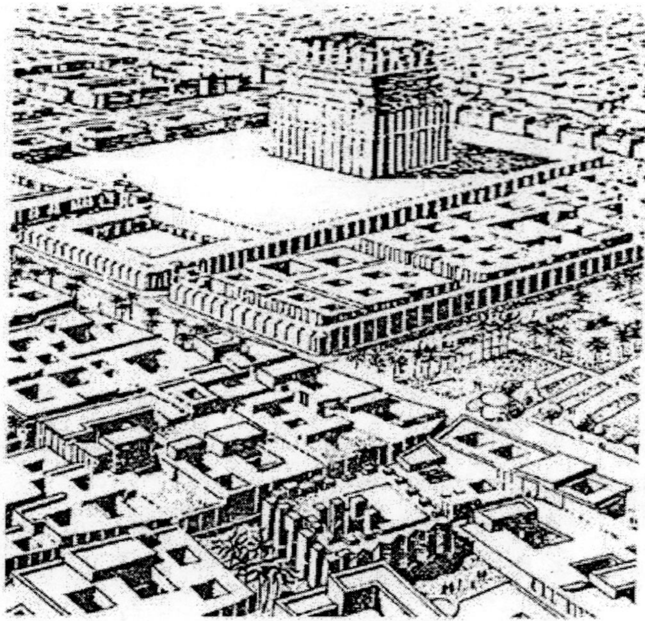

Fig 2.16: Babylon Ziggurat (200-323 BC)

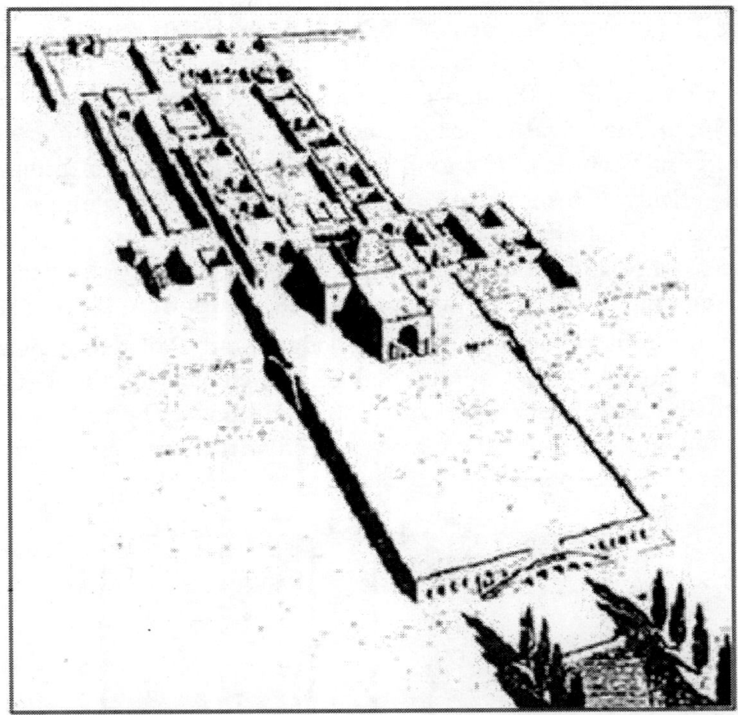

Fig. 2.17: Reconstruction of the Imarat-i Khusraw at Qasi-i Shirin in Iran, showing the beginning of the great pool and the arched openings of the passageway beneath the terrace. The palace was built for Khusraw H. between AD 591 and 628 and was encircled by a large park.

Persian Culture

Persian cities were developed in opposition to harsh and arid landscape of the Iranian Plateau. Their ethereal and delicate qualities emphasized their intrinsic response to the hot and arid environment. The water was an important element in the design of the cities and gardens. Irrigation was provided via a form of underground tunnel called a qanat, that transported water from a local aquifer. Well-like structures were connected to the qanat, enabling the drawing of water. Animal-driven Persian wheels also drew sub-soil water to the surface. In Persia, Darius the Great developed "paradise garden" and the Hanging Gardens of Babylon were renowned as a Wonder of the World.

At the beginning of the ninth century, Baghdad was reputed to be the wealthiest city in the world, famous for its tiled buildings and houses with gardens and pools. It was the fairy-tale city of Arabian Nights. Tenth-century visitors describe the palace as having two gardens, pools lined with shiny pavilions with lawns with numerous trees. The Arabs had maintained the existing Persian canal systems, so the Euphrates River basin had remained well-populated and prosperous. However, due to the capricious whims of rulers, Baghdad declined when abandoned by the Caliph Mutasim (833-842 BC) who built a new city at Samarra.

Before building his palace at Samarra, Caliph Mutasim constructed a system of waterways and planted groves of date palms with an irrigation network. Spread over four hundred acres, of which 172 acres were gardens, the Jawsaq Palace had vaulted halls, extensive quarters for a large harem and luxurious private quarters for the king. The largest palace ever constructed in the Islamic world and occupied for only a few years, it was built of unbaked brick with a flat mud roof and quickly became a ruin when abandoned. The remains reveal chambers decorated with murals and built around courts with fountains and aromatic plants. Arab historians describe a large garden on the opposite bank of the river linked to the palace by a bridge of boats. For this garden, the Caliph imported plants from all corners of the empire.

The early Caliphs built palaces as hunting lodges and Pairidaeza near royal hunting grounds. The Arab conquerors had succumbed to the charms of the Persian garden and absorbed them into the new Islamic culture. The tradition of the enclosed Persian garden with its crossed watercourse and symbolic trees spread with Islam throughout Egypt and the Maghrib to India, Sicily and Spain.

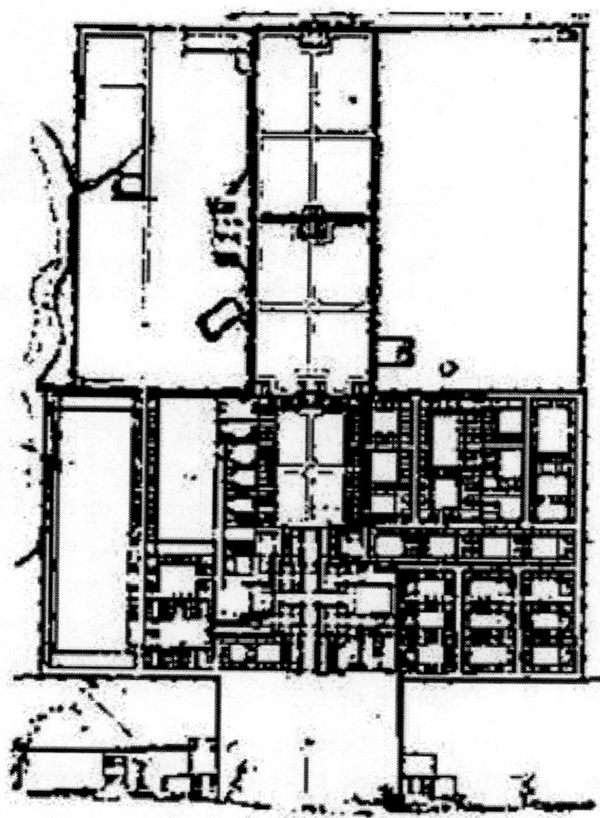

Fig. 2.18: Samarra, Bulkawara Palace (849-859 BC), of which J.D. Hoag has written: "Besides the river a quadripartite garden flanked by pavilions overlooking the water was probably on international evocation of the Koran's paradise suggested also by the mosaic vines of the nearby portal". This is one of the earliest example of Chahar Bagh concept.

Ancient China (2000 BC-800 BC)

The dawn of civilisation in China is associated with many mythological as well as historical facts. The Xia Dynasty 2000 to 1600 BC marked an evolutionary growth between Neolithic culture and the typical Chinese urban civilisation of the Shang dynasty. Shang Dynasty (1700-1027 BC) and the Zhou dynasty (770-221 BC) were considered to be the founders of Chinese culture, politics and economic development.

City of Beijing was founded in 800 BC as the capital of China, which was located in the Northern part of China. The city now extends over an area of 10,000 sq. km with a population of over 8 million. The original city had a layout similar to the one in the Ming Dynasty. In the center lies the group of palaces called the forbidden city, where entry of common people was not allowed. Imperial palaces lie to the south of it. Surrounded the imperial palaces is a square called the inner city, which is criss-crossed by main streets intersected by lanes called hutongs. The north-south and east-west streets divide ancient towns in blocks performing the functions of social control.

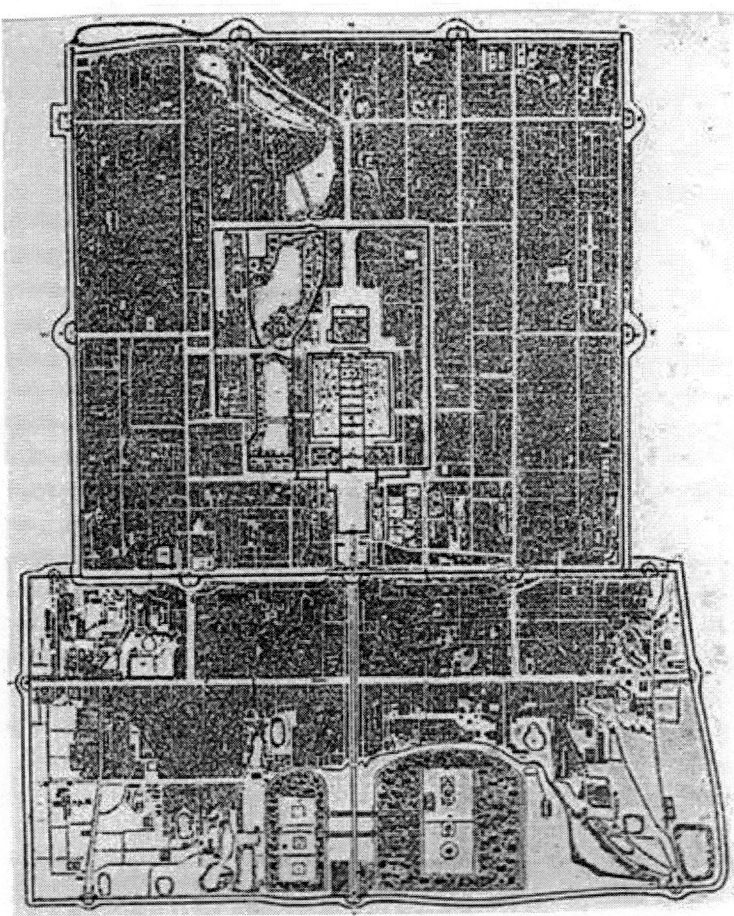

Fig. 2.19: Beijing 1st Century BC

Fig. 2.20: A Traditional Beijing Park

South American Cities

The Mississippian culture developed in the central portion of the American continent from 500 to 1400 AD where various urban cultures emerged. The most notable among the cities was Teotihuacan, which had at least 125,000 residents in 500 AD. This city was

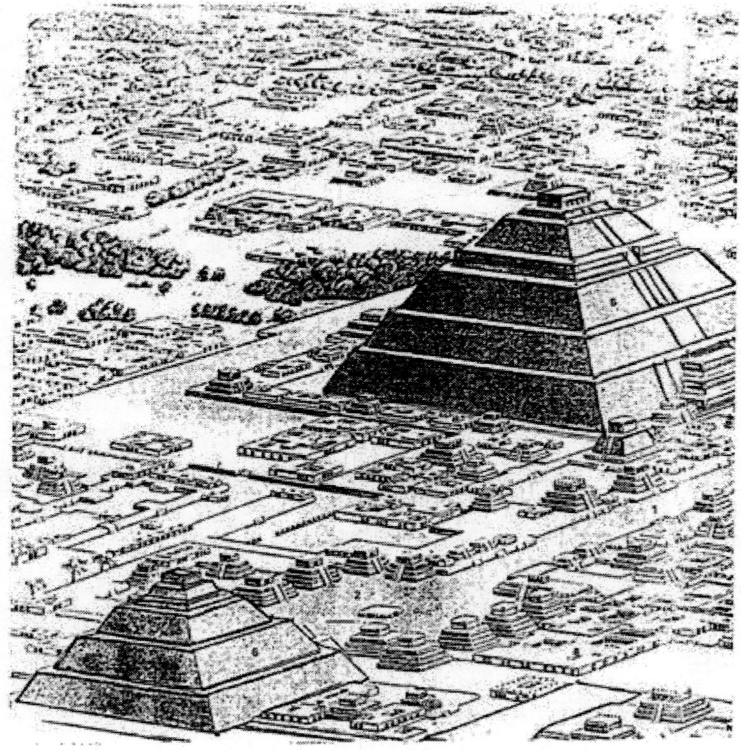

Fig. 2.21: Ziggurats at Teotihuacan, Mexico (500 BC)

organized on a grand plan centred upon a main street which now referred as the Street of the Dead. This 300 feet wide thoroughfare connected ceremonial pyramids and public structures with a market and ruler's residence. To the west and east of the street residential blocks were laid out following a precise, pre-planned grid pattern.

The Aztac, Incas and Maya civilizations are known by their cities, such as Mexico and Tenochtitlan. The Inca civilization stretches from north to south along the high mountainous Andean range from Colombia to Chile and reached west to east from the dry coastal desert called Atacama to the steamy Amazonian rain forest. The city of Cuzco had massive masonry buildings. The Mayas from southern Mexico developed agriculturally intensive city centred empire. The Mayan cities were dictated by the topography of each location and orientation of temples and conservatories was in accordance with interpretation of the orbits of the stars. At the heart of the Maya city existed the plaza surrounded by the government and religious buildings, the royal acropolis, great pyramid temples and occasionally ball courts. Tikal was the one of the largest cities of this period. Mayan culture declined in 8th and 9th centuries AD due to number of reasons like severe famine, revolts, etc.

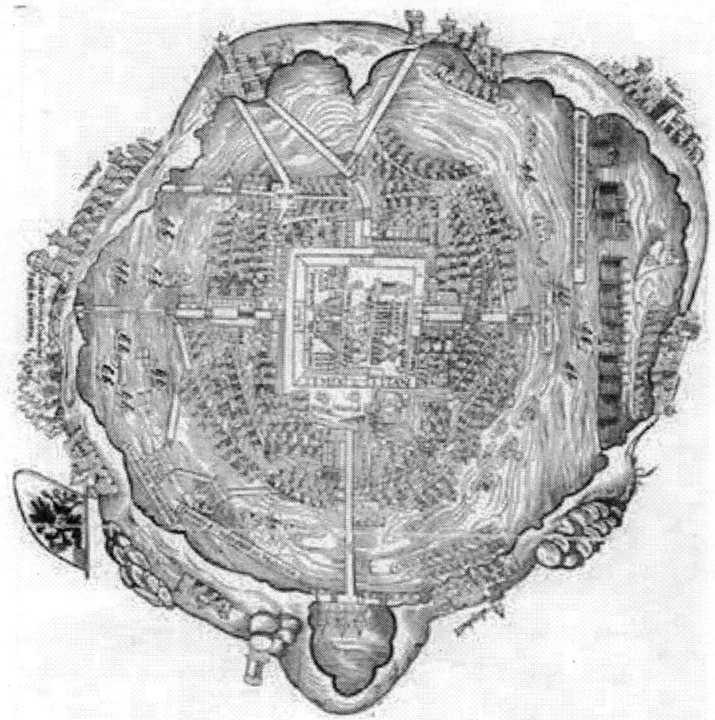

Fig. 2.22: Ancient Mexico – Tenochtitlan Correns Plan

The Aztecs adopted the planning principles of Teotihuacan (Mexico) City. They built Tenochtitlan on an island in the no longer extant Lake Texcoco, with a series of causeways extending from the major streets of its grid plan to the surrounding mainland. At the center of the city, two major streets crossed at the location where the temples, plaza of the city, mercantile and ceremonial functions were located. On the perimeter of the island and on adjoining shorelines of the mainland the Aztecs refined the chinampa field system for agricultural production. The Mississippians developed Cahokia which follows several planning principles found at Teotihuacan. The city was laid out in a grid having modules of 57 meters, as Teotihuacan Cahokia lacked a ceremonial street, but had a Grand Plaza, enclosed by a series of smaller mounds, which was adjacent to Monks Mound. Cahokia's residential areas were clustered into neighbourhoods around small plazas.

Fig. 2.23: Machu Picchu in Peru is a UNESCO world heritage site and a symbol of Inca civilization

Buddhist Period (6th Century BC) and Mauryan Empire (324-187 BC)

In the 6th Century BC Buddhist period began, which correspond to the period when Persia invaded India and ruled for 200 years over Northern part of India, Alexander, the Great, invaded India in 4th Century BC and the contacts between Greek and Indian were established. Thereafter the Mauryan Empire (324 BC to 187 BC) was at its glory under Samrat Ashoka and covered almost the whole of India (except Assam and some southern parts), Afghanistan, Baluchistan, Kashmir and Nepal, Buddhism flourished during this period. The Mauryan Empire divided the settlements into cities and municipalities.

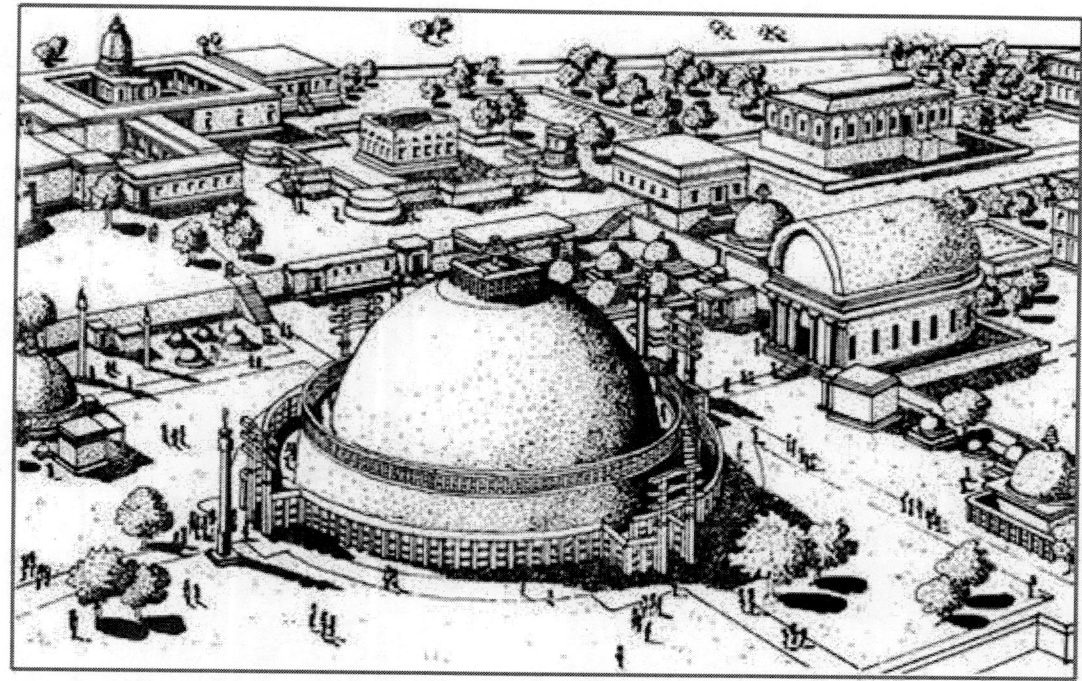

Fig. 2.24: The Budha Stupa, Sanchi, Madhya Pradesh (First Century), the circumambulation determines the form of the stupa

Fig. 2.25: Sanchi, Mahastupa, Torana reliefs of village and town scenes

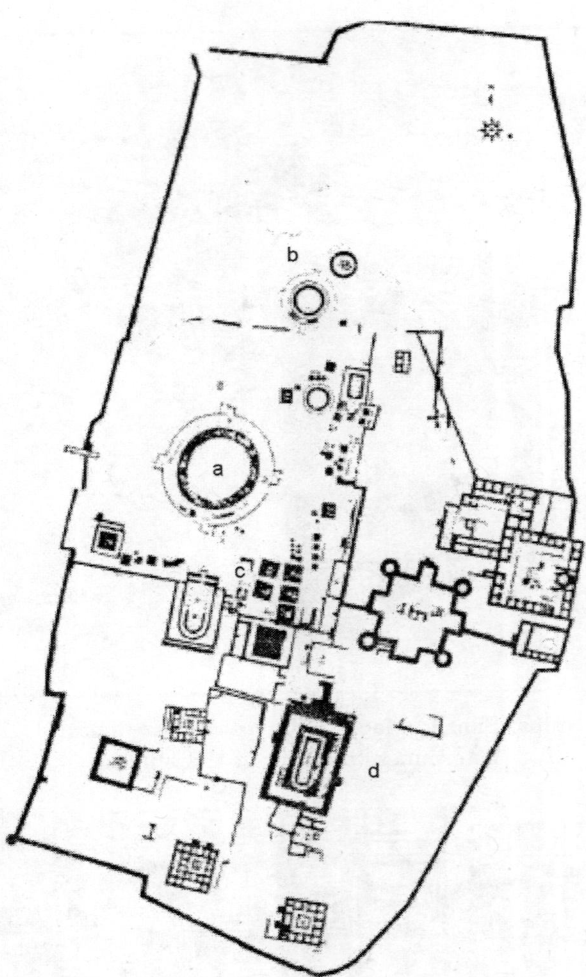

Fig. 2.26: Sanchi Plan (a) Mahastupa, (b) Smaller Stupa and (c) Temple

Fig 2.27: Ajanta Chaitya Griha

Fig. 2.28: Great Kailasa (Cave 16) Ellora caves, Aurangabad, Maharashtra, Photo HH Maha Chakri Sirindhorn

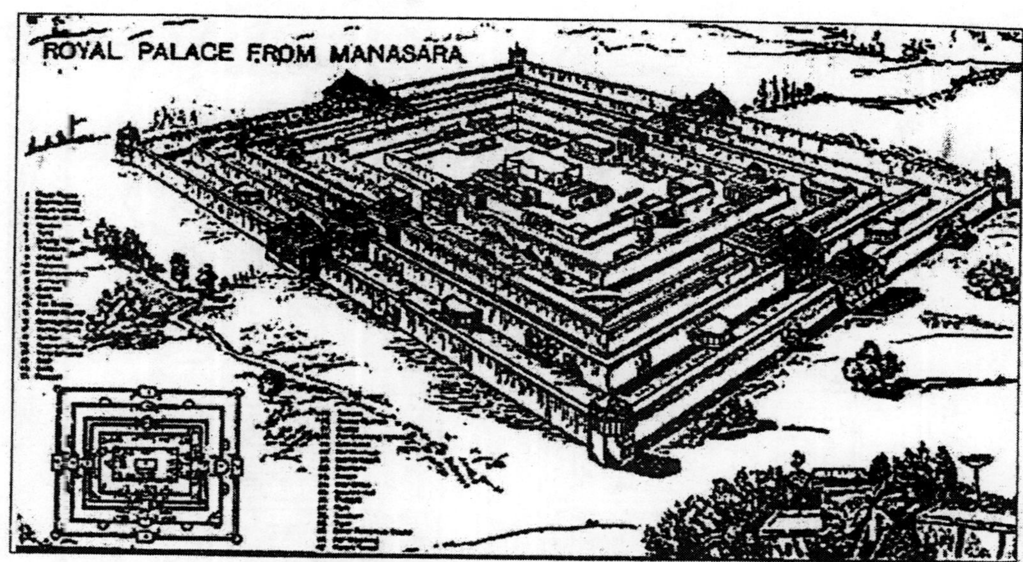

Fig. 2.29: Royal Palace from Mansara

Source: Prasanna Kumar Acharya, Hindu Architecture in India and Abroad, J K Publishing, Bhopal

Arthashastra written by Chankya of the Mauryan Empire laid down guidelines in respect of the duties of government, administration and also on town and country planning and housing. The Mansara of the 6th Century A.D. prescribes 8 different types of towns and villages.

The form of a city was derived on the principle of Vãstu Purush Mandal. It established an interrelationship of physical form of a settlement with the spiritual, cosmic and behavioural system. It determined the basic form, its location and orientation of various functions in a settlement. It was interrelated with the surroundings, like the planets in the astrological chart. A system of ashtha (8), Navgrah (9 planets), 24 matrika pithas, etc. was devised as a numerical symbolism and for orientation and linkages of the settlement system. The Vãstu-Purush-Mandala had been so universal that it could be applied to an altar, a temple, a house, a city or the entire cosmos. The symbol relates physical form with the outer form and the inner-vision. The Mandala is not only a spatial axiom but a temporal process as well. It is a module encompassing the principles of organicity – interrelationship of parts, inter-dependence of systems, resonance and synchronicity. The five elements of nature were tied with the cosmic system.

In the overall urban fabric, the generic morphology manifests a labyrinthine hierarchy of social organization. It contains an introvert spatial organisation with a system of courtyards and chowks, which enhance frequent contacts and social participation among the residents. These also served as an efficient means of security, privacy and social control.

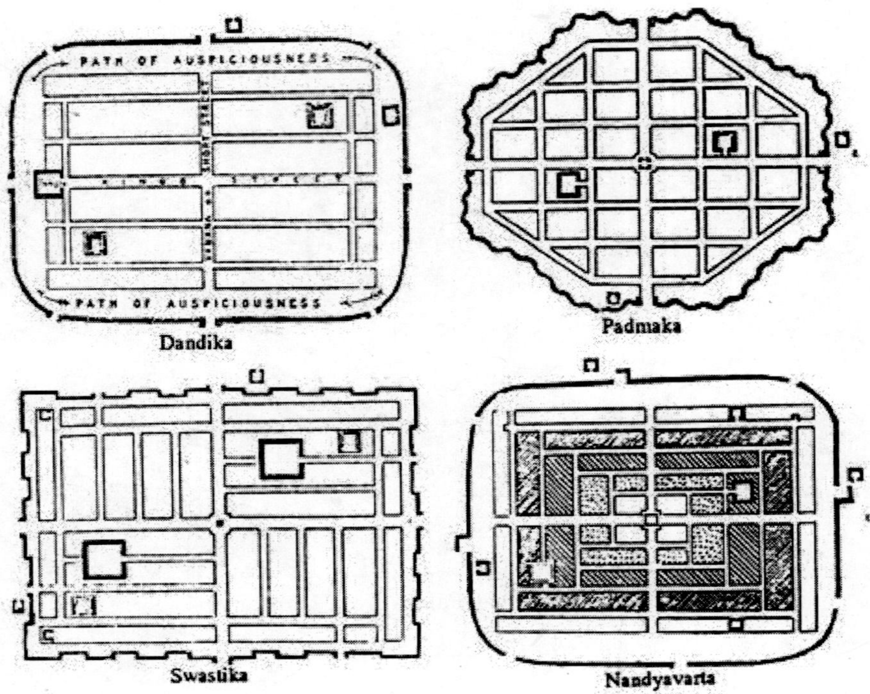

Fig: 2.30: City Patterns According to Mansara. The basic shape of a city was a square with a temple or a palace at the centre and different quarters for people around it.

Fif. 2.31: The Purana Qila excavations established the existence of settlement from Late Harappan to Medieval period covering about 2500 years of history.

Source: ASI/INTACH, Delhi—A Living Heritage, 2010

Indraprastha-The Legendary City of Pandavas

Indraprastha, the legendary city of Mahabharat dates back between 1000 BC to 1800 BC. It was located on the western bank of River Yamuna, where now Purana Qila in Delhi stands. The legend says that the capital of Pandavas, named after God Indra, was built by Maya Danav. According to Mahabharat when the relations between Pandavas and Kauravas became strained, Dhratarashtra, the father of Kauravas, gave away the region of Khandavaprastha on the bank of the river Yamuna to the Pandavas. There they built the city surrounded by the ditches and provided a high defensive wall. Indraprastha was a part of the Khandavaprastha empire, where the Pandavas ruled. There is also a reference in Mahabharat about the five villages demanded by the Pandavas, which are Indrapat, Baghpat, Tilpat, Sonipat and Panipat. The excavations of these settlements have yielded painted grey earthenware which dates back to 1000 BC, and are similar to those found in the excavations at the Purana Qila. These are simple in design and black in colour. The village of Indrapat, which is derived from Indraprastha, did exist in the Purana Qila in the beginning of the 20th century. When New Delhi, the Imperial capital, was constructed, it was cleared alogwith other villages like Raisina, Jaisinghpura, Narsinghpura, etc. Indraprastha was stated to be a district Pratigana as mentioned in a Sanskrit inscription dated 1328 AD, which is preserved in the Red Fort museum. On the basis of the evidence, it can be said that the society that time was quite advanced and used iron and copper. Tools were made of stone, iron, bones, glass, etc. Clay was used to make pots and precious stones were used for the ornaments. The houses were built of mud bricks, wattle and daub.

In the Mahabharat, the description of the Indraprastha is as follows:

"*....The fortress sported massive iron wheel and well laid plan of streets that avoided collision with fate; and it had beautiful buildings of many kind. Thus Indraprastha shone like the image of heaven, like a mass of packed clouds that are encircled by lightning.... Lovely gardens surrounded the city with mango trees, Amratakas, Nipas, Ashoka, Kadambs, Bakulas and Jasmine.... Swarming of the birds of all kinds, always joyous cuckoo. There are houses white like mirrors and all kind of pavilions, lovely painted houses and pleasure hillocks; and many ponds filled with pure water. And most charming lakes redolent with the fragrance of lotuses and water lilies, colourful with wild geese and ducks.... lotus ponds of all shapes and broad and big tanks of great beauty. As they dwelled in their great realm, which was peopled with honest folk, the joy of the Pandavas, great king grew externally, and thus the Pandavas, when Bhishma and the king had displayed the law, became inhabitants of Khandva tract.....*"

In the Mahabharat there is also a reference of the palace built by Pandava which was designed by Maya Danava. It was so beautiful that Duryodhan was envious. Its floor and walls were made of crystal, which gave illusory effect. By this, it was a unique building and looked like a mirror. At the end of Mahabharat war, the Pandavas shifted to Hastinapur and handed over the Indraprastha to the Yadavas. Thereafter the city went into oblivion and became deserted as a mere village. However, the excavations have shown the remains of Maurya, Gupta, Sultanate, Tughlak and Mughal dynasties. The city fort was once again rebuilt by Shershah Suri in the middle of sixteen century and the city was rechristianed as Shershah's City.

The city was planned according to the canons of Mansara, the treatise on town planning and architecture. As a basic principle, a city would be planned within an integral system of broad cosmic cycle. It was inter-related with the surrounding cities, like the planets in the astrological chart. The five elements of nature were also signified by the settlement system. Perhaps the five cities namely, Indraprastha, Bagpat, Panipat, Sonipat and Tilpat signified the 5 elements of nature, namely air, earth/vegetation, water, fire and space.

Today the lofty remains of Indraprastha are surrounded by the Purana Quila, zoo, Nizamuddin, Humayun Tomb, Exhibition ground, Sunder Nagar and Millennium Park along the river Yamuna and Ring Road. The reign of King Vikrmaditya is identified by the celebrated Kalidas, poet and dramatist. Cities like Ujjain, Patliputra (Patna), Mathura and Shravsti became great centres of learning and culture. Fa Hein, a Chinese traveller who visited India during the 4th Century AD wrote that the government was liberal and people had enough food, clothes and housing. Caves at Ajanta and Ellora with unique famous paintings belongs to this period. The famous Iron Pillar at Delhi near Qutab Minar was cast in the 5th Century AD. King Harshvardhan was the ruler of north India from 606 to 647 AD. Chinese pilgrim Hiuan Tsang who visited in India during this time recorded that the world renowned university of Nalanda, Bihar had 8500 students and 1500 teachers.

Gupta Period (320 AD to 570 AD)

The fall of Maurya Empire was followed by a period of political instability, which is known as the Gupta Period (320 AD to 570 AD). The reign of Samundragupta and his son Vikrmaditya. King Vikramaditya patronized advancement of learning and culture. The period is characterised by growth of trade and industry, which brought in wealth. Caves of Ajanta and Ellora belong to this period and demonstrate the classical Indo-Greek and Gandharva styles of arts and architecture.

Byzantine and Islamic Culture

The Byzantine empire spanned a period of more than 1000 years (330-1453 AD) and a geographic area from modern day Spain and Britain to the Middle East and North Africa. Due to this temporal and geographic spread, there is no single dominant style that can be labeled "Byzantine style". However, the cities are full of pleasure gardens, parks and mosques. Constantinople, Madrid, Córdoba in southern Spain, the Morocco and Naranjos are the examples of Byzantium cities established during 8th century onwards.

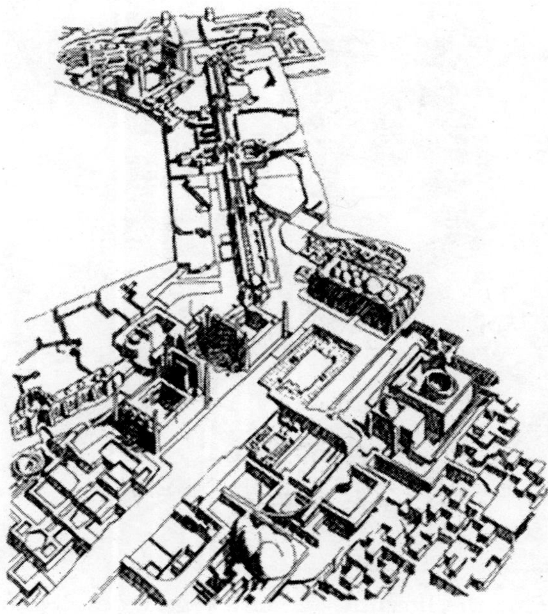

Fig. 2.32: Isfahan: One of the earliest classical city with a central vista and large open spaces around public buildings

Isfahan

The centre-piece of Isfahan, Shah Abbas city, was the central square known as the Maydan-i-Shah or imperial square. It was used for markets and ceremonies, including wild beast fights, court pageants and the playing of polo. Around this square are the major buildings and the great royal mosque Masjid-i-Shah. This is magnificent structure with a jewel like finish encrusted with mosaic. To the north, royal bazaar linked the old city. On the east is a magnificent mosque for the royal ladies, the Masjid-i-Shaykh Lutfullah, facing the Ali-qapu or lofty gateway, a seven storey building which acted as a state gateway to Shah Abbas paradise garden beyond. On top of it was an audience chamber and grandstand overlooking the maidan. The Ali-Qapu linked the palace complex with the public maidan.

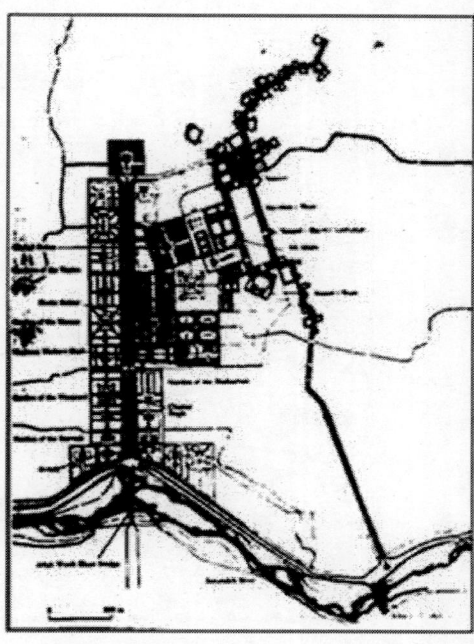

Fig. 2.33: Isfahan in 17th Century

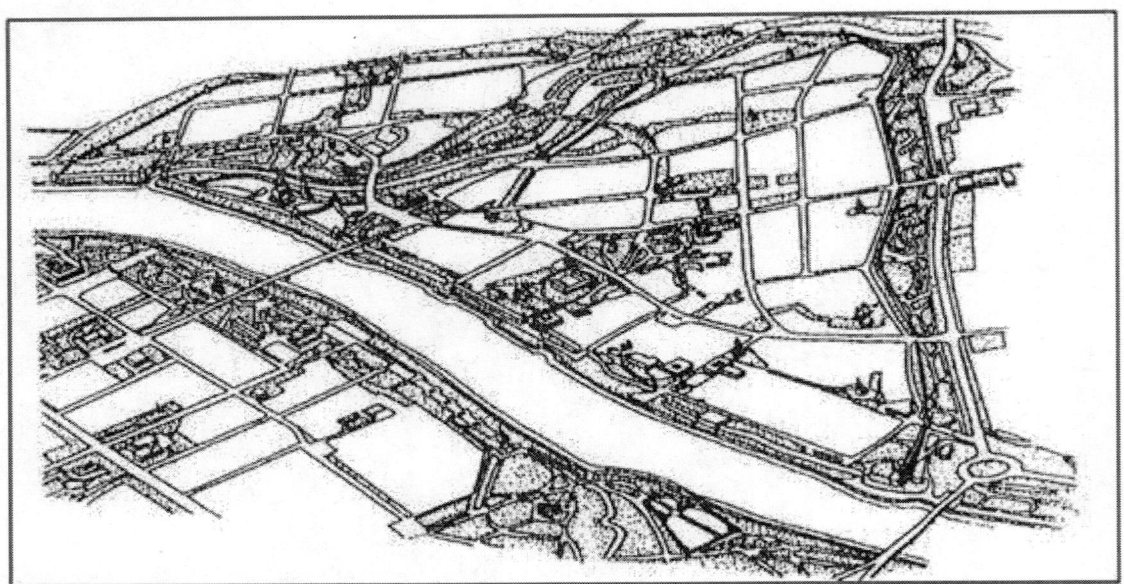

Fig. 2.34: Water being the life line, the cities were developed along the rivers

Fig. 2.35: Istanbul, 3rd Century AD

Hellenistic and Roman Culture

In Greece and Roman culture, Hippopotamus, Vitruvius, Pythagoras and other stalwarts developed the principles of town planning and architecture. Priene, perched on a precipice above the meander valley has a sequential placement of architectural elements. Temples, theatres, shops, streets, and ways conform to grid arrangement. East-west streets run parallel to contours which had public spaces, like the agora, temples and shops. Persian influences extended to post-Alexander's Greece. Around 350 BC there were several cities and gardens at Athens and other parts of Greece.

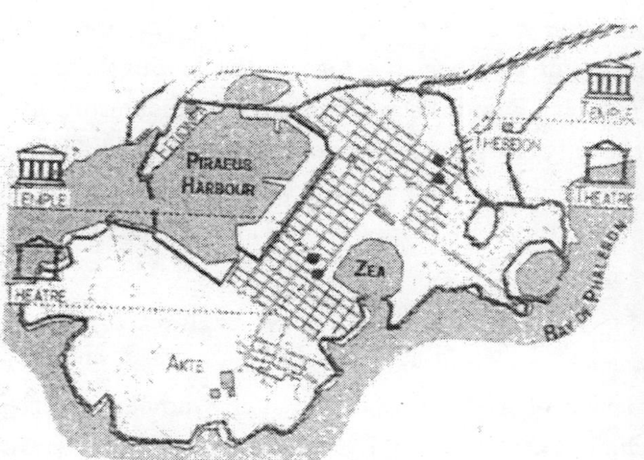

Fig 2.36: Ancient Athens Plan

Fig 2.37: Vitruvius Diagram of the Winds (from Rivius, G.H. (1548), Vitruvius Ieutsch, in Rosenau 1959)

Vitruvius believed that "since the city would face the eight winds, let the direction of your streets and alleys be laid down on the lines of division between the quarters of two winds so no wind would blow directly down them, and would be dispersed." Vitruvius prescribes locations of major temples, the forum, the basilicas, which should be in the warmest possible quarter. The city would be walled with defensive towers. Access roads should slope upwards towards the city gates which should be approached from the right so that enemies, carrying their shiels in their left hands, would expose their unprotected flanks to the defenders. Vitruvius suggested that towns should be laid out in circular form to give views of enemy from many points.

The later Crete cities were characterised by fortress towns due to increasing invasion form Greece and Asia Minor. The cities in Greece developed from 6th century BC till Alexander's period (4th Century BC), which was characterised by dominance of nobles and emergence of democracy, philosophy, science, mathematics and law led to the development of House of People or council chamber, the Assembly House, Open Air Theatre and Agora. Town planning was based on gridiron pattern.

Fig 2.38: Countryside in Greece-pristine and organic landscape

Source: www.visitgreece.01

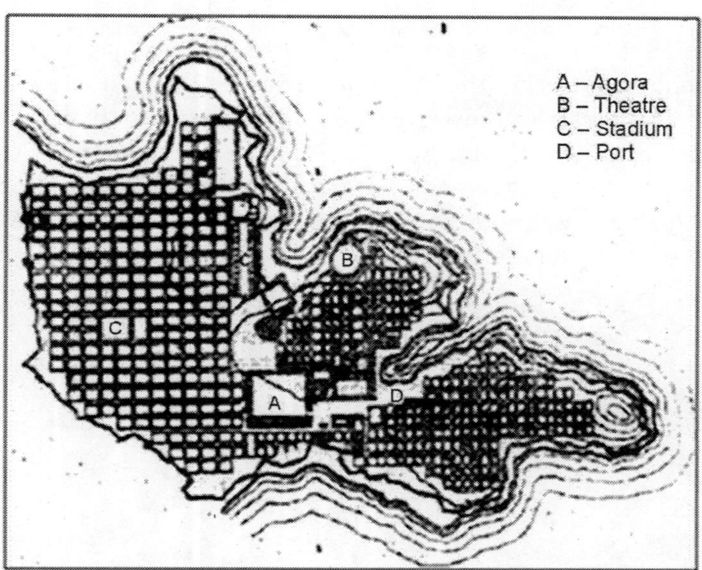

Fig. 2.39: Miletus (700-500 BC)

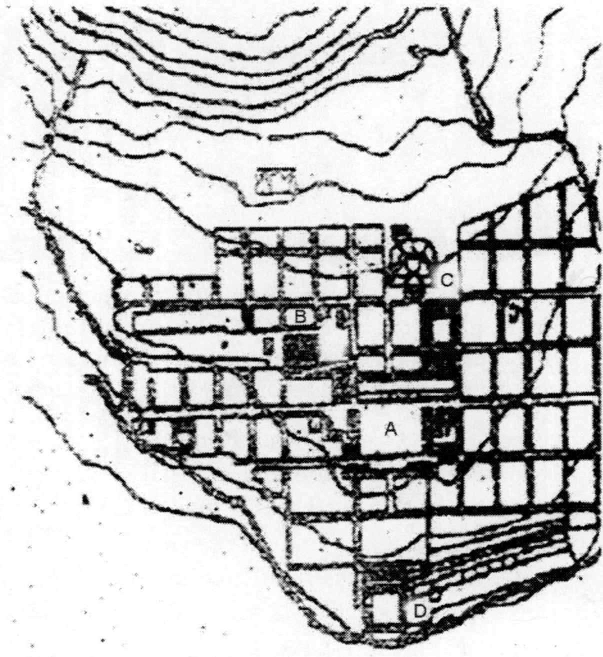

Fig. 2.40: Plan of Priene (6th century B.C) Greek Colonial City

The ancient cities were full of gardens and the tradition was brought to Rome by Lucullus. Wall paintings in Pompeii attest to elaborate development later. The wealthiest Romans built extensive villa gardens with water features and topiary. Archaeological evidence survives at sites such as Hadrian's Villa.

During the Roman Empire, the Greeks and Etruscan groups, who occupied different regions of Italian peninsula during the eight centuries established cities and city states. By 500 BC the Roman monarchy was overthrown and replaced with republic. Julius Caesar annexed many States of Africa, Spain, France, England and other smaller coutries. Roman cities became highly developed as the administrators of the Roman Empire (c.100 BC - 500 AD) actively pursued their development. The Gardens of Lucullus (Horti Lucullani) on the Pincian Hill on the edge of Rome about 60 BC introduced the Persian garden to Europe.

Fig. 2.41: Piazza del Campo, Siena, Italy. 700-year-old plaza was originally the site of a Roman forum. The square has acted as the cultural heart of the city since the construction of the town hall in the 12th century. It functions superbly as a civic and social space, with active edges around it. The Piazza del Campo is a champion of the place making Credit: Ricardo André Frantz.

Borrowing from the Greeks, the Romans improved the construction techniques, applied mechanics, metal and built thermae for games and bathing, circuses, amphitheatres for gladiatorial contests, theatres, basilicas and temples. Vitruvius developed the famous Ten Books of Architecture, which gave the basic principles and norms for town planning, architecture and technical considerations. Most of the Roman cities were characterised by their commanding position, enormous scale, impressive architecture, chess board planning of the streets, aqueducts, sanitation and public health considerations.

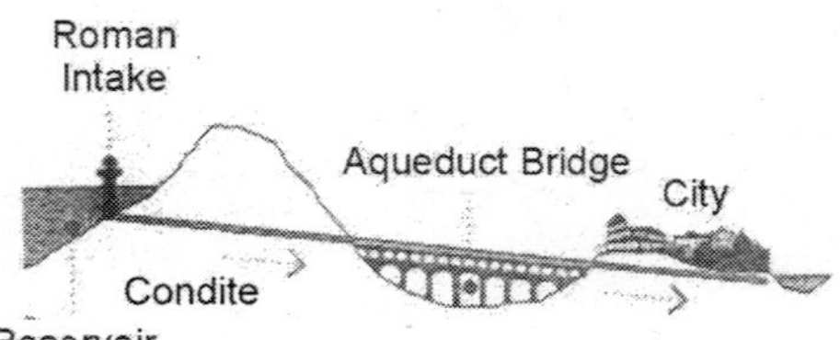

Fig. 2.42: Aqueducts, roads, bridges, public buildings, classical order of columns, arch and dome are some of the innovative and greatest achievement of the Romans. They constructed around 50,000 miles of roads. Colosseum is a perfect example of marvelous engineering and architecture of the Roman civilization.

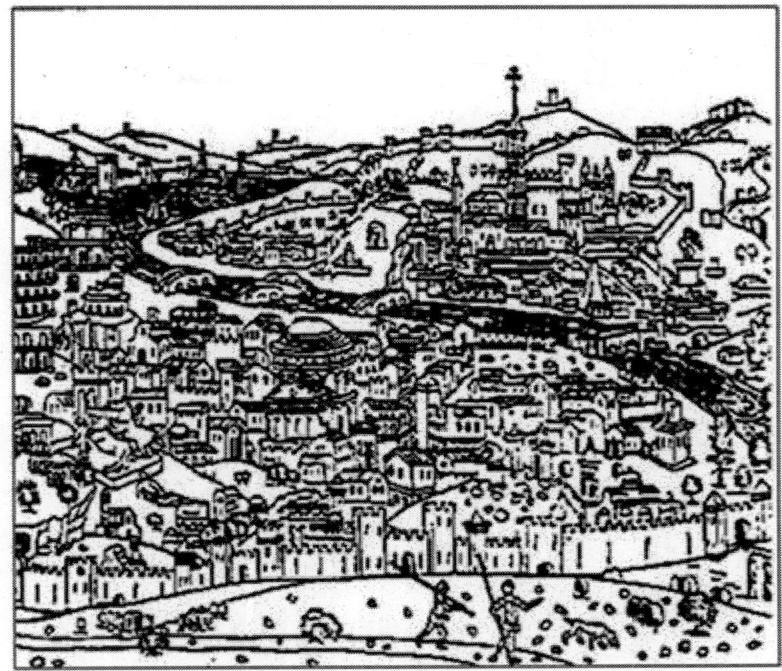

Fig 2.43: Rome- the City on Seven Hills

Fig 2.44: Florence (1420). Cathedral Dome, designed by Brunelleschi provided Florence with a visual expression of the Renaissance.

Source: Bacon, Edmund N., The Design of Cities, Penguin Books

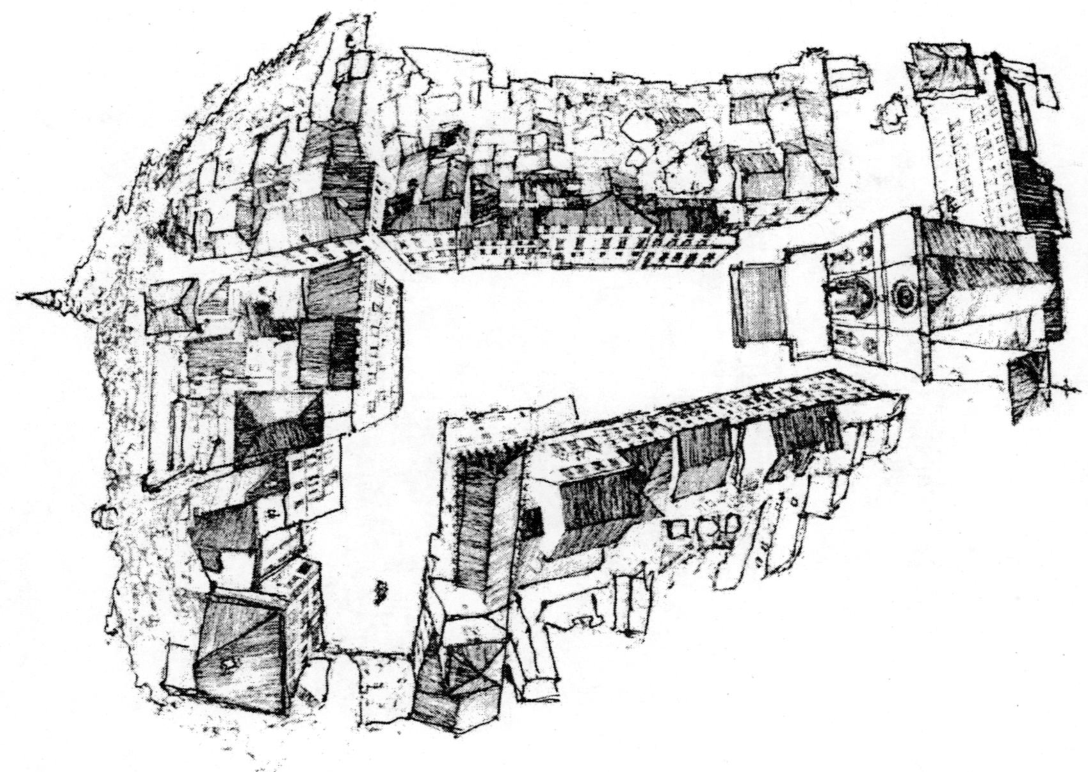

Fig 2.45: Todi, Italy is a medieval city with interlocking squares. The simplicity of design is such that the citizen never looses his relationship with the city. Drawing by JH Aronson.

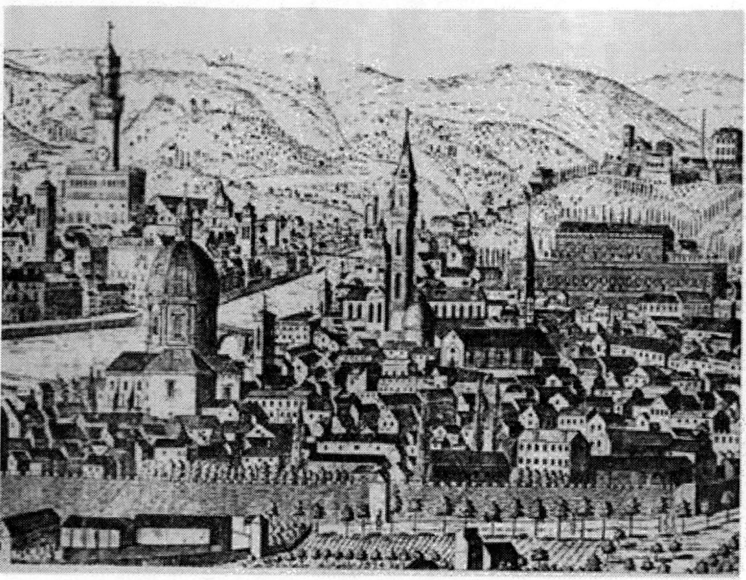

Fig. 2.46: Rome (18th Century)

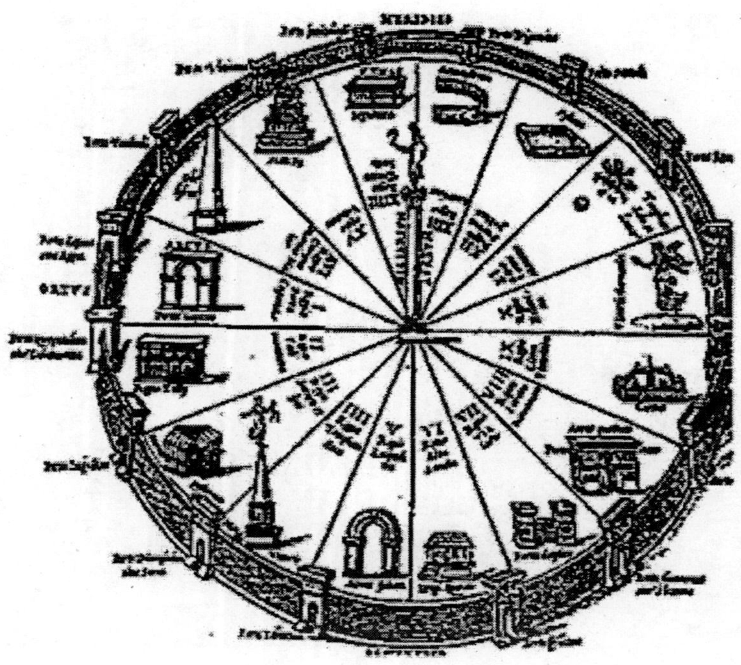

Fig. 2.47: Rome (1527 AD)

There was a continued trade relationship between ancient India and Rome, which gave rise to the Indo-Roman culture. The Mauryan Empire (324 B.C. to 187 B.C.) under Samrat Ashok, who extended his empire to Afghanistan, Baluchistan, Kashmir and Nepal witnessed the exchange of Indian and Roman art, architecture and culture.

The Dark Age saw the shift of Roman capital from Rome to Byzantium (Constantinople). 7th to 10th century saw the rise of Muslim Civilisation all over the northern Africa and much of South East Europe which challenged Christianity. City planning was guided by the defense needs with heavy fortifications. Church controlled all fields of knowledge leading to revival of classical knowledge. The physical size of towns was restricted by the girth of fortifications. The exalted position and glory of nobles was reflected in the monumental vistas, royal gardens, palaces of nobles. The Italian Renaissance inspired a revolution in urban development. The period between 1400-1750 AD was the golden age of Italy, where public buildings, cathedrals, markets, roads, stadia, theatre, canal, waterways, gardens luxurious villas were built in and around Venice, Milan, Florence, Rome and other cities. Some of these include Tivoli and the Villa d'Esta (1549), at Frascati and the Villa Dobrandini (1518), Torlonia (1621), Mondragon (1567), at Bagraia and the elegant Villa Lente (1566). The Roman culture spread to Britain, Switzerland and many other European countries.

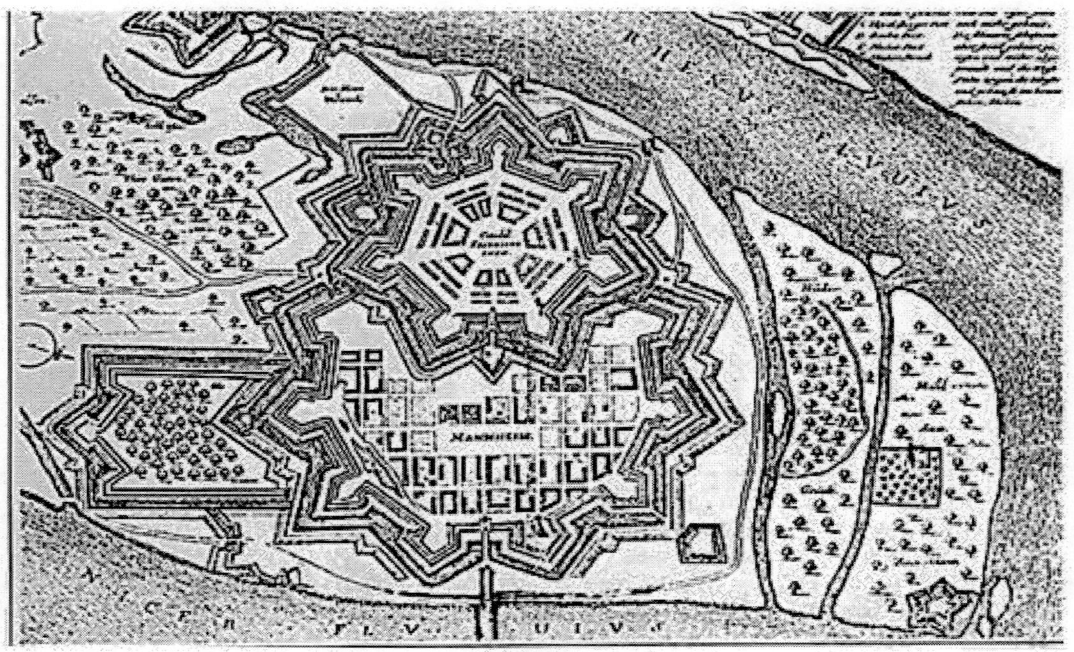

Fig 2.48: Mannheim- A Military Cantonment in Germany

Fig. 2.49: Milan (1548 AD)

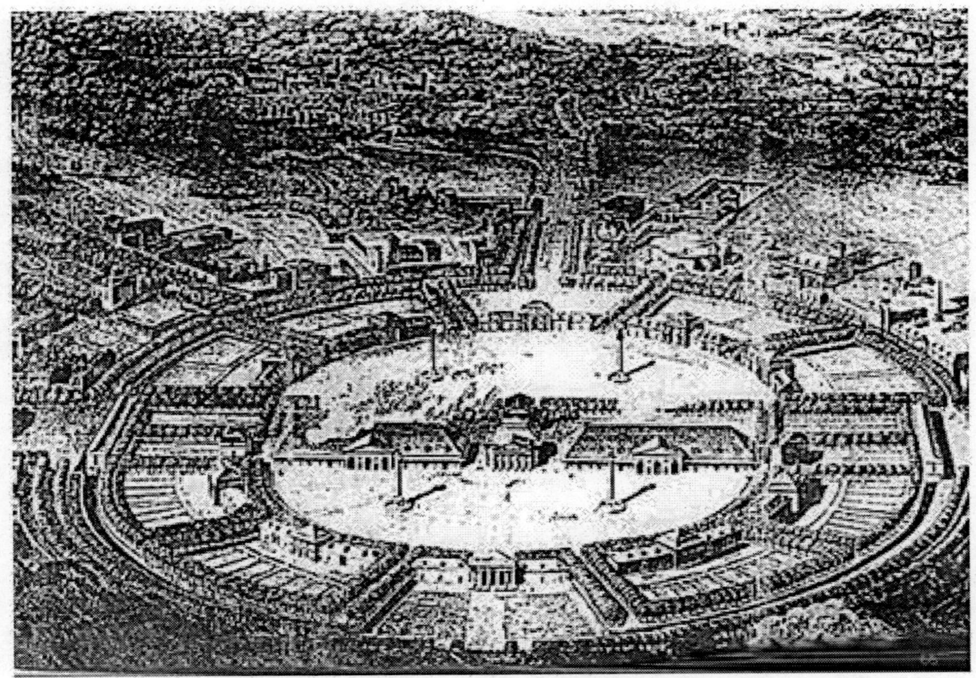

Fig. 2.50: Chaux Ideal Town (18th Century)

Fig. 2.51: Venice-Piazza de St. Marco

Fig. 2.52: Piazza del Campo Siena, Italy

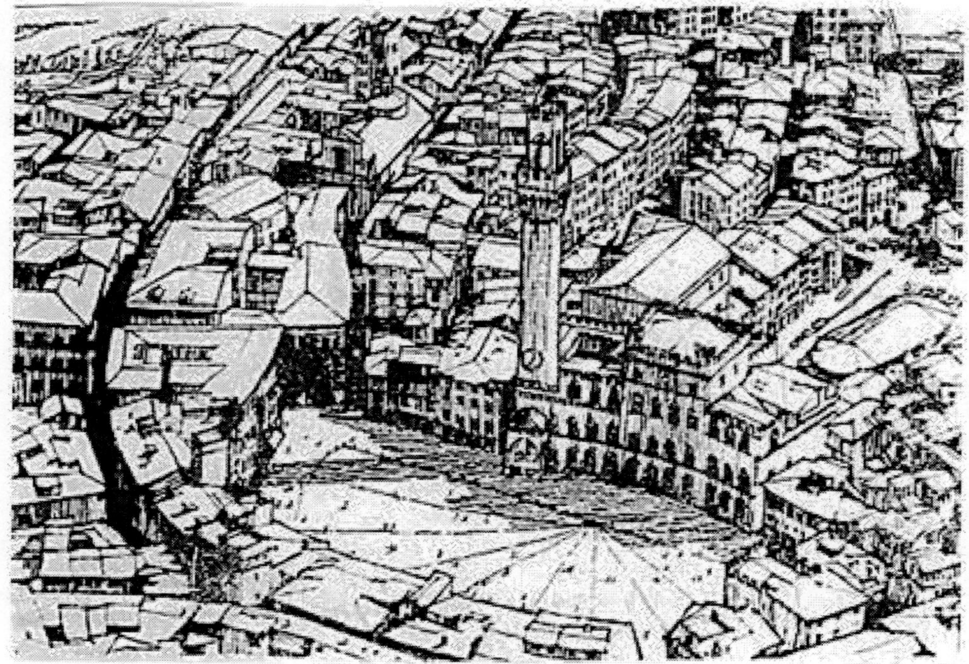

Fig. 2.53: Piazza del Campo Siena, Italy

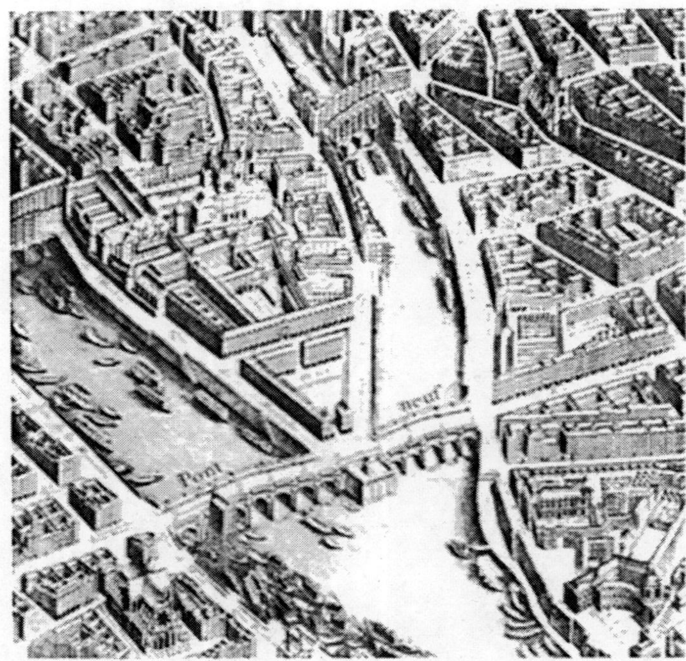

Fig 2.54: Medieval Paris (early 17th century print from Hiorns)

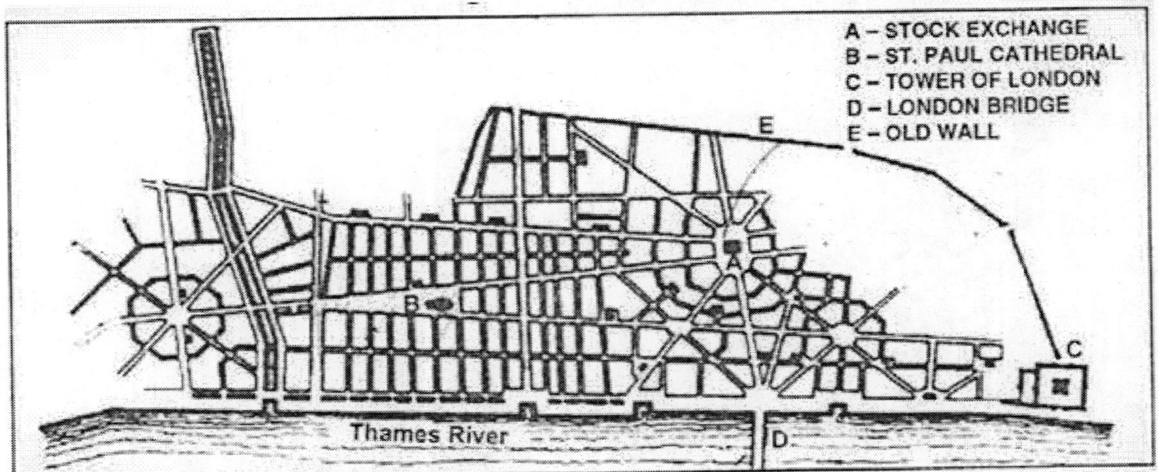

Fig 2.55: London was built on the river Thames which was dominated by cathedrals and churches, the circus, royal crescent and parks. The present London is credited to Christopher Wren (1666) who restructured the city after great fire.

Fig. 2.56: Monument to Victor Emmanuel II (1885-1911), with which many architects, including Sacconi, Koch Piacentini, Manfredi and Bernini were associated

Fig. 2.57: Canale Grande layout with Church of Antonio di Padova at end of Vista Trieste, 1826-49 (Peter von Nobile)

Fig. 2.58: Amsterdam-Network of canals developed mainly for trade and transport.

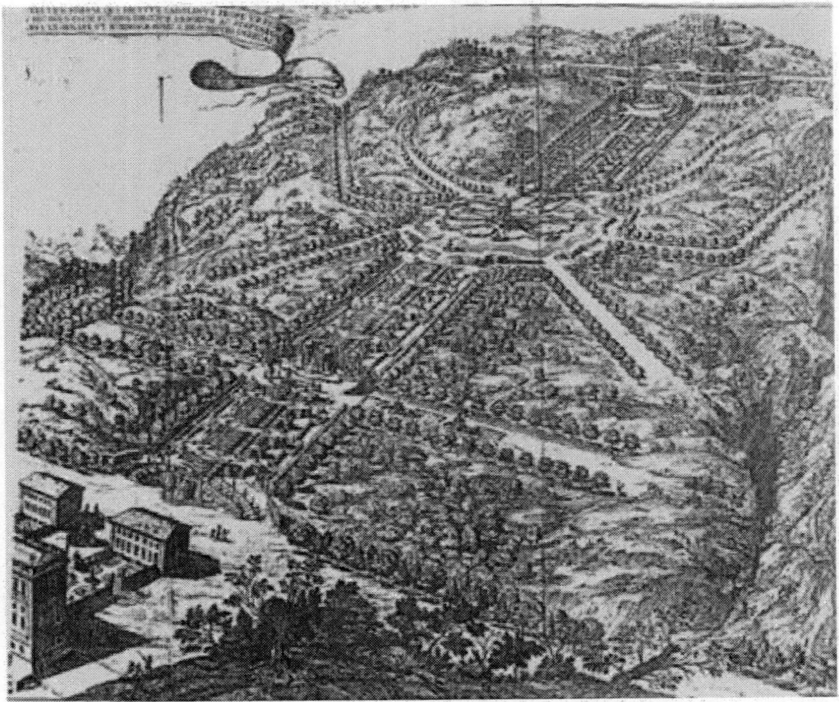

Fig. 2.59: This 1706 engraving by Alessandro Specchi of Wilbelmshahe, Hesse-Kessel, shows the huge array of cascades, of which only the upper third was completed.

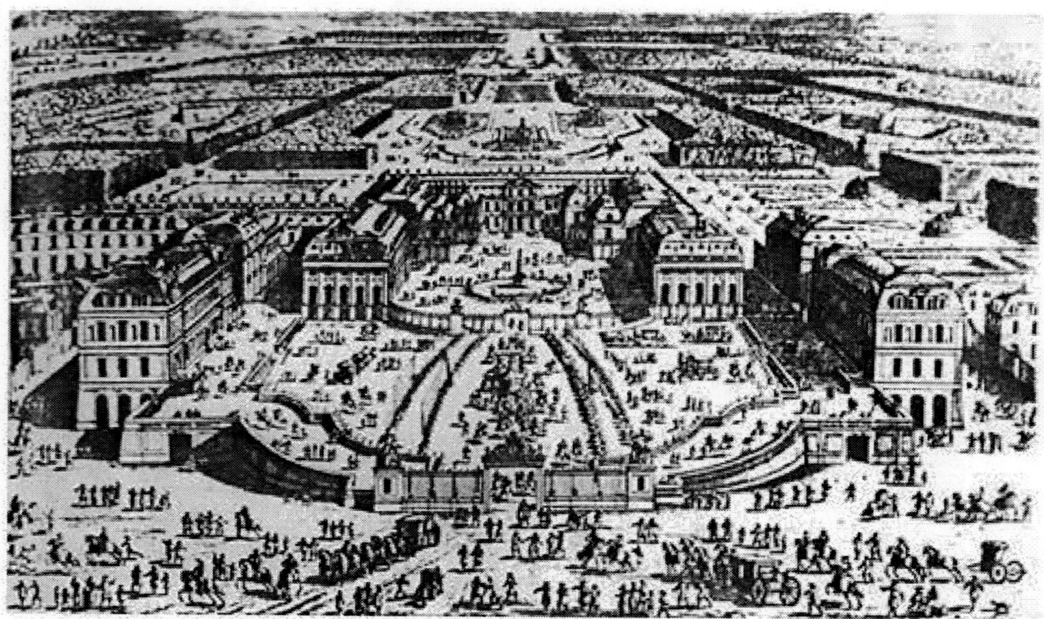

Fig. 2.60: Park and Palace Ensemble, Versailles, France

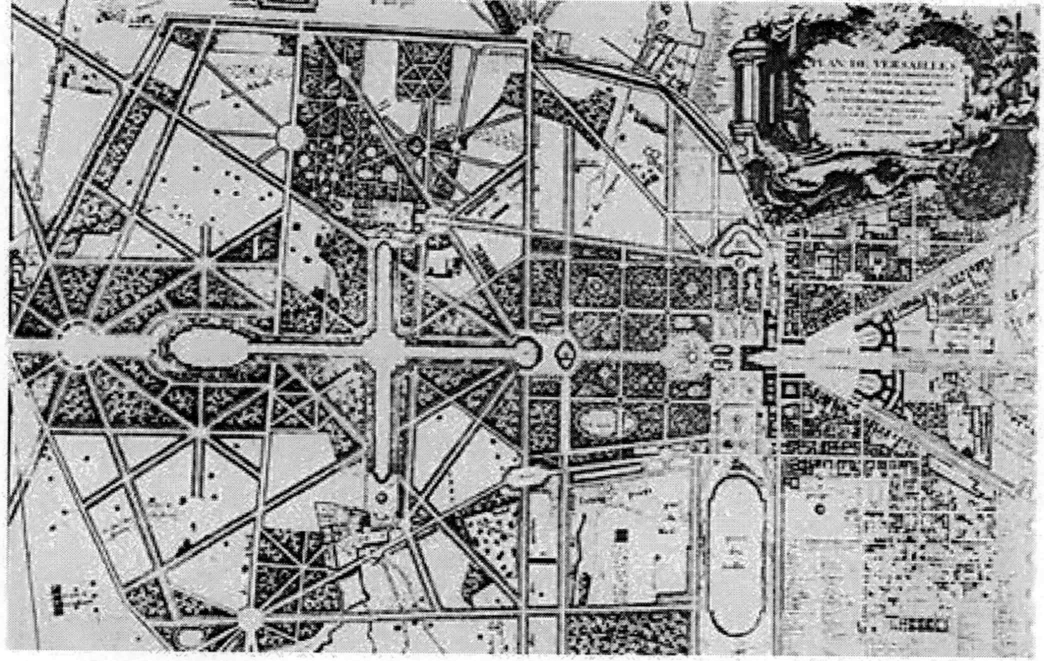

Fig. 2.61: Gardens of Versailles (1746) : The Vaux le Vicomte André Le Nôtre. The garden spans more than 1,000 acres and encapsulates the essence of a Baroque-era landscape in the French formal style asserted monarchical power and taste.

Fig. 2.62: Karlsruhe was designed to radiate from the Palace de la Concorde which is the most magnificent feature of the city, designed by Jacques Ange Gabriel during reign of Louis XV

Syncretic Cities in India

India's connection with Iran goes back to the third century BC when the Mauryan Empire modelled itself on Achaemenid Empire of Iran. In Patliputra, the Capital of Maurya Dynasty, a royal palace was erected on a plan inspired by that of Achaemenid palatial hall at Takht-e-Jamshid (Persepolis). In the wake of Alexanders's conquest the Achaemenid and Greek legacy gave rise to the syncretic art in India. This is reflected by the third century BC capital Rampurva in Bihar and Achaemenid capital with sculptures of lions and humped bull. During this time Buddhism extended to East Iranian land under Kushans, besides other countries. Buddhism absorbed Iranian concepts and figural iconography from Hellenistic Iran. This gave birth to a remarkable syncretism in arts, sculpture and architecture.

During the 6th to 8th centuries the traders from Africa and Middle East arrived in Kerala and Gujarat where they established themselves as a part of the fishing and trading community. In the North, the Muslims from Central Asia established themselves by way of conquest that triggered the spread of Islamic cultures.

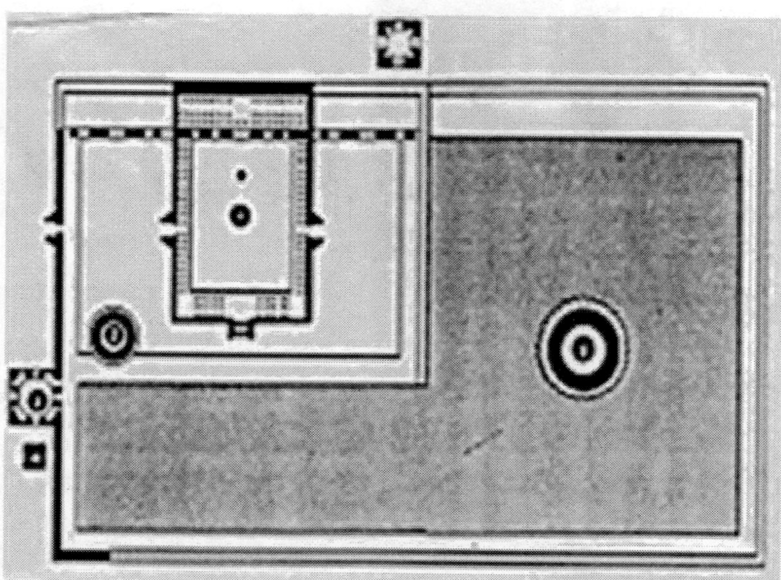

Fig. 2.63: Plan of Qutab Minar Complex, Mahrauli, Delhi

Fig. 2.64: Mosque built from recycled pillars of Hindu Temples at Mehrauli (Qutab Complex), Delhi

In the 11th Century, a ruler of Eastern Iran, Mahmud of Ghazna invaded North-Western India and integrated part of it into Ghaznavid Sultanate. Vernacular traditions of the sub-continent are visible in the early mosques, minarets and mausoleums. The Qutb Minar in Delhi, an iconic pillar built in the late 12th century, does not look Iranian. The Arhai din ka Jhompra at Ajmer built in the early 1200s and the tomb of Iltutmish in Delhi which dates back to 1235 AD are the torch bearers of syncretic arts and Indo-Iranian aesthetics, where aisles supported by intricately carved pillars adapted or recycled from broken Hindu temples.

Fig. 2.65: Qutab Minar at Mehrauli, Delhi

The Mughals

The Mughals, derived from Mongols, traced their ancestry to Chengiz Khan. The Mughal Empire began with Zahir-ud-Din Muhammad Babur (1483-1530) who descended from Taimur. He captured Kabul in 1504 and occupied Delhi and Agra in 1526 after defeating the Lodhis. His father Omar Sheikh Mirza was the ruler of the Fergana Valley, Uzbekistan and brought Timrid heritage as well as the Persian architecture of Samarkand and Herat. Babur's son Humayun (1530-40, 1555-56) and his grandson Akbar (1556-1605) stretched the empire from Kandhar in the north and Bengal in the east. Akbar built the ephemeral capital Fatehpur Sikri (1571-85), besides many other forts, gardens, mosques and tombs. Mughals introduced new ways of city planning, as Emperor Babur upon seizing Delhi declared that "everywhere that was habitable, should be constructed with waterwheels to create running water and make planned, geometric spaces."

The Mughals borrowed frequently from other cultures, adapting elements to their new settings. The resultant Mughal forms of arts and architecture became over time closely interrelated with the wider urban artefacts of its period. Delhi, Lahore and Kabul pre-dated the Mughals, but they were significantly transformed in part during the 16th to early18th centuries. These cities became torch bearer of a cosmopolitan culture that embraced diverse facets of society, trade and commerce, arts, architecture and culture. The second Mughal emperor Humayun and his successor Akbar were influenced by Nasir-al-Din Tusi's well known treatise Akhlaq-i-Nasiri (1235). It taught respect for diversity and values of justice, tolerance and the pursuit of cultural excellence in the creation of a pluralistic society.

Fig. 2.66: Persian Wheel

Their finest surviving examples, such as Humayun Tomb in Delhi, Shalimar Garden in Lahore and Kashmir, Taj Mahal in Agra, Fatehpur Sikri and Red Fort in Agra, remain enduring expression of beauty in the built environment. These monuments and gardens have fascinated and attracted people from all walks of life for centuries. These are the bold juxtaposition of Iranian and Indian designs melting seamlessly. With the accession of Akbar's son Jahangir to power in 1605, these ideals continued to prevail.

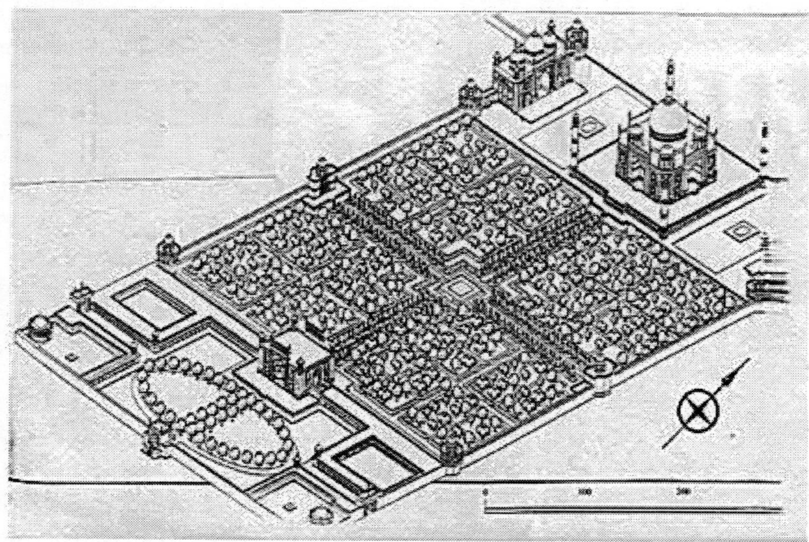

Fig. 2.67: Plan of Char Bagh, Taj Mahal, Agra

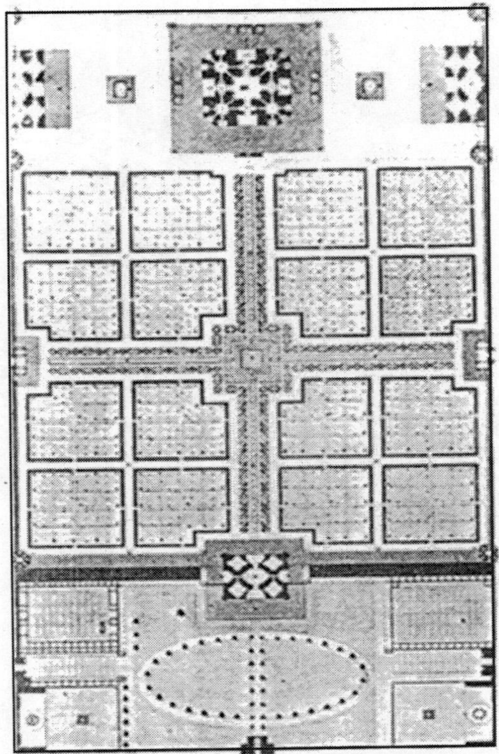

Fig 2.68: Agra: Plan of tomb and gardens of the Taj Mahal. Garden is 800 feet wide and 975 feet from the gate to the tomb

Source: Archaeological Survey of India drawing by J.H Hodgston (1828)

The Mausoleum of Atgah Khan in Delhi built during Akbar's rule is a fine example of the Hindustani-Iranian styles. The stone polychromy, calligraphy and geometric patterns are handled with perfection.

Fatehpur Sikri (the city of victory), where Akbar's son Jahangir was born in 1569, was the Capital of Hindustan until 1585, when Akbar moved his seat of empire to Lahore. The Jami Masjid retains elements of Iranian architectural model with rich colours of stone and numerous chattris, which provide an Indian touch. Buland Darwaza, 40 m high gateway has a pink and white palette of tile masonry with the chhatris on its top. The Panch Mahal with its five superposed levels draws on the vernacular heritage of Sind. The colonnaded structure open on all sides acts as a transition building between the semi-public spaces that surround the Daulat Khana courtyard.

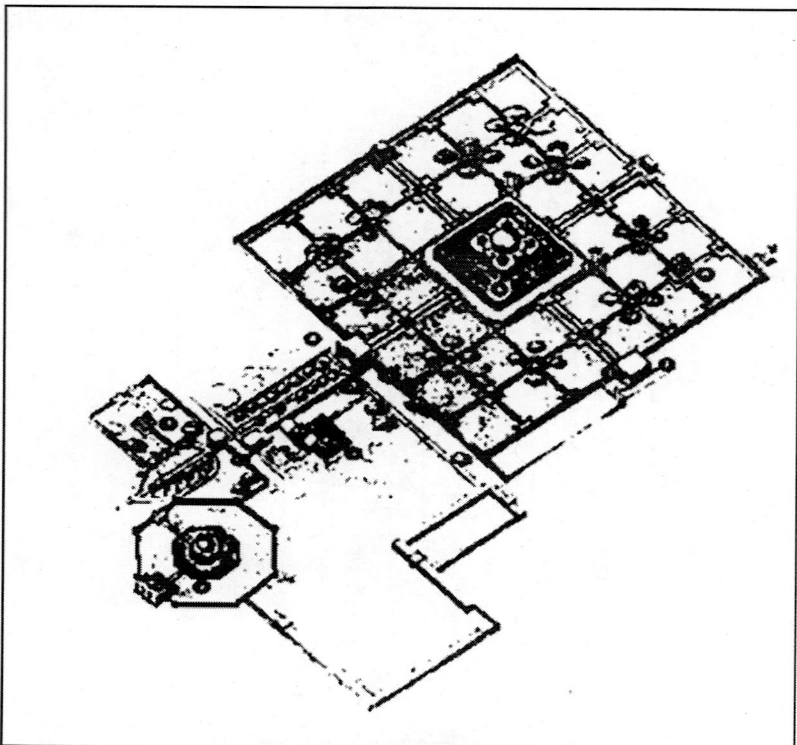

Fig. 2.69: Humayun Tomb Complex

Fig. 2.70: Humayun Tomb, New Delhi

Set within the Jami Masjid, the white marble Salim Chishti tomb occupies a prominent position opposite the Buland Darwaza, which was built to honour the Sufi Saint, who predicted the birth of Jahangir. The Anup Talao is profusely ornamented chamber, referred to as a pavilion of the Turkish Sultana. Akbar used this structure to receive visitors and honoured guests. The Anup Talao or peerless pool was built on wide platform to the north of the imperial apartments (mahal-i-khas) courtyard. The mini tank and canal cools the air in the vicinity of the royal living quarters. Diwan-i-Khas is a small building with a massive ornamental column at its centre upon which sits a massive capital with four jali lined bridges. It is said that this structure was used for religious discussions or as a music house. Diwan-i-Aam (public audience hall) was the place where the emperor made his daily public appearance and was also used for court ceremonies and the reception of guests.

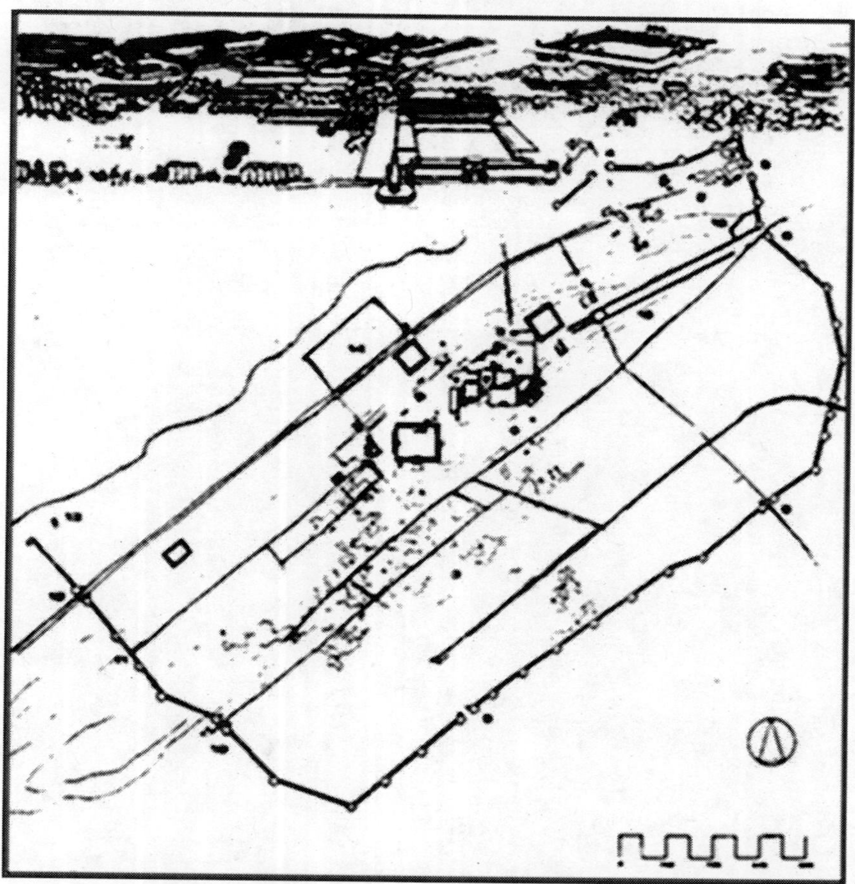

Fig 2.71: Plan of Fatehpur Sikri

Fig. 2.72: Panch Mahal, Fatehpur Sikri

Fig. 2.73: Agra Fort, Agra

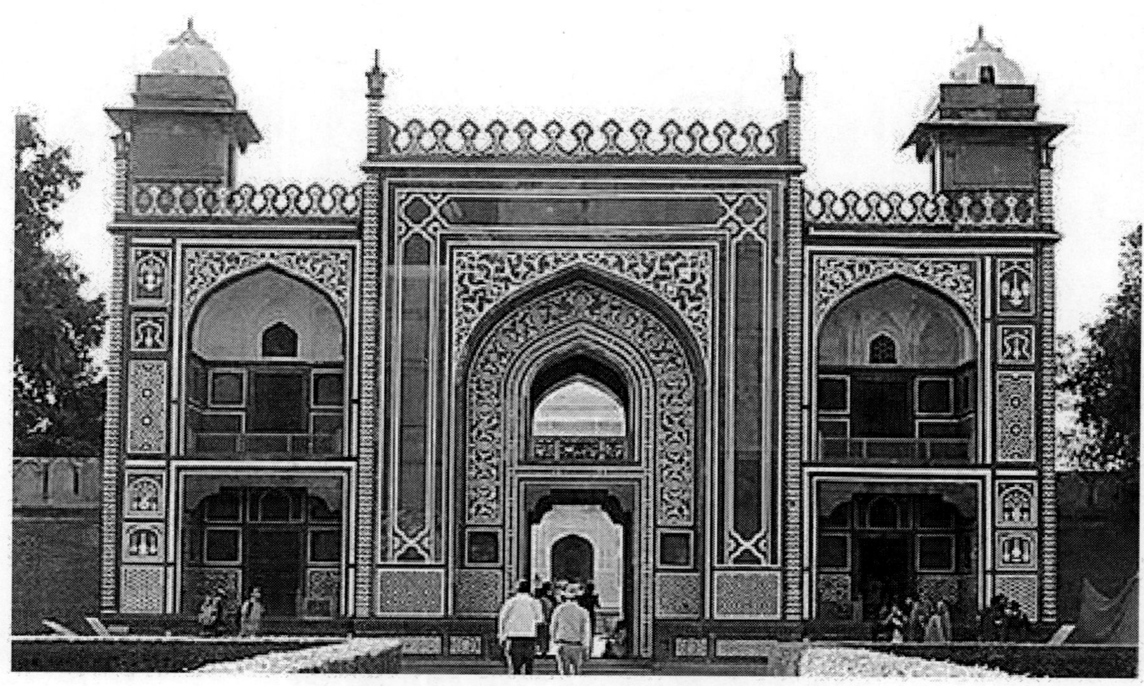

Fig. 2.74: Itmad Daula's Tomb, Agra

The ultimate example of this metamorphosis is the mausoleum, known as Taj Mahal, erected in 1631 over the Shahjahan's Iranian spouse Mumtaj Mahal. The Taj Mahal garden continued the chahar-bagh model initiated by Humayun's Tomb. Its main garden space has a fourfold plan as does the Taj Ganj village associated with it to the south and the mahtab garden to the north. The tomb itself is sited on a high riverfront plinth. The Mahtab bagh across the river was part of the original composition within a larger landscape.

After the conquest of India by the Muslims a hybrid urbanscape started. Various cities such as Lahore, Shahjahanabad, Fatehpur Sikri, Adilabad, Bhopal, Golconda, Hyderabad, Lucknow, Murshidabad and Aurangabad came up. The Taj Mahal (1650) in Agra is a climax of Mughal architecture. Agra on the banks of the Yamuna had as many as 42 river facing gardens. At the Taj Mahal, Shah Jahan's wish to build a lasting memorial to his wife, Mumtaz Jahan, overwhelms the senses in its extravagance. The plan conforms to a char bagh (four square) order, with a main axis connecting a red sandstone entry pavilion. Along both major and cross axes are water channels; the main axis is delineated by rows of cypress trees.

Fig. 2.75: Qutab Minar drawn by John Luard

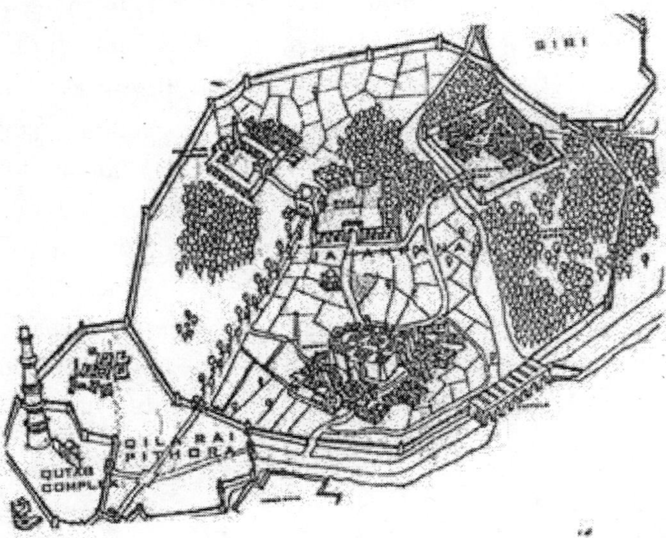

Fig. 2.76: Historical cities of Delhi, like Mehrauli, Quila Rai Pithora, Jahanpanah and Siri had large parks within and around them

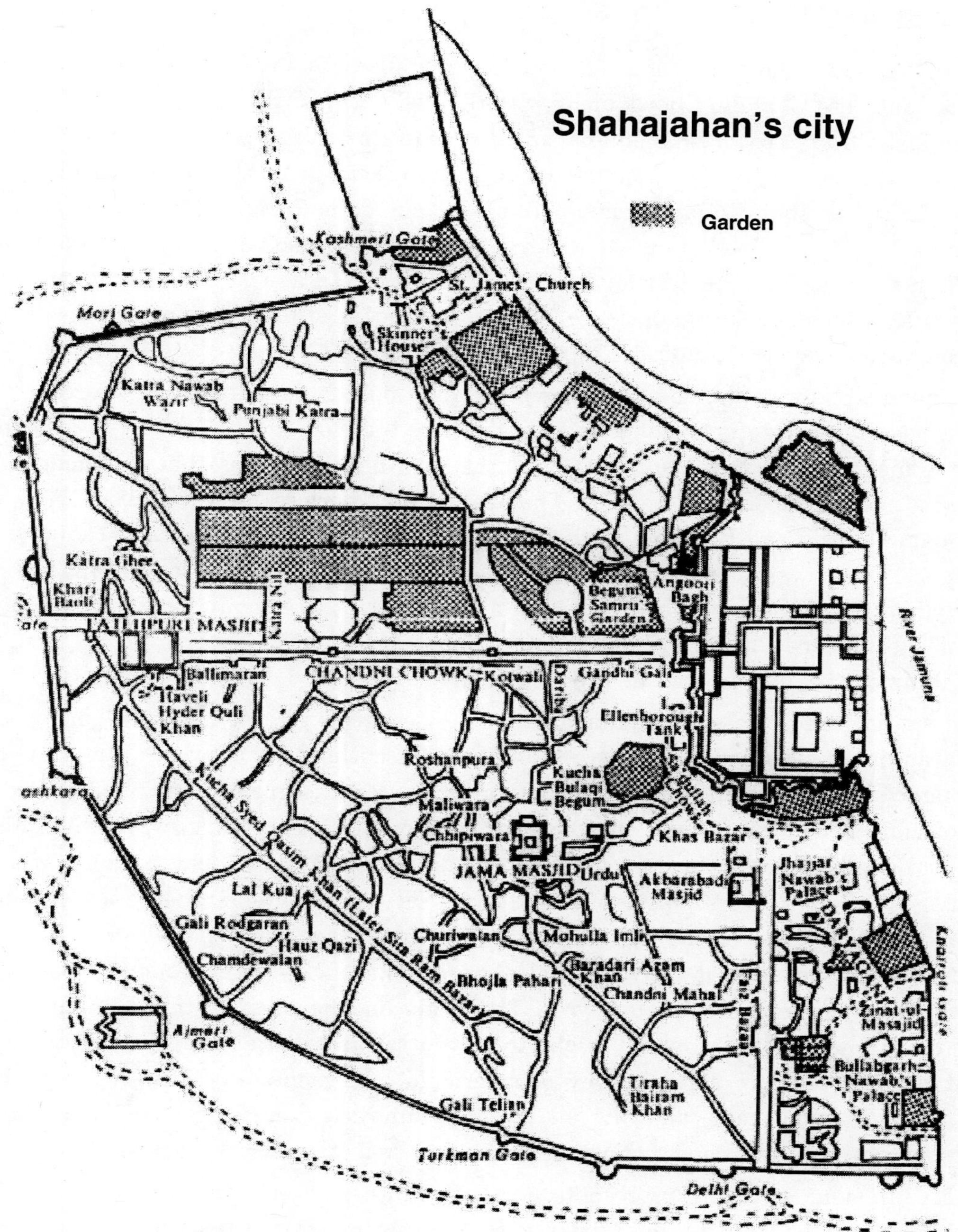

Fig. 2.77: The traditional cities in India, like the Shahjahanabad had been structured on the basis of mohallas or the communities according to the occupations. The residential units (katra, havelis) invariably had a courtyard. These form a network of introvert open spaces, which could be about one third of the built up area. The public gardens were usually in the royal segments and around public buildings.

Source: India Office Library, London

Shahjahanabad

Shahjahanabad, built during 1638-1656, immortalises Shahjahan. Its centrepiece was shopping boulevard Chandni Chowk along with the Red Fort and the Jama Masjid. Shahjahan built the magnificent city of Shahjahanabad with wide streets and parks, which were located along the river and to the north of the Indraprastha, said to be the city of the Pandavas, around which Ferozshah Kotla, Humayun Tomb, Nizamuddin, Purana Kila, Tughlakabad and Mehrauli exist. The city wall had 14 gates connecting it to various highways leading to Agra, Kabul, Lahore, Ajmer, Calcutta, Delhi (Mehrauli), Kashmir, etc. and other gates commemorated its great predecessors (Turkman, etc.). Shahjahanabad is still a thriving city, which has embraced various syncretic cultures during last 380 years.

Shahjahanabad was planned along the river Yamuna, which was a major source of water and was used for navigation, connecting Agra, where the earlier Mughal capital existed. Ali Mardan Canal supplied water to the city and the river had numerous ghats all along. It also provided a natural defence to the city. The Walled City encloses an area about 1700 acres having Jama Masjid and Red Fort as the nodal points. Three main boulevards radiated from Red Fort. The first was Chandni Chowk with a canal in the middle; the second was the Jama Masjid while the third one led to Delhi Gate. The other three main streets radiated from Jama Masjid towards Chandni Chowk, Ajmeri Gate and Turkman Gate. It was reputed to be one of the most beautiful cities in the Orient.

The spatial form of the Shahjahanabad comprises introvert open spaces, narrow lanes, compact and high density. The variety of land uses has richness of activities round the clock. The organic character of the city is striking, strongly reminiscent of pattern of nature. The power of indigenous form of the walled city derives from a spatial context where the intimacy of physical expression results from a close packing of components. Behind blank walls and dark narrow alleys 30 to 40 per cent of the spatial envelope is in the series of internal courtyards, where most of the activities of living take place. The spatial structure of the community corresponds to its occupational division. The unclean occupations cluster on the periphery-low lying areas or in the west. The trade and business of the dominant groups occupy the prime locations, usually high lands, central areas or north side. The patches of occupational clusters are separated by open ground and community facilities, e.g. chowk, chopal, temple and bazaar, allowing all levels to interact. Sometimes the boundaries are simply common walls of houses, courtyards, or streets between groups of houses.

The settlement structure represents a closely knit orthogonal fabric with an introvert character. The clusters are clearly defined in terms of social structure. An inhabitant traditionally relates to his Mohalla, i.e. a geographical area that defines the spatial pattern of the community. Increasing social mobility now makes it difficult to relate the occupation of a man to his Mohalla, but groups related by practice or customs and geographic origin continue to cluster in specific Mohallas.

Fig. 2.78: Delhi and Surrounding Country by A. Maclure, 1857, showing the integration of Shahjahanabad with River Yamuna on one side and the Aravali Ridge on the other.

Fig 2.79: Jama Masjid (Shahjahanabad) , 19th Century Lithograph by John Daniel

Source: Jain A.K., 2010, Lutyens' Delhi, Bookwell, New Delhi

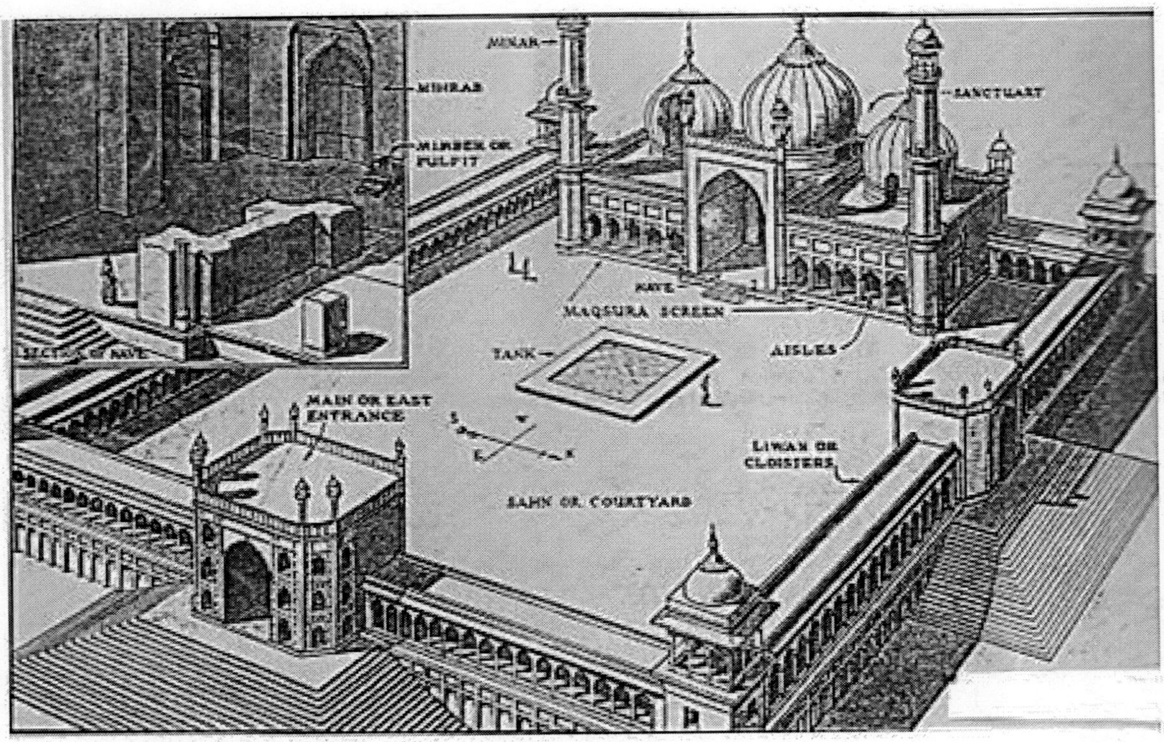

Fig 2.80: Jama Masjid, Shahjahanabad, Delhi (1650-56), was not only one of the largest mosques in the world, but also a prototype.

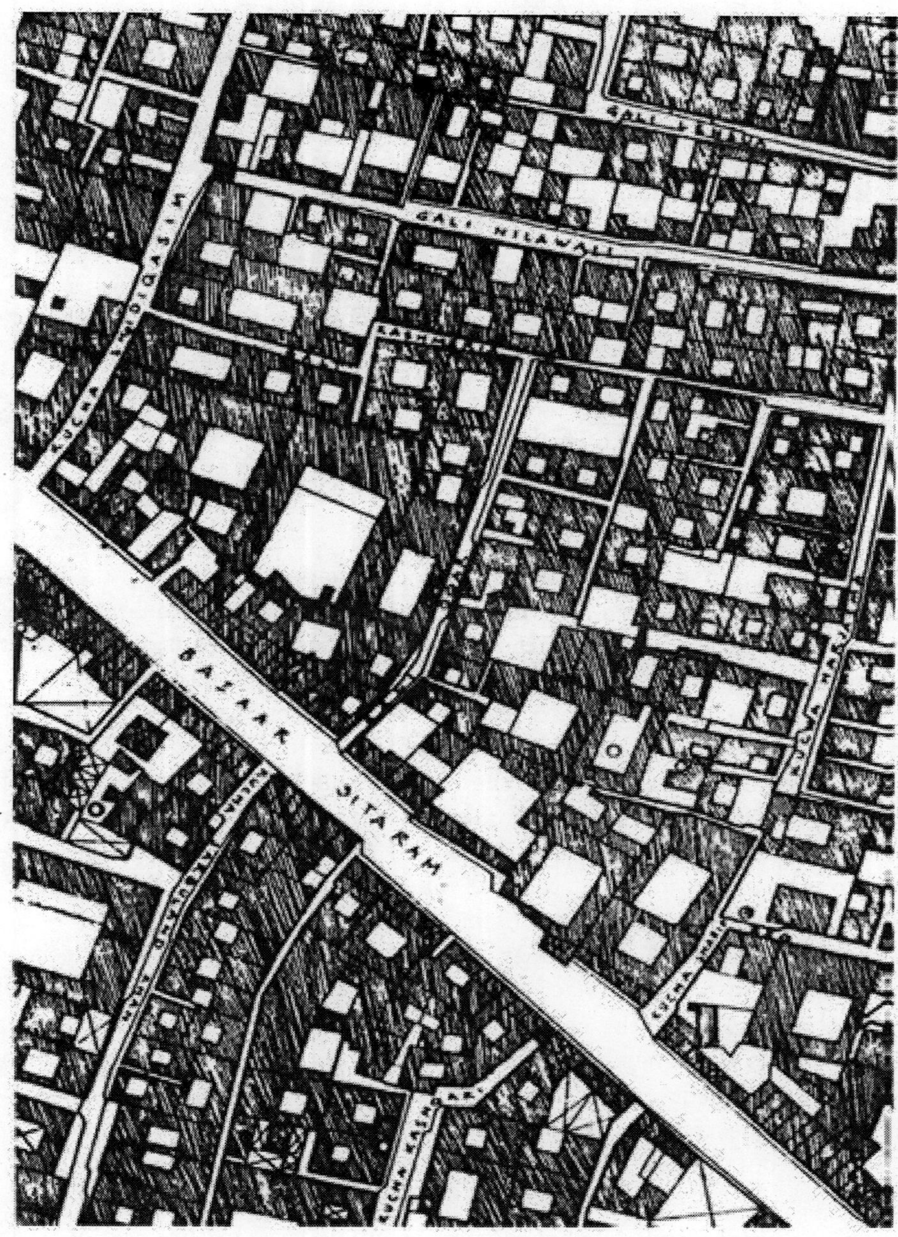

Fig. 2.81: Shahjahanabad: one third of the area is under courtyards that cool the mohalla and houses

Source: Rory Fonseca, 1976, The Walled City of Delhi, in Shelter and Societies.

Fig 2.82: Chandni Chowk, Delhi (1957)

The traditional spatial structure has a sieve like porous form. Closely knit fabric of structures help to keep out the harsh sun and provides shaded courtyards and streets. During the night, the open courtyards radiate out the heat and creating a cooling effect. Thus the form, based upon the principle of thermal comfort through passive means, presents a framework of energy conscious design. The indigenous settlement is a working model of closely knit and self-contained community. Its spatial structure is a logical outgrowth of viable set of social and economic norms governing the community and individual behaviour. The focal point of mohalla in this traditional morphology is the chopal. This is often a semi-public open space at the junction of streets, or at the termination of gali, which acts as a connector between different mohallas and communities. Though chopals apparently appear as left over spaces in a confined environment, the fact that there is no encroachment is an indication of the great value that the community attaches to them. The chopal has a sacrosanct and symbiotic imagery, where the elders and community leaders often meet to take the decisions and to exchange information. Its sanctity is accentuated by a temple or a mosque, invariably located adjacent to the chopal. Around the chopal there is generally a communal or service activity (like a well) serving to daily needs. There is general community agreement and unwritten principle of its use and sequence of events: washing of clothes, playing, smoking hookah, meetings or occasional festival, marriage or other rituals. The temple or a mosque is not only a place of worship but serves as an institution of learning and a centre of community activities.

The custom of purdah required that women be shielded from the gaze of passers-by, as such a street face high blank walls, and women's courtyards are located in the rear. The privacy is protected by a series of spatial envelopes according to the spatial continuum. First degree of privacy is provided by the interior courtyard which is the exclusive domain of women. Second degree of privacy is defined by the land outside the door, which is accessible to the members of family and their relations. Third level of privacy is the boundary of the Mohalla, which is the domain of the local residents. These zones of privacy are reflected in a sequence of public, semi-public and private domain of spaces, including streets, chowks and the chopal. The degree of privacy increases with the depth. Within a house, the privacy increases on upper floors and intermediate terraces offering exclusive privacy.

Fig 2.83: Red Fort, Delhi

An outside observer sees the irregular streets as a pattern of dark voids between buildings and is apt to arrive at an erroneous conclusion. Behind the narrow dark lanes, bounded by blank walls, are sunny courtyards where most of the activities take place. The courts act as the node of horizontal and vertical circulation. The transitional elements, e.g. veranda, entrance and gate are highly pronounced, while the services are located on the periphery of the houses.

After the arrival of East India Company, the Mughal empire started flickering. After the defeat in 1803, the Mughal Emperor. Akbar II (1806-37) was a protectorate of East India Company. Shahjahan's jewel Peacock Throne had left India. Bahadurshah II was the last Mughal Emperor enthroned in Red Fort, below the emblematic scale of justice carved into white marble wall. The king of the world was now simply powerless king of Delhi. With the uprising of 1857 his reign and Mughal empire came to an end. The East India Company was replaced by British Crown. As Mughal rule waned and British authority gradually assumed control of India. Besides exploiting the country's resources, they introduced industries, a new pattern of irrigation for agricultural, canal systems, communication, railways and other transportation systems.

Some Other Cities

Besides Mughal cities, many other cities were coming up in various parts of the country, e.g. Rajasthan (Ajmer, Jaipur), Central India (Mandu, Burhanpur, Aurangabad), Gujarat (Ahmedabad, Baroda, Surat), South India (Hyderabad, Golconda, etc.).

Fig. 2.84: Palitana, the holy place of Jains, presents a unique sight with over 800 temples crowned with marble aspires dotting the hill slope. Having faced destruction from the invaders, the hill was enclosed with high wall.

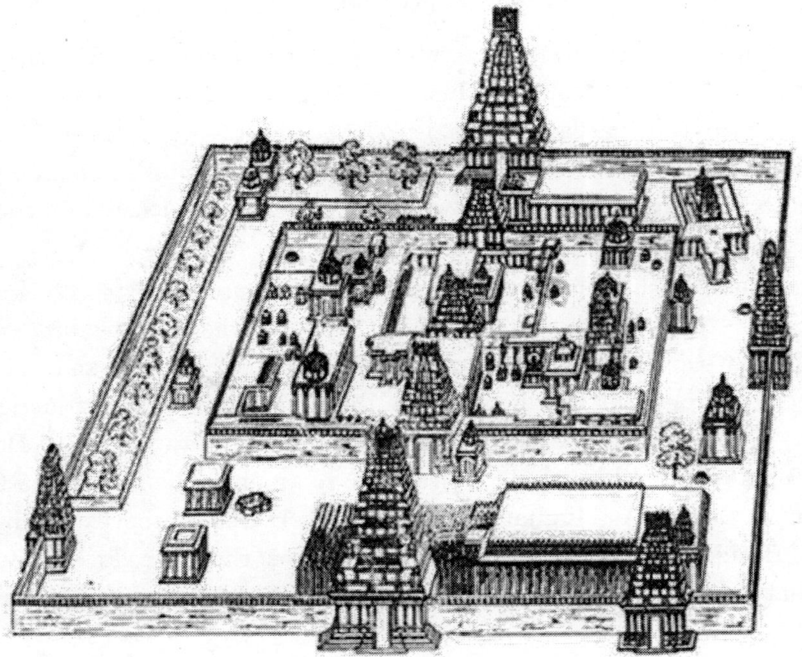

Fig. 2.85: Temple Town of Thiruvanamalai, Tamil Nadu, Sketch by Sitaram, 1832.

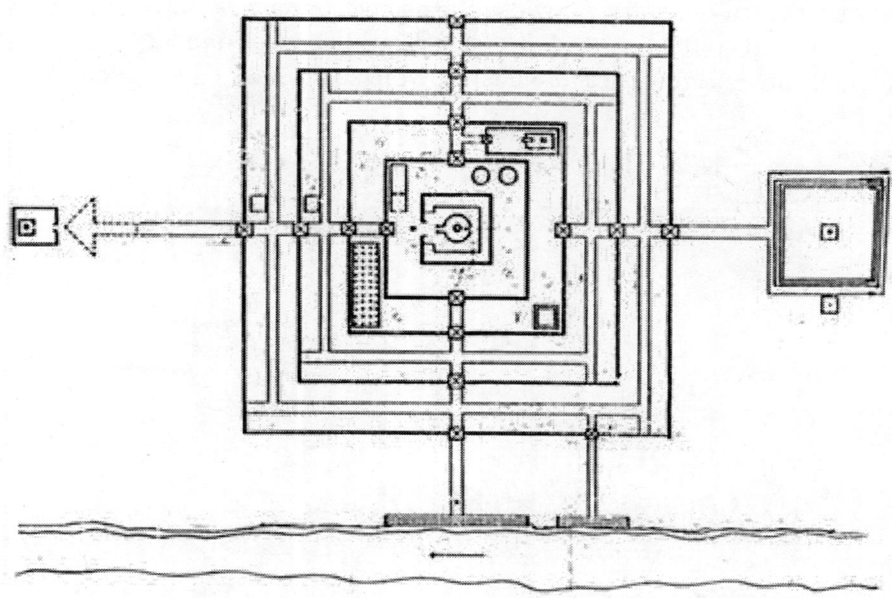

Fig. 2.86: Schematic Plan of a Temple City according to Mansara

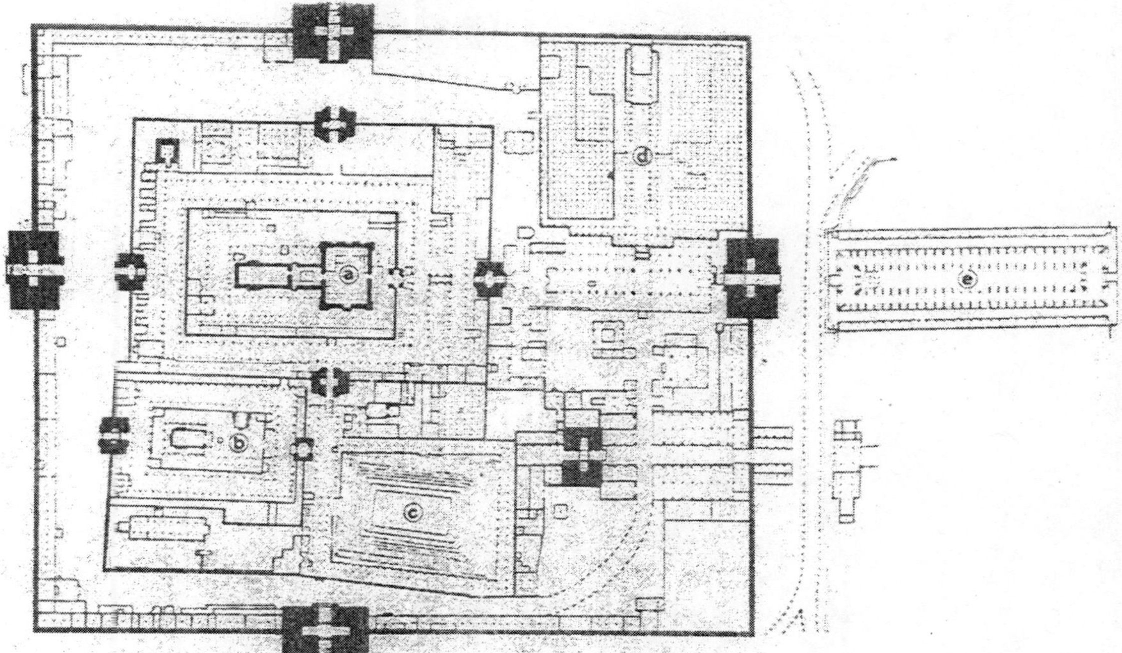

Fig.: 2.87: Temple city of Srirangam, Tamil Nadu (14th century), comprises seven concentric enclosures, each with a gopuram of receding size, all focusing towards the inner sacred shrine

Source: Vistara, The Architecture of India (1986)

The Manasara (Vastu Shashtra) provides the geometric concept of vastu purush mandala, which translates prakriti into physical form. The Vāstu Purusha Mandala depicts the position of various planets on a time-space dimension which provides basic principles of spatial organisation.

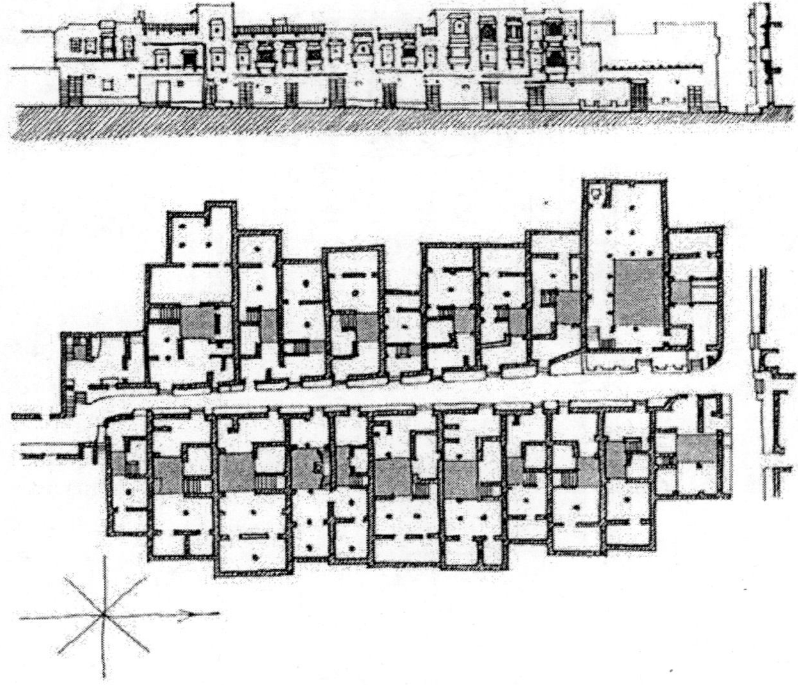

Fig. 2.88: Jaisalmer: Typical residential street (after Kulbhushan Jain)

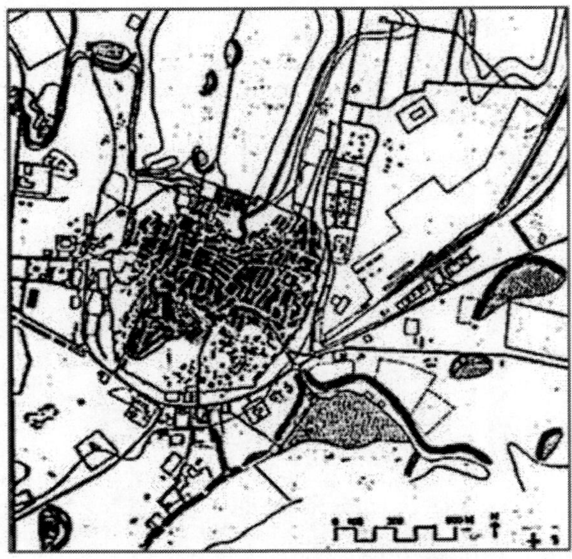

Fig. 2.89: Plan of Jaisalmer

Fig. 2.90: Jaisalmer: Narrow compact streets with courtyard buildings provide cool, shaded space and streets

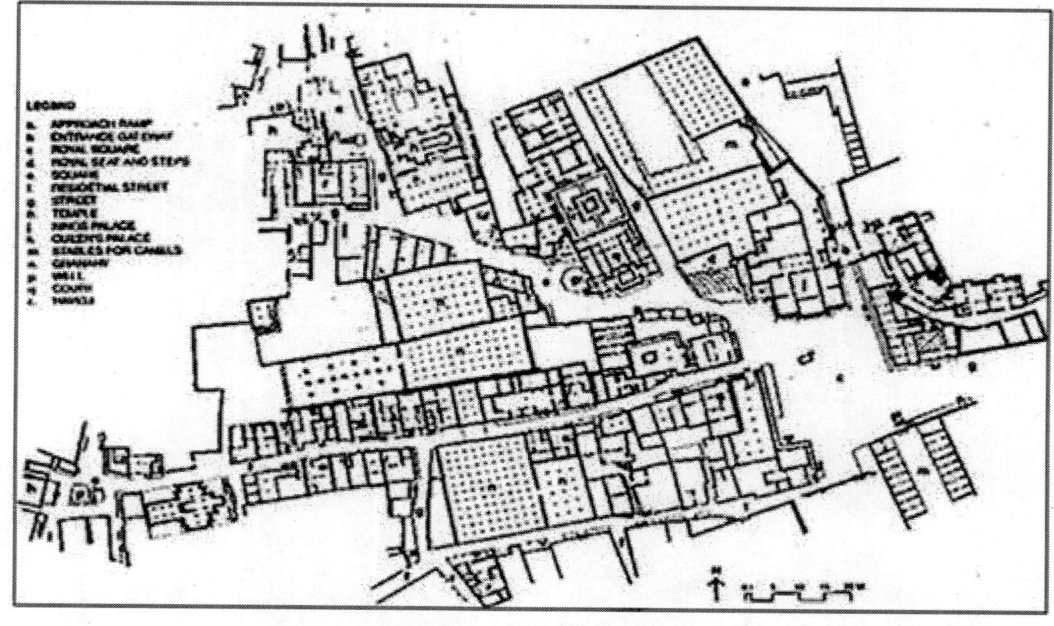

Fig. 2.91: Jaisalmer Fort

Fig. 2.92: Jaisalmer: the urban pattern responds to local culture and micro-climate

Pig. 2.93: Royal Complex, Jaisalmer

Fig. 2.94: Himmatramji Adinath Temple Bahurandhra Jalas, Jaisalmer, 1872 AD

Fig. 2.95: A Street in Jaisalmer - Intimate, Cool and Indigenous

The form of a city was derived on the principle of Vāstupurush Mandal. It established an interrelationship of physical form of asettlement with the spiritual, cosmic and behavioural system. It determined the basic form, its location and orientation of various functions in a settlement. It was interrelated with the surroundings,like the planets in the astrological chart. A system of ashtha (8),Navgrah (9 plantes), 24 matrika pithas, etc. was devised as a numerical symbolism and for orientation and linkages of the settlement system. The Mandala is a module encompassing the principles of organicity: interrelationship of parts, inter-dependence of systems, resonance and synchronicity.

In the overall urban fabric, the generic morphology manifests a labyrinthine hierarchy of social organization. It contains an introvert spatial organisation at the city level, with a highly extroverted system within the residential cluster. The extrovert spatial character is accentuated by courtyards and chowks, which enhance frequent contacts and social participation among the residents. These also serve as an efficient means of security, privacy and social control.

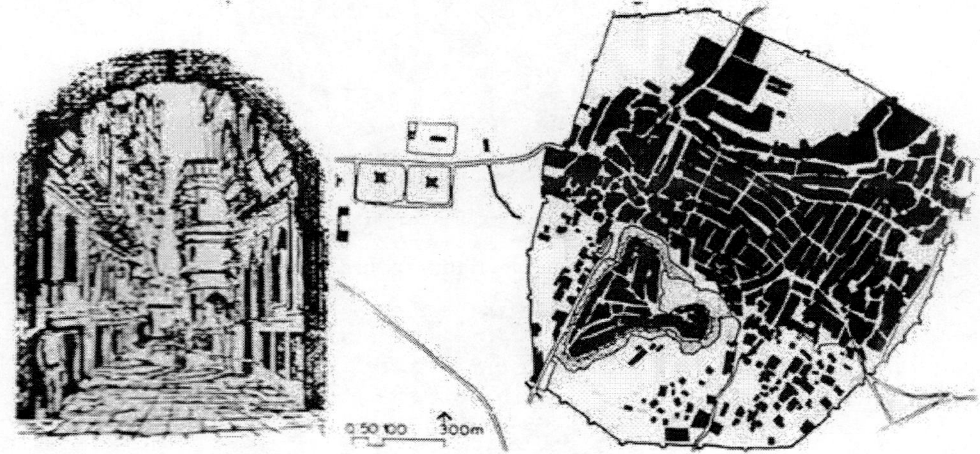

Fig. 2.96: Jaisalmer street network and facade control (Sketch by Ramesh N. Dengle)

Fig. 2.97: Street and gate, old Jaipur (B.V. Doshi)

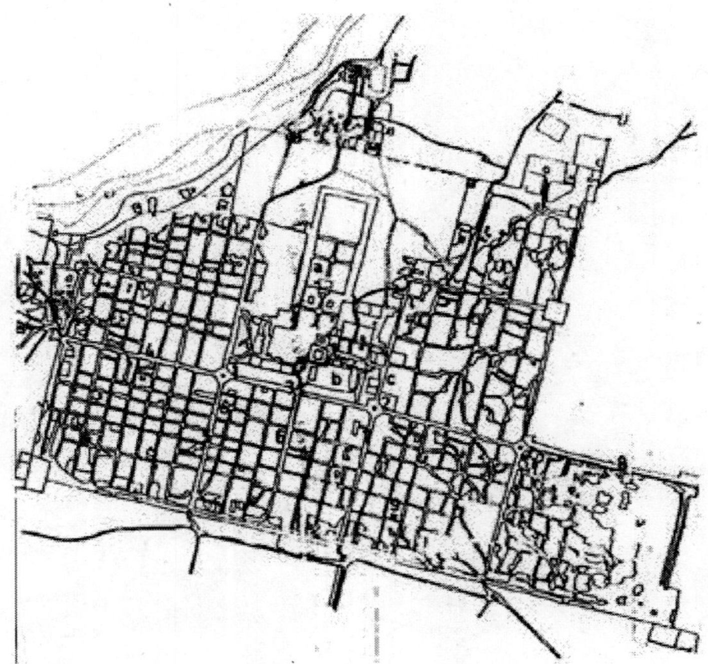

Fig. 2.98: Plan of Jaipur (1725 AD)

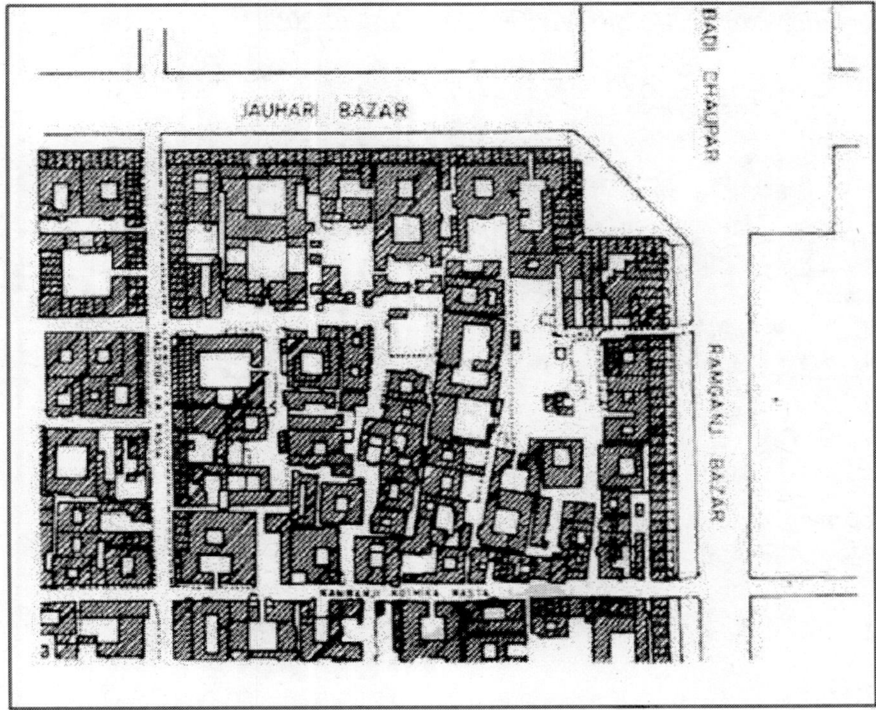

Fig 2.99: Inner city of Jaipur (Yatin Pandya)

Fig 2.100: Jantar Mantar, Jaipur

Source: Discovering Jaipur, Jaipur Virasat Foundation, 2006

Fig. 2.101: Pritam Niwas Chowk, The Palace, Jaipur

Source: Discovering Jaipur, Jaipur Virasast Foundation, 2006

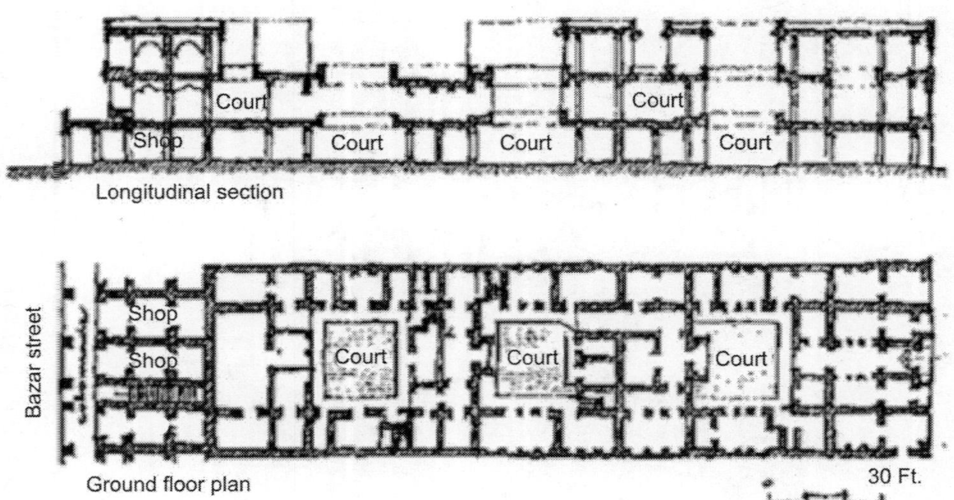

Fig. 2.102: A Large Haveli with shops on roadside and multiple courtyards, Jaipur

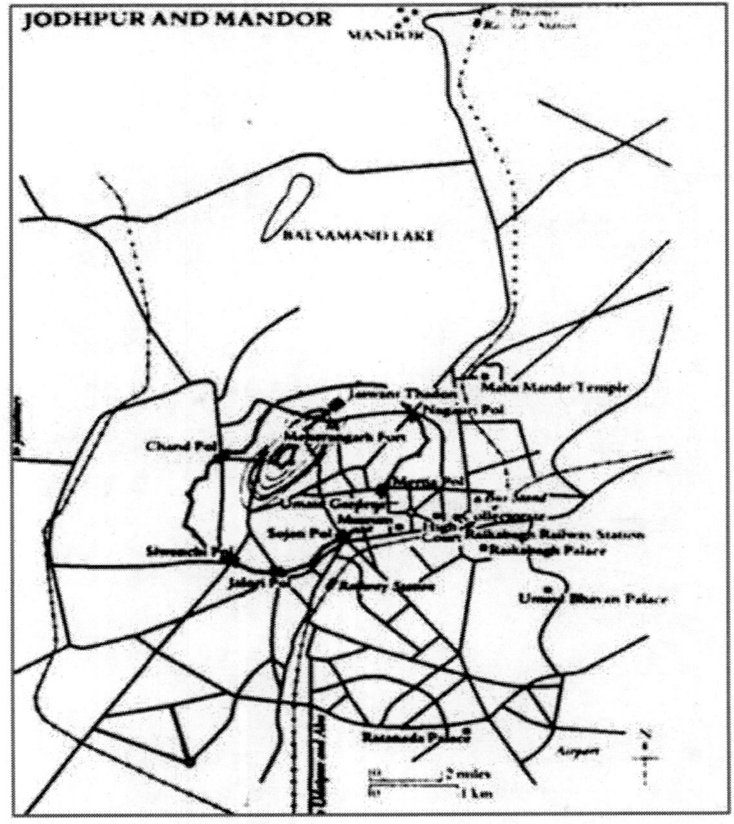

Fig. 2.103: Jodhpur and Mandor

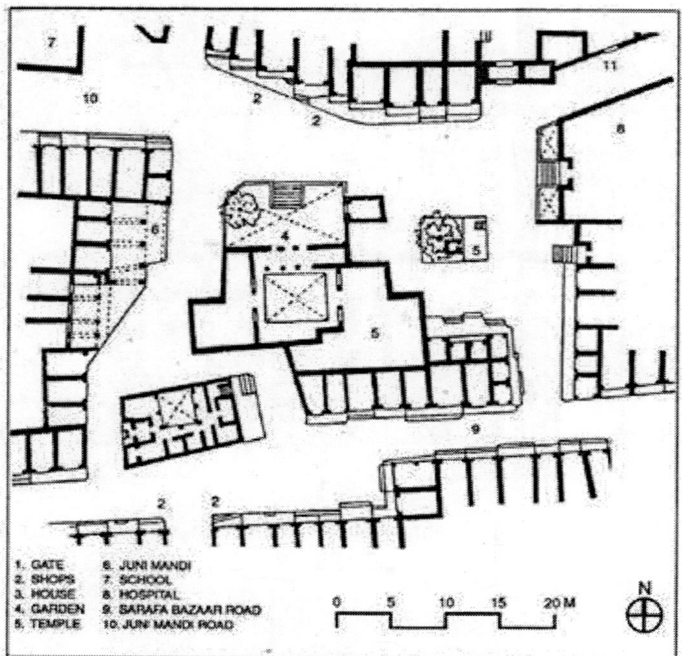

Fig. 2.104: Juni Mandi Square in Jodhpur

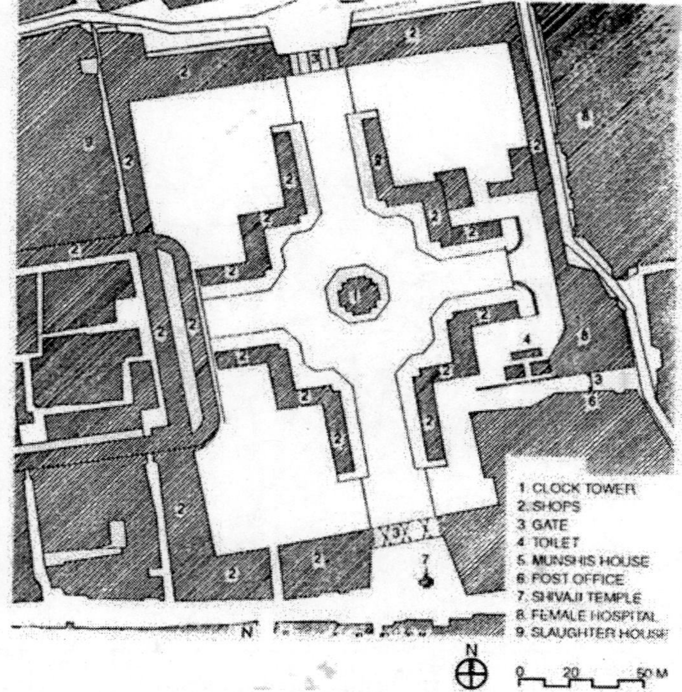

Fig. 2.105: Sardar Market Square in Jodhpur

Source; Jain, Kulbhushan

In traditional Indian cities courtyards and squares have been important climatic and socio-cultural space. There are city squares, chaurahas, and neighbourhood squares. In Jodhpur, Sardar Market square is the largest square, built by Maharaja Sardar Singh with shops and five-storey clock tower in the centre. Juni Mandi Square is a neighbourhood chowk, which is informal and organic.

The centre of city is Brahm-sthan, the divine space according to the concept of Vãstu Purusha Mandala. Surrounding the temple were the residences of Brahmins, the priests the higher castes and went on decreasing towards the boundary. All the roads originated from the temple towards the periphery. The character was maintained as per importance of the street and the inhabitants in it. The individual dwelling units were based on the category and occupations of people.

Preindustrial settlements usually developed with a coherent and balanced set of forces, endogenous and exogenous. As a life-support system, it did not often reach optimal levels of amenity, but it did produce furnishings, buildings and communities of great aesthetic consistency.

Industrial Revolution and New Urbanism

The industrial revolution saw profound influence of science and technology. Changes in building technology, invention of the steam engine and railway, motor car, telegraph, radio, electricity during the industrial revolution changed the concepts of city planning.

Fig. 2.106: The Fleet Ditch (1844) Behind the Red Lion, London Polluting the River Thames.

After the Industrial Revolution, Britain's cities faced severe problems of workers' housing, services and pollution. The advent of railways and motors changed the concept of urban mobility which needed a new type of infrastructure and wider corridors. The rapid urbanisation was not in pace with the city planning.

The industrial revolution saw the opening up of new industrial areas and cities. It led to decline of nobles and landlords and rise of industrial entrepreneurs and middle class. Changes in building technology, invention of steam engine and railway, motor car, telegraph, radio, electricity and other technologies led to development of suburbs, peri-towns and dense cities. It also gave rise to rapid urbanisation with congested shacks and shanties of the workers and the problem of pollution and public health. By 1870s many of the large cities like London, Sheffield, New York, Paris, etc. had high densities, poor services and became unhealthy with polluted and congested environment.

In response, the Garden City Movement attempted to offset negative industrial effects such as pollution. Sir Ebenzer Howard pioneered the concept of Garden City, which was applied in several new towns in UK and also in planning of Imperial Delhi by Edwin Lutyens in the early 20th century.

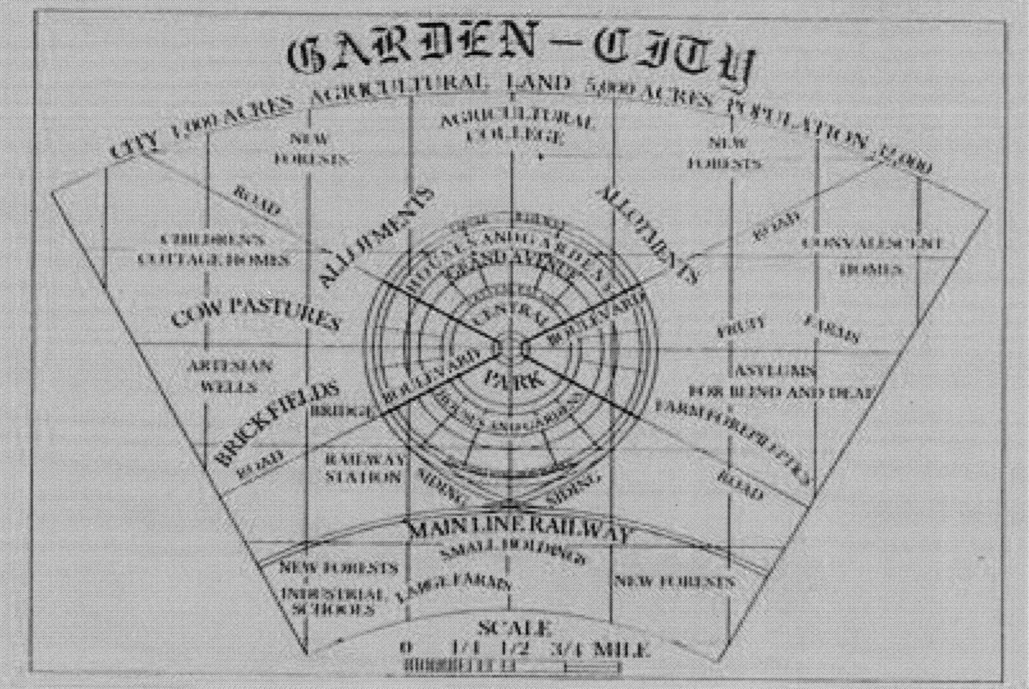

Fig. 2.107: Sir Ebenezer Howard's Garden City: The Garden City and Rural Belt cover about 1,000 acres at the center of a 6000 acre tract. It was planned for a population of 32,000. Six magnificent boulevards-each 120 feet wide traverse the city from centre to circumference, dividing it into six equal parts or wards. In the centre the circular space containing of five and a half areas, laid out as a beautiful and well-watered gardens. Each ward has ample grounds, and the larger public buildings-town hall and principal concert and lecture hall, theatre, library, museum, picture gallery and hospital.

Source: Ebenezer Howard, Garden Cities of Tomorrow (Cambridge, MA: MIT Press, 1965)

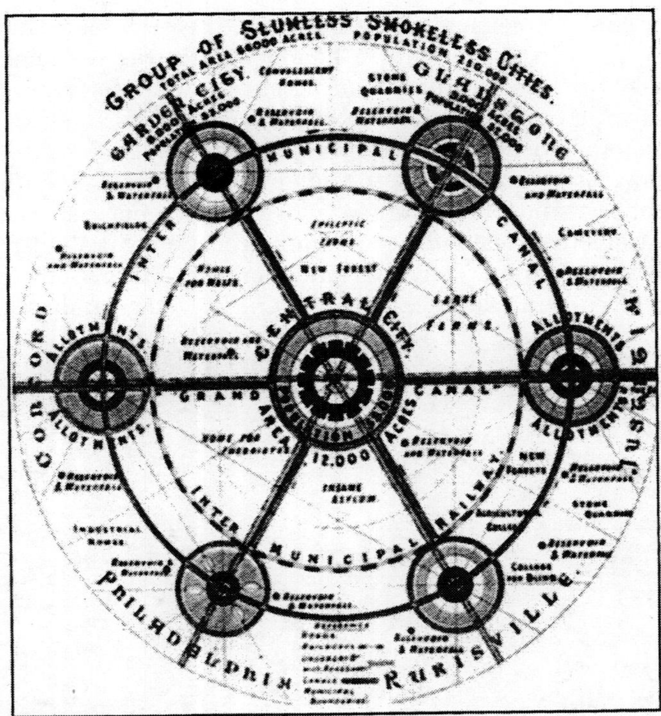

Fig. 2.108: Sir Ebenezer Howard's group of slumless, smokeless cities (1898)

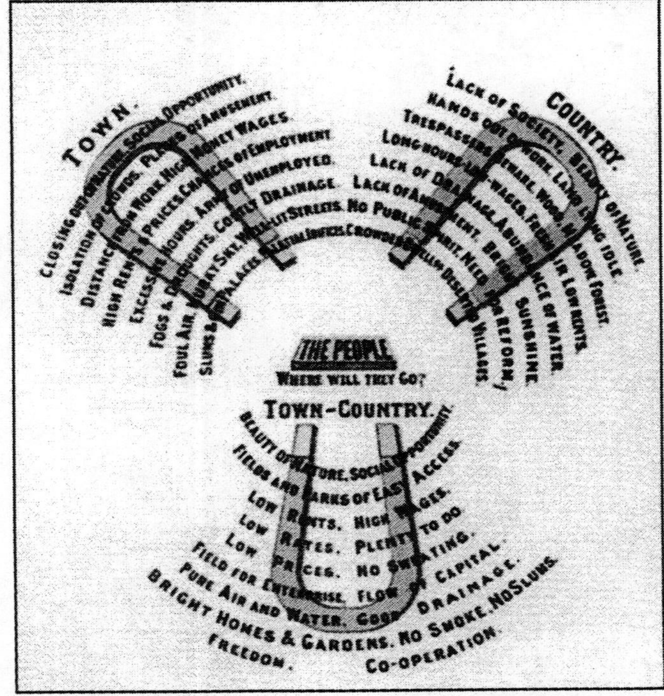

Fig. 2.109: The Three Magnets: Town-Country-People (Ebenezer Howard, 1898)

In the America, a chain of settlements grew along the east coast such as Virginia, New Port and New Amsterdam in the Manhattan Island, which was renamed as New York. The era of great metropolis witnessed a number of inventions and discovery of iron frame, steel structure and elevator which changed the face of American cities. The development of electric power and automobile, telephone, computer technology helped in sub-urbanisation of the cities. The chaotic growth of the cities led to the development of regulations and application of restrictions for light, air and plot coverage and the emergence of garden city concept by Ebenezer Howard. Various theories and city planning concepts were put forward by a number of visionaries like Patrick Geddes, Tony Garnier, Soria Y. Mata Ludwig Hilbersiemer , Le Corbusier, Lewis Mumford and Clarence Stein to enhance the quality of life in the cities.

Fig. 2.110: Paris Musee Del Ecoutes with Underground Services Tunnel (19th Century)

Fig 2.111: Frank Llod Wright's St. Mark's tower (left) and Eliel Saarinen's Tribune building

Fig 2.112: Le Corbusier's Plan Obus

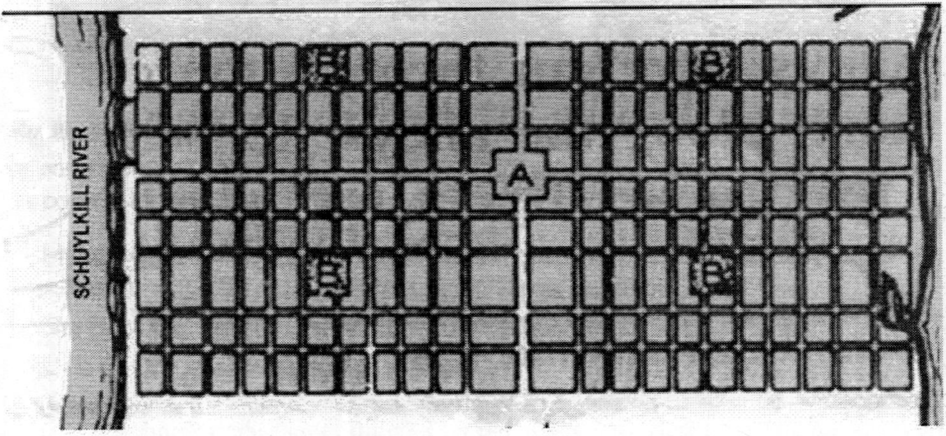

Fig. 2.113: Philadelphia was planned by William Penn/Thomas Holman (1882) on a gridiron pattern, markets, parks (B) and a public square (A) in the centre of the city

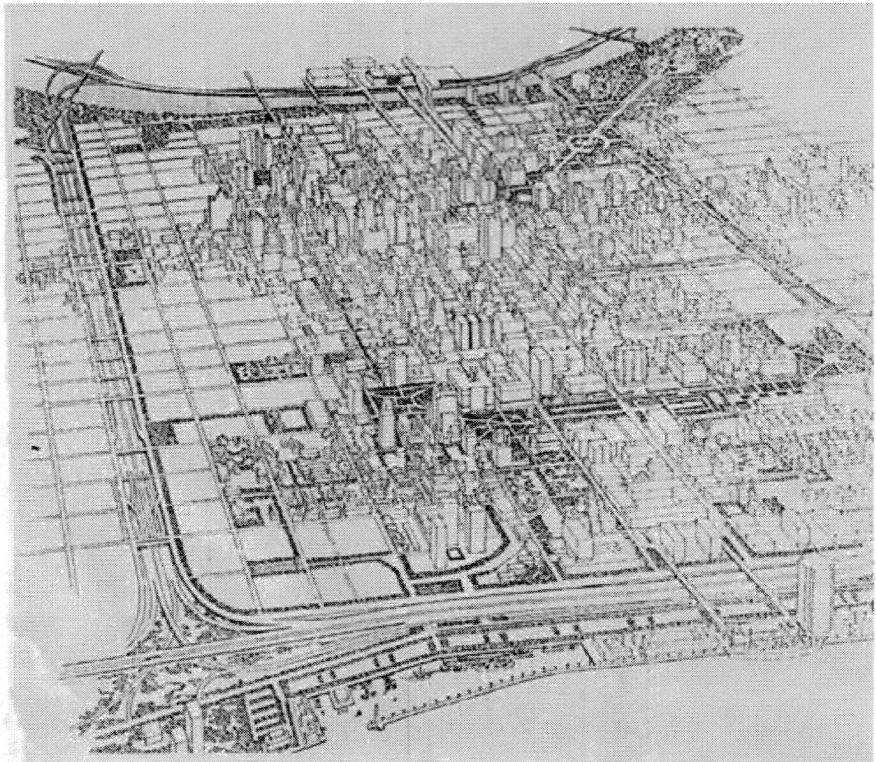

Fig. 2.114: City Center, Philidelphia (USA)

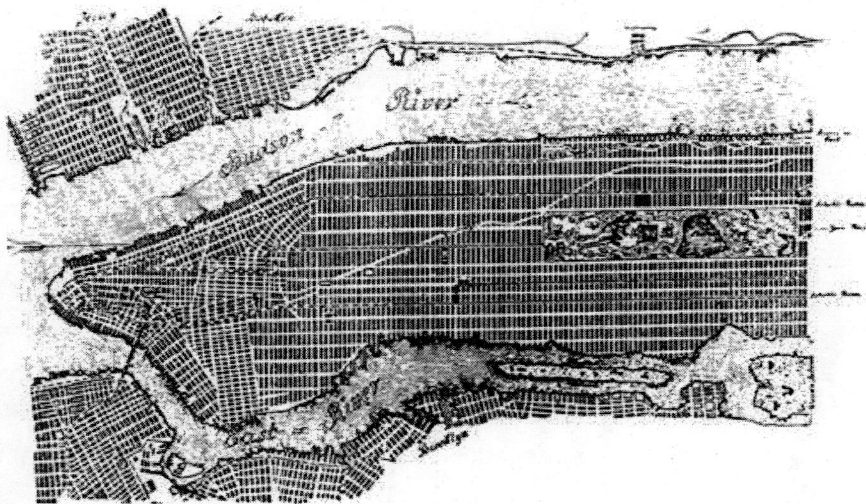

Fig 2.115: The Commissioner's Plan for Manhattan Island (1811) New York. Planned by City Surveyor and Architect Joseph Mangin, City had two major north-south streets with squares and plazas and one major angular street-the Broadway. Open space was not generously allocated and city became cramped with only five small parks, a military parade ground and a market. Ultimately in the middle of 18th century Central Park was established.

Fig. 2.116: New York City, Broadway near Cortlandt Street and Maiden Lane- The urban street was chaotic, foul smelling and congested, though it was the public meeting and market place, until the automobile made it dangerous and inaccessible (Lithograph by J.J. Fogerty).

The colonial era of America (1600-1800) was marked with the formation of a chain of settlements along the east coast. Important cities of this period are Virginia, Boston, Newport and the New Amsterdam in the Manhattan which was named New York in 1664. The era of growth and expansion (1800-1870) was characterised by trade and industrialisation, that led to unprecedented growth of cities between 1820 and 1860. The era of great metropolis (1870-1940) witnessed a number of inventions, such as frame, steel structures and elevators, which changed the skyline of American cities and development of suburbs. The City Beautiful Movement in 1893 emphasised the need for a city that would be big, broad and beautiful. The plans were of colossal scale with monumental proportion failed to meet the needs of the common man. Boston-Washington was the first America megalopolis. Office towers multiplied very fast and many residential areas of the cities got totally transformed.

This was beginning of a new era of 'modern' style cities. The buildings were being designed with an eye toward innovation and streamlining their functional roles, removing unnecessary references and embellishment. The building design, followed the philosophy of "form follows function". In post-war United States people's residences and domestic lives became more outdoor oriented.

Besides the garden city concept by Ebenzer Howard (1898-1915), various innovative concepts of the city design emerged. Saria-Y Mata, a Spanish engineer counterpoised a linear city structure in place of conventional closed plan. During the early 1920s Ladovsky and Milyutin, the Soviet planners, proposed functional zoning of urban territory combining the linear city and radical concentric forms. These became the basis of planning of a number of new cities in the erstwhile USSR. In 1924 Le Corbusier, the celebrated French-Swiss Architect, proposed a high rise city of 3 million known as Radiant City. His design was much ahead of the time and predicted new forms of the city and integration of greenery, building and transport. Main traffic highways were defined with separation of local and through traffic and pedestrian circulation. Further to the concept of La Ville Radieuse-the Radiant City, Le Cobusier focussed on organic growth for the city, and the traffic pattern follows an orthogonal system with superimposed diagonals and a network of subways.

Congress International Architecture Modern (CIAM) in 1928 proposed four basic elements of the urban biology: sun, space, vegetation, steel and concrete, where Le Corbusier played a major role. It affirmed that town planning is the organisation and linking of functions of collective life, comprising dwellings, work, recreation and transportation. Le Corbusier in CIAM organised an Assembly of Constructors for an Architectural Renovation (ASCORAL) which set forth the Three Human Establishments:

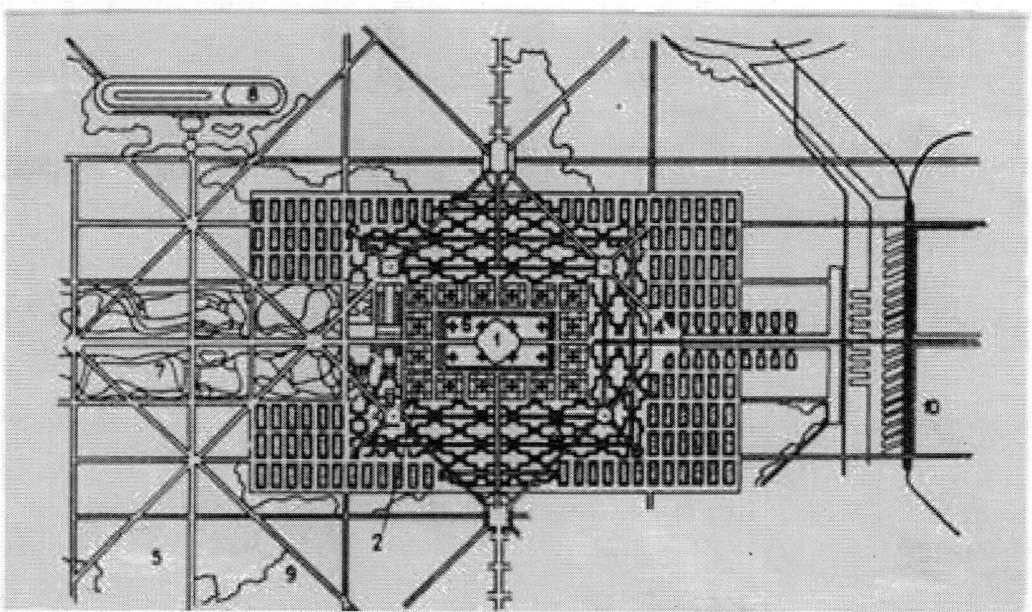

Fig. 2.117: Le Corbusier: Radiant City for 3 Million People

(a) The Radiant City

(b) The Linear Industrial City

(c) The Farming Unit (the cooperative village for agricultural production)

The new industrial communities are located along the main arteries of transportation-water, rail and highway connecting the existing cities. Factories are separate from the residential section. A green strip includes the horizontal garden town houses and vertical apartment buildings with civic centre, sports, entertainment, shopping and office facilities.

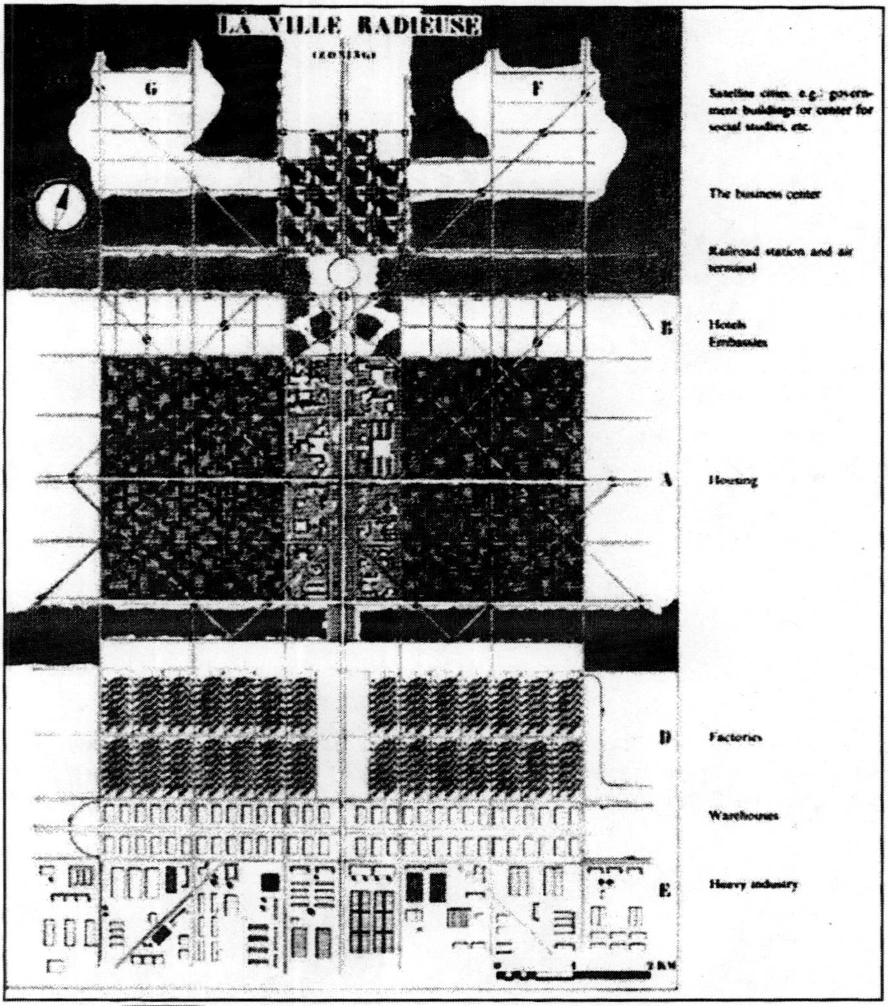

Fig 2.118: Plan of La Villa Radieuse-Le Corbusier (1933)

The most famous American architect Frank Lloyd Wright planned the Broadacre City, where he tried to satisfy the inner urge of city dwellers for vast spacious openness and rural ambience. He proposed plot of one acre to each family, and 1mile high skyscraper. Frank Lloyd Wright demonstrated his interpretation for the modern building and homes, which were in harmony with natural surroundings. Taliesin and Falling Water are both examples of careful placement of architecture in nature so the relationship between the built and natural environment becomes seamless.

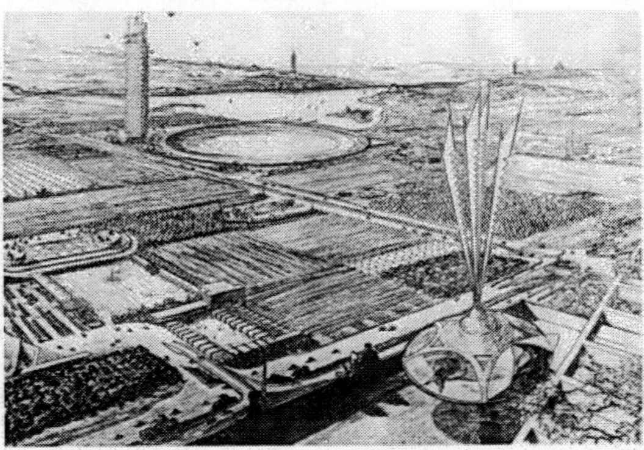

Fig. 2.119: Frank Lloyd Wright: Broadacre City

In 1953, the famous Greek planner C.A. Doxiadis formulated the concept of Dynapolis, that is monocentric city form developing along with population growth in one direction. The basic concept was applied by him in the planning of Islamabad, the new Capital of Pakistan.

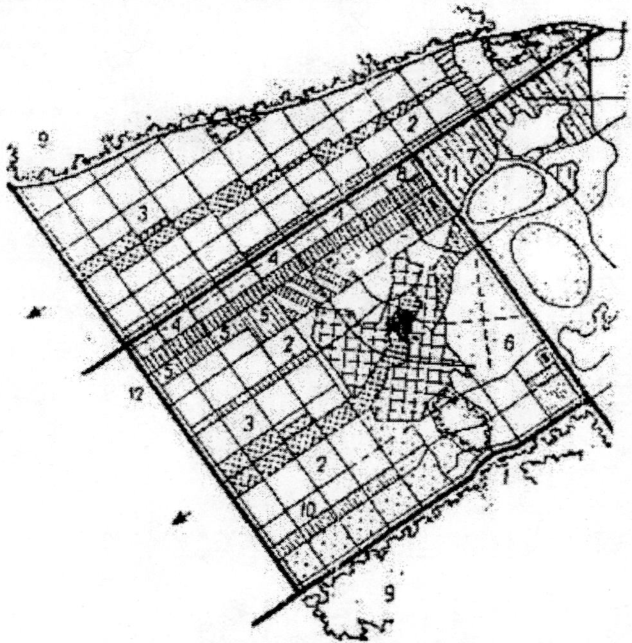

Fig. 2.120: C.A. Doxiadis: City Plan of Islamabad (Pakistan): 1) Rawalpindi Town 2) Residential District 3) Dynamic Developing Centre, 4) Military Zone, 5) Embassies, 6) Airport, 7) Old City, 8) Bus Terminal, 9) Green Space, 10) Industrial Area, 11) Railway Area. Arrows show direction in which the city grows.

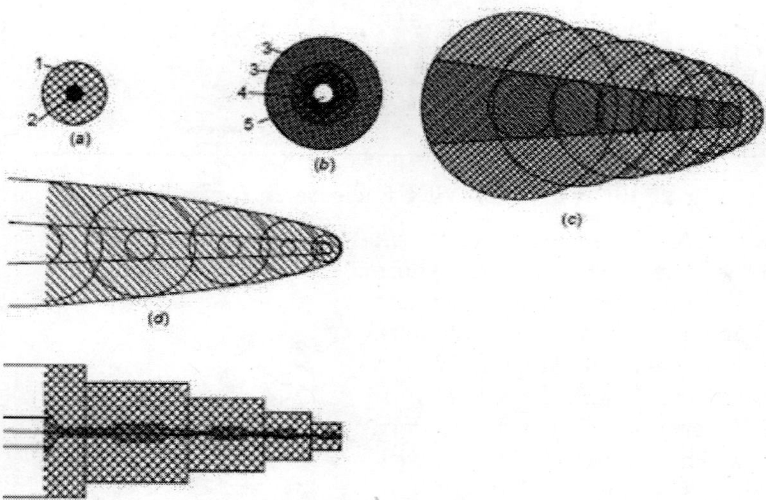

Fig. 2.121: Concept of Evolving City by C.A. Doxiadis (a) static city of the past: (b) concentric development of city in which the crowded centre absorbs other areas; (c) free "monocentric" development of city and centre the city of the future; (d) development of city in one direction on parabolic or rectangular form; 1-city; 2-centre; 3-expansion zone of centre; 4-expanding city; 5-old centre

Brazilian architects Lucio Costa and Oscar Niemeyer prepared a cruciform plan of Brasilia, the new Capital of Brazil. Kenzo Tango of Japan developed the plan of Skopje (Yugoslavia), which reinterpreted the concept of city wall, city square and other elements of urban design. Earlier he had prepared a plan for Tokyo (1960) which was based on a system of linear growth with civic axis and mega structures for housing and other activities. It was proposed to utilise the sea for extension of the city. Also in Japan, the Metabolism Group suggested revolutionary proposals for new urbanism which were published in their book- Marine City (1960). The architect Kiyonori Kikutake and Noriaki Kurokawa proposed an urban design scheme incorporating the concepts of artificial ground, helix form and the wall city, Yona Friedman of France proposed spatial town based on the concept of mobile architecture so that it adapts with the changing society. Eckhard Schulz-Fielitz further developed the spatial city of Yana and called it a Scientific Fiction of Town Planning. Many of these concepts are no more fantasises, but are becoming feasible. Buckminster Fuller in USA developed the concept of Geodesic Dome. It encloses maximum area within minimum surface and has controlled environment and climate. Italian-American architect Paolo Solari developed a new form of city which he called Arcology. This is being developed in Arizona.

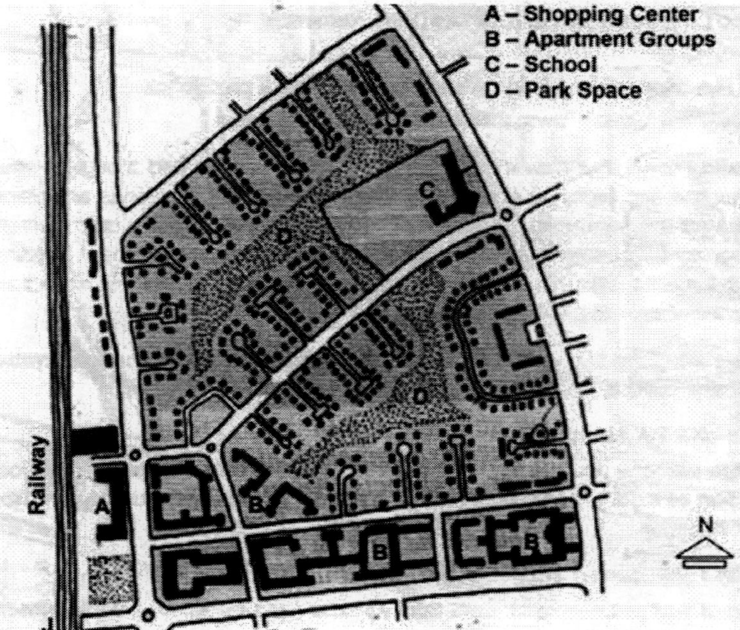

Fig 2.122: Layout Plan of Radburn. Housing plots are situated on narrow, quiet cul-de-sacs that connect with the green spaces. The cul-de-sac arrangement reduced street area and the length of utility lines by 25 percent.

Lewis Mumford in his seminal book, The Culture of Cities (1930), advocated the neighbourhood unit as a building block for a city. Its size is determined by the walking distance between the house and the school and playground. To safeguard the school and home from the noise and traffic, no major traffic arteries must run through which may be at its boundaries. Whatever traffic enters into the neighbourhood must be that which sub-serves it directly.

The town of Radburn adopted the concept of neighbourhood which was developed by the City Housing Corporation of New York and was adopted in New Jersey. Radburn, Henry Wright and Clarence Stein introduced the concept of super block ranging from 30 to 50 acres in size. Traffic streets surrounded rather than traversed the area and dwellings were grouped around the cul-de-sacs. Pathways provided uninterrupted pedestrian access to a continuous park strip, which led to large common open spaces at the centre.

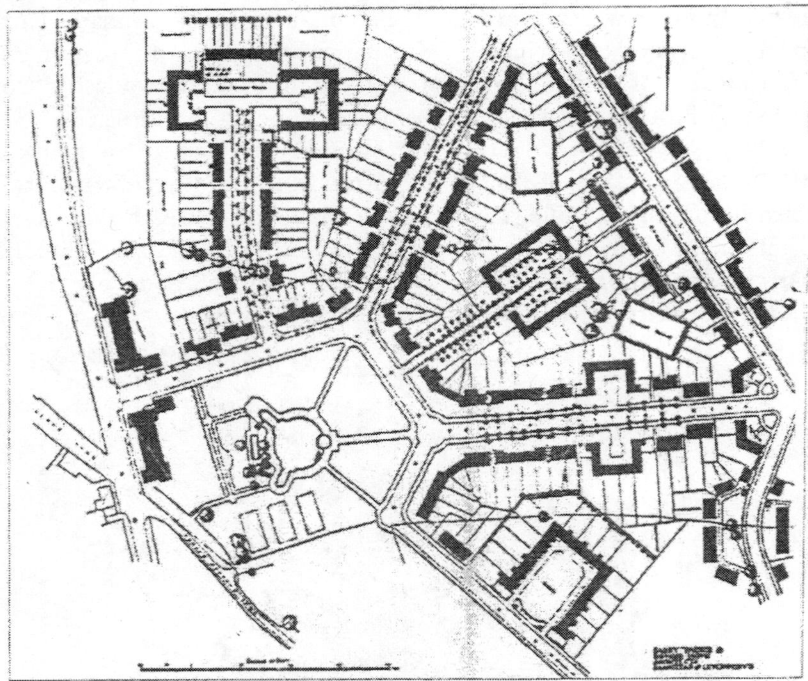

Fig 2.123: The layout of Hampstead Garden Suburb avoided the rectilinear grid and utilized numerous cul-de-sacs and courts to create quiet pedestrian-oriented residential enclaves.

Source: Raymond Unwin

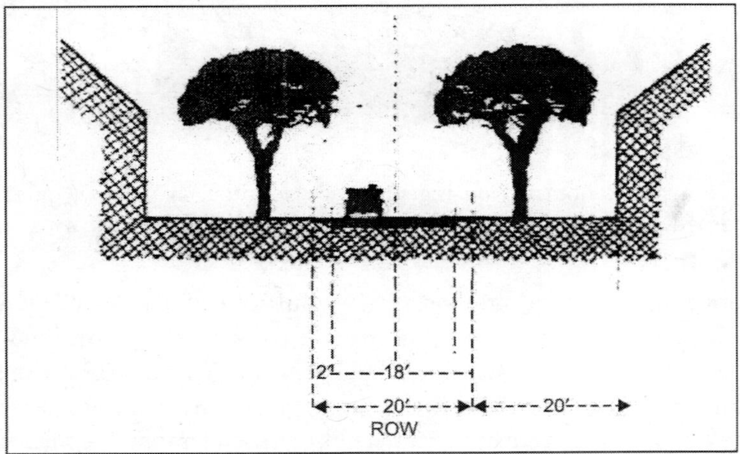

Fig 2.124: Road Section at Hampstead Garden Suburb

Source: Eran Ben-Joseph

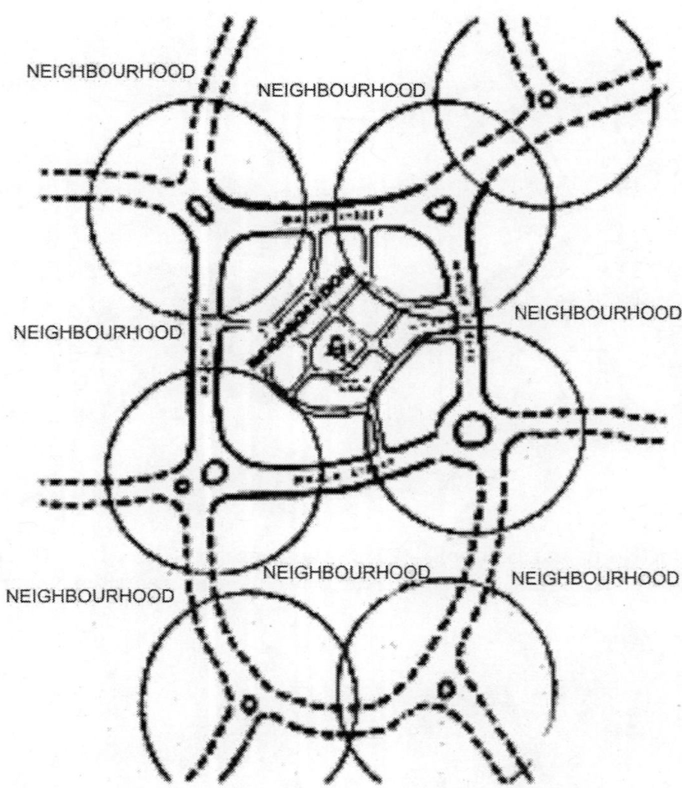

Fig. 2.125: Layout of a Neighbourhood Unit according to Clarence Stein provides elementary school at the centre within half-mile of all residences and a shopping centre near the school

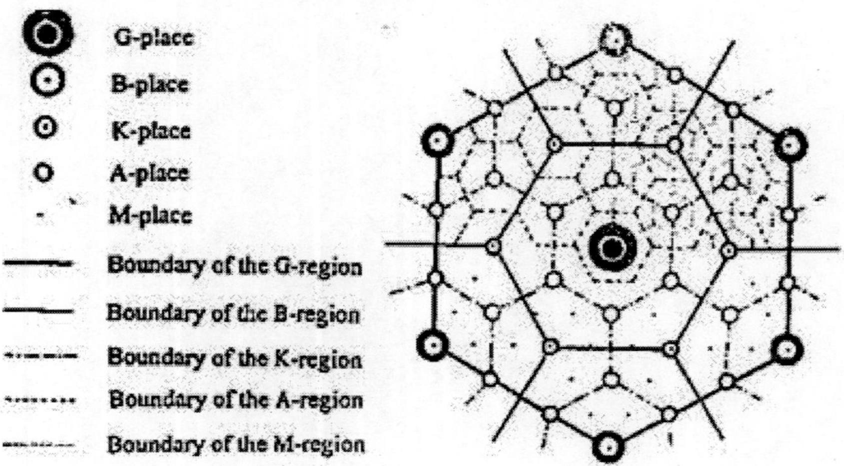

Fig. 2.126: Christaller Theory of Urban Settlements

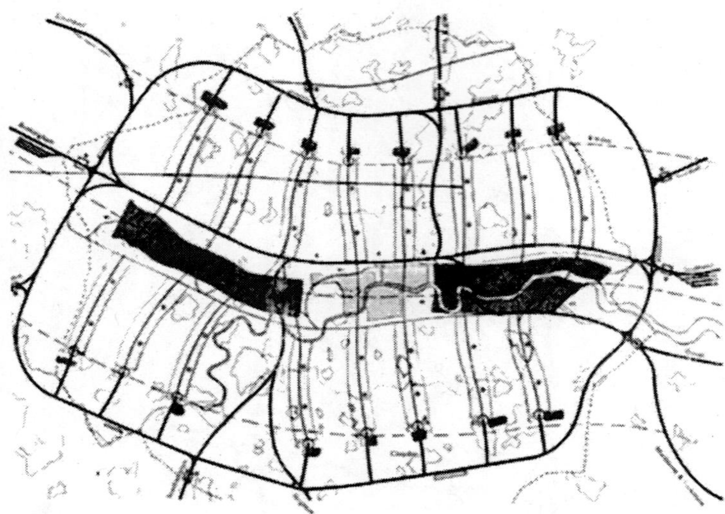

Fig. 2.127: Mars Plan (Korn and Samuelly, 1942) the concept is based on the rational movement of people and goods, public transport and consequential reduction of private cars

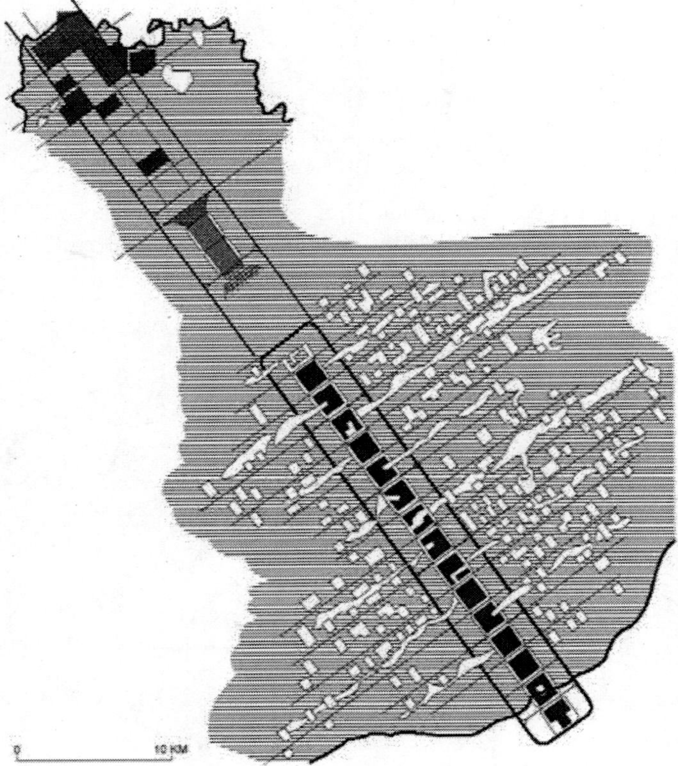

Fig. 2.128: Plan of a linear city by Le Corbusier (1922) the city develops along a central spine served by public transport. The central spine is primarily a commercial / industrial / institutional zone which is flanked by residential neighbourhood, accessible by pedestrian corridors as well as by public transit and private vehicles

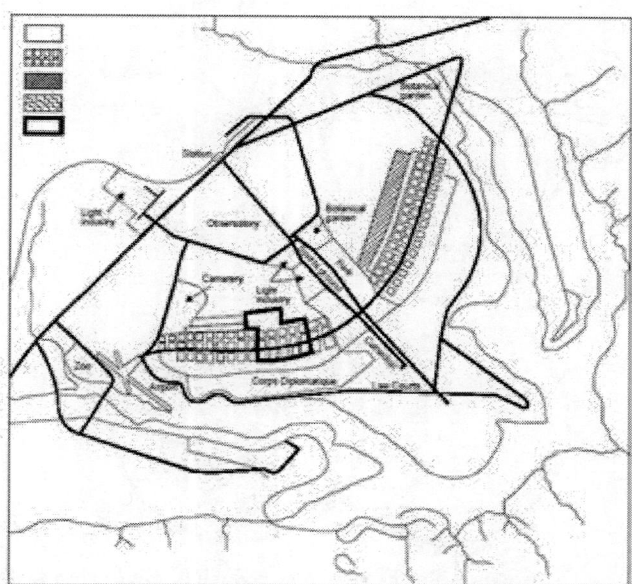

Fig. 2.129: Brasilia, the new capital of Brazil, had been planned by Lucio Costa in the shape of a cross, as was used in the ancient city of Alexandria. This form provides an efficient pattern of transportation, segregating residential and non-residential traffic to a large extent

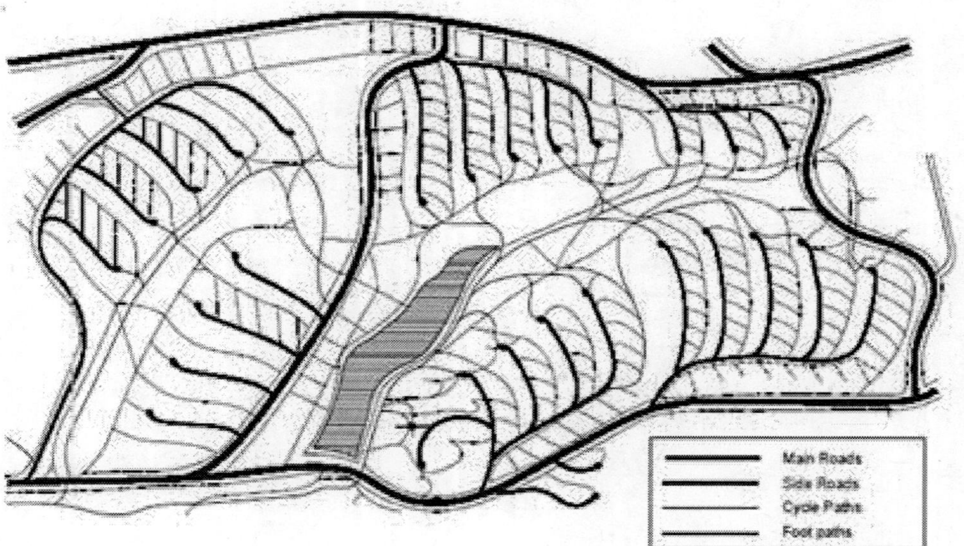

Fig. 2.130: Plan for Leverkusen-Steinbuchel (near Cologne): at first the layout appears to be haphazard, but a clear organic leaf vein-like pattern can be discerned (H. B. Reichow, Dic Autogenechte Stadt).

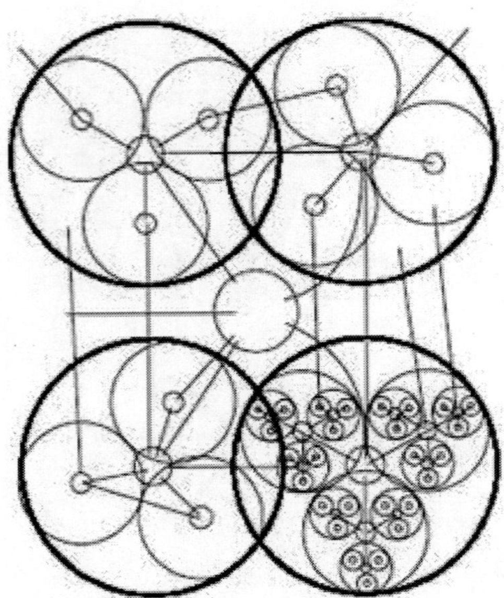

Fig. 2.131: Diagram of Egli's proposal for Furttal near Zurich, Switerland. The proposal follows Egli's description of Bardet's concept of urban hierarchy comprising hierarchy of family, neighbourhood, group, district, town and city.

Source: Egli, E. Geschichte des Stadtebaues Erlenbach-Zurich Eugen Rentsch Verlag 1967

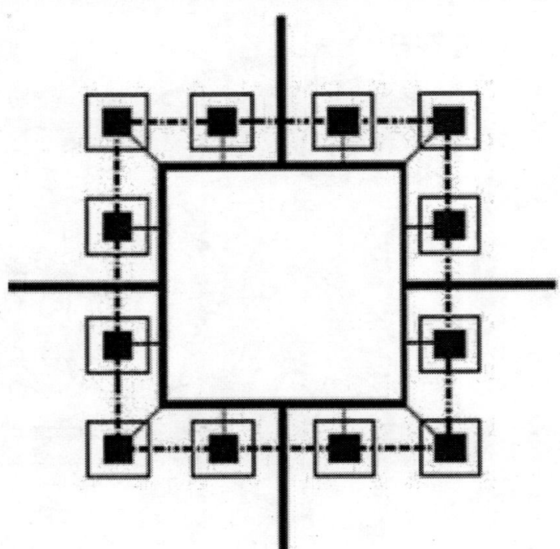

Fig 2.132: Diagram showing a 'Mencian' approach towards arranging twelve balanced communities, public transport circuit and road links to each other and a rational road network. The 'Mencian' centre typically contains symbols of unity and culture.

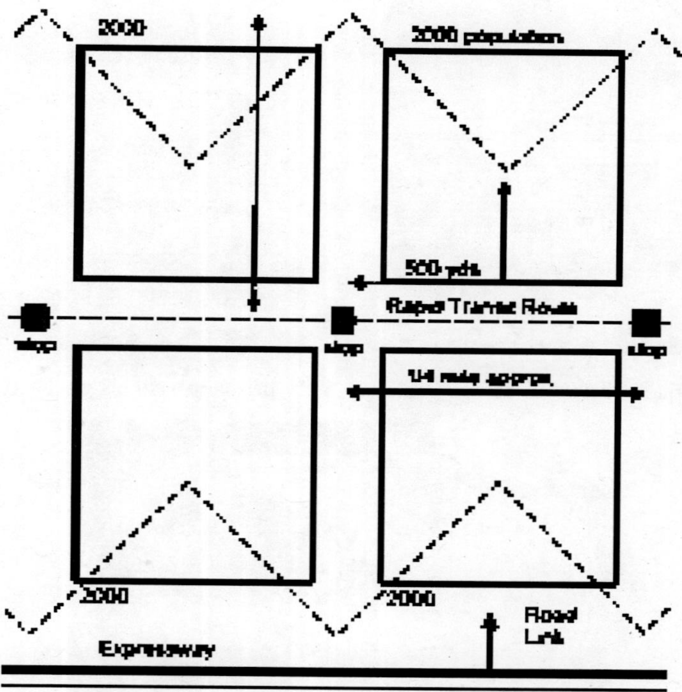

Fig. 2.133: Runcorn New Town Plan evolved on the basis of module of neighbourhood accessed by rapid public transit route

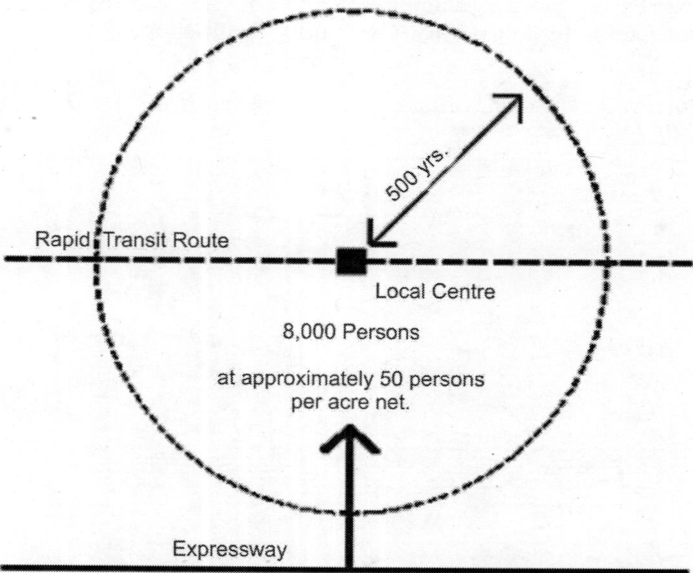

Fig. 2.134: Population Related to Walking Distance

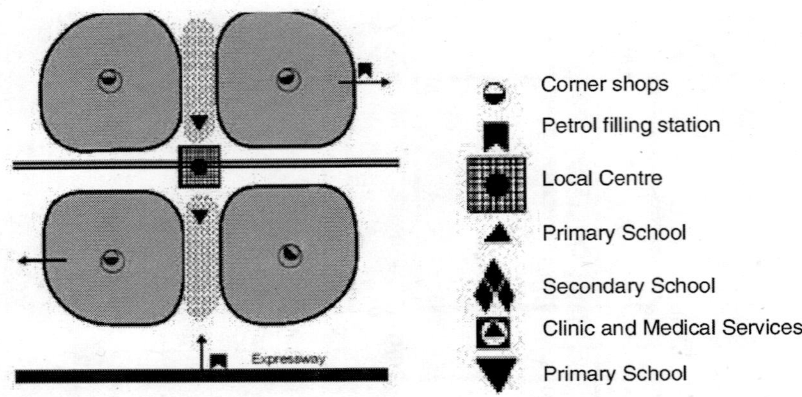

Fig. 2.135: Location of social facilities with primary schools at local centre.

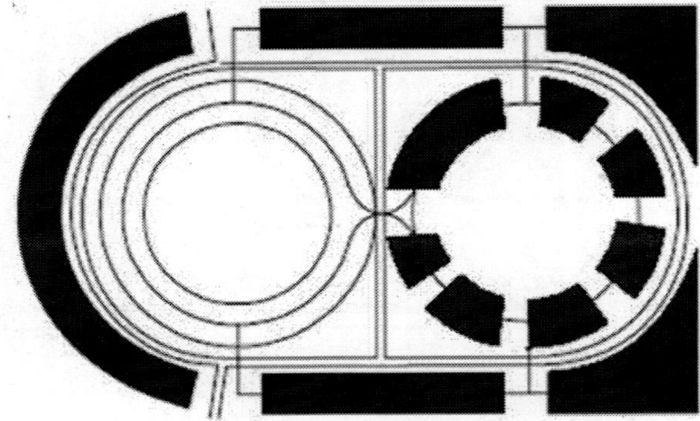

Fig. 2.136: Diagram showing the figure 'eight' network of the public transport system. This leads to a simplified hierarchy comprising communities and only one centre, at the intersection of the loops. The public transport interlinked with community facilities, work centres and neighbourhood road system.

Source, Ling, A. Runcorn New Town: Master Plan Runcorn, Runcorn Development Corporation, 1967 Runcorn New Town (UK).

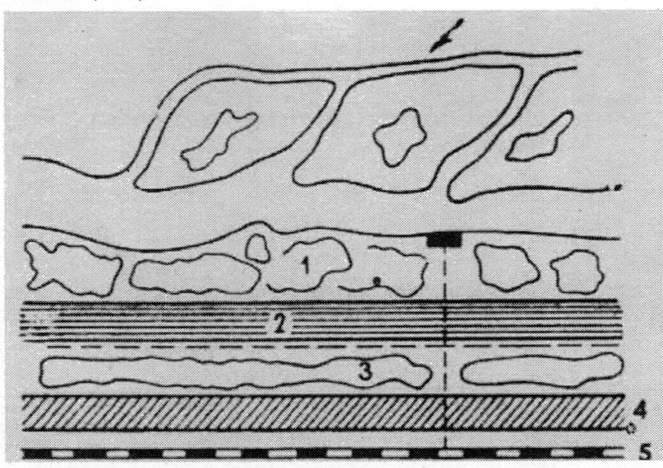

Fig. 2.137: N Milyutin Functional/linear Zoning of the Urban Territory 1. Park Area, 2. Housing Zone, 3. Protective Green Belt, 4. Industrial Area, and 5. Railroad Terminal

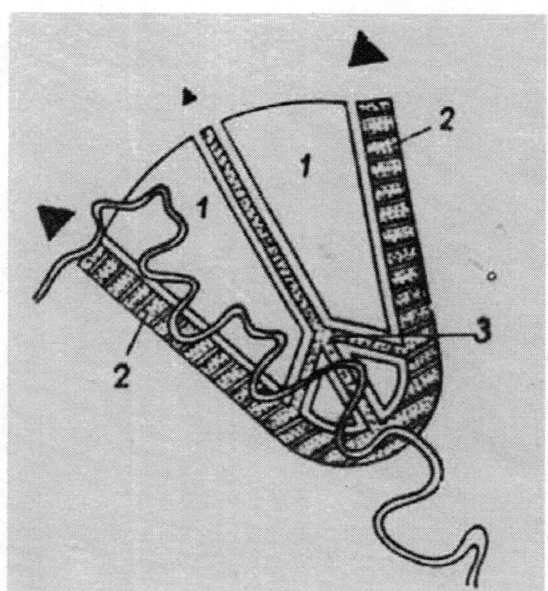

Fig. 2.138: N Ladovsky: Diagrammatical Plan of a Developing Town 1. Residential Area, 2. Industrial Area 3. Administrative Centre

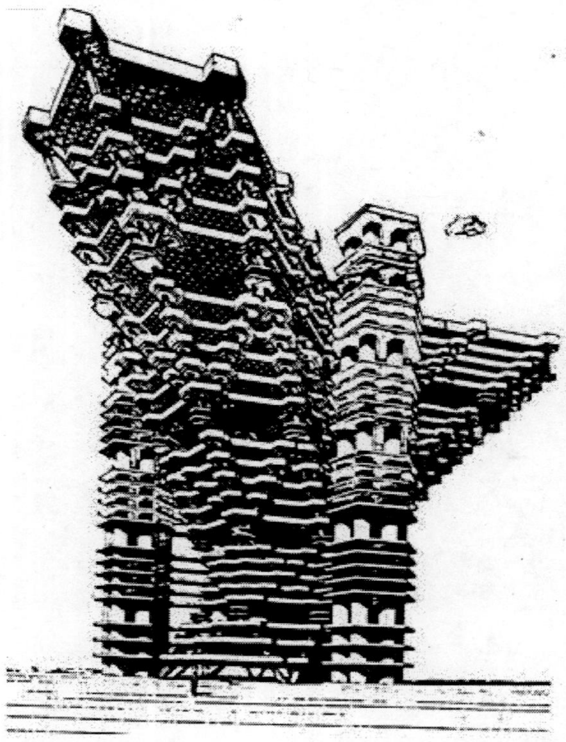

Fig. 2.139: High Density Compact City, 1961 (Architect Wilhelm Holzbauer)

Fig. 2.140: Floating City, 1959 (Architects : Kiyonori Kikutake and Arata Isozaki)

Fig. 2.141: Archigram's Plug in City, 1961 (Architect Peter Cook)

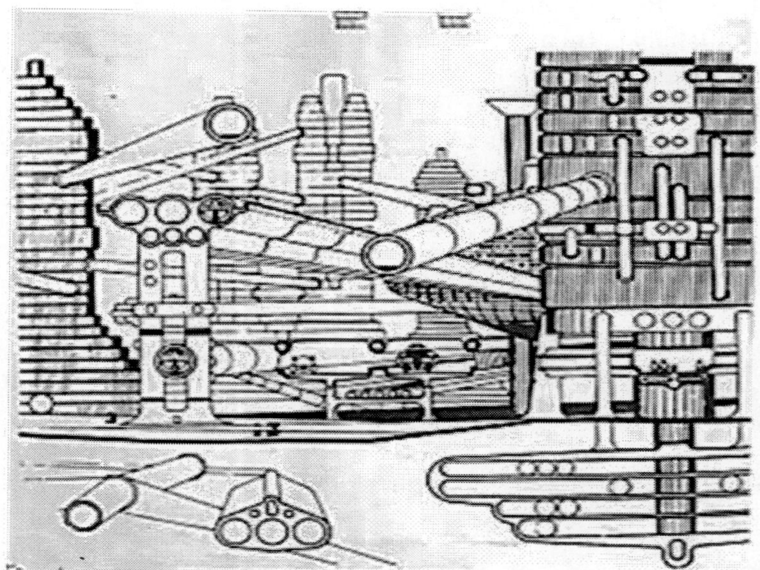

Fig. 2.142: Ron Herron and Warren Chalk, Interchange Project, 1965

Presidency Cities of India

During 1608-1757, the East India Company set up factories and trading posts in India, mostly in coastal areas. Surat, set up in 1608 was the company's first headquarters town. It was followed by a Machilipatnam on the Coromandel Coast, and other coastal cities. During 1757-1858, the Company gradually acquired sovereignty over large parts of India, and established

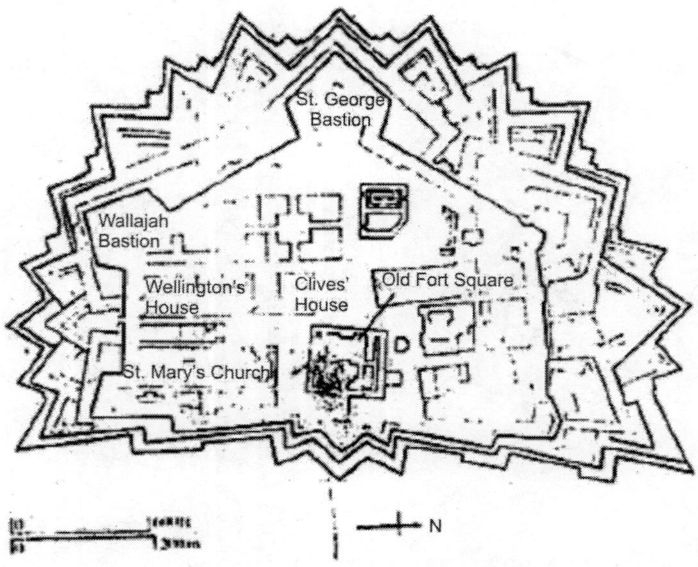

Fig. 2.143: Madras: Fort St. George (1785 AD)

Presidencies at Madras, Bombay and Calcutta. North-Western Provinces was added later with its headquarter at Allahabad, then at Agra from 1834 to 1868. Hooghly, Calcutta was founded by Job Charnock in 1686, where the Presidency of Fort William was established. Fort St. George was established as the headquarter of Madras Presidency. Their provinces increased after the British and Company defeated local rulers in the wars and annexed their empires.

Fig. 2.144: Madras: Fort St. George (1785 AD)

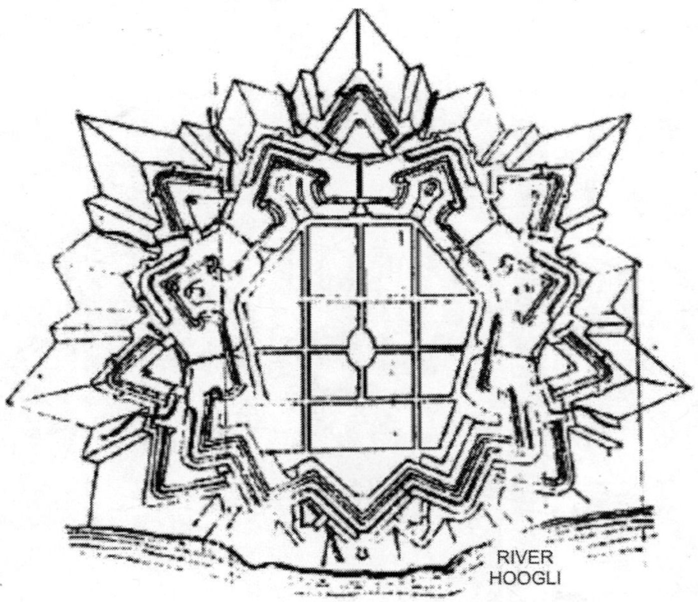

Fig. 2.145: Fort Williams, Calcutta (1686 AD)

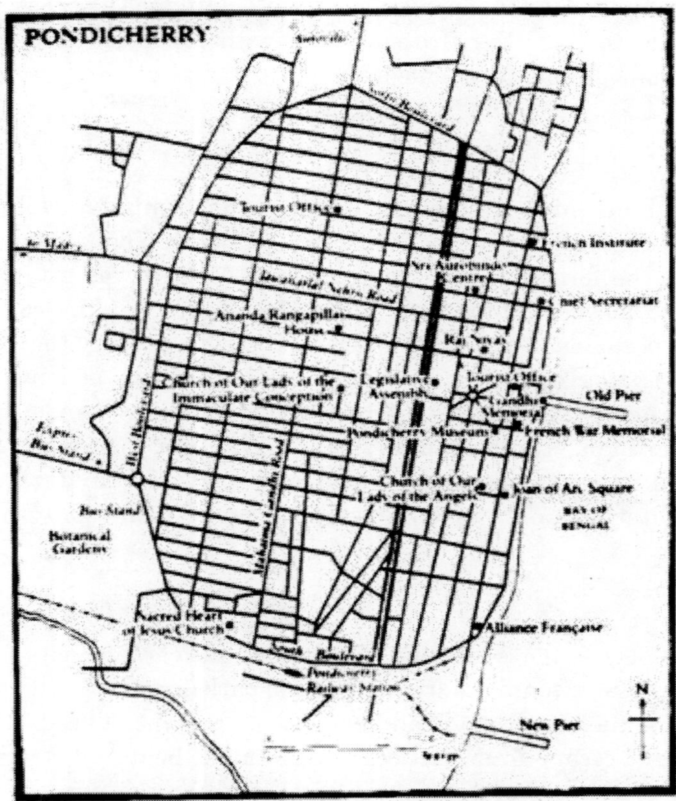

Fig. 2.146: Pondicherry

Fig. 2.147: Mayo College Ajmer, 1888

This was the beginning of a new approach to town planning. The cities and buildings built by the British were mainly for the British rulers with fortified cantonments and had no relationship with Indian people, dust and heat, poverty and culture.

Cantonments

Many cities such as Meerut, Pune, Rawalpindi, Ambala, Belgaum, Bangalore, Secunderabad Delhi, Kanpur, Bathinda,Peshawar, Ramgarh, Sialkot and Trichy contained large cantonments of the former British Indian Army. Meerut was established in 1803 and was for 150 years the biggest cantonment in the region. Earlier the cantonments in India were viewed as semi-permanent, but by the turn of the 20th century they became permanent garrisons, and were further entrenched via the military reforms of Lord Kitchener in 1903 and the Cantonments Act of 1924. At present 62 notified cantonments and 44 unlisted Garrisons/ Cantonments exists in India. These generally have a grid iron pattern, large parade grounds, parks, bungalows and barracks, mess and clubs, mall roads, Sadar Bazar, schools, hospitals and dispensaries, military training centres, barracks, etc. General pattern is of low-rise low-density development.

Hill Stations

The British rulers also developed several hill stations and cantonments and a new landscape of race courses, cricket clubs, tennis courts and public parks emerged. The pattern of classical, decorative gardens, avenues, mall roads and boulevards was introduced. After the uprising of 1857 the British sought escape from the locals and Indian heat and return to home country without leaving India. The hill stations were developed for the purpose with the object to reproduce the home country in India. This is illustrated by Lord Lytton's statement about Ootacamund, in the 1870s, – *such beautiful English rain, such delicious English mud.* Shimla was made the summer capital of India in the 1860s and hill stations served as vital centers of political and military power, besides providing refuge as "*places to rest and recuperate from the arduous life on the plains*". The hill stations reached their zenith in the late nineteenth century, which were as many as 40 in numbers.

New Delhi

On December 12, 1911 at the historic Delhi Durbar, King George V, Emperor of the British Empire proclaimed that the capital of India would henceforth be Delhi instead of Calcutta. A temporary capital complex was built in the area now known as Delhi University and the Old Secretariat during 1912-15. Delhi Town Planning Commission (DTPC) was constituted to plan the new capital, comprising of G.S.C. Swinton, Edwin Lutyens and J.A. Brodie. There was continued debate regarding whether the city should be located north or south of Old Delhi, and finally it was decided to locate the new city on Raisina Hill, between the Ridge and the River, towards South of Shahjahanabad. The reasons were primarily a healthy and naturally drained site, as compared to low lying northern site at Kingsway Camp and also that the new city at a higher ground will dominate the urban landscape.

Imperial Delhi was laid out by Edwin Lutyens as a garden city covering 8,200 acres to accommodate a population of 65,000. It was accessible from the Walled City only through two underpasses, Minto and Harding Bridges. Beyond this, New Delhi was laid in a geometric pattern over a triangular base formed by the Connaught Place, Viceroy House and India Gate. With its wide avenues, double row of trees, the Central Vista called Kingsway (now Rajpath) was the centre-piece of the new city. The residential areas were planned with lower and middle income employees to the north of the vista and senior British officials to the south, in an hierarchical pattern.

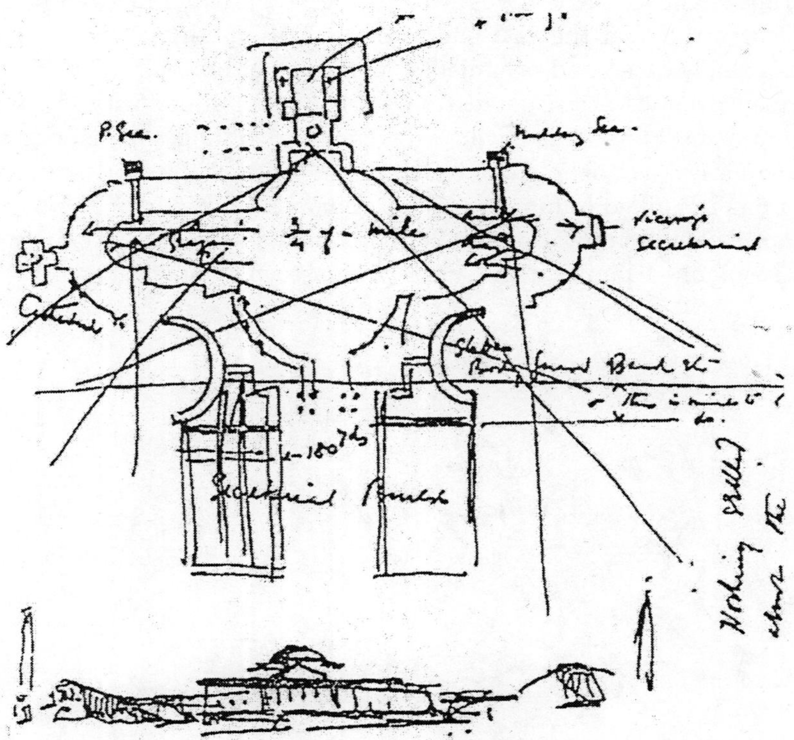

Fig. 2.148: Edwin Lutyens' initial sketch of Capital Complex (June 1912)

Source: Jain A.K., 1994, The Cities of Delhi, Management Publishing Co.

Imperial Delhi lent India a place of pride among the countries with great capitals, like, Washington, Paris and Canberra. Lutyens' design of New Delhi is an architect's tribute to India's greatness. The new city was planned adjacent to Shahjahanabad, yet separated from it by an open space buffer and railway embankment. Beyond this, New Delhi was laid in a geometric pattern over a triangular base formed by three major functions, viz., commercial, governmental and recreational. Connaught Place, Government complex (Viceroy Palace and Secretariats) and the India Gate were the respective centres of these major activities. The Connaught Place was conceived as the city centre, with its location in the geographical centre of Old and New Delhi. It was to act as a link between two Delhis and a Railway Station was laid adjacent to it in order to link the city to the region. The Viceroy Palace on the Raisina Hill was the focal point for the entire city. To the south of the fashionable shopping centre of Connaught Place and along river Yamuna, the India Gate, National Stadium and recreational activities were planned.

The plan of New Delhi is geometrical in shape with hexagonal and triangular patterns. The plan can be viewed in 2 parts – a rectangular grid or main central axis that has the monumental government buildings and the hexagonal layout that focuses on the local and residential aspects of the city. The central axis, which was known as Kingsway and now called Rajpath, runs through the layout of the new city with several avenues and streets radiating from it. It was designed by Lutyens as a processional avenue that linked the Viceroy's Palace now the Rashtrapati Bhavan at the west end to the War Memorial Arch or India Gate and the canopy of George the V at the east end of the axis. Rajpath is a picturesque, broad road flanked by large, shady trees and ornamental ponds on either side of it. The Central Vista and the vast green avenues accentuated the grandeur and superiority of the new city. The panorama of monumental buildings enveloped within a rich landscape is unique. The Central Vista has become almost symbolic of New Delhi as a stage of the world's largest democracy. The grand vista has remained to function as a ceremonial path during the celebrations of the Republic Day Parade held annually on the 26th of January when the avenue comes alive. The Secretariats were planned flanking the Viceroy House on two sides.

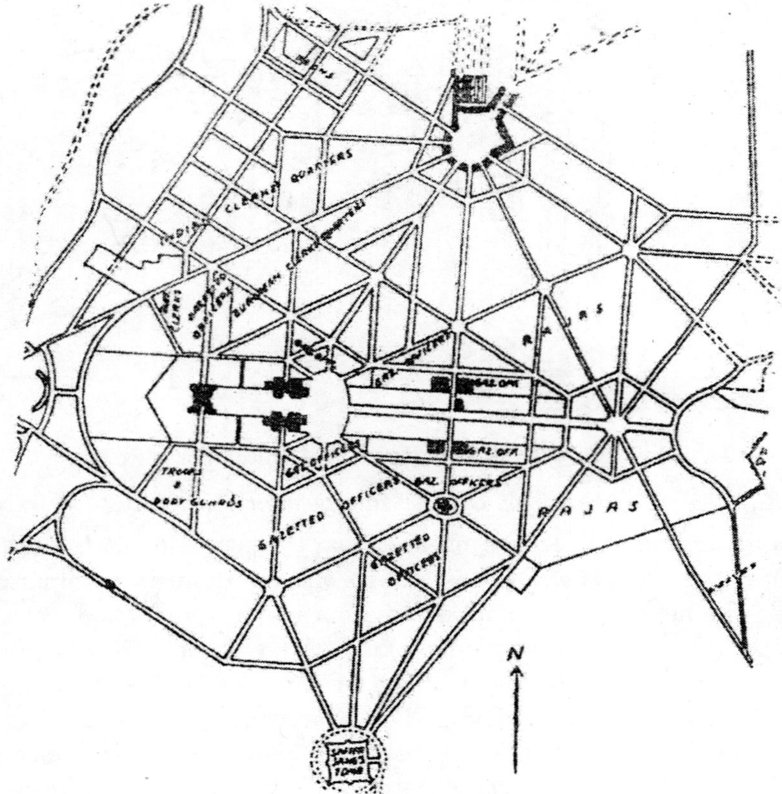

Fig. 2.149: Imperial Delhi: Plan by Lutyens (1913)

Source: A.K. Jain (2010) Lutyens' Delhi, Bookwell, New Delhi

Fig. 2.150: Elephantine Security Post, built in red sandstone at Viceroy House, designed by Edwin Lutyens

Photograph by A.K. Jain

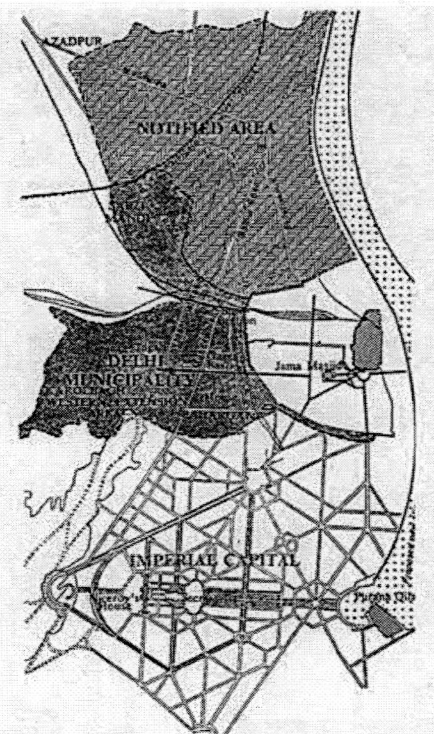

Fig. 2.151: *Delhi Municipality Notified Area, Imperial City and Western Extension, 1914*

Source: Jain A.K., 2010, Lutyens' Delhi, Bookwell, New Delhi

The capital complex is an architectural ensemble of unique value. Lutyens visualized a grand vision, highlighting the supremacy of the British rule. A hexagonal pattern linked the major activities of the triangular base, viz., governmental, commercial and recreational, at the apex of the triangle and the residential areas in the hexagonal. This provided a visual continuity of the new city with the monuments of ancient capital, like the Purana Quila, Jama Masjid, Safdarjung Tomb, Ferozshah Kotla, Lodhi Tombs, etc. The city was nestled between two ecological features of the site, which were river Yamuna on the East and the Aravali ridge on the West. Lutyens' plan was to landscape a vast expanse joining the river Yamuna and the Ridge. The water pools of the India Gate were surrounded by a number of palaces and a stadium. The city was conceived as a vast park with buildings hidden by trees.

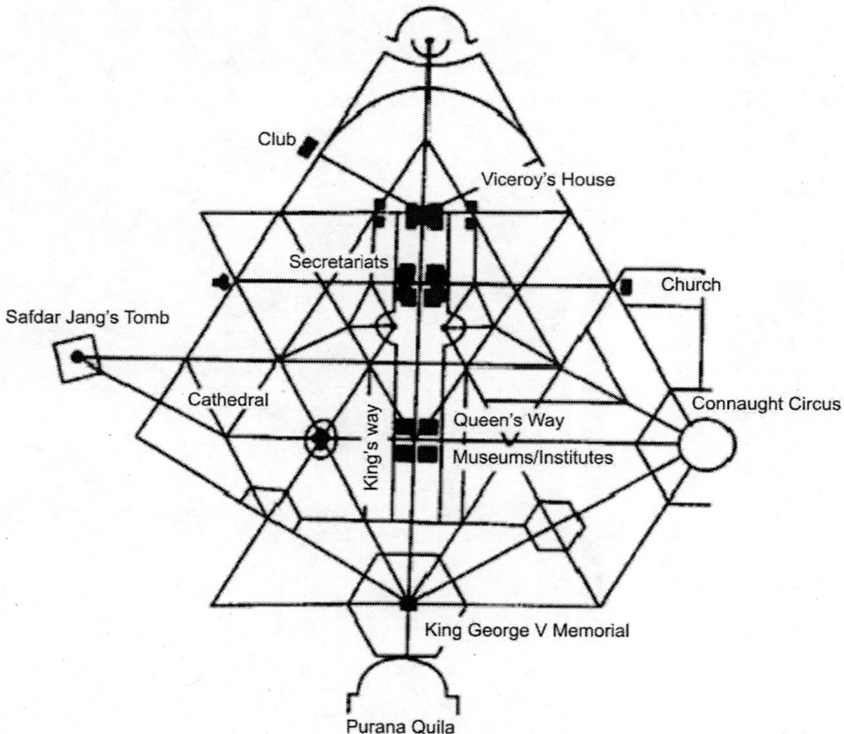

Fig. 2.152: While planning New Delhi, Lutyens conceived a garden city with buildings below tree height except the buildings in the monumental grid i.e. along the Central Vista. India Gate and Government Complex were linked by a monumental grid, known as the Central Vista. The India Gate, symbolic city gate was planned on the river side, while the Capital Complex dominating the skyline was placed at the Raisina Hill. A hexagonal grid provided visual continuity of the city with the ancient monuments, like Purana Qila, Jama Masjid, Safdarjung Tomb, Ferozshah Kotla, Lodhi Garden, Humayun Tomb, etc. The new Capital was carefully placed between two natural features of the site, viz. River Yamuna on the East and the Ridge towards the West.

Fig. 2.153: Central Vista, the centerpiece of New Delhi

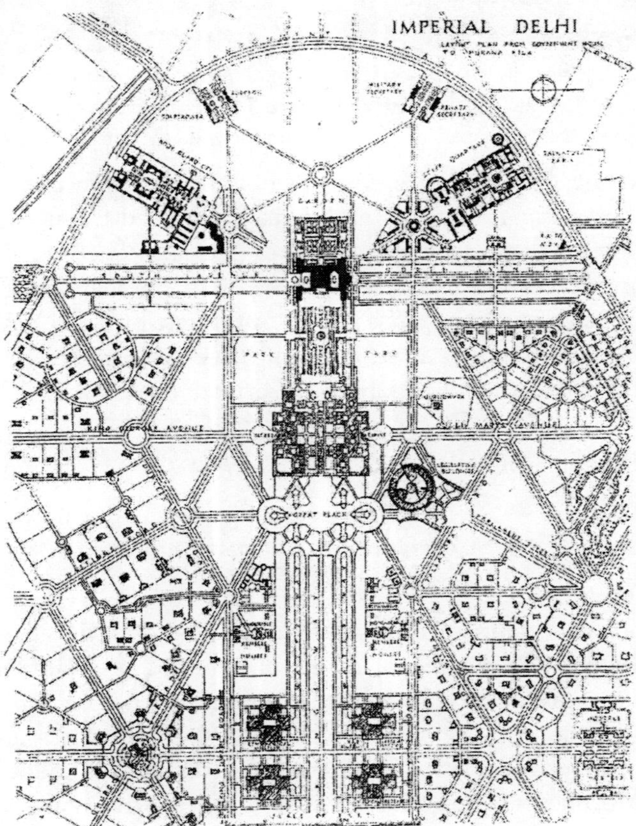

Fig. 2.154: Detailed layout of the Viceregal Estate Capital Complex at Raisina

Source: Central PWD, New Delhi

Fig. 2.155: Landscape had been an integral part of the design of Imperial Capital (New Delhi) by Edwin Lutyens. The Mughal Garden at Viceroy House combines the concepts of British Garden and Mughal Char-bagh

Lutyens enjoyed using geometrical shapes in his designs and architectural plans. In his plan for New Delhi, the triangle, hexagon and square are used frequently. These geometrical forms were also used by Lutyens' predecessors, the Mughals. The hexagon is commonly used in Mughal architecture, a perfect example of which can be seen in the inlay work in red sandstone and white marble at Humayun's Tomb. Although Lutyens never had much respect for Indian cities and its architecture, it seems, that gradually he began to appreciate India's greatness, as reflected by the following lines inscribed on Jaipur Column at the Viceroy Palace:

"Endow your thoughts with Faith
Your deeds with courage
Your life with sacrifice So all men may know
the greatness of India:"

Various roads cross this main avenue at right angles, but the general street pattern is diagonal to the main axis. The system of diagonal avenues in Delhi provides directness of movement for vehicular traffic which has much to commend it. In contrast to a compact and introverted Walled City, the new city was designed on an extrovert and low density pattern. With a maximum density of 25 persons per acre, no attempt was made to relate the new to the old city. The plan proposed large plots of 1 to 6 acres (with some plots even bigger) for residential development. However, the city remained deserted and looked barren for decades. In attempts to populate the deserted New Delhi, housing allowance given to government employees working in New Delhi was refused to those residing outside it. Businessmen were given incentives to open their shops in the Connaught Place. To service and maintain the new city, the New Delhi Municipal Council was constituted in 1916, but it did not become effective until 1925.

When the Imperial Delhi was formally inaugurated in 1931, it indeed was discerned to be an Anglo-Indian Rome. Lutyens, who was deeply influenced by the Greeco-Roman roots of city planning and architecture faithfully followed them in the design of New Delhi. In spite of the fact that in the West "modern architecture", with new materials, functional emphasis and changing concepts of structural engineering, was raising a storm, Lutyens ignored it while planning and building the New Delhi. However, despite Lutyens' own ignorance of Indian architecture, it is intriguing that the plan of New Delhi is not very alien to the principles of Mansara.

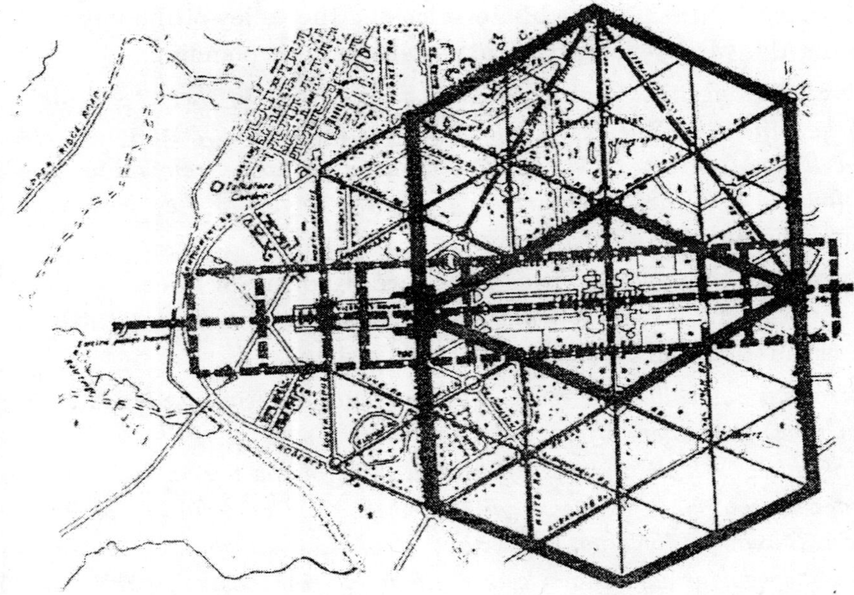

Fig. 2.156: The plan of New Delhi is formed by the superimposition of two separate and distinct geometric systems. The narrow rectangular grid is monumental and relates to the major scale of the region and Government buildings. The other, the hexagonal system is local and devoted to the residential city.

Source: A Greenburg, 1969, Lutyens' Architecture Restudied, in Perspecta,12, Connecticut

The location of the city, its zoning and functional classification coincide quite well with the traditional principles. The mythology and rituals of Greece and Rome suggest some similarities with the Vedic culture.

In the 'Politics', Aristotle makes explicit recommendations for a site:

"The land upon which a city is to be sited should be sloping that we must just hope to find, but we should keep four considerations in mind. First and most essential the situation must be a healthy one. A slope facing east, with winds blowing from the direction of sunrise, gives a healthy site, rather better than the lee side or north, though this gives good weather. Next it should be well situated for carrying out all its civil and military activites."

Vitruvius makes similar recommendations:

"The choice of a healthy site must come first. Such a site will be high, neither misty nor frosty, the climate neither too hot nor too cold, but temperate. There should be no marshes in the neighbourhood. If the town is on the coast and exposed either to the south or the west it will not be healthy... In founding towns, in short, beware of districts where hot wind can blow on the inhabitants."

In the fifth century BC, Hippocrates formulated the basic principles of city planning. These might have been a revolutionary period as earlier cities were more organically developed. It was after Hippocrates that the selection of site of a city, its orientation, topography and health aspects of ground became important considerations, besides its military necessities. Rome was founded on the Palatine hill, overlooking the valley of the forum. Street layout to the direction of the winds emerged an important facts of planning.

Vitruvius, following his Greek preceptors, warns that *"if the streets run straight in the direction of the winds then their constant blasts rush in and ...... sweep the streets with great violence. The lines of houses must therefore be directed away from the quarters from which the winds blow, so that they may strike against the angles of the blocks and their force be broken up and dispersed."*

Vitruvius described a sixteen rayed-tablet arrangement for orienting the main streets at an oblique angle in the strongest winds. 300 years after Vitruvius, Oribasius modified the principle of orientation and recommends the following:

"When streets are parallel in a town, some in length and some in breadth, the first running from east to west, the others from south and north, so that they pierce the town through length and breadth without any obstacles, and none of the winds meet any building which might obstruct its course.... (the town will be) well aired and sunlit, healthy and clear. For all the winds, Boreas and Notus, Eurus and Zephyrus, which are the dominant and most regular winds, sweep through the streets without meeting obstacles and pass freely without causing any disturbance... This kind of plan also makes the town a good suntrap because at sunrise and sunset, and sun lights up the streets which run east-west, and at midday those that run north south..."

However, the logic continued to be interspersed with faith, rituals and symbolism. Lutyens' geometry conveyed a monumental classical style combined with the concept of Ebenezer Howard's Garden City, which was making waves in England during that time. Several Maharajas also engaged the British architects and engineers for planning their capital cities and palaces such as Mysore, Baroda, Jaipur, Jodhpur, Indore, Hyderabad, etc. These were the show pieces of splendour and royal affluence with a few lone voices, such as Patrick Geddes, a natural and social scientist, who maintained the indigenous metaphor of city design in his "conservative surgery" approach.

Patrick Geddes in India

Patrick Geddes was in India from 1915 to 1919. Before arriving in India, Patrick Geddes had no specific knowledge of the culture of India. Soon he learnt about it and his work reflects his perceptivity about the Indian city, revealing the deepest insight and the sympathy for the people. Four years before he arrived at Gateway of India, Bombay, the great durbar in Delhi in 1911 marked the apex of imperial rhetoric, created by plan of Lutyens and architecture of Baker, a city of bungalows, fountains, avenues, palaces and esplanade. The Imperial style got the Colonialist message and it left the borrowed cultural heritage. The old city was seen as a slum fit for clearance.

However, method adopted by Geddes was based on an analytical approach to the issues of urban planning based on social humane concerns. Patrick Geddes' approach was based on the understanding of the spirit of the place and small adjustments, not magniloquent clearances, on rationalisation of the existing, rather than grandiose works of engineering. His plans were moderate in terms of cost and population in planning. He was disturbed by the cities growing without the concern of health, clogging up all their common spaces, overcrowding and segregation of different castes. British planners overcame the problem of congestion by cutting broad boulevards through the crowded districts, while using traditional city gardens for railway stations, industry and power houses. However, Patrick Geddes stated that *'Architecture always claimed to be regulator of the arts, and rightly so, town planning in its turn claims to be regulator of architecture. If this is true, then another truth is also inescapable that Civic is the regulator of Town Planning-----so to perceive the ideals that create the city and keep it alive is supreme task of a civic awareness matured through historical studies and transformed into a science.'* For Geddes, people become the principal term of reference in town planning. If it is to be successful it must be folk planning. This means its task is not to coerce people into new places against their associations, wishes and interests. Instead its task is to find the right places for each sort of people, places where they will really flourish. To give people, in fact, the same care that we give when transplanting flowers, instead of harsh evictions and arbitrary instructions to move on, delivered in manner of officious amateur policeman, Geddes did not favour either the Romantic conservatives linked to Sir Walter Scott of the Oxford movement, Ruskin Morris, and Sir Gilbert Scott, aggressive architects inspired by Haussmann and led by Stubben. Geddes suggested that city planning must be based on Civic and Diagnostic Surveys. In a brief note on Ahmedabad, where he was asked to give his opinion on circle of city walls, a careful analysis of ring of walls is essential, with precision of a botanist and sensitivity of an architect.

In 1915, Patrick Geddes gave a report on planning of the Walled City of Delhi (Shahjahanabad). He advocated the 'civic survey' as a tool of 'Conservative Surgery' to improve the dilapidated, congested city. Intensive surveying led to working out the minimum number of the most dilapidated houses to be pulled down for creating open spaces within the congested areas and also allowing ventilation for each surrounding house. The few families displaced were to be resettled with a basic standard of housing and environmental hygiene. Thus he advocated slum rehabilitation and improvement, in place of clearance, and greenfield development. He strengthened the need for creating urban Improvement Trusts.

Fig. 2.157: Indore: Expansion of the New Industrial City in the North-East Quadrant under Geddes Plan

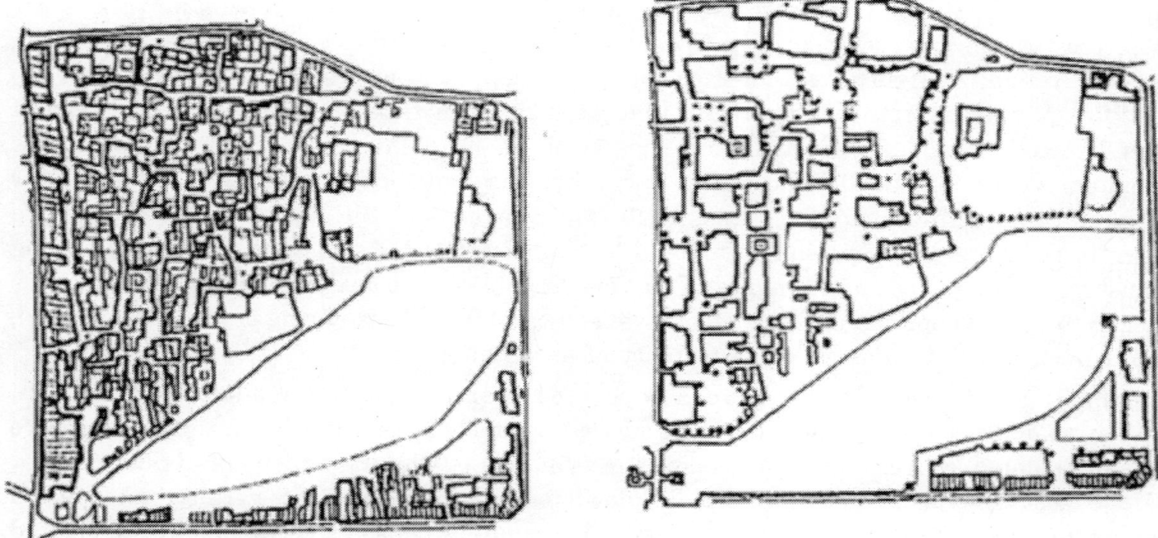

Fig. 2.158: Conservative Surgery applied to Balrampur, 1917

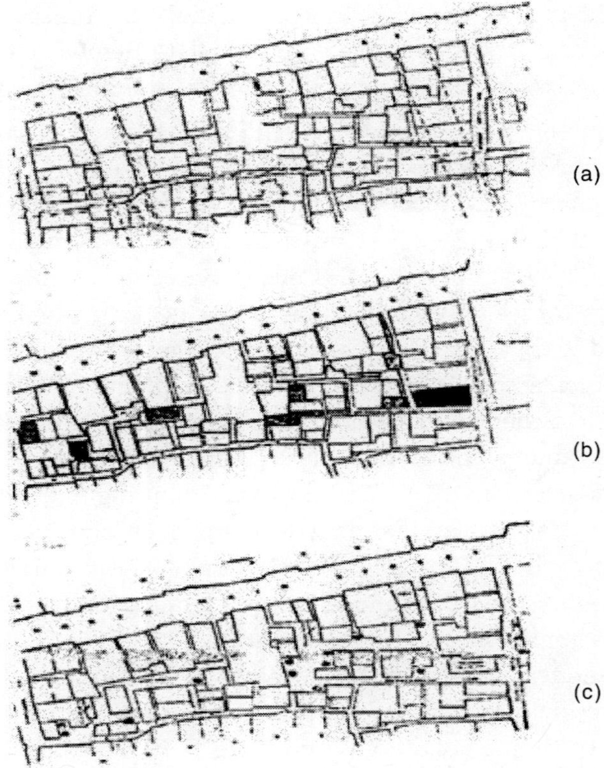

Fig. 2.159: Tanjore: (a) Municipal Council Plan, (b) and (c) Geddes plan with application of the theory of conservative surgery

Improvement Trusts

Under the Bombay Improvement Trust Act, 1898, Improvement Trust was established with the object of improving some of the badly congested areas in the city with roads, open spaces and reservation of plots for schools, hospitals and other amenities. The Bombay Improvement Trust prepared 71 different schemes in Mumbai and also constructed residential tenements for low income groups. It also took up the schemes of municipal services- water, sewerage, drainage, electricity and roads. However, the costs could not be recovered in most of the cases and the Trust could not survive. Ultimately, in the year 1937 all the assets, liabilities and functions were transferred to the Bombay Municipal Corporation. Improvement Trusts were also established in Delhi, Punjab, United Provinces, Agra, Kanpur, Calcutta and many other towns.

Town Planning Acts in India

The first town planning legislation came in the year in 1915 when the Bombay Town Planning Act was passed. This was only applicable to the areas under Bombay Province and even the city of Bombay was excluded in the original Act, unless special permission from government was obtained. It was first made applicable to Bombay city in 1944 after explosion of a ship in Bombay Harbour with heavy damages to buildings in Mandvi area.

The Act was inspired by the British Town Planning Act, 1909, with several similarities and differences. Both Acts provide for making Town Planning Schemes for areas under process of development by the local authorities. Against the elaborately described social objectives in the Town Planning Act in UK, the objective of Bombay Act was more physical-orderly development, provision of amenities and services, including roads, sewer and drains. The British T.P. Act provides only zoning of areas for housing, shopping, etc and not detailed planning of each and every plot. There is provision for recovery of betterment charges but hardly any such charges are recovered from owners of lands falling in the T.P. Scheme. The main drawback of T.P. Schemes in Bombay had been the inordinate delays involved in the laid down procedures under the Act. Besides Bombay, Punjab Town Improvement Trust (1920), UP Improvement Trust (1919), Madras Town Planning Act, 1920. Many States in India modelled or modified their Town Planning legislation on the basis of Town and Country Planning Act, (1947) of United Kingdom. A Model Town and Regional planning and Development Act (1962) was drafted by the Town and Country Planning Organisation (TCPO) and Urban Development Plan Formulation and Implementation Guidelines (1996) were prepared by the Institute of Town Planners, India for the Ministry of Urban Development, Government of India. The UDPFI Guidelines have been revised as the Urban and Regional Development Plans Formulation and Implementation Guidelines (URDPFI) in 2014–15. In view of 74th CAA, Right to Fair Compensation in Land Acquisition, Resettlement and Rehabilitation Act 2013, a revised Model Town and Country Planning and Development Law has been drafted, as a part of URDPFI guidelines.

New Cities in Independent India

After the Independence of the country in 1947, there was a zeal to build a new India. Several new cities and industrial townships were taken up such as Chandigarh, Bhubaneshwar, Gandhinagar, Bokaro, and Faridabad.

Chandigarh, the capital of Punjab and Haryana, was designed by Le Corbusier. It was based on his concept of city as a human system, comprising the head, heart and hands, with roads as the veins. It echoes Corbusier's vision of the city, its human engagement and urban landscape. In the great Indian cities of Mughals, the water flowing from the mountains and rainwater was collected into lakes, reservoirs and channels, where the gardens were located (e.g. Shalimar Bagh in Srinagar). Le Corbusier applied the same principle in Chandigarh Plan. Corbusier's plan for Chandigarh established lake Sukhna that impounds the water flowing from the Shivalik hills and a leisure valley along an existing stream cutting across the city. It cuts through the city, bringing the landscape in the midst of the city, which has become an ecological asset for the city, besides a source of drainage, recreation and protection of bio-diversity.

The capital complex was located at the head of the city, with the hill landscape in the backdrop. A hierarchical system of V-7 roads, streets and pathways provided mobility to its citizens. The City Centre was at the heart of the city. The industrial zone was buffered by a 'invioable' green belt.

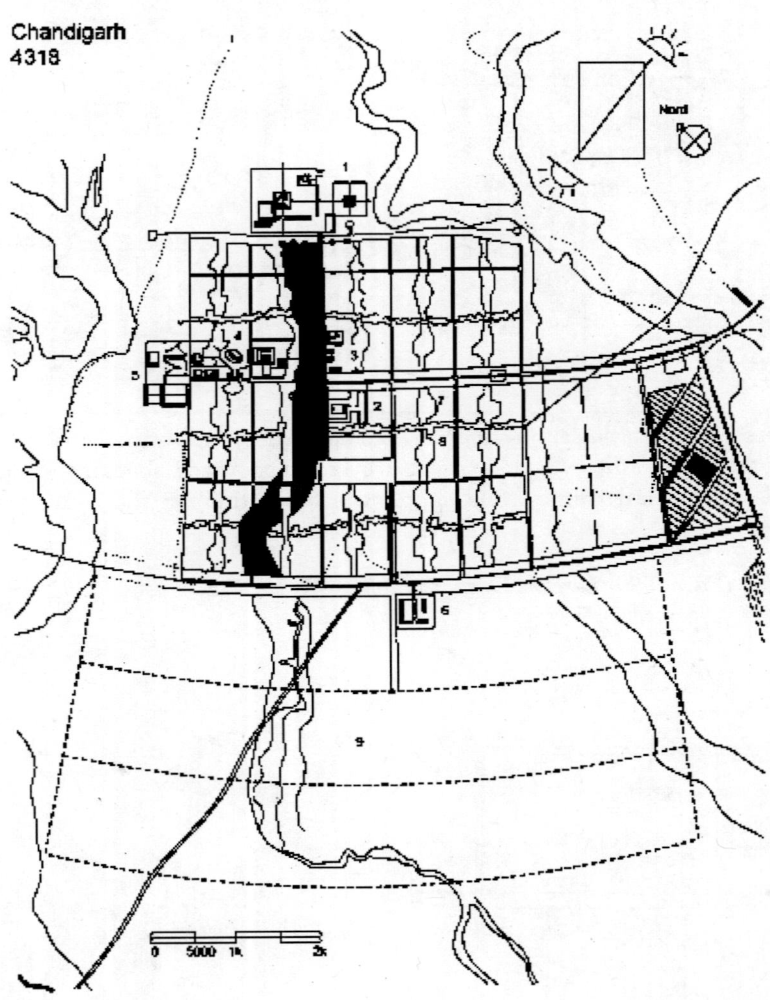

1. Capitol complex
2. Central business district
3. Hotels, restaurants and visitors' center
4. Museums and stadium
5. University
6. Wholesale market
7. Park through residential areas
8. Shopping Street (V4)
9. Area for expansion of the city

Fig. 2.160: Plan of Chandigarh by Le Corbusier, 1951

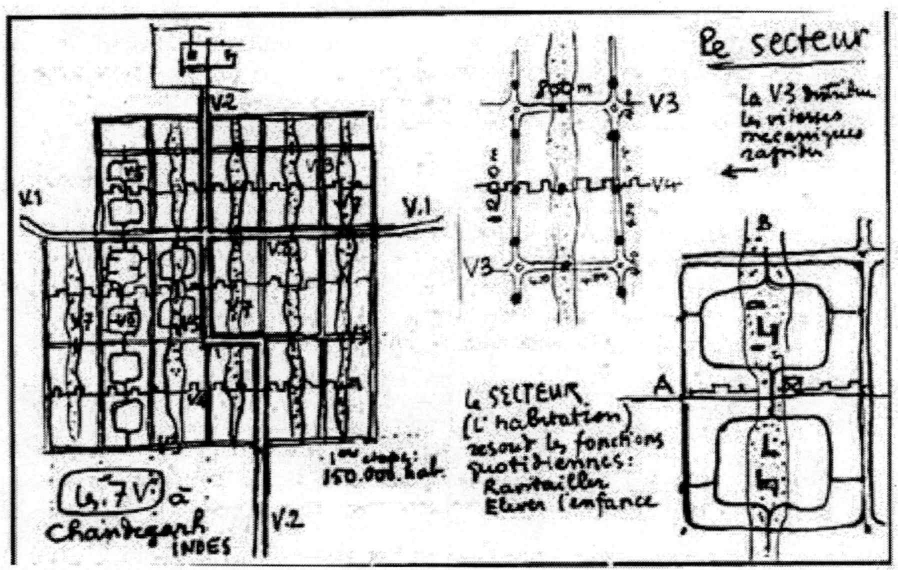

Fig 2.161: Studies by Le Corbusier in 1951 for Chandigarh. A residential sector is surrounded by streets carrying through traffic (V3) and bisected by neighbourhood shopping street (V4 and V5). Loop roads distribute local traffic while parkland extends through the sector providing sites for schools, etc.

Source: Boesiger, W. (Ed.) 1999, Le Corbusier- Complete Works, Birkhauser Publishers, Basel

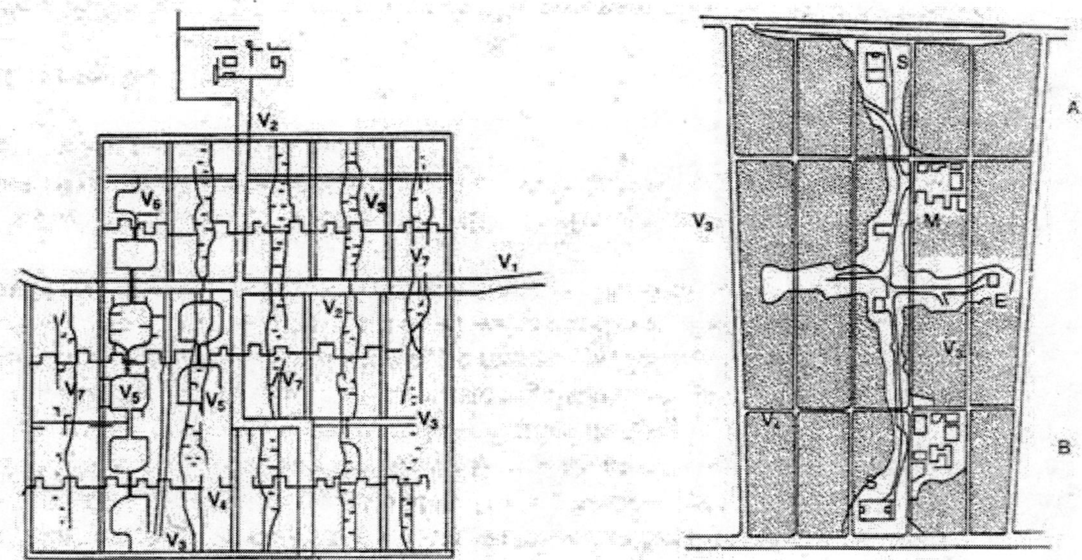

Fig. 2.162: Le Corbusier's road classification, V1 cross country, V2 branch to city, V 3 sector divide, V 4 sector connector, V5 local spine, V6 buildings, V 7 pedestrians through interlinked greens

Source: Boesiger, W. (Ed.) 1999, Le Corbusier- Complete Works, Birkhauser Publishers, Basel

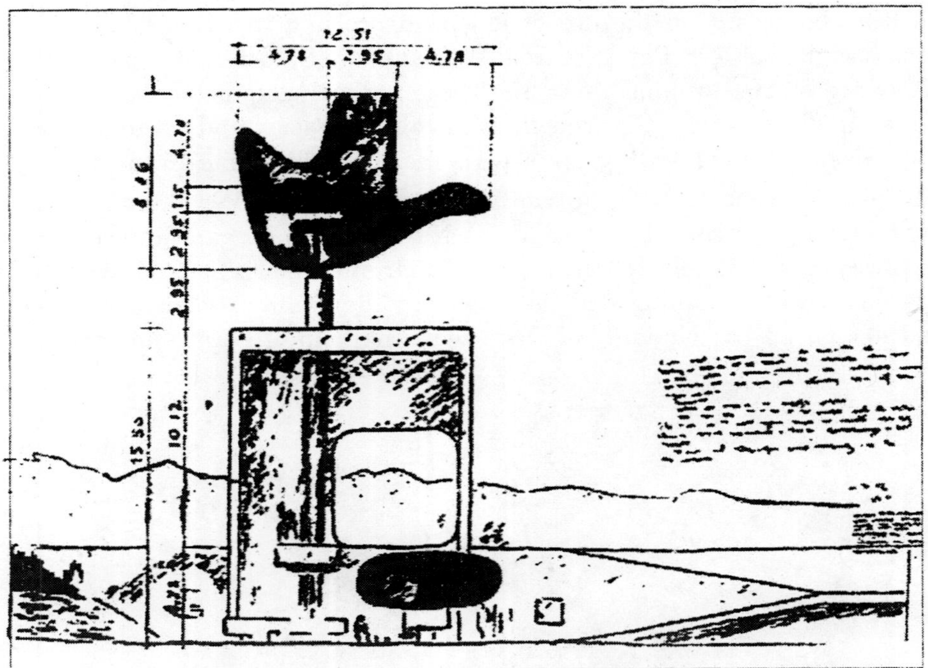

Fig. 2.163: Open Hand Monument in Chandigarh by Le Corbusier is based on philosophy of man as a giver with an open hand

Fig. 2.164: The Capital Complex by Le Corbusier

After the independence, Indian cities witnessed unprecedented in-migration. Delhi for example witnessed an estimated half a million refugees seeking shelter. Delhi's population was thus doubled up in just two months. Tents were pitched to house these uprooted people.

Communal riots broke out on the eve of independence and there was mass movement of population across the borders. Refugees from West Punjab, Baluchistan, Sind and North West Frontier Province started coming to Delhi. These were the uprooted families who sought shelter in the lap of free India. Government rose to the occasion and set up numerous camps and took up development of setting up of permanent rehabilitation townships.

In Delhi 36 Rehabilitation townships sprang up which include Nizamuddin, Lajpat Nagar, Kalkaji, and Malviya Nagar, the three Patel Nagars, Moti Nagar, Ramesh Nagar, Tilak Nagar, Kingsway camp, Gandhi Nagar, Kalkaji, Tihar and Sheikh Sarai. However, for a more comprehensive citywide planning and development, the Delhi Development Authority was created and it took up the planning of Delhi with the help of Ford Foundation.

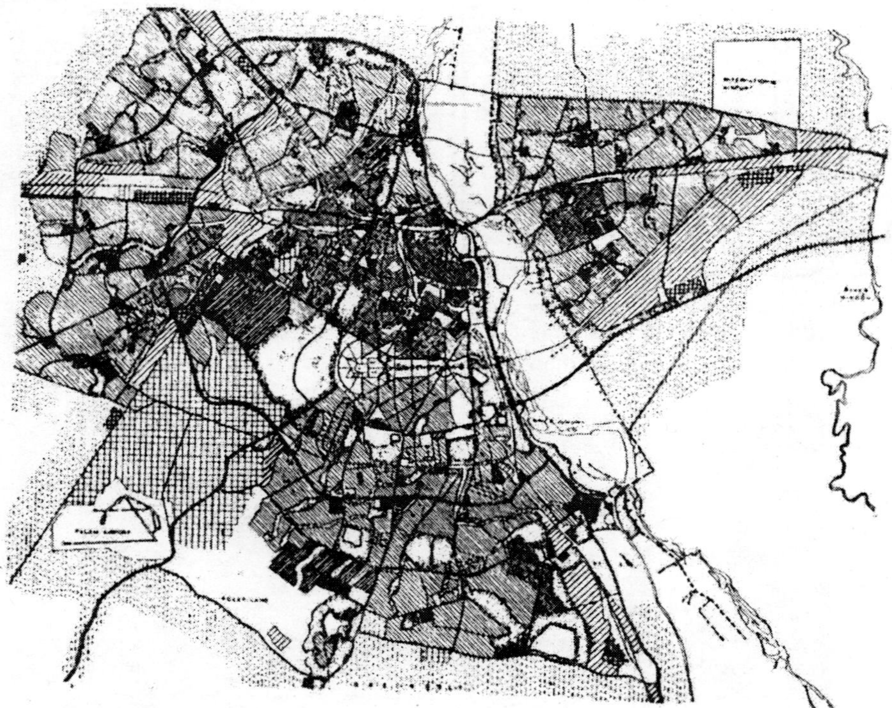

Fig. 2.165: Master Plan for Delhi-1962 was first statutory Master Plan in India. It was planned for a population of 5.7 million (1981) covering an urban area of 44,000 Ha.

The Master Plan for Delhi was given statutory shape on September 1st 1962. It assessed the existing deficiencies in housing community facilities, services, etc. and projected the requirements of 4.6 million (revised to 5.3 million) population in 1981. The Delhi Master Plan earmarked the Old City for Urban Renewal, comprising redevelopment, rehabilitation and conservation. The Master Plan for Delhi-2001 projected the concept of Special Area Plan, which covered an area of 2600 Ha., comprising the Walled City, Karol Bagh and other Areas. The Master Plan for Delhi-2021 (MPD-2021), notified in 2007, stipulates the conservation of various Heritage Zones of Delhi, including Shahjahanabad and Lutyens' Bungalow Zone (LBZ).

The development of State Capitals, industrial townships, port towns, etc. was also initiated in 1950s. As per Town and Country Planning Organisation the Master Plans of about 1500 cities have been prepared by the State Town Planning Departments. After the economic liberation policies (1991), the Parliament enacted the 73rd and 74th Constitutional Amendment Acts (1992), which provided for the constitution of District and Metropolitan Planning Committees and decentralisation and democratisation of the planning process. However, there had not been much progress on this count, except in few States.

From time to time the Ministry of Urban Development floated schemes, such as Integrated Development of Small and Medium Towns which covered 235 cities and towns across the country. The Regional Plans of various metro cities were also prepared, such as Mumbai, Delhi, Kolkata, Chennai, Hyderabad, Bangalore, Ahmedabad, etc. Under the Special Economic Zone Act, 2003, about 200 SEZs have been developed. Several private sector townships have also come up, which include Amby Valley and Lavasa in Maharashtra.

The existing metro cities also added large sub-cities, e.g. Rohini, Narela and Dwarka in Delhi, Kalyan , Jadavpur and Rajarhat in Kolkata, New Mumbai, Vashi, Belapur and other townships in Mumbai, and Vidhyadhar Nagar in Jaipur.

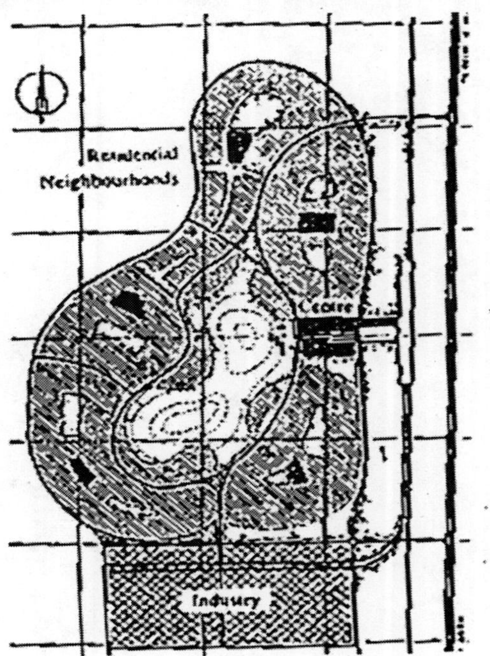

Fig. 2.166: Development Plan of Faridabad (O.N. Konigsberger)

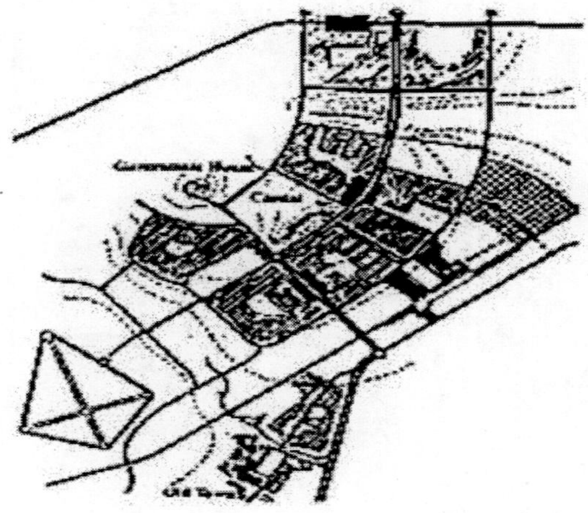

Fig. 2.167: Development Plan of Bhubaneshwar (O.N. Konigsberger)

Fig 2.168: Town and Country Planning Organisation identified 235 small and medium towns in India for integrated development

Source: Town and Country Planning Organisation

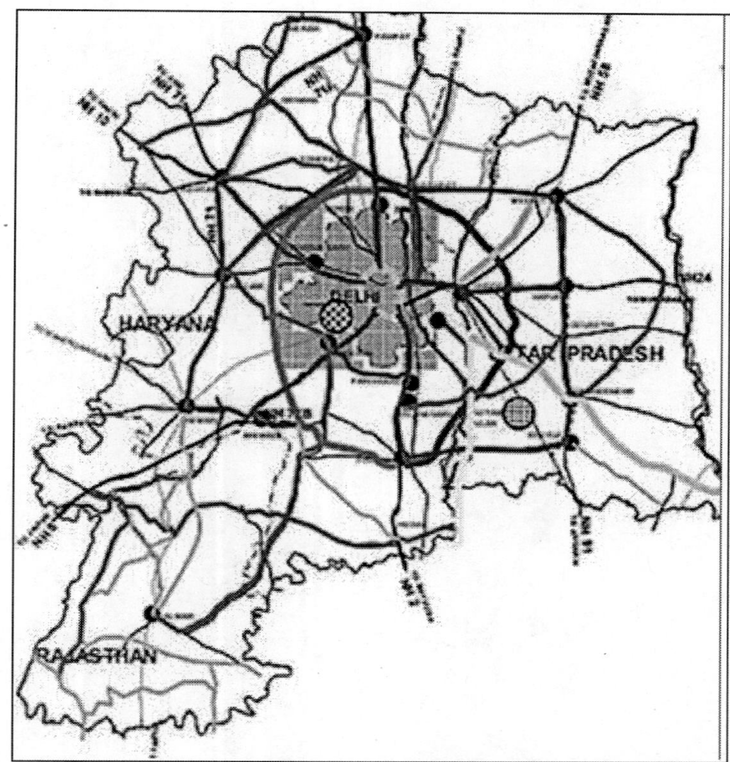

Fig. 2.169: National Capital Region-Proposed Transport Network (Roads)-2032

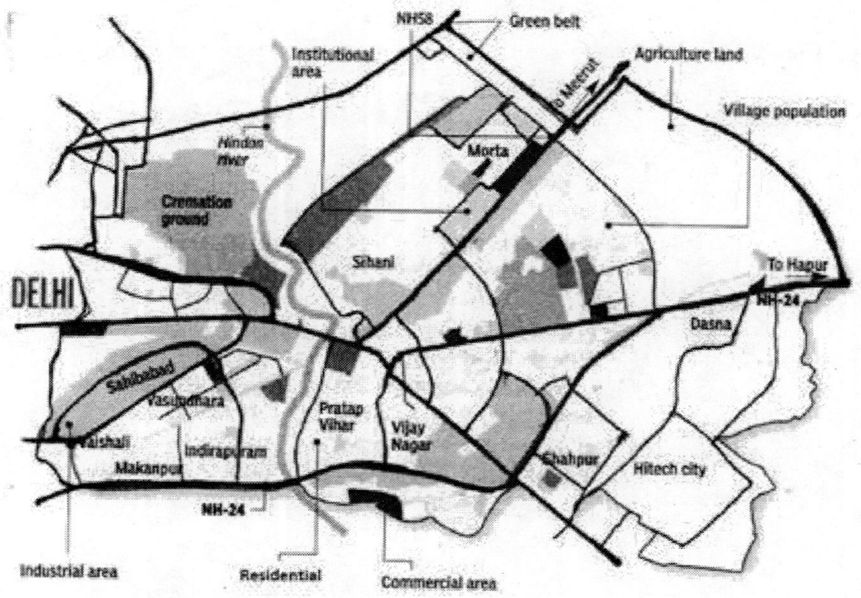

Fig. 2.170: Ghaziabad Master Plan 2021

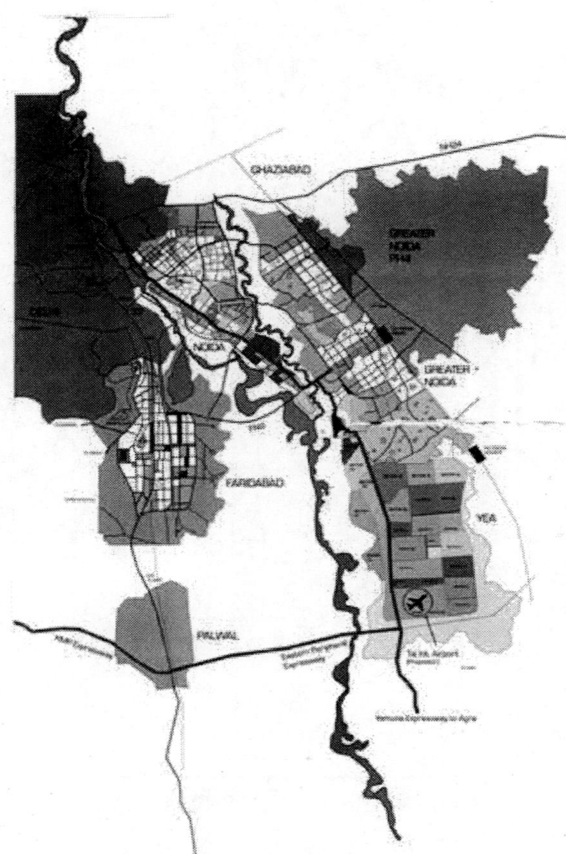

Fig. 2.171: Composite map of Noida, Greater Noida and Faridabad

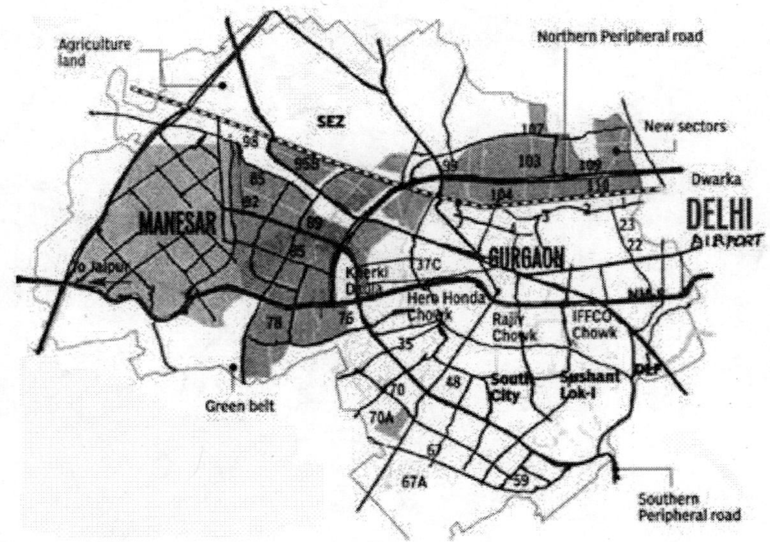

Fig. 2.172: Gurgaon-Manesar Master Plan 2025

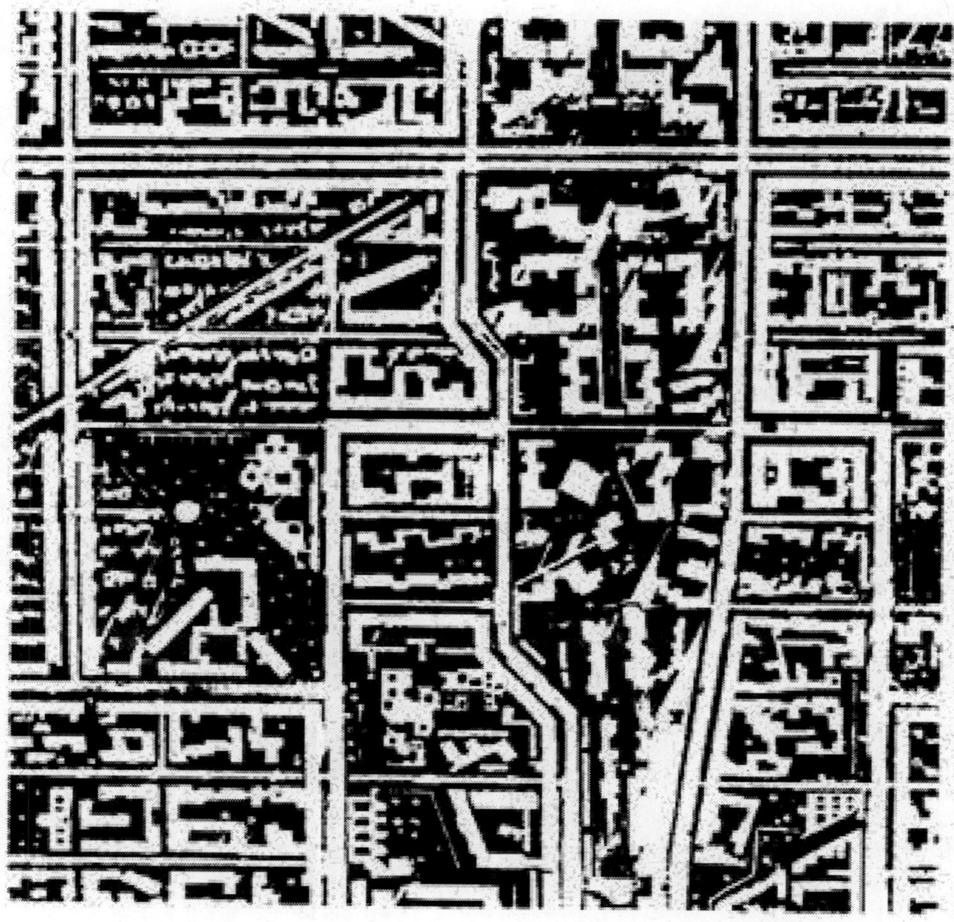

Fig. 2.173: Plan of Vidyadhar Nagar (New Jaipur) (Architect B.V. Doshi)

The new pattern envisages a partnership approach for housing and infrastructure projects including ports and airports, rail freight corridors and industrial regions. The emergence of transport corridors with a substantial increase in industrial investment, services, flow of goods and people along them has been a significant feature of spatial change in recent years. The "Golden Quadrilateral" network of National Highways linking Delhi, Mumbai, Chennai and Kolkata as well as North-South and East-West Corridors, promote this type of growth. One of the recent initiatives is Western (1,483 kilometres), Delhi-Mumbai Industrial Corridor (DMIC) and Eastern (1,279 kilometers) Delhi-Kolkata Rail Freight Corridor. A separate corridor for freight trains would enable the Railways to achieve higher speed, facilitate guaranteed transit time that will reduce cost of transportation.

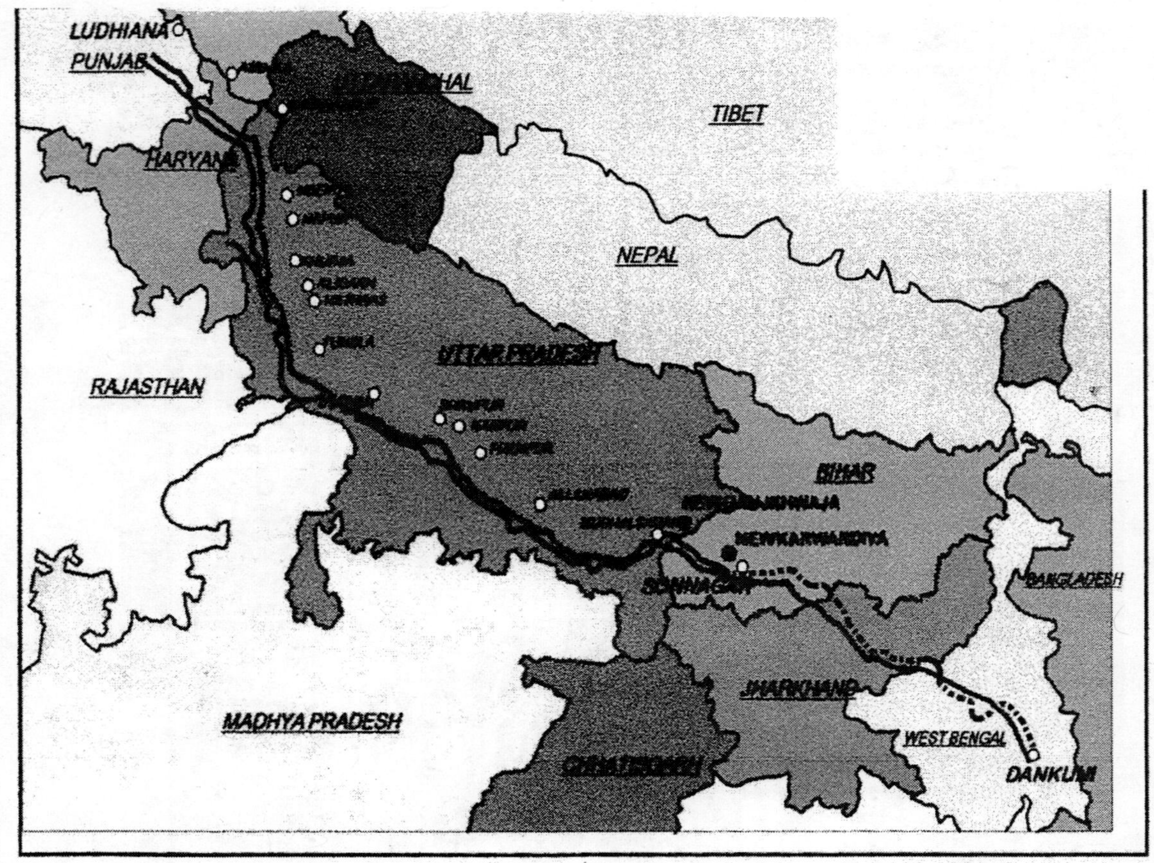

Fig. 2.174: Eastern Corridor

Source: DFCC

The Delhi-Mumbai Industrial Corridor (DMIC) is Asia's biggest urban development project, which is expected to create 24 smart cities (7 Industrial Regions) spanning six Indian States, including Uttar Pradesh, Haryana, Rajasthan, Madhya Pradesh, Gujarat and Maharashtra. The key features of these cities include digital planning and governance, compact, vertical development, efficient public transportation system, technology for smart grids and better management of civic infrastructure, recycling of sewage water for industrial use, green spaces and easy access to goods, services and other community activities. This project has the potential to be a benchmark in smart urban infrastructure and low carbon development.

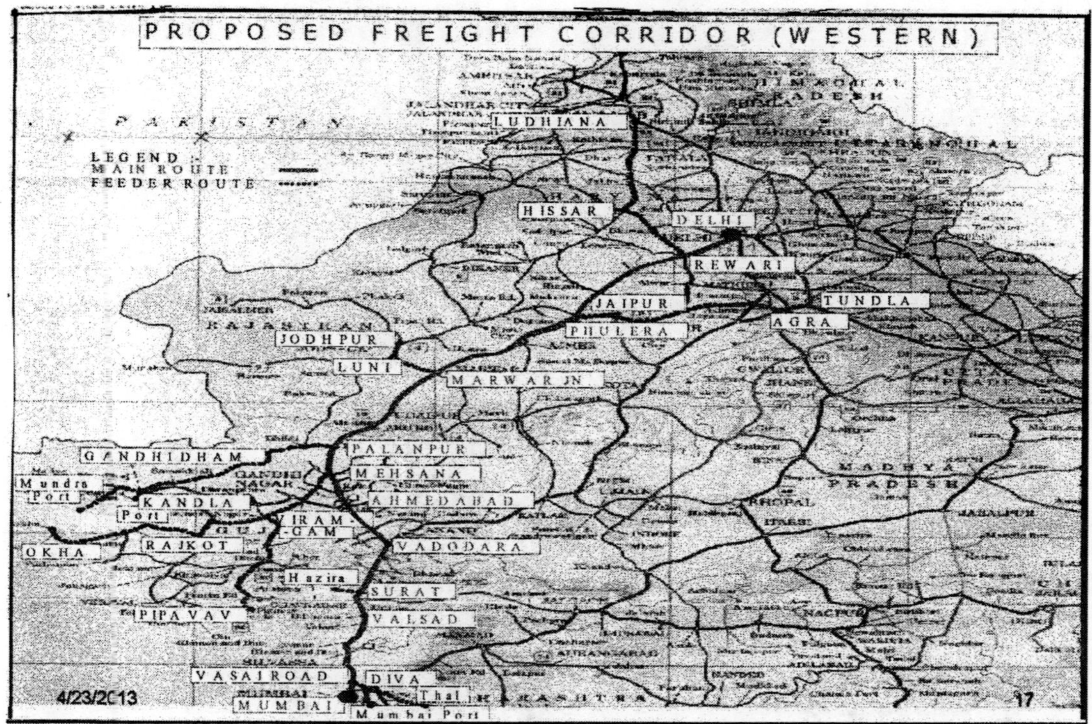

Fig. 2.175: Delhi Mumbai Industrial Corridor

Source: DMIC Ltd.

GIFT Gandhi Nagar Smart City: Gujarat International Finance Tec-City (GIFT) is an upcoming Smart city at Gandhi Nagar in Gujarat. It covers 886 acres (359 Ha) of area. It provides high quality physical infrastructure (electricity, water, gas, district cooling, roads, telecoms and broadband), special economic zone (SEZ), international education zone, an international techno park, shopping malls, stock exchange and service units. The Gujarat Urban Development Company Limited (GUDCOL) and Infrastructure Leasing & Financial Services (IL&FS) have established a Joint Venture Company. Gujarat International Finance Tec-City Company Limited (GIFTCL) for development of the project. The estimated cost of the project is ₹ 70,000 crores.

It will be a globally benchmarked smart city having an ultimate built up area of 85,000,000 sq ft (7,900,000 m^2), in which state of art connectivity, communication, technology, security and other services have been planned. It is envisaged to become a model of smart and sustainable city. It will provide a safe and clean environment, and ecological integrity through low energy consumption, smart energy grids, piped gas. Internet Gateway, District Cooling System. pneumatic waste management and intelligent/bionic. systems. Recycling and reduction in wastes will help to protect the natural environment. The city has been planned by East China Architectural Design & Research Institute (ECADI) and Fairwood Consultants India.

A multi-modal mix of transport systems (MRTS/LRTS/BRTS, etc.) connect the city with Ahmedabad, Airport, Gandhinagar and other cities. Walk-to-work has been used with a modal split of 10:90 between private and public transport. Besides Bus Rapid System (BRT), Metro and electric personal rapid transit systems are planned for intra-mobility.

Fig. 2.176: GIFT Smart City Gandhi Nagar

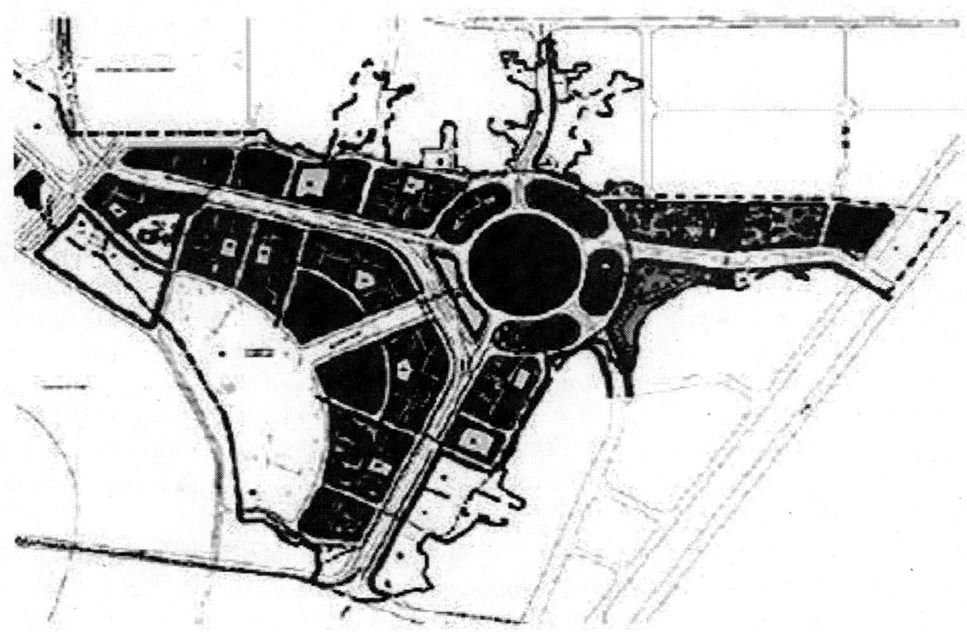

Fig. 2.177: Plan of GIFT Smart City Gandhi Nagar

However, it lacks human scale, local identity, inclusive housing and spaces for informal sector. International style, glass and chrome buildings apparently do not respond to hot-dry climate of Gandhinagar and look transplanted. More important than international style glass buildings are the greens, public places, health and education facilities, affordable housing and public transit. The Indian cities have to be liveable for all and engage with people, their traditions and diverse cultures. An Indian city has to be inclusive and focus on the jobs, livelihood, services, mobility and social housing. It should reserve space for slum dwellers, informal sector and provide dedicated facilities for the pedestrians and non-motorised transport. This means evolving a new paradigm and design of a city which is based on place making and responds to local culture, climate and poverty, rather than the buildings, corporate business and land use zoning. Let us learn from the past while planning and building smart cities, which can be a turning point in India's urban growth.

New Urbanism

New Urbanism also called Smart Growth, New Community Design, Neo-traditional Design, Traditional Neighbourhood Development, Location Efficient Development and Transit Oriented Development is a set of development practises to create more attractive, efficient and liveable communities. These can significantly improve accessibility and reduce per capita automobile travel. New urbanism focuses on the community has a discernible Activity Centre. This is often a plaza, square or green, and sometimes a busy or memorable intersection. A transit stop should be located at this centre. Special attention is paid to protecting the public realm and creating quality public spaces, including sidewalks and paths, parks, streetscapes and public buildings. This helps create more community identity and cohesion, leading to stronger and healthier communities. Buildings at the centre are placed close to the sidewalk and to each other, creating an urban sense of spatial definition. Buildings towards the edges are placed further away and further apart from each other, creating a more rural environment. Most dwellings are within a five-minute walk (a quarter mile) from the center. Streets are designed for walking and cycling, with sidewalks on both sides, bike lanes where needed, good crossings, traffic calming features used to control motor vehicle traffic speeds and other features to encourage non-motorized travel. There are a variety of dwelling types. These take the form of houses, row houses, and apartments, such that younger and older, singles and families, the poorer and the wealthier can find places to live. There are places to work within and adjacent to the neighbourhood, including shops, office buildings and live-work units. Other specific features of new urbanism include the following:

- There are shops sufficiently varied to meet common household needs, such as convenience stores, a post office, a bank, ATM and a gym.
- A small ancillary building should be permitted within the backyard of houses. It may be used as a rental apartment, or as a place to work.
- There should be a primary school close enough so that most children can walk from their dwelling. This distance should not be more than one kilometer.
- There are parks, trails and playgrounds near every dwelling. Their distance should not be more than one kilometer.
- Network of highly connected roads and paths provide multiple routes between destinations, increasing accessibility and reducing problems, if one route is closed. Access points into neighbourhoods may be highlighted with a gateway or signs.
- Thoroughfares are relatively narrow and shaded by rows of trees that slow traffic and create an appropriate environment for pedestrians and bicyclists.

- Parking lots and garage doors rarely end at the front of the thoroughfares. Parking is relegated to the rear of the buildings and usually accessed by alleys or lanes.
- Certain prominent sites are reserved for public buildings. A building must be provided at the centre for neighbourhood meetings.
- The neighbourhood should be self-governing, deciding on matters of maintenance, security, and physical evolution.

New Urbanism and Transit Oriented Development reflect local level planning, while access management, location-efficient development and clustering reflect similar principles at the site and block level, even sometimes at the regional level. New Urbanism has gained increasing attention among development professionals and the general public, particularly in regions experiencing growth-related conflicts. Many see the New Urbanism as a way to accommodate growth while enhancing community and environmental objectives.

City Typology

The cities in India have evolved over a long period of time, which accelerated during last 300 years. The typology of the cities in India can be categorised as given below:

Typology	Examples
1. Military	Amber (1037 AD)
2. Capital /Military	Dausa, Tonk (1006 AD)
3. Capital /Trade	Shahjahanabad (Delhi), Jaipur (1727 AD), Agra, Lahore, Ahmedabad, Baroda, Gwalior, etc.
4. Mercantile	Sanganer (16th Cent.), Jaisalmer, Udaipur, Bangalore, etc.
5. Religious/Pilgrim	Ranakpur, Palitana, Ajmer, Amritsar, Badami, Dwarka, Gaya Kanchipuram, Somnath, Mathura, Madurai, Tirupati, Badrinath, Kedarnath, Bhubaneshwar, Amravati, Haridwar, Varanasi, Warangal, etc.
6. Out Grown Villages	Muzzafarnagar, Muzzafarpur, Gazipur, Sohna, Neemrana, Baghpat, Shamli, etc.
7. Colonial/Presidency	Bombay (Mumbai), Calcutta (Kolkata), Madras (Chennai), Pondicherry, Panjim, Kochi, Capitals/Port Cities, Ahmedabad, etc.
8. Cantonments	Fort Williams, Alipore, Kohima, Allahabad, Banaras, Meerut, Agra, Delhi, Mhow, Jabalpur, Jhansi, Sagar, Satna, Solan, Jalandhar, Ludhiana, Amritsar, etc.
9. Hill Stations	Nainital, Mussorie, Simla, Darjeeling, etc.
10. New Cities	Chandigarh, Bhubaneshwar, Gandhinagar, Amravati, etc.
11. Industrial Cities	Faridabad, Kanpur,Bokaro, Dhanbad, Bhilai, etc.

Understanding the Heritage Significance of Cities

The cities are the interaction of people, places and time. As such understanding of the process of their evolution helps to appreciate them as a heritage resource. However, these are subject to development pressures and globalisation threats. This demands a sensitive and futuristic vision to manage the past, that includes natural and built heritage and conserve the symbiotic relationship between the natural and the built heritage. This requires that the whole range of components of a cultural landscape which include the cities, rivers, hills, mountains, streams; drains, agricultural areas, ponds, tanks, lakes, canals, villages, pilgrimages and religious centres, historic cities, etc. be identified and conserved.

A systematic study of a city or a village can help in conservation of its cultural significance. This should be done with the help of maps, surveys and photographs.

1. **Baseline Information:**
   - Name of the City/District/Zone/Area
   - Demographic Profile
   - Physical Surveys/Maps
2. **Chronology/History**
3. **Heritage Significance, Structures and Functions:**
   - Built
   - Natural
   - Non-tangible
4. **Socio-cultural Profile**
5. **Economic Conditions, Employment, Informal Sector**
6. **Land Use Survey, Analysis and Proposals**
7. **Profile and Inventory of:**
   - Infrastructure Services (Status, Issues, Jurisdiction/Responsibility) for Water Supply, Electricity, Sanitation, Sewerage, Drainage, Solid Waste Management, Roads
   - Mobility Networks, Nodes and Parking Areas
   - Housing
   - Open Spaces, Forests, Boulevards, Parks, Sports, Playgrounds
   - Water Bodies, Rivers, Canals, Drains, Lakes, etc.
   - Heritage Zone, Parks and Structures (Archaeological) Listed/Others/Unprotected
   - Visual Survey
8. **Findings and Abstraction:**
   - Significant Heritage and Historic Value
   - Areas where planning interventions are required

Debriefing and Review

1. Explain the purpose and relevance of study of historic human settlements.
2. Briefly explain the chronology, form and salient features of 3 settlements, one each from mythology, nekropolis and Mughal era cities.
3. Give comparative highlights (Social/Cultural/Economic and Environmental) of traditional Indian and European cities.
4. Write short notes:
   - The Radiant City
   - Garden City
   - Brasilia
   - Patrick Geddes
   - Jamshedpur
5. How the industrial revolution changed the urban paradigm?
6. How will you structure the study of a living traditional city for its planning and conservation.
7. What lessons a planner can draw from the following cities:
   (a) Shahjahanabad/Delhi
   (b) Rome
   (c) Nalanda
   (d) Jaipur
   (e) Florence
   (f) Isfahan
   (g) Venice
   (h) Athens
   (i) Beijing

CHAPTER

3

Town Planning Surveys, Mapping and Analysis

Town planners use variety of techniques at different stages of the planning. These relate to physical and socio-economic surveys, collection of data for assessment of existing conditions in a settlement, as well as analysis and projections of future requirements in respect of various activities. Substantial proportions of these techniques are highly elaborate and demand intensive data inputs. Considerable time is lost in collecting the required data causing delay in the plan preparation process. Further with rapid urbanisation, planners need simplified techniques for analysis and plan preparation.

Surveys and Land Information Systems

Surveys are the pre-requisites to town planning. Various kinds of surveys are conducted according to the need, purpose and resources:

- Field Surveying, Total Station Survey by electronic equipment.
- Global Positioning System, Photogrammetry and Aerial Photography
- Satellite Imagery and Remote Sensing
- Geographic Information System (GIS)
- Cadastre/Spatial Data Infrastructure
- Air Borne Laser Terrain Modelling (ALTM)
- Radar Informetry.
- Transmitting graphic and digitised (map) information on-line by application of internet, compression of data

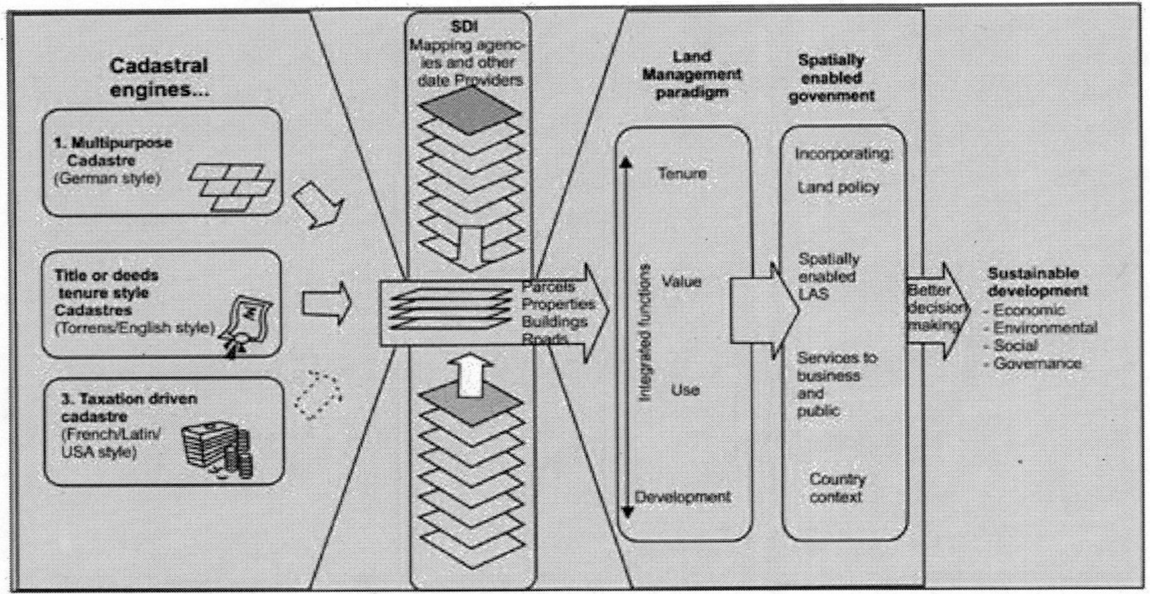

Fig. 3.1: Significance of the Cadastre (Williamson and Wallace, 2007)

The survey maps (Survey of India, etc.) can be superimposed and corrected by ground surveys, administrative revenue maps, aerial maps, satellite imagerises and other available maps, such as environmental, groundwater, etc. All these should be mechanically enlarged or reduced to the same scale (preferably 1:4000, which corresponds to revenue maps 1″ = 330 feet). These provide useful vector base maps for planning without the need for elaborate, time consuming fresh surveys.

Mapping

A map can be defined as representation of earth's pattern as a whole or part on a plane surface with conventional signs, drawn to a scale and projection so that each and every point on it corresponds to the actual terrestrial position. No matter how large or small a community is, a planner has to deal with spatial information required for planning land parcels, zoning, landuse, transportation networks, housing stock, as well as to monitor multiple urban and regional indicators, forecast community needs, and to plan accordingly. Mapping activities are valuable in understanding and communicating planning issues.

Scale of Map

The scale of map used depends upon the size of the planning area, the coverage and extent of the information to be shown. The scale of maps for different types of planning exercises at various levels may be selected out of the range indicated in the table 3.1. Scale of Maps provides the basis for planning. It is the spatial dimension of development. For various levels of planning, appropriate kinds and scale of map are essential. Apart from field surveying, maps are now available through internet, satellite, geographic information system and aerial photography. New technologies are emerging which map hidden/ underground information (like service lines, minerals, geology, sub-soil water, temperature, etc.). For town planning purpose, a map will have the following characteristics:

- **Geometry, positioning and height:** The geometry of a map is achieved through a set of ground control points, called stations and leveling Bench Marks (BMs). These stations may have the utmost accuracy of a geodetic station. BMs are, presently, being provided by the Survey of India (SOI). The position of these stations is given in the form of coordinates expressed in terms of latitude and longitude. In most of the cases, accurate information about the stations and the BMs is restricted.
- **Contents of a map:** The earlier technology of the ground based methods (plane tabling, etc) has been replaced by the aerial photography (photogrammetry) and satellite imagery. The resolution of the modern day satellites has reached a level of one metre. This enables contents of the map to be based on high-resolution satellite imagery on most of the scales of mapping.
- **Updating the map:** It is a natural desire of a map user that the map is up to date. Here also the satellite imagery is of great utility because satellite visits the same spot at a regular interval of say, one month or so. Therefore, the problem of updating the maps, to large extent, can be solved.
- **Scale:** The scale of a map can be chosen according to its purpose, such as given below:

Table 3.1: Scales and Contours of Maps for different users

Functions	Scale	Height/Contour Interval(CI)
Regional Plan	1:40,000	20-50m
Master Plan/Structure Plan	1:20,000	10-20m
Zonal Plan/Sector Plan	1:10,000	5-10m
Planning Industrial Sites/SEZ	1:4000 to 1:500	2m Contour Interval(CI)
Engineering Plans	1:2000 to 1:500	1m CI +Benchmarks
Housing	1:2000 to 1:500	1m CI +Benchmarks
Transportation	1:5000 to 1:500	1m CI +Benchmarks
Traffic	1:1000 to 1:500	Traffic intersection levels
Services/Utilities	1:1000 to 1:200	Levelling along the alignment
Water Supply and Sewerage, Waste Disposal	1:1000 to 1:5000	1m CI
Road	1:1000 to 1:2000	1 m Contour Interval

Revenue/Land related records	1:2000 to 1:4000	Correlation with Revenue maps (usually 1:4000)
Local Area Plan	1:2000 to 1:4000	
Jhuggi Jhompri Clusters/Basti /Slums	1:1000 to 1:2000	1m CI
Ground water	1:5000 to 1:1000	5m CI
Drainage, Surface Water	1:5000 to 1:1000	5m CI
Inventory of vegetation, trees, parks etc.	1:2000 to 1:500	1m CI
Heritage sites, monuments	1:500 to 1:200	1m CI

Standard Layout of the Maps

The size of the map is largely influenced by statutory requirements of the plan. However, availability of infrastructure for mapping also influences the decision of map sizes. In order to standardise the size of the maps, Bureau of Indian Standards (BIS) has also made an attempt in simplifying the numerous size of the maps. Keeping in view the requirements of urban development plan and recommendation of the BIS, the following sizes of maps/drawings could generally be used:

Table 3.2: Standard sizes of maps

Sl. No.	Category	Size
1	AOO	1710 mm × 1230 mm
2	AO	1230 mm × 880 mm
3	A1	880 mm × 625 mm
4	A2	625 mm × 450 mm
5	A3	450 mm × 330 mm
6	A4	330 mm × 240 mm

Souce: UDPFI Guidelines

The layout of map should facilitate convenient reading of essential infomaion as given below:

Margin

- A trimming margin of 10 mm all around or the purpose of trimming and edge binding.
- A second margin with thick firm line indicating the outer limits of the drawing. Such margin of filing edge could be 25 mm while on other three sides it could be 15 mm for all sizes of maps.

Title

The title of the map should be as short as possible and should include the general title as well as sub-title. Size of letters used for the sub-titles should be generally one to two sizes smaller than the size of letters used for the main title.

Normally, the title block should contain the following particulars:

- Name of the office
- Drawing number and the title of the drawing
- Signature of the dealing officer
- Date of preparation / revision / alteration / approval

Title block should be located at the bottom right hand corner of the sheet in a simple manner. Recommended size of title block is 150 mm × 100 mm for sizes A2 and larger and 150 mm × 75 mm for size of A3.

North Point

Indication of north point is essential on the drawing and it could be located immediately above the title block. Wherever possible, north point should be shown along with the windrose. The north point on a map should, as far as possible, point upwards.

Scale

- Graphic scale: Graphic scale is one of the essential requirements of map and preferably it should be given in metric system for the convenience of reproduction. The graphic scale could be drawn above the title block.
- Spatial scale: In addition to graphic scale, the spatial scale should also be given on all plans. The spatial scale should consist of square with metric sides and the area covered by the square should be given inside the square. Such spatial scale could be located above the graphic scale in the drawing.
- Numeric scale: A numeric scale giving representation fraction (R.F.) e.g. 1:10,000 should be given below the graphic sale. This requirement of the planning level is usually expressed in this scale.

Numbering

A systematic numbering of maps / drawings would be convenient for reference. The respective department/ organization may allow its own numbering system based on standardised methods such as:

- Systematic numbering
- Consecutive numbering
- Sectional numbering

Map Enlargement and Reduction

Maps are generally available in different size and scales from different sources. All these maps could be brought in a required uniform scale by employing any of the following methods:

- Square method
- Similar triangle method
- Pantograph (mechanical method)
- Optical pantograph method
- Photographic method (optical)
- Digital method

The last three methods require sophisticated equipment, but they are rapid and produce more accurate maps.

Map Notation

Planning exercise of settlements requires preparation of maps to depict on ground conditions and variety of data relating to physical and socio-economic aspects which play crucial role in decision making and showing plans in spatial context. Broadly, these maps could be grouped under 2 categories.

- Survey and study maps
- Development Plan/Proposal maps

Source: MoUD (2015) URDPFI Guidelines

Map Analysis Techniques

Map related softwares contain maps from official sources such as NRSC, NIC having locations of infrastructure and services and boundaries of urban/rural centres plotted on them through GIS overlays. They also contain an interface in which numerical data could be inserted through excel sheet following which data is displayed on map. Some initiatives of such software applications are by Gram +++ (which converts numerical data into visual outputs) and Ridhisofts Whizmap (GIS platform for local planning). These and other platforms of GIS can be used for the preparation of different plans.

The above mentioned data collection, analytical and mapping techniques are comprehensive in nature and can be appropriately adopted during the course of the project. Some of the specific techniques for city planning are covered in the following section. City planning has lately taken encompassed innovative concepts of land and resource management. For sustainability, the National Sustainable Habitat Mission (NSHM) recommends that to plan high density development, it is necessary to undertake carrying capacity analysis.

For appropriate location of activities, optimum use of land and protection of natural conservation areas, land-suitability analysis plays an important role wherein land for particular use is selected after considering range of factors.

Source: Integrated District Planning Manual by Planning Commission and National Mission on Sustainable Habitat (MOUD).

Procedue of Collecting Data

Procedure to retrieve data by permissions, which is not available in the public forum are given below:

1. Toposheets

Unrestricted, topographical/ city guide maps published by Survey of India are available for sale. The standard topographical maps on scale 1:25,000, 1:50,000 and 1: 250,000 and city guide maps published for selected towns/cities are useful for urban development plan purpose.

All the topographical maps along the external boundary/coastline of India, as indicated in the Topo Index Map of Survey of India are categorised as restricted maps. The restricted category maps can be procured by State and Central Governments / private individuals / organisations/commercial firms by following a prescribed procedure. Private individuals and organizations / commercial firms can also obtain restricted maps with prior approval from Ministry of Defence through the State Government to whom they should apply.

Aerial photography

The available information regarding area of interest, its scale and cost rates can be obtained from Surveyor General's Office, Dehradun or the Directorate of Survey (Air), New Delhi. Survey of India (Sol) has a dedicated web portal for presenting the meta data information available with Sol from various aerial photography tasks commenced. Web Aerial Photography Transaction Registry (APTR) provides transparent indenting process based on instructions issued by Ministry of Defence.

Indentor can obtain the existing photography by marking the area of interest on 1:250,000 scale topographical map, indicating purpose, identifying the type (B&W, colour, colour infrared), scale and the photographic product required (contact prints, enlargements, mosaic, etc.). If the existing photography does not cater to the requirements of indentor, process for fresh aerial photography can be initiated. The National Government agencies, which provide fresh aerial photography, are:

- Indian Air Force (through Survey of India)
- National Remote Sensing Centre, Hyderabad
- Air Survey Company, Kolkata.

For indenting fresh aerial photography the indentor may approach any of the flying agencies with specific information. The indentor may mark the limit of the area to be photographed on 1:250,000 scale toposheet. If photography is required on scale smaller than 1:50,000 scale or on 1:20,000 or 1:40,000 scale, the specific requirements should be mentioned.

Satellite Imagery

National Remote Sensing Centre, Hyderabad is the nodal agency for supply of current and archived satellite data products from all contemporary satellites namely Ocenasat-1, Ocenasat-2, Resourcesat, Cartosat-1, Cartosat-2, and from older satellites like, IRS-IA, 1RS-IB-, IRS-IC, IRS-ID, IRS-P3. These can be processed to various levels and supplied on photographic media or on digital computer compatible media. Satellite data (processed and raw), aerial products, visualisation services can be assessed from the NRSC Data Centre, Hyderabad. Standard Satellite Data provided by NRSC (as on 2014) is presented in the following Table:

Table 3.3: Satellite Data Provided by NRSC (2013)

Sensor	Product	Scale	(Accuracy)
High Resolution			
PAN (1 m)	System corrected Geo-referenced Mono (9.6 km x 9.6 km)	-	(100m)
	Ortho kit with RFC AOI	-	(100m)
PAN - A/F (2.5m)	Geo-reference Mono (27.5 km × 27.5 km)	-	(250m)
	Stereo Ortho kit (27.5 km × 27.5 km)	-	(250m)
		-	(250m)
	Ortho Corrected (7.5′ × 7.5′)	25,000	(25m)
LISS-4 MX (5m)	Standard (23.5 km × 23.5 km)	-	(500 m)
	Standard Full Scene (70 km × 70 km)	-	(100 m)
	Full Scene Ortho Rectified (70 km × 70km)	-	(10 m)
MICRO WAVE (RISAT) (1m - 50m)	Standard RISAT SAR		
Medium Resolution			
LISS - III (24m)	Standard Full Scene (141 km × 141 km)	250,000	(500 m)
	Full Scene Ortho Rectified (141 km × 141 km)	-	(24m)
AWiFS(56m)	Standard Full Scene (740 km × 40 km)	-	(500 m)
	Full Scene Ortho Rectified (740 km × 740 km)	-	(56 m)
	Standard Quadrant (370 km × 370 km)	500,000	(500 m)
	Quadrant Ortho Rectified (370 km × 370 km)	-	(56 m)
Low Resolution			
OCM (360m)	Full Scene (1420 km × 1420 km)	-	(1.5 km)

Souce: National Remote Sensing Centre

Remote Sensing and Geographical Information System (GIS)

Geographical Information System (GIS) is increasingly being applied for plan formulation, analysis as well as for proposal. GIS is a computer based system, capable of input, storage, manipulation, analysis and geographic data useful for planning, decision making and implementation decision. As a powerful tool, GIS helps the planners to view different scenarios and their outcome so that an optimal strategy can be chosen for planning and development. Besides this, using Remote Sensing and GIS platform for planning have the following advantages:

- Benefits of Analytical techniques in GIS platform
- Ground points and geo-referenced data base for plan preparation
- Dynamic features can be incorporated from RS data
- Regular Database updating and Plan Revision without hassle
- Provides decision making support
- Promotes collaboration among public agencies.
- Automated tasks reduce human errors
- Long Term Investment
- For *Bhuvan* - Increase access to government and efficient approval procedures.

Once the spatial and attribute data are generated in GIS frame, their applications are many and varied. These include resource inventory and management, planning and monitoring, land records for taxation and ownership controls, facilities and services management, and environment impact assessment. GIS is being used for planning of various cities in India lately. Development Plan is a level of plan for which GIS could be used very successfully. Preparation of Development Plan using RS & GIS can be classified under following parts for easier understanding and implementation.

- Base map preparation process
- Preparation of existing land use plan
- Analysis of the study area
- Proposed land use plan
- Revision of the plan

Base Map Preparation Process

Preparation of Master Plan starts with base map preparation before which relevant data of all the information which is to be presented via base map is collected. For base map preparation, *Bhuvan* Land use sheet and/or National Urban Information System, (NUIS) can be used.

Bhuvan Land use sheets provide administrative boundaries, infrastructure, water bodies, watershed boundaries, soil resources, wasteland, groundwater prospect and land use/land cover data. NUIS database comprises thematic mapping and attribute data. Thematic mapping database consists data of; urban land use/cover, physiography, geomorphology, geological structures, lithology, soils, drainage, surface water bodies, road, rail, canal and transportation nodes. Attribute data has spatial layers as, administrative boundaries, forest boundary, settlement and village locations/names of villages and cities, and city/town boundaries and non-spatial data. Other sources of licenced/authentic versions of interpreted satellite imageries can also be used for preparation of base map.

Alternatively, for detailed base map preparation more than one satellite imageries can be merged to provide appropriate information through fused imagery. For preparing thematic maps, under NUIS, Cartosat-1 (panchromatic) and Resourcesat-1 (LISS-IV/ multispectral data) satellite imageries were used, which produced fused (PAN+LISS-IV) image consisting data from both the images.

At this stage, scale-of the map should be decided. Thematic data available with NUIS is at the scale of 1:10,000 and with *Bhuvan* is at the scale of 1:10,000, 1:50,000 and 1:250,000.

Once the base from the Satellite Imagery is prepared, other information can be superimposed on the imagery from the sources other than satellite. Such information could be cadastral maps, revenue records, plans of government agencies and bodies like Industrial Development Corporation, Public Work Department, Railways, National Highways Authority, etc.

Once the base map is prepared, the process of preparation of draft existing land use plan can be started which is next stage.

The existing land use map incorporating the land use features from the satellite interpretation, revenue records is taken for ground verification. The amount of information or area verified under this stage varies from settlement to settlement. In rural area, 15-20 percent of ground verification should be appropriate given the predominance of agriculture, wasteland or forest land cover. While in urban areas ground verification could be 20-50% or even up to 100%, if settlement is very dense.

Once ground verification is over and incorporated in the existing draft land use map, final land use map is produced. In the final existing land use map, the date on which map was approved should be mentioned.

Bhuvan GIS Application for Planning

Bhuvan is a geoportal of Indian Space Research Organisation (ISRO), which coordinates the Indian Earth Observation data and services. *Bhuvan* provides interpretated satellite imageries, thematic data and other services to all, apart from base for urban and regional planning for the authorised government agencies.

Bhuvan provides access to ULBs, development authorities and government administration for urban and regional planning. The three tier system of *Bhuvan* data provides login to draughtman and Town Planning Offices.

The ULB and the State governments by utilising the *Bhuvan* portal can create new data layers for the non-conforming land uses to assess the deviation between the proposed land use plan and the existing situation. Since the mapping has been done on GIS, temporal variation from the latest remote sensing imagery can also be earmarked. This deviation can be addressed during the revision of the plan.

Each level has different powers to access *Bhuvan* database, which is described below:

- Draughtsmen have access to all database for planning purpose, which is indexed in temporary folders. At this level personnel can create new spatial files or edit the existing files and upload data for approval.
- Town planning officer (TPO) can work on urban database. The maps, analysis on existing data, uploaded data and reports by draughtsmen are posted in temporary folder and requires TPO approval to move these files to the database.

After planning activity is over such data can be uploaded on *Bhuvan* portal for public viewing. *Bhuvan* portal has user interface at three levels:

- Viewing: Citizens and governemnt departments can view the spatial plan that is uploaded on *Bhuvan* portal.
- Data creation: Urban Planning authorities can create and upload data on the Portal.
- Feedback on the uploaded Plans: Citizens, government departments and planning authorities can give feedback of uploaded data/plans.

Bhuvan provides Mobile platform to collect data and upload data on web portal, which can be used for urban and regional planning exercise. '*Bhuvan* App' can be downloaded on compatible mobile softwares. Both attribute data and pictorial data can be collection from the field through the app, and uploaded on *Bhuvan* to develop a centralized data base and thereafter can be viewed by all.

Source: MoUD (2015) URDPFI Guidelines.

Collecting the Data for Town Planning

There are two kinds of data sources; primary and secondary. Primary data are first hand information, gathered from original sources, for instance through interviews or going out and directly observing the phenomenon that is being studied. Secondary data are second hand data that someone else has gathered but that are available and may fit one's needs. Data collected by the Census of India, published and stored in the library, becomes a secondary source for everyone's use.

Interviews

They can be face-to-face or by internet or telephone. Face-to-face interviews are more accurate, but any sort of interviewing is expensive. Interviewers must be trained and since one-shot surveys cannot hire full time interviewers, staffing for a survey is difficult. However, survey research centres, often affiliated with universities or with large businesses with experienced staff, are frequently used for major survey and research jobs.

Direct Inspection

The direct inspection of conditions or activities is employed in making traffic counts, recreation area use surveys, housing quality studies, and many other kinds of surveys where human communication is not required to elicit the information directly. However, this is not always as easy as it sounds.

A well known direct technique is participant-observation. The technique was developed by anthropologists in the study of community life. The surveyor becomes a resident of the community and lives among the people, learning their way of life by participating in it. It has been very effectively used by social scientists to investgate problems of middle class and ethnic life.

The question of choice of techniques rests primarily on two criteria—time and cost, both of which we always want to minimise but often reducing one results in increasing the other. The choice of technique is a problem of striking a balance of these two criteria. The mode of observation is often largely determined by either the form or the substance of the question being asked. The questions of a survey are also called the variables of the survey. This means that each question constitutes an item for which we seek information about variation in the population being surveyed. Family income, as a variable or question in a survey, tells us how family income varies among those being surveyed. There are three basic structures that are used in structuring the questions of a survey. These are the basic kinds of measurement scales : nominal, ordinal and interval.

A sample, properly chosen of some fraction of the whole, is usually adequate to estimate the information accurately for the whole population. Where estimates from samples cannot be trusted, and adequate resourcaes are available, the whole population can be surveyed. This is called a 100% sample. But a smaller sample is often the only feasible alternative. The problem is to make certain that the sample accurately represents the population. A sample that is not representative is called a biased sample. If the population to be surveyed is very large and the sampling proportion is small then the test can be done with the target population. Otherwise, as not to bias the real sample, an alternate but similar population should be used for the test. The test run will allow one more accurately to estimate costs in terms of time per interview or per question, allowing final adjustments in sample size or number of questions. It will also help one to spot the ambiguous questions, areas of misinterpretation, poor layout of the form and will help in formulating the special instructions and training that must be given to the survey persons. When surveys are conducted by a staff of interviewers or observers, some system of monitoring is advisable to discourage and eliminate improper practices.

Multiple Index Surveys: To assess the particular aspect or condition, such as poverty, the multiple index system can be adopted by means of a sieve map (or quantitatively by calculating average multiple index). This may help to determine the areas having worst (shown by incidence of all the bad factors in that areas), moderate (few bad factors) or fair (no bad factors) conditions.

Some of the factors chosen for the purpose may be, for example:

- No bath room
- No latrine
- No electricity
- Number of rooms per family
- Rooms excessively small
- Structural condition

Average Multiple Index is calculated for different areas, which can be given different weight depending upon the gravity of a factor in contribution to condition of buildings, poverty or environment.

Transect: Transect as a schematic device can be extremely useful to obtain an overview of a particular area and its problems and issues. This is a diagrammatic illustration and record of major characteristics, events, profiles or issues. While conducting windscreen or triangulation reconnaissance, freehand transects can be prepared, which can supplement the diary or records.

Proxy Indicators: Proxy Indicators are short-cut to time consuming data collection and an alternative to unstructured observations. Information about these indicators may be readily available, which has to be applied on the basis of past experience, common sense and certain assumptions. For example, the growth in the number of banks in an area may indicate its economic base or a greater number of fast food restaurants may represent a youth dominated society or business.

Selection of Areas: After a rapid, synoptic and windscreen survey one can identify areas of representative nature on basis of the criteria for selection of case studies. Depending upon the objectives, the following could be the basis for selection of study areas:

(a) category of settlements/sectors;

(b) level of consolidation;

(c) representative nature of the area.

Search for Questions and Indicators

Accuracy, timeliness, reliability and cost effectiveness are important qualities determining the usefulness of data for formulation of policies. These factors should be kept in view while deciding the data that needs to be collected for a study. It is always useful to deliberate over the question as to what data needs to be collected. To collect quality information, the key informants should be selected carefully, so that those who are knowledgeable in the field are approached. In addition to public agencies, other sources of information, viz., cooperatives, residents groups, women's organizations, traders associations, etc. can also be useful to augment information obtained from primary and official sources. Secondary sources of data, such as, reports and literature can also provide useful information.

Triangulation: Triangulation is an important method to cross-check information obtained from different sources. Multi-disciplinary teams are useful in triangulation, so that the data and information can be cross-checked by observation, discussions and by inter-disciplinary perspectives. This way, the reliability of information obtained through rapid surveys/ appraisal can be enhanced.

Exploration: A preliminary visit can be very helpful to work out a handy semi-structured check list and a framework of indicators for actual survey. Simultaneously, a semi-structured questionnaire for interviews with people and organizations concerned can be prepared. The information thus obtained should be triangulated from time to time to make sense out of it. Information related with observations can be transformed into abstractions in order to make use of it. The information gathered should be crisp and clear so that it can be digested, codified, analyzed, and then synthesized to arrive at the conceptualization.

Triage: Triage is a useful method for assessing social, economic, institutional and technical performance of alternative options, systems or technology. It is particularly concerned with the technical aspects and design process and therefore, is relevant for project planning and design. Under this method, various components of a system are given a score and a screening criteria is evolved. For this, the results of technological systems and performance are reviewed and scored as low, medium or high, as case may be.

Impact Analysis

The purpose of impact analysis is to assess the impact of a particular service, project or facility. A preliminary impact analysis may be essential at the planning stage. For this, the intended or planned activity is placed at the centre and its direct and indirect, positive and negative results are listed in the boxes around the activity. The arrows linking various boxes indicate the linkages, directions and causes. The effects may be comprehensive, which can be categorized under physical, environmental, social, economic, political, institutional, legal and other impacts. For example, the impact of intended regularization of unauthorized colonies can be analysed by evolving a set of Impact Diagrams.

Sustainability Analysis

Amongst various planning alternatives, sustainability is a key consideration in making a viable selection. For this, various stages and steps involved in implementation are listed. Against each major problems are systematically located with their possible solutions. This allows exploration of possible solutions at various stages of implementation. This exercise can help to arrive at logical decisions or conclusions among various alternatives and options.

Strategic Issues Identification

Many enterprises, whether infrastructure, industrial or business end up in failures. While the success stories become the talk of the town and the media, no one knows what happened to other 90% of failures. It is common to blame the political system, interference, corruption or red-tape for the failures and troubles, while the planning and management pitfalls are underplayed. The failure of Tata's Nano project at Singur, West Bengal to take off had been largely due to the political reasons, but 'politics' in a democratic set up is part of the management and cannot be wished away. It works both ways-political alignment and intervention can speed up the project or kill it. The fact is that initiating a large infrastructure projects involves a complex cohort of risks, clearances and interventions, such as obtaining licences, loans, land, labour, technology, public services(like power, water), environment impact assessment, etc. There are still about 40 clearances, approvals and licences required in India for putting up a large project.

In order to obviate the unforeseen problems and red lights, which may adversely delay or stall the project, it is necessary for the project proponent to make a detailed study of the strategic issues which are critical for smooth operation of the project. It is accordingly necessary to work out an action plan in order to obviate and troubleshoot the critical problems that could be anticipated. Some of the critical problems can be nipped in the bud through initial legal framework, company memorandum, rules and regulations, agreements, etc. A classic example is that of Delhi Metro Rail Corporation(DMRC), a joint venture company of the Central Government and Delhi Government. Sensing the problems of land acquisition in heavily built up area of Delhi, long time taken by the local authorities in giving the approvals of new buildings and structures, getting project clearances from multiple authorities, obtaining finances for a project with no profit, the DMRC framed its legal frame, documentation and agreements with the concerned authorities so as to obviate these problems. As a result, within a span of 20 years, Delhi is served by a world class metro covering a stretch of more than 225 km, as compared to Kolkata metro, which covers only a stretch of 27 km after 48 years of existence.

Analysis of Existing Land Use Map

Base data such as population, transportation, infrastructure, area under conservation/ preservation, ecologically sensitive area, developable areas, etc. can be obtained and analysed for planning purpose. Thematic layers from Bhuvan series providing data of geomorphology, geology, lineaments, DEM, land transformation atlas can be selected. After giving weightage to the chosen indicators, these layers can be superimposed to generate maps showing land suitability or its potential for development or conservation. Here the parameters for selection are to be chosen carefully suiting the planning requirement of the region. Through the weightage given for analysis, the resulted map can be categorised into suitability layers, such as:

- Land most suitable for development
- Land suitable for development
- Land moderately suitable for development
- Land not suitable for development

Landuse Plan

Development strategy can be prepared from the analysis of the situation after surperimposing it on the existing land use map. Development strategy could be focussed on pertinent issues such as urban nodes, key infrastructure, transport links or industrial development. The development strategy and land suitability analysis is to direct the landuse zoning and the proposed plan. The existing land use plan are overlaid and refined for detailing the plan. Analysis on GIS also allows planners to prepare the Disaster Management Plan, which can be integrated with the proposed draft land use map.

By efforts from the State and Local Governments, window on Bhuvan can be utilised for planning on a digital platform. The approved proposed land use plan could be uploaded on *Bhuvan* website. Feedback can be given on such plans on *Bhuvan* website by public or by State officials. Based on objections and suggestions received, the proposed land use plan can be modified and uploaded on *Bhuvan* website again. The process of objections and suggestions, approvals and uploading of the Plan can be repeated for a number of times as per the statutory provisions, until the Final Plan is approved.

Information/Matrix Analysis

There are various ways and means to analyse the information/data to visualize the strategic issues in development, as given below:

Matrix Analysis helps in identifying the critical strategic issues, potential barriers and bottlenecks, which the project is likely to encounter, while on one side verticals are identified.

1. Physical: such as land required, location, access, land ownership power and water,services, raw material, markets, etc.
2. Investments/ Finances and other resources, such as budget, bank loans, institutional/ finance, taxes, human resource, subsidies, cost benefit, market potential, pricing, etc.
3. Environment factors: such as, pollution, EIA, carbon emissions and reduction, waste management, water recycling, energy efficiency, etc.
4. Organisation / Management/ Legal issues, such as laws, rules, regulations, labour organizations involved, contracting, completion, regulatory system, political support, timelines, etc.
5. Technology: level, import potential, skills, safety retrofitting, repair, maintenance, impact, etc.
6. Service Delivery and Marketing: consumers, society, local community benefit, jobs, etc.

On the other side Critical Strategic Issues are listed, which may be external or internal. By fuzzy logic these can be given a conceptual weightage and then accordingly action required to tackle the issues is outlined. This way matrix chart provides a clear picture of the future troubles, difficulties and risks which need to be tackled. In certain cases, the situation could be:

1. Impossible
2. Can be remedied with additional inputs/efforts, but with risk, and,
3. Can be nipped in the bud by pre-planning, or by internal action. In most of the large infrastructure projects, a congenial relationship with the political and bureaucratic apparatus and local community becomes necessary which can be achieved by proper PR, communications, through the NGOs and CSR in terms of offer of jobs to the locals, cultural promotion, religious, healthcare and educational programmes, etc. For certain critical issues, it may be necessary to appoint the consultants, peer advisory group or outsource the difficult components of work.

Table 3.4: Identifying strategic issues, causes and possible reforms

Strategic Issue	Basic environmental causes	
	Infrastructure and services	**Possble Reforms/Action**
Serviced land, shelter	Poor functioning urban land and housing markets, Highly regulated prices, lack of affordable housing for the poor	Reform property rights; Develop mortage financing; introduce affordable standards and target subsidies to the poor; Reduce unneeded regulations, government interventions and subsidies
Water supply, sanitation, drainage, solid waste collection/transport	Supply side dominated by government monopoly, Prices heavily regulated; Heavy subsidies	Reconsider subsidies; Move toward decentralisation, privatisation and participation Introduce pricing and Demand Management
Pollution from urban wastes and emissions:		
(a) Water pollution	Uncontrolled municipal and industrial discharges: Excessive water use and waste generation; Failure to link water quantity and quality issues	Introduce water pricing and effluent charges: Subsidise sewage treatment; Strengthen regulations and capacity for monitoring and enforcement; Prepare comprehensive basin plans,
(b) Energy use and pollution • Ambient air pollution • Indoor air pollution	Increased motorization and transportation congestion; Energy supply side dominated by government monopoly, Heavy energy subsidies; Household and cottage industry use low quality fuels	Introduce energy and fuel pricing, road charges emission charges, Reduce automobile subsidies, fuel subsidies; Integrate transport and land use planning;
(c) Solid and Hazardous waste Management	Poor municipal management; Lack of disposal facilities; inadequate regulation and enforcement	Promote clean technologies, fuel substitution and vehicle maintenance, Introduce regulations, licensing and charges;

Resource losses:		
(a) Ground water depletion	Unsustainable extraction linked to unclear property rights and treatment	Clarify property rights; Introduce extraction charges, Rain water harvesting.
(b) Land and ecosystem degradation	Low-income settlements pushed onto fragile lands by lack of access to affordable serviced lands. Lack of control over damaging economic activities.	Co-ordinate land development; Remove artificial shortages of land; Develop sustainable uses of sensitive areas; Monitor and enforce land use controls
(c) Loss of cultural and historic property	Lack of property rights regulations enforcement, maintenance; Failure to reflect social values in land prices	Introduce tax incentives for preservation; Use redevelopment planning, zoning and building codes, Develop property rights
Environmental hazards:		
(a) Natural hazards	Poorly functioning landmarks, ineffective land policies, poor construction practices	Enable land markets Provide disincentives to construction practices occupation of high-risk areas incentives for using disaster resistant construction techniques.
(b) Man made hazards	Inadequate equation and enforcement, Low income settlements alongside hazardous activities.	Introduce and enforce environmental zoning, formulate disaster management plans and revisit the organisational, financial and legal/procedural frameworks

Source: Delhi Urban Environment and Infrastructure Improvement Project,2001, Status Report for Delhi

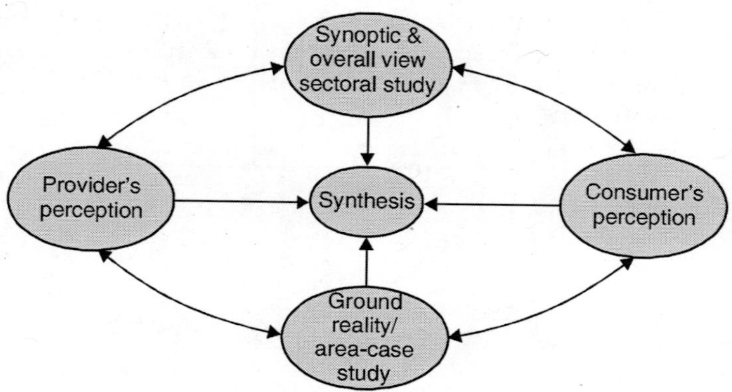

Fig. 3.2: Integration of Synoptic/Sectoral Study with Ground Reality/Area Studies and Triangulation of Provider's Perception by Consumer"s Perception

Force-field Analysis

Force-field Analysis is a well established management tool. It allows the analysis of a problem, or an opportunity in a manner that helps to generate innovative but realistic actions. The actions generated may range from use of certain technology to manpower development and choice of partners in development. As such, it has become increasingly recognized as an appropriate tool to develop innovative actions to help in solving urban management problems. In the context of better use of private sector participation to improve urban service delivery and accessibility, it can be used to develop appropriate line of action.

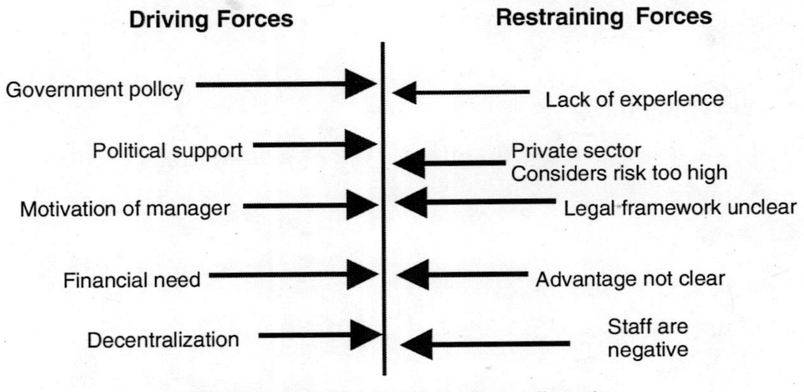

Fig. 3.3: Force-field Analysis

Impact Analysis

Impact analysis aims to assess whether the plan is likely to be implemented and what will then happen if the plan is implemented. Broader consequences include:

- Economic—How is the plan likely to impact economically? This includes its effects on employment and on business in the plan area and also at a broader level, e.g. the city or region.
- Social—What will be the impact on social organization?
- Political—Is the plan likely to have political repercussions?
- Environmental—What will be the environmental impact of the plans-both within the site and at a broader level?
- Cultural—Are the plans sensitive to existing culture? Are they likely to have an impact?

All these elements have to be questioned both in terms of short term impact and long term impact.

Debriefing and Review

1. What are the common types of surveys for town planning?
2. Explain the following:
   (a) Geometry (positioning and height in a map)
   (b) Contents of a map
   (c) Scale of a map

3. What is understood by Digital Land Information Surveys?
4. Explain various methods of data collection and analysis for town planning.
5. Write short notes on:
   (a) Triangulation
   (b) Exploration
   (c) Triage
   (d) Community mapping
6. How would you determine land suitability for various areas for urban development?
7. Write short notes on:
   (a) Force–Field Analysis
   (b) Swot Analysis
   (c) Impact Analysis
   (d) Traffic Surveys

CHAPTER

4

TOWARDS A NEW PLANNING FRAMEWORK

The 20th century had been an era of change, progress, urbanization and development. The first half of the century was underlined by the World Wars, destruction and new polarizations. The highlights of second half of the century have been decolonisation, democratization, reconstruction, industrial/technological developments, scientific-educational progress and rapid growth of the tertiary sector of the economy. While on the one hand, colonial regimes collapsed giving independence to several major countries, at the same time the world witnessed widening gulf between the rich and poor nations and political and socio-economic polarisations, which are reflected by the human settlements. Since the Independence of the country in 1947, India has achieved a remarkable technological, economic and organizational capacity; yet, it has not been able to realize its potential for the masses. The majority of population suffers a growing sense of loss and frustration as their lives and hopes for the future disintegrate. Millions of people lack secure and adequate shelter and basic services, livelihood and sustenance.

During the last century urban population of India increased ten folds, to some 377 million. Cities today are in the centre-state of environmental pollution, land degradation and loss of bio-diversity. Concentration of intense economic processes and high levels of consumption in cities increase their resource demands.

While there have been significant demographic, governance, financial, economic, technologial and ecological changes, the concepts of urban planning have not changed much, and do not align with the increasingly complex urban environment and developmental challenges. Some of the major changes which impact urban development that have taken place during last three decades in India are the following:

Table 4.1: Some Milestones in Urban Policies

1990s	—	Democratic Decentralisation (73rd and 74th Constitutional Amendment Acts), District and Metropolitian Planning Committees, Panchayat Raj, Strengthening of Municipal Bodies, etc

	—	Economic Liberalisation Policy; high level economic growth, rise of secondary and teritiary sectors, China factor, quantam leap in production of cars, motorization, rise of middle class
	—	Environmental Issues: pollution of air, water and land
	—	Climate change
	—	Terrorism, crimes, disasters
	—	Information Technology, wi-fi, internet, mobile, smart phones, etc.
2000s	—	MG National Rural Employment Guarantee Act
	—	National Urban Transport Policy (2006)
	—	National Urban Housing and Habitat Policy (2007)
	—	Rajiv Awas Yojana
	—	Jawaharlal Nehru National Urban Renewal Mission
2010s	—	Right to Fair Compensation and Transparency in Land Acquisition, Rehabilitation and Resettlement Act, (2013)
	—	Real Estate (Regulation and Development Act, 2016)
	—	Swachh Bharat Mission, Smart Cities Mission, Atal Mission for Rejuvenation and Urban Trasformation, Pradhan Mantri Awas Yojana (Housing for All), Historic City Development and Augmentation Yojana (Hriday Mission), Rurban Mission.

In India, the Parliament took a very significant step in 1992, by passing the 73rd and 74th Constitutional Amendment Acts thereby transferring many administrative and financial powers to Local Bodies. This makes urban local bodies as the most important functionary in the provision of the urban services. India has the distinction of having the largest number of democratically elected local governments in the world having more than 250,000 rural and urban local bodies with almost 3 million elected representatives.

As per the 12th Schedule of the 74th Constitutional Amendment Act of India, 18 tasks have been defined as the functional domain of the ULBs, which are the following:

1. Urban planning including town planning
2. Regulation of land-use and construction of buildings
3. Planning for economic and social development
4. Roads and bridges
5. Water supply for domestic, industrial and commercial purposes
6. Public health sanitation, conservancy and solid waste management
7. Fire service
8. Urban forestry, protection of the environment and promotion of ecological aspects.
9. Safeguarding the interests of weaker sections of society, including the handicapped, aged children and women
10. Slum improvement and upgradation
11. Urban poverty alleviation

12. Provision of urban amenities and facilities such as parks, gardens, playgrounds
13. Promotion of cultural, educational and aesthetic aspects
14. Burials and burial grounds; cremations, cremation grounds and electric crematoriums
15. Cattle pounds: prevention of cruelty to animals
16. Vital statistics, including registration of births and deaths
17. Public amenities, including street lighting, parking lots, bus stops and public conveniences
18. Regulation of slaughter houses and tanneries.

These Constitutional amendments mandate the preparation of district and metropolitan development plans, which integrate investments and their spatial implications, and align with the changes in the policy context.

Table 4.2: Changes in Policy Context

Conventional	New
Centralised System	Decentralised System, District and Local Planning
Command Economies	Market economies, Privatisation, leveraging
Low Environmental Awareness	High Environmental Awareness, Climate change adaptability and mitigation, Disaster Resilience
High Deficit Spending	Structural Adjustment
Government Domain over Infrastructure and Housing Development	Incentives for Privatisation, PPP, Infrastructure Investments and Housing
High Subsidy Regime	Users Pay Principle, Low Subsidy
Closed-Circuit Departmental Working	Information Technology, Participatory Decision Making, Capacity Building

The Indian federal has a three-tier institutional system with the Central government, state governments and local governments. The responsibility for providing basic services and implementing development programmes is mainly of the local government.

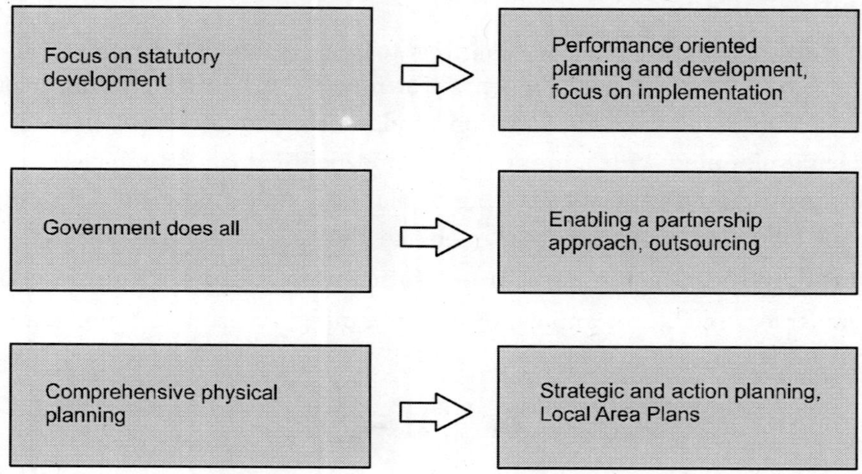

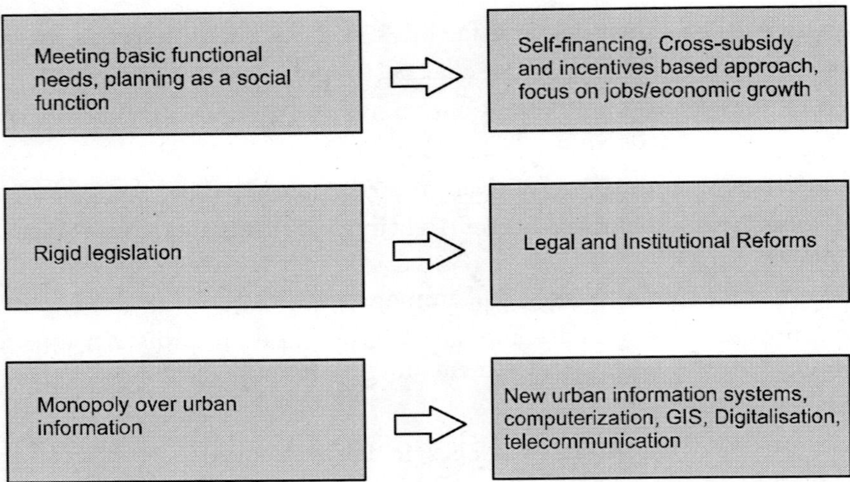

Fig. 4.1: Paradigm Shifts in Urban Sector

An Agenda for Planning Reforms

The urban local bodies give a general impression of being deficient in planning and implementation and are poorly administered. Their aims are obscure and there is little evidence of their achievements. This has inhibited economic opportunities and failed to meet the development objectives, which address the peoples' problems and popular preferences. The basic concern of planning to create a pollution free environment, provide efficient services, housing and social services for the poor have not been achieved. This requires a major reform in planning and municipal governance, that ensures environmental protection, welfare of the population and is more responsive to the needs of the population.

In order to complement the ongoing policies of economic reform and democratic decentralization, there is a need to embark upon several basic changes in the planning approach. The focus is to remove the barriers created by outdated planning, encouraging service delivery on the ground with speed and efficiency. The key areas where changes are necessary are given below.

Decentralized Planning

- From statutory/comprehensive planning to integrated district, local and strategic planning, with focus on environment, brown-fields, urban renewal and conservation.
- Locationalisation and decentralization of planning and development
- Interfacing planning with administrative and political constituencies.
- Corporatisation and capacity building of planning and municipal organizations.
- Strategic planning with a view to mobilise the resources/investments.
- Integrating physical planning with institutional, financial and infrastructure plans.
- Government as facilitator and catalyst in planning; creating an apparatus for people-centred planning.

Economy and Employment Oriented Planning

- Economic potential as the criteria of urban planning.
- Preparation of local economic development plan, circular economy.
- Incentives for infrastructure and housing investments.
- Release access to land, housing, services, finance and information by public-private partnerships.
- Focus at the grass roots and a pro-poor perspective.
- Planning to promote micro-enterprises and micro-banking.
- Mixed land-use as a tool of planning for poverty reduction.
- New methods of land assembly, pooling and development.
- Regularization of land tenure; simplify and expedite land registration.
- Review and simplify property taxation.
- Emphasise cost recovery and "user pays".
- Upgrading of infrastructure in slums and lower-income population areas.
- Identify and provide incentives to community and joint sector institutions.
- Target subsidies to the poor, empower the community.
- Encourage self-build housing and small businesses.
- Eliminate monopoly practices, including government monopolies.
- Make urban development self-financing and self-sustaining by developing the concepts, such as, Excess Condemnation, TDR, Accommodation Reservation, land pooling and readjustment, development and conversion charges, betterment levy, additional FAR charges, BOT, franchising, contracting out, etc.

Environmental Concerns

- Developing local environmental standards, environment impact analysis.
- Transit Oriented Development and Travel Demand Management
- Waste management and recycling.
- Services upgrading.
- Cyclic renewal.
- Urban form and housing appropriate for environment and ecological compatibility.
- Energy saving, adoption of non-conventional sources of energy; rainwater harvesting.
- Industrial zoning; microclimate, pollution, dust and noise minimization.
- Public transport policy, innovations and technology for environmental protection.

- Health concerns of planning, housing, services and slum/inner city renewal.
- Conservation of heritage.

Simplification of Planning and Regulatory Controls

- Reduce the number of approvals required.
- On-line approvals, One window system.
- Devolve and delegate powers
- Replace lowest tendering system by alternative/project management contract systems.
- Replace building approval by development centre planning permission
- Resort to white zoning (flexible land use zoning).
- Invoke concepts of Transferable Development Rights (TDR) and Accommodation Reservation (AR).

Information Technology

- Smart systems approach; digital planning, development of Information Technology System based infrastructure and transit system.
- Computerise land/property records and digitize plans, layouts; develop GIS and computer aided design and planning.
- Human resource management and capacity building.
- Assets management.
- Community/CBO/NGO networking.
- Online planning and property information.
- Flexible zoning and dynamic networking.
- Computerised system of approvals/planning permission.
- Intelligent services, buildings and transport.
- Environment monitoring.

Legal and Management Reforms

- Review all planning/building legislations and scrap outdated ones.
- Remove unnecessary controls.
- Simplify procedures.
- Reduce regulatory complexity and deregulate wherever possible.
- Establish regulatory authority for urban development and privatization.
- Minimize legal complexity, maximize enforcement and empower the community.
- Effective horizontalisation among actors, organisations and people.

The above reforms aim at urban transformation in concert with emerging economic development, ecology and technology. It is imperative that the planners and urban managers reconsider their approaches, ways and procedures and their impact on the economy, infrastructure and housing. The planners will have to redefine their roles so that they provide necessary support to the growing importance of market philosophy, while safeguarding the interests of the poor sections of the society.

This requires a fundamental change in the approach towards understanding and addressing the urban problems and issues. The old assumptions have to be re-assessed to develop a new vision.

Table 4.3: A New Vision for Urban India

Old Assumption	New Vision
1. Economic development as a vehicle for social progress.	Economic development is not a substitute of socio-cultural integration. Focus on poverty alleviation, sustainable habitat, infrastructure development and social mobilisation.
2. Social equity by downward filtration	Focus at the grassroots and evolve a pro-poor perspective.
3. State intervention for creating a civil society.	State itself is not a creation of civil society.
4. Poverty as indicator of socio-cultural unrest and law and order problems.	Majority of the poor have the 'values of patriots and perseverance of pioneers.'
5. Globalization of urban development	Decentralization and localization of habitat planning and development.
6. Political intervention as a hindrance.	Political apparutus as an essential part of planning and development.
7. Trade-off between development and conservation.	Conservation as the basis of development.
8. Population distribution and decentralization by regional policies and planning.	Guide population distribution by incentives and integrated economic development.
9. City planning and governance as expert domains.	Bottom-up, participatory approach, rather than top down.
10. Centralized and strong apex organizations for coordinated city management.	Decentralised management, devolution and effective horizontalization among actors, resources and people.
11. Government as provider of housing and jobs to the poor.	Government as facilitator and catalyst of community and private sector partnerships.
12. Regulate and control access to land, housing, building, services, finance and information window approach.	Deregulate, decontrol and public-private partnerships.
13. Large cities as problems (limit city size).	Large cities are engines of innovation, social equity and economic growth.

14. Migrants are 'dregs of the barrel'.	Migrants are the 'Cream of the Crop'.
15. Squatters are a burden on urban services.	Squatters return more to the city than they receive.
16. Slums are the blots on city portrait. services which sustain a city.	Slums provide cheap labour and essential services.
17. High density is a problem for urban services. affordability and other factors.	Density by itself does not indicate much until related with FAR, land economics,
18. Planning for an egalitarian society with modern education.	Promote and preserve local semantic values and heterogeneity.
19. Legal systems for social justice and gender equity and to control social unrest, crimes, corruption, landuse-building bye-laws violations. community. Devolve planning powers.	Many of the problems arise due to complex and too many legislations. Simplify procedures, minimise legal complexity, maximise enforcement and empower the community.
20. Statutory Master/comprehensive Planning.	Flexible strategic and action planning focussed on performance.
21. Single land use zoning.	Mixed land use/flexible zoning.
22. Planning and development of mass housing and new areas.	Facilitate housing by the masses and concentrate on urban renewal/inner city.
23. Large scale land acquisition for planned development.	Land as a key resource, adopt alternatives of land assembly, such as transferable development rights, accommodation reservation, excess condemnation, etc.
24. Focus on spatial and physical planning.	City being a social and economic system, integrate habitat planning with socio-economic, environmental, institutional and legal aspects.
25. Meeting basic functional needs through habitat planning.	Emphasis on quality and innovation, demand driven planning.
26. Environmental issues subsidiary to habitat planning.	Ecology and environment (including land, water, air, energy, sanitation, waste management, drainage, transport, building materials, industry and technology) as the basis of habitat planning and development.
27. Design and develop 'City Beautiful'.	Encourage incremental and brown-field development, which serves the need of the people, largely poor and informal sector.
28. Disaster and climate change management as the peripheral concerns	Security, resilience and gender safety as the core issues.

29. Controlling the city development, land use, urban form, etc.	Promoting diversity and removing/ minimising controls. Reduce gap between ideas and practice.
30. Formulate minimum planning, housing and services standards and parameters.	Develop incremental standards and norms linked with affordability.
31. Conventional property management inventory and management.	Resort to digital/computerised property/assets management.
32. Monopoly over urban information.	Resort to GIS, GPS, tele-communications, internet, web, virtual conferencing, networking, intelligent systems, etc.
33. Government as service provider	Government as the entrepreneur and partner with Community/Service Agencies
34. Subsidize the poor. Maintenance as a post project activity.	User pay principle, differential pricing, capture value addition, use land and FAR as resources. Maintenance integral to planning, design and urban management.
35. Create specialized organization for specific urban tasks	Capacity building of govt./local bodies/ community groups.
36. Accountability and transparency as part of code of conduct.	Mandatory performance management system, monitoring and MIS.
37. Learn from faults and failures.	Learn from successes

Urban Governance

Of India's 7936 towns and cities, only 107 have municipal corporations, while 1438 have municipal committees or councils. It is necessary to review the institutional structure and redefine their roles keeping in view the 73rd and 74th CAA. Simultaneously there is a need to redefine and reform the role and legal framework of the development authorities, Cantonment Boards and other urban local bodies in India. An important legislative instrument is the regulation of public private partnerships in urban infrastructure provision, financing and management. The sustainability of infrastructure project depends on the success of policy planners in implementing a strong techno-financial and techno-legal regime based on viably rates of return for private sector participation. The techno-financial and techno-legal regime should support each other so that a conducive and sustainable environment is maintained to attract investments in the sector.

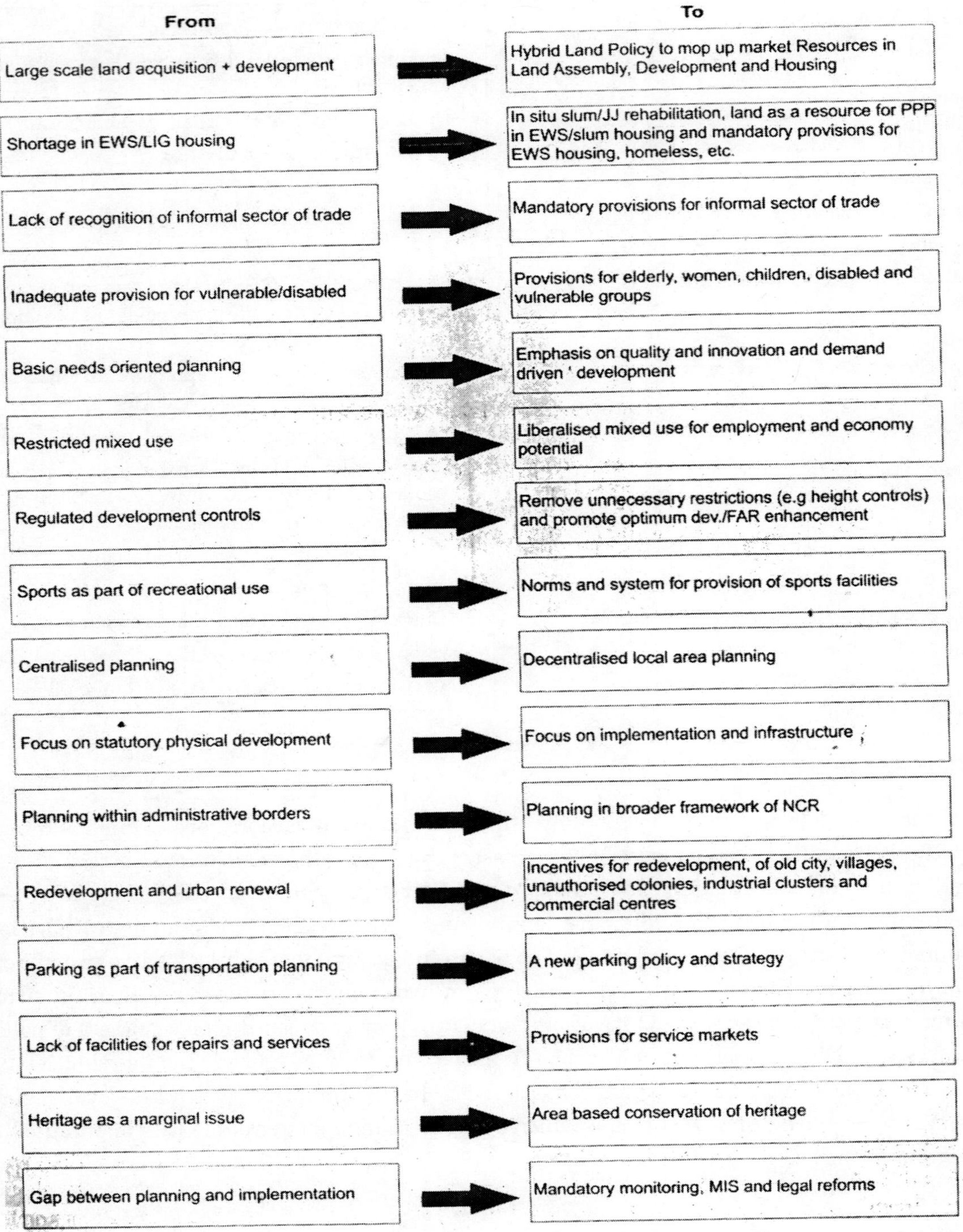

Fig. 4.2: Paradigm Shifts in Urban Planning and Governance

The process of urban development is intimately linked with the system of governance, which articulates the participation of civil society, issues of transparency and ethics and democratic decentralization of decision making process. It has direct bearing on the aspects of the environment, urban poverty, infrastructure/basic services, equity, resources and capacity building. This calls for reforms in legal and institutional framework and adopting a new paradigm of urban management, where people are integral part of the planning and development process. The watchwords are environment, equity, efficiency, energy and excellence. So that urban planning acts as a powerful tool of economic growth and social justice, there is a need of urban and legal reforms facilitating strategic initiatives and action planning approach.

A major area of reform should be reworking the maze of archaic legislation which govern urban sector and municipal bodies. There is an urgent need of transition towards a post-modern, post-European civilisation for people centrered planning approach. There is a need to give up old assumptions and embrace a new vision. These should combine the principles and values, viz, ecological, social, political, cultural, economic and environmental dimension.

Accordingly, an urban index can be evolved the principles of effectiveness, equity, participation and accountability of services. This will help in 'actualising' the process of new governance model on the ground. For this a set of 'tools' are to be identified for phasewise preparation, planning, management and implementation. These should be based on local priorities, profiles and situation (e.g., poverty, environment, safety and community). The strategy formulation and implementation should be derived on the basis of city consultation process.

The critical factors of urban governance can be evaluated by giving weightage to indicators, as below:

Table 4.4: Urban Governance Index System

1. Effectiveness	Local Government revenue Expenditure in basic services Share of transfers Travel Time
2. Equity	Poor households Access to water Access to sanitation Women councillors
3. Participation Index	Adult literacy Voters participation, Residents' Associations/NGO and CBOs Public participation in projects Formal Participatory budgeting
4. Accountability Index	Elected Mayors, Councillors/population Publication of contracts, tenders, budget and accounts

5. Security Index	Under five mortality+ Environmental action plan+ Crime prevention policy+ Inaccessible areas to police+ Domestic violence policy

Urban Governance Index (Effectiveness index+ Equity index + Participation index + Accountability index + Security Index/5)

Source: Adapted from Institute of Housing and Urban Studies (IHS, Netherlands), and UNCHS (UN Habitat), 2002.

Indian cities are at the cross roads. With the initiation of new policies and programme, it is as rare moment to transform the urban scenario, which can be smart, inclusive and sustainable, that leverages the economic growth and social equity. This is an opportunity to indigenise urban planning and make it part of larger eco-system of sociology. This implies thinking afresh in order to reorient planning to address our own demographics, culture, humanity and local geography. Gautam Bhatia puts it succinctly:

'Today India is at the crossroads of some serious choices: to either enter the world market as a shameless imitator of China and the West, competing with them on expanding highways, ports, and racing restlessly to compare GDP figures. Or we choose a different destiny, a path of serious discovery and inventiveness, directing our energies to more imaginative forms of architecture, planning and urban living, that produce altogether different - but relevant - models - ideas that may even do away with inessential and expensive Western-type infrastructure. Whatever their final form, new cities could accommodate a wide swath of diverse citizens and lifestyles, and give everyone that much-needed uplift that comes with living in a place they love. Surely the choice should not be difficult'. (Times of India, 25th May 2014).

The current planning is, by and large, reactive, which should gradually move towards transformative action. This involves moving from incremental to radical actions, that include alternative ways of land assembly and management, local planning, transit oriented development (TOD), infrastructure development and urban renewal. This needs strategic planning and a balance between regulation and collaborative partnerships.

Community empowerment, governance reforms and participatory communications are vital for equity and inclusive development. This needs legal and institutional reforms, along with local planning, which responds to the local ecology and geography and addresses the issues of livelihood, land, services and mobility. This necessitates reforms in the legal, institutional and regulatory frameworks.

Debriefing and Review

1. What are the domain areas of the urban local bodies under the 74th Constitutional Amendment Act?

2. Write short notes on the following:
   (a) District Plan
   (b) Metropolitan Area Plan
   (c) Local Area Plan
   (d) Municipal Area Plan
3. What planning reforms are necessary to address the issues of
   (a) Democratic decentratisation
   (b) Economic liberalisation
   (c) Environment and climate change, and
   (d) Information technology
4. Write a note on Urban Governance Index System.
5. How public participation in planning can effectively deal with the local issues?

CHAPTER

5

Planning Policy and Process

After the independence of India in 1947 a new era of planning started. It reflected the political commitment to build a new India. With socialist vision of mass production, centralized governance and comprehensive planning, it laid emphasis on rural and regional development agriculture, industrial development and slum clearance. New industrial towns were developed in the hinterland, and the plans for capital cities were prepared.

The post-independence era denotes various milestones in the process of planning. With a Socialist model, various Five Year Plans sought the intervention of the welfare state through planned development. However, the thrust of the Five Year Plans had been economic development, and no conscious efforts were discernible in respect of spatio-economic integration and translating the policies into spatial plans. In spite of numerous, laudable programmes

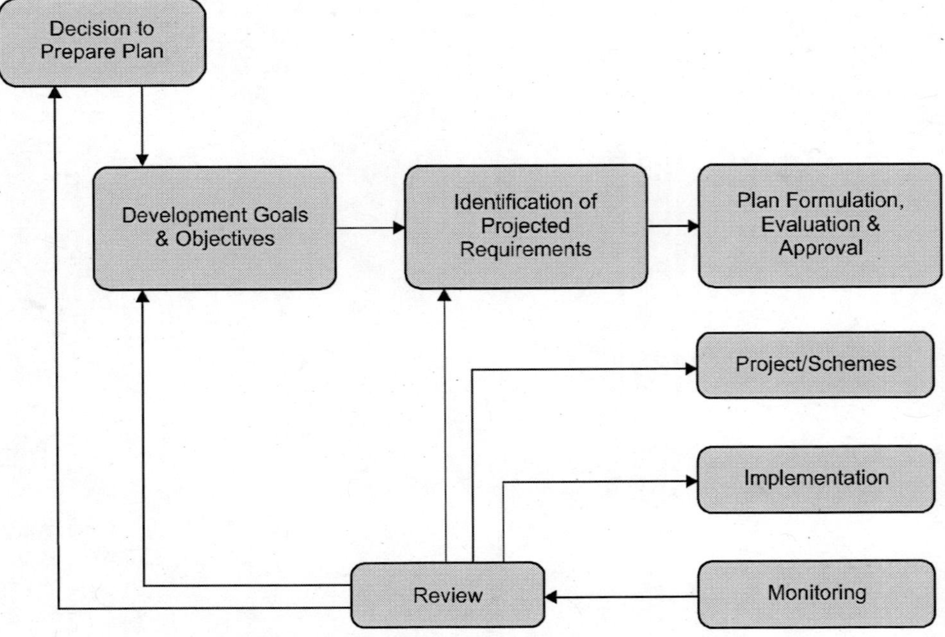

Fig. 5.1: General Process of Planning

and huge investments, the state of infrastructure is rather dismal. There is a persisting lack of the basic amenities and services, like roads, transport, communications, drinking water supply, power, sanitation, healthcare, and jobs. The decision making power is concentrated in the hands of few and the concepts of citizen empowerment, participatory governance and decentralization are often confined to the seminars and papers. The decision making is often piecemeal, disjointed, ad-hoc, motivated and lacks an overall perspective. A lion's share of subsidies is eaten up by the administration/establishment structure and their salaries. The programmes are too many, so are the departments involved in each one of them. Often there is lack of clarity about the organizations and their accountability. The programmes frequently exceed the time and financial allocations.

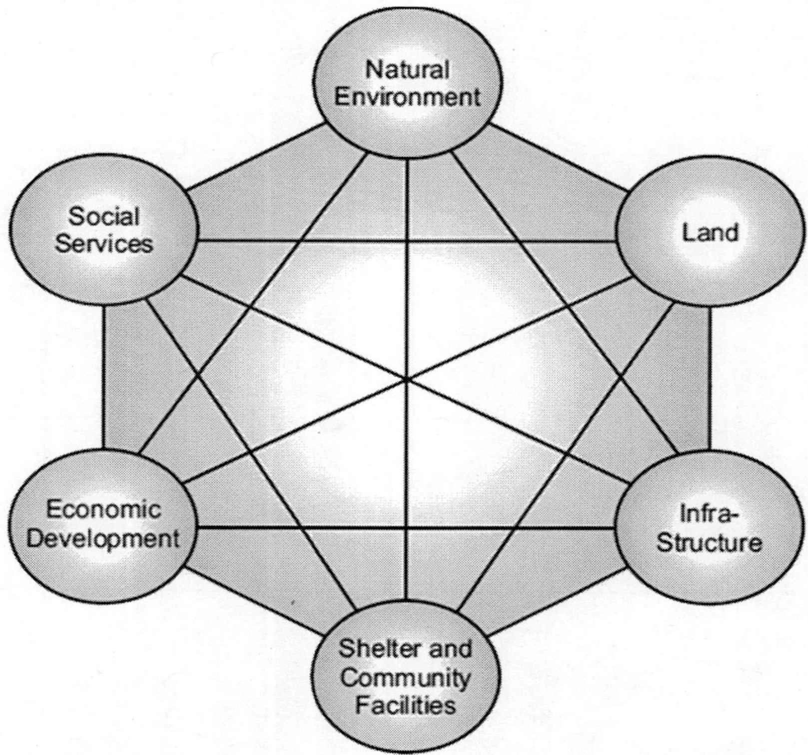

Fig. 5.2: The planning attempts to synthesise the resources (natural environment, water land, humans) with infrastructure services, shelter, community facilities, social services and economic development. Governance and urban management provide the linkages among the resources and development.

Purpose of Planning

Planning attempts to strike a balance among various scales and levels of development with political, economic, financial, social, environmental and governance, structures. The traditional planning paradigm- 'survey, analyse and plan' has become redundant. Planning involves:

(a) organizing timely and relevant information,

(b) identifying the pertinent issues and problems,

(c) conceptualizing options, solutions and plans,

(d) converting the plans into action, implementation, enforcement, monitoring and feedback.

Levels of Planning

Planning can be seen as a matrix or intersection between the 3 levels of planning, i.e., policy, strategic and action planning, and 5 spatial scales as given below:

(i) Regional/sub-regional

(ii) City

(iii) Zone/Sub-Zone/Sector

(iv) Ward/Local Area

(v) Projects.

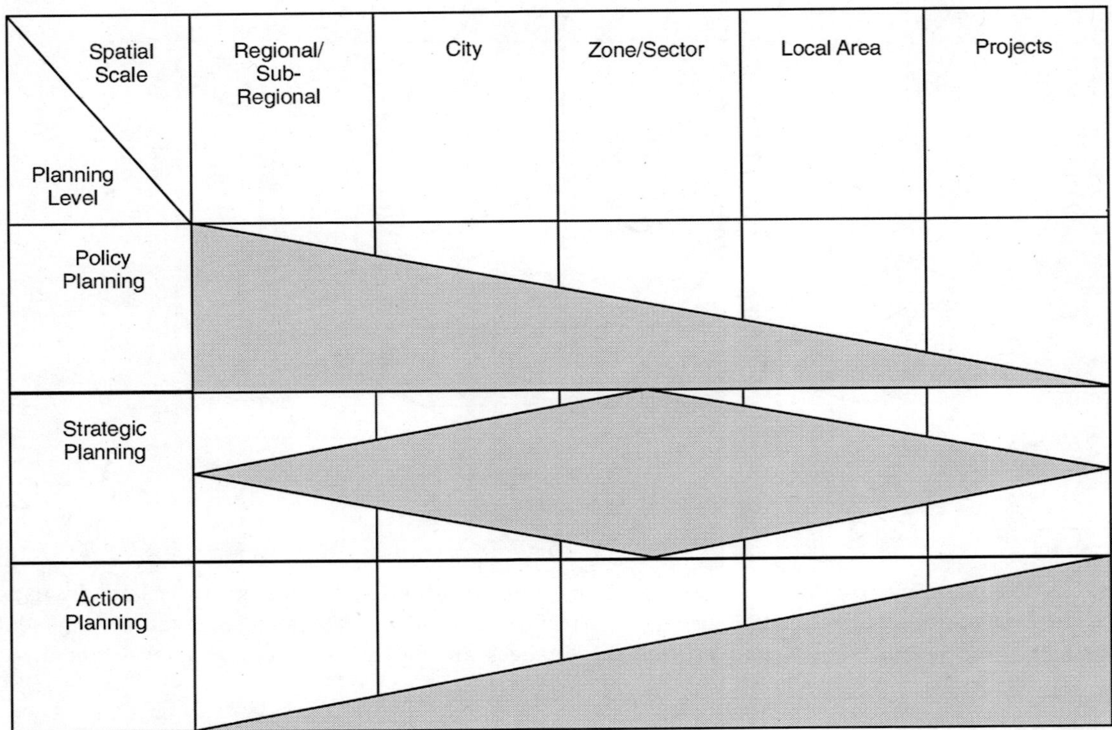

Fig. 5.3: Matrix of planning levels and spatial scale. Shaded area shows the predominant interventions

Planning can be divided into 3 interconnected phases-Long term, Short term and Annual. Long term plans are usually the vision and policy plans, short term are strategic plans (usually for 5 years) and project Plans are operational, action plans.

Planning Cycle

Linkage of these phases is obtained by planning cycle comprising Survey and Analysis, Plan Preparation, Plan Approval, Plan Implementation, Plan Monitoring and Plan Review.

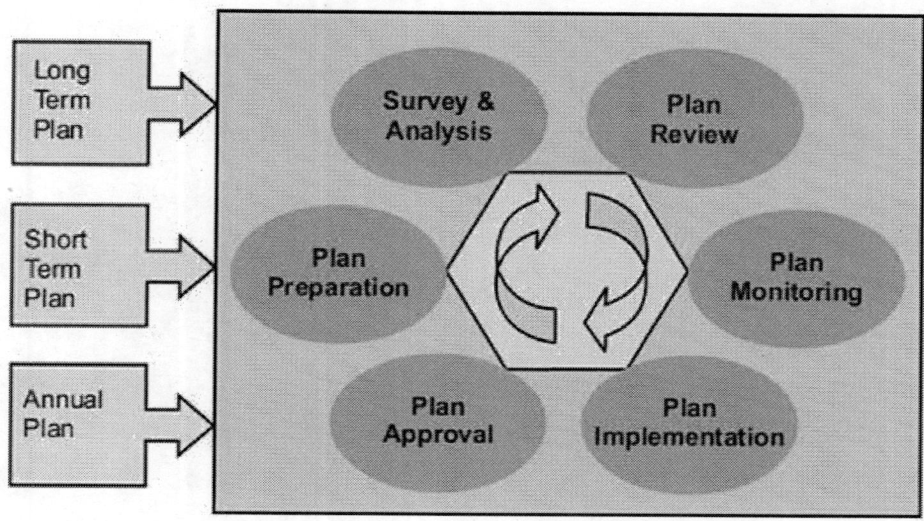

Fig. 5.4: Integration of Time and Planning Process

The inter-linkages among development planning and projects aim to achieve social welfare through inclusive economic growth, employment, equity and social justice. National Development Plans are the blue-prints in organizing population, economy, resources and mobility over space. Regional Development Plan aims at orderly development, efficient functioning and enhancement of the quality of life. A Sub-regional/District Development Plan attempts and translates activities, life sphere systems, transport, social and physical infrastructure in terms of space and time.

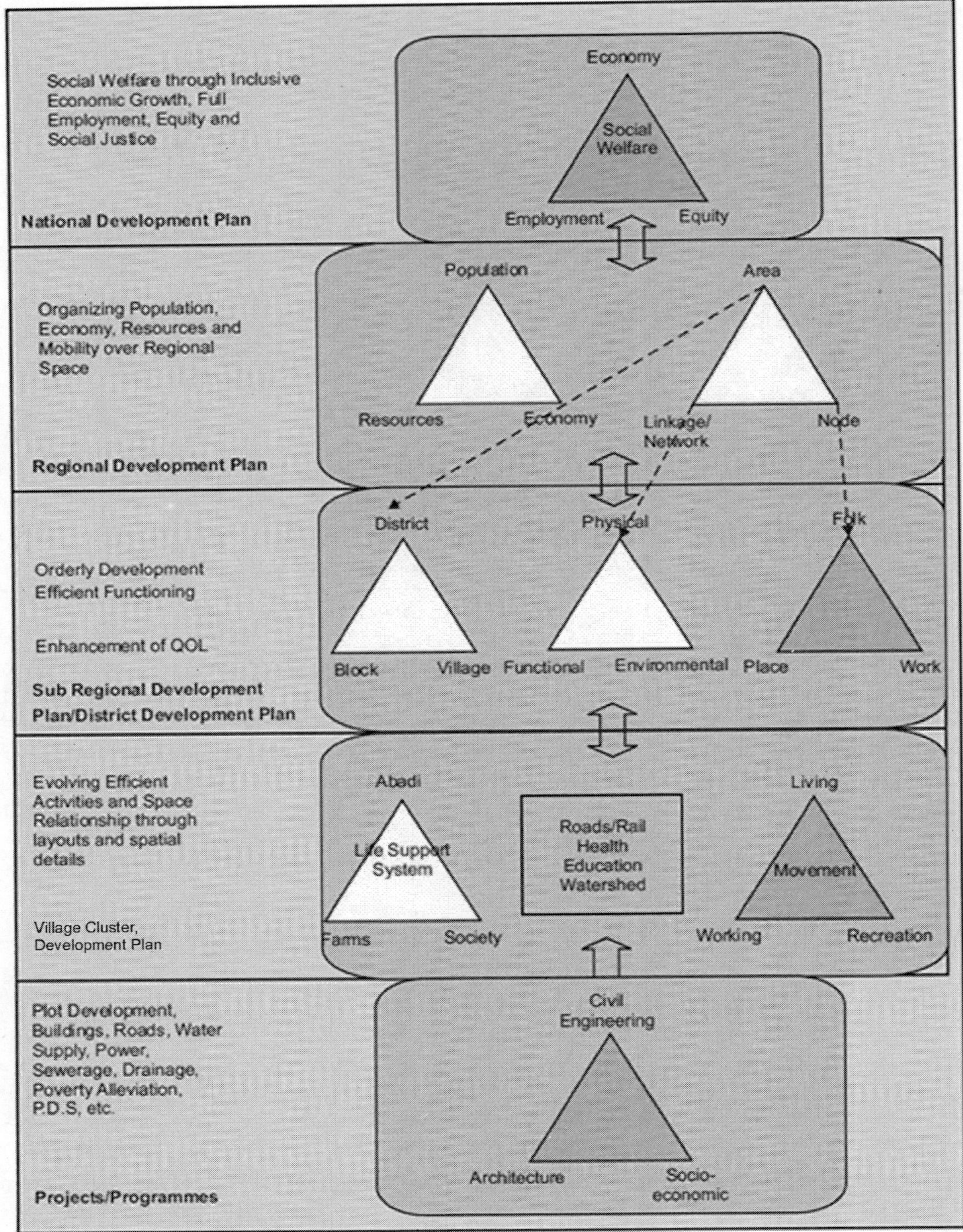

Fig. 5.5: Inter-linkages between Development Planning and Projects

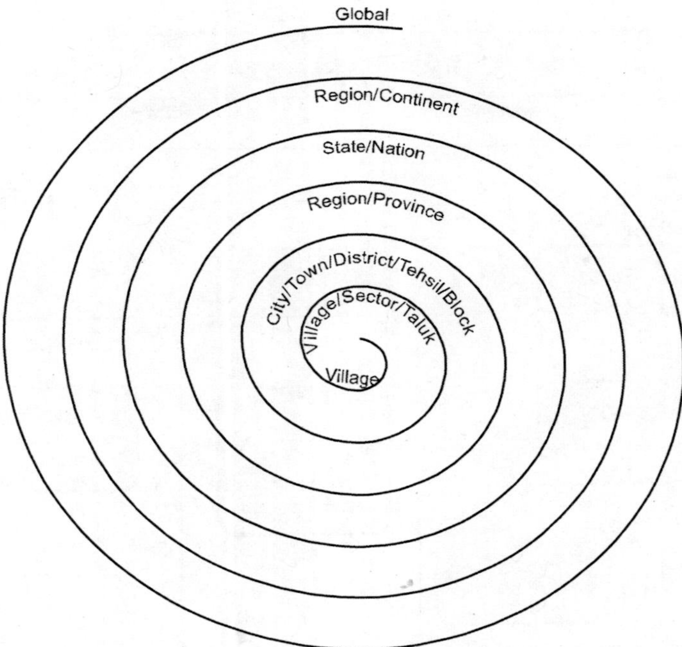

Fig. 5.6: In an era of globalization, the Indian settlements are linked with the spiral of development of the state, nation, continent and the globe. However, care is to be exercised that they do not lose their cultural values.

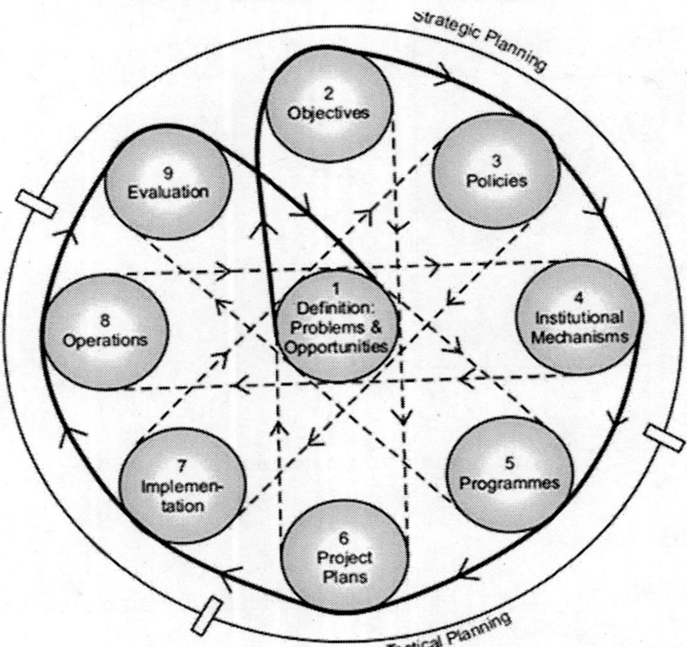

Fig. 5.7: Planning comprises a continuous and inter-linked cycle of Problem Definition, Objectives, Policies, Strategies, Institutional Structure, Programmes, Projects, Implementation, Operation and Evaluation.

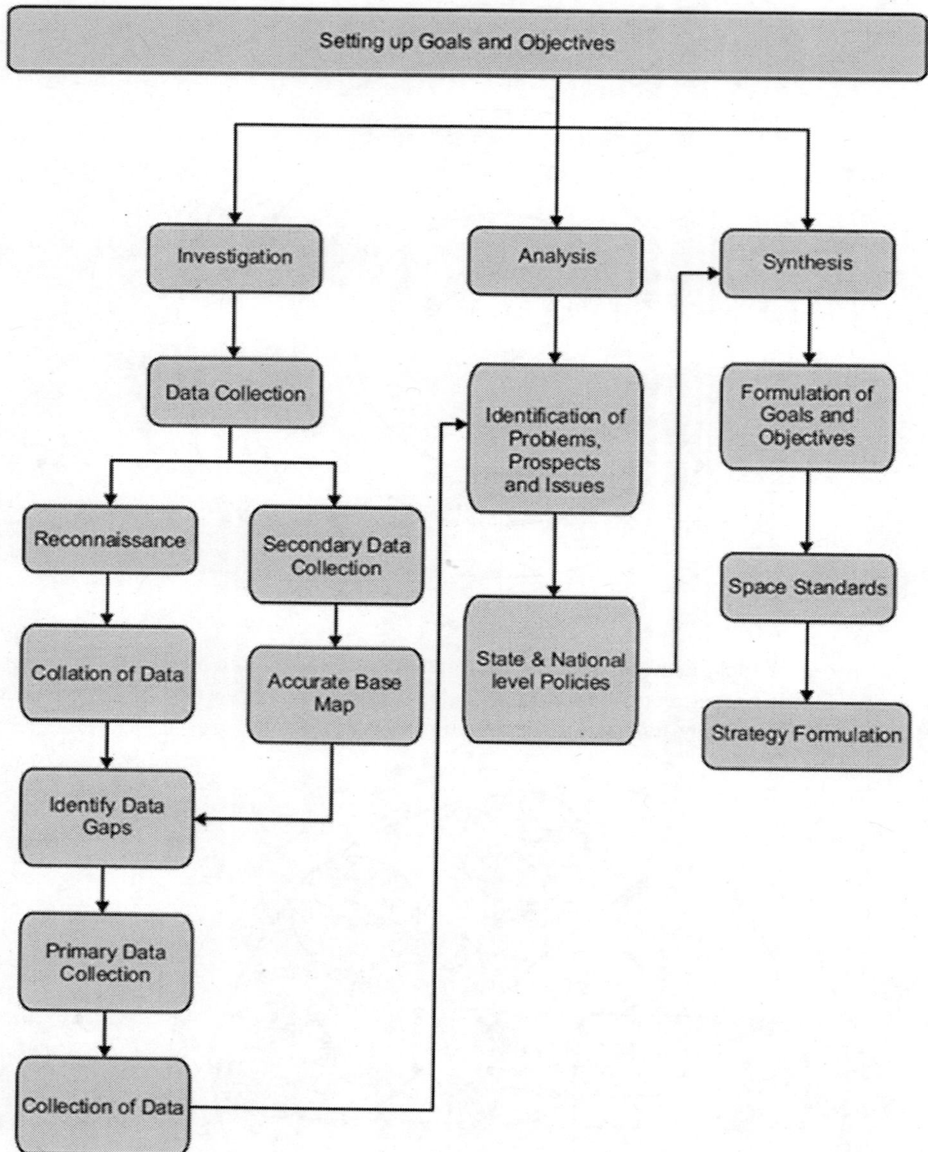

Fig. 5.8: Setting up Goals and Objectives

Planning Pyramid

The process of planning can be graphically explained as a pyramid, comprising the following sequence:

1. Mission Statement and Objectives.
2. SMART Goals.

3. Baseline Information and participatory learning.
4. Identifying the issues and Key Action Areas.

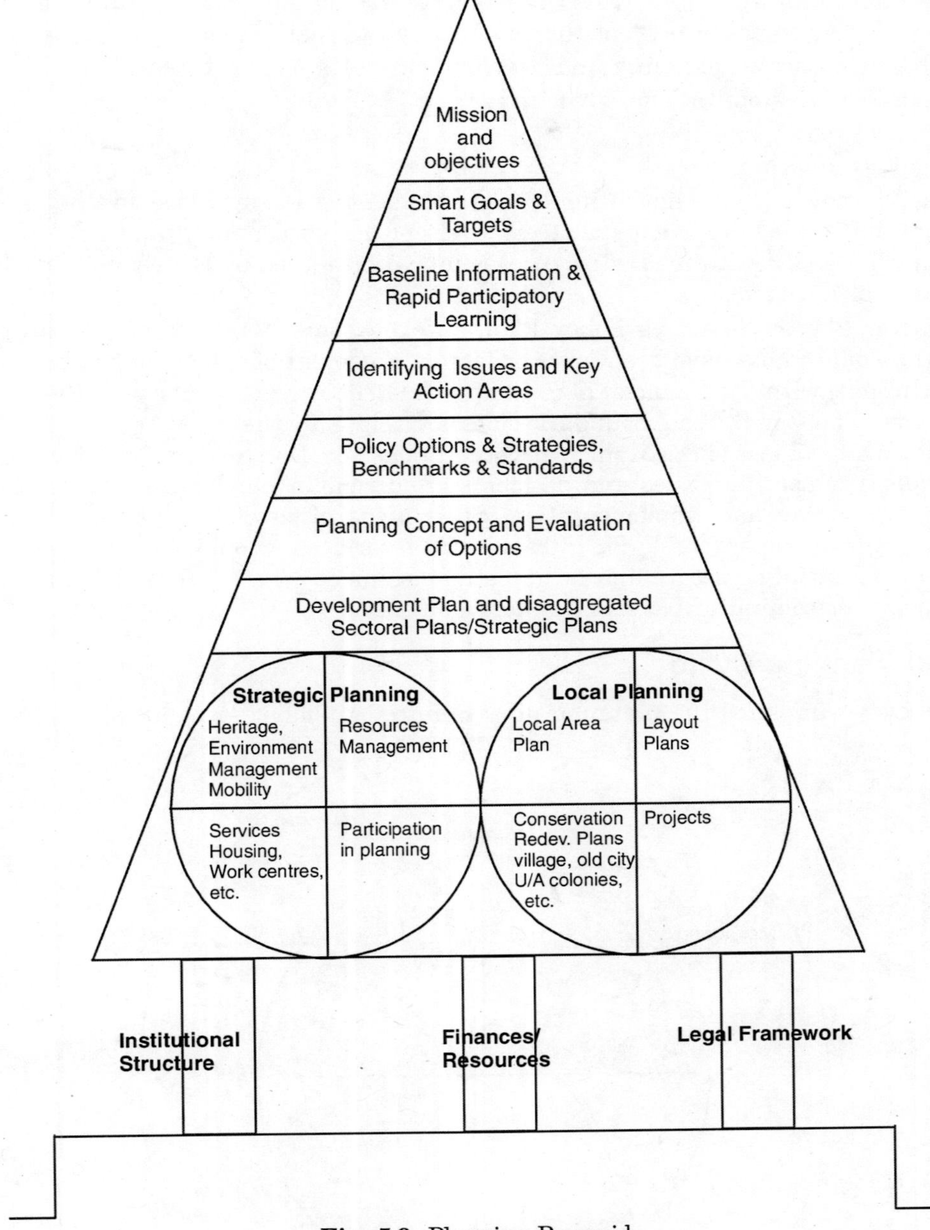

Fig. 5.9: Planning Pyramid

5. Conceptual framework, policy options, strategic planning, benchmarks and standards.
6. Evaluation of planning options by SWOT analysis, financial implications, cost benefit analysis, feasibility and viability assessment.

7. Development Plan disaggregated into sectoral plans for various services and key action area.
8. Resource Planning and Governance; identifying key issues via-a-vis resource assessment, empowerment of the community and participatory planning

The superstructure of planning and development rests on the three pillars :

- Organisational/institutional structure;
- Finances; and
- Legal Framework.

No Plan, however good, can be implemented unless it is supported by the people and stakeholders who have to participate at all levels of decision making and implementation. Spatial, financial and institutional structures can be coordinated by clearly defining the roles and resources of all agencies.

The Master Plan is broadly a Policy Plan, and the Zonal Plan acts as 'Strategic Plans'. However, the Zonal Plans have been more or less enlargement of the Master Plan. The Plans do not synchronise with the financial plans, and infrastructure plans, nor with the 5 year and Annual Plans. The Zonal Plan boundaries do not relate to the constituencies of Election Commission, Wards, Zones of the Municipal Corporations, etc. Due to lack of public participation at local levels, the specific issues and problems often remain unaddressed. There is a wide gap between planning and implementation. Such plans often do not provide area-specific strategies for development of land, infrastructure services, mobility, TOD, environment management, financial structure and heritage management. The absence of Local Plans has been a major shortcoming of planning system and mandate.

Simplified Planning Cycle

Baum's cycle simplifies the planning process into four major steps as shown in fig. 5.10

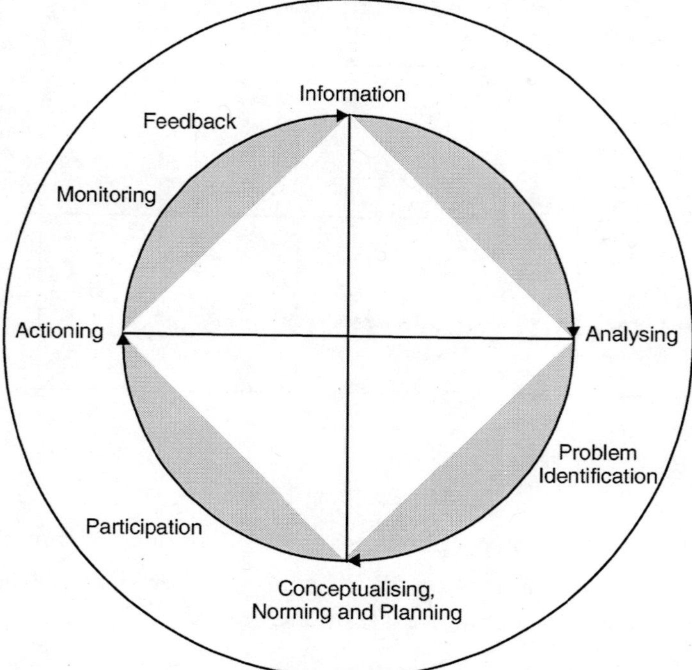

Fig. 5.10: Simplified Planning Cycle (after Baum)

Planning is an attempt to synthesize the diverse activities, perspectives, aspirations and resources into a composite whole. The process of planning depends upon the political, socio-economic, physical, infrastructural and administrative realities. During last decades the peoples' aspirations and the purpose of planning have become enlarged-from the spatial, infrastructure, housing and functional aspects to global, environmental, organizational, governance, conservation of heritage, urban aesthetics, employment and poverty alleviation, human dignity, empowerment and participation. It sets into motion a more activist orientation of planning practice than the regulatory/technocratic approach which had dominated the profession emulating the British Town and Country Planning tradition. The strategic and action planning have gained a wider acceptance as the new ways of dealing with both localised issues and larger social objectives (environmental, transport, social, poverty, etc.). These are synonymous with problem solving rather than problem defining.

Strategic and Action Planning

The origins of strategic action planning can be traced back to the period when international donor organizations begun to consider the financing of the urban sector, either as a series of large scale projects or as "sector loans" that aimed to establish national level financial intermediaries to provide an assured flow of capital. The urban investments were scrutinised for how their equity and efficiency of urban growth as well as for its replicability in the future. This approach of stimulating a sustained capacity of urban growth management differed sharply from the prevailing practice. The effective utilization of the capital injected in the urban system requires the following preconditions :

- Rapid assessment of prevailing problems and priorities, leading to project identification;
- Strengthening or creation of institutional structures which could oversee the detailed planning and implementation of a set of major projects which often incorporated technical, financial and management innovations;
- Resource mobilization which ensured that the benefits created by the project will be translated to finance streams that directly or indirectly will cover the cost of investments leading to sustained replicability.

Existing planning practices, the outdated master plans devoid of resource implications and assessment of institutional management capacity were not suitable tools to guide the application of this massive capital inflow. The alternative approach of action planning has been advocated with the following generic features as given in a monograph of the World Bank :

"The Action Planning approach supplements development planning and implementation techniques in improving institutional capacities for effectively plan and manage the implementation of their development programmes. It is a powerful means for achieving seven fundamental objectives:

(a) *Identifying local perceptions of problems and constraints to be addressed by development programs / projects;*

(b) *Revealing values and attitudes to which the program / project approach must be adapted;*

(c) *Arriving at a procedural, analytical and operational framework that meets the development goals of the country;*

(d) *Mobilizing a critical mass of local supporters and implementors for the development strategy as a whole or particular program / project elements of the strategy;*

(e) *Generating sufficient commitment and ownership by appropriate supporters and implementors;*

(f) *Starting a process for team functioning to be used throughout planning, implementation and evaluation; and*

(g) *Improving the capacity of project or program management teams to plan and manage on an ongoing basis during implementation.*"

Action planning aims to address to the problems which are self-evident, persistent and where sufficient social committment exists for their solution.

The solutions are sought by a coordinated involvement of number of agencies through a synchronised scenario of various options. 'Local involvement' is a key to success of planning, alongwith the political expediency of implemention. These plans are remedial, localised, participatory, implementation focussed. This needs an assessment of the perceived urgency, political support and resource allocation to translate planning into action. The visibility of implementing capacity also enhances the prospects of attracting additional resources. Local and action planning operate on a short gestation period in preparing alternatives and draw upon "learning by doing" attitude which places premium on developing an institutional, legal and financial structure for implementation.

Action planning seeks to break new grounds in technical, managerial and financial areas where conventions in the past prevented solution generation. It avoids institutionalising techno-bureaucratic routines, but looks at each situation as one. In action planning explicit attention is paid to the financial implication of macro-developmental projects, their contribution to sustainable expansion of programmes on the basis of their resource mobilizing impact. 'Affordability' at the user, institution or broader governmental level is the elementary justification for investment commitments which allow linkage between planning and implementation.

It aims to introduce the element of 'changing course', both in terms of existing practices and opening new opportunities. The feasible vision of alternative futures (urban growth, technological and administrative innovations) will require the adjustment and change management of existing practices. Action planning recognizes the essential ingredient of political support, and builds upon the participatory process of its own planning through the mobilisation of institutions, individuals and media. This become the motivating force, reinforcing the commitment by a number of institutions to contribute to the implementation of the projects.

With people and resources in place, the plan needs to set a strategic direction for growth in a manner acceptable and supported by the people. There must be a good match between the planner's perspective and the people's aspirations. This can be expressed by the planning perspective, which converge to become an all-round set of shared values and sustainable development (Fig. 5.11).

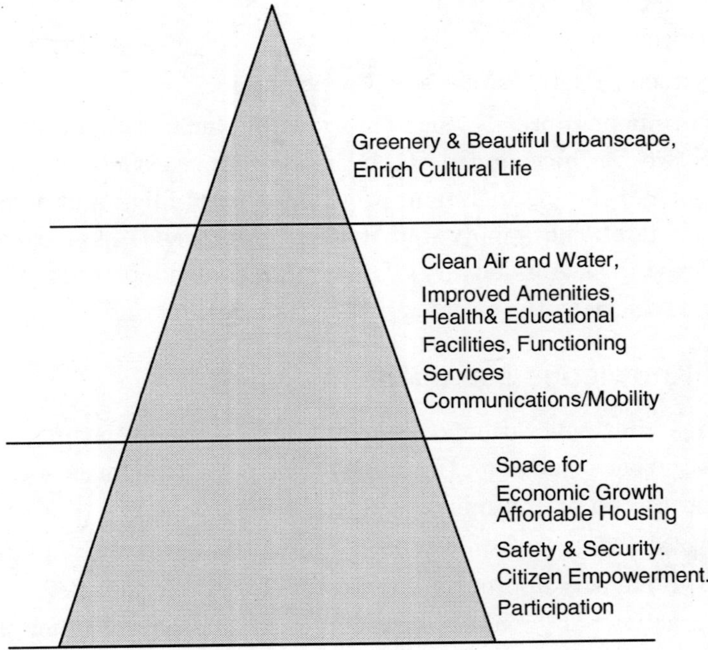

Fig. 5.11: The Aspirations Pyramid

Sustainable development synthesizes various components of environment, such as:

- The conservation of natural resources and minimizing ecological footprint of urban system.
- Economic development, livelihoods, jobs and poverty related challenges.
- Education, health and other social infrastructure
- Energy, transportation, water resources, drainage, sanitation and other services.
- Environment, pollution control, climate change, disaster resilience related challenges.
- Heritage and cultural conservation.
- Governance and institutional capacity.

In other words, the sequence of planning can be expressed in the following words, starting with "P":

1. Position, Perceptions, People and Projections
2. Problems
3. Possibilities
4. Proposals, Policy, Principles, Parameters
5. Plan Options
6. Process/Procedures/ Programmes
7. Practice/Performance
8. Projects, Products, Partnerships and Participation.

Planning is a continuous process, which embraces implementation and delivery. It has to strikes a balance between whole and part and grasps an overview as well as the ground reality. The perceptions of the planners and providers should align and engage with those of the people and consumers. The supply and demand approaches should converge with the needs of the people, resources and delivery. This implies that the policies and specific projects are triangulated so as to meet the peoples' needs and perceptions.

Information and Knowledge Management

Planning requires the exploration of relevant indicators by posing "who, how, what, where, and when" as the basic questions. Framing of 'correct' questions is of utmost importance, as no answer can be correct if the question itself is not correct.

Operationally useful and time bound information is the basis of the planning process. As such, it is important to identity appropriate indicators and their sources as integral elements of developing an interactive and flexible approach for information collection, rather than rigid statistical methods. This involves working out flexible check lists and semi-structured cross examination of various sources of information. The salient features of such an approach are as follows:

(a) to collect information as an incremental learning process.

(b) to relate information and inputs with reflective observation, conceptualization and experimentation.

(c) to recognize the limitation of optimal ignorance and appropriate in precision.

(d) adoption of triangulation process for a three-dimensional perception

(e) proxy indicators as an aid to information and perceptive understanding,

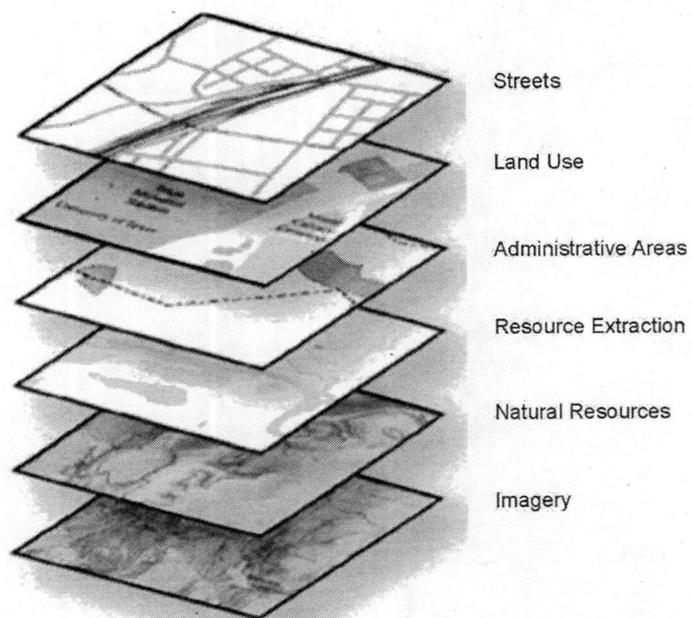

Fig. 5.12: Digital Planning and Resource Management

(f) quality control vs quantitative/statistical approach.

(g) use of GIS and digital tools

(h) recognizing the principle of "less is more" (time/information/resources).

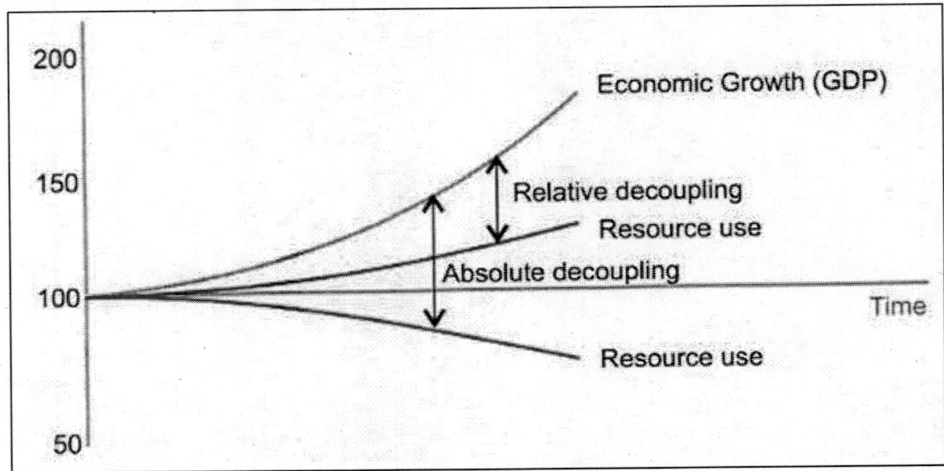

Fig. 5.13: Less is more: Reduce the use of Natural Resources and Ecological Footprint by Decoupling Economic Growth and Environmental Sustainability. India is annually using 462 million tonnes of oil equivalent of energy, of which 40 per cent is used by the cities. Construction uses 40-45 per cent of steel, 85 per cent of paint and 65-70 percent of glass. 56 percent of cities are dependent on ground water.

Source: Development Alternatives, 2016

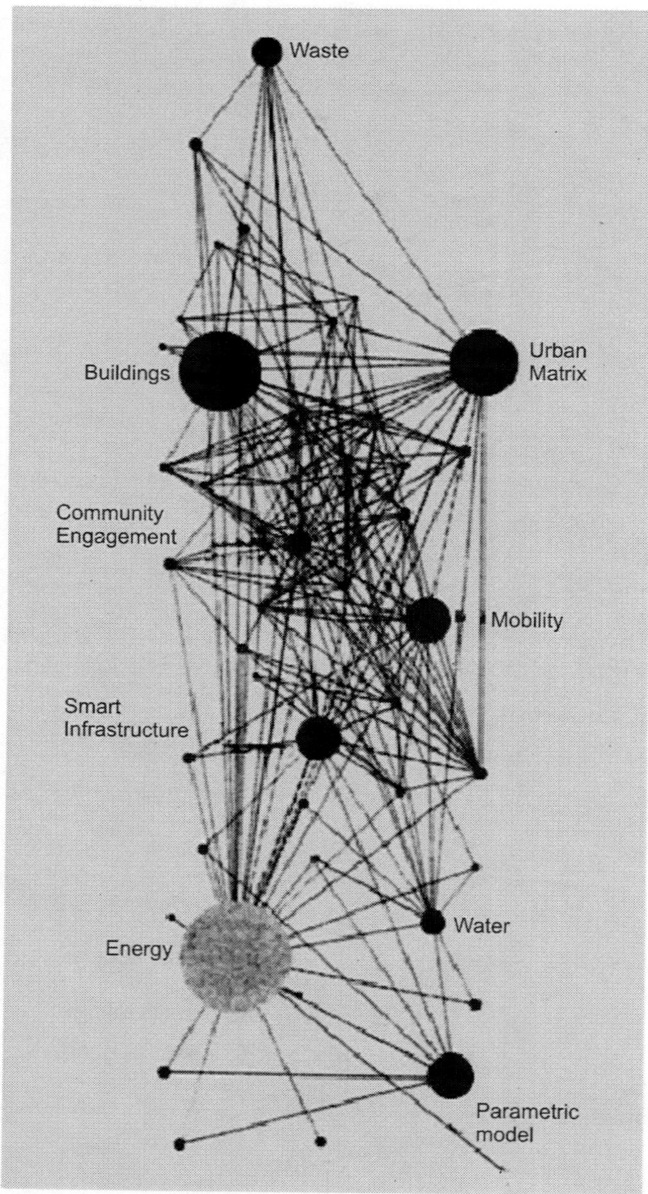

Fig. 5.14: The urban matrix encompasses ecology, infrastructure services, energy, greenery, water and waste management, mobility and community engagement

Source: Adrian and Gordon Gill, 2011, Towards Zero Carbon, Image Pub., Australia

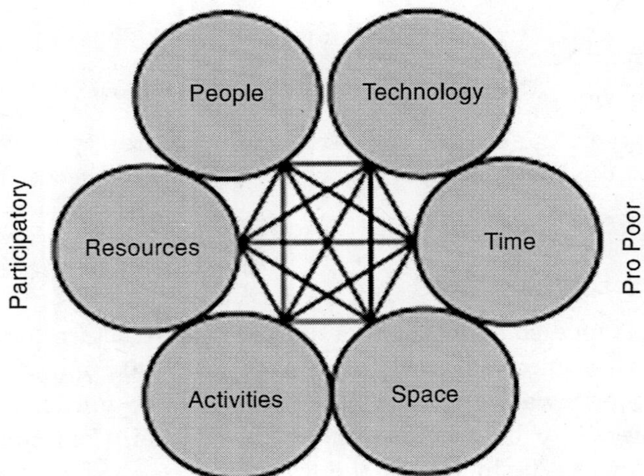

Fig. 5.15: Components of Planning Process

The Concept of Carrying Capacity

Carrying capacity of an area can be defined as the maximum number of population that can be supported by the environment of that area through optimum utilization of the available resources. The pattern and extent of resource usage affects the carrying capacity. This indeed depends on the:

- Socio-economic status of the people
- Use of technology

If technology is used in a positive manner then the carrying capacity is measured to increase manifold. Planners usually define carrying capacity as the ability of the natural or artificial system that can absorb the population growth or physical development without considerable degradation or damage.

The techniques can be translated into policies, strategies and action plans at the local level towards augmentation and sustenance of urban environment resources in terms of their supportive and assimilative capacities on one hand and size, nature and distribution of urban economic activities and their concomitant demands on environment, and on another.

The evaluation of urban carrying capacity is a complex process as it is determined from basic needs such as food requirements, various kinds of resources consumed and many kinds of wastes generated, different kinds of landuse conversions leading to ecological imbalance and the great variability in technology, institutions and lifestyles created. There are 6 types of carrying capacities that can be evaluated:

- Infrastructure capacity
- Institutional capacity
- Perceptual carrying capacity,

- Environmental capacity
- Sustainable capacity, and,
- Bio-centric capacity level.

Among these six types, the critical ones are infrastructure capacity level,environmental capacity level and sustainable capacity level, which are more relevant to urban planning.

Source: MOUD (2015) URDPFI Guidelines

Hierarchy of Urban Development

A city should be planned so as to create a hierarchical structure for self-sufficiency. The smallest planning unit is conceived as Housing Area for 5000 population with convenience shopping, green area, anganwadi and milk booth as minimum infrastructure provision. The higher level of facilities is to be provided at Neighbourhood, Community, District, Zonal, Subcity and Regional levels. The hierarchy of development on the basis of population is given below:

Table 5.1: Hierarchy of Urban Development

Sr.No.	Planning Unit	Population
1	Housing Cluster/ Neighbourhood	5000
2	Neighbourhood	5000-15,000
3	Community	Up to 100,000
4	District	5 Lakh
5	Zone	10 lakh
6	Subcity centre	25 Lakh - 50 Lakh
7	City	50 Lakh +

Sources: UDPFI Guidelines, 1996; MPD 2021 and Jaipur Master Plan.

The provision of amenities in the hierarchy of urban development can be planned according to the standards requirements and resources.

Land use Classification

Land use is classified into;

(a) Categories, such as residential, industrial, commercial, recreational, government, etc

(b) Land Use Zones: The sub-categories of each land use, e.g. public and semi-public facilities include educational, health, safety and security, utilities, etc.

(c) Land use premise, which is exact use of a particular site. This is usually shown on the layout plan. For example, residential use zone may have parks, primary schools community health, etc. which are shown and referred in a layout plan.

Table 5.2: Urban Land Use Classification

Level I			Level II		
N	**A-N**	**Use Category**	**N**	**A-N**	**Use Zone**
1.	R	Residential	11	R-1	Primary Residential Zone
			12	R-2	Unplanned/ Informal Residential Zone
2.	C	Commercial	21	C-1	Retail Shopping Zone
			22	C-2	General Business and Commercial District/ Centres
			23	C-3	Wholesale, Godowns, Warehousing/ Regulated Markets
			24	C-4	Service Sector
			25	C-5	Regulated/ Informal/ Weekly Markets (TCPO Study on Zoning Regulations)
3.	I	Industry	31	I-1	Service and Light Industry
			32	I-2	Extensive and Heavy Industry
			33	I-3	Special Industrial Zone - Hazardous, Noxious and Chemical
4.	PS	Public and Semi-Public	41	PS-1	Govt./ Semi Govt./ Public Offices
			42	PS-2	Govt. Land (use undetermined)
			43	PS-3	Police Headquarter/ Station, Police Line
			44	PS-4	Educational and Research
			45	PS-5	Medical and Health
			46	PS-6	Social Cultural and Religious (inc. Cremation and Burial Grounds)
			47	PS-7	Utilities and Services
5.	M	Mixed Use	51	M-1	Mixed Industrial use Zone
			52	M-2	Mixed Residential Zone
			53	M-3	Mixed Commercial Zone
6.	P	Recreational	61	P-1	Playgrounds/ Stadium/ Sports Complex
			62	P-2	Parks & Gardens – Public open spaces
			63	P-3	Multi-open space (Maidan)
7.	T	Transportation and Communication	71	T-1	Roads/ BRTS
			72	T-2	Railways/ MRTS/
			73	T-3	Airport
			74	T-4	Seaports and Dockyards

Level I			Level II		
N	A-N	Use Category	N	A-N	Use Zone
			75	T-5	Bus Depots/ Truck Terminals and freight Complexes
			76	T-6	Transmission and Communication
8.	A	Primary Activity	81	PA-1	Agriculture
			82	PA-2	Forest& Horticulture
			83	PA-3	Poultry and Dairy Farming
			84	PA-4	Rural Settlements
			85	PA-5	Brick Kiln and Extractive Areas
			86	PA-6	Others (fishing, pottery etc.)
9.	E	Protective and Undevelopable Use Zone	91	E-1	Water Bodies
			92	E-2	Special Recreation Zone / Protective Areas such as sanctuaries/ reserve forests and Eco-sensitive zone
			93	E-3	Undevelopable Use Zone
10.	S	Special Area	101	S-1	Old Built-up (Core) Area
			102	S-2	Heritage and Conservation Areas
			103	S-3	Scenic Value Areas
			104	S-4	Government Restricted Area (such as Defence)
			105	S-5	Other Uses/ Spot Zone*

N: Numeric Code A–N: Alpha Numeric Code

Source: UDPFI Guidelines, 1996 & Study on Zoning Regulations, TCPO, 2004.

Notes: Overall, there could be 42 use zones at the Development Plan level within 10 land use categories at the Perspective Plan level as given in the above table.

- Areas of informal activities may be identified in the above land use categories at Level II for 1to 7 Level I Use Zones only.
- Mixed use zone shall be identified at the Development Plan level, having dominant use and mixed use.
- Use permissions for different activities can be provided at the project/action plan level or with the approval of the Statutory Authority as the case may be.

The process of changing/relaxing/modifying land use of part or "Spot" of a "zone" in a particular land use is termed as "Spot Zoning". Spot Zoning can be done for comparatively smaller area in a particular land use zone in such a way that it does not affect the overall Development Plan.

- Use zone regulations for the use permissibility (from the suggestive list) could be decided by the town planner depending upon the requirement/ feasibility.
- Appropriate code in terms of both numerical and alphabetic (letter) are provided to facilitate the reference and to have a simplified procedure to follow.
- Mixed use in an area of provides and a better option for urban form, facilitates a more equitable mix of social classes, makes city safer, and fosters walk-ability by reducing the distances.

Many urban centers in India have heritage value, preserving the history and aesthetics of earlier developments within a city creates a more livable space and can boost economy and tourism. Special attention must be given to lower-income housing. Mixing housing for various income levels provides increased educational and opportunities for lower income families.

Land use classification for Regional Planning

1. **Urbanisable Zone:** In a Regional Plan, the areas under existing development and those armarked for future development shall be termed as 'U Zone'. This zone is envisaged at three levels U1, U2 & U3.
   - 'U1' zone shall primarily cover the existing areas where more intensive urban development and economic activity are expected in future.
   - 'U2' zone shall cover the new town areas/ satellite towns/counter-magnet/growth/ centres where urban development and economic activity is expected or proposed.
   - 'U3' zone shall be zone outside the existing or proposed urban zones, which have potential for urban development such as lands around major roads and corridors, railway stations, etc. No formal development plan may be prepared for U3 zone but the development shall be regulated on the basis of road widths and development promotion regulations.

   In U Zone all residential, commercial, light and service industry, public and semi-public buildings, transport zones and recreational area may be permitted depending upon the compatibility of the uses.
2. **Industrial Zone:** The areas earmarked for industrial use - service and light industry, extensive and heavy industry, special industrial zone or development of SEZ, IT zones, etc. shall be termed as 'I Zone'.
3. **Transport and Communication Zone:** The areas earmarked for transport and communication use shall be termed as 'T Zone'. This zone can be sub-divided into Roads/ BRTS: T1, Railway/MRTS: T2, Airport: T3, Seaports/ Dockyard/ Dry ports: T4, Bus depots/ truck terminals and freight complexes: T5, Transmission and Communication T6.
4. **Primary Activity Zone:** The areas earmarked for primary activity use shall be termed as 'PAZone'. This zone can be sub divided into Agriculture: PA1, Forest: PA2, Poultry and dairyfarming: PA3, and Brick kiln and extractive areas: PA4.
5. **Open Area Zone:** The areas earmarked for leaving open shall be termed as 'O Zone'. This zone can be subdivided into Recreation Area: O1, Green Buffer Zone: O2. Green

buffer zone shall be provided, so as to restrict the peri-urban areas from unauthorised development. For peri-urban areas special regulations and development control regulations shall be determined in the development plan.

6. **Protective and Eco Sensitive Zone:** The areas earmarked as Protective and Eco-sensitive Areas shall be termed as 'E Zone'. This zone may comprise Water bodies: E1, Special recreation zone/ protective areas such as sanctuaries/ reserve forests: E2, Forest Zone: E3,Coastal Zone: E4 Undevelopable use zone: E5. Undevelopable use zone identified as Earthquake/ landslide prone, cliffs and environmentally hazardous area, areas adjacent to fault lines, areas with slope higher than 45°, areas adjacent to major drainage lines and other areas identified by the national or State Disaster Management Authority as environmentally sensitive.
7. **Special Area Zone:** In addition to the above listed zones, zones may also be specified keeping inview the special characteristic of such areas/pockets. Such areas shall be termed as 'S Zone'.This zone may comprise of old built-up areas with architectural or historical importance : S-1, areas of scenic value, S-2 which need to be preserved without spoiling the character by putting up various kinds of structures, the area restricted for development by Government, S-3, or it may be area under other uses/ spot zones, S-4. Therefore, it is necessary that use/activity permissibility in special areas should be carefully thought of in the development plan when it is being formulated.

Source: URDPFI Guidelines 2015, MOUD

Average Densities

The land use distribution norms depends upon densities and work force. The Gross Population Densities are defined as person per unit area (in hectares) for developed area only. The calculation includes population of the settlement on the developed land of the settlement.

Fixation of density norms should be based on carrying capacity analysis focusing on parameters such as space per person, access to facilities, available piped water per capita, mobility and safety factors. The task should be settlement specific. However, for overall planning approach, density ranges are suggested below:

Table 5.3: Developed Area Average Densities

Settlement Type	Persons per Hectare(pph) in	
	Plain Areas	Hill Areas
Small Towns	75-125	45-75
Medium Town	100-150	60-90
Large Cities	125-175	60-90
Metropolitan Cities	125-175	100-150
Megapolis	More than 200	--

Source: MOUD, URDPFI Guidelines, 2015

Density, expressed in terms of persons per hactare are suggestive densities as per the settlement size. However, while planning the compact and TOD development these densities should be modified to suit the requirement.

This Urban Strategic Planning should in consonance with the income distribution structure of the city region with the urban poor located near public transport nodes/links and specially providing space for the urban poor in master/development plans for living, selling and working at city, zone and local levels.

Overall, the social indicators allow the planner to understand the city, link it with the city spatial form and its behaviour pattern. In short, unlike the traditional approach to zoning, social parameters can be used for creating zones and its functions. This can directly point at the urban facilities such as bus service, dedicated transportation corridors, facilities of social infrastructure and physical infrastructure.

The work force ratio is as given below:

1. Work force participation can be considered as 33% of total population. In the industrial town it can be as high as 75%.
2. The participation of industrial workers as percentage of total work force can be taken as:
   (*a*) For small and medium town : 20
   (*b*) For large cities : 25
3. The industrial workers density can be : 100 pph to 125pph

The ratio of employment to land allocation should be case to case specifically for the sector of investment. With the advanced technology, the investment intensive development would alter the employment and space ratio.

Land use Structure

The proposed land use structure for urban centres is given below:

Table 5.4: Land use Structure for Urban Centres

S.No.	Land use Category	Percentage of Developed Area			
		Small	Medium	Large Cities	Metropolitan Cities & Megapolis
1	Residential	45-50	43-48	36-39	36-38
2	Commercial	2-3	4-6	5-6	5-6
3	Industrial	8-10	7-9	7-8	7-8
4	Pub. & Semi-Public	6-8	6-8	10-12	10-12
5	Recreational	12-14	12-14	14-16	14-16
6	Transport & Communication	10-12	10-12	12-14	12-14
7	Agriculture, Water bodies and Special areas	Balance	Balance	Balance	Balance
8	**Total Developed Area**	**100**	**100**	**100**	**100**

Source: UDPFI Guidelines, 1996 and URDPFI Guidelines 2015

Industrial City/Special Economic Zone

An industrial township should provide for a judicious mix of land uses / activities in such a way that it is not dependant on the neighbouring or other city. The norms and standards for distribution of land use may be as under:

Table 5.5: Land use structure for Industrial towns

Sl. No.	Land use Category	Percentage of Developable Area
1	Residential	20-25
2	Commercial	3-4
3	Industrial	30-35
4	Public and Semi-Public	6-8
5	Recreational	12-15
6	Transport and Communication (including logistics)	10-12
7	Water bodies & Special areas	Balance
	Total	100

Note: The above landuse distribution is indicative, and may vary as per the size of SEZ, industrial town, cluster development.

Source: Draft SEZ Guidelines by TCPO, URDPFI Guidelines, 2015. Ministry of Urban Development

The industrial town should primarily be a modern state of the art township having world class infrastructure, high quality living, working and entertainment provisions, which are particularly suited to the flexible uses and space demands of modern technology and knowledge based activities. The World-class infrastructure would consist of twenty four hour water-supply, unintrupted power supply, efficient and pollution free transport and modern solid waste management, sewerage treatment and communication network.

Stipulations for Infrastructure Development

(a) All industries shall be responsible for treating the effluent generated as per the CPCB regulations for small and medium size industries infrastructure of Common Effluent Treatment Plants(CETP). Special care is to be taken in cases where the effluent after treatment is discharged into a water body.

(b) Solid waste disposal to be as per CPCB/SPCB regulations, specifically for hazardous waste disposal.

(c) To meet the power supply, alternative source of energy to be explored to meet the domestic and commercial demand.

(d) Logistics and Parking requirement of industrial area, transportation infrastructure, including RoW and speed design is to be as per the norms.

(e) To ensure safety from high tension power line, reduce disruption and for increasing life, infrastructure lines are to be well designed within the Right of Way (RoW) for infrastructure corridors, by allocating Right of Use as per regulations of each facility.

Source: MoUD URDPFI Guidelines, 2015

Strategic Issues in Urban Development: Very often, many urban projects, whether infrastructure, industrial or others end up in failures. Such failures are often attributed to the political interferance, but 'politics' in a democratic set up is part of the management and cannot be wished away. It works both ways-political alignment and intervention can speed up the project or kill it. The fact is that initiating a large project involves a complex cohort of risks, clearances and interventions, such as obtaining licences, loans, land, labour, technology, public services (like power, water), environment impact assessment, etc. There are still about 40 clearances, approvals and licences required in India for putting up a large project.

In order to obviate the unforeseen problems and red lights, which may adversely delay or stall the project, it is necessary for the project proponent to make a detailed study of the strategic issues which are critical for smooth operation of the project. There are various ways and means to visualize and tackle the strategic issues in urban projects, such as given below:

Matrix Analysis: Matrix Analysis helps in identifying the critical/strategic issues, potential barriers and bottlenecks, which the project is likely to encounter, while on one side verticals are identified-

(i) Physical: such as land required, location, access, land ownership power and water, services, rawmaterial, markets, etc.

(ii) Investments/Finances and other resources, such as budget, bank loans, institutional finance, taxes,human resource, subsidies, cost benefit, market potential, pricing etc.

(iii) Environment factors: such as pollution, EIA, carbon emissions and reduction, waste management,water recycling, energy efficiency, etc.

(iv) Organisation, Management and Legal issues, such as law, rules, regulation, labour , organizations involved, contracting, completion, regulatory system, political support, timelines, etc.

(v) Technology: level, import potential, skills, safety retrofitting, repair, maintenance, impact, etc.

(vi) Service Delivery and Marketing: consumers, society, local community benefit, jobs, etc.

Critical Strategic Issues are listed on the matrix chart which may be external or internal. By fuzzy logic these can be given a conceptual weightage and then accordingly action required to tackle the issues is outlined. This way matrix chart provides a clear picture of the future troubles, difficulties and risks which need to be tackled. In certain cases, the situation could be–

(i) Impossible

(ii) Can be remedied with additional inputs/efforts, but with risk, and,

(iii) Can be nipped in the bud by pre-planning, or by internal action.

In most of the large projects, a congenial relationship with the political apparatus and local community becomes necessary which can be achieved by proper PR, Communications, through offer of jobs to the locals, cultural promotion, religious, healthcare and educational programmes, etc. For certain critical issues, it may be necessary to appoint the consultants, peer advisory group or outsource the difficult component of work.Triangulation technique can be adopted to co-relate the critical factors (verticals) and project aspects (horizontals).

Conceptualising, Norming and Planning

In India the settlements can be grouped as below:

7936	→	Cities and Towns (377 m people 31.15%)
53	→	Metropolitan area (160 m 42.6% of urban population)
640	→	Districts
476	→	Urban Agglomeration (157 m people)
6.41 lakh	→	Villages (833 m people)
Total		1,210 m people

Spatial planning, land, housing, slum improvement, local self government, physical and social infrastructure, urban transport are in States list. Environment and heritage protection, education, health, regional transport, bulk services, industrial growth and tourism are in concurrent list. The 74th CAA requires that Metropolitan Planning Committees (MPCs) be created for metropolitan areas. The 73rd CAA requires that District Planning Committees (DPCs) be created for all districts. However, the track record in creating MPCs and DPCs is dismal. As a result, planning functions are performed under State Urban and Regional Planning Acts and State LSG or Development Authority Acts.

The Urban and Regional Plans usually have top down approach and leave out the planning at the ward and local levels.The Municipal bodies neither consider this as an obligatory functions nor have developed capacity for this task. Ward plans can be the refreshing canvas for not only the ward councilor but the entire community to understand, participate and address the issues and problems at local levels. Wards of around 50,000 persons (10,000 families) constitute ideal communities that make up the larger urban matrix for working out a spatial- financial framework of community development.

Policies and vision are converted into strategic and action plans for development of priority areas and to mobilize the resources. The Local Area Plans provide a road map to achieve these goals. These establish the requirement of the resources and detail out the exact manner in which a certain activity must be accomplished in a chronological sequence. A Local Area Plan will have a programme which combines goals, policies, procedures, rules, assignments, steps to be taken, resources to be employed and other elements necessary to carry out a given course of action.

Local Area Plan should address the specific issues of a ward or area and synchronise with the political apparatus, administrative system and financial allocations. The Local Area Plan aims to preserve the urban design, heritage and eco-sensitive character of an area/zone. It should attempt to ensure adequate supply of water and other facilities such as, sewerage, public toilets, transportation, schools, security (police, fire, emergencies, etc.) and parks and sports, besides taking care of the vendors and informal sector and livelihood.

The Local Area Plan acts as a link between Master Plan/Zonal Plan and is to be prepared by the urban local body. The governance and investments through local planning enjoins a state-citizen partnership. It implies peoples' involvement in the development process at neighbourhood, ward and colony levels and make the municipal bodies and ward councilors accountable to the people and responsible for implementation.

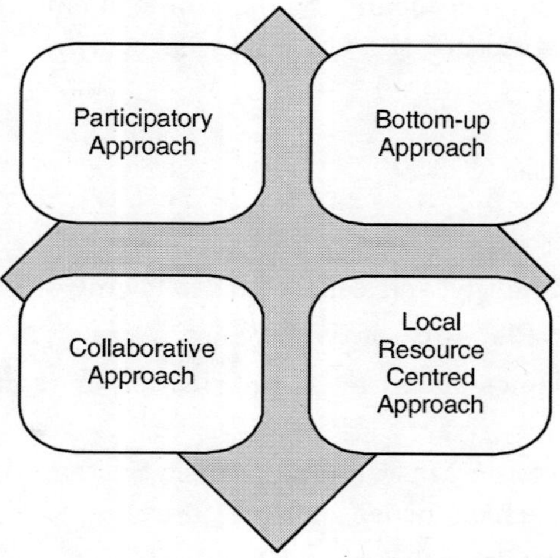

Fig. 5.16: The 74th CAA empowers the Urban Local Bodies for planning and implementation at local levels.

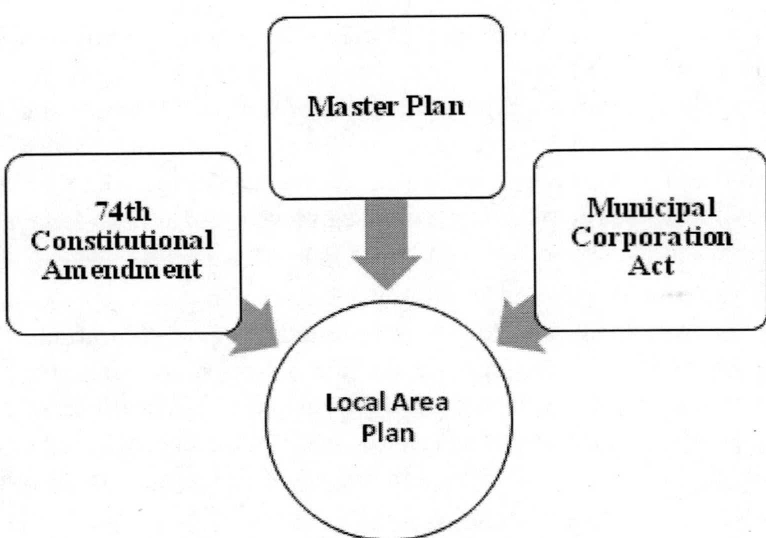

Fig. 5.17: Local Area Planning (LAP) for a defined locality and electoral wards (with population of approximately 50,000) envisages assessment of public needs and their participation in the planning process

Preparation of local area plan involves comprehensive documentation and base maps of the municipality and wards, socio-economic profile, profile of environment and health services, and status reports on infrastructure services as given below:

- Base Map (survey)
- Google Maps
- Census Data
- LAP/ Ward Boundary

An LAP is expected to identify and collate the following:

- All approved Layout Plans in the Ward/Local Area
- All unauthorized colonies slated for regularization or regularized as per government records and policy
- The influence zone of the Mass Rapid Transit System (MRTS) and other transport corridors, terminals, depot, nodes, parking areas, etc.
- Low density areas available for redensification
- Slums and JJ (Jhuggi Jhompri) clusters
- Villages in the city
- Status of Infrastructure- water supply, sewerage, waste collection, electricity, water harvesting, drainage, public toilets, etc.
- Status of facilities- educational, health, safety, security, etc.
- Open spaces, sports facilities and water bodies
- Mixed use streets and commercial streets

- Spaces for service markets, tehbazari, weekly markets, informal shopping, night shelters, etc.
- Industrial clusters slated for regularization, if any
- Hoardings, street furniture and signage
- Facilities for pedestrians and physically challenged
- Gas godowns and petrol pumps
- Heritage buildings and precincts protected notified, listed and unlisted.

The information is analyzed and digitized, and in consultation with the concerned agencies, local people, etc. and the following maps and draft proposals are prepared:

- Land use map showing important uses such as, residential, commercial, mixed use, slums parks, open areas, water bodies, etc.,
- Identifying the problems in spatial context,
- Municipal resources, investments and their sources,
- Environmental and infrastructure services and their location, including traffc and transport,
- Other proposals, specific to the character and potentials of the area.

For public participation, hearings, discussions and dialogues on community and local concerns are done during the process of preparing local plans. On the basis of the information on key problem areas, opportunity areas and potential resources, plans are evolved integrating the land use, physical and socio-economic infrastructure including environment and health services, pollution control and opportunity areas and also areas for preservation and conservation.

Priority is given to the needs of local communities; promote their social and economic development; and contribute to the progressive realisation of the fundamental rights with provision for education, health, informal sector of trade, slum rehabilitation, redevelopment of villages and Old City, energy efficiency, conservation of water bodies, zero polluting industries, etc.

The LAP also addresses the common issues of infrastructure services, parks/playgrounds, community facilities and transport networks. A Local Area Plan may designate any part of the city/municipal area as an action area for development, redevelopment or improvement, along with the proposals for the development controls. The LAP contains a written statement, land uses, development controls, boundaries of designated areas, such as heritage sites/zones, conservation areas, redevelopment areas, influence zone along major transport corridors, infrastructure services, etc.

The following aspects may be considered in arriving at the broad delineation of boundaries for the LAP:

- Ward/municipal boundaries/composite administrative area.
- The character of the area enabling the formulation of area specific proposals;
- Similarity of concerns, development needs;
- Physically recognizable boundaries (e.g. edge of water bodies, roads, railway lines, and existing compounds, etc.);
- Historicity, homogeneity and domain.

As far as possible, the boundaries of the planning area should be co-terminus with ward/ administrative/Zonal Plan boundaries to facilitate involvement of elected representatives in the planning process. However, each Local Area Plan should overlap and include about 100-200 meter of adjacent ward for maintaining continuity and inter-relationship of circulation, services, urban form, etc.

Contents of LAP: A Local Area Plan should be based on local needs and characteristics and indicate area specific configuration of plots/properties, basic amenities; existing built up area infrastructure services, etc.

- The Local Area Plan (LAP) shall aim to meet the specific development needs, including the upgradation of Physical and social Infrastructure and amenities such as housing, water, power, roads, drainage, solid waste management, sewerage, sanitation, etc.
- Upgrading of Social Infrastructure-health, schools, sports, dispensaries,community centers, cultural centers, etc.
- Livelihood and inclusive development, especially for the informal sector, slum dwellers, vending zones, weekly markets and re-development of degraded areas.
- Mobility Planning and Integration of different modes of transport- public transit, parking, cyclist, rickshaws/ NMVs and pedestrians.
- Preserving and Upgrading the Environment- greenery, water bodies, wet lands and parks,preservation of heritage.

The Local Area Plans endeavour to bring informal, unplanned areas into planning fold, gradually facilitating their conversion into planned development with safe buildings, adequate facilities, services and transport. Additional FAR against public green/facilities, redevelopment, mixed land use, in-situ redevelopment and infill development can be the tools to achieve this transformation.

A LAP should be based on Urban Design approach and a comprehensive framework of development controls, height of the buildings, setbacks, Floor Area Ratio (FAR), margins, parking space, signage, beautification of public spaces, etc.

A Local Area Plan should have the following:

(i) Title, its legality, plan approval details.

(ii) Purpose and context: The plan should mention in the introduction its purpose and briefly explain the planning framework and policies within which it is prepared. A brief explanation should be included of the plan's relationship with the other policies, programmes and management strategies.

(iii) Vision, strategy, aims, objectives and target: A local area plan should include in the introduction a clear and concise statement of its main aims, objectives and targets, and the strategy for achieving them, having regard to the likely level of resources available, both public and private sector. Taken together, the strategy, aims, objectives and targets should provide a clear vision of what will be achieved by the implementation of the plan, and make clear the priorities at the outset. A clear indication of how the policies and proposals will be implemented, by which agency and over what period, will assist monitoring of both implementation and the effectiveness of policies.

The Local Area Plan should be clear, succinct and easily understood by all those who need to know about the planning, policies and proposals which apply in the area. The needs of different groups should be carefully considered in determining the approach and style proposals. The use of a plan summary and a full index will help to make the plan more accessible. Jargon should be avoided as far as possible. Where it is necessary to use technical terms, these should be explained in a glossary.

The written statement should be clear and concise and should be limited to those policies and proposals which provide a strategic framework for local plan and development controls. The proposals should be clearly and unambiguously expressed, with sufficient precision to enable them readily to be implemented and their performance measured. In the event of a contradiction between the written statement and the map/ diagram, the written statement prevails.

Organisational Set-up: For the preparation of the LAP, the Local Body are the nodal agencies. For each LAP Working Groups, comprising elected representatives of public, RWA, Traders Association, service agencies, industries, revenue/L&B/Urban Development Department, health, education, transport infrastructure, environment, finance, etc. may be constituted. Each Working Group may consist of elected representatives, government officials, NGOs, etc. A Core Committee of these Working Groups may be formed as Spatial Integration Committee (SIC). SIC has a key role in the preparation of the LAP and has the overall responsibility right from data collection to plan preparation and report writing. An integrated

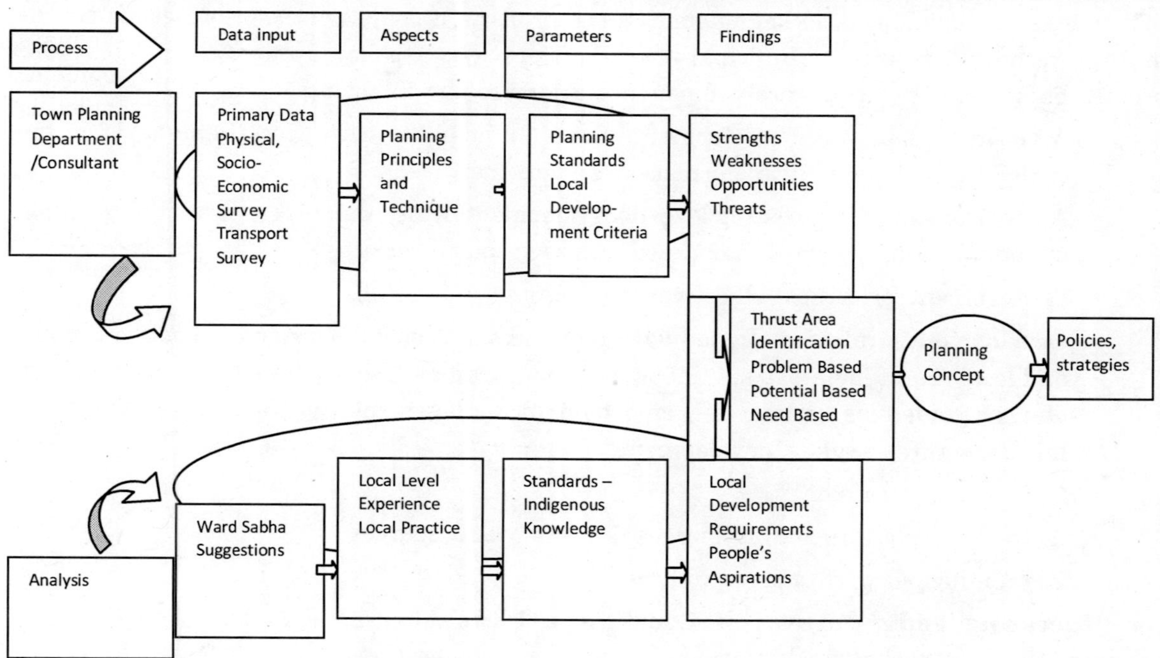

Fig 5.18: Planning Process for Local Area Plan

analysis will result in identification of thrust areas, followed by planning concept, policies and strategies and finally Draft LAP. These are formulated jointly by Planning Department of

Local body, Consultants and Spatial Integration Committee. The findings and the analysis form an input for the identification of the thrust areas of the LAP. The various LAPs provide the input for the formulation of an Integrated Municipal Plan.

For the preparation of the LAP, a Technical Advisory Committee (TAC) may be constituted, comprising the elected representatives, heads of government departments, NGOs, representatives of research wings/educational institutions, etc. The members of various departments- Forests and Environment, Industries, Transportation, Housing, Health, Water and Sanitation, Education, Finance, Social Welfare, Power, Communications, Tourism, Culture, Sports, etc., ensures that the LAP is in synchronization with their own budgets and Annual/ Five Year Plans. The Technical Advisory Committee may be convened by a Senior Town Planner. Finally, infrastructure/LAP and Integrated Municipal Plan are approved by the Municipal Planning Committee, headed by Municipal Commissioner.

The Local Area Planning process brings various departments, RWAs and Councilors, etc. on a common platform. It enables the translation of annual and five year financial plans on ground.

The Municipal Area Plan

The Municipal Area Plan establishes horizontal and vertical linkages among various levels of planning and also among various stakeholders/ departments/ agencies/ RWAs/ Councilors, etc. It provides a strategic framework for development within a timeframe and integrates spatial, financial, socio-economic and other plans, considering the priorities, potentials and the resources required. Municipal Area Plan provides a policy framework and basis for annual budget. As such, its core components comprise the following:

- A vision for long term development of the municipality with special emphasis on the critical development, transformation and reform needs;
- An assessment of the existing level of development, which must include an identification of communities which do not have access to basic services;
- Development priorities, objectives and aims;
- Development strategies aligned with regional/sub-regional/Master Plan,sectoral plans and local requirements; a spatial development framework which includes the provision of basic guidelines for land use; environment management, heritage management and infrastructure services development.
- Operational strategies;
- A financial plan, including budget projection and sources
- Key municipal performance indicators

Processing and Approval of Local Area Plan: After a draft local Area plans is prepared, it is to be published inviting objections and suggestions from the public. The draft LAP is accordingly modified and forwarded for sanction of the local body concerned and the Government. In case of any Master Plan changes/ modifications it is referred to the government for approval and processing of such changes under the relevant Act.

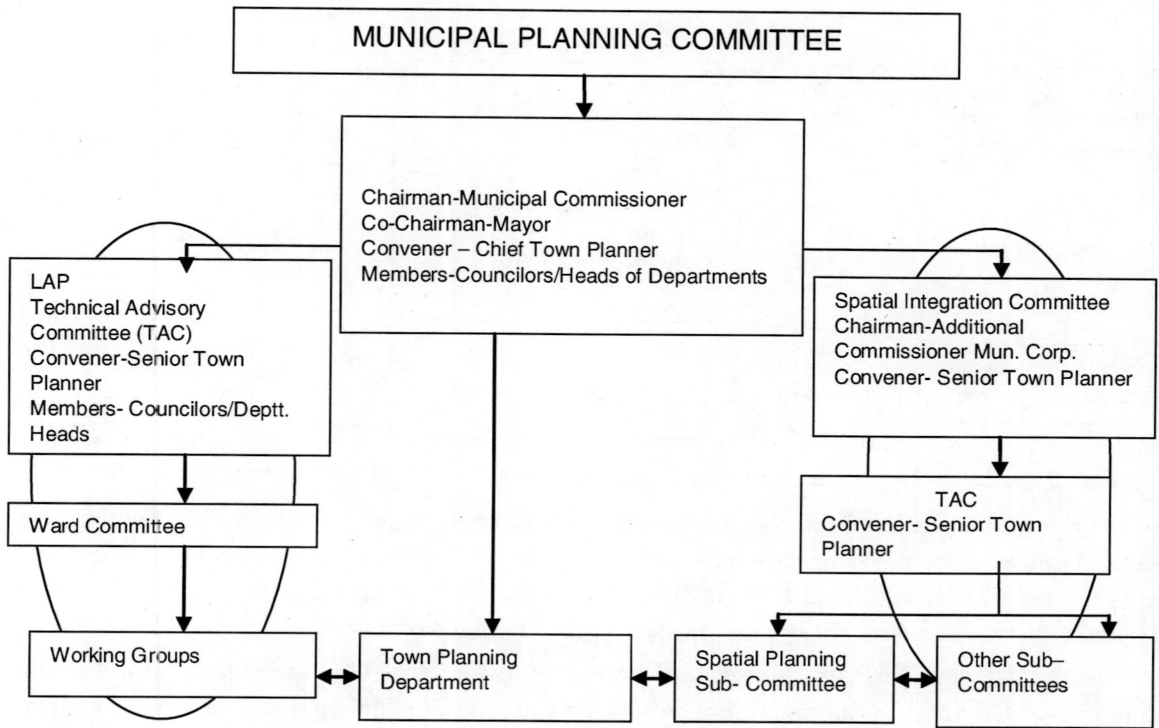

Abbreviations: MAP -Municipal Area Plan, LAP - Local Area Plan, TAC - Technical Advisory Committee

Fig. 5.19: Organisational Set-up for the Preparation of Integrated Municipal Area Plan and Local Area Plans

The organizational set-up of for preparation of Local area Plan envisages setting up of a Municipal Planning Committee for the preparation of LAP and MAP, which is interdisciplinary and participatory. The Municipal Planning Committee (MPC) is the apex body with the department of town planning acting as the nodal agency for the preparation of the plans. The coordination committee comprises mainly elected committees heads of local self-government institutions (LSGI) and service agencies.

For the preparation of the LAP, ward committee of the municipality is the apex body, which is supported by various sub-committees/groups. The working groups consist of elected representatives, government officials, NGOs, etc. A Spatial Integration Committee (SIC) plays a key role in the preparation of the LAP and has the overall responsibility right from data collection to report writing. The process of the data analysis will result in identification of thrust areas, followed by planning concept, policies and strategies and draft LAP. These are formulated by Town Planning department with the help of consultants and guidance of Spatial Integration Committee. Draft LAPs will be inputs for the preparation of MAP.

A Technical Advisory Committee (TAC) is constituted, which comprises the elected representatives, heads of government departments and service agencies, NGOs, representatives of research wings and educational institutions, etc. It plays a key role in the plan preparation.

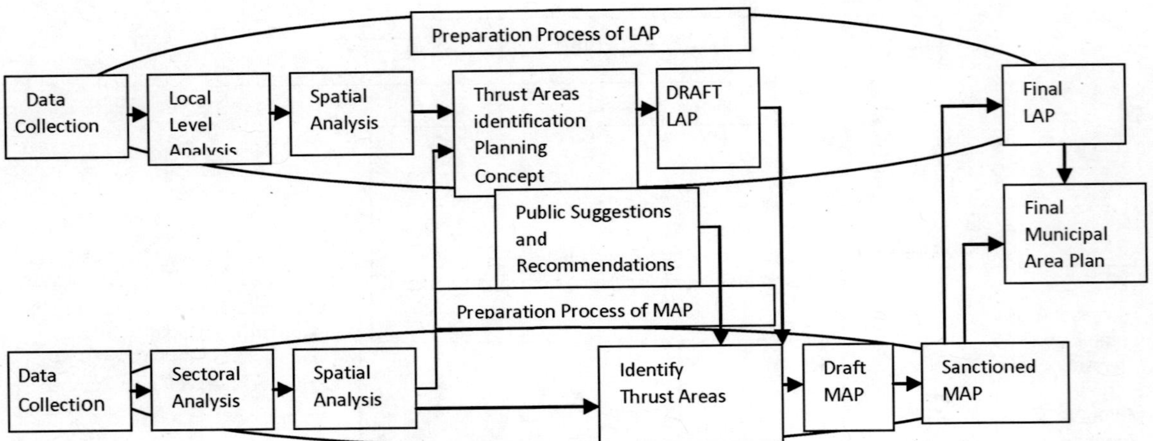

Fig. 5.20: Local Area Plan (LAP) and Municipal Area Plan (MAP): Synchronization Process

At the municipal level the Town Planning Department, which is headed by the chief town planner plays a coordinating role in the preparation of the Municipal Area Plan and Local Area Plans. The Local Area Plan is finalized only after the consultations with concerned departments and stakehodlers and incorporation of their comments.

Draft MAP and LAP are placed and presented before the TAC and Spatial Integration Committee. On their recommendation, the plans are put up for approval of the Municipal Planning Committee. Thereafter the plans are forwarded to State Government for final approval and notification. After the approval of the plans follow up projects, schemes, programmes and resources plans and action plans are formulated.

The Local Area Plan would enable the ULBs/Municipal Corporations to grant planning permissions, incentive and additional FAR for redevelopment and transit oriented development, mixed land use, Transferable Development Rights (TDR) and Accommodation Reservation (AR). This would release a new stream of financial sources to the Corporations by way of capturing the Development charges, Land Use Conversion charges, Betterment levy, Mixed Use charges, FAR charges, etc. As such, the preparation of Local Area Plans may also build up financial capacity of the local bodies.

Strategic and Action Plans

Strategic Plan is usually a mid-term (3-5) year plan which focuses on achieving a limited number of priority objectives. It normally comprises a number of programmes and projects which are closely tied into the commitments- personal, institutional and investment, which are necessary for its implementation. These programmes and projects should incorporate a locational dimension, i.e. where they take place. To certain extent administrative and management bottlenecks, vested interests and political intervention can be mitigated by Strategic and Action Planning.

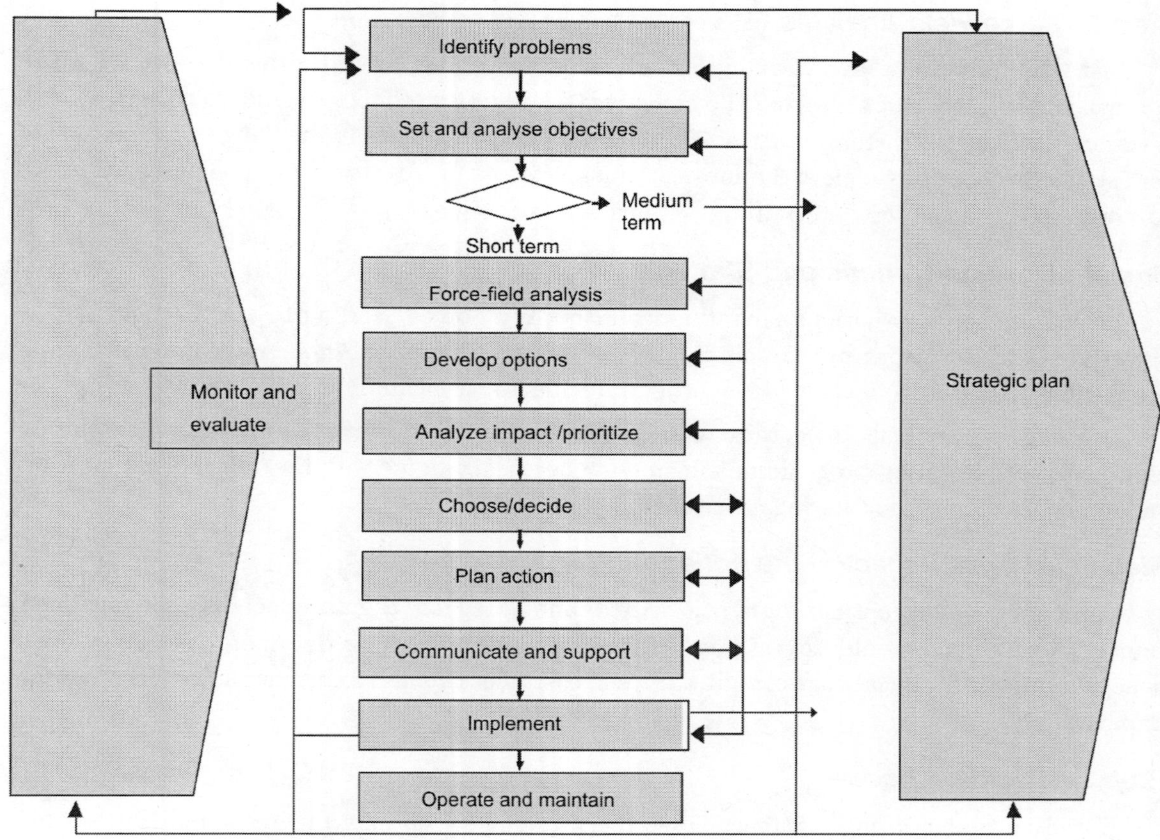

Fig. 5.21: Links to Strategic Planning

Source: Forbes Davidson (1994), Action Planning, IHS Rotterdam

The Action Plan is an operative plan defining goals and clearly indicating how these goals are to be carried out. It involves a series of steps as given below:

Step 1 : Identify Problems

Scanning survey to get overview and base information. This includes an overview of organizations and problems as seen by key actors. SWOT analysis helps to "talk" with the problem, to determine whether it really is a problem according to action planning criteria. If more than one problem is apparent, find out whether the problems are in any way 'interlinked'.

Step 2 : Set and Analyse Objectives

Formulate objectives for the problems that appear SMART at this stage: Specific, Measurable, Attainable, Realistic and Time bound. Divide objectives into short term (say one year), and medium term-3-5 years.

Step 3 : Force Field Analysis

List the Restraining and Driving Forces, constraints and opportunities that would work against and in favour of achieving the objectives. Categories of forces would be related to, for instance, institutions/actors and resources. Make notes of solutions that already come up in this stage, for later use. Select the most promising forces to further work on. The Force Field Analysis is the basis for determining options and strategies.

Step 4 : Develop Options and Strategies

Formulate solution-options for influencing the Key Forces, leading to achievement of the objectives and contributing to solving the problem. Check whether solution-options are compatible with those developed for other interlinked problems.

Convergence analysis to coordinate and integrate, to avoid overlaps, wastage of resources and incompatible action programmes. It may be necessary to identify the 'feasible action sets' or 'decision schemes' for various interlinked problems.

Step 5 : Analyze Impact of the options

Compare feasible options and prioritize them based on their impact assessment. The Impact Assessment would cover detailed assessments of goal achievement, economic cost benefit analysis; financial cost benefit analysis; cost effectiveness analysis and environmental impact analysis.

Step 6 : Decide/Choose

Based on a comparative impact assessment of review options the recommendations for the preferred options/ strategy may be developed for a decision and approval by the authorities.

Step 7 : Define Tasks/Plan Action

Break down the finalise action programme(s) into tasks to be implemented within a specified time frame and people responsible. One of the tasks must be monitor progress for which time schedule should be specified.

Step 8: Communicate, Get Support

Communication with/among actors is be one of the major tasks. This involves sharing the plans, programs and implementation, organizational set up, financing plans and to get support for implementation. The implementation and monitoring of tasks, may bring up new problems to tackle. It may also provide a learning experience and adjustment in action plan.

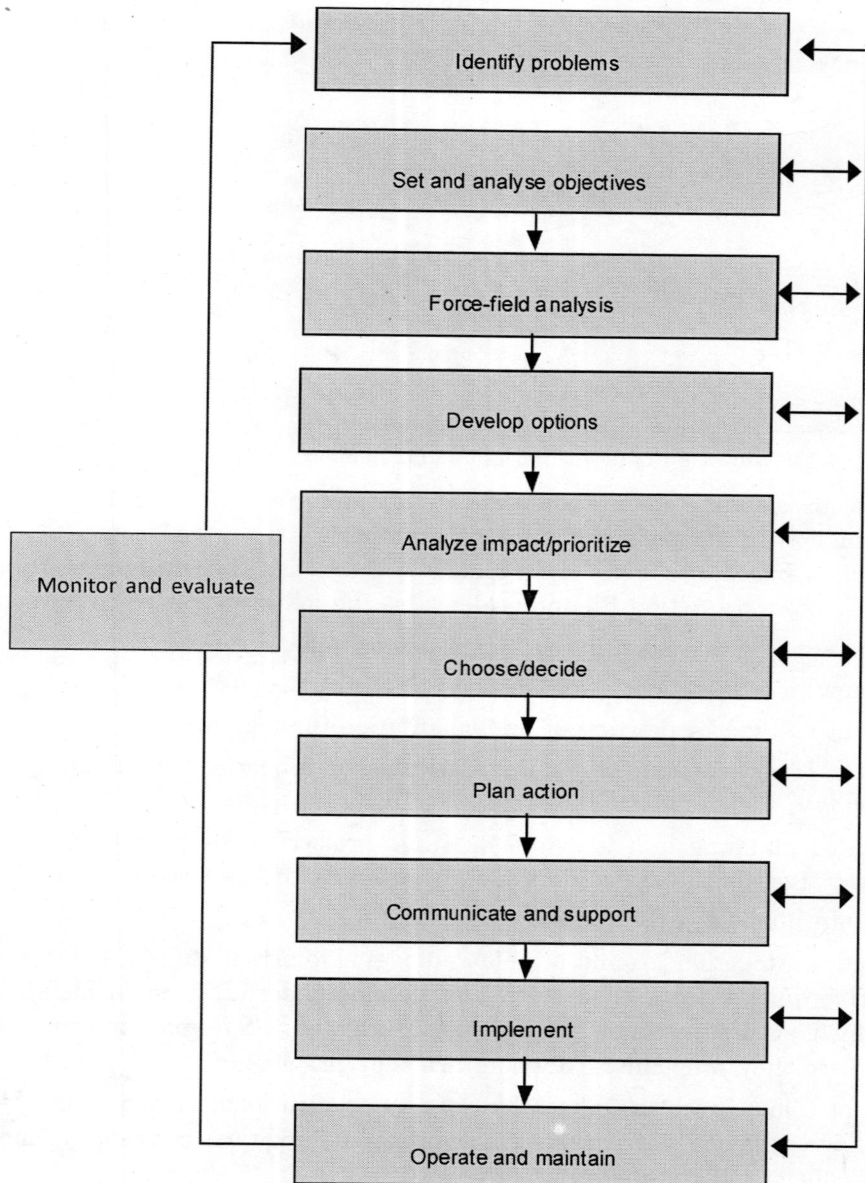

Fig. 5.22: Process of Action Planning

Plan Implementation

Implementation of plans is a key issue, as wide gaps exist between intended and realized strategies. This is due to lower attention and ad-hoc approach to implementation, lack of investments and revenue generation, shortfall in institutional capacity and lack of time-bound programmes. For successful implementation of the projects, community involvement may be essential. During the last few years, the costs of land and its development have increased disproportionately. It is necessary to make optimum use of land and services besides lowering the cost of land and development.

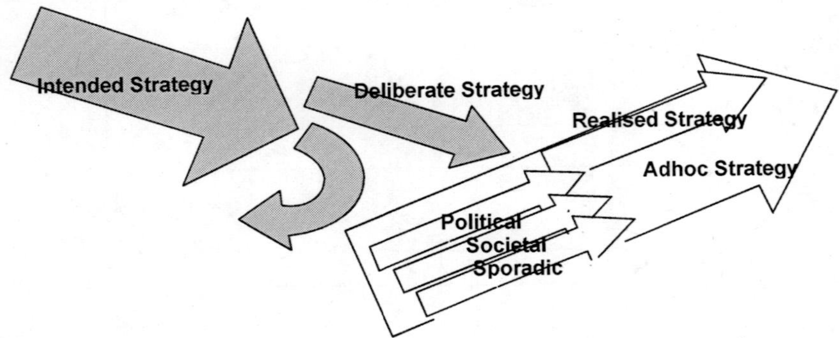

Fig. 5.23: Wide Gap between Intended and Realised Strategy

Action planning focuses on implementation and delivery and involves the communities to implement and manage their own development programmes. Its key characteristics are participatory, community-based, problem-driven and fast. Developed by Nabeel Hamidi and Reinhard Goethert, Community Action Planning identifies the following phases:

1. Deciding what was needed (identifying key problems and priorities)
2. Sorting out how to achieve what was needed (preparing proposals)
3. Assessing what will get in the way of implementation (project viability)
4. Building a plan of action (tasks, partners, schedules, organizations, etc.) and getting projects going.

For this a dedicated planning unit is established and project coordinators are selected from the community to pursue the tasks identified, grouped in the key result areas.

The following quote illustrates the process :

"...the group sits down together around a table and begins to articulate its thoughts and feelings. The "experts" quickly loose their aura and become cheerful, humble facilitators asking questions which at first are not too difficult to answer : 'So what are the main problems here. Why are they problems? To whom are they problematic?'

Implementation of plans involves financial resources, institutional capacity and legal back-up and reforms. Accordingly a matrix chart can be prepared for various critical components of plans, identifying causes and possible reforms needed.

Participants are urged to see the host of issues which spring to mind as opportunities rather than problems. Large sheets of newsprint and fat felt-tip pens obligingly record long lists of apparently insurmountable hurdles as groups cluster around tables, heads bend in communal concentration. Emerging at last from their huddles after a short hour, the newsprint is put against the wall and one spokesperson is democratically press-ganged into presenting the findings.

'Well, it's the water supply, as you all know, the pipes are leaking and we can only draw water twice a day and then the water has little things floating in it.'

The representatives of the other groups follow with similar tales in a depressed living environment. 'Right! Get back into your groups and let's have some solutions', comes the slightly shocking response. 'Divide your next sheet into four columns and describe a series of projects which will deal with these problems.'And so the process carries on for four days - huddle, present, discuss, agonise, rethink, present, rework, re-present-until gradually the action plans take shape."

The concept of CQT (Coordination, Quantum, Time) analysis with a focus on targets vis-a vis resources, agencies involved, data and time based management information system (MIS), and monitoring of programmes can help in performance orientation, which catalyse planned development. Priority areas should be worked out so as to deliver the services in the shortest possible time, with a sense of competition between public and private sectors. The planning approach, standards and procedures should be evolved on the basis of realistic assessment, which are implementable.

Green Township Rating System

A critical consideration in planning is to enable the design of a green township. IGBC Green Township Rating System addresses various features under the following categories:

- Site Selection and Planning
- Land Use Planning
- Transportation Planning
- Infrastructure Resource Management
- Innovation in Design and Technology

A green township should meet certain mandatory requirements which are non-negotiable. Different levels of green township certification are awarded based on the total credits earned. The credit on 'innovation in design and technology' is to recognize innovative ideas that are not addressed under the rating system of the project and demonstrates exemplary performance. The threshold criteria for certification levels are as under:

Table 5.6: Green Township Rating System

Certification Levels	Points for Green Township	Recognition
Certified	100–119	Best Practice
Silver	120–139	Outstanding Performance
Gold	140–159	National Excellence
Platinum	160–200	Global Leadership

Source: IGBC

Green Townships are typically characterized by long periods of construction in phases. The Certification of IGBC Green Township is divided into three stages depending upon the percentage of development completed:

Stage I: 50% of total project infrastructure development is constructed

Stage II: 75% of infrastructure and 25% of residential development of the total project in constructed and is in operation.

Stage III: Township completed in all aspects; 100% infrastructure and residential development. Infrastructure includes roads and streets, footpaths and pathways, public bus, power cables, street lighting, traffic lights, drinking water and sewage distribution systems, water storage tanks, sewage treatment plants storm, water drains, rain-water harvesting facilities, etc.

Township development generally covers:

- Roads and streets
- Bus stops, MRT station
- Fuel recharging stations
- Footpaths and pathways
- Street lighting, traffic lights
- Motors and pumps in public areas
- Common waste-water treatment ad distribution system for reuse
- Rain water harvesting system in public areas
- Common growing spaces for vegetables and fruits
- Public landscaping areas, parks, open spaces, and,
- Public common areas such as community hall, club house, auditorium, sports club, sports facilities, etc.

Documentation for certification has to be submitted in three stages —two at design stage and one at construction stage. The Stage I & II submissions involve those credits which can be evaluated at the design stage. Each design submission is assessed by third party assessors and review comments are provided within 50 working days.

Table 5.7: Checklist for IGBC Green Township Rating System

Site Selection and Planning		
SSP MR I	Local Regulations	Required
SSP MR 2	Avoid Development of Inappropriate Sites	Required
SSP MR3	Soil Erosion Control Plan	Required
SSP Credit 1	Preserve Existing Trees and Water Bodies	6
SSP Credit 2	Retain Natural Topography	6
SSP Credit 3	Public Landscape Areas	6
SSP Credit 4	Redevelopment of Contaminated Areas	6
SSP Credit 5	Local Fruits and Vegetable Produce	8
SSP Credit 6	Urban Heat Island Effect	8

Land Use Planning		
EP MR 1	Land Use Optimisation	Required
EP MR 2	Basic Facilities for Construction Workforce	Required
EP MR 3	Basic Amenities within the Community	Required
EP Credit 1	Mixed Use Development	10
EP Credit 2	Housing Typologies	8
EP Credit 3	Green Buildings	12
EP Credit 4	Employment Opportunities (Post-occupancy)	8
EP Credit 5	Social & Cultural Initiatives	6
	Total	44

Transportation Planning		
IP MR 1	Long Term Transportation Plan	Required
IP MR2	Design for Differently Abled	Required
IP Credit 1.1	Public Transportation Facilities	6
IP Credit 1.2	Eco-Friendly Transportation Services	6
IP Credit 2	Road & Street Network	6
IP Credit 3	Bicycle Lane Network	6
IP Credit 4	Pedestrian Network	6
Total		30

Infrastructure Resource Management		
IRM MR 1	Rainwater Harvesting, 50%	Required
IKM MR2	Segregation of Waste (Post-occupancy)	Required
IRM Credit 1	Rainwater Harvesting, 75% to 95%	6
IRM Credit 2	Waste Water Treatment, 100%	6
IRM Credit 3	Waste Water Reuse, 75% to 95%	6
IRM Credit 4	Energy Efficiency in Infrastructure Equipment	8
IRM Credit 5	On-sile Renewable Energy	16
IRM Credit 6	Off-site Green Power	12
IRM Credit 7	Construction Waste Reduction (Civil Works)	6
IRM Credit 8	Recycled Content (Civil Works)	8
IRM Credit 9	Measurement & Verification Plan (Post-occupancy)	2

Innovation in Design & Technology		
IDT Credit 11	Innovation in Design & Technology	3
ID! Credit 1.2	Innovation in Design & Technology	3
IDT Credit 1.3	Innovation in Design & Technology	3
IDT Credit 1.4	Innovation in Design & Technology	3
IDT Credit 2	IGBC Accredited Professional	4
	Sub-Total	16
	Total Points	200

Source: www.igbc.in

Definitions and Short Notes

Agriculture: includes horticulture, farming, raising of crops, fruits, vegetables, flowers, grass, fodder, trees or any other kind of cultivation, dairy, animal husbandry, breeding and keeping of live-stock, including cattle, horses, donkeys, mules, pigs, fish, poultry and bees; and use of land which is ancillary to the farming of land or any other agriculture purposes, but shall not include the use of land attached to a building for the purposes of a garden to be used alongside such building.

Amenities: include roads and streets, open spaces, parks, recreational grounds, playgrounds, water and electric supply, street lighting, sewerage, drainage, public works and other utilities, services and conveniences.

Development: The carrying out of building, engineering, mining or other operations in, on, over or under land or the making of any material change, in any building or land, or in the use of any building or land and includes sub-division of any land.

Development Plan: A plan for the development or redevelopment or improvement of an area within the jurisdiction of a Planning Authority and includes a Regional Development Plan, a Metropolitan Development Plan, Area Development Plan, Town Development Plan, Zonal Development Plan, District Development Plan, or any other plan or scheme prepared under relevant Act by what-so-ever name known.

Domestic Sewage: All forms of wastewater derived from residential properties, as well as black water and grey water from commercial and institutions buildings.

Floor Area Ratio: The quotient or the ratio of the total covered area of all floors to the total area of the plot, multiplied by 100.

Infrastructure: Any project, public amenity or public utility or service, which is required for smoofh, productive and efficient functioning of the Planning Area such as trunk infrastructure, access from or to the nearest major road, bulk supply of drinking water (surface water and ground water with trunk line), power (electric substation and network), health, education facilities, transport (major roads such as national highways, state highways, major district roads, other district roads, bridges, bypasses and underpasses), common effluent treatment plant (CETP), sewage treatment plant (STP), solid waste disposal system and receptacles, communication network, shopping, institutional buildings, malls and multiplexes, cinema halls, community halls, open air theatres, playgrounds, civic and cultural facilities, public parking areas, etc.

Land Use: The major use for which a land is being used on any specified date.

Local Authority: A municipal corporation or committee or board or district board or other authority legally entitled to, or entrusted by the government with the control or management of a municipal or local fund or which is permitted by the government to exercise the powers of a local authority, and includes a town improvement trust; and a local authority is a Local Authority Concerned, if any land within its local limits falls in the area of a plan prepared or to be prepared under relevant Act.

Plan: The statement of proposals, policies and development briefs for securing, promoting and regulating development in a Planning Area, and includes a map or maps or set of documents or all of them.

Planning Area: A territorial unit demarcated and declared by the Government for the purposes of planning under *relevant* Act and shall be known by such name as the Government may decide.

Public Place: Any place or building which is open to the use and enjoyment of the public whether it is actually used or enjoyed by the public or not and whether the entry is regulated by any charge or not.

Residence: Includes the use for human habitation of any land or building or part thereof, the use of gardens, grounds, garages, stables and out-houses, if any, appertaining to such land or building, and "Residential" shall be construed accordingly.

Sanitation: Interventions usually construction of facilities such as latrines that improve the management of excreta and promote sanitary (healthy) conditions.

Scheme: A Development Scheme includes a plan or plans together with the descriptive matter, if any, relating to such a scheme.

Septage: Mixture of wastewater and sludge removed from a septic tank during cleaning operations.

Septic tank: A form of on-plot sanitation for the anaerobic treatment of sewage/black water.

Sewage: A mixture of wastewater from all urban activates from residential, commercial properties. It may also contain a component of industrial wastewater.

Sewerage: A network of interconnected sewers in an area, district or town.

Utility: Services such as roads including approach roads, bridges, bypasses and underpasses, street lights, water supply system, sewerage system, storm water drainage system, electrical network, communication network, sewage treatment plants, percolation wells, solid waste disposal system, collection, treatment, discharge and disposal of industrial, institutional and township waste, gas pipeline, common effluent treatment plant (CETP), spaces for informal services, and any other as may be delineated by the Government.

Wastewater: Liquid waste from households or commercial or industrial.

Debriefing and Review

1. Explain how Urban Planning can synthesise the resources, economic development and social transformation?
2. What do you understand by the matrix of 5 spatial scales and 3 levels of planning?
3. Explain town planning cycle.
4. Explain the planning pyramid and 3 pillars of planned development.
4. Write notes on
   (i) Strategic planning
   (ii) Action planning
   (iii) Digital planning and resource management
   (iv) Environmental sustainability
5. What do you understand by carrying capacity?
6. Explain urban Land Use classification.
7. Give the average distribution of land uses for urban centres.
8. Write short notes on:
   (i) Physical infrastructure
   (ii) Social infrastructure
   (iii) Participatory planning
   (iv) Urban and Regional Development Plans Formulation and Implementation Guidelines of the Ministry of Urban Development, Govt. of India.

CHAPTER

6

Town Planning and Social Infrastructure

Town Planning aims to achieve sustainable and inclusive development by a process of organizing people and their activities over space and time, while considering resources and technology. It envisages optimum use of land and siting of buildings, together with communication routes to secure the maximum degree of economy, convenience and beauty. It manifests collective intelligence and foresight to chart direction, order, harmony and progress in public activity relating to the environment and community welfare.

The planning is a multifaceted process where various aspects are simultaneously considered. It is a process of rational decision-making. It is a continuous, time oriented and cyclic process, where planning, implementation, monitoring and review go on as a dynamic process.

Planning can be seen as a matrix or intersection between the 3 levels of planning, i.e. policy, strategic and action planning, and 5 spatial scales as given below:

(i) Regional/Sub-Regional
(ii) City
(iii) Zone/Sub-Zone/Sector
(iv) Ward/Local Area
(v) Project Area.

Planning is usually divided into 3 interconnected phases-Long term, Short term and Annual. Long term plans are usually the vision and policy plans, short term are strategic plans (usually for 5 years) and Annual Plans are operational, action plans. The continuity and linkage of these phases is obtained by planning cycle, comprising Survey and Analysis, Plan Preparation, Plan Approval, Plan Implementation, Plan Monitoring and Plan Review.

City Development Plan

Policies and vision are converted into a City Development Plan, which provides a road-map to achieve the vision. These establish the requirement of the resources and detail out the exact manner in which a certain activity must be accomplished in a chronological sequence.

A spatial plan combines goals, policies, procedures, rules, assignments, steps to be taken, resources to be employed and other elements necessary to carry out a given course of action. The Master Plan or City Development Plan provides a broad planning framework at city level.

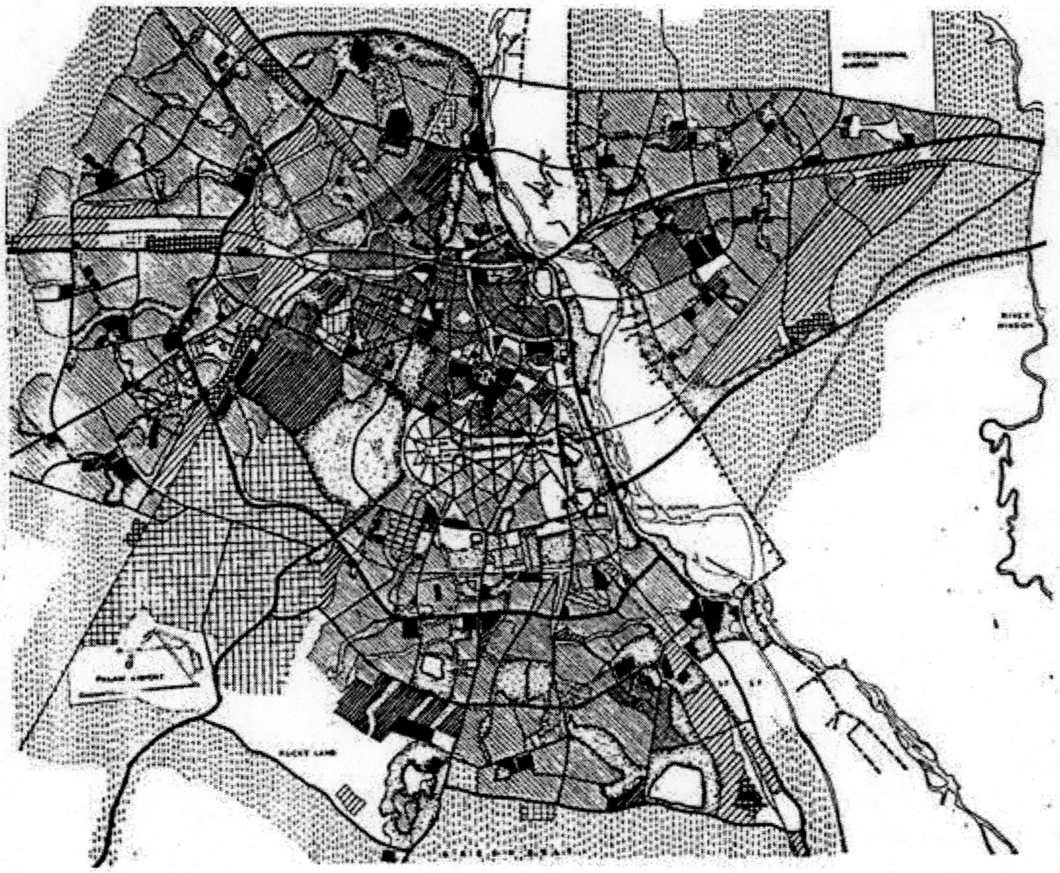

Fig: 6.1: Delhi Land Use Plan (1962-1981) covering 44000 Ha of urban area for a population of 5.7 million (1981) provided a policy framework and development controls for various categories of land uses viz. residential, commercial, industrial, recreational, government, infrastructure services, transport, public and semi-public, agriculture and water bodies. It also proposed policies of regional decentralisation, urban renewal, housing, slum rehabilitation, urban economy and conservation of built and natural environment.

Source: Delhi Development Authority

Zonal Plan

A zonal plan is a strategic plan which stipulates the strategies and programmes for development of a zone of a city within the framework of Master Plan. It provides mandatory guidelines and identifies areas for the preparation of local area plans, layout plans, regularisation plans, redevelopment plans of villages and other areas, TOD schemes, housing and slum rehabilitation, commercial centers, public and semi-public facilities, greens, etc, and sectoral plans (water supply, electricity, transport, sewerage, solid waste management, conservation of heritage, environment management, etc.).

It is not simply an enlargement of Master Plan but addresses the specific issues as per the characteristics of a zone. For example, strategies for conservation of New Delhi Zone (Zone 'D') comprise largely of Lutyens' Bungalow Zone which needs to be preserved. The zonal plan being statutory document provides a strategy and legal back up for conservation and development of such areas.

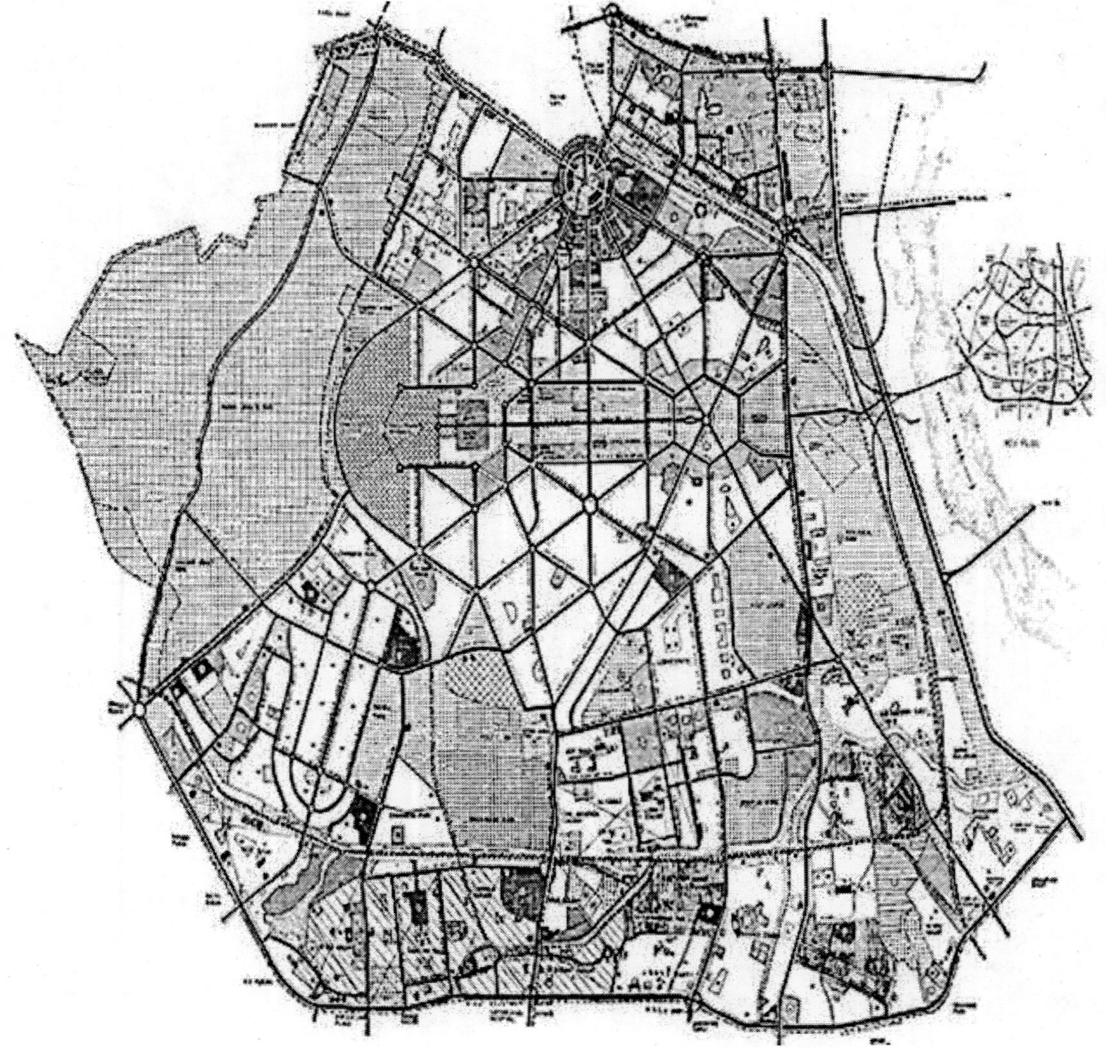

Fig. 6.2: Land Use Map of Zone 'D' (New Delhi)

Source Delhi Development Authority

The main residential area of New Delhi zone (Lutyens' Bungalow Zone) consists of about 3000 single or double storey bungalows. The average bungalow size varies between one and three acres and the status of allottees/occupants corresponds with the bungalow sizes. In the North-West side of New Delhi Zone were the quarters for Indian assistants, stenographers and clerks were planned. Adjoining this, towards the South, were quarters for European clerks, while peons, sweepers and dhobis were located along the boundaries of the old and new cities.

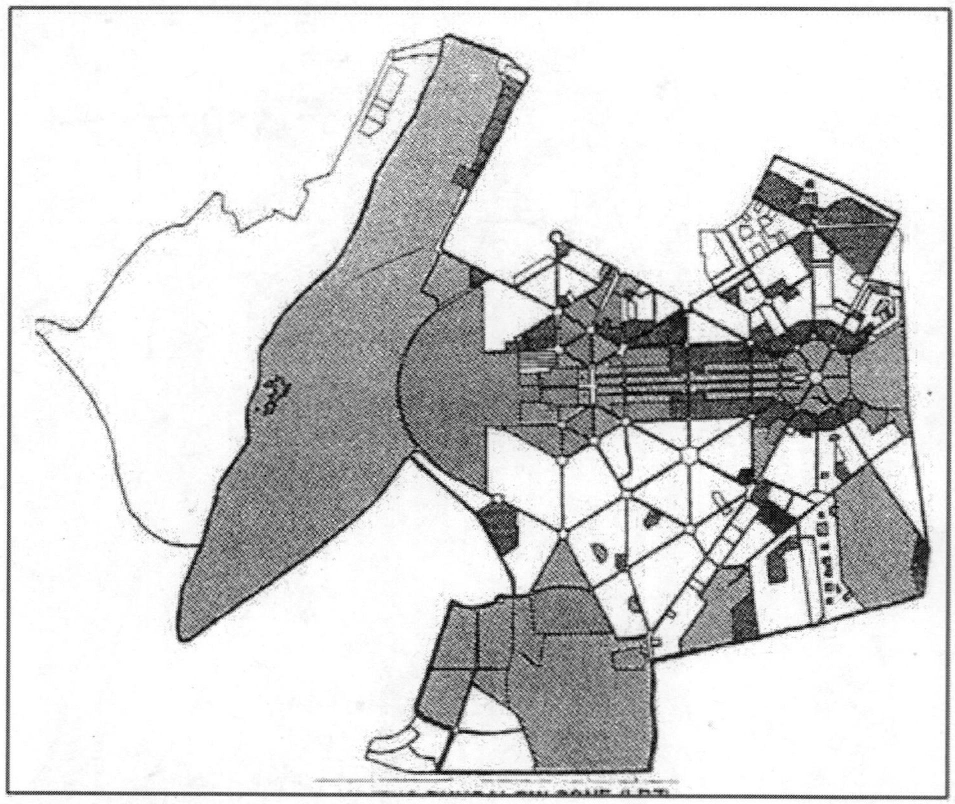

Fig. 6.3: Lutyens Bungalow Zone (LBZ)

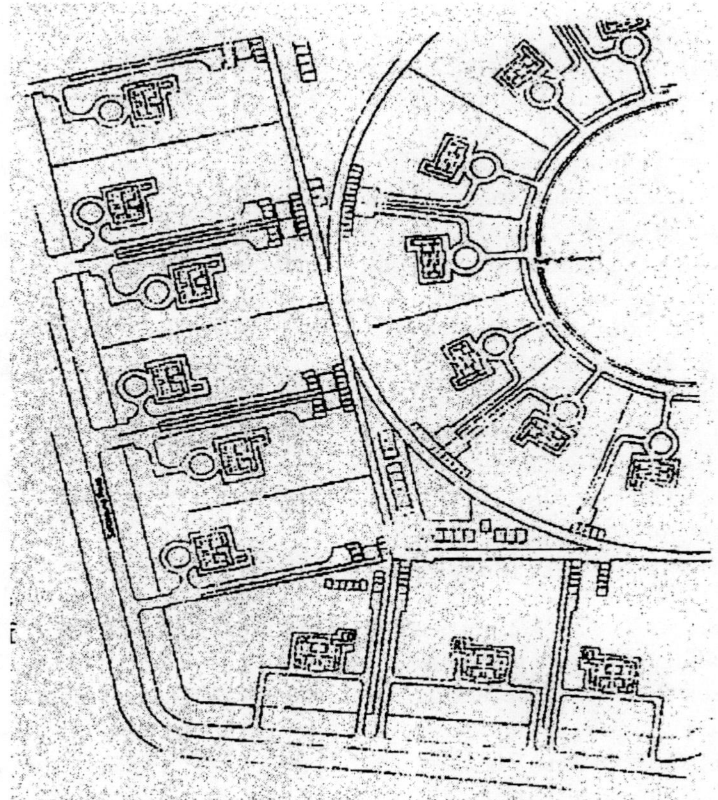

Fig. 6.4: Layout Plan of Bungalows, varying between 1 to 10 acres plot size, New Delhi

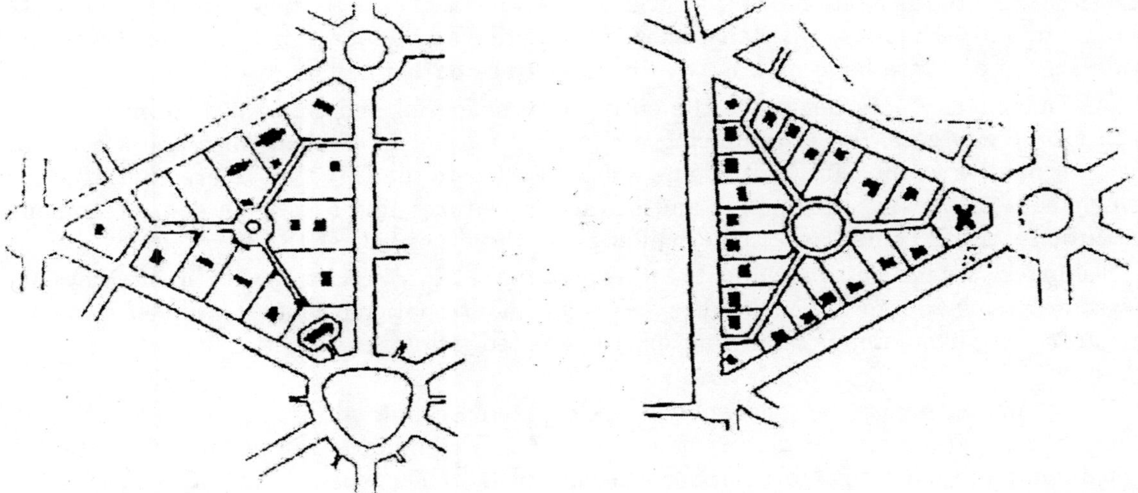

Fig. 6.5: Bungalows towards South and North of the Kingsway (Rajpath), New Delhi

Sub-city Planning

A zone in a mega-city may be as large as a sub-city, comprising a population of about one million. It may be built-up area requiring upgradation of services, social facilities, connectivity, better public transport and redevelopment or infill development of certain areas. On the other hand, it may comprise the urban extension, i.e. green-field development. The examples of sub-cities in Delhi are Rohini, Narela and Dwarka. The initial planning of Dwarka sub-city (earlier known as Papankala) is explained below.

The Papankala Project (Dwarka) is an endeavour to integrate the efficiency of man-made environment with the beauty, freedom and informality of organic and natural ambience. The sub-city has been planned for a projected population of over a million and covers an area of about 56 sq kms. The site is situated in south-west Delhi, along the western border of the Indira Gandhi International Airport. Of this, 1688 hectares was already built up with an estimated population of about 3 to 4 lakhs. 1,964 hectares of land up to the Mathura-Jullunder oil pipeline falls in the first phase and 2,100 hectares in the second phase.

Detailed ecological and environmental studies had been carried out which form the basis of land use planning. These studies point to the conservation of natural features such as the drainage pattern and water basins. This lead to the identification of rolling greens in natural and accentuated form, and offers important clues for the proposed drainage system of the area which aims to enhance and exploit the natural potential. The air funnels of the adjacent International Airport and noise contours are the other basic determinants of the land use concept. The area affected by the air funnels and noise has been primarily proposed for the development of greens and is to be kept free of residential development.

Delineation of green areas is one of the basic determinants of the concept. To check the effect of dust storms and to act as a barrier against the invasion of the desert from Rajasthan and Haryana, a thick forest belt all along the Najafgarh Drain is essential to serve functional and climatic needs. Besides, this green belt provides for harvesting and storage of storm water. Pollution of the Najafgarh Drain is proposed to be controlled so that it acts as a waterfront and the recreational belt for the scheme. To tackle the particular problems of dust storms and air-borne noise, special species of plantation and undergrowth will be grown. The roads are proposed to have at least two rows of trees on both sides.

A symbolic city gate celebrates the entry, with memorial and cultural buildings around it. From the city gate, the vista, having a city level market in a linear form and a cultural node, terminates at the City Centre. The areas adjacent to the City Centre are envisaged for development of housing, distinctive and attractive features like a rock garden, prestigious institutions, a golf course and iconic buildings as the cynosures of the city.

Taking advantage of its proximity to the airport, the sub-city is planned with an international character having an international centre for sports, an international centre for higher learning, an international conference centre, an export oriented industrial complex and other related activities.

The planning envisages a network of self-contained communities. The composition and delineation of community module is accessible by 5 to 8 minutes walk from a bus stop. A typical community, having 3 to 4 neighbourhoods (about 15,000 population each) is surrounded by the public transport system. Work centres have been planned in all directions to encourage and a balanced distribution of traffic on all the roads in various directions. Uninterrupted flow of pedestrian green linkages and exclusive cycle tracks are important features of the concept. At the nodal points, that is intersection of major roads, community centres, which have a high volume of pedestrians and cyclists, underpasses have been planned. An underpass created by raising metalled roads by 3 to 4 metres, provides greens, pedestrian and cyclist linkages at the intersections. Pedestrians do not have to cross major roads, nor do they have to move up and down on sub-ways.

By planning green belts, public and semi-public activities and commercial centres along the roads, an attractive street picture would be obtained. A departure from conventional planning is that all along the major roads, community land uses have been proposed. This would provide corresponding benefits of major infrastructural routes to the community. While the residential sectors will have underground drains, at the city level the system of rolling greens and balancing reservoirs is proposed for stormwater drainage. These reservoirs will be situated on low-lying ground parallel to the Najafgarh Drain. The proposed system of balancing reservoirs will have distinct advantages over conventional drainage, and affords huge savings in construction of drains, while replenishment and enrichment of the underground water table. The greens, recreational areas and water bodies also provide climatic comfort, and act as a dust and noise buffer.

The project team led by A. K. Jain included JDS Sodhi, R R Mukku, Ritu Kapila, R K Jhingan, Sujata Kohli and H C Gupta, Project Engineer, Delhi Development Authority.

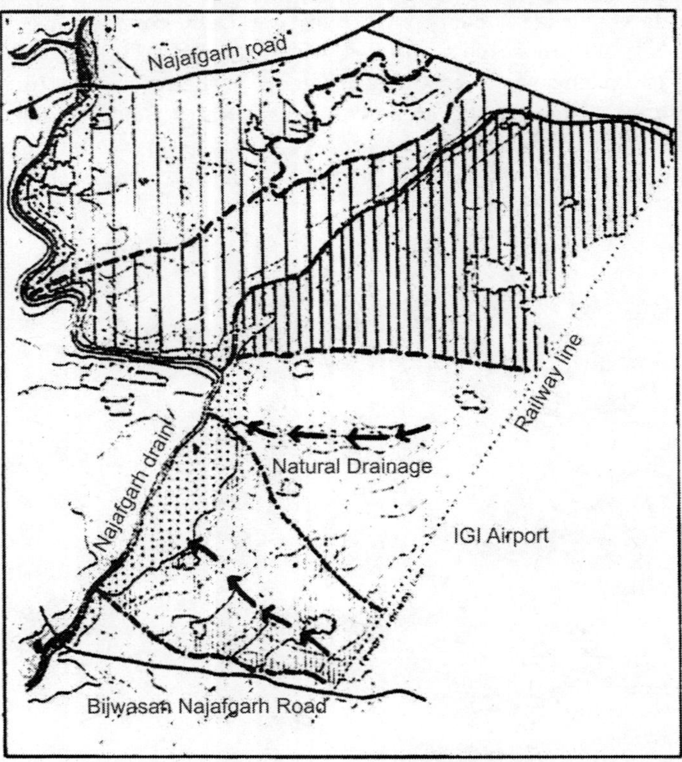

Fig. 6.6: Balancing Lakes and Rolling Greens worked out on the basis of natural drainage pattern are ecologically more appropriate and enrich surface and underground aquifers.

Fig. 6.7: The Papankala (Dwarka) Sub-city project in New Delhi covering about 56 sq. km of area was based on ecological and landscape principles. The study of valleys and ridges indicated the natural drainage pattern and water basins. This helps in identifying the proposed greens in natural form and drainage system of the area. This storm water would be fed into artificial lakes and reservoirs planned for this purpose. The concept plan was presented by the author to the Prime Minister, who observed: "a beautiful concept, which will become pride of Delhi" (1989).

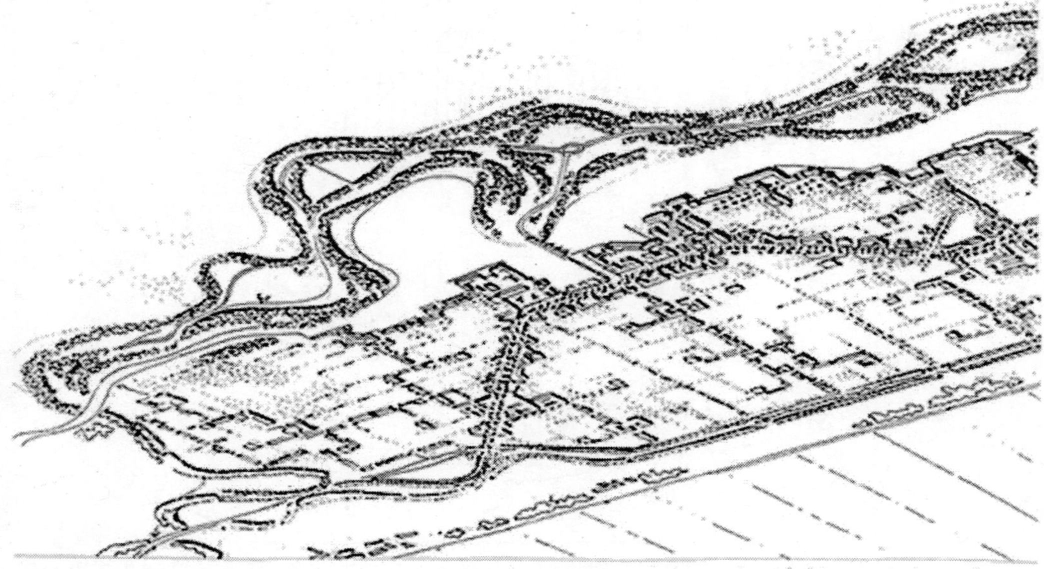

Fig. 6.8: Papankala Project is bound by Najafgarh Drain, which used to be Sahibi River, on its West. The project plans to revive the river by pollution control, provision of boating and cycle tracks along it.

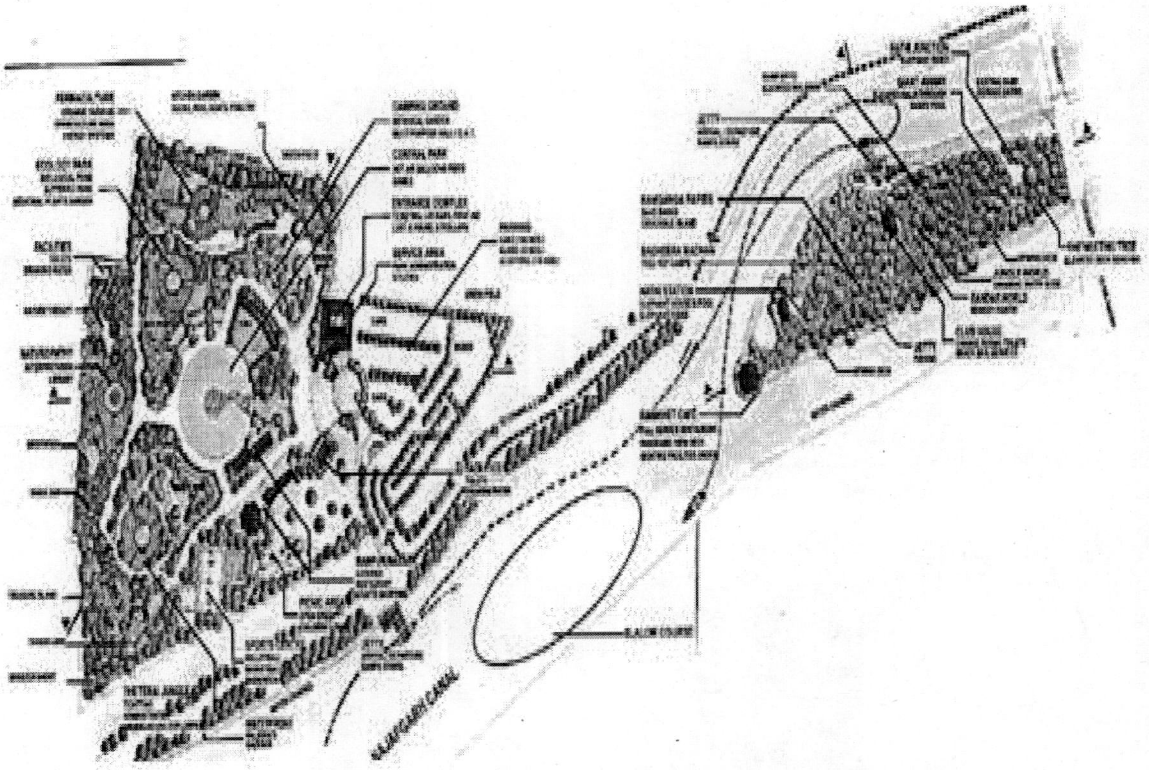

Fig. 6.9: The section of 100m wide Najafgarh drain proposed with native woodland, aquatic vegetation, bicycle road, boating and other facilities (DSIIDC).

Fig. 6.10: The cycle track proposed with a swale all along

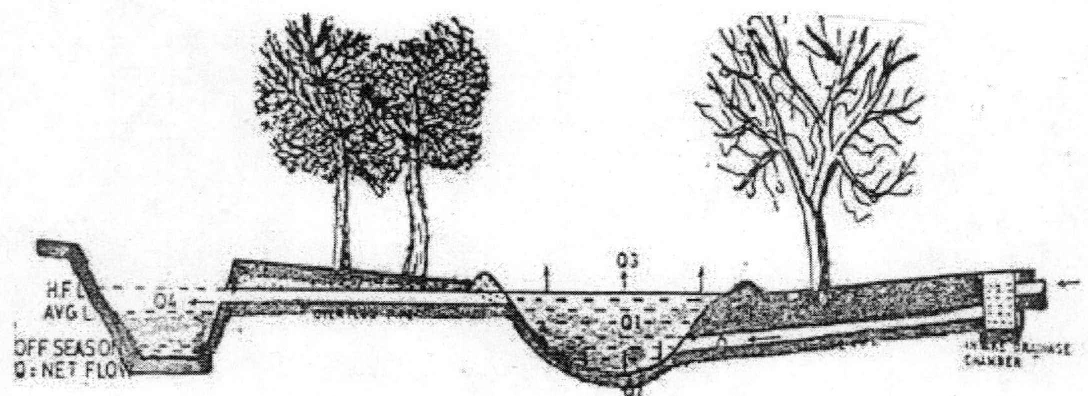

Fig. 6.11: The concept of balancing reservoirs envisages harvesting of the storm water in low lying catchment areas within the sub-city and along Najafgarh drain.

Fig. 6.12: About one fifth of the land of Dwarka (Papankala) project has been planned for organized parks and playground, aggregating to about 10 sq.m per capita, distributed at the city, district, community, local/neighbourhood and cluster levels.

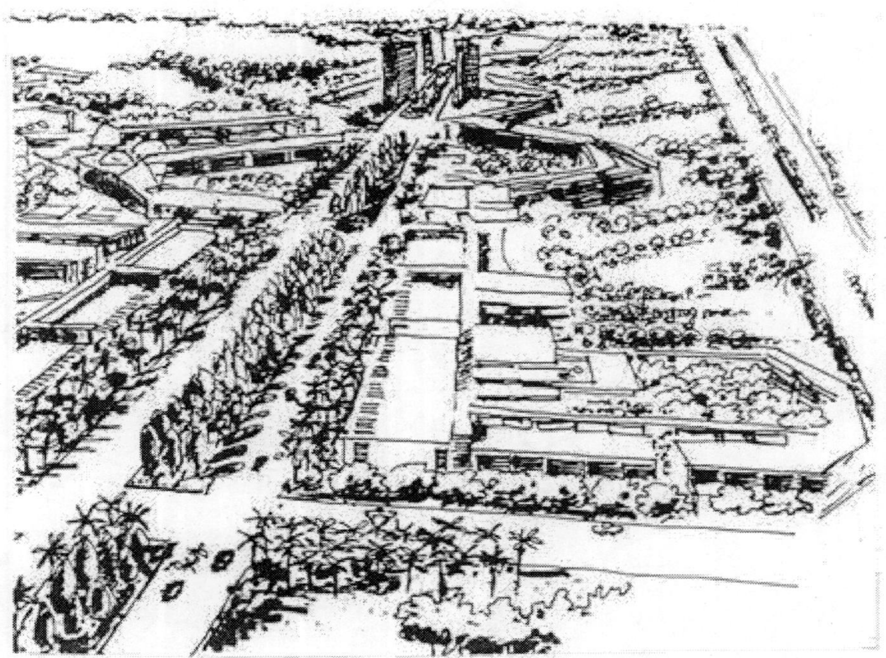

Fig. 6.13: Roads as Boulevards

Fig. 6.14: Housing Area Park

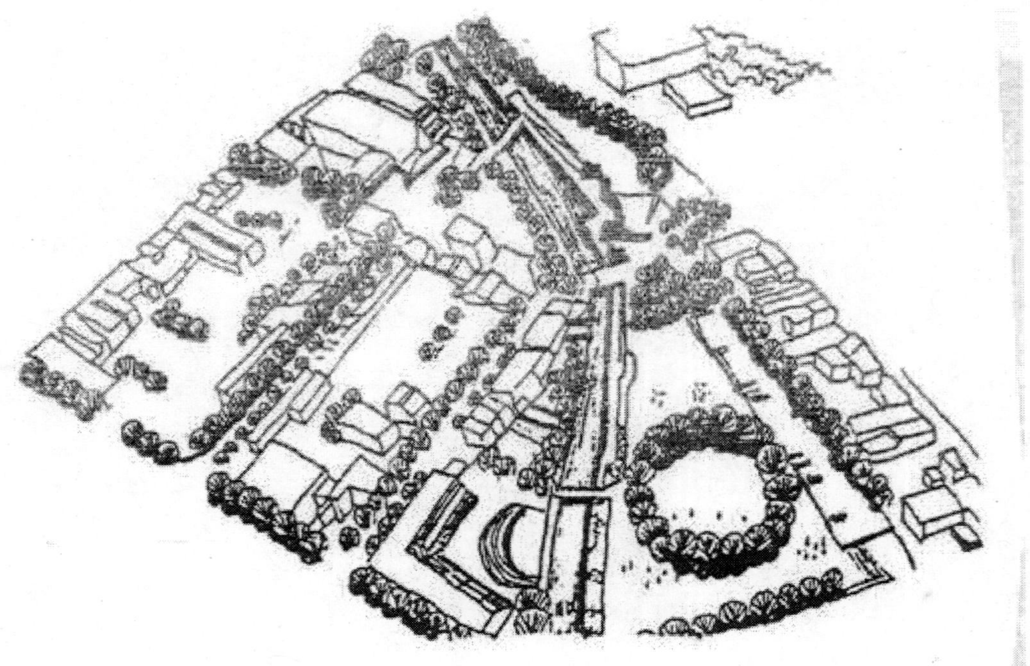

Fig. 6.15: Palam Drain is proposed to be cleaned by bio-remediation, desitting and blocking falling of untreated waste water and garbage, and developed as an attractive green trail, which had been the backyard and corridor of insanitation and filth
(A K Jain)

Fig. 6.16: The City Centre has a linear pattern which forms a central vista for the Dwarka Sub-city with a symbolic City Gate, Millennium Park and a Cultural Complex.

Fig. 6.17: Pedestrian green linkages and cycle tracks have been planned with underpasses by raising metalled roads by 4 metres for safety and uninterrupted movement of pedestrians and cyclists..

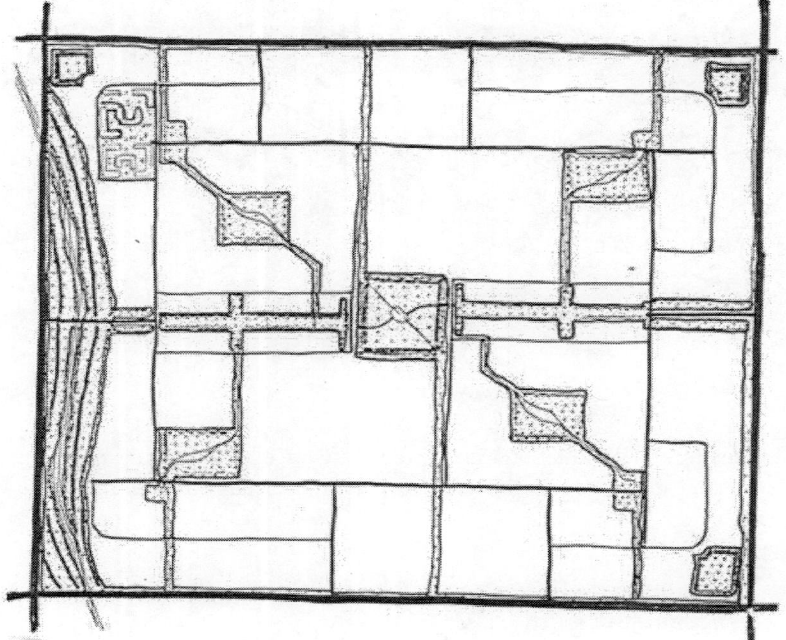

Fig. 6.18: A typical sector comprises four neighbourhoods

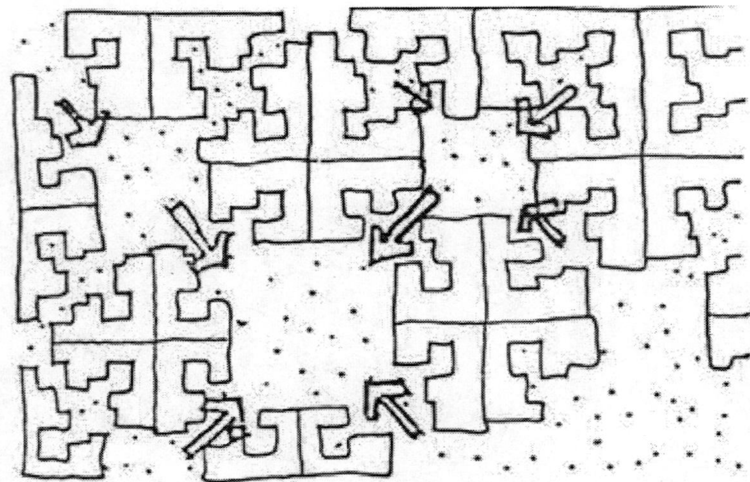

Fig. 6.19: Hierarchical Organisation of open spaces and housing clusters

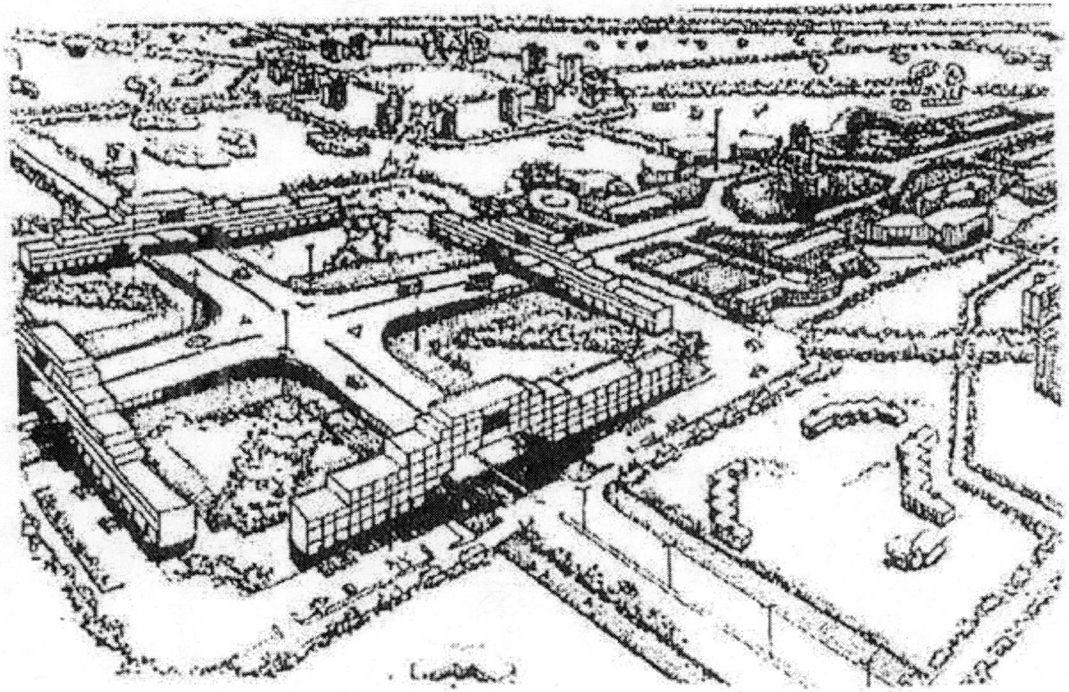

Fig. 6.20: The roads at the junctions are lifted by 6 m which provide pedestrian, cyclists, and green connectivity to surrounding areas (A K Jain)

Local Area Plans

A Local Area Plan addresses the specific issues of a ward or area and synchronise with the political apparatus, administrative system and financial allocations. The Local Area Plan aims to preserve the urban design, heritage and eco-sensitive character of an area/zone. It should attempt to ensure adequate supply of water and other facilities such as, sewerage, public toilets, transportation, schools, security (police, fire, emergencies, etc.) and parks and sports, besides taking care of the vendors and informal sector and livelihood.

The Local Area Plan should aim at visual integration of built, natural and heritage environment. This involves providing unhindered access, movement, parking and pedestrian realm, and controlling the hoardings, street furniture and signage.

The Local Area plans should spearhead infrastructure services, which catalyse planned development. Priority areas should be worked out to deliver the services in the shortest possible time, with a sense of competition between public and private sectors. The planning approach, standards and procedures are evolved on the basis of realistic assessment, which are implementable. Local Planning dovetails urban development, revenue generation, institutional organisation, capacity building, multi-year programme and technology upgradation. The priorities can be fixed on the basis of community demand and importance from the people's point of view.

It is necessary to strike a balance and integrate physical growth and environmental sustainability. Eco-balance and social health integrate social, economic and environmental aspects of development. It includes provision of adequate greenery, lung spaces, sports facilities and play fields, disaster mitigation, industrial location, waste management, drainage, conservation and other physical and social infrastructure.

An enviromentally sustainable plan focuses upon various factors, such as given below:

(i) Landuse and density pattern.

(ii) Norms and standards of community facilities and greens

(iii) Social Infrastructire

(iv) Physical infrastructure, water supply, sewerage, solid waste management, drainage, etc.

(v) Circulation network

(vi) Provision for informal sector, vulnerable sections, women, aged, children, disabled, etc.

The cities manifest a variety of both-planned and unplanned developments. These include plotted residential schemes and planned and unplanned markets, unauthorised colonies, slums and squatter settlements. One such area studied by DUAC and Ashok B. Lall is Malviya Nagar, Hauz Rani, Greater Kailash II and Shahpur Jat (Municipal Ward Nos. 161, 162, 189 & 191) in New Delhi. These areas witness chaos due to the advert of a mix of conditions akin to the rest of Delhi/NCR. These are areas of extremely high volume of vehicles on roads and rampant horizontal growth largely. The services, parking and amenities are substandard which are unable to sustain increasing population and socio-economic growth of the city. Planning of such area requires a focussed approach addressing the specific issues and ground level difficulties faced by the people. Different types of areas need to be studied in detail so as to address the problems faced by them, whether in an urban village, a market or a transport corridor.

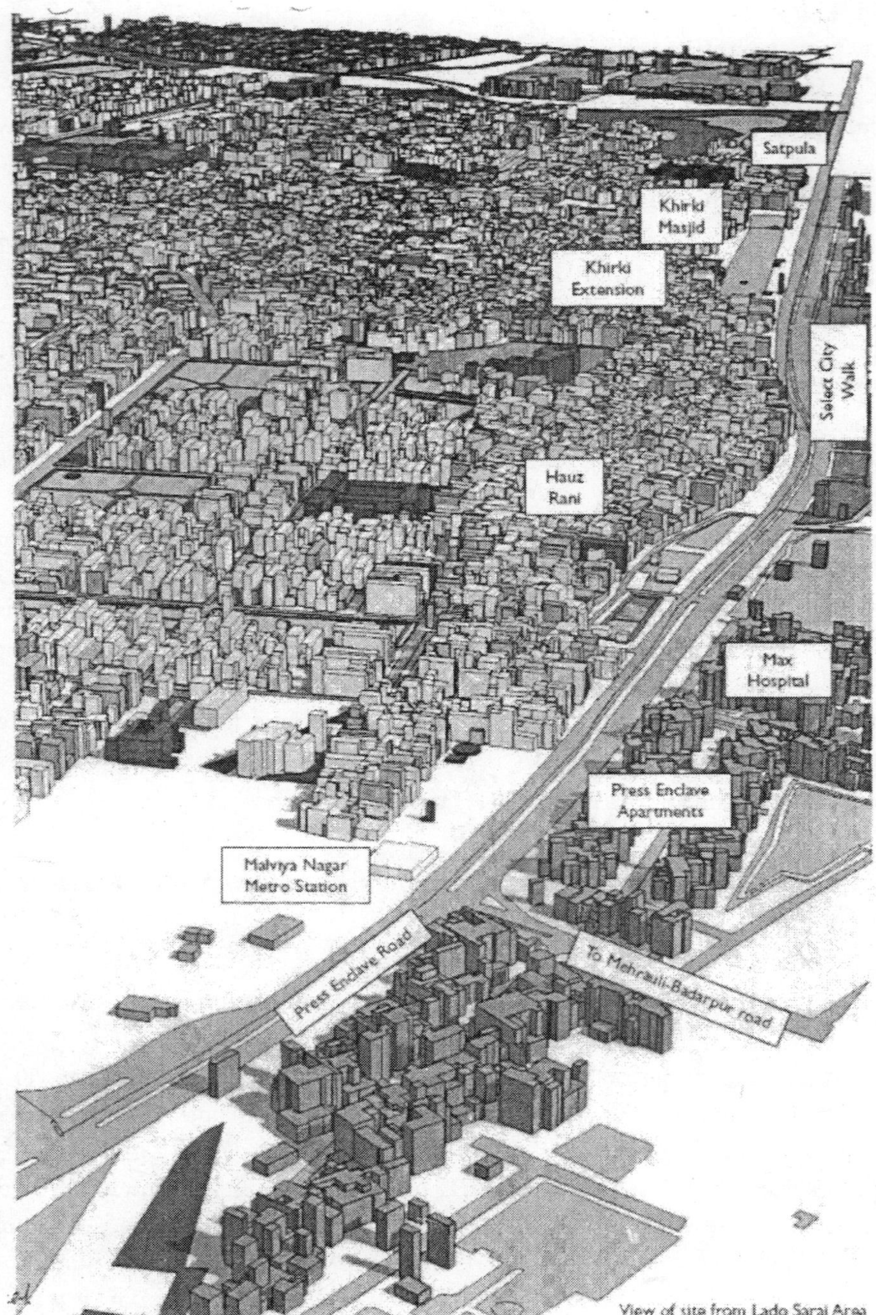

Fig. 6.21: Composite Local Area Development Malviya Nagar, Hauz Rani and Khirki Extension.

Source: DUAC/Ashok B. Lall (2016), Malviya Nagar, Hauz Rani and Khirki Extension Site Specific Project for Ward Nos. 161, 162, 189, 191, New Delhi.

Fig. 6.22: Malviya Nagar, Hauz Rani and Khirki Extension. Site Specific Design for Ward Numbers 161, 162, 189 and 191.

Source: DUAC/Ashok B. Lall (2016), Malviya Nagar, Hauz Rani and Khirki Extension Site Specific Project for Ward Nos. 161, 162, 189, 191, New Delhi.

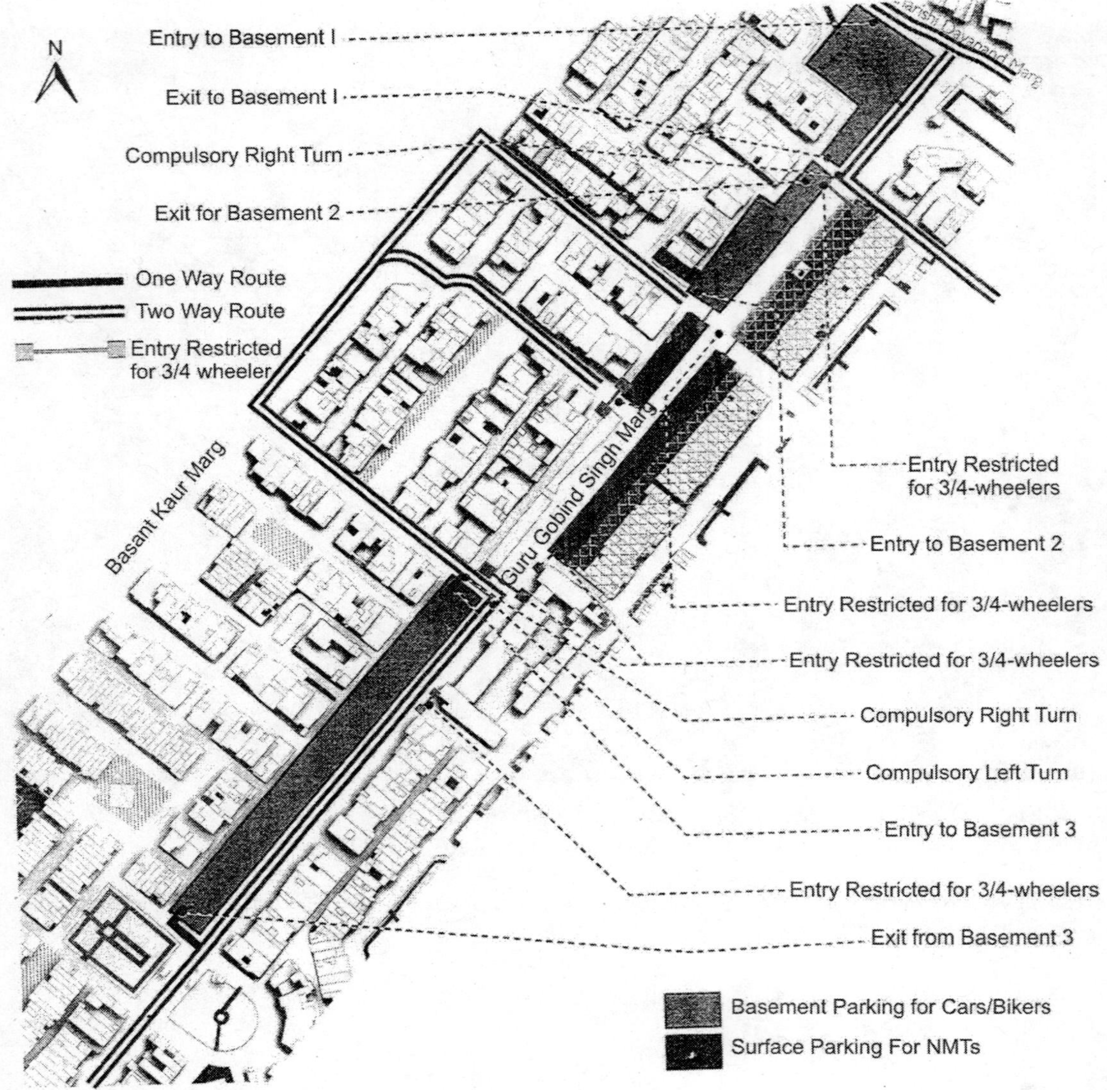

Fig. 6.23: Location of basement car/bike parking and surface parking in Malviya Nagar Market.

Source: DUAC/Ashok B. Lall (2016), Malviya Nagar, Hauz Rani and Khirki Extension Site Specific Project for Ward Nos. 161, 162, 189, 191, New Delhi.

Hierarchy of Urban Areas and Land Uses

A city plan envisages the organisation of space based on a hierarchy and modular pattern of community space which starts with a housing cluster as the building block. The objective is to create conditions conducive to a healthy, social living. The housing cluster may comprise about 750 to 1000 persons which is analogous to the traditional "mohalla". Three to four such units form a residential unit with a population of about 5000, which is planned around a primary school and convenience shopping. At the next level, the residential planning area with a population of 15,000-20,000 can be planned around a senior secondary school, community facilities and a local shopping centre. A Sector with a population of 30,000-40,000 can be organised around a Community Centre; and a transit hub. A Planning Division is conceived as a self-contained sub-city for a population of 5 to 10 lakhs, with a District Centre, University and cultural hub.

The concept of community planning, therefore, attempts to create within the city, physical and social units of smaller and manageable sizes of community. The concept of the neighbourhood has diverse origins. As Mumford (1954) points out its origin is in the various 'quarters' of the medieval city. As a planning concept, the neighbourhood unit signifies the natural human tendency for relationships to have a territorial expression.

Community planning is generally accepted as the basis for the planning of urban areas. The idea is to conceive a city composed of a number of sizeable units, each unit as a comprehensive entity by itself. This intends to allow the growth of a community spirit fostered by sustained social interaction and at the same time function as a modular unit of a greater whole. Used in the physical sense, a sector is a minimum geographic and planning unit, which contains the basic utilities, services and community facilities, required by the residents. It provides a physical form suitable for the development of an individual, his family and the community living together.

Though the sector is a physical concept, it has social implications, and is recognized as a social entity. It aims at social stability and cohesion amongst the residents, by promoting their participation in the community activities and by sharing community facilities and urban infrastructure. The common use of schools, shopping facilities, health centres, parks and playgrounds, community centres, etc. brings about a certain degree of social cohesion among the residents. It is planned in a manner so that it relates with the larger urban context in respect of jobs, industry, higher education, cultural facilities, etc.

It provides shops for day to day shopping, parks and open spaces, institutional sites and transportation network for the movement of people and goods which discourage through traffic to enter the sector. Chandigarh provides an excellent example of sector planning (800 × 1200 m) with a systematic distribution of community facilities and housing for various groups.

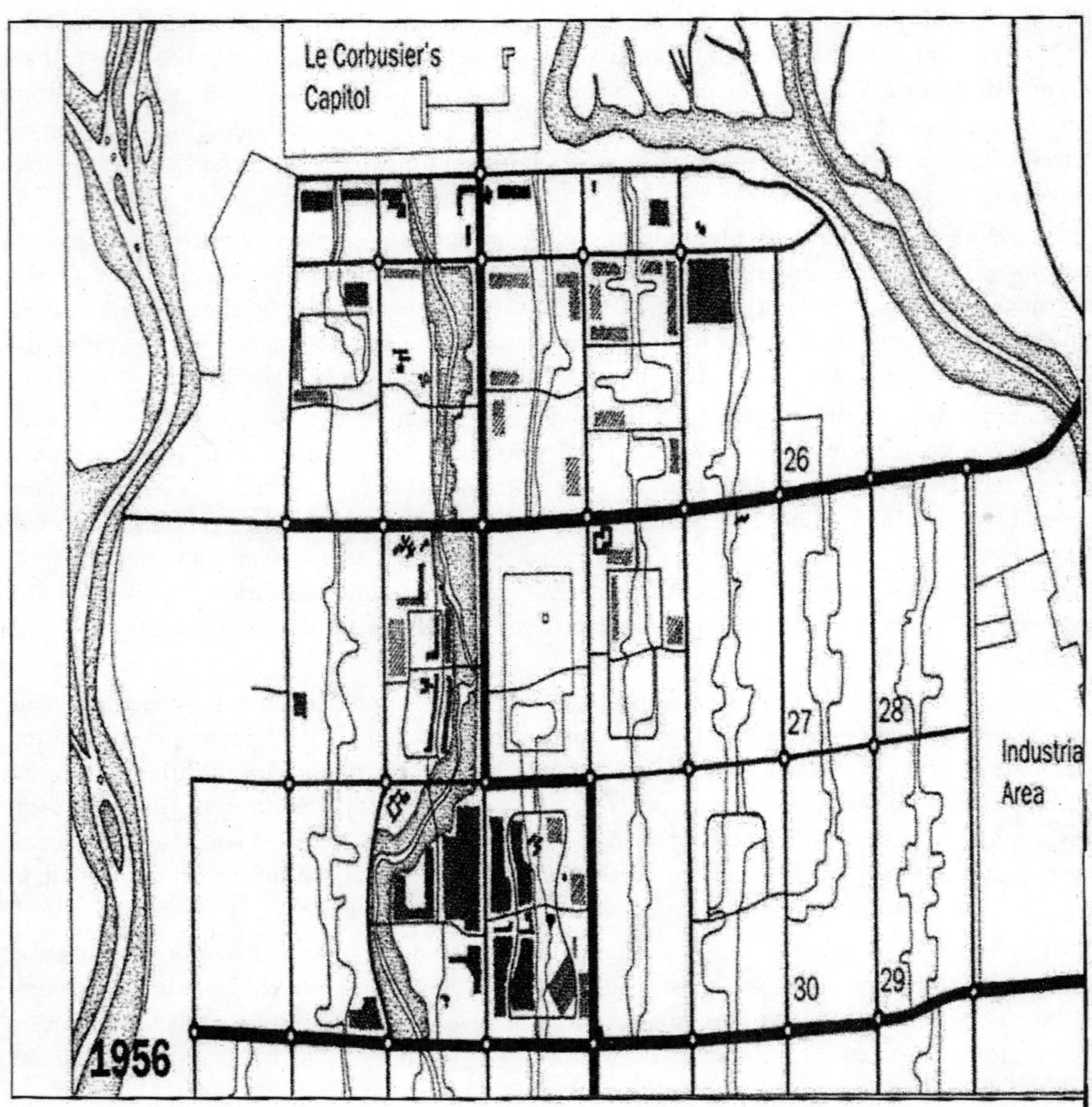

Fig. 6.24: Plan of Chandigarh, 1956 (Le Corbusier)

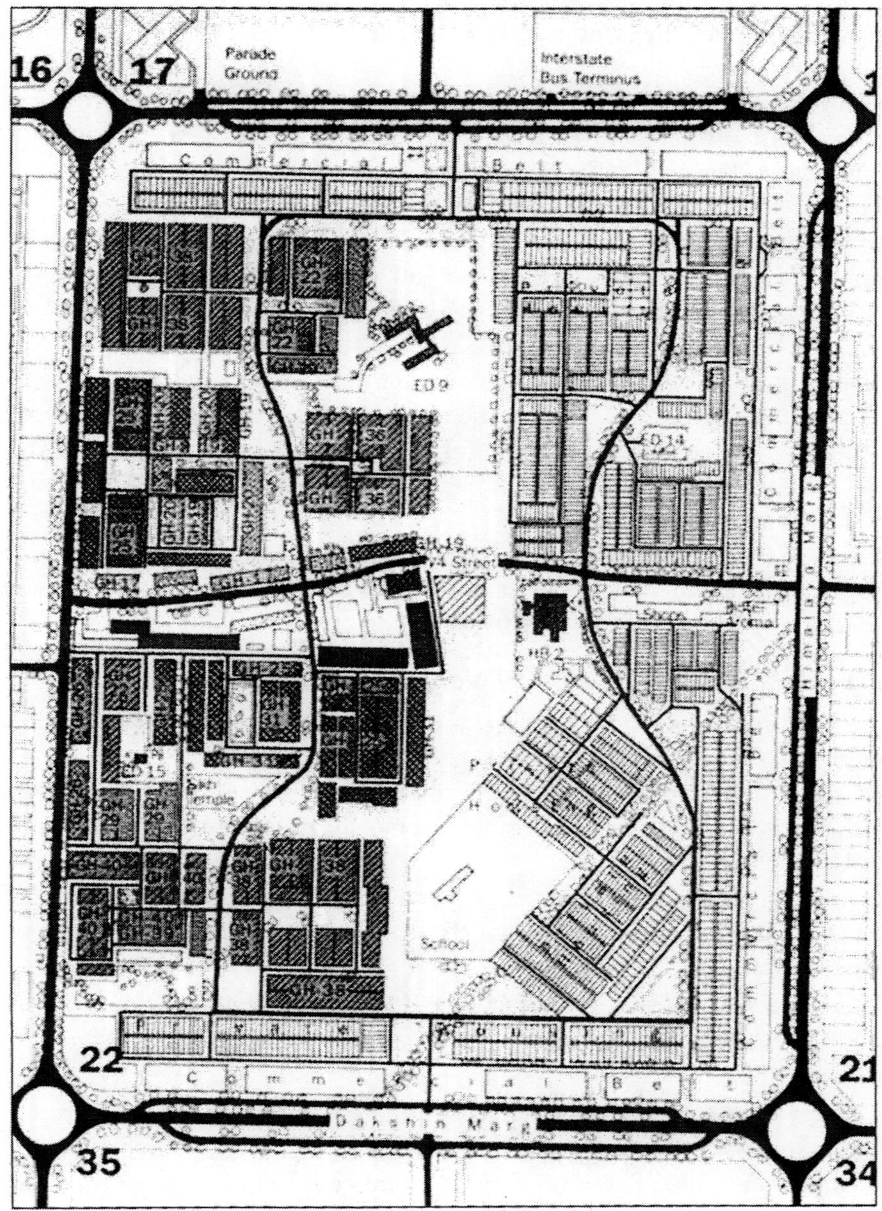

Fig. 6.25: Plan of Sector 22 (800 × 1200 m) has been Planned with variety of housing, and a systematic distribution of educational, recreational, health, cultural and commercial facilities for a population of 15,000 and three density groups of 25, 50 and 75 ppa.

Environmental Planning

Redevelopment of existing areas and development of green-fields have to be based on the principles of environmental sustainability, rejuvenation of water bodies, solid waste management, energy efficiency and road network design.

The environment is composed of both natural and cultural elements. The natural environment includes land, air, water, plants and animal life. A clean and varied natural environment is valuable both for self and for its importance to the quality of human life. The cultural environment is shaped by human activity and includes the built environment, housing, industries, offices and infrastructure. It also includes resources like parks, trails and the architectural heritage. The ways in which we maintain and develop this environment have profound effects on the health of the population.

The equal system approach provides model for planning and decision making focusing upon the inter-relationships between all the elements of urban planning while respecting natural processes. Human beings are an integral part of the environment in which they live.

The development activity should not deplete non-renewable resources, harvest renewable resources at an unsustainable rate, pollute the environment or irreparably disrupt ecosystem, health and stability (the ecological web of life); the economic activity must also not deplete "social capital", and communities through exploitation, disempowerment and disintegration of social web of life.

Principles of Environmental Planning: The Accord signed on environment day on 5th June 2005 at San Francisco provides a template of environmental planning, which can be adapted according to local problems and priorities:

Energy: Renewable Energy, Energy Eficiency and Climate Change

Action 1: Adopt and implement a policy to increase the use of renewable energy to meet 10 percent of the city's peak electrical load within seven years.

Action 2: Adopt and implement a policy to reduce the city's peak electric load by ten percent within seven years through energy eficiency, shifting the timing of energy demands, and conservation measures.

Action 3: Adopt a citywide greenhouse gas reduction plan that reduces the jurisdiction's emissions by twenty five percent by 2030, which includes a system for accounting and auditing greenhouse gas emissions.

Waste Reduction: Zero Waste, Manufacturer Responsibility and Consumer Responsibility

Action 4: Establish a policy to achieve zero waste, *i.e.* no need of landfills and incinerators by 2040.

Action 5: Adopt a citywide law that reduces the use of a disposable, toxic or non-renewable product category by at least ten percent.

Action 6: Implement "user-friendly" recycling and composting programs, with the goal of reducing by twenty percent per capita solid-waste disposal to landill and incineration.

Urban Design: Green Building, Urban Planning and Slums

Action 7: Adopt a policy that mandates a green building rating system standard that applies to all new municipal buildings.

Action 8: Adopt urban planning principles that advance higher density, mixed-use, walkable, bikeable and disabled accessible neighbourhoods which coordinate land use and transportation with open space systems for recreation and ecological restoration.

Action 9: Adopt a policy or implement a program that creates environmentally beneficial jobs in slums and/or low-income neighbourhoods.

Urban Nature: Parks / Habitat Restoration / Wildlife

Action 10: Ensure that there is an accessible park or recreational open space within half-a-kilometre of every city resident.

Action 11: Conduct an inventory of existing canopy coverage in the city; and then establish a goal based on ecological and community considerations to plant and maintain canopy coverage in not less than fifty percent of all available sidewalk/planting sites.

Action 12: Pass legislation that protects critical habitat corridors and other key habitat characteristics (e.g. water features, food bearing plants, shelter for wildlife, use of native species, etc.) from unsustainable development.

Transportation: Public Transportation, Clean Vehicles, Reducing Congestion

Action 13: Develop and implement a policy which expands affordable public transportation coverage to within half-a kilometre of all city residents in ten years.

Action 14: Pass a law or implement a program that eliminates leaded gasoline (where it is still used); and that phases down sulfur levels in diesel and gasoline fuels, concurrent with using advanced emission controls on all buses, taxis, and public fleets to reduce particulate matter and smog-forming emissions from those fleets by fifty percent.

Action 15: Implement a policy to reduce the percentage of commute trips by single occupancy vehicles by ten percent.

Environmental Health: Toxics Reduction, Healthy Food Systems and Clean Air

Action 16: Every year identify one product, chemical or compound, that is used within the city that represents the greatest risk to human health and adopt a law to provide incentives to reduce or eliminate its use by the municipal government.

Action 17: Promote the public health and environmental benefits of supporting organic foods. Ensure that twenty percent of all city facilities (including schools) serve locally grown and organic food within seven years.

Action 18: Establish an Air Quality Index (AQI) to measure the level of air pollution and set the goal of reducing by ten percent in seven years the number of days categorized in the AQI range as "unhealthy" to "hazardous."

Water: Access & Eficiency, Conservation and Wastewater Reduction

Action 19: Develop policies to increase adequate access to safe drinking water, aiming at access for all by 2015. For cities with potable water consumption greater than 100 litres per capita per day, adopt and implement policies to reduce consumption by ten percent by 2015.

Action 20: Protect the ecological integrity of the city's primary drinking water sources (i.e. aquifers, rivers, lakes, wetlands and associated eco-systems).

Action 21: Adopt municipal wastewater management guidelines and reduce the volume of untreated wastewater discharge by ten percent in seven years through the expanded use of recycled water and the implementation of a sustainable urban watershed planning process that includes participation of all affected communities and is based on sound economic, social, and environmental principles.

Physical Infrastructure: The quality of livability and health are dependent upon the level and standard of physical infrastructure, i.e. water, power, sewerage, drainage and solid waste management. However, the level of urban infrastructure is reaching a stage of crisis. There is a wide gap between its availability and demand. The quality of water is posing a serious health hazard. Large areas in the cities, especially those of the poor, are without sewerage and solid waste management. Sanitary landfill sites are at their saturation level and there is skepticism regarding the method of solid waste disposal in open landfill sites.

The proposed strategy for solid waste management will be based on the principle of 3 Rs - Reduce, Reuse, Recycle. Solid-waste management is a step by- step process and each step holds equal importance. As the first step, it is essential to reduce waste generation. The next step is to segregate waste which can be achieved by keeping colour-coded segregated waste bins. Storage and collection of this waste from households should be done in segregated chambers. The waste can then be transported and treated to be reused or recycled according to its category.

The people in urban areas suffer from a high level of air borne and water borne diseases. It is estimated that 2.5 lakh children in Delhi suffer from asthama and chest ailments which are 12 times higher than the national average. Gastro-entritis and cholera break up frequently in various parts of the city. This is largely due to percolation of leachate and pathogens into the water supply system, especially sub-soil water on which large segments of population of unauthorized colonies and slums survive.

It is necessary to adopt a health oriented and environment friendly approach, particularly in respect of solid waste management, water supply, drainage and sewerage. In place of public toilets, it is necessary to encourage construction of individual toilets in the Resettlement Colonies and slum clusters. In case of solid waste management, adoption of recycling is necessary for improving the situation. Decentralised systems of sewerage, water supply, and waste management with community participation offer practical solutions for unauthorized colonies, villages and other areas without municipal service networks.

By proper sanitation, development and maintenance of community toilets in the localities of the poor and promoting installation of water closets (WCs) by tax reliefs, the Gandhian ideology of scavenger free society would be achieved.

To check services related health hazards, it is necessary to fix and upgrade obsolete water supply and sanitation system, replace old pipes and make the joints water tights. There has to be proper segregation of water supply and sewerage pipe lines. There should be safe distance between cess/pool/exidation pond/septic tanks and water pumps/water storage.

The practice of disposal of waste water together with storm-water and garbage in open drains should be discontinued and waste water and rainwater disposal systems must be segregated. Proper landscaping and covering of open drains will help in achieving a better environment. To discourage breeding of mosquitoes in water bodies, fountains and other ways of aeration of water can be effective. The heat generated from sewage treatment and incineration should be captured for generation of electricity and cooling of buildings.

The quality of water in most of the rivers and water bodies in urban areas is unfit for human consumption and a health hazard. To regenerate the rivers and control water pollution, it is necessary to develop an integrated approach towards water-sanitation-sewage and drainage. This involves inter-departmental coordination and an integrated approach.

The concepts of watershed development and rainwater harvesting, together with recharging of underground water table can substantially resolve the water crisis and improve the micro-climate. A system of connected greenways can act as a recreational and health reservoir and act as air filter for vehicular pollution. These concepts are being increasingly adopted in the planning of new areas. These have a direct bearing on improving the environment and making the city healthy and liveable.

Every city has drains, canals and derelict streams. However, with urbanisation these have become the backyards and corridors of insanitation, mosquitoes, encroachments and garbage dumping. These can be revived to provide valuable open space, ghats and greenery to the people.

Conservation and Connecting Waterways with People

Fig. 6.26: Stepped paved edge of the waterway with shady trees i.e Ghat System for visitors and pedestrians

Fig, 6.27: Waterway with shady trees and a combination of green and an interactive green space on the upper edge.

Fig. 6.28: Waterway edge with shade and trees on the slope with a combination of green and an interactive green space on the upper edge.

Fig. 6.29: Waterway edge with shade and trees on the upper edge and lower edge, a segregated cycle/pedestrian track with dense green buffer on water edge

Fig. 6.30: Waterway edge with a sloped lawn on the edge, and a pedestrian/cycle bridge for people to cross over from one edge to the other

Fig. 6.31: Waterway edge with dedicated path for cyclists and pedestrians with lawns and plantation of trees

Source: DUAC/Rahoul B. Singh (2014), Rejuvenation of Najafgarh Waterways, New Delhi

Rejuvenation of Water Bodies

Urban ponds and water bodies, lakes are very important part of eco-system as they recharge groundwater. Filter water is aesthetically pleasing, provides space for recreational activities, prevents floods and allows sediment retention. These are venues for religious and cultural activities and help to promote bio-diversity and stabilise climate, However, urban lakes are under constant threat due to degradation of quality of waters, undertreated sewage discharge, solid-waste disposal, eutrophication, floating vegetation, etc. There is over-abstraction of water for variety of uses. Encroachments, squatters and silt influx from degradation of catchment areas are continuously endangering the lakes. There is a need to prevent disposal of municipal and/or industrial effluent, solid-waste, idol immersion, etc. The encroachments and over-exploitation of resources like fish, sand and water need to be checked.

The following flow chart represents the process for lake rejuvenation from initial data collection, treatment options to planning and action.

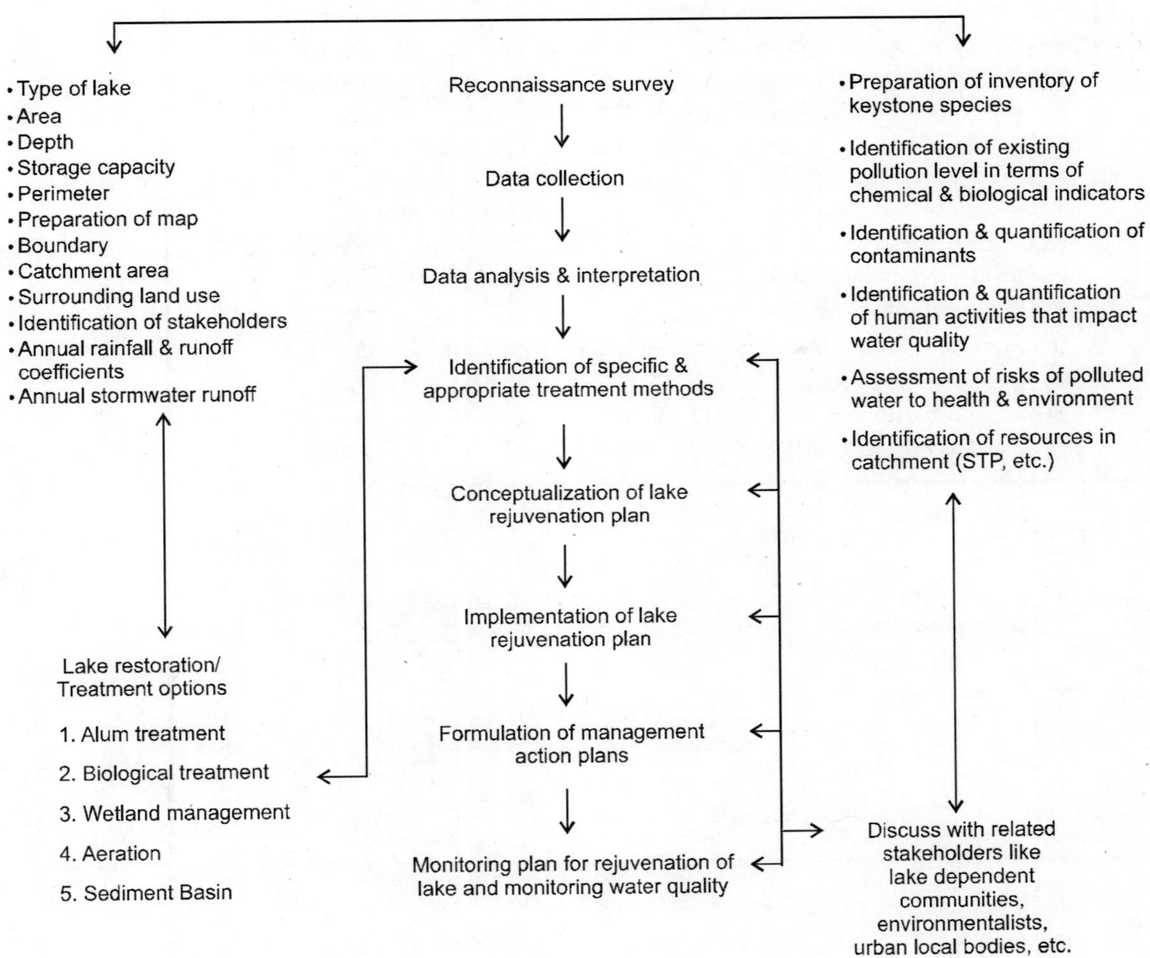

Fig 6.32: Methodology of Rejuvenation of Lakes

Source DUAC and Amit Ghosal, 2016

Storm Water Management

Usually there are no gratings on drain inlets and de-silting chambers due to which silt, leaves and a lot of garbage flow directly into the storm water drains. The drains get clogged due to garbage and silt and result in water overflowing on to streets. Cleaning these drains is a tedious process as it involves the cleaning of the whole length of the drain. They are not being maintained and cleaned regularly which causes waterlogging on the streets. The condition of the drains can also result in health problems.

Strategy for storm water management:

- Based on natural topography, catchment zones may be identified.
- The parks and green strips can have bio-swales and recharging pits which will receive water from all hard paved areas.
- The storm water will flow into the de-silting chamber with grating, where the silt settles down and can be easily cleaned. As the chamber has a grating over it, the other waste like leaves, etc. will not enter the drain.
- From the storm water drain, the water will flow into a bio-swale (located in parks and green strips), where it will be retained and infiltrated.
- This water can then be recharged into the ground.
- In case of space constraints, the water from the drain can directly flow into the recharging pit.
- This would allow storm water to be managed within each locality of a ward, thus ensuring complete storm water management within a year.

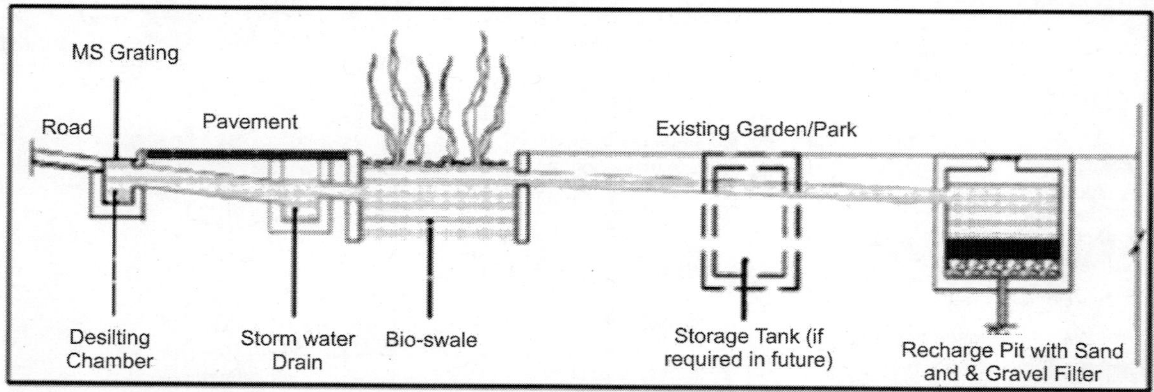

Fig. 6.33: Proposed Strategy for Stormwater Management

Source DUAC/Amit Ghosal 2016 , Punjabi Bagh , Ward 103, New Delhi

Fig. 6.33: Rainwater harvesting, porous paving and raingarden landscape.

Wastewater Treatment

The drains become polluted due to inflow of untreated waste water. Treated wastewater generated from the dwelling units can be used for irrigation/gardening and for flushing of toilets. Instead of mechanically treating the wastewater, it is also possible to install decentralized wastewater treatment systems on-site. These treatment plants can be located in the green areas or along the drains.

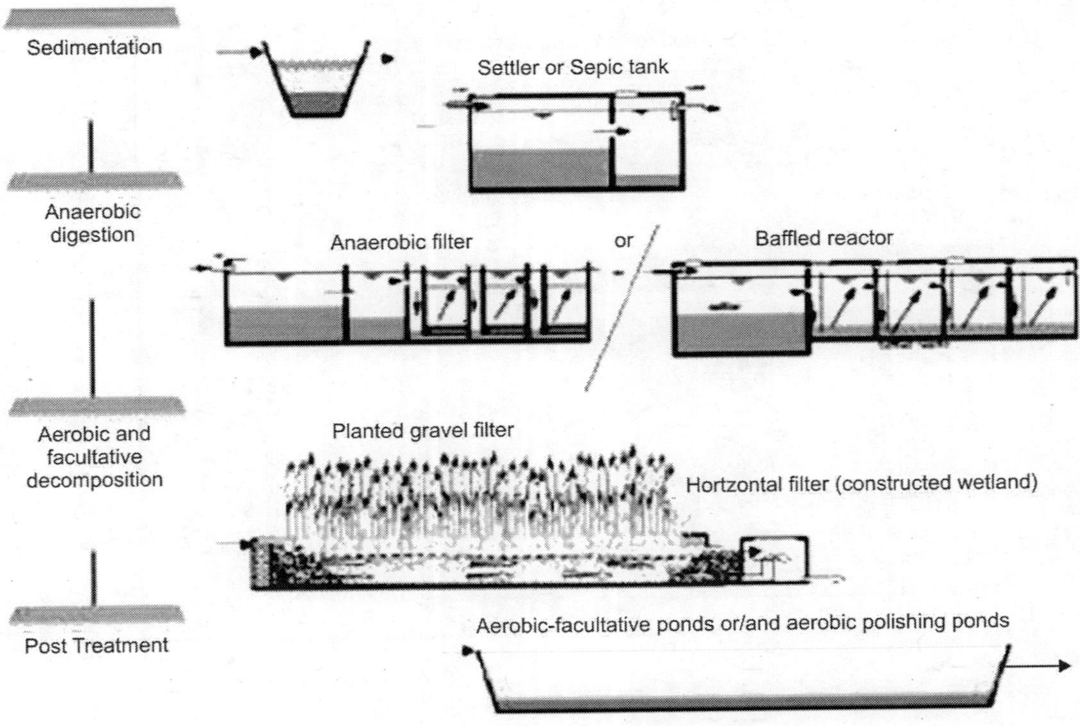

Fig. 6.35: Decentralised Wastewater Treatment System

Source DUAC/Amit Ghosal 2016 , Punjabi Bagh , Ward 103, New Delhi

Decentralized Wastewater Treatment Systems (DEWATS) are self-sustainable, easy to maintain and run. In this system the wastewater first goes into a two-chamber settler. After primary treatment the wastewater goes to the Anaerobic Baffled Reactor which is a nine-chambered system. Then it flows to the planted gravel filter, and finally to the polishing pond. From the polishing pond the treated wastewater can be reused for landscaping of urban greens or for flushing of toilets and for cleaning roads.

Energy Efficiency

For environmental sustainability, it is necessary to adopt energy efficiency and renewable energy at household levels. This requires adoption of green building guidelines which include shading, renewable energy, wall insulation, green roof, energy efficient lighting and equipment, etc., which help in reducing the energy load of the building. The buildings should be compliant with energy efficiency codes and mandates.

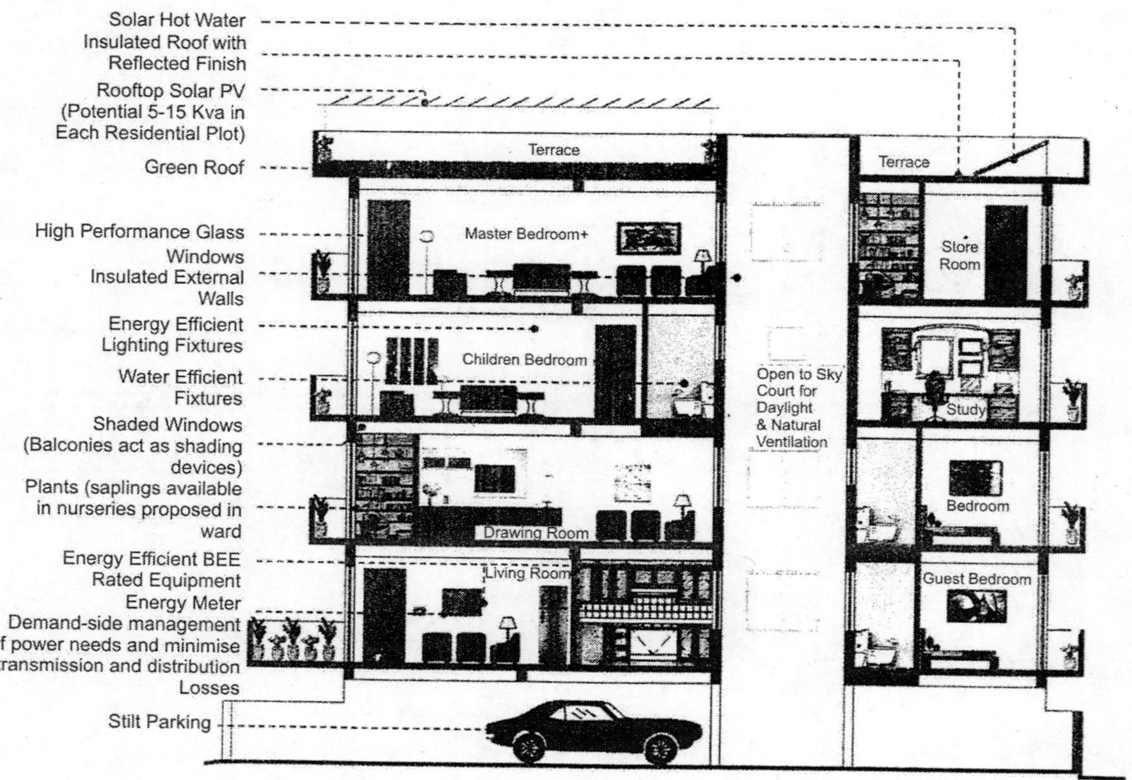

Fig. 6.36: Typical Section of a Residential Building in Compliance of Energy Efficiency Building Code

Source DUAC/Amit Ghosal 2016, Punjabi Bagh, Ward 103, New Delhi

Planning of Residential Areas

In deciding the size of the residential module the following are considered.

- School and its catchment area considering the age structure of the residents.
- Maximum walking distance to the service area should be generally upto 400 meters. It is possible to plan the densities, layouts and types of housing accordingly.

The size of a residential module is governed by

(a) the area required for various land use components;

(b) the population required to support the sector level services and facilities;

(c) accessibility to such facilities; and

(d) the existence of physical boundaries.

The sector must be large enough to support the community facilities such as the primary school, secondary school; local shopping centre, health centre, park, etc. At the same time, it should not be so large as to loose the advantages of a compact and integrated community life. A sector is defined as a physical planning unit comprising an area required for housing about 10,000 families with the required facilities and services.

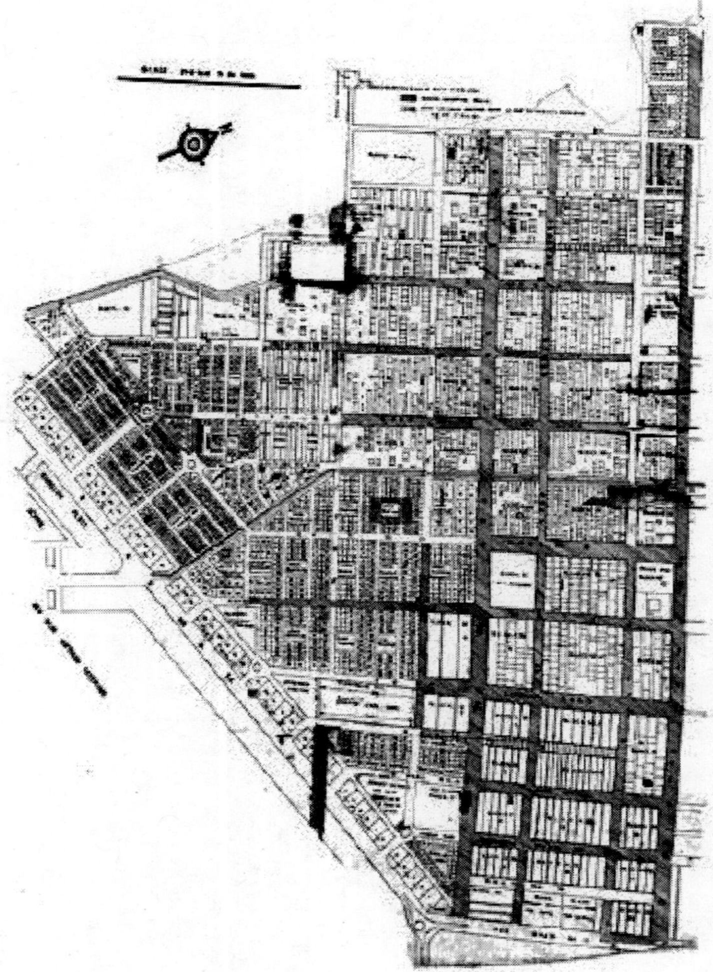

Fig 6.37: The development of Western Extension, Karol Bagh was initiated during the planning of New Delhi (1914). The Delhi Improvement Trust after its formation in 1937 took over and expanded the schemes to decongest Old City, Paharganj, etc.

Source DIT Archives

With ever increasing urbanisation, the planning of residential areas has been a core function of town planning. In the earlier times plotted residential schemes had been popular, some of which provided shops on the ground floor. These were generally based on a modular, grid iron pattern.

However, with the increasing demand, the size of the plot descended to 60 to 80 sq. yd. in the residential colonies planned to house the half million refugees who came to Delhi in 1947. It was further reduced to 25 sq. yd. and thereafter 18 sq. yd. during the 1970s for resettlement of slum dwellers in Delhi. In 1990s, the policy of plotted development was changed in favour of group housing.

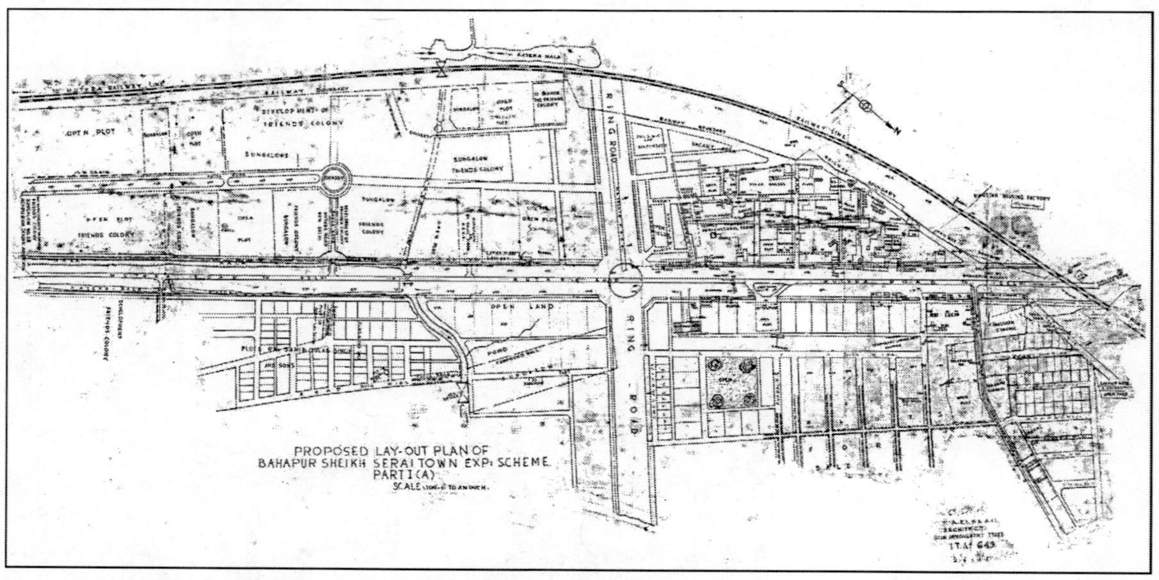

Fig. 6.38: Layout Plan of Sheikh Sarai Town Expansion Scheme

Source : DIT

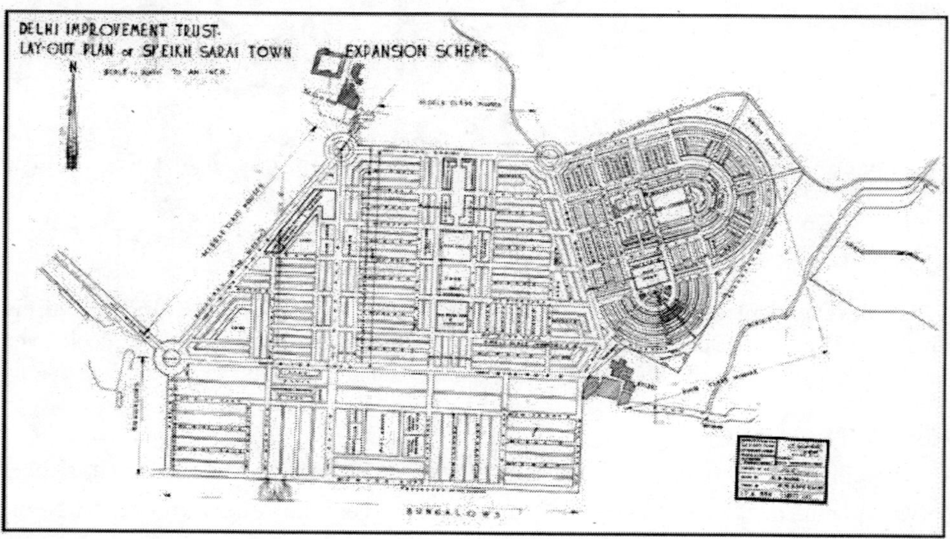

Fig. 6.39: Layout Plan of Sheikh Sarai Town Expansion Scheme

Source: DIT

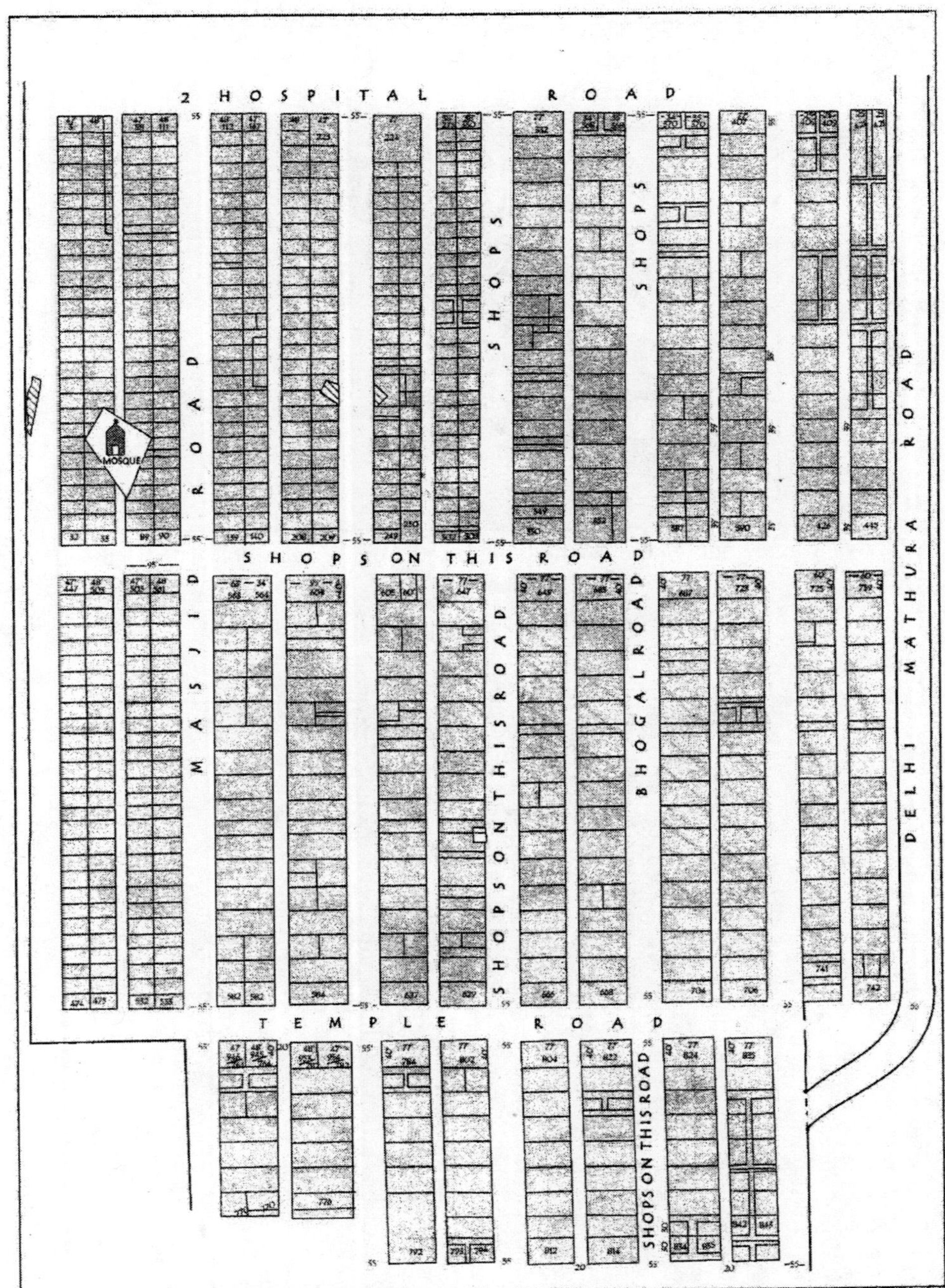

Fig. 6.40: Layout Plan of Jangpura Colony developed by Delhi Improvement Trust

Source: Redrawn by Guerrieri, Pilar Maria (2018) Negotiating Cultures, Oxford Univ. Press, New Delhi

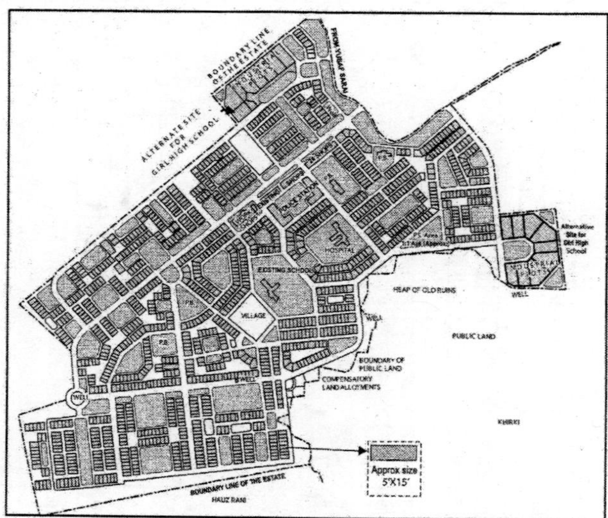

Fig. 6.41: Malviya Nagar, one of the 36 Rehabilitation Colonies developed in Delhi after 1947 for the refugees with 60 to 80 sq. yd. plots

Source: Guerrieri, Pilar Maria (2018) Negotiating Cultures, OUP, New Delhi

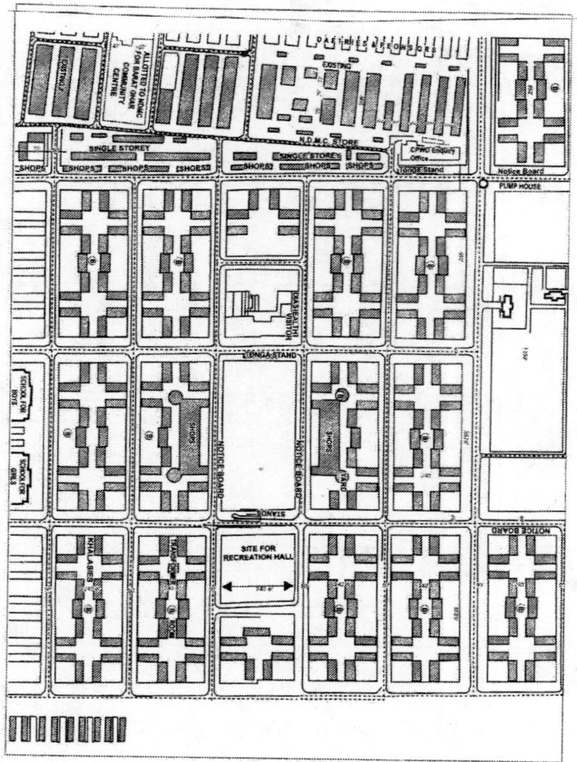

Fig 6.42: Layout Plan of Lodi Colony

Source: Guerrieri, Pilar Maria (2018)

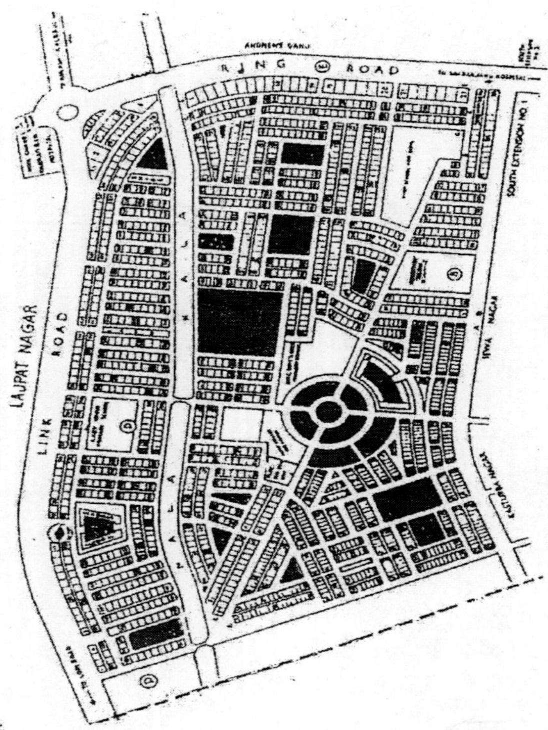

Fig. 6.43: Defence Colony: Besides 36 Rehabilitation Colonies, and other schemes by the Ministry of Rehabilitation and Delhi Improvement Trust, the private sector also undertook several residential schemes, such as Model Town and Shakti Nagar

Source: DIT

Slum Rehabilitation

A major challenge of town planning is slum rehabilitation, where bulk of the poor seek shelter and livelihoods. Slum Rehabilitation started with the Slum Areas (Clearance and Improvement) Act, 1956. Initially, the thrust had been on slum clearance and resettlement in small plots (25 sq. yards to 18 sq. yds). In Delhi, about 4 lakh such plots had been developed during 1960-1995. However, keeping in view the shortage of land, cost involved and physical, socio-economic and political implications of their shifting, now the policy advocates in-situ rehabilitation. This involves low-rise, high density and mixed use development. As per the Master Plan for Delhi 2021, a density of 900 dwelling unit per hectare and a FAR of 400 is permitted for slum rehabilitation. Minimum 60% of land and FAR should be utilised for slum dwellers, whereas 40% can be used for market sale housing, including 10% for commercial activity.

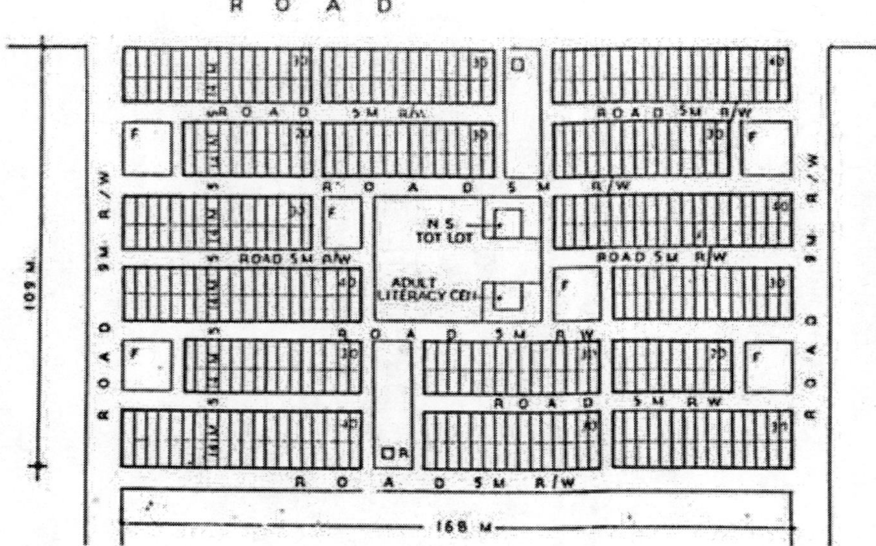

Fig. 6.44: Typical layout Plan of a Site and Services Scheme, (1976), whereby about 4 lakh slum/ squatter households were resettled in Delhi during 1960-1996. Back to back 25 sq. yd. plots provide a high density development. However, with the paucity of land and large number of slum dwellers, the policy now advocates group housing at 500 to 900 dwellings units per Ha

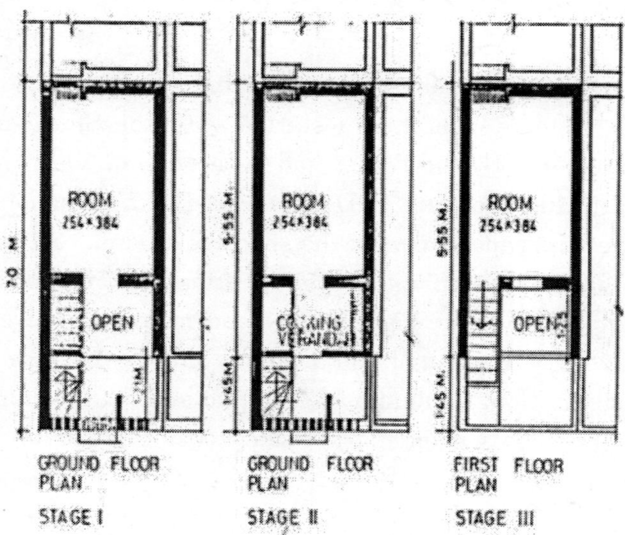

Fig. 6.45: Standard design for a 21 sq.m. (25 sq. yd.) plot

Fig. 6.46: Ambedkar Nagar Site and Services/Resettlement Scheme (1977). The initial horizontal pattern has gradually transformed into high density walk-ups.

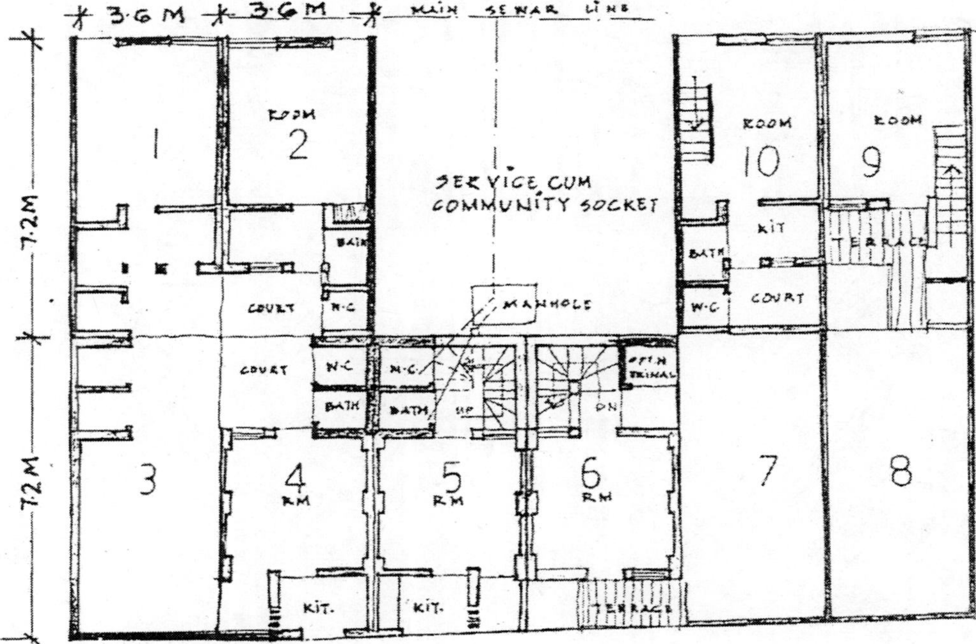

Fig. 6.47: Slum Rehabilitation -Module of 10 families with a Service-cum-Community Socket, (Delhi Development Authority)

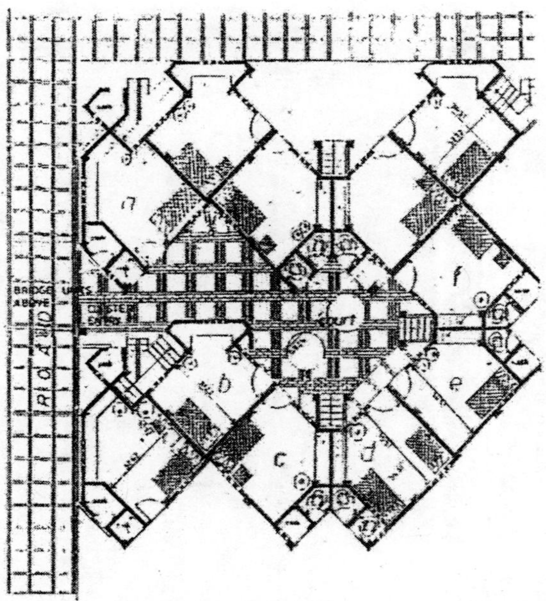

Fig. 6.48: A typical slum tenement cluster developed by the Building Centre and Slum Wing, DDA (Architect: Anil Laul)

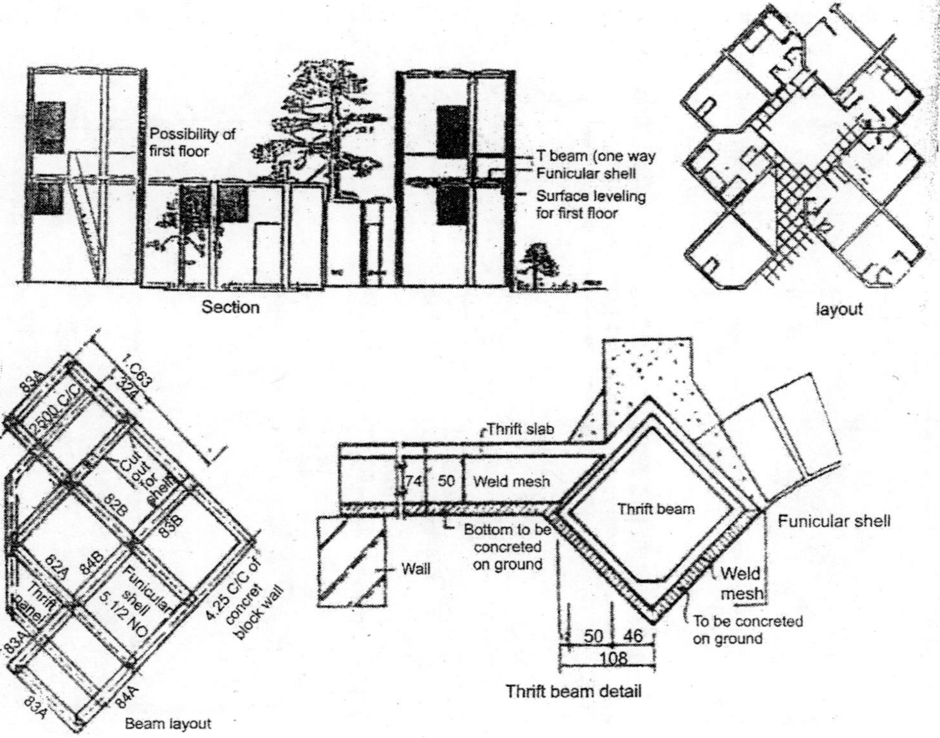

Fig. 6.49: A cluster built with funicular shell and thrift beams (Architect: Anil Laul)

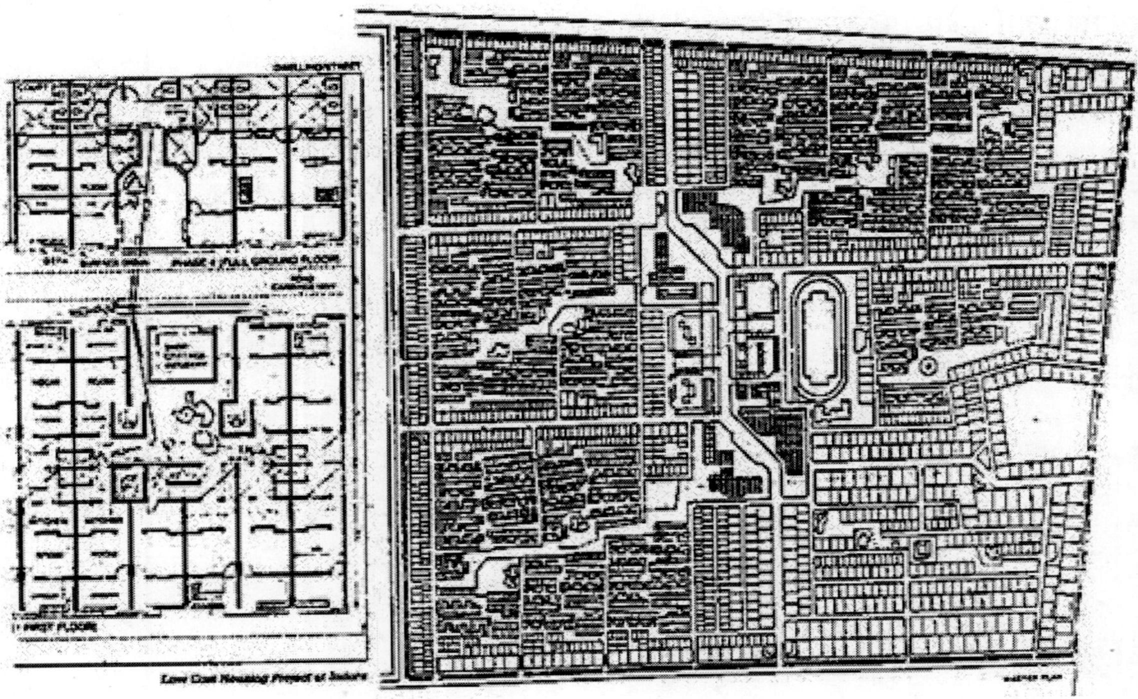

Fig. 6.50: Aranya Township, Indore (Architect: B.V. Doshi)

Fig. 6.51: Self -help housing at Aranya Township, Indore, which allows building of units built according to household's resources, needs and priorities

Patparganj Slum Rehabilitation

The concept of Patparganj Slum Rehabilitation Scheme takes into account the existing social fabric and connections that residents have created over decades of living. It generates a hierarchy of areas comprising public, semi-public, semi-private and private spaces within the layout and residential units, creating secure spaces and a feeling of ownership. Spaces have been designed so as to encourage outdoor activities like walking, cycling and social activities among all age groups.

Commercial and institutional buildings are located at road edges and junctions to create quiet and safe residential pockets, with access to parking.Residential units are organized around a courtyard which provides natural light, ventilation and safety.

The EWS units are designed on modular basis and can be adapted according to site variations, with building heights of G+4. As vehicular movement is restricted to the periphery, with access only during emergencies, the distances between buildings inside the cluster varies between 5-7 m.

Fig. 6.52: Land Use map of Patparganj Slum

Source: DUAC/Dr Aruna Ramani Grover and Satish Khanna, 2016, Patparganj Redevelopment Scheme, Ward No. 220, New Delhi

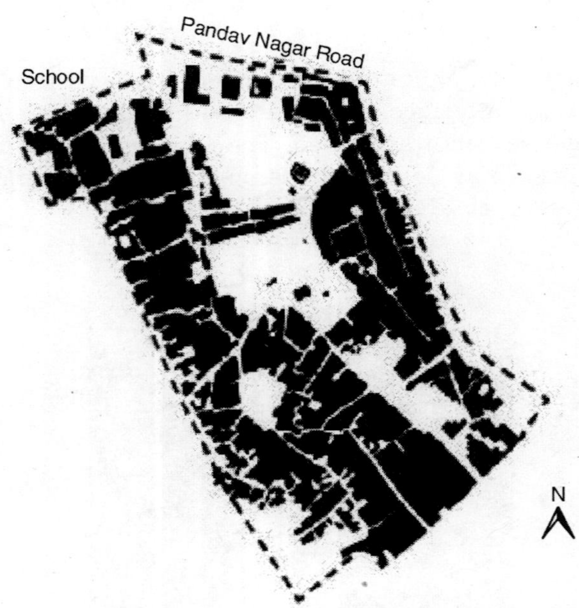

Fig. 6.53: Existing Ground Map

Source: DUAC/Dr Aruna Ramani Grover and Satish Khanna, 2016, Patparganj Redevelopment Scheme, Ward No. 220, New Delhi

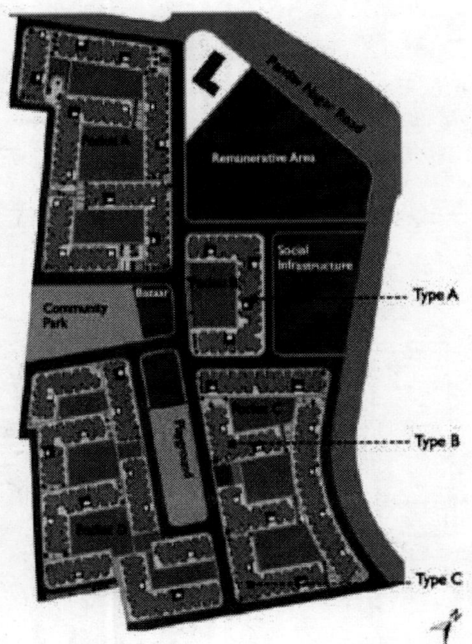

Fig. 6.54: Layout Plan. Commercial and institutional buildings are located at road edges and junctions to create quiet and safe residential pockets

Source: DUAC/Dr Aruna Ramani Grover and Satish Khanna, 2016, Patparganj Redevelopment Scheme, Ward No. 220, New Delhi

Urban Renewal

The cities have a composite, organically developed urban pattern with a high degree of socio-cultural and physical interface, However, with indiscriminate urbanisation, and modernisation, these have became fragmented. The strategy of urban renewal is advocated to transform and upgrade such areas so that these align with changing lifestyles and enable upgradation of physical and social infrastructure.

Fig. 6.55: The landuse pattern of Shahjahanabad, Delhi depicts a closely packed, self-generated, high density housing and mixed land-use.

Source: Rory Fonesca, 1976, The Walled City of Delhi in Shelter and Society

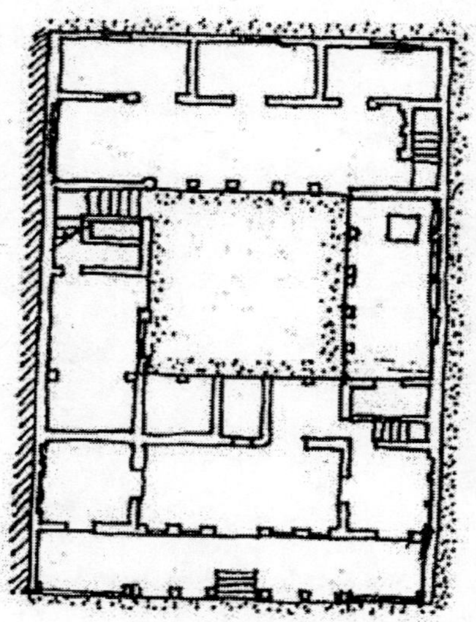

Fig. 6.56: Plan and Elevation of a Haveli

Source: Shikha Jain, Haveli: A Living Tradition of Rajasthan

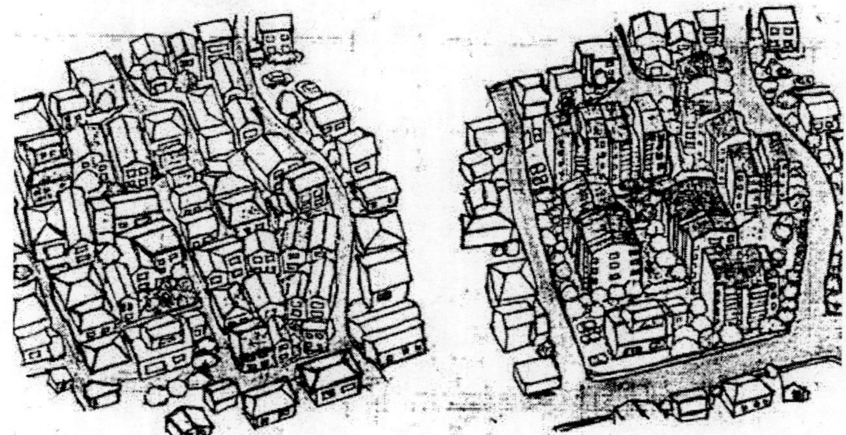

Fig. 6.57: Urban Renewal in Japan: Congested housing areas with single/double storied houses were replaced by multi-storied housing releasing ground for roads, parks and common facilities. Special regulations enabled combination of properties for joint development, with certain exemptions from general building bye-laws

Redevelopment of Urban Villages

Every city has a number of villages around which urban development has taken place. These settlements are usually unplanned and remain disintegrated from the benefits of development, although they provide valuable land for urbanisation and cheap services to the city. These villages pose a major challenge of planned development and require a differentiated planning strategy principles.

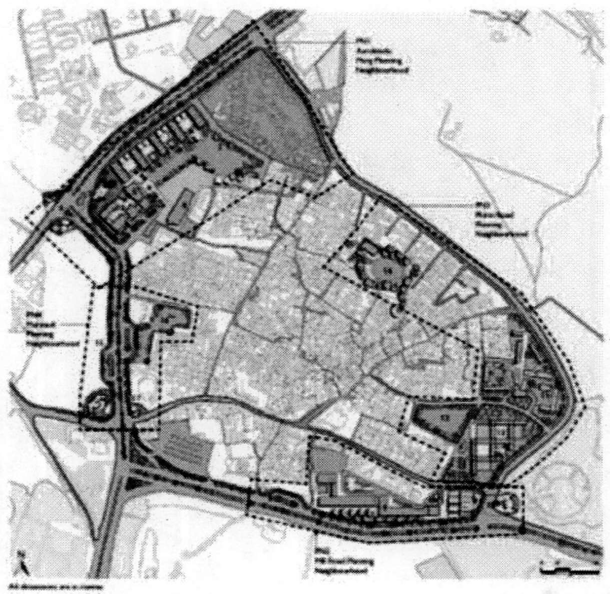

Fig. 6.58: Lado Sarai Village, New Delhi

Source: DUAC/ Ashish Ganju (2014) Lado Sarai, Site Specific Design for Ward 169

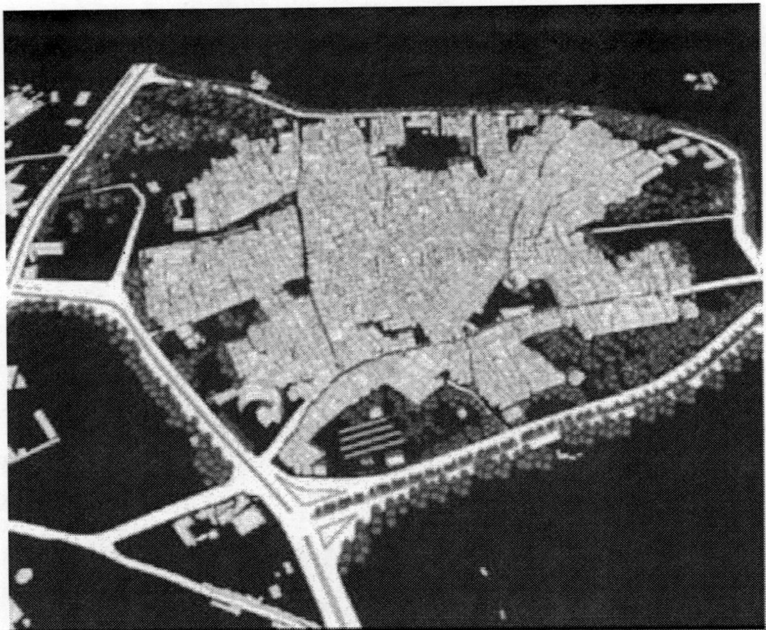

Fig. 6.59: Lado Sarai Urban Village

Source: DUAC/ Ashish Ganju (2014) Lado Sarai, Site Specific Design for Ward 169

Urban Context

Lado Sarai is located within a large green area containing many important historical monuments. The immediate surroundings include forested areas, an archaeological park, traces of historic cities, a golf course and neighbourhood parks.

Important roads connect Lado Sarai and Mehrauli with New Delhi, Shahjahanabad, Badarpur, Gurgaon and the adjoining states of UP, Punjab and Rajasthan.

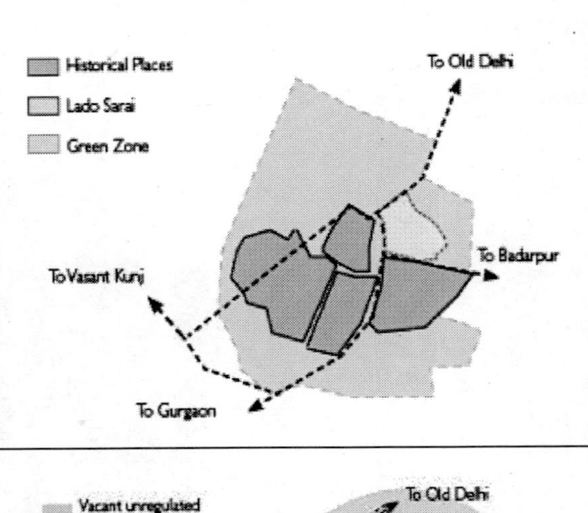

City Level Interface

The Delhi Master Plan proposed arterial roads, which while providing city level accessibility, enclosed the habitation to make it an urban island. These roads generated open spaces on the edge of the built fabric which have become areas of unregulated urban growth. The urban habitation interfaces with the city at only a few places through vehicular traffic junctions.

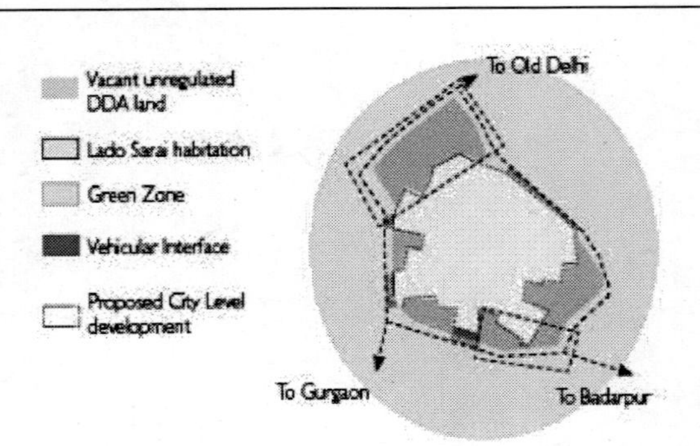

Neighbourhood Interface

The unregulated edges of the existing habitation are proposed for planned development which can help in decongesting the existing built environment. The movement structure is designed to ease connection with Mehrauli and adjoining areas by developing sunken courts/gardens to cross under the major vehicular junctions. These will connect Lado Sarai with the surrounding public places, such as the DDA children's park, Mehrauli community park and Sanjay Van.

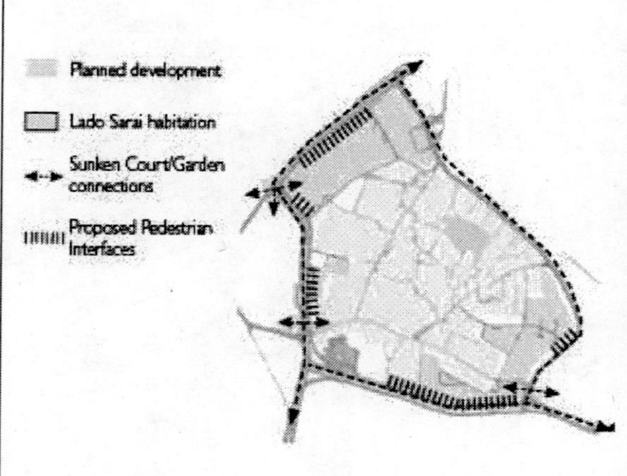

Community Facilities

The existing built fabric is becoming congested with the inlux of new inhabitants renting built space for a host of new activities, like designer studios, art galleries and handicraft showrooms. Increase in population and vehicular traffic has added pressure to the existing community facilities and infrastructural amenities.

The proposed development contains public amenities and facilities which augment the existing facilities.

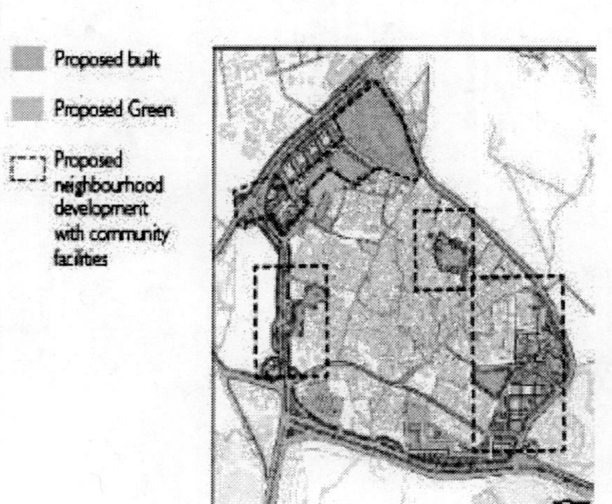

Fig. 6.60: Urban Design Principles

Source: DUAC/ Ashish Ganju (2014) Lado Sarai, Site Specific Design for Ward 169

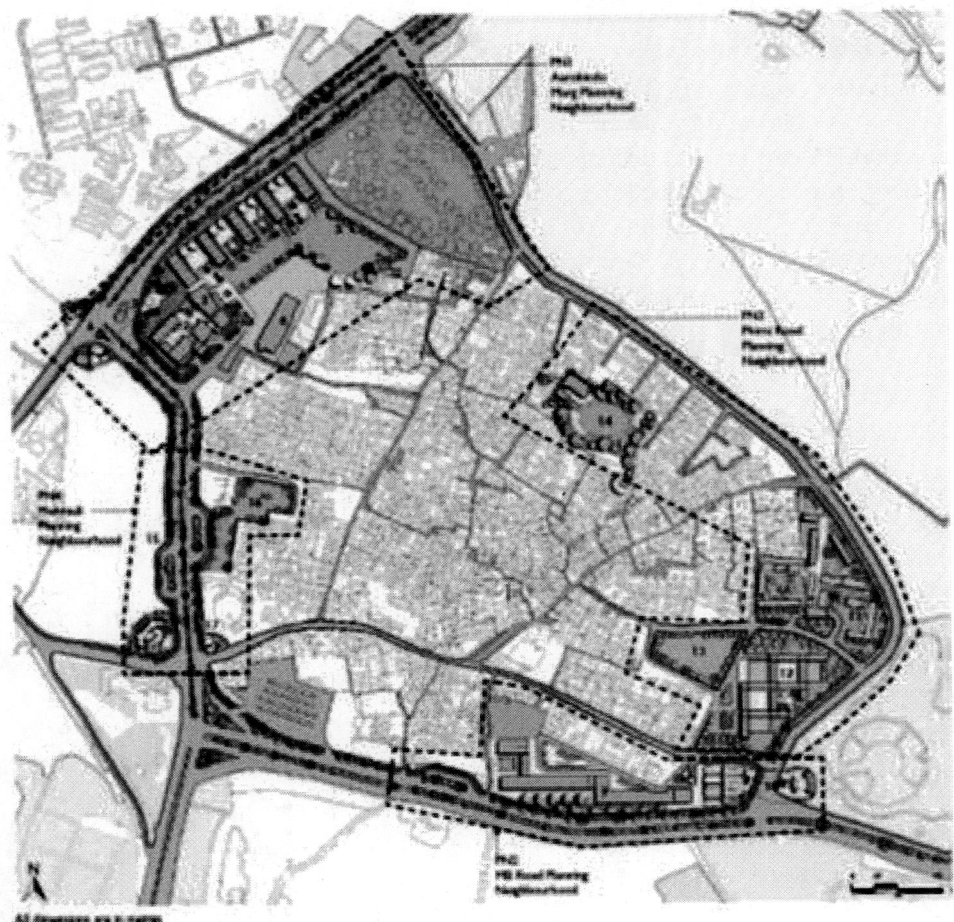

Fig. 6.61: Redevelopment Plan of Lado Sarai

Source: DUAC/ Ashish Ganju (2014) Lado Sarai, Site Specific Design for Ward 169

The redevelopment plan comprises the following specific areas:

1: Aurobindo Marg Planning Neighbourhood

The following proposals form the structure of the neighbourhood:

1. The mixed-use development along Aurobindo Marg is the city scale interface.
2. The cultural centre along Anuvrat Marg is designed to provide spaces for cultural events, exhibitions and design galleries.
3. A vehicular road is proposed between the mixed-use development on Aurobindo Marg and the existing DDA nursery, which is retained as a major green area in keeping with the overall character of the surroundings. The proposed road will connect the village with the underground parking adjacent to the new development.

4. The DDA has allotted a land parcel for a private hospital on the western edge of Lado Sarai village habitation. Access from Anuvrat Marg and a public green area separates the building from the new development.
5. Another public amenity is a set of banquet halls between the cultural centre and the public green area facing the hospital building.
6. Under the road junction of Aurobindo Marg and Anuvrat Marg, a sunken court/garden connects the new development as well as the existing village with Mehrauli and the Qutab complex.
7. This road junction at present is a traffic safety hazard because of a petrol pump on the corner of Aurobindo Marg. It is proposed to relocate the petrol pump and shops on the corner to ease traffic flow at this junction. The revised road alignment gives space for an open air theatre to be integrated with the sunken court/garden.

2: MB Road Planning Neighbourhood

8. A redesigned bus stop for city level transport is proposed at the junction of the inner roads of Lado Sarai connecting old MB Road and new MB Road.
9. A mixed-use development is proposed between new MB Road and existing commercial development along the old MB Road.
10. The development is contiguous with the sunken court/garden connecting Lado Sarai with DDA park under the junction of Phirni Road and MB Road.

3: Phirni Road Planning Neighbourhood

11. The existing MCD school is to be upgraded to senior secondary level.
12. The second entry from the Phirni Road into Lado Sarai village is realigned to serve the MCD school and a proposed museum complex adjoining it.
13. A public park with multi-level car parking below is located at the realigned entry.
14. Adjoining DDA housing on Phirni Road, a community centre with a club and public playground is proposed.

4: Mehrauli Planning Neighbourhood

15. Along Anuvrat Marg, a number of city level bus services have their bus stops. These bus stops have been relocated contiguous with the DDA park at the Mehrauli side and within the Lado Sarai residential area.
16. A newly designed public park with underground car parking is proposed adjoining the existing CNG station and relocated bus stop.
17. Pedestrian movement between Lado Sarai and Mehrauli is facilitated by sunken court/garden connecting under the junction of Anuvrat Marg and old MB Road.

Redevelopment of Unauthorised Colonies

A major challenge in the cities is regularisation and redevelopment of unauthorized colonies. The unauthorised colonies are broadly characterized by the following:

- Buildings are usually structurally unsafe and dilapidated, do not conform to the building bye laws and are deficient in basic services, facilities and open space.
- Encroachments and appropriation of public lands, roads, railways, and land earmarked for parks, public facilities and utilities.
- Illegal conversion of green areas and agricultural land in contravention of the Master Plan/Zonal Plan and DCR;
- Transactions of lands by Power of Attorney, non-legal tenure and non-payment of stamp duty.
- Violation of various Acts, such as, ULB/Development Authority Acts, Town Planning Act, Land Reforms Act, Stamp Duty Act, Property Registration Act, etc.

The regularisation and redevelopment of unauthorised colonies involves improvement and provision of physical infrastructure, social infrastructure and community facilities, open spaces, parks, etc.

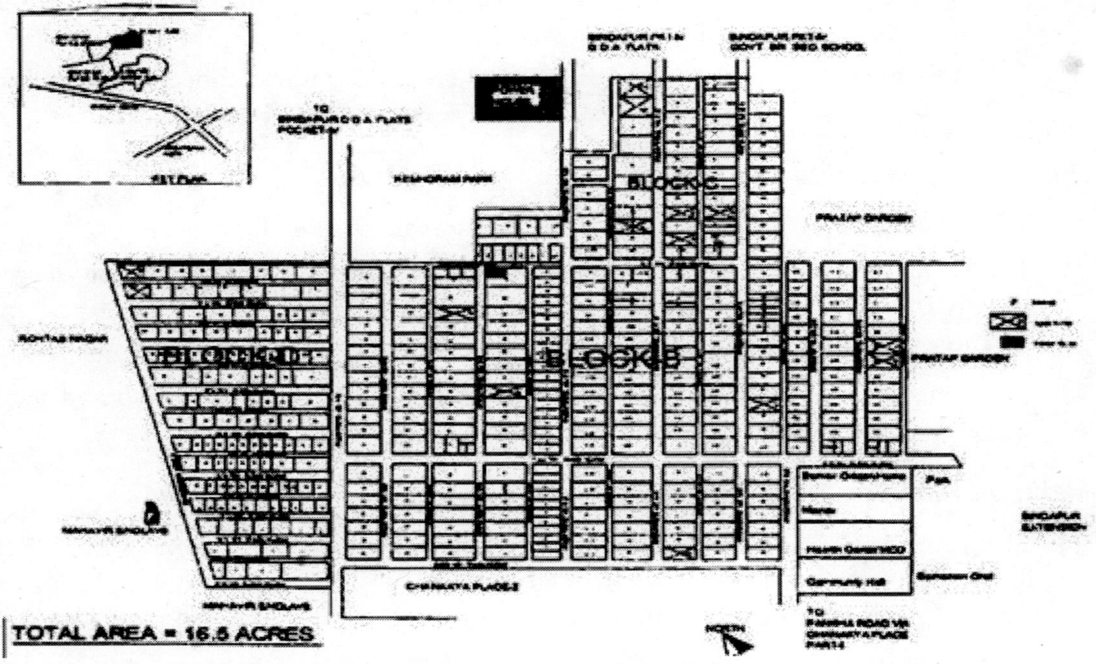

Fig. 6.62: Existing Layout Plan of Janakpuri Unauthorized Colony, Average Plot Size 100 to 200 sqm

As per the Master Plan for Delhi 2021, redevelopment areas must conform to a minimum area of 4 ha and should include a cluster block with a minimum area of 3000 sqm. The redevelopment incentives include:

- An increase in FAR by 50%
- Allocation of 10% of the area for commercial use
- Allocation of 10% of area for community facilities.

Commercial development in the area is permissible along plots that abut 18 m wide roads. Mixed-use and commercial activity up to one plot depth is permissible. The small shops are permitted with a maximum of 20 sq m area each, restricted to maximum permissible number of DUs in the plot or four, whichever is lesser. Parking standards prescribed in the Master Plan require 2 ECS to be provided per 100 sq m of built-up area within the premises.

The DUAC has taken up studies of redevelopment of Adarsh Nagar and Uttam Nagar (ward 127) on the basis of norms as prescribed by the Master Plan for Delhi-2021.

Fig. 6.63: Redevelopment of Adarsh Nagar Unauthorised Colony

Source; DUAC/Amit Ghosal, Adarsh Nagar Unauthorised Colony

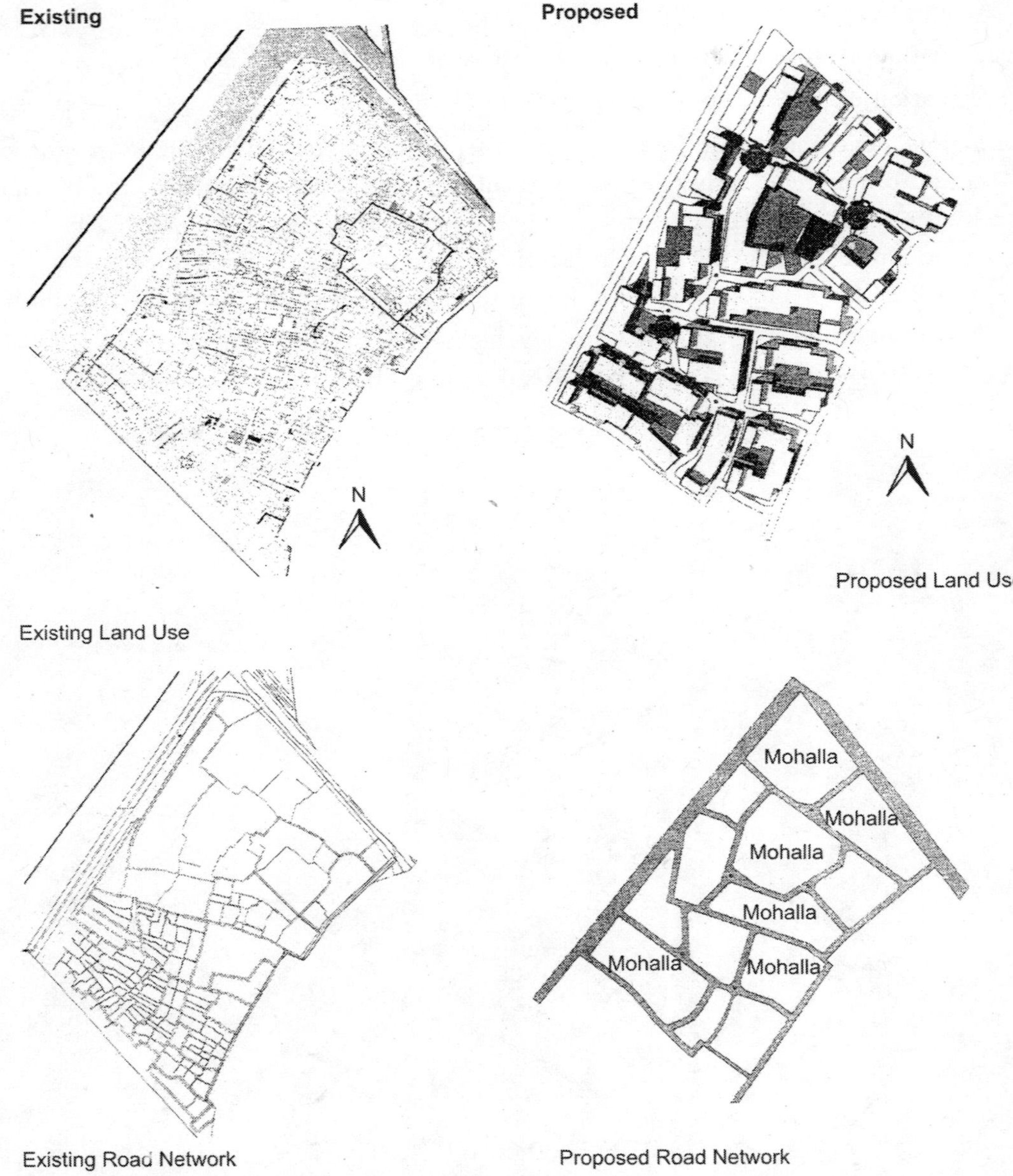

Fig. 6.64: Concept Design: Redevelopment of Adarsh Nagar

The Existing Situation

- Organic, haphazard growth, plotted development.
- The nodes are not defined and often encroached upon by parking or vendors, thus no space is left for any public/recreational activities.
- Each pocket is further divided by narrow, dark lanes with no proper widths and light and ventilation, thus creating unsafe living conditions.

- Rampant redevelopment going on with builders bringing down old houses and raising new floors for sale or for rental with stilt parking and four floors

Proposed Design Solution

- Existing pockets to be redefined, treated as a mohalla where the pocket size varies from 2500 sq m to 10,000 sq m.
- The mohalla pocket holds a certain number of population and serves its basic needs.
- The nodes to be identiied and designed so that they can be used as small congregation/ public spaces, a typical character of the village.
- The existing 3.5 m roads are proposed to be widened to 7.5 m with segregation of vehicular and pedestrian movement

Source; DUAC/Amit Ghosal, Adarsh Nagar Unauthorised Colony

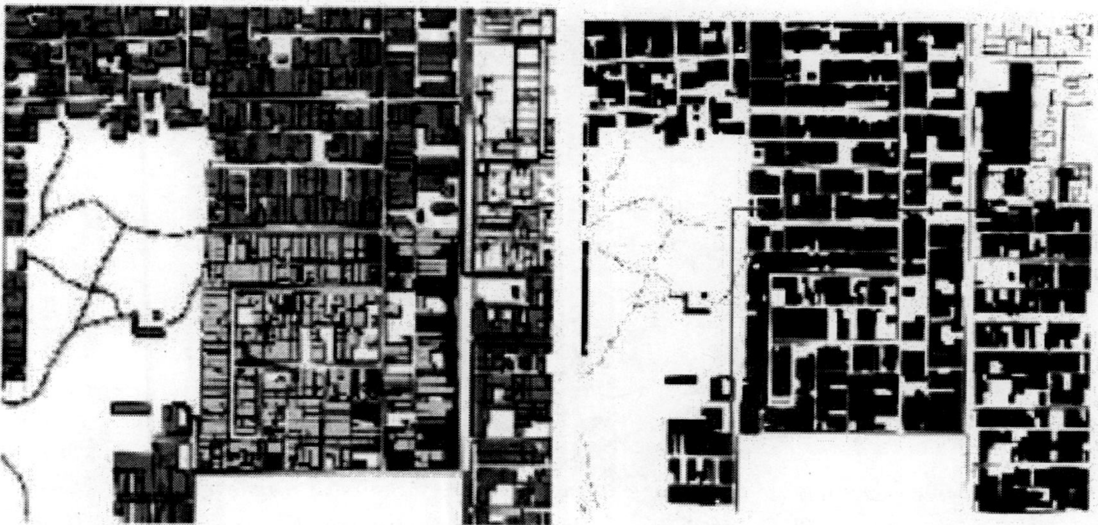

Fig. 6.65 Landuse distribution of the existing block

Fig. 6.66: Built/open space map of existing block

Source: DUAC/Arun Rewal (2016) Uttam Nagar Site Specific Design for Ward No. 127, New Delhi

Fig. 6.67: Proposed section through Commercial Zone

Source: DUAC/Arun Rewal (2016) Uttam Nagar Site Specific Design for Ward No. 127, New Delhi

Fig. 6.68: Key Map showing the proposed block that respect the existing road/block pattern of Uttam Nagar Ward

Source: DUAC/Arun Rewal (2016) Uttam Nagar Site Specific Design for Ward No. 127, New Delhi

Fig. 6.69: Providing for higher density and FAR as incentives to redevelopment

Source: DUAC/Arun Rewal (2016) Uttam Nagar Site Specific Design for Ward No. 127, New Delhi

Fig. 6.70: Creation of open spaces, Uttam Nagar

Source: DUAC/Arun Rewal (2016) Uttam Nagar Site Specific Design for Ward No. 127, New Delhi

Standards of Social Infrastructure

The quality of life in any urban centre depends upon the availability of quality social infrastructure. These include the following:

(a) Educational facilities

(b) Healthcare facilities

(c) Socio-Cultural facilities

(d) Recreational facilities

(e) Sports Facilities

(f) Distribution Services

(g) Police, Safety and Security

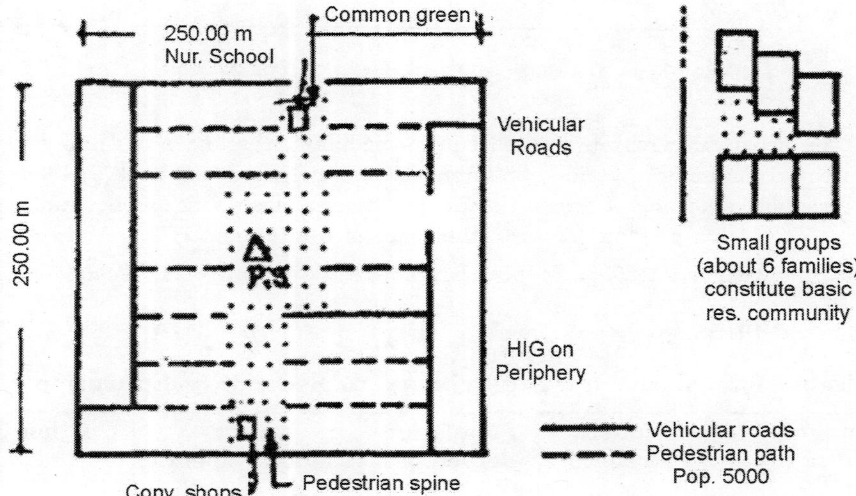

Fig. 6.71: Primary Community Unit with about 5000 population (1000 families) acts a building block of urban planning.

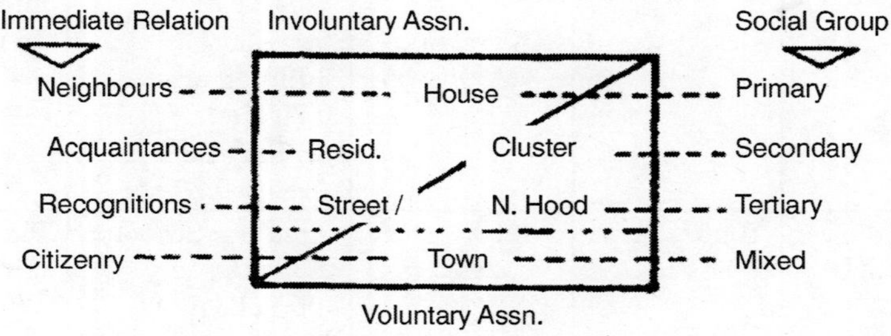

Fig. 6.72: Community planning is closely related with the levels of Association, which gradually shift from voluntary to involuntary.

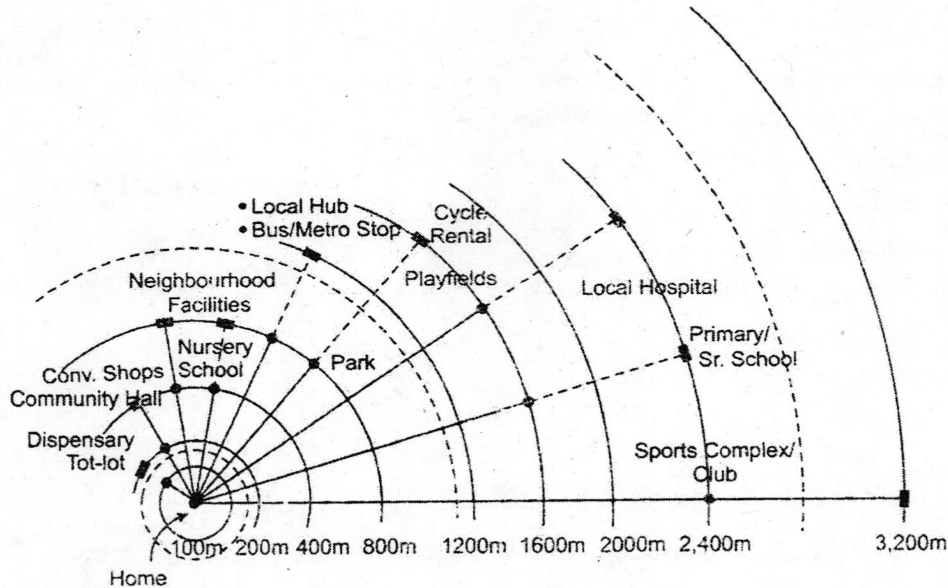

Fig. 6.73: The urban hierarchy is worked out on modular basis and accessibility to various functions so that communiy, especially children, women and aged can walk to their places of education, recreation, shopping or work. As the distance increases, the public transport should provide access to the place of destination.

Source: Adapted from Barton H. (2003) Shaping Neighbourhoods, Spon Press, London

Educational Facilities

Table 6.2: Norms for Pre-Primary to Secondary Education

Sr. No.	Category	Student Strength	Population Served per unit	Area Requirement	Other Controls
1.	Pre-Primary, Nursery School	—	2500	0.08 ha	To be located near a park
2.	Primary School (class I to V)	500	5000	Area per school =0.40 Ha (a) School building area = 0.20 Ha (b) Play field Area = 0.20 Ha	Playfield area with a minimum of 18 m × 36 m for effective play
3.	Senior Secondary School (VI to XII)	1000	7500	Area per School = 1.80 Ha (a) School building area = 0.60 Ha (b) Playfield Area = 1.00 Ha (c) Parking Area = 0.20 Ha	Playfield area with a minimum of 68 m × 126 m for effective play

4.	Integrated School without hostel facility (Class I-XII)	1500	90,000 – 1 lakh	Area per School = 3.50 Ha (a) School building area = 0.70 Ha (b) Playfield Area = 2.50 ha (c) Parking Area = 0.30 Ha	To be located near a sport facility
5.	Integrated School with hostel facility (Class I-XII)	1500	90,000 – 1 lakh	Area per School = 3.90 Ha (a) School building area = 0.70 Ha (b) Playfield Area = 2.50 Ha (c) Residential Hostel Area = 0.40 Ha (d) Parking Area = 0.30 Ha	To be located near a sport facility.
6.	School for Physically Challenged	400	45,000	Area per School = 0.75 Ha (a) School Building Area = 0.20 Ha (b) Playfield Area = 0.30 Ha (c) Parking Area = 0.25 Ha	To be located near a park or sport facility.
7.	School for Mentally Challenged		10 Lakh	0.20 Ha	To be located near a park and non-noise polluting zone
Other controls: The schools should preferably face service road and roads with less traffic intensity.					

Source: NBC 2005 Part 3 and MPD 2021.

Fig. 6.3: Norms for Higher Education Facilities

Sr. No.	Category	Student Strength	Population Served per unit	Area Requirement
1.	College	1000-1500	1.25 lakh	Area per college = 5.00 Ha (a) College Building Area = 1.80 Ha (b) Playfield Area = 2.50 Ha (c) Residential including Hostel Area = 0.30 Ha (d) Parking Area = 0.30 Ha

2.	University Campus	—	City/Sub-city level (say 10 Lakh pop.)	10 to 60 Ha area (a) Residential (if included) = 25% of total land area. (b) Sports and Cultural Activities = 15% of total land area (c) Parks and landscape including green belt = 15% of total land area.
		Technical Education		
3.	Technical Education Centre (A) – to include 1 Industrial Training Institute (ITI) and 1 Polytechnic	ITI = 400 Polytechnic = 500	10 Lakh	Area per Technical Education Centre = 4.00 Ha (a) Area for ITI = 1.60 Ha (b) Area for Polytechnic = 2.40 Ha
4.	Technical Education Centre (B) – to include 1 ITI Technical Centre and Coaching Centre	—	10 Lakh	Area per Technical Education Centre = 4.00 Ha (a) Area of ITI = 1.60 Ha (b) Area for Technical Centre = 2.10 Ha (c) Area for Coaching Centre = 30 Ha
		Professional Education		
5.	Engineering College	1500	10 Lakh	Area per College = 6.00 Ha
6.	Medical College	—	10 Lakh	Area per College = 15.00 Ha Area of site including space for general hospital
7.	Other Professional College	250 to 1500	10 Lakh	(a) Area of site for student strength up to 250 students = 2.00 Ha (b) Additional area for every additional 100 students or part thereof up to total strength of 1000 students = 0.50 Ha (c) Area for strength of college from 1000 to 1500 students = 6.00 Ha
8.	Nursing and Paramedical Institute	—	10 Lakh	Institute Plot area = 2000 sqm (subject to Nursing Council of India/Ministry of Health Norms)
9.	Veterinary Institute	—	—	As per Veterinary Council of India/ Ministry Norms (subject to availability of land)

Source: NBC 2005 Part 3 and MPD 2021.

Education facilities not only depend on the population, but also on the socio-cultural and economic characteristics. Considering that there is wide variations in the levels of literacy, and form of built-up areas, the norms can have the variations. The threshold population for schools is determined on the State policy and development/density and character of development. The norms could be differentiated accordingly.

Health-care Facilities

The size of a hospital depends upon the hospital beds requirement, which in turn is a function of the size of the population it serves. As per the Indian Public Health Standards (IPHS), 2012, the calculation of number of beds is based on:

- annual rate of admission as 1 per 50 population
- average length of stay in a hospital as 5 days

For the purpose of convenience the average size of a district is taken as one million population. Based on the assumptions the number of beds required for 10,00,000 population are:

- No. of bed days per year: (10,00,000 × 1/50) × 5 = 1,00,000
- No. of beds required with 100% occupancy: 1,00,000 / 365 = 275
- No. of beds required with 80% occupancy: (1,00,000 / 365) × 80% = 220

According to the recommendations of the World Health Organization (WHO), the hospital bed ratio to be achieved had been 5 per thousand population, whereas in most cities in India the bed population ratio had been around 1.5 to 3.0 per 1000 population.

The norms and classification of healthcare facilities are given below.

Table 6.4: Standards for Healthcare Facilities

Sr. No.	Category	No. of beds	Population served per unit	Area requirements
1.	Dispensary	—	15000	0.08 to 0.12 Ha
2.	Nursing home, child welfare and maternity centre	25 to 30 beds	45000 to 1 lakh	0.20 to 0.30 Ha
3.	Polyclinic	Some observation beds	1 lakh	0.20 to 0.30 Ha
4.	Intermediate Hospital (Category B)	80 beds, Initially may be for 50 beds including 20 maternity beds	1 lakh	Total area = 1.00 Ha (a) Area for Hospital = 0.60 Ha (b) Area for residential accomodation = 0.40 Ha
5.	Intermediate Hospital (Category A)	200 beds, Initially the provision may be for 100 beds	1 lakh	Total Area = 3.70 Ha (a) Area for hospital = 2.70 Ha (b) Area for residential accommodation = 1.00 Ha
6.	Multi-Speciality Hospital	200 beds, Initially the provision may be for 100 beds	1 lakh	Total Area = 9.00 Ha (a) Area for hospital = 6.00 Ha (b) Area for residential accommodation = 3.00 Ha

7.	Speciality Hospital	200 beds, Initially the provision may be for 100 beds	1 lakh	Total Area = 3.70 Ha (a) Area for hospital = 2.70 Ha (b) Area for residential accommodation = 1.00 Ha
8.	General Hospital	500, Initial provision may be for 300 beds	2.5 lakh	Total Area = 6.00 Ha (a) Area for hospital = 4.00 Ha (b) Area for residential accommodation = 2.00 Ha
9.	Family Welfare Centre	As per requirement	50,000	Total area = 500 sqm
10.	Diagnostic centre	—	50,000	Total area = 500 sqm to 800 sqm
11.	Veterinary Hospital for pets and animals	—	5 lakh	Total area = 2000 sqm
12.	Dispensary for pet, animals and birds	—	1 lakh	Total area = 300 sqm
13.	Rehabilitation Centre			As per requirement

Source: UDPFI Guidelines, 1996, NBC, 2016 and MPD-2021.

Socio-cultural Facilities

The provision of socio-cultural facilities shall correspond to the urban demography, cultural background and local demand.

Table 6.5: Norms for Socio-Cultural Facilities

Sr. No.	Category	Population Served per unit	Land Area Requirements
1.	Anganwadi – Housing area/cluster	5000	200-300 sqm
2.	Community Room	5000	750 sqm
3.	Community hall, mangalkaryayala, barat ghar/library	15000	2000 sqm
4.	Music dance and drama centre	1 lakh	1000 sqm
5.	Meditation and spiritual Centre	1 lakh	5000 sqm
6.	Recreational club	1 lakh	10,000 sqm
7.	Old age home	5 lakh	Max. 1000 sqm, subject to availability of land

8.	Religious Facilities		
8a.	At neighbourhood/housing cluster level	50000	400 sqm
8b.	At sub-city level	10 lakh	4.00 Ha
9.	Other facilities		
9a.	Orphange/Children's centre (One each)	10 lakh	Max. 1000 sqm subject to availability of land
9b.	Care centre for physically/mentally challenged	10 lakh	Max. 1000 sqm subject to availability of land
9c.	Working women – men hostel	10 lakh	Max. 1000 sqm subject to availability of land
9d.	Adult education centre	10 lakh	Max. 1000 sqm subject to availability of land
10.	Socio-Cultural Centre/ Exhibition-cum-fair ground	10 lakh	15 Ha
11.	Science Centre	10 lakh	As per requirement
12.	International Convention Centre	City level	As per requirement

Source: UDPFI Guidelines, 1996 and MPD 2021.

For lower income group population, the maintenance and management of formal community buildings is a challenging task. Thus to ensure optimum utilisation, maintenance and management of community buildings, the use of such facilities shall be planned and designated for multi-purpose activities. Activities such as adult education, training programmes for economic generation activities, child and family welfare programmes, etc. can be organised in such spaces.

Orphanage and Old Age Homes can be developed with appropriate green spaces to promote social relations between the two dependent age groups. The facility could include the following:

(a) Common recreational facilities such as sports facilities, walking tracks, reading rooms, etc.

(b) Opportunity for part time work for old people. This shall promote their active involvement with other social groups.

(c) Adequate social security of vulnerable groups such as women, children, elderly and orphans.

It has generally been observed that the religious buildings come up on public sites and especially those meant for open spaces. Effort should be made by the development agencies with the assistance of NGOs in the area to ensure that the places of worship come up as planned with the participation and preferences of the community itself. On a general basis, separate religious sites (2 for 15,000 population) may be provided so that places of worship do not get established on encroached sites.

Open Spaces and Greens

The open spaces include the following three categories, namely:

(a) Recreational space, playfields and sport grounds

(b) Organised green

(c) Other public open spaces (such as flood plains, forest cover, etc.)

For all the above mentioned categories, provision may be made @ 10 to12 sqm per person. However, in hilly areas the protected zones and ecological conservation areas shall be considered to be over and above this open space requirement. In the built up area (excluding recreational space, vacant land, flood plain, forest) the NBC suggests 3 sqm/ person as minimum norm.

The hierarchy for organised green such as parks, play fields and other open spaces like specified park, amusement park, maidan, a multi-purpose open space, botanical garden and zoological parks, traffic parks, etc. are as under:

Table 6.6: Hierarchy of Organised Greens

S. No.	Planning Unit	Number of Organised green spaces
1.	Housing Cluster	3-4 housing Area Parks
2.	Neighbourhood	3-4 local parks and playgrounds
3.	Community	2-3 community level park and open space
4.	District/Zone	1 district level park and sports centre, maidan
5.	Sub-city centre	1 city park, sports complex, botanical/zoological garden, maidan

Source: UDPFI Guidelines, 1996.

Table 6.7: Norms for Organised Greens

S. No.	Category	Population served per unit	Area Requirement (Ha)
1.	Housing Area park	5000	0.50
2.	Neighbourhood park	15000	1.00
3.	Community park	1 lakh	5.00
4.	District park	5 lakh	25.00
5.	Sub-city park	10 lakh	100.00

Source: UDPFI Guidelines, 1996 and DDA, MPD, 2021.

Open spaces should be spatially distributed for multiple functions—marriage, religious ceremonies, exhibitions, etc. In any layout or sub-division of land measuring 0.3 Ha or more in residential and commercial zones, the community open space shall be reserved for recreational purposes which shall as far as possible be provided in one place. The minimum recreational space provided shall be 450 sqm. The minimum average dimension of the recreational space shall not be less than 7.5 m and the length shall not exceed 2.5 times the average width. Each recreational area and the structure on it shall have an independent means of access. Any building line has to be at least 3 m away from the boundary of recreational open space.

Fig. 6.74: A playground can be developed as a mini-stadium-cum-amphitheater

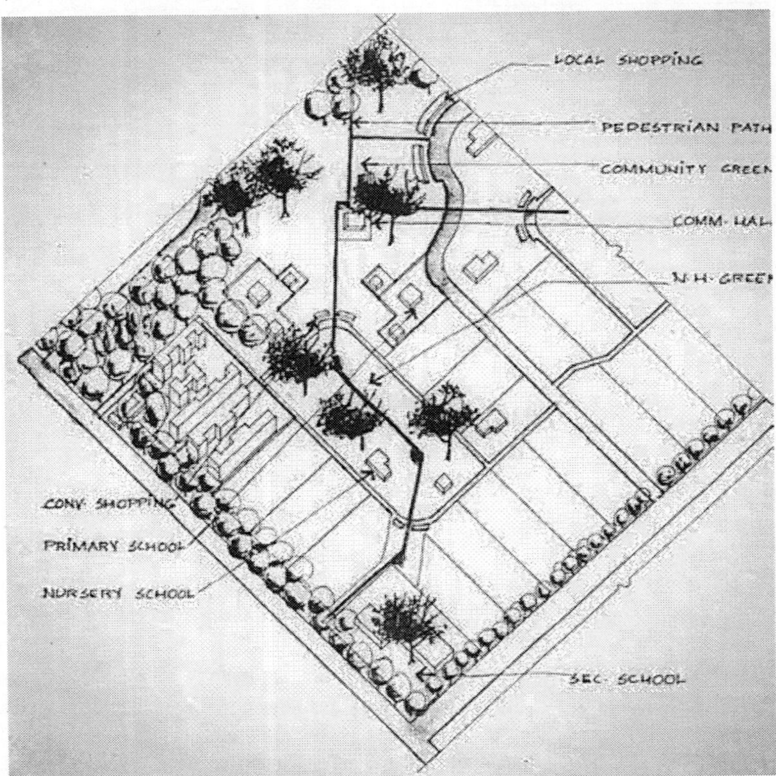

Fig. 6.75: Axonometric showing the neighbourhood park merging with community green and green buffers. The pedestrian greenways diagonally cut across neighbourhood through the greens and community facilities

Table 6.8: Norms for Multi-purpose Ground

S. No.	Category	Population served per unit	Area Requirement (Ha)
1.	Sub-city multi-purpose ground	10 lakh	8
2.	District level multi-purpose ground	5 lakh	4
3.	Local level multi-purpose ground	1 lakh	2

Source: MPD-2021.

In light of the standards recommended by various bodies, it is suggested to provide 1.0 to 1.2 ha of greens/open space per 1000 persons at city level. These can be distributed for different residential pockets uniformly. Some of these open spaces are to be developed with educational, socio-cultural and commercial facilities so that they can serve multiple purposes. The area under facilities like community halls, etc. can be merged with the open spaces. The older parts of the cities are usually deficient with respect to the availability of open spaces, which may be compensated by additional provisions in the adjacent new development.

Table 6.9: Norms for Sports Facilities

S. No.	Category	Population served per unit	Area Requirement
1.	Residential unit play area	5,000	5000 sqm
2.	Neighbourhood play area	15,000	1.50 ha
3.	District Sports Centre	1 lakh	8.00 ha
4.	Divisional Sports Centre	10 lakh	20.00 ha

Source: NBC, 2005

Table 6.10: Norms for Distribution Services

Sr. No.		Land Area Requirement		Other Controls
		Type of facility	Area requirement	
1.	**Petrol/Diesel filling and Service Centre** Permitted in (a) Central District (b) Sub-Central District (c) District Centres (d) Community Centre (Only Filling Station) (e) Residential and Industrial Use zone in Urban Area	(i) Only filling station (ii) Filling cum Service station (iii) Filling cum service station cum worksshop (iv) Filling station only for two and three wheelers	30 m × 17 m 36 m × 30 m 45 m × 36 m 18 m × 15 m	• Shall not be located on road having Right of Way less than 30 m. • Special cases in old city areas may be considered based on the approval by statutory authorities

(f) Along National and State Highways (g) Village identified as growth centre (h) Freight Complex (i) Proposed major roads (j) Police/security force services (for captive use only)			• Shall be approved by the explosive/ fire department.
2. Compressed Natural Gas (CNG)/filling centre Permitted in: (a) All use zones (except in Regional Parks and Development District Parks) (b) Along National and State Highways (c) Village identified as growth centres (d) Feight Complex (e) Proposed major roads.	CNG mother station (Including building component-control room/office/ dispensing room/ store, pantry and W.C.)	1080 sqm (36 m × 30 m)	• Shall not be located on road having Right of Way less than 30 m • Shall be approved by the explosive/ fire department.
3. LPG Godown/Gas Godown One each per 40,000 to 50,000 population	Capacity = 500 cylinders or 8000 kg of LPG	Area (inclusive of guard room) 520 sqm (26 m × 20 m)	Location shall be away from the residential areas and shall have open spaces all around as per the Explosive Rules.
4. Milk Distribution	One/5,000 population	Area inclusive of service area 150 sqm	—

Source: NBC, 2005.

Notes:

1. Super Kerosene Oil/ Light Diesel Oil for industrial activity shall be provided separately.
2. Large petrol/diesel storage centres to be located outside city jurisdiction.

Police, Civil Defence and Home Guards

Table: 6.11: Norms for Police Facilities

S. No.	Category	Population Served per unit	Land Area Requirement
1.	Police Post	40,000–50,000 (area not served by Police Station)	0.16 Ha (area inclusive of residential accommodation)
2.	Police Station	90,000	1.50 Ha (area inclusive of residential accommodation) Additional area to be provided for civil defence and home guards.
3.	Traffic and Police Control Room	—	As per requirement
4.	District office and battalion	10 lakh	Total area = 4.80 Ha (a) Area for district office = 0.80 Ha (b) Area of battalion = 4.00 Ha
5.	Police Lines	20 lakh	4.00 to 6.00 Ha
6.	District Jail	10 lakh	10.00 Ha
7.	Civil defence and home guards	10 lakh	2.00 Ha
8.	Police Training Institute/ College	City level (to be located in fringe areas)	5 Ha
9.	Police Firing Range	City level (to be located in fringe areas)	Up to 10 Ha
10.	Police camp including Central Police Organisation/Security Forces (Including Central Security Forces)		Up to 10 Ha
11.	Police Booth (at major road intersections)	—	10–12 sqm

Source: NBC 2005 and MPD 2021.

Table. 6.12: Norms for Safety Facilities

S. No.	Category	Distribution or Population Served per unit	Area Requirement
1.	Sub-Fire Station/Fire Post	Within 3-4 km radius	0.6 Ha (with residential accommodation)
2.	Fire Station	2 lakh population or 5-7 km radius	1 Ha (with residential accommodation)
3.	Disaster Management Centre	One in each administrative zone	1 Ha, along with soft parking, temporary shelter, parade ground, etc.
4.	Fire Training Institute/College	City level	3 Ha

Source: MPD - 2021.

Guidelines for locating fire stations and other fire fighting facilities

- Fire stations should be located so that the fire tenders are able to reach any disaster site within 3 to 5 minutes
- Fire stations should be located on corner plots as far as possible and on main roads with minimum two entries.
- In the new layouts, concept of underground pipelines for fire hydrants on the periphery exclusively for fire fighting services should be considered.
- Necessary provisions for laying underground/ over ground fire fighting measures, water lines, hydrants, etc. may be kept wherever provision of fire station is not possible.
- The concerned agencies shall take approval from Fire Department for fire fighting measures while laying the services for an area.

Source: DDA, MPD-2021.

Commercial Activities: Hierarchy of Commercial Centres

Hierarchy of commercial centres corresponds to the hierarchy of planning units in an urban area. Normally an urban area shall have some or all of the following, depending upon its size:

Table 6.13: Hierarchy of Commercial Centres

S. No.	Planing Unit	Class of Settlement			Population served	Hierarchy of Commercial Centres
		S	M	L		
1.	Housing Cluster	✓	✓	✓	5000	Convenience Shopping
2.	Neighbourhood	✓	✓	✓	15000	Local shopping centre
3.	Community	✓	✓	✓	100000	Community Centre
4.	District	-	✓	✓	500000	District Centre
5.	Sub-city	-	-	✓	25 lakh – 50 lakh	Sub-city Centre
6.	City	-	-	✓	50 lakh	City Centre

S: Small Town
M: Medium Town
L: Large City, Metropolitan City, Megapolis

Source: National Building Code

Norms for Commercial Centres

The norms for planning of commercial centres are as given in table below:

Table 6.14: Norms for Commercial Centres

S. No.	Category	Population Served per unit	Land Area Requirement
1.	Convenience Shopping	5,000	1,500 sqm
2.	Local Shopping (including service centre)	15,000	4,600 sqm
3.	Community Centre with service centre	1,00,000	5 Ha
4.	District Centre	1 at District level/5,00,000 population	40 Ha
5.	Sub-city Centre	25 lakh to 50 lakh	As per requirement
6.	City Centre	50 lakh	As per requirement
7.	Local Wholesale market/Mandi	10 lakh	10.00 Ha
8.	Weekly Markets 1. Parking and other open spaces within the commercial centres could be so designed that weekly markets can operate during non-working hours.	1 to 2 locations for every 1 lakh population with 300 to 400 units per location.	Area per location = 0.40 HA

	2. The informal market should have public conveniences and solid waste disposal arrangements.		
9.	Organised Informal eating spaces	1 lakh	2000 sqm

Source: NBC, 2005

The standards of areas of commercial centres and the number of shops are given below:

Table 6.15: Area of Commercial Centres

S. No.	Category	Area per 1000 persons (sqm)	Number of shops
1.	Convenience shopping	220	1 for 110 persons
2.	Local shopping including service centre	300	1 for 200 persons
3.	Community Centre with service centre	500	1 for 200 persons
4.	District Centre	880	1 for 300 persons

Source: UDPFI Guidelines, 1996

Distribution of Activities

The following activities are allowed in the hierarchy of Commercial Centres.

Table 6.16: Distribution on Commercial Activities

Hierarchy of Commercial Centres						
S. No.	**Activities**	**City or Sub-city Centre**	**District Centre**	**Comm-unity Centre**	**Neigh-bourhood Centre**	**Convenient Shopping Centre**
1.	Shopping (retail service, repair)	✓	✓	✓	✓	✓
2.	Limited wholesale	✓	✓	-	-	-
3.	Informal shopping	✓	✓	✓	✓	✓
4.	Commercial Offices	✓	✓	✓	✓	-
5.	Cinema	✓	✓	✓	-	-
6.	Hotel	✓	✓	✓	-	-
7.	Guest House	✓	✓	✓	-	-
8.	Bank/ATM	✓	✓	✓	✓	✓
9.	Nursing Home	✓	✓	✓	-	-
10.	Service Industries	✓	✓	✓	✓	✓

11.	Auditorium	✓	✓	✓	-	-
12.	Museum	✓	✓		-	-
13.	Library	✓	✓	✓	-	-
14.	Reading room	✓	✓	✓	✓	
15.	Science Centre, Art/Craft/Music/ Dance School	✓	✓	-	-	-
16.	Weekly markets	✓	✓	✓	✓	-
17.	Local Government Offices	✓	✓	✓	-	-
18.	Bas Terminal	✓	✓	-	-	-
19.	Fire Station	✓	✓	-	-	-
20.	Police post/station	✓	✓	-	-	-
21.	Telephone Exchange	✓	✓	-	-	-
22.	Electric sub station	✓	✓	✓	✓	✓
23.	Post office	✓	✓	✓		
24.	Petrol pump	✓	✓	✓		
25.	Convenience shopping centre	✓	✓	✓	✓	✓
26.	Essential Residential	✓	✓	-	-	-

Source: UDPFI Guidelines, 1996 and MPD 2021 (DDA,2007)

Fig. 6.71: Connaught Place—A Bird's Eye View: The character of commercial center like the Connaught Place changed over time with commercial activities having grown manifolds together with increasing demand of parking and services. Such areas need to be restoredto their pristine glory.

Mandis and Wholesale Markets

Small and medium towns hvae to give emphasis on the weekly markets, mandis and wholesale markets. Integration of the rural and small and medium towns can be achieved through the provision of Mandis.

According to the recommendations of the National Farmers Commission (2004), availability of regulated markets should be within 5 km radius (area served approx. 80 sq km). The agricultural produce can be categorised under two heads (a) Perishable produce consisting of fruits, vegetables and flowers and (b) Non-perishable produce consisting of grains and pulses. The planning for the mandis shall depend upon the following parameters:

- Number of food items
- Perishability of food items
- Volume to be handled
- Type of storage/ cold chain facilities.
- The mandis shall be preferably adjacent to arterial roads.

The government initiatives for promoting regulated markets are:

1. **Direct marketing** by promoting farmers' markets in various forms, such as Apni Mandis in Punjab, Rythu Bazaars in Andhra Pradesh, *Uzhavar Santhai* in Tamil Nadu and Shetkari Bazaar in Maharashtra, promoted by state agencies.
2. **E-trading:** Various states have adopted the Model APMC Act, which provides for e-trading.
3. **Terminal market complex:** proposed to be implemented through Public Private Partnership (PPP) mode by establishing the Hub (Main Market) and Spokes (Collection Centres) in the States who have amended their APMC Act.

Cremation / Burial Ground

Table 6.17: Norms for Cremation/ Burial Ground

S. No.	Category	Population served per unit	Min. Land Area Requirement
1.	Electric Crematorium	1 for large size towns	2.00 Ha
2.	Cremation Ground	5 lakh	2.50 Ha
3.	Burial Ground	5 lakh	4.00 Ha

Source: NBC, 2005.

Dhobi Ghats

Table 6.18: Norms for Dhobi Ghat

Category	Population served per unit	Min. Land Area Requirement
Dhobi Ghat with appropriate arrangements for water and drainage facilities. It may be ensured that the water bodies are not polluted as a result of such activities.	1 lakh	5000 sqm

Note: Mechanical laundry may be provided in basement of group housing, guest houses, hotels, hospitals, etc. with an area of 40 sq. m per 10 machines.

Communication Facilities

Table 6.19: Norms for Communication Facilities

S. No.		Category	Population served per unit	Area Requirement
1.		**Telephone and communications**		
	1a	Telephone exchange of 40,000 lines	4 lakh	4 Ha
	1b	Radio/TV Station	5-8 lakh	1,700 sqm
	1c	Remote subscriber unit	1 for 3 km radius	300 sqm
2.		**Postal**		
	2a	Post office counter without delivery (Floor area to be provided in local shopping centre)	15,000	85 sqm
	2b	Head post office with delivery office	2.5 Lakh	750 sqm
	2c	Head post office and administrative office	5 Lakh	2500 sqm
3.		**Banking**		
	3a	Bank with extension counters with ATM facility	15000	
	(i)	Floor area for counters		75 sqm
	(ii)	Floor area for ATM		6 sqm
	3b	Bank with locker, ATM and other banking facilities	1 lakh	2500 sqm

Source: NBC, 2005 and Study on Zoning Regulations, TCPO, 2004.

Circulation Network

The circulation pattern of a local area /sector must be designed so as to fit into the overall road pattern of the city. The road system should be such that no road within the sector can be used as a shortcut for a thoroughfare. The circulation system should give safe and easy access to residences, shops, schools, public buildings and recreational facilities. The peace of the sector must be preserved by avoiding traffic hazards, noise, glare, automobiles and pollution. The mass-transit system of the city should be so planned so that the buses, metro monorail, suburban trains, etc. run on the major traffic arteries and feeder streets, but not on the residential access streets of a sector. Special attention should be paid to silence and safety zoning. Cul-de-sac, loop streets and footpaths may be laid out to link residential areas with community facilities and to connect the sectors with one another so that cyclists may be free from the hazards of vehicular traffic.

In Transit Oriented Development, along the major transport corridors there is considerable mixing of residential and commercial uses on the edge of a sector. In order to eliminate the possibility of the misuse of residential areas along the edge of residential sectors, such plots should be pre-planned for institutional buildings, commercial, organised open spaces, socio-cultural facilities, services, parking, etc.

The internal road network of the sector should be detailed out with a view to discourage through traffic. Traffic other than public transport which does not have its origin and destination within the sector should not pass through the sector. The road network should have a clear hierarchy in terms of collector/distributor, access roads and pedestrian paths. The arterial and sub-arterial roads should form the boundaries of the sector and should not subdivide it. The road network should be designed keeping in view the segregation of vehicular traffic and pedestrian movement. Sub-arterial roads should form the boundaries of the sector and should not subdivide it. The width of a collector/distributor road should be 30 m and an access road can be 20 m or 12 m wide depending upon the expected traffic load. All pedestrian paths will have a minimum width of 1.5 m. As far as possible, intersections and Y-junctions should be avoided. Maximum use should be made of T-junctions. The junctions of collector/distributor roads with arterial/sub-arterial roads bounding the sector should be in the form of T-junctions. Staggered junction of arterial/sub-arterial road with the collector/distributor will discourage entry of external through traffic.

The distributor and collector roads within a sector must make separate provisions for cycle tracks. As far as possible, the cycle tracks should connect other sectors through underpasses, so as to enable the cyclists to move comfortably without obstacles. The road network should be detailed out keeping in mind the facility of serving the area with public transport buses.

Minimum spacing of junctions within the sector should be 300 m along the arterial and sub-arterial roads bounding the sector. Cross-sections of access roads should be designed with adequate provision for roadside parking. Geometric design details of roads, cross-sections, junctions and intersections, grade separators, along with associated details such as spacing, camber, gradients, super-elevations, turning radius, siting distance, widening on curbs, shoulders, median strips should adhere to IRC standards. Liberal use of cul-de-sacs should be made to enable the designing of open spaces with surrounding residential buildings undisturbed by vehicular movement. Parking areas should be provided in conformity with the standard road width and for next 2 decades. The width of the roads and streets and the number of traffic lanes should depend upon the anticipated volume of traffic during the peak hours projected for next 2 decades, and also composition of traffic. The following table shows the road standards as recommended by the Indian Roads Congress (I.R.C.):

Table 6.20: Road and Street Standards

Types of Road	*Right of Way*	*Number of Lanes*
Major road	25 m to 30 m	Two lanes to start with and four lanes ultimately
Neighbourhood road	14 m to 18 m	Two lanes
Residential street	9 m to 14 m	Two lanes
Cul-de-sac (not to exceed 180 m length)	8 m to 9 m	Two lanes
Loops	3 m to 5 m	As may be necessary
Service lane (to be provided in case of row housing).	5 m to 6 m	--do--
Cycle track	2 m to 3 m	--do--
Footpath	1.5 to 3 m	--do--

Source: Indian Roads Congress

Note: Footpaths of adequate width should be provided on the arterial roads, major roads and some of the sector roads. Cycle tracks may be provided along major roads.

Accessibility Standards

Recommendations for minimum and maximum distances to be covered for gaining access to schools, recreational areas, parks, shops and various public buildings in a residential sector made by the Committee of Plan Projects (COPP) are given below:

Table 6.21: Access Standards for Community Facilities

Community Facilities	**Suggested Walking Distance**
Nursery School	0.40 km
Primary School	0.40 to 0.60 km
Secondary School	0.80 to 1.60 km
Tot-lot	0.20 km
Children Park	0.40 to 0.50 km
Playground	0.80 to 1.60 km
Neighbourhood Park	0.80 to 1.60 km
Local Shopping	0.40 to 0.80 km
Health Centre	0.80 to 1.60 km

Source: Committee of Plan Projects, Govt. of India

Principles of Road Designing

1. Safety: Roads should be safe for users, which should have slow zone for pedestrians and in smaller roads, entire roads can be slow zone.
2. Mobility: Larger roads can have mobility zones for faster vehicle movement. They should be physically separated from slower zones for pedestrians and cycle tracks. Dedicated bus lanes are an added advantage.
3. Pedestrian Accessibility: All streets need to have continuous footpaths or safe shared spaces with minimal grade differences. These should have adequate clear width for pedestrian movement.
4. Liveability: Elements such as tree lines, landscaping, and furniture enhances a street's slow zone, creating space for relaxation, vending, and other activities.
5. Sensitivity to Local Context: Street design should factor on local street activities, patterns of pedestrian movement, and nearby land uses.
6. Creative Use of Street Space: for example, the width occupied by a parking lane can accomodate occasional bulb-outs for street vending or street furniture.

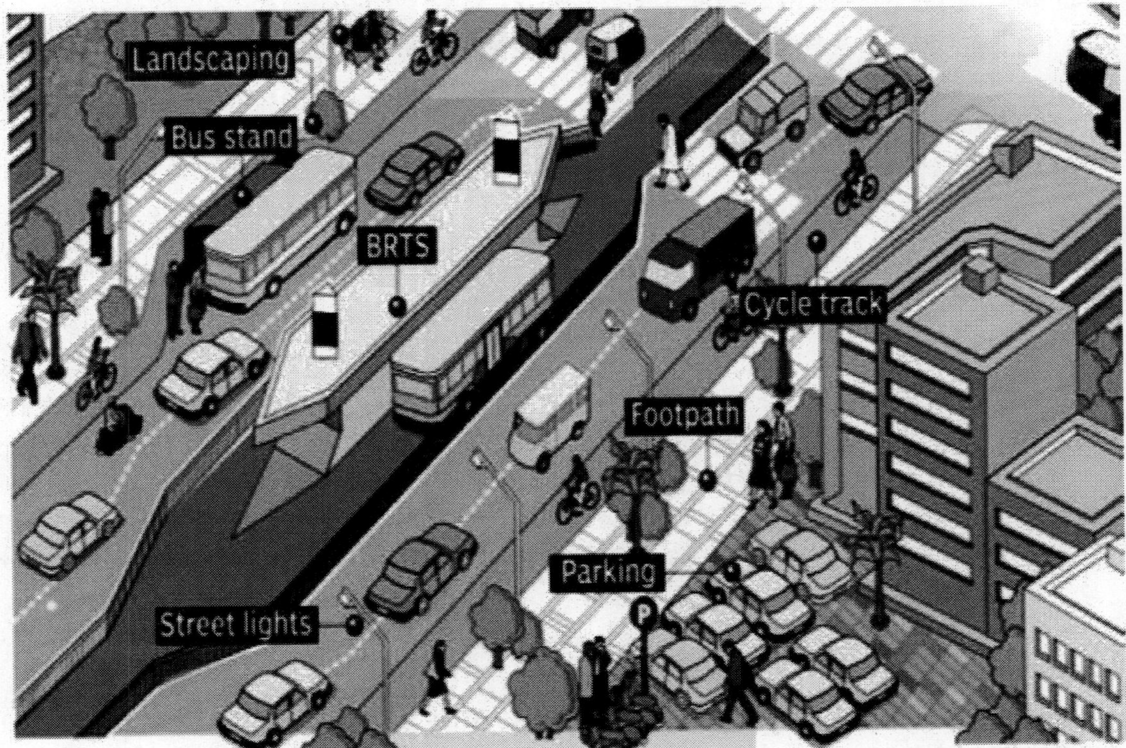

Fig. 6.77: Elements of Street Design are the footpaths, cycle tracks, carriageway, storm water drainage, Bus Rapid Transit System, bus stop, street vendors, pedestrian crossing, underground utility, street furniture, median, service lane, trafic calming elements, parking, landscaping and street lights. Priority of transport mode is determined on the basis of emission, capacity and cost.

Source: DUAC/Amit Ghosal, Punjabi Bagh Ward No. 103, New Delhi

Transit Oriented Development (TOD) Norms

With the introduction of public transit system such as BRT and metro, the cities in India have opened up the potential for the compact and smart growth. In Delhi, the MPD 2021 recognizes 500-m-wide belt on both sides of the MRTS/Major Transport Corridor as influence Zone or TOD Zone. The norms recommend that the entire scheme will be included in the zone if more than 70% of the plan area falls inside the Influence Zone. The norms recognize that higher FAR and heights can be availed through the preparation and approval of a comprehensive integrated scheme.

The Master Plan TOD policy recognizes high density, FAR and mixed use development. The policy focuses on shorter commutes and travel time and to bring about equity for all sections of society. The policy promotes efficient use of land in TOD zones, maximizes the population holding capacity and prevents low density development.

Densification through redevelopment and infill within existing brownfields is to be prioritized over development in the greenfields. The policy advocates maximum permissible FAR and densities in various TODs to be based on the capacity of public transport modes, circulation networks and the physical infrastructure thresholds of the area.

In the Transit Oriented Development (TOD) Zone, the following development control norms shall apply:

(i) TOD norms of FAR and density may be availed through the preparation and approval of comprehensive integrated scheme of minimum 1 Ha with maximum ground coverage of 40%. In case of MRTS/Government Agencies, the minimum plot size for development shall be 3000 sq.m., but all other development norms shall apply.

(ii) Cluster Block approval may be given for a minimum area of 3000 sq.m. only if an approved influence zone plan or integrated scheme for the area exists.

(iii) For an integrated scheme, a maximum FAR of 400 and a maximum density of 2000 persons per hectare (PPH) is permissible. The entire amalgamated plot will be considered for calculating the FAR and density. FAR utilization shall not be less than 400. Mandatory EWS FAR of 15% over and above the maximum permissible FAR shall be applicable. Additional FAR may be availed through TDR only for schemes larger than 1 Ha.

(iv) All residents residing in that scheme area shall have to be accommodated within the same scheme, with no induced displacement of existing residential population.

In all TOD schemes, a minimum of 30% of overall FAR shall be mandatory for Residential use, a minimum 10% of FAR for commercial use, 20% for greens/parks and minimum 10% of FAR for community facilities. Mix of uses and FAR utilization for the remaining 50% FAR shall be as per the land use category designated in the Zonal Plan.

The Informal/Un-organised Sector

Scholars have given various definitions of the informal or unorganized sector. The following criteria have often been used in identifying the informal or the unorganized sector using the data from secondary sources :

(a) The household based activities as identified by the Census and the National Sample Survey (NSS) or the 'own account enterprises' as defined by NSS may be taken to comprise the sector.

(b) 'Own account enterprises' and 'non-directory establishments less than six workers, may be taken to constitute the organized sector. As per this classification scheme, all public sector units, directory enterprises that employ six or more workers and the industries registered under the Factories Act, 1948 are treated as components of the organized sector.

(c) The units covered under the programme of collection of Employment Exchanges may be considered as belonging to the organized sector. Under EMI, the Director General of Employment and Training compiles data on units employing 10 or more workers. Unorganized sector may then be defined as a residual category.

(d) The units not recovered by formal legal stipulation and, therefore, not maintaining or submitting regular accounts to any government agency can be taken to constitute the unorganized sector, as stipulated by CSO. This implies that the manufacturing and repair units registered under the Factories Act, 1948, for which data are tabulated systematically by the Annual Survey of Industries would form the unorganized sector. In the sectors like, trade, hotels and restaurants, storage and warehousing services, all non-public operating units constitute the unorganized segment on consideration of non-availability of regular accounts of their activity.

Informal Sector activities are usually grouped into the following broad categories:

1. Petty Trade and Vending (such as vegetable / Fruit Seller, Feriwala, Tailor, Salesman, etc.)
2. Transport (Rickshaw Puller, Auto-rickshaw Driver, Bus Conductor, Bus and Taxi Driver, Truck Driver, etc.)
3. Services (such as cobbler, domestic servant, cycle and rickshaw repairing, sweeper, cycle repairing, mechanic, peon, home guard, watchman, barber, porter, etc.)
4. Factory / Manufacturing/ Construction (Binder, Carpenter, Labour, Electrician, Plumber, Painter, Machine Operator, Blacksmith, etc.)
5. Casual Labour - Daily Wage Labour
6. Domestic Workers; It is estimated that there are 90 million unorganized domestic servants in India. (Jeanne Devos)

Street Vendors

The National Policy on Urban Street Vendors, 2009 defines Street Vendor as 'a person who offers goods or services for sale to the public in a street without having a permanent built up structure'. The three basic categories of street vendors are a) Stationary, b) Peripatetic and c) Mobile.

As per Street Vending Act, 2014: "Street Vendor" means a person engaged in vending of articles, goods, wares, food items or merchandise of everyday use or offering services to the general public, in a street, lane, side walk, footpath, pavement, public park or any other public place or private area, from a temporary built up structure or by moving from place to place and includes hawker, peddler, squatter and all other synonym terms which may be local or region specific; and the words "street vending" with their grammatical variations and cognate expressions, shall be construed accordingly.

"Vending zone" means an area or a place or a location designated as such by the local authority, on the recommendations of the town vending committee, for the specific use by street vending and includes footpaths, side walk, pavement, embankment, portions of a street, waiting area for public or any such place considered suitable for vending activities and providing services to the general public.

Street vendors as per the National Policy for Urban Street Vendors, constitute about 2 per cent, or 8 million of India's urban population, who support a rising number of the urban poor with their cheap meals and wares. A study by National Alliance of Street Vendors of India (NASVI 2000) estimates that 30 per cent of Mumbai's workforce has at least one meal a day from hawkers, with an average middle income Mumbai household buying around Rs. 1500 worth of goods from them. In Kolkata 82 per cent people buy vegetables from vendors, as do 83 per cent in Bangalore. According to various estimates, Mumbai had about 200,000 hawkers at the turn of the decade, which is now variously estimated to be around 400,000, while the Supreme Court (SC) puts the number in Delhi at about 3,00,000.

Writing about home-based enterprises and hawkers in Delhi, Surbaya and Pretoria, Graham Tipple concludes that "they should be accorded more attention by policy makers - not to control them, but to find ways of cooperating with entrepreneurs to assist them to be effective and efficient". Other reasons why cities need vendors on streets and not in designated food courts is because hawkers are the eyes of the street and prevent violent crime. Our city roads are safer because of them.

Norms for Informal Sector and Street Vendors

A survey conducted by the Directorate of Economics and Statistics in Delhi on unorganized trading activity in Delhi estimated the total number of unorganized trading activity in Delhi as 2 lakh and the number of persons employed around 3.18 lakhs. The contribution of this sector in terms of gross value added to the economy of Delhi was estimated at Rs. 1.01 lakh per enterprise per annum. Broadly about one third of the city GDP is contributed by the unorganized/ informal sector, which also provides about two-thirds of jobs.

Large sections of unemployed and under employed population look forward for self-employment in the informal sector. They bring forth multitude of small enterprises, petty trading and casual labour. As such there is a parallel economy in the form of informal sector. This vernacular and disorganized sector with highly reduced needs of space, services and investments is a major source of employment in the economic fabric of a city. Realising this fact, the Master Plan for Delhi-2021 has adopted the following multi-pronged approach to cater to this sector:

- Earmarking of 'Hawking' and 'No Hawking' zones. Specific areas be marked for stationary and mobile street vendors by the concerned local authority. Reservation of 10 percent of space for street vendors, hawkers, etc. in every shopping centre.
- The existing prominent weekly markets/haat to be identified and replanned.
- New areas for informal trade in form of Janta markets, repair shops and workshops be developed and provided with basic amenities in housing, commercial, institutional and industrial area.
- Provision of common basic services, like solid waste disposal, urinals/toilets, water point and lighting.
- Institutionalising this sector by adopting mandatory norms of space for hawkers/vendors.
- To evolve innovative designs of stalls, push-carts and mobile vans of various sizes and with cleaning facilities.

Table 6.23: Norms for Informal Units for Street Vendors

Sr. No.	Category	No. of Informal Units
1.	Retail Trade	3 to 4 units per 10 formal shops
1a.	Central Business District	
1b.	Sub-Central Business District	
1c.	District Centre	
1d.	Community Centre	
1e.	Convenience Shopping Centre	
2.	Government and Commercial Offices	5 to 6 units per 100 employees
3.	Wholesale Trade and Freight Complexes	3-4 units per 10 formal shops
4.	Hospital	3-4 units per 100 beds
5.	Bus Terminal	1 unit per 2 bus bays
6.	School	
6a.	Primary	3-4 units
6b.	Secondary/Senior Secondary/Integrated	5-6 units
7.	Parks	
7a.	Regional/District Parks	8-10 units at each major entry
7b.	Neighbourhood Parks	2-3 units
8.	Residential	1 unit/1000 population
9.	Industrial	5-6 units per 1000 employees
10.	Railway terminal	To be based on surveys at the time of preparation of the project

Source: UDPFI Guidelines, 1996.

Demarcation of Vending Zones

City/ Town Development Plan shall demarcate the zones as 'Restriction free vending zones', 'Restricted Vending Zones' and 'No vending zones' as per the following guidelines:

(a) Spatial planning should take into account the natural prospersity of street vendors by providing locations in response to the patterns of demand for their goods/ services. For this, competent institutions recommend photographic digitised surveys of street vendors and their locations.

(b) A policy for regulating entry of street vendors into the identified street vending zones on time sharing basis shall be formulated by Municipal Authorities.

(c) The 'vendor markets' may be established at suitable locations keeping in view demand for the wares/ services of street vendors. Time restrictions on vending should be in accordance with the need for ensuring non-congestion of public spaces/ maintaining public hygiene without being ad hoc, arbitrary or discriminatory. Attempts should be made to provide ample parking areas for mobile vendors for security of their vehicles and wares at night on payment of suitable fees.

(d) Mobile vending should be permitted in all areas even outside the 'Vendors Markets', unless designated as 'No vending zone' in the zonal, local area or layout plans. 'Restricted Vending zones' may be notified in terms of both location and time. Locations designated as 'No vending zones' shall be fully justified.

Provision of Civic facilities

The following basic civic facilities shall be provided in Vending Zones/ Vendor's markets:

(a) Solid waste disposal

(b) Public toilets to maintain cleanliness

(c) Aesthetic design of mobile stalls/ push carts

(d) Electricity

(e) Drinking water

(f) Protective covers to protect wares of street vendors as well as themselves from heat, rain, dust, etc.

(g) Storage facilities including cold storage for specific goods like fish, meat and poultry, and

(h) Parking areas

The vendor markets should to the extent possible, also provide for crèches, toilets and restrooms for female and male members.

For other aspects of the street vending norms such as organisation and participatary processes, promotional measures, action plan for stakeholders, monitoring and review, etc. the provisions of the policy shall be referred to as updated from time to time.

Repair Shops/ Workshops

On an average, the rate of growth of vehicles in Indian cities is twice the rate of their population growth. The number of vehicles per 15000 population in Delhi is around 5000 (1500 cars, 3000 two wheelers & 500 other vehicles. On an average 50% of these need vehicles servicing/repair, i.e. 2500 vehicles once in a month per 15,000 population. As such about 20 lakh vehicles in Delhi every month need repair and servicing. At an average of 200 vehicles per workshop there are nearly 20,000 automobile repair establishments operating in the city. In some areas specialised markets for automobile repair have come up. Most of the workshops tend to locate in areas of maximum traffic, e.g. adjacent to bus terminals, commercial centres, main roads, highways, adjacent to flyovers, industrial areas, open parking areas, fruit and vegetable markets and densely populated area. About 50% of the petty repair shops are running within the road right of way who pay tehbazari to the MCD (Rs. 30 to 45/- for an area of 6' × 4', 3' × 5' or 3' × 4').

Conventionally the Service and Repair shops/ workshop are permitted only in commercial centre, petrol pumps and industrial use. However, these have not been adequate, nor economically viable for the small business. As such, the proliferation of unplanned automobile repair shops causing traffic and environmental problems continues. Besides lack of provision of service/repair shops in the commercial centres and their non-affordability, the growth of unauthorised repair shops, within the road right of ways and on public lands could not be checked.

Mandatory norms are necessary for provision of at least 10% of industrial and commercial areas for service and repair shops. In all commercial centres in order to meet the shortfall, 10% of space should be reserved for repair shops/ workshops and some of the local shopping areas may be redesigned for repair and service shops and ancillary facilities like motor parts shops, etc. The average area of repair shop may be 15 to 30 sq. mts. with common open space for repairs @7.5 to 15 sq. mts./shop. Informal repair shop area may be average 2.16 sq. mts. (1.8 X 1.2 m) with provisions for disposal of solid waste, metallic oil, paints, and liquid wastes, lighting, signage and noise control. Informal repair shops can also be provided in large parking areas.

Dairies and Resettlement of Cattle

Dairies are scattered all over the urban areas in a haphazard manner causing insanitary conditions and traffic congestion. Because of their incompatibility within the urban areas, it is essential to resettle these dairies in suitable areas in the outskirts of the city for improving the environment. Milch cattle from the urban area should be shifted to the dairy colonies at suitable places.

There are about 3 lakh cattle in Delhi, as estimated by the MCD and Director (Animal Husbandry), GNCTD. Out of these, approximately 35,000 cattle (cows/buffaloes) are in 281 unauthorized dairy colonies in urban areas and approximately 40,000 cattle are in the authorized dairy colonies. In addition there are about 180,000 cattle in rural areas of Delhi.

Lessons can be drawn from the experience of the shifting of dairies in Amritsar and Kolkata. In Amritsar, due to the unhealthy conditions and the location of dairies within the urban areas, few sites were selected for locating 2133 dairies consisting of 33000 cattle in an area of 136 acres in the outskirts. The frontage of the plot was kept at a multiple of 25 feet so that shed could be built in half of the rear portion of plot and remaining half could be utilized for outdoor feeding and resting of the cattle. In order to avoid choking of drains, services like sewerage, surface drainage and water supply plans were prepared and implemented. For disposal of dung and waste, adequate space was provided for installing a biogas plant. Plot area per cattle and facilities and services had been worked out as per BSI Norms. Collection centres for the collection of milk and distribution network for the supply of milk was done through a centralized agency/co-operative society.

In Kolkata, the growth of cattle created number of problems in the city with regard to environment, health, traffic, drainage, sewerage, etc. In order to create a healthy living environment, the khatas (cow sheds) were resettled on the urban fringes at Ganganagar, Garden Reach (north) and East Kolkata. The cattle resettlement site at Ganganagar is about 25 kilometers away from Kolkata. The project area is well connected by the road and the Railway Station is not very far. Attempts were made to incorporate updated infrastructure within resettled area. Space was provided for the construction of gobar gas plants to utilize cattle dung to generate gas. Total area acquired for the purpose of resettlement of 3,000 cattle was about 19.62 acres (26 sq. m. per cattle). Garden Reach (North) cattle schemes is close to the water treatment plant at Garden Reach. The area of the land is about 24 acres. Around the site there are villages and agricultural land for grazing. Instead of milk reception unit, a milk chilling plant was installed in the site. The sullage water is discharged to an artificial lake closeby, after proper treatment in a resettling tank. The cattle resettlement at East Kolkata was developed alongwith the area development programme of East Kolkata Township.

Standards for Livestock/Cattle

In order to ensure primary economic activities and food security, sustainable development of agricultural sector and associated activities is necessary. Livestock management and addressing the problem of street animals calls for a dedicated space.

The National Livestock Policy, 2013 provides a policy framework for improving productivity of the livestock sector in a sustainable manner taking into account the provisions of the National Policy of Farmers, 2007 and the recommendations of the stakeholders, including the States. The policy recommends the following with respect to urban and regional planning:

1. Inclusive planning of livestock management services such as veterinary institutions, vaccine and diagnostic production units, semen stations and artificial insemination breeding farms, feed and fodder production units, etc. at regional and community level for generation and delivery of these services in rural and urban areas.
2. Integrated land use planning with livestock as a component should be encouraged through Panchayati Raj Institutions to ensure production potential of pastures and grazing community lands.

Along with the livestock management, adequate provisions for street animals shall also be planned for by provision of animal management centres in the villages, urban and regional areas. The other facilities to be provided here are:

- Veterinary facilities and hospitals
- Gaushala with primary milk packaging facilities

- Bio-degradable solid waste disposal and decomposition facilities
- Biogas plants
- Open/green spaces and nurseries
- Essential residential spaces.

Debriefing and Review

1. Write short notes on the following:
   (a) Master Plan/City Development Plan
   (b) Zonal Plan
   (c) Sub-city Plan
   (d) Hierarchy of Urban Areas
   (e) Urban Design
   (f) Environmental Planning
2. Explain the concept of sector, neighbourhood and community planning.
3. Write short notes on the following:
   (a) Land use vis-a-vis density and FAR
   (b) Norms and standards for various community facilities
   (c) Planning of Greens/Open Space/Parks
   (d) Local Area Plan
   (e) Provisions for informal sector, street vendors, etc.
4. How rejuvenation of water bodies can be done by town planning?
5. Explain the relevance and process of Urban Renewal.
6. How would you undertake the planning of an urban village?
7. Write a note or slum rehabilitation.
8. Write short notes on:
   (i) Hierarchy of Commercial Facilities
   (ii) Principles of Road Design
   (iii) Transit Oriented Development
9. Explain why norms and standards for social infrastructure are necessary and how these are worked out?

CHAPTER

7

Zoning Regulations and Development/Building Controls

Zoning regulations and development controls are emerging as the new legal tools for guiding the sustainable use of land, promoting inclusive development and also for hassle free acquisition/ assembly of land. In the present scenario, when private sector has an enhanced role in urban development, zoning regulations have assumed an important role.

Zoning regulations are legel tools for guiding the use of land including, placement, size of buildings, circulation. services requirements, parking and protection of public health, welfare and safety. Zoning was developed as a tool to protect residential environment from polluting and noise generating industrial and commercial activities and to secure good living conditions.

Objectives of Zoning Regulations

- To promote quality of life by organizing the most appropriate development of land in accordance with the development policies and the land use proposals contained therein.
- To provide regulations for development of a particular area to serve the desired purpose efficiently and to preserve its character.
- To regulate land use in hazard prone areas to minimise the damage caused by natural hazards, viz. earthquakes, cyclonic storms, landslides, floods, etc.
- To define use of premises/property and limitations upon shape, size and type of buildings that are constructed or occupy the land. These provide both horizontal as well as vertical use of land.
- To preserve the "character" of a community.

Purpose of Zoning Regulations

- Orderly development consistent with utility, location/capacity, street network, public services.

- To protect residential areas from the harmful invasion of commercial and industrial uses.
- To promote business and industry by providing planned and orderly development of areas.
- To ensure continued and adequate supply of water and other services and facilities, such as sewerage, transportation, schools and parks.
- Economic development (planned commercial and industrial areas), compatibility of land use, quality neighbourhoods and their stability.
- Preservation of property investments and city's tax base.
- Community aesthetics and development quality.
- Protection of "sensitive" land uses (e.g. schools, churches, hospitals, water supply and other environmental resources, historic/cultural sites).
- Management of land use transitions/evolution over time.
- To ensure the safety and well being of the citizens.

Types of Zoning

There are numerous types of zoning techniques for better site design, including open space residential design (OSRD), watershed-based zoning, overlay zoning, floating zones, incentive zoning, performance zoning, urban growth boundaries, large lot zoning, infill/ community redevelopment, transfer of development rights, and limiting infrastructure extensions. The table below describes each of these zoning techniques.

Table 7.1: Zoning Regulations and Land Use Planning Techniques

Land Use Planning/Zoning Regulations	Description
Open Space Residential Design	A method of planning residential development that conserves open space in a new subdivision.
Watershed-Based Zoning	Watershed and sub-watershed boundaries are the foundation for land use planning.
Overlay Zoning	Superimposes additional regulations or specific development criteria within specific mapped districts.
Impervious Overlay Zoning	Specific overlay zoning that limits total imperviousness within mapped districts.
Floating Zones	Applies a special zoning district without identifying the exact location until land owner specifically requests.
Incentive Zoning	Applies bonuses or incentives to encourage creation of amenities or environmental protection.
Performance Zoning	Specifies a performance requirement that accompanies a zoning district.
Urban Growth Boundaries	Establish a growth limit and where agricultural or rural land is to be preserved.

Large Lot Zoning	Land subdivision at very low densities.
Infill/Community Redevelopment	Encourages new development and redevelopment within existing developed areas.
Transfer of Development Rights (TDRs)	Transfers potential development from a designated "sending area" to a designated "receiving area."

Land Use/Activity Control

"Land Use Plan" is ideally made on the basis of in-depth analysis of urban activities, social and physical infrastructure. Designations for the use of land are provided in a master plan or a zonal plan, which usually intend to ensure the following:

- Transportation Flow
- Economic Development
- Historic Preservation
- Recreational Space/Parks
- Environmental/Wildlife Protection
- Businesses and residential communities.

Accessibility is the key of land-use. Businesses are more suitable downtown while manufacturing centers are most accessible for shipping at an interstate or a port. When designing residential developments, planners generally focus on developing close to or directly above commercial areas. These form a broad zoning for the city.

The lifeline of an urban area is flow of transportation. Before any development can happen, there must be an infrastructure suitable to the needs of future growth. Infrastructure includes sewer, water, electricity, roads and floodwater management. The master plan of any urban region has the potential for guiding growth in a way that will generate a fluid movement of people and commerce, especially in emergency situations. Public investment through taxes and fees is the cornerstone for developing an infrastructure.Most major urban centers have been around for a long time. Preserving the history and aesthetics of earlier developments within a city creates a more livable space and can boost tourism in the area.

Tourism and liveability are also boosted by growing the city around major parks and recreation areas. Water, mountains and open parks offer citizens an escape from the city's hub of activity. National parks and wildlife sanctuaries are perfect examples of preservation and conservation.

One of the most essential parts of any plan is the ability to provide citizens with an equal opportunity. Communities cut off from urban centers by railroads, interstate or natural boundaries have difficulty in accessing employment. When planning for development and the use of land, special attention must be given to lower-income housing projects. Mixing housing for various income levels provides increased opportunities for lower income families.

Transfer of Development Rights

Transfer of development rights, or TDR, is a certificate from the city administration that the owner of a property gets for developing public utilities such as parks, schools and hospitals. Under the TDR policy, builders are compensated in kind if they surrender some of their land to the government for public purposes, such as widening a road, creating a park or for slum rehabilitation. These rights can be sold to other builders or can be used for development by the builder himself in the suburbs in lieu of the plot that he has surrendered. TDR is a powerful tool that when used in the right manner works to revitalize existing city centres and neighborhoods, preserves historic landmarks, provides opportunities for low-income housing, reduces the burden on limited infrastructure capacity and encourages land use patterns that promote a better quality of urban living.

Advantages of TDR

- TDR programs compensate property owners: Local governments use TDR programs to mitigate the economic impact of land use regulations, specifically to compensate land owners for perceived partial takings. This planning tool offers land owners a way to recapture some lost economic value when a property is downzoned from residential use to green agricultural use or for preservation purpose.
- TDR programs are an easier way to implement zoning: TDR programs do not replace zoning, but make strong land use regulations more politically feasible and easier to implement. Local officials feel less political pressure if landowners are compensated for their "lost" rights. A well-constructed TDR program reduces the demand for zoning variances, since developers will use the market, not their connections to the local zoning commission, to secure additional development rights.
- TDR programs provide private funding for protection: Finding public funds to protect open space and historic buildings is increasingly difficult as governments carefully watch their bottom lines. One reason local governments created TDR programs was to leverage market monies to achieve such goals.
- TDR programs make development more predictable: Developers benefit from the clarity and consistency that TDR programs offer. Instead of incurring the costs and risks of negotiating for variances, developers can exceed certain zoning regulations simply by purchasing development rights from other property owners.
- TDR programs are more permanent than zoning: Since TDR uses deed restrictions or conservation easements to sever and extinguish development rights, public values such as open space and historic buildings are permanently protected. In contrast, zoning rules can change over time and with new administration.

Incentive Zoning

Incentive zoning allows developers more FAR and density in exchange of community improvements. An increase in density encourages high density development supportive of compact development. In exchange, the developer would be encouraged to include some community improvements in their projects. Community improvements may include additional open space, affordable housing, special building features, or public art.

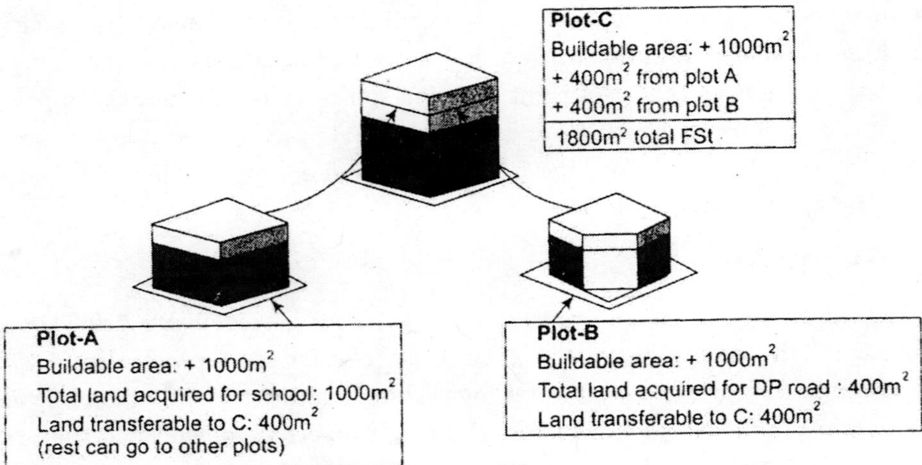

Fig. 7.1: The Concept of Transferable Development Right

Process of Incentive Zoning

1. **Assemble stakeholders.** Get ideas for incentives from the people who will be using them. Stakeholders should also help determine the target areas for incentive zoning. This group may include:
   - Builders, developers, and real estate business owners, local officials.
   - State officials.
   - Schools, colleges and universities.
   - Local residents, neighborhood groups, civic groups, and non-profits.
   - utility providers (electricity, gas, phone, wi-fi, sewer/water)
2. **Determine the specifics of the incentive zone.**
   - Areas for new higher density development,
   - Benefits provided by the developers in exchange for the density increase
   - Enhancement of the infrastructure in the incentive zone
   - To determine the right type of incentive (i.e. housing unit allowance, FAR increase,etc.)
3. **Determine what community benefits the developer in each area should provide.**
   - Lack of parks or affordable housing units
   - Sidewalks or street lighting

- Small businesses with mixed-use buildings or live-work units

4. **Amend planning documents such as zoning ordinance and comprehensive plan.**
   - Establish an overlay zoning district for a quality growth and prepare incentive zoning.

Incentive/Inclusionary Zoning

- Inclusionary zoning, also known as incentive zoning, refers to municipal planning ordinances that require a given share of new construction to be affordable by people with low to moderate incomes.
- Inclusionary zoning is becoming a common tool for local municipalities to help provide a wider range of housing options than the market provides on its own.
- The term inclusionary zoning indicates that these ordinances seek to counter exclusionary zoning practices, which aim to exclude low-cost housing from a municipality through the zoning code.
- The mix of "affordable housing" and "market-rate" housing in the same neighborhood is seen as beneficial by many.
- Inclusionary Zoning is a way for the public and the private sectors to share the responsibility for providing affordable housing to all.

Strengths of Incentive Zoning

- Shifts some of the burden for providing affordable housing from the public sector to the private sector.

Weakness of Incentive Zoning

- Where mandatory programs are not possible, incentive programs may have limited effectiveness.
- Requires significant amount of administrative oversight
- Can increase the cost of market rate units

Prerequisite Tools: Zoning Ordinance, Functional Plan (Housing)

White Zoning

The White Zoning had been introduced by the Urban Redevelopment Authority (URA) Singapore. It allows for the development of a variety of different uses like commercial, residential and hotel within the zone. The White Zoning gives the market greater flexibility and creativity in planning for developments that provide a mix of uses like residential and retail.

Planned Unit Development (PUD)

Planned Unit Development (PUD) is a tool municipalities use to encourage or require flexibility, creativity, and innovation in the planning and design of development to achieve a variety of objectives. A PUD may include varied and compatible land uses, such as housing, recreation, and commercial centers within one defined development or subdivision. PUD can be used to encourage certain types of development, based on goals and objectives in the municipal plan. Development can range from affordable housing to certain forms of development such as transit-oriented or traditional neighborhood design, PUD provisions are often intended to convey benefits to developer in the form of higher densities, lower development costs and reduced infrastructure costs.

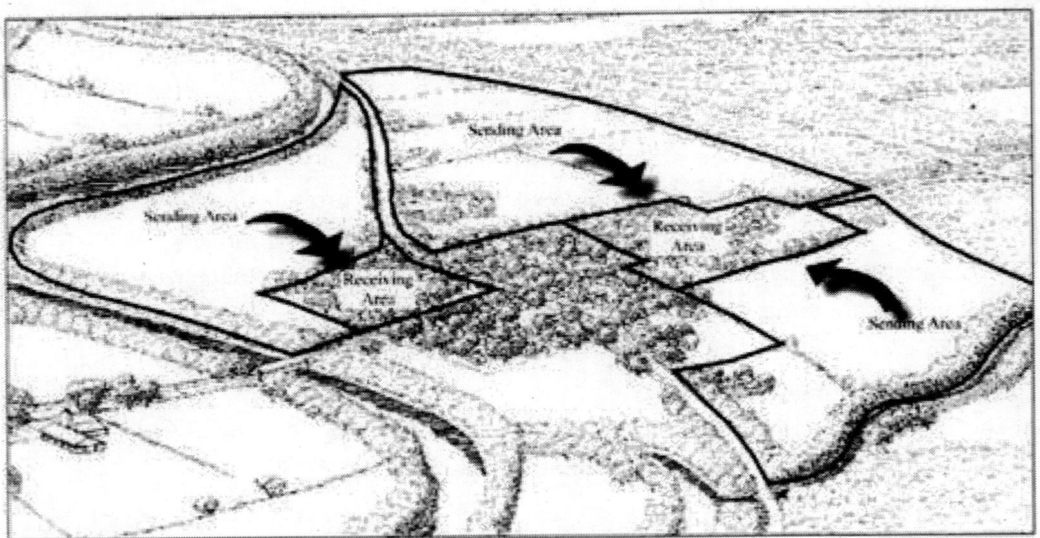

Fig. 7.2: PUDs are normally used to shift the permitted density from one portion of a property to a smaller area to enable more efficient and concentrated development on a single parcel of land.

Role of Planned Unit Development (PUD)

- To accommodate the planning and development of "new communities" that include a variety of uses, densitites, and building styles such as garden apartments, town houses, and single-family houses.
- To encourage clustered development, open space protection, and an overall low density of residential development
- PUDs are increasingly used in rural setting to protect farmland and open space
- To promote compact, pedestrian-oriented, mixed-use development
- To provide affordable housing
- Flexibilty in site design for design of buildings, parking and circulation, open areas
- For efficient use of public facilites and infrastructure
- To promote energy-efficient forms of development
- Preservation of natural areas
- Quality site planning and design

Fig. 7.3: PUDs can be created to encourage compact, mixed-use neighbourhoods, where private homes and public amenities are part of a single master plan

There are three types of PUDs :

1. Residential PUDs
2. Non-Residential PUDs
3. Mixed Use PUDs

1. **Residential PUDs—**Planned Residential Development encourages mix of housing types and promote a more pedestrian-oriented neighbourhood design that incorporates moderate to high densities of development, street, trees, side-walks and parks
2. **Non-residential PUDs—**Non-residential PUDs include commercial centers and industrial parks. It emphasises compact layout and design, a pedestrian scale of development, urban streetscapes with pedestrian amenities, high-quality landscaping, and shared, unobtrusive parking areas. It can also be used to promote a more "campus" style of development with consistent design elements, landscaping, dispersed parking and loading facilities, public transit facilities, employee amenities such as recreational and community facilities, and to minimize physical and visual impacts to neighboring properties and uses.

3. **Mixed Use PUDs**—It is most common use of PUDs for integrated mix of residential and non-residential uses at moderate to higher densities of development.

Overlay Zoning

Overlay zoning ordinance is made to protect particular natural or cultural features, such as historic districts, steep slopes, waterfronts, scenic views, agricultural areas, aquifer recharge area, wetlands, watersheds, or downtown residential enclaves.

Overlay zones build on the underlying zoning by establishing additional or stricter standards and criteria; the standards of the overlay zone apply in addition to those of the underlying zoning district. Overlay zoning can be an effective tool for communities to use in protecting specific resources from development pressures. For example, an overlay zone can be instituted for a specific neighborhood to preserve its character and design by encouraging new construction, and additions to existing buildings, that are compatible with the neighborhood's building types and character. An overlay zone can also be designated in areas to promote mixed-use development, such as near community centers. Additionally, municipalities can use overlay zones in existing low density, single use areas to encourage mixed-use or higher density development. An overlay zone may be used near a certain intersection or street which is served by transit, in order to increase the amount of housing to support that transit corridor. Overlay zones could also be used to allow affordable housing as a use by right in areas selected by the community, regardless of the current zoning.

Potential Uses of Overlay Zoning

- Create a walkable community,
- Connect pathways
- Preserve/enhance a special district
- Encourage economic development
- Preserve/enhance the character
- Protect quality of surface water
- Protect groundwater quality and quantity
- Manage stormwater
- Preserve forestry integrity
- Preserve sensitive area/wildlife habitat
- Protect aesthetics of the natural environment
- Preserve farmlands

District zoning overlay is prepared for the following issues:

1. To guide new development and redevelopment along the arterials, highway corridors by designating permitted uses.
2. To establish enhanced standards for the design, appearance and placement of building and other site improvements, landscaping, utilities, lighting, fences and screening.

3. To create a desirable transportation corridor ideal for travelers and also serving as a source of retail, entertainment, dining and employment opportunities for residents and visitors
4. To protect residential neighbourhoods
5. Hardscape and landscape features with combination of grass, ground cover, berms,trees, shrubs or other native and drought-tolerant vegetation selected by local feedback
6. To enhance right of way.
7. To promote excellence in land use and the image of built and natural environment
8. To establish higher standards for landscaping, building design, site design and other development requirements for property along highway.
9. To improve the visual impression of the community
10. To provide safe pedestrian connections between parking areas and buildings

Floating Zone

Floating Zoning is a zoning tool, which involves the creation of a zoning district that defines a use, such as an office, mixed use, reuse of a vacant mill, or attached housing. The floating zone is a zoning district, which does not have any specific geographic relationship at the time of adoption, and can only be used in conjunction with a Master Plan. A "floating" zone is a zoning district that is described in the zoning ordinance but "floats" over the community, with no land assigned tot he district. The floating zone is not assigned to any particular location, until the zoning map is amended by an application for rezoning. Such a zone then provides flexibility to both developers and elected officials in determining the most appropriate locations for uses.

Strengths of Floating Zoning

- Provides flexibility in the location of uses.
- Allows scrutiny of the location of a use throughout the rezoning process
- Considers current conditions when determining uses to be permitted.

Weakness of Floating Zoning

- No enabling legislation exists
- Failure to allow rezoning to the floating zone may result in exclusion of a use
- Cannot depend upon initial proposal to be built.
- Cannot place conditions upon the approval of the rezoning.

Exclusive Agricultural Zoning

The goal of exclusive agricultural zoning is to protect and preserve agricultural land and farming. The exclusion of other uses from the district is intended to limit conversion of prime farmland to non-agricultural use and to prevent conflicts between farm and other uses. Agricultural and non-agricultural uses, especially residential uses, can have negative impact on each other.

Strenght of Exclusive Agricultural Zoning

- A straightforward approach to protecting agriculture and prime farmland.

Weakness of Exclusive Agricultural Zoning

- Requires extremely strong farm economy and relatively low development pressures,often difficult to obtain political support for enactment in communities that do not meet this requirement.
- Provides limited options for use of parcels within the districts that have poor soils,too small or oddly shaped for farming; therefore district boundaries should be delineated with care.

Urban Design Controls

A city is reflected by the development happened in it by periods of the assemblage of buildings, streets, system of communication and utilities, places of work, transportation, leisure and meeting places. The developed and preservation of its urban form needs urban design controls for holistic development. Urban Design guidelines are used to control the form of the built environment. They help in preserving, developing and maintaining the aesthetic quality of urban and environmental design. The urban design control instrument is only a part of the broad spectrum of urban design theory that deals mainly with the process of managing and controlling the implementation of the urban design in actual practice. The following aspects need to be considered to arrive at the basic for policies affecting the urban fabric:

1. Areas of significance in built environment
2. Visual integration of the city
3. Policy for tall buildings, Urban Design based development controls to specific areas, commercial centres, heritage areas, etc.
4. Policy on unhindered access movement, parking and pedestrian realm
5. Policy on hoardings, street furniture and signage
6. Urban Design Scheme
7. Policy for design of pedestrian path
8. City structure plan and Urban Design objectives
9. Policy for conservation of Heritage Precincts, Buildings and Zones

Environmental Controls

Environmental controls are the tools which help in improving quality of life by creating a sustainable physical and social environment. Development and globalization bring enormous pressure on the physical environment with a severe adverse impact in terms in pollution and cities like Delhi are considered to be among the most polluted cities in the world. The city's environment can essentially be seen in terms of two components - the environment per se, or the habitat, and services management. The former pertains to the natural features and resources, including the elements of air and noise, water (water bodies, river, lakes, drains, ponds and ground water) and land with reference to open spaces, green areas and other surface and sub-surface conditions. The latter is related to the built environment and includes the environmental infrastructure - water supply, sewerage, solid waste disposal and the transportation network. The following approach and strategy are adopted for environmental controls:

1. Management of Natural Resources and the related environment infrastructure and services in a manner that would lead to optimization of use of natural resources (surface water, ground water, air and noise), and reduction/abatement of pollution
2. Conservation and Development of the natural features with a view to enhance the environmental value; and
3. Development and preservation of open spaces, greens and landscape/ recreational areas.

Mixed Land Use

Land use is essentially a physical and graphical representation of the allotment of the typology of uses assigned to certain areas in an urban agglomeration. Land use is more like a guideline that allows people to ascertain the kind of use the land in question can be put into currently or for any future project. The land use map usually has different classifications, namely residential, commercial, industrial, institutional, public uses, green areas, etc. Planners and policy-makers assess the demands of an urban area based on certain premeditated rules and figures and thereby assign certain percentages of land areas for certain designated uses. The land use plan essentially captures the basic necessity of the people and the kind of uses that they may have and then spatially distributing them on the map of the urban area.

Land use plans are necessary to ascertain and regulate the form the city takes and to ensure that market pressures do not result in a lop-sided development.

However, land use has its limitations in being exhaustive in its content thereby restricting the necessary manoeuvering needed to make an area more pleasant and liveable. Moreover, to make the management and implementation of land use easy, planners have taken resort to single use zoning, this in turn has led to decrement in the vibrancy and vivacity of the community life, which was otherwise present in the traditional areas.

Land use plan as documented in a notified Master Plan is a legal document that enforces the people to develop the city in a certain trajectory as envisaged by the planners and designers. Any development ranging from a small residential apartment to a large SEZ have to be in tandem with the land use plan.

In most of the traditional urban areas in the ancient times, most of the streets were a vibrant mix of work and live conditions. Cities like Jaipur, Varanasi, etc are living examples of those times when mixed land use was the order of the day and these traditional fabrics have stood the test of time and are still the most active part of their modern extended city.

However, with the industrial revolution and the consequent deterioration of the living conditions in the urban areas it became an exigent concern of the planners and the social activists to look into the matter and ensure segregation between the polluting uses such as industries and living areas. Therefore, arose the concept of land use zoning ensuring that there was a zone demarcated for each kind of activity.

Again in the 1960's and 70's city thinkers like Jane Jacobs eulogised the concept of MLU which would foster vibrant streets and safer communities, thereby harbouring a much healthier way of living. Social equity and rationality in the built environment was also envisaged to be dealt with the implementation of MLU. Today, MLU is a much hyped and favoured form of urbanity.

Mixed land use is essentially a typology of land use where variegated uses are located in close proximity and sometimes in the same building thereby fostering a holistic approach towards urban form. Mixed land use encompasses a conjugal existence of commercial, institutional and other public uses in residential pockets making the community more liveable and augmenting accessibility of the people.

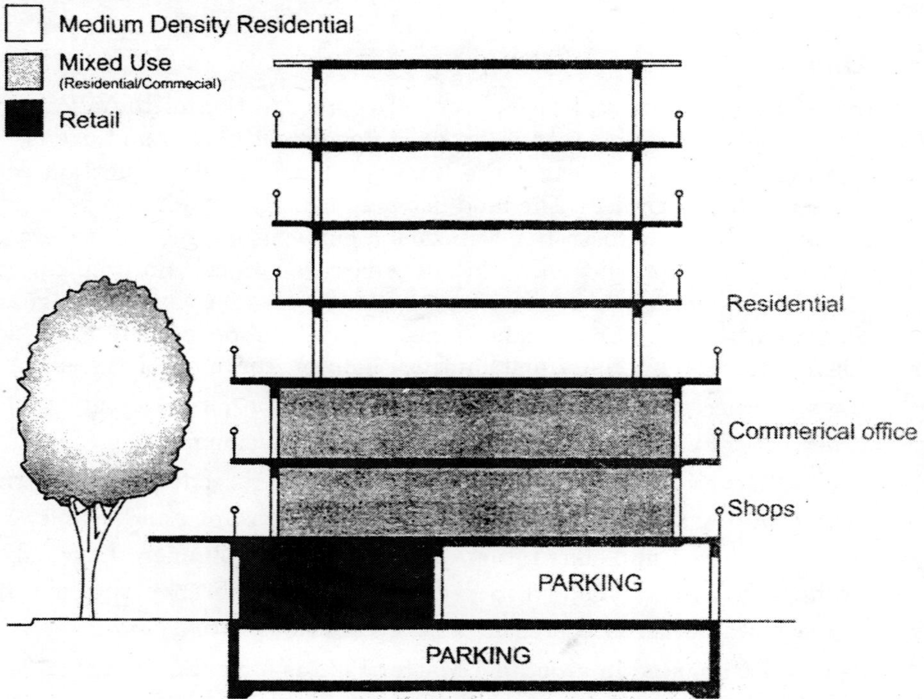

Fig. 7.4: Mixed land use in a building allows different uses

A balanced land use mix will contribute the following:

- o Economic and environmental sustainability and synergies that combine individual elements into neighbourhoods that are more than the sum of the parts
- o Transportation efficiencies by making the neighbourhoods more walk-able and increasing accessibility
- o effective use of infrastructure investment by people
- o The mix and overlap of populations will add life on the streets
- o 24/7 instead of 9 to 5, with increased safety and walkability
- o Integration with surrounding neighbourhoods
- o Distinct sub-areas with uses that reinforce uniqueness

Though the current real estate market is inclined toward mixed use development, there is still a need for guidance and direction, potentially including development incentives, to achieve the right mix of uses in the right locations.

<table>
<tr>
<td>Vertical Mixed-Use:
• Different uses in same building.
• Lower Floors - Public Uses.
• Upper Floors - Private Uses.
Advantage: Can have any number of revenue producing and mutually compatiable activities and uses.</td>
<td>
</td>
</tr>
<tr>
<td>Horizontal Mixed-Use:
Single-Use buildings on distinct parcels in a range of uses in a planned development project.
Advantage: Avoids the financing and code complexities of vertical layered uses.</td>
<td>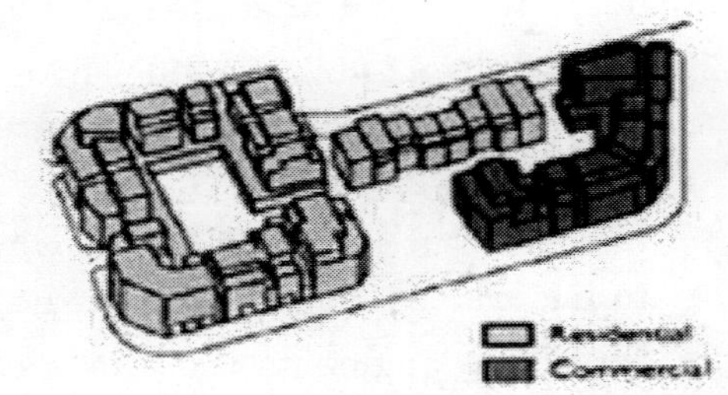
</td>
</tr>
<tr>
<td>Mixed-Use Walk-able Areas:
Combine both Horizontal and Vertical mix of uses in an area ideally within a 4-minute walking distance or a 400 m radius of activities.</td>
<td>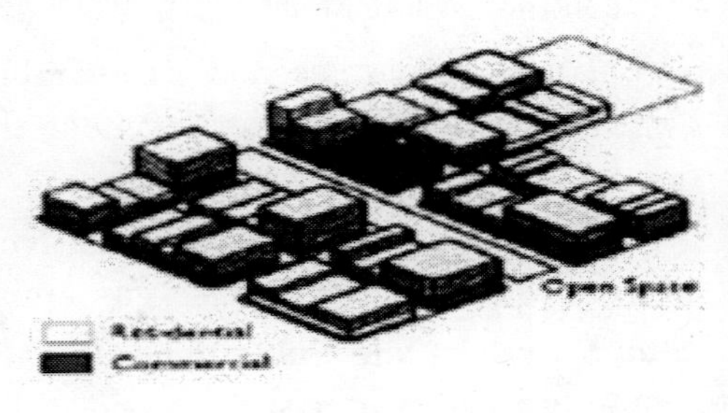
</td>
</tr>
</table>

Fig. 7.5: Typologies of Mixed Land Use

Successful mixed use areas can be achieved through:

- locating development within easy walking distance (400 metres) of high quality public transport corridors or other public transport operating at a frequency of four or more services per hour in the off-peak
- providing a range of development types that allow for a mix of day and night time activities supported by dense residential activity that aids natural surveillance and provides a 'base load' of activity

- ensuring that surrounding transport networks and adjoining development are integrated with the new development
- providing high amenity open space and recreation areas, and ensuring that lighting, street furniture, signage, footpath treatment and safe road-crossings provide a safe and convivial urban realm for all users.Combine both Horizontal and Vertical mix of uses in an area ideally within a 4 minute walking distance or a 400 m radius of activities.

Some of the most notable issues where the mixed land use poses a better option for an urban form, are as follows:

- MLU makes a more equitable mix of social classes
- MLU ensures more people on the streets for more number of hours thereby making it safer than the Single Use Zoning (SUZ) residential areas where the place becomes desolate when the residents go out for work.

MLU fosters walk-ability options by reducing the distance to access the regular necessities, where in SUZ the segregation led to greater distances to be travelled.

- MLU ensures higher densities thereby enabling a more intensive usage of the infrastructure by more people, whereas in SUZ more infrastructure has to be provided to ensure that it reaches all the remote parts of the settlement.
- MLU also augments the intangible issues that add to the flavour of urban life such as cultural vibrancy, characteristic zones, sense of place, diversity and beauty, whereas SUZ forms more sterile environments of monotonous housing estates and mammoth commercial centres.
- MLU is a more economically viable model for urban form since it ensures the return of investments for development through long term commercial ventures established in proximity.
- MLU has an enormously positive effect on the ecology. By fostering walkability it reduces the green house gas emissions made by unnecessary vehicular trips.

Smart Growth and Sustainable Urban Form support the integration of mixed land uses into communities as a critical component of achieving better places to live. By putting uses in close proximity to one another, alternatives to driving, such as walking or biking, are again becoming viable. MLU also provides a more diverse and sizeable population and commercial base for supporting viable public transportation. It can enhance the vitality and perceived security of an area by increasing the number and attitude of the people on the street. It helps streets, public spaces and pedestrian oriented retail again become places where people meet, attracting pedestrians back onto the street and helping to revitalize community life. There are innumerable opportunities with the implementation of MLU and some of them have been enumerated as follows:

Civic Sites: Clearly identified and at a prominent location should attract residents to that location where they can meet neighbours or have scheduled community events. They also lead to a "sense of place", which increases pride in one's community.

Walkability: A modified grid design with sidewalks, mixed with linear parks and parkways, encourages residents to move around other than in automobiles. This is particularly important for children and the elderly and reduces the burden on "chauffeur moms", as well as reduces fuel consumption on unnecessary vehicle trips.

Connectivity: Plentiful connections between different communities within a development reduces traffic on "connector" routes, by allowing for traffic to flow on a greater number of local streets.

Live-Work Concept: One of the recent pioneering trends of the mixed-use concept is the "Live-Work" concept. This trend started in the 1970s and 1980s, when many urban factories and warehouses in central city locations were converted into residential lofts, with zoning that allowed for the operation of a business as well. This trend has gained momentum outside of the major industrial cities and is now emerging in newer cities with the construction of new warehouse style structures, or the conversion of older structures in downtown locations. However, their locations are still generally limited to Central Business District locations, as more liberal zoning in those locations has been enacted to spur redevelopment. It is rare to see this type of development outside of central business districts or other central city locations, and there are a few signs that this type of development will expand into suburban locations in the near future, especially older suburbs.

Diverse Housing Types: Single family, townhouses, multi-family apartments and condos can be integrated into one development, as long as the scale and design of adjacent uses is compatible with each other. A mix of housing types ensures that people of various socio-economic classes may live in proximity to one another and share a common pride in one's community.

High Quality Architecture and Urban Design: Should reflect classic elements, including vernacular, or local styles. However, overly prescriptive architectural standards raise the cost of housing construction and should be argued against in the name of work force housing. Builders know what kind of design elements to incorporate into housing to attract buyers. This should not be the realm of local government zoning codes.

Increased Density: More units on smaller lots allow for preservation of open space, reduce infrastructure and maintenance costs, and allow for a more diverse mix of housing stock. Increased density is being perceived as a panacea to "urban sprawl".

Environmental Sensitivity: If possible, preservation of natural areas such as wetlands and woodlands should be utilized and used a community amenity and as buffers. These open space areas should also be counted toward, not in addition to other open space requirements, such as setbacks, park dedication and water bodies. This mainly applies to suburban locations that have existing natural features on site, but there are opportunities even in more urban settings, particularly for restoration of natural features.

Public Transportation: The connectivity, walkability, and higher density make existing and potential public transportation services more accessible and feasible than conventional sub-divisions.

Transit Oriented Developments (TODs) provide the best opportunity to better serve future residential areas with efficient public transportation. A TOD is typically a master planned development that has as a focus a rapid transit station that provides service to other major employment, shopping, and entertainment centers. Ideally, rapid transit station should be no greater than a 10-minute walk, or 500 m from all residential housing units, This close proximity necessitates higher residential density.

With the advent of cars in the early 20th century the city form came to celebrate the automobile and consequently it manifested the urban sprawl. The society transformed rapidly into a car dependent one; thereby increasing pressure on the infrastructure and more importantly on the environment. But now since the understanding of the deep relationship between the urban form and climate change has been extricated and established beyond the shadow of doubt, urgent steps are being taken to remediate the damage by rethinking the urban form. A paradigm shift from vehicular dependency to walk-ability, cycling, non-motorised means of transportation and public transit system has to be necessitated.

Mixed land use, higher densities, transit oriented development, etc are the new magic mantras that are being facilitated by the planners and policy makers at large. MLU goes a long way in ensuring a socially equitable urban form that also helps negotiate with negative environmental impact. MLU is definitely a gigantic step forward in addressing issues of a more sustainable urban form.

Planning and Building Plan Approval Process

A plan for development of urban land and building construction requires governmental/ ULB's approval. This begins with schematic design and planning steps based on permissible land use, zoning controls, development control norms, Floor Area Ratio, Road Right of Way, orientation to the street, parking, loading,circulation, height, setbacks, etc. The zoning entitlements vary according to land use and location. The ownership rights of the site or legal arrangement with the owners is a basic pre-requisite. Other mandatory regulations, viz. planning controls, heritage, environmental, airport zoning, etc. should be considered when a development plan/layout plan is prepared for approval and planning permission.

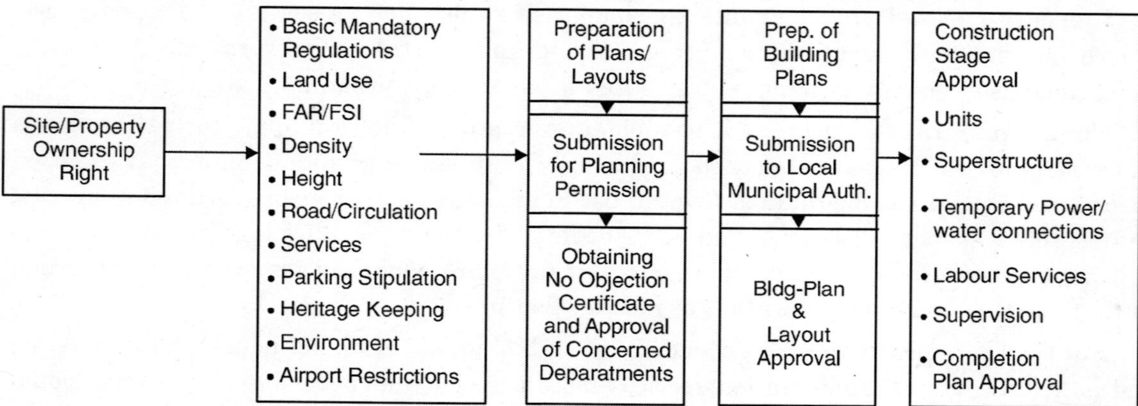

Fig. 7.6: Broad Sequence of Development Plan Approval.

The plans must conform to zoning, or the studies may be required to seek zoning and entitlement changes to meet the site constraints and opportunities. The site plan is developed showing the streets, utilities, lots, building footprints and landscape plan to meet the requirements of the site approval process. Once a basic plan is in place, a project must seek the approved by a wide variety of agencies. Required government approvals may include:

- Land use and land ownership documents
- Utility/services plans
- Environmental clearances
- Traffic and Transportation/Parking Plan
- Urban Design/Heritage approval
- Fire/Security and Airport Clearances
- Zoning and Planning Approvals
- Layout plan approval, and
- Building Permit. This is usually granted when all other clearances/approvals are obtained by the project proponent.

The design process requires that all issues related to planning and building regulations are addressed which are explained below:

Area and Height Limitations

The limitation of area and height of buildings shall be specified in terms of Floor Area Ratio (FAR). The FAR shall take into account the following aspects:

1. Population Density
2. Occupancy Class
3. Type of construction
4. Width of street fronting the building and the traffic load
5. Locality where the building is proposed and the density
6. Parking facilities
7. Local fire fighting facilities
8. Water supply and drainage facilities
9. Earthquake prone zone
10. Land use zone
11. Carrying capacity (estimated population on above based inputs)

Minimum Setbacks

The setbacks in a building layout are provided subject to requirements of building height, the ventilation and fire safety requirements. Setbacks can be provided in two ways, i.e.:

1. Based on plot sizes
2. Based on abutting road widths.

These two methods may be adopted for providing setbacks. However, the provisions shall also conform to the local building bye-laws.

The following table may be referred for deciding the minimum setbacks for different size plots in various use zones. The size of plots should be decided after taking into account the provisions of National Urban Housing and Habitat Policy and Urban Land (Ceiling and Regulation) Act. The setbacks, if necessary, may be changed depending upon the local situation and specified in the Development Plans and Building byelaws. Details indicated in UDRPFI Guidelines (2015), National Building Code (2016) and other sources are presented in the table below.

Table 7.2: Minimum Setbacks

Sr. No.	Plot size (in sqm)	Front (m)	Rear (m)		Side (m)	Side (m)
			Plains	Hill Towns	Plains	Hill Towns
1.	Upto 60	0	0	2	0	1.5
2.	Above 60 and upto 150	3	0	2	0	1.5
3.	Above 150 & upto 300	3	3	3	0	1.5
4.	Above 300 & upto 500	3	3	3	3	3
5.	Above 500 & upto 1000	6	3	3	3	3
6.	Above 1000 & upto 2000	9	3	3	3	3
7.	Above 2000 & upto 4000	9	6	6	6	6
8.	Above 4000 & upto 10000	9	6	6	6	6
9.	Above 10000	15	9	9	9	9

Source: UDRPFI Guidelines (2015) and other sources.

Notes:

(i) In case the permitted coverage is not achieved with setbacks, the setbacks of the preceding category may be followed.

(ii) In case a layout is sanctioned with more than the minimum prescribed setbacks, the same shall be followed in the sanction of the building plans.

(iii) The building plan sanctioning authority may relax setbacks in special circumstances.

(iv) In case of compact city planning, the margins to be altered upto at least 50%.

Setbacks with respect to Abutting Road Width

A. Front Setback

The norms for setback, as per National Building Code, are indicated in the following table:

Table 7.3: Front Setbacks with respect to Abutting Road Width

Sr. No.	Front Setback (m)	Width of street fronting the plot (m)	Remarks
1.	1.5	Upto 7.5	For Buildings upto a maximum height of 7 m
2.	3.0	7.5 to 18	For Buildings upto a maximum height of 18 m
3.	4.5	18 to 30	- do -
4.	6.0	Above 30	- do -

Source: NBC, 2005/2016.

Note: For streets less than 7.5 m in width, the distance of the building (building line) shall be at least 5m from the centre line of the street.

B. Rear and Side setback for building height up to 10 m

Rear setback: the rear setback shall be minimum 1.8 m

Side setback: the side setback shall be as follows:

For detached buildings: Minimum 3 m on both sides,

For semi-detached buildings: Minimum 3 m on one side,

For row type buildings: No side setback is required.

C. Rear and Side setback for building heights above 10 m

Table 7.4: Rear and side setbacks with respect to abutting road width

Sl. No.	Height of Building (m)	Side and Rear setbacks (m)	Other Controls
1.	10	3	• For building above 24 m in height, the minimum front setback shall be 6 m. • Where rooms do not derive light and ventilation from the exterior open space, the width of such space shall be reduced by 1 m subject to a minimum of 3 m and maximum of 8 m. • Alternative setbacks for tower like structure. – Upto height of 24 m with one setback Minimum 6 m. – Between 24 m and 37.5 m with one setback Minimum 9 m. – Above 37.5 m with two setbacks; Minimum 12 m
2.	15	5	
3.	18	6	
4.	21	7	
5.	24	8	
6.	27	9	
7.	30	10	
8.	35	11	
9.	40	12	
10.	45	13	
11.	50	14	
12.	55 and above	16	

Source: NBC, 2005/2016.

Note: The building plan sanctioning authority may relax setbacks in special circumstances and in case of compact city and TOD development

Distance from Electric Lines

Following clearances shall be maintained between the building and overhead electric supply line in accordance with the current Indian Electricity Rules as amended from time to time:

Table 7.5: Distances from Electric Lines

Sr. No.	Description	Vertical Distance (m)	Horizontal Distance (m)
1.	Low and medium voltage lines and service lines	2.5	1.2
2.	High voltage lines upto and including 11 kV	3.7	1.2
3.	High voltage lines above 11 kV and upto and including 33 kV	3.7	2.0
4.	Extra light voltage line beyond 33 kV	3.7 (plus 0.3 m for every additional 33 kV or part thereof)	2.0 (plus 0.3 m for every additional 33 kV or part thereof)

Source: NBC, 2005.

Residential Use Zone: The minimum dwelling units size may vary from State to State and region to region, owing to various factors, including the terrain and soil type, etc. However, a thumb-rule could be noted from the following table:

Table 7.6: Indicative Minimum Dwelling Unit Sizes

Number of rooms	Dwelling unit size (sqm)
1 BHK	60-80
2 BHK	80-120
3 BHK	120-160
4 BHK	160-200
5 BHK	200-260

Source: Naya Raipur Master Plan.

The residential areas are developed either as (a) plotted development or (b) group housing/ flatted development. The density pattern (i.e. high density, high medium density, low medium density or low density) are followed for working out the pattern of development with respect to the size of plot to number of dwelling units on each plot, setbacks, FAR and the number of storeys/ height of the building.

Table 7.7: Norms for Low Density Residential Area (Farm House)

Minimum Plot	Maximum FAR	Maximum Height	Other Controls
4000 sm	20 including mezzanine floor, 30 subject to payment of additional Floor Area charges	12 m	• Setback of the dwelling house should be 15 m in the front and 5 m on three sides. • Where the property abuts urban road, the building setback from the centre line of that road should be 30 m. Where property abuts the village road, building setback from the centre line of that road should be 15 m. • No dwelling unit should be built within 400 m of the right of way of any National Highway.

Source: DDA (MPD - 2021) modified in 2013.

Table 7.8: Norms for Primary Activity

Type	FAR	Ground Coverage	Max. Building Ht.
Agro based use	5	5%	15 m
Poultry Farm	25	25%	10 m
Religious, Educational, Hospital, Slughter house, cold storage, transport related activities and truck terminal, Govt/Semi-govt/FCI godown and warehouses	As per Development Code/Zoning Regulations/BBL		

Source: Ahmedabad Development Plan (part III, page 103).

Building Norms for Natural Habitat

The land uses identified as Natural Habitat covering water bodies, forest and vegetation, green open spaces, coastal zone, wetlands, etc., shall be protected and adequate buffer shall be provided from the planned establishments. For planning around these areas,the building norms and regulations as stipulated by the respective statutory bodies such as MoEF and State Environment and Forests Department shall be applicable.

Special Requirements for Disabled

External Ramps: Min. width 1200, Max. gradient 1:12, When gradient exceeds 1:20 an unobstructed platform minimum 1200 × 1200 should be provided at top of ramp. When gradient exceeds 1 : 15 a handrail should be provided both sides. When ramp exceeds 2000, a central rail may be substituted.

External stepped approach: goings should be not less than 280 and riser should be not higher than 150. The vertical rise of any flight should not exceeed 1200. Handrail should be erected each side.

Entrance doors: minimum clear opening of 800.

Lifts: minimum depth 1400 and width 1100. Door clear opening of 800. Clear space in front of doors 1500 × 1500.

Doors in buildings: minimum clear opening of 750 plus 300 clear wall space to edge of door.

Passageways: minimum1200 wide.

Internal stairs: goings should be not less than 250 and risers not more than 170. Vertical rise of flight should not exceed 1800. Switches and controls: light swtiches should align with door handles. No higher than 1400 above floors.

Signage: Should have large characters or numerals contrasting with the background.

Note: All dimensions are in millimeters (mm).

Building Permit Procedure

The Building Bye-Laws 1983 as adopted by Delhi Development Authority are applicable for the development areas of the Authority within the National Capital Territory of Delhi as declared under Section 12 of Delhi Development Act, 1957 in exercise of powers conferred under sub-section 1 of Section 57 of Delhi Development Act, 1957. No development shall be allowed in the development area of Delhi Development Authority without prior sanction.

Application for sanction/Addition/Alterations/Revised plan of residential plot/ other buildings:

If a person intends to erect or re-erect or make alterations in a building he/she shall give notice in writing in the prescribed form and such notice shall be accompanied by necessary permit fee and the following documents:

1. Application form
2. Specifications Form of proposal signed by owner and Architect/Engineer.
3. Certificate of supervision-1 by Architect/Engineer.
4. Certificate of Supervision-II by Plumber/Engineer.
5. Appointment letter of Architect/Engineer.
6. Copy of valid registration certificate of Architect/Engineer.
7. Copy of valid registration certificate of Plumber/Engineer.
8. Affidavit for ownership and plot lying vacant.

9. Affidavit/undertaking for non-stacking of building materials on public property.
10. Time Extension, if required, up to the date of submission of building permit.
11. Indemnity Bond in case of proposal for construction of basement.
12. Undertaking under Section 29(1) of Delhi Development Act, 1957.
13. Copy of possession plan and Lease Deed.
14. Copy of NOC issued by Lessor.
15. Building Plans including water harvesting proposal duly signed by Owner & Architect.
16. Landscape Plan duly signed by Owner & Architect.
17. Parking Plan duly signed by Owner & Architect.
18. Layout Plan, wherever applicable duly signed by Owner & Architect.
19. Certificate by owner, Architect/Engineer and structural engineer for safety from natural hazards.
20. Qualification Certificate of Structural Engineer.
21. Certificate by owner and Architect/Engineer for water harvesting in prescribed format.
22. Undertaking for balance peripheral charges in case of Group-IV Cooperative House Building Society.
23. Certificate from the Secretary of the Cooperative House Building Society that all the damages, etc. to the services shall be made good by the Society before handing over services to Government Agency.
24. NOC from Society (Group-IV-Cooperative House Building Society).
25. Any other document/information that the authority may deem fit. Additional documents required in case of buildings other than residential-plotted development:
26. No objection Certificate from competent authority regarding land use as per Master Plan/Zonal Plan, if required.
27. Approval from Chief Inspector of Factories in case of Industrial Buildings.
28. Approval from Chief Controller of Explosives, Nagpur in case of hazardous buildings.
29. Approval of Chief Fire Officer, Delhi Fire Services. In case of schools, guidelines of Directorate of Education, GNCTD are to be followed.
30. Alongwith these documents additional sets of plans are to be submitted, if these require the clearance from Delhi Fire Services and DUAC.

Additional Documents Required for Sanction of Building/Layout Plan for Group Housing, Public and Semi-Public (PSP), Institutional, Commercial, Industrial Schemes, etc.

1. General Body Resolution for appointment of Architect and Structural Engineer.
2. List of members of Managing Committee and office bearers of Society, duly approved and attested by Registrar of Co-op Societies, wherever applicable.

3. Authorization letter for signing the documents.
4. Approved list of members duly approved and attested by Registrar of Co-op Societies, wherever applicable.
5. Delhi Urban Art Commission (DUAC) proforma
6. Chief Fire Officer (CFO) proforma
7. Undertaking from the owner for contribution towards Economically Weaker Section (EWS) Housing Fund
8. Copy of allotment letter.
9. Copy of approved Layout Plan of area
10. Architectural Control Drawings, wherever applicable.
11. Approval from the Chief Inspector of Factories in case of Industrial Buildings.
12. Approval from the Chief Controller of Explosives, Nagpur and Chief Fire Officer, Delhi in case of hazardous buildings.
13. Height Clearance frm Airports Authority of India
14. Electric Sub-stations (ESS) location clearance from local power company/Discom.

Revalidation of Plans: The original sanctioned plan is required to be submitted with requisite fees and a letter of request for revalidation along with time extension letter from the Lease Department, if necessary

B-1 Permit: Plinth Level: On completion of construction up to plinth level, Architect/ Owner will apply in Appendix 'B-1' for plinth level checking along with requisite fees and documents.

Completion-cum-Occupancy Certificate: Every owner/builder has to submit a notice of completion of the building with the following documents:

1. The Certificate by the Owner, Architect, Engineer, Structural Engineer and supervisor.
2. One set of structural drawings, as executed, duly signed by owner, Architect and Structural Engineer.
3. Copy of Lease-deed.
4. Valid extension of time up to the date of applying for Completion Certificate; and in case completion is applied in phases, valid extension of time would be required up to the last phase.
5. Revalidation of plan up to the date of application of completion certificate.
6. Valid Certificate of Architect, Engineer.
7. Qualification Certificate of Structural Engineer.
8. Certificate regarding deviations from Architect/Engineer.
9. One set of building photographs.
10. Completion Plans (Layout Plan, Building Plan, Sections & Elevations) along with actual area at site i.e. ground coverage, FAR, Greens, Parking with other details duly signed by owner and Architect.

11. Superimposed Layout and Building Plans wherever applicable.
12. Sewer connection permission wherever applicable.

Additional Documents for Public and Semi-public (PSP/Institutional) Buildings

1. No objection Certificate for occupancy from Chief Fire Officer.
2. Clearance from Chief Controller of Explosives, wherever applicable.
3. Clearance/NOC from BSES/local power company regarding provision of transformers, Electric Sub-Stations, Ancillary Power Supply System, etc., wherever applicable.
4. Certificate from the Lift Inspector, GNCTD, wherever applicable.
5. Certificate from Air-Conditioning Engineer, Manufacturers, wherever applicable.
6. Undertaking regarding day/night marking as per standard, wherever applicable.
7. Valid clearance from Airports Authority of India (AAI),
8. Approval of Sewerage, Water Supply and Storm Water Drain Schemes from DJB/ MCD/DDA, as applicable.
9. DUAC Proform
10. Model Photographs coloured (8"×10") signed by owner & Architect.
11. Building photographs coloured (8"×10") signed by owner & Architect
12. External Finish Certificate signed by owner & Architect
13. Certificate regarding deviations from Architect
14. One set of attested copies of Sanctioned Plan.
15. Clearance from Chief Fire Officer, Delhi wherever applicable.
16. 5 sets of Completion Plans(Layout Plan, Building Plans, Sections & Elevations) along with area calculations i.e. ground coverage, FAR, mandatory Green, Parking details, duly signed by owner & Architect.
17. Two sets of super-imposed layout and Building Plans, wherever applicable.
18. Any other document/information that the authority may deem fit

Documents Required for Provisional Occupancy Certificate (POC) for Cooperative Group Housing Societies, Govt. Departments, Govt. Institutions, Charitable Trust and Wakf Board

1. The Certificate by the owner, Architect/Engineer, Structural Engineer and supervisor.
2. One set of structural drawings as executed duly signed by owner, Architect and Structural Engineer(as defined in NBC of India).
3. Copy of Lease-deed duly attested by Owner/Architect.
4. Valid extension of time up to the date of applying for Completion Certificate; and in case completion is applied in phases, valid extension of time would be required up to the last phase.
5. Revalidation of plan up to the date of application of completion certificate.
6. Valid Certificate of Architect and Engineer.

7. Qualification Certificate of Structural Engineer.
8. Clearance from Chief Fire Officer, Delhi, wherever applicable.
9. Clearance/NOC from local power company regarding handing over/taken over of electric sub-station), wherever applicable.
10. Certificate from the Lift Inspector, GNCTD, wherever applicable.
11. Undertaking regarding day/night marking as per ICAO standard, wherever applicable.
12. Sewer connection permission.
13. Superimposed layout and building plans
14. Confirmation of draw of flats duly attested by Registrar of Co-op. Societies(RCS) for group housing schemes.
15. Approval of Sewerage, Water Supply and Storm Water Drain Scheme from DJB/ MCD/DDA, wherever applicable.
16. Numbering plan for group housing schemes.
17. Three sets of Completion Plans (Layout Plan, Building Plan, Sections & Elevations) along with actual area at site, i.e. ground coverage, FAR, mandatory Green, Parking and other details.

Documents required for Completion-cum-Occupancy Certificate for Cooperative Group Housing Societies, Govt. Departments, Govt. Institutions, Charitable Trust and Wakf Board.

1. The Certificate by the owner, Architect/Engineer, Structural Engineer and supervision.
2. DUAC Proforma
3. Two sets of building photographs(coloured) (in size of 8"×10").
4. Two sets of model photographs (coloured) (in size of 8"×10").
5. External Finish Certificate from Architect.
6. Certificate from the Architect regarding deviations.
7. One set of attested copies of sanctioned plans.

Mitigating Construction Nuisance

(i) The mulba during the construction will be removed on weekly basis. If the same is not done, in that case the local body shall remove the mulba and the cost shall be borne by the owner of the plot.

(ii) During construction, it is mandatory on the part of the owner to properly screen the construction site off the main road by means of erecting a screen wall not less than 8 ft. in height from ground level which is to be painted to avoid unpleasant look from the road side. In addition to this, a net or some other protective material shall be hoisted at the facades of the building to ensure that any failing material remains within the protected area.

(iii) Noise related activities will not be taken up for construction at night after 10 P.M. Further, it will be ensured that construction/demolition work shall be carried out in such a manner that no disturbance/nuisance is caused to residents of the neighborhood.

Validity Period of Building Permit

The building permit shall remain valid from the date of sanction as mentioned below:

(a) For Residential, Institutional, Industrial & Commercial (upto 4 storeyed bldgs.) 5 yrs.

(b) For large complexes and multi-storeyed building and institutional building 5 years.

Note: (i) No building activity can be carried out after the expiry of building permit.

(ii) The building permit can be revalidated for a period of one year at a time from the date of expiry of validity of the original permit.

Procedure during Construction of Building

The owner/applicant who has been granted such building permit shall intimate the Authority in writing within 7 days of starting of construction work at site. He shall obtain an acknowledgement from the Authority of this notice.

Procedure for Obtaining Form B-1

The owner/applicant who has been granted the building permit shall intimate about completion of work up to 'plinth level' through his appointed licensed Architect/ Engineer/ Supervisor in form B-1. The documents required for this permit will be as under:

I. Processing fee

II. Completion Certificate upto plinth level from the Architect/Engineer

III. Copy of valid certificate of licensed Architect/Engineer/Supervisor.

IV. Plan, indicating plinth level construction at site in relation to plot dimension, area and set back, duly signed by owner and licensed Architect/Engineer/Supervisor.

V. Extension of time for construction, valid up to date, if required.

Authority will inspect the site and intimate the objection, if any, to the owner/Architect/ Engineer/Supervisor within 30 days in form B-2 (in case deviations of non-compoundable nature are noticed).

In case construction of plinth level is found in accordance with the sanctioned plan/ compoundable limit, there is no need for intimation as per notification. It will be the responsibility of the owner and Architect/Engineer/Supervisor to ensure that further construction of building is in accordance with the sanctioned building plan.

Procedure of Obtaining Completion-cum-Occupancy Certificate

No person shall occupy or allow any other person to occupy any building or part of a building for any purpose until such building or part of a building has been granted the occupancy certificate.

The owner shall submit the notice of completion along with the required documents and plans. The Authority on receipt of the notice of completion shall inspect the work and communicate the sanction/refusal, or objection thereto within 60 days from the date of receipt of notice of completion. Time for an inspection shall be communicated to the Owner/Applicant/

Architect. After inspection of completed building, the objections and compounding fee, if leviable, shall be intimated to the owner/Architect. On compliance and fulfillment of all formalities, the Occupancy Certificate shall be issued.

Reviewing the Building Regulations

The building regulations now encompass a complex range of controls, such as given below:

Planning Controls/DCR

- Development Controls
- Land use zoning
- Sub-division Regulations, infrastructure services, traffic/mobility and parking plan, landscape plan, etc.

Building Controls

- Height
- Ground coverage
- Setbacks
- Floor Area Ratio
- Density
- Parking/road in front

Architectural Controls

Fire safety, earthquake and structural safety

Airport Regulations

Environment Regulations

Urban Design Regulations

Heritage Regulations and Archaeological Stipulations

Currently a builder requires as many as 34 kinds of permits before starting construction which takes anywhere between six months to three years. The developer has to run to over two dozen Government ministries and agencies, including Environment and Forests, Archaeological Survey of India, National Highway Authority, fire department, electricity department, Airports Authority of India, Ministry of Labour, Ministry of Mines, Central Ground Water Board, etc. to get no objection certificates.

Table 7.9: Number of Approvals Required and Time Taken

Country	No. Of Approvals Required	Time Taken
India	34	6 months to 3 years
Hong Kong	6	About two months
Singapore	11	26 days

The development control regulations and building bye-laws are made primarily for green-field development and not for redevelopment which is a major thrust of Housing for All, AMRUT and other programmes of urban development. Regulations have to respond to the need of redevelopment and provide a facilitating framework. The constraints of redevelopment are the requisition of proof of land ownership, mechanism for approval of plans, joint ownership and development of small plots being amalgamated together. The regulations do not provide any system of assembly of small plots, so that the old dilapidated areas can be developed with proper layouts, adequate roads, services, amenities, parking and open spaces.

The building regulations act as exclusionary devices, excluding slums, hutments, poor households, small vendors and manufacturers. The development control regulations and building bye-laws often ignore the vital aspect of public importance, like public toilets, dustbins, drinking fountains, footpath design, street furniture, locating street vendors, utility booths, signage, public spaces, conservation of cultural heritage, etc.

Building bye-laws are based upon an absolute normative set of regulations, and do not permit location specific variations and flexibility. This is due to general apprehension that discretion leads to rent seeking behavior. On the contrary rigid regulations impel developers to bypass the regulations by rent paying.

The bottlenecks and overlapping regulatory jurisdictions can be reduced by a careful mapping of the regulatory jurisdictions, regulatory authority and regulatory laws. The Real Estate (Regulation and Development) Act, 2016 seeks to provide a uniform regulatory environment, creation of Real Estate Regulatory Authority and a unified regulatory framework to fast track and re-engineer the process. The Act provides for a uniform regulatory environment and help speedy adjudication of disputes by the establishment of a Real Estate Appellate Tribunal. The Act is expected to significantly reduce frauds and delays, and enhance the efficiency, professionalism and standardization. The Act covers both residential and commercial real estate and envisages:

- Establishment of Real Estate Regulatory Authority
- Registration of Real Estate Projects and Registration of Real Estate Agents
- Mandatory Public Disclosure of all project details
- Adherence to declared plans
- Fast Track Dispute Settlement Mechanism
- Establishment of Central Advisory Council
- Establishment of Real Estate Appellate Tribunal
- Bar of Jurisdiction in Courts, and,
- Power to make Rules and Regulations.

Reforms in Building Regulations

The Government of India has initiated certain reforms to fast track clearance for construction which include the following:

- The Union Ministry of Environment, Forests and Climate Change has come out with revised and simplified environmental laws. These would be notified after the consultation with the Ministry of Urban Development. Urban local bodies and State governments will be empowered to accord approvals at their level.
- The Ministry of Civil Aviation has asked the Airports Authority of India to standardize the norms for building heights around airports. The authority has issued Color-Coded Zonal Maps (CCZMs) for 12 airports which account for 58 per cent of such applications and make them available to the respective urban bodies. The Ministry also commissioned an improved version of online NOCAS (No Objection Certificate Application System), eliminating human interface and expediting issues of NOC through automatic calculation of permissible height in airport zone and also enabling the applicants to track the status of their applications.
- Online filing and NOC for buildings falling outside restricted areas of national monuments can be obtained using 'app' developed by ISRO. Heritage bye-laws of 281 for major monuments have been fast tracked by the Ministry of Culture.
- Local military authorities and units have been directed to provide details and maps of restricted and unrestricted areas.
- Formulation of Model Building Bye-laws by the Ministry of Urban Development, together with on-line approvals on single window (2015).

The Expert Committee appointed by Government of India for Streamlining Approval Procedure for Real Estate Projects (SAPREP) has come up with six areas for reforms:

- Bring transparency, predictability and accountability to protect consumer interest
- Review existing systems and procedures by removing duplicity and conflict between regulations, bringing in automation process and delegation of approvals.
- Single window or 'one-stop shop' enabled by IT
- Reforms to promote affordable green housing/buildings
- Sharing of best practices, and incentivizing States and cities
- Creating capacities in public (ULBs and UDAs and TP Departments), private sector and professionals (architects, engineers, urban planners, structural and other specialists) to carry out development responsibility and be empowered.

In view of the complexity of getting building permit, loss of time and corruption involved, there is a need to consider on-line processing, simplification and deregulation of planning and building controls, including the following reforms:

- Reduce the number of approvals required
- Time limit for grant of the approvals
- Devolve and delegate powers
- One window system, a computerised portal/platform for Building Plan approvals
- Replace building bye-laws by Planning and Development Permission

- Resort to a more flexible and local Development Zoning and White Zoning
- Invoke concepts of Transferable Development Right (TDR) and Accommodation Reservation (AR)

A graded and differential approach may be a possibility, comprising the following stages:

- No sanction/waiver
- Instant Sanction (on-line)
- Sanction of architectural plan and structural design by Registered Architects and Structural Engineers under intimation to the ULB, and within BBL, NBC and DCR of Master Plan
- Planning and development permissions by the ULB

This involves the devolution of powers and responsibility to registered Architects/ Engineers and deletion of micro-details from the Building Regulations, which can be attended by the architects and engineers.

The role of the urban local body (ULB) should be redefined, who should primarily deal with Planning and Development Permission, which are concerned only with the external and broad aspects of buildings. The Planning and Development Permission Regulations comprise three sections: i) Planning and Development Control Regulations, ii) Building Design, and iii) Building Safety and Structural Design. For (ii) & (iii) the registered panels and agencies of architects and engineers can be delegated the powers of deemed sanctions. The development controls to be regulated by the ULB should cover the following aspects only:

- Land use zoning, layout plan, redevelopment plan, housing cluster plan, Sub-division Regulations, Mixed Use, mandatory provision of social housing, social and physical infrastructure, urban design and heritage control, etc.
- Floor Area Ratio, density, parking and road in front, height, urban form
- Ground coverage, setbacks and mandatory green/open space be regulated as per the area specific character of the area on the basis of the local development plan and area specific urban design guidelines. All these plans and details should be available on the web site.

Larger plots (say 4 Ha and above) may involve the approval of Services Plans, Transport and Parking Plans, urban design, heritage, environmental and other clearances. The Planning & Development Regulations should also cover the approval of land pooling schemes, sub-division plans and building proposals, including mandatory social housing component.

For Planning and Development Permission, an interdisciplinary platform representing Architects, Planners, Engineers, Service Agencies, representatives of Fire Department, Civil Aviation, NMA/ASI, Pollution Control Committee and other concerned authorities can be created. The power for approval and clearance under various Acts may be delegated to such an interdisciplinary platform.

For the unplanned areas (unauthorized colonies, urban villages, etc.) Planning and Development Permission can help to gradually bring them within the fold and framework of planned development. This will need evolving comprehensive guidelines for amalgamation of plots, infill development, and conversion of isolated plots into development of group housing, with proper facilities, parks and parking.

The local authorities should ensure that on-street parking, congestion and traffic bottlenecks are avoided and greens, mixed land use, utilities and amenities are adequately provided in all built up areas.

The architectural design of the buildings up to 8 storied (height 26 m) and up to 1000 sqm plot in a planned colony may be approved by the registered architect under intimation to ULB. The Structural Design, Civil and Services Plan may be approved by a registered engineering, professional or such an agency under the delegated powers. The reform in Building Regulations should make it redundant for an inspector to enter a private building, and the regulations concerning the internal features, like room size, ceiling height, ventilation; sanitary fittings, etc. may be the mandatory responsibility of the Architect.

However, in the unplanned areas, unauthorised /regularised colonies, village abadi, etc. the Completion Plan / Occupancy Certificate may be issued only by the concerned local body. The devolution of powers to registered panel/ agencies of architects and engineers would not work unless they are made responsible and accountable to the local body, who delegate them with such powers.

The city should not have any unsafe building irrespective of status of a colony, land ownership or land use. As such, it is necessary to delink building safety from the process of the planning and development permission or approval of building plan. Every building should have a Structural Safety Certificate which need not be linked with land use, approved layout and ownership. This approach has been mandated in the Master Plan for Delhi-2021 (MPD 2021), which requires that a structural safety certificate be submitted for all buildings in the planned and unplanned built-up areas, including the unauthorized colonies, villages and Special Area. However, this mandate could not be enforced due to lack of qualified engineers with the ULB. The Local Bodies can proactively help the building owners in making available the services of a panel of structural engineers/ institutions for guiding the owners to ensure the structural safety of non-engineered buildings.

Online Building Plan Scrutiny System

The computerised scrutiny system named "AutoDCR" is being brought in use by various municipal corporations in India. The system has been adopted by Pune Municipal Corporation, Thane Municipal Corporation, Meera Bhayandar Municipal Corporation, Kolhapur Municipal Corporation in Maharashtra. The SUDA, AUDA, Hubli-Dharwad Municipal Corporation and Delhi Municipal Corporations are also implementing the system. Products are designed to get faster and accurate approval of building proposals. It brings uniformity and standardization of drawings and process to eliminate lengthy manual process and human errors. It reduces the time and effort of the architect and the authority.

BPAMS and Auto DCR integrate documental data with drawing. Auto DCR reads data from CAD drawing, establishes relationship between various entities, imposes specific proposal conditions, geometrically maps each and every entity by corresponding with complex and interlinked rules. By using AutoCAD objectivity, users can maintain the objectivity and speed.

Analysis is done as per Development Control Regulations by AutoDCR. Tables and reports are saved with the drawing. It takes about 3-5 minutes to save a file. Reports are sent to BPAMS for making status available online. In order to save time and hassles in obtaining NOCs from various departments, the soft copies of the proposal are forwarded by the Local Authority itself to the concerned departments for scrutiny and on-line response/NOC.

Auto DCR generates various scrutiny reports dynamically based on the DC rules described by the respective authority. Generated report shows the failed/passed items with their rules in a very user friendly viewable/printable format. Reports can also be generated in local regional language. Customization of reports can be made by user defined templates.

Software can be customized/upgraded as per the local requirements and specifications. Special features include user friendly manual, context sensitive help, signage, graphics and toolbars. Auto DCR/BPMAS is integrated with data and photographs, web interface data flow management with regular notification through SMS during the scrutiny of building proposal.

Pune Municipal Corporation (PMC), like many other cities, was facing the challenges of haphazard development, lack of proper monitoring system leading to inefficiency and corruption and eroding accountability due to delay in permissions. PMC implemented single window for architects and licensed engineers to submit the building proposal online for approval. The single window user reads a CD from architect or files the proposal/information, and calculates scrutiny amount to be deposited at PMC. The Auto DCR checks for mandatory and conditional mandatory documents submitted along with proposal. A challan is issued for scrutiny fee, if documents submitted are in order for on line payment. SMS is sent to both Building Inspector (BI) and architect mentioning the site visit date and time. Thereafter document validation scrutiny as per DC rules is carried on the computer. Auto DCR creates entities like plot, building layout, roads, etc. from drawings based on layers and colours, geometrical mapping and reports of scrutiny. These are examined for approval.

The main goal of the reform was that citizens could submit their building permission proposals online, know the status of their proposals, and receive sanctions without any delay via electronic channels. As a result, time required for sanction of building proposal reduced to 21 days from 45-50 days and revenues of the PMC have also increased.

The task of ensuring compliance in simple structures can be entrusted to professional agencies, where the enforcement agency only needs to carry out random checks to prevent abuse of the system. This necessitates empanelling and empowering agencies of the professionals and charging them with the responsibility of ensuring compliance. An effective system for testing competence and empanelling professionals and institutionalising a system for penalizing them in case of violations are essential.

It is also important that administrative procedures are simplified, streamlined, and are time bound. For this, it is imperative to rely on modern management practices and best technological tools that are available. It will be necessary to improve the format of all forms and applications and demand digitized drawings and photographs of constructions, institute random checking procedures, build the capacity of enforcement staff, and publication and interactive workshops. The task of reforming administrative procedures is crucial for the new model of enforcement to be effective.

Definitions and Short Notes

Building Area

- Carpet area refers to the area on which a carpet can be laid. Builders generally sell on the basis of the super area that includes the entire built-up area and common spaces such as cooridors, lifts and stairs.
- Plinth area refers to the entire carpet area along with the thickness of the external walls of the apartment. It obviously includes the thickness of the internal walls and the columns, if any, lying within the four walls of an apartment

Super built-up area refers to the plinth area of an apartment as added by the balconies, etc.

Building Types

Assembly building—A building or part thereof, where groups of people congregate or gather for amusement, recreation, social, religious, patriotic, civil, travel and similar purposes and these includes buildings of drama and cinemas theatres, drive-in-theatres, assembly halls, city halls, town halls, auditoria, exhibition halls, museums, mangal karyalayas, skating rink, gymnasia, restaurants, eating or boarding houses, places of worship, dance halls, clubs, gymkhanas and road, railways, air, sea or other public transportation stations and recreation piers.

Business building—Includes any building or part thereof used principally for transaction of business and/or keeping of accounts and records therefore including offices, banks professional establishments, court houses, etc. if their principal function is transaction of business and/ or keeping of books and records.

Education building—Includes a building exclusively used for a school, college, recognized by the appropriate Board or University, or any other competent iority involving assembly for instruction, education or recreation incidental to educational use, and including a building for such other uses as research institution. It shall also include quarters for essential staff required to reside in the premises, and building used as a hostel captive to an educational institution, whether situated in its campus or not.

Hazardous building—Includes a building or part thereof used for. -

(i) Storage, handling, manufacture of processing of radioactive substances or of highly combustible or explosive materials or of products which are liable to burn with extreme rapidity and/or producing poisonous fumes or explosive emanations;

(ii) Storage, handling, manufacture or processing of which involves highly corrosive,toxic or noxious alkalis, acids, or other liquids, gases or chemicals producing flame, fumes and explosive mixtures, etc. or which result in division of matter into fine particles capable of spontaneous ignition.

Industrial Building—Includes a building or part thereof wherein products or material are fabricated, assembled or processed, such as assembly plants, laboratories, power plants, refineries, gas plants, mills, dairies and factories, etc.,

Institutional Building—Includes a building constructed by Government, Semi-Govemment organizations or Registered Trusts and used for medical or other treatment, or for an auditorium or complex for cultural and allied activities or for an hospice, care of persons suffering from physical or mental illness, handicap, disease or infirmity, care of orphans, abandoned women, children and infants, convalescents, destitute or aged persons and for penal or correctional detention with restricted liberty of the inmates ordinarily providing sleeping accommodation, and includes dharmashalas, hospitals, sanatoria, custodial and penal institutions such as jails, prisons, mental hospitals, house of correction and detention, reformatories, etc.,

Mercantile Building—Includes a building or part thereof used as shops, stores or markets for display and sale of wholesale or retail goods or merchandise, including office, storage and service facilities incidental thereto and located in the same building.

Multi-storeyed Building or high rise building—A building above 4 storeyes, and/or a building exceeding 15 meter or more in height above the average level of front road.

Multi level car parking building—A building may be partly below ground level having two or more basements or above ground level, primarily to be used for parking of cars, scooters or any other type of light motorized vehicle.

Office Building—includes a building or premises or part thereof whose principal use is for office purposes or clerical work. "Office purpose" includes the work of administration, clerical work, handling money, telephone, telegraph and computer operation; and clerical work includes writing book-keeping, sorting papers, typing, filling, duplicating, punching cards or tapes machine calculations, drawing of matter for publication and editorical preparation of matter for publication.

Special Building—Includes assembly, industrial, hazardous buildings, buildings used for wholesale establishments, hotel, hostels, centrally air conditioned buildings and which exceed 15mts. in height and have a total built up area exceeding 600 sq.m.

Storage Building—A building or part thereof used primarily for storage or shelter of goods, wares, merchandise and includes a building used as a warehouse, cold storage, freight depot, transit shed, store house, public garage, hanger, truck terminal, grain elevator, barn and stables.

Wholesale establishment—An establishment wholly or partly engaged in wholesale trade and manufacture wholesale outlets, including related storage facilities, warehouses and establishments engaged in truck transport, including truck/transport booking agencies.

Residential Building—Includes a building in which sleeping and living accommodation is provided for normal residential purposes, with cooking facilities and includes one or more family dwellings, apartment houses, flats, and private garages of such buildings.

Detached building—Includes a building with walls and roof independent of any other building and with open spaces on all sides within the same plot.

Semi-detached building—A building detached on three sides with open space as specified in building regulations.

Mixed Landuse Building—A building partly used for commercial activities and partly for residential purpose.

Unsafe Building—Includes a building which:

(iii) Is structurally unsafe, or

(iv) Is unsanitary, or
(v) Is not provided with adequate means of ingress or egress, or
(vi) Constitutes a fire hazard, or
(vii) Is dangerous to human life, or
(viii) In relation to its existing use, constitutes a hazard to safety or health or public welfare by maintenance, dilapidation or abandonment

Note: All unsafe buildings/structure will require to be restored by repairs, demolition or dealt with under the relevant provisions of the Building Bye-laws in taking action against such buildings.

Building Line—The line upto which the plinth of building adjoining a street or an extension of a street or on a future street may lawfully extend and include the lines prescribed, if any, as per an approved scheme/development plan.

Front air plane—The air plane contained between the ground in front of the building and the straight lines drawn downwards and outwards from the line of intersection of the outer surface of any front wall of the building with the roof perpendicular to that line, and at en angle of 63-1/2 degrees to the horizontal;

Note: The 63-1/2 degrees angle has a tangent of 2:1 so that if the ground is the level, the air plane reaches the ground at a distance from the exterior wall equal to half the height of the above level of that ground for the purpose of the definition of light plane, the outer surface of any verandah abutting on an interior or side open space shall be considered to be the exterior wall of the building.

Rear air plane—The plane contained between the ground behind the building and the straight line drawn downwards and outwards from the line of intersection of the outer surface of rear wall of the building with the roof perpendicular to that line and at an angle 63-1/2 degree to the horizontal.

Betterment Levy: It is a self-financing mechanism and means of recovering infrastructure development costs in a short period. The unearned increase in capital values of properties serviced by new infrastructure is recovered by the implementing agency as one time levy.

Compounding Fees: The fee charged on the building or part thereof which have been constructed unauthorisedly or without obtaining the requisite building permit from the enforcement agency.

Conforming Uses: The use premises which are consistent with the landuse of a development plan.

Development Charges/Fees: The Charges/Fees which are required to be paid by the owner developers at the time of approval of the building plans for the provision of infrastructural facilities.

Equivalent Car Space: The space occupied by a car to be provided for parking purposes.

Floor Area Ratio: The quotient of the ratio of the combined gross floor areas to total area of a plot:

$$\text{FAR} = \frac{\text{Total Floor Area} \times 100}{\text{Total Plot Area}}$$

By using FAR as a resource and by promoting formation of cooperative societies of slum and squatter clusters, the residents can be activated in resettlement and self-help upgradation programmes. An incentive FAR may be allowed for social housing alongwith commercial activity by which social housing schemes can become self-financing and provide self-employment. Permission may be granted to build more or larger units than otherwise allowed by the existing zoning/development controls to compensate developers for revenue that may be lost due to a zoning ordinance that obliges him to provide a share of social dwelling units. As a basic principle, FAR and Density bonuses are granted as incentives to encourage owners to provide affordable units. Optimum utilization of scarce urban land through higher FAR and densities shall promote housing development, in the high potential areas. There is a need to gradually give up the plotted development and in no case, any plot should be more than 200 sqm in any city in India, as has been proposed in the National Urban Housing and Habitat Policy (2007).

Group Housing: A premises of size not less than 3000 sq.mt. (in NCT Delhi) comprising residential flats with basic amenities like parking, park, convenience shops, public utility, etc.

73rd Constitutional Amendment Act

The 73rd Constitutional Amendment Act (also referred to as 73rd CAA,73rd Amendment or the Panchayati Raj Act) was passed in 1992 and came into force on April 24, 1993. It is meant to provide constitutional saction to establish democracy at the grassroots level, similar to the state and national levels. This initiative was undertaken in response to a growing recognition that the development initiatives of the preceding decades had not delivered, that the extent of rural poverty was still much too large, and thus the existing structure of government needed to be reformed. The primary changes envisaged under the 73rd CAA include:

- The Gram Sabha or village assembly as a deliberative body to decentralize governance and to be regarded as the foundation of the Panchayati Raj System.
- A uniform three-tier structure of Panchayats at village (Gram Panchayat-GP),intermediate (Panchayat Samiti-PS) and district (Zilla Parishad-ZP) levels.
- To promote bottom-up-planning, the District Planning Committee DPC, in every district is to be accorded constitutional status.

74th Constitutional Amendment Act

The 74th Constitutional Amendment Act (also referred to as 74th CAA, 74th Amendment or the Nagarpalika Act) for decentralization of urban local governance came into force in 1993. One of the requirements under the 74th Amendment is the formation of Ward Committees in municipal corporations in cities with a population of more than three lakh (300,000), and making them responsible for the planning and implementation of local services.

Key tasks to be accomplished by urban local bodies (ULBs) under the 74th CAA are, inter alia:

- Urban Planning, including town planning
- Regulation of land use and construction of building

- Planning for economic and social development
- Roads and bridges
- Water supply for domestic, industrial and commercial purposes
- Public health, sanitation conservancy and solid waste management
- Urban forestry, protection of the environment and promotion of ecological aspects
- Slum improvement and upgradation
- Urban poverty alleviation
- Promotion of cultural, educational and aesthetic aspects
- Constitution of District Planning Committee

District Planning Committee

District Planning Committee (DPC) is the committee created under 73rd and 74th CCA, for planning at the district level. The Committee in each District consolidates the plans prepared by the Panchayats and the Municipalities in the District and prepare a draft development plan for the District. The Plan includes issues like spatial planning, sharing of water and other physical and natural resources, development of infrastructure, environmental conservation and the extent and type of available resources, both financial or otherwise.

Metropolitan Planning Committee

Metropolitan Planning Committee (MPC) is the committee created under the 74th Constitutional Amendment Act for a Metropolitan area. Its purpose is to prepare a draft development plan for the Metropolitan area as a whole. The legislature of a State can work out the composition of the Metropolitan Planning Committees and the manner in which people would be elected to it.

Parastatal organisations

Parastatal organisations are state-run establishments or enterprises, legal entities created by a government to undertake commercial or service-provision activities on behalf of the government. Development authorities and service providers found in most large cities and towns, e.g. Delhi Development Authority, (DDA); Mumbai Metropolitan Region Development Authority, MMMRDA); Delhi Jal Board (for water and sanitation), etc fall under this designation. These bodies often drive the development agenda and control large amounts of resources (such as land), despite being unelected órganisations.

Urban Local Bodies (ULBs)

ULBs in India are the constitutionally mandated administrative units that provide basic infrastructure and services in cities and towns. According to Census of India 2011, there are 3893 ULBs in the country classified into three main categories:

- *Nagar Nigams,* or Municipal Corporations, which govern large urban areas. The area under a Corporation is further divided up into wards. Individual wards or collections of wards within a corporation sometimes have their own administrative body known as ward committee, as also described under the 74th CAA.

- *Nagar Palika,* or Municipal Councils, which govern smaller urban areas. Municipalities are also divided into wards, which may be grouped together into ward councils.
- *Nagar Panchayats,* for very small towns, or peri-urban and semi-rural areas.

Urban Renewal

The concept of urban renewal first gained currency in India in the 1970s and 80s as a process of land re-development in moderate to high density urban areas. It is a policy based approach that aims to regenerate the central business districts, with a strong focus on retaining the existing communities and their livelihoods. Although urban renewal has been on the agenda of many master plans and development programmes, it has only achieved limited success in Indian cities, where the over-arching focus has been on horizontal expansion and development of greenfield sites in the suburbs.

Urban Revitalisation

Revitalisation is a process combining the architectural and urban rehabilitation of historical centres while at the same time enhancing the urban activities therein. Urban revitalisation encompasses projects aimed at renewing the economic and social life of a run-down part of a town.

Bringing back new vitality and life a building, a community, a neighbourhood, activities, business, etc. may involve allocation of new uses. The term is the opposite of a "museum city" and does not include revitalisation of an existing social/economic dynamism, but its proper order and dimension, including the informal sector rehabilitation consists in giving the urban and architectural heritage its full capacity to play a useful role for society. It should contribute to the continuity of urban and agricultural enrichment.

Urban Policies and Plans

Urban policy and urban planning are concerned with the management of urban transformation. They are activities that seek to influence the distribution and operation of investments and consumption processes in cities for the "common good".

Urban planning is a forecasting and organising method that allows public authorities to guide and control urban development by drawing up and implementing urban planning documents. It is principally expressed in two separate documents: Master Plans and Landuse Maps. These documents establish the basic guidelines for the organisation of the land concerned, taking into account both the need for urban expansion and agricultural activities as well as the protection of sites and landscapes.

Slums

According to UN-HABITAT, a slum household is defined as a group of individuals living under the same roof lacking one or more of the following conditions: access to improved water; access to sanitation facilities; sufficient living area (not more than three people sharing the same room); structural quality and durability of dwellings; and security of tenure.

According to the Government of India, an area can be designated as a 'slum' under the State Slum Clearance/ Improvement Act when the competent authority is convinced that the area is a source of danger to health, safety and convenience, or when buildings are found to be unfit for human habitation due to dilapidation, overcrowding or lack of ventilation, light or sanitation facilities. According to the 2011 Census, the slum population of India in cities and towns with a population of 50,000 and above was 65.50 million. As urban development is a state subject, state governments have the responsibility of notifying an area as a slum. Notified slums are recognized slums by the Government of India and are eligible for improvement of services under the programmes sponsored by the government.

World Heritage Site (WHS)

This is a site (such as monument, groups of buildings, city, forest, mountain, etc.) designated by the UNESCO World Heritage Committee as being of outstanding universal value and significance. As of 2008, 878 sites have been included in the World Heritage list comprising 678 cultural, 174 natural, and 26 mixed properties, in 145 countries. Each World Heritage Site is the property of the country on whose territory the site is located, but it is considered in the interest of the international community to preserve each site.

The World Heritage Convention provides the following definitions of different types of heritage:

- Cultural Heritage, which includes monuments, groups of buildings or sites which are 'of outstanding universal value';
- Natural Heritage, which includes natural features (physical or biological formations or combinations of these), geological and physiographical formations and other natural sites, also of outstanding universal value;
- Mixed Cultural and Natural Heritage, which includes a combination of the two types of heritage described above.

Chawl

A chawl is a residential building typically found in western India, especially Mumbai. These are usually 4-5 floors high with about 10-20 tenements on each floor, originally constructed to house the migrant worker population. A typical tenement in the chawl consists of a single multipurpose room (living and sleeping) and kitchen, with shared/ common utilities for each floor. In Mumbai the chawls typically provide housing for new migrants of low-income strata, who cannot afford the high rents and house prices in the city.

Haveli

Haveli is the term used to denote private mansions in north and west India. The word haveli is of Persian origin, meaning an enclosed place. The havelis are usually closed from all sides with a single large main entry and exit gate with living spaces inside. They typically consist of one or two courtyards with rooms around. They are traditionally energy efficient and climatically sound structures especially suited for the dry and hot climate of north and west India. The havelis of Shekhawati, Rajasthan are famous for the beautiful frescoes that adorn their external walls and internal ceilings while the havelis of Jaislamer are noted for their richly carved stone jaalis (screens) and jharokhas (windows).

Katra

A katra is the spatial organisation of neighbourhood typically found in the inner/walled city areas of northern India, especially Delhi. These neighbourhoods are entered through a single arched gateway (main entry and exit point) and consist of two-three storey houses along narrow streets, surrounded with markets on all sides.

Pol

A pol is a cluster of traditional houses in inner city areas wherein a number of families live together and are linked together by caste, profession or religion. Pols are typical of traditional walled cities in Gujarat, still visible in Ahmedabad. The word pol is derived from the Sanskrit word pratoli meaning entrance to an enclosed area. A typical pol normally has one or two entrances and contains beautiful wooden carved houses inside with internal courtyards and fresco work done on courtyard walls and/or ceilings.

Debriefing and Review

1. What do you understand by Zoning Regulations and what is its purpose?
2. What are the types of zoning regulations?
3. What do you understand by development control regulations?
4. Write short notes on the following:
   (i) Transfer of Development Rights
   (ii) Accommodation Reservation
   (iii) Incentive Zoning
   (iv) White Zoning
5. Explain the concept of Residential Planning Unit Development.
6. Explain the purpose and scope of environmental controls.
7. Write a note on mixed land use.
8. Explain the planning permission process.
9. Write a note on building plan approval process and digitised on-line plan approval system.
10. Write short notes on the following:
    (a) National Monuments Authority
    (b) Heritage Conservation Committee
    (c) Delhi Urban Art Commission
    (d) Real Estate Regulatory Authority
    (e) 73rd Constitutional Amendment Act
    (f) District Planning Committee

CHAPTER

8

INFRASTRUCTURE DEVELOPMENT AND MANAGEMENT

Infrastructure is generally defined as "services, roads, mass transportation, water and sewer systems, solid waste management, drainage and flood protection, electric installations and telecommunications, traditionally supported by the public sector, to enhance quality of living, work and consumption".

Infrastructure is also defined as the physical framework of facilities, utilities and support system through which goods and services are provided to the public. Infrastructure facilities are generally grouped into two major categories (i) physical infrastructure comprising of water supply, drainage, sewerage, water disposal system, transportation power and (ii) social infrastructure, which includes education, health, telecommunication secutiry, fire-fighting services, socio-cultural, recreation parks, banks and financial institutions, housing and other services. Various components of physical and social infrastructure, facilities and services indicate the status of development.

Infrastructure is the basic requirement of urban life and its adequacy and accessibility are two important ingredients and key contributors in the upgradation and enrichment of quality of urban life. The extent and the nature of problems faced by different towns vary by size, geographical conditions, and local natural resources: state/regional differentials in the resource availability and the policies, resource base of local authorities and several such factors directly or indirectly affecting the population of cities/towns.

The High-Powered Expert Committee under the chair of Isher Ahluwalia (2010-11), covered the following components of urban infrastructure: water supply, sewerage, solid waste mangement, storm water drains, urban roads, urban transport, traffic support infrastructure and street lighting.

According to the Reserve Bank of India (RBI) circular on Infrastructure, a credit facility is treated as "infrastructure lending" to a borrower company which is engaged in developing, operating and maintaining, or developing, operating and maintaining any infrastructure facility that is a project in any of the following sectors, or any infrastructure facility of a similar nature:

- A road, including toll road, a bridge or a rail system;
- A highway project, including other ancilliary activities;
- A port, airport, inland waterway or inland port;
- A water supply project, irrigation project, water treatment, sanitation and sewerage system or solid waste management system;
- Telecom services whether basic or cellular, including radio paging, domestic satellite service, trunking, broadband and internet service.
- An industrial park or special economic zone;
- Generation and distribution of power;
- Transmission or distribution of power by laying a network of new transmission or distribution lines.

The Eleventh Finance Commission's index of infrastructure included economic, social, and administrative infrastructure indicators. These were (i) agriculture, (ii) banking, (iii) electricity, (iv) transport, (v) communications, (vi) health, and (vii) civil administration. The index of infrastructure indicates that generally States with high infrastructure index have low incidence of poverty. Infrastructure defined by the Housing and Urban Development Corporation (HUDCO) covers the following:

1. Utility Infrastructure

1.1 Water supply	— Unserviced areas
	— Rehabilitation of existing supply systems
	— Augmentation of existing supply
	— Improvement of water quality
1.2 Sewerage and Drainage	— Unserviced areas
	— Rehabilitation project
	— Augmentation of existing systems
1.3 Low Cost Sanitation	— Conversion of dry latrines
	— Construction of new latrines
	— Community latrines/Pay-and-use toilets
1.4 Solid Waste Management	— Collection and Conveyance
	— Treatment and Disposal
	— Energy/Material recovery
1.5 Ecologically Appropriate Infrastructure Projects	— Projects envisaging utilisation on Liquid and Solid waste (recycling of waste water, fuel pellets, bio-gas, etc.)
	— Development of City Forests
	— Development of Water Bodies

1.6 Integrated Area Development Scheme	— Development of new towns and urban extensions
	— Integrated development of small and medium towns
	— Growth centres
	— Mega-cities
1.7 Transportation	— Roads, bridges, flyovers, subways, by-passes
	— Transport Nagars/Terminals, Parking Complexes
	— Ports, Airports and Railway infrastructure
	— Jetties/Pipelines
	— Purchase of Public Transport vehicles
2. Social Infrastructure	— Schools/Colleges/Hostels
	— Health Centres/Library
	— Nursing Homes/Hospitals, including Medical Equipment
	— Community Centres/Barat Ghars, Clubs, etc.
	— Parks and Playgrounds/Stadia
	— Creches/Rehabilitation Centres
	— Electric Crematoria
	— Old-age Home, Anangwari, etc.
3. Economic/Commercial Infrastructure	
	— Shopping centres
	— Market Complexes
	— Office buildings/Software Technology Parks
	— Theaters/Auditoria
	— Trade and Business Centres
	— Industrial and Business Infrastructure
	— Warehouses, Industrial Estates
	— Tourist and Health Resorts

Urban Plans and Town Planning Acts generally cover the following components of Infrastructure.

A. Utilities

1. Water supply
2. Sewerage, drainage
3. Solid waste managment
4. Distribution of electricity, gas, fuels, etc.

B. Facilities

1. Healthcare
2. Educational
3. Sports and recreational
4. Socio-cultural

C. Services

1. Telecommunications
2. Public transport
3. Transport terminals: airports, sea ports, railway station, bus/truck terminals.
4. Road network
5. Warehousing
6. Fire protection
7. Burial/cremation grounds

In Indian cities the status of infrastructure services is generally poor, as indicated below:

Water Supply

- As per 54th round of NSS, 70% of urban households reported being served by tap water and 21% by tubewell or hand pump.
- 66% of urban households reported having their principal sources of water within their premises while 32% had it within 0.2 km.
- 41% had access to their own sources of drinking water and 59% were sharing a public source.

Sewerage and Waste Water

- 54th round of NSS reported 26% of households are having no latrines, 35% using septic tank, and 22% using sewerage system.
- In urban areas sewerage connections varied from 48% to 70%.
- According to Central Pollution Control Board, the waste water generated in 300 Class I cities is about 15800 million litres per day while the treatment facilities exist for hardly 3750 million litres per day.

The coverage of underground sewerage system varies between 24% in Nagpur and 85% in Pune with a weighted average of 60%. In the metropolitan cities 100% of the sewage is not subject to treatment before disposal. Sewage treatment facility is available for a total flow of 960 mid. which is 22% of the flow rate generated. Although nearly 300 urban centers have sewerage system and only 70 towns/cities have sewage treatment facilities. Of the total garbage generated in urban areas only 60% is being collected by the municipal authorities while the rest remains un-collected. As far as sanitation facility is concerned about 35% of urban residents have access to sewerage system, 15% have septic tank system, 20% have service latrines and the remaining 30% use the open spaces. For garbage collection and disposal 1.16 sweepers are employed per thousand of urban population as against the norm of 3-5 sweepers /1000 urban population.

On an aggregate, 21 percent of India's urban population is living in slum and squatter settlements, where access to basic services is extremely poor. Although 90% of urban population is reported to have access to safe drinking water, there are severe deficiencies in quantity and quality of water available to urban residents. About 49% of urban population is covered with sanitation facilities while rest of the urban population is devoid of such services. Nearly 46% of urban household have water borne toilets but only 36% of the urban households are connected to the public sewerage system. As per the survey conducted by the Central Pollution Control Board (CPCB) even among metros only 5 metropolitan cities have proper wastewater collection system. Ten metropolitan cities have reported to have sewage treatment facilities of which four each have partial primary and partial secondary treatment facilities while the remaining two have secondary treatment facilities only. A survey of mode of disposal conducted by CPCB for 142 class-I cities reveals an interesting picture. In about 30% of the surveyed class-1 cities mode of disposal is on agricultural land, another 30% discharge into rivers either directly or through drains. About 22% cities followed mode of disposal both on agricultural land and into rivers while rest discharged to other recipient system such as sea, lakes, ponds etc. Similar situation for mode of disposal of wastewater is prevalent in Class-II towns. The problem of wastewater management is acute even in mega cities. In none of the mega-cities 100% wastewater is treated. In Delhi out of 1634 mld wastewater generated about 78% is treated. While in Bangalore, Chennai and Kolkata the proportion of wastewater treated is about 75, 63 and 50 percent respectively. In respect of Hyderabad and Mumbai the position is still worse. As such effective steps for collection, treatment and disposal of wastewater from urban communities need to be taken up to control environmental pollution and water degradation.

Solid Waste Management

The position with regard to solid waste management is no better. It is estimated that about 1,70,000 metric tonnes of solid waste is generated every day in the urban centers of India. About 60% of the solid waste generated is collected for proper disposal. Per capita waste generation in cities varies between 0.2-0.6 kg per day and it is increasing by 1.3% per annum. With the growth of urban population, the increase in solid waste is estimated at 5%. The solid waste generated by the million plus cities varies from 1200 metric tpd in cities like Ahmedabad and Pune to a maximum of 10,000 metric tpd in cities like Delhi and Mumbai. The per capita solid waste generation varies from 300 gm per capita per day in Bangalore to 500-550 gm in Mumbai and Delhi. Out of total waste generated in the million plus cities, hardly 30% is treated before disposal. The uncollected solid waste is generally disposed of either to fill the open space in and around the locality or into the drains and along the roads thereby causing insanitary conditions and spread of diseases in the towns and cities, it is reported that on an average Rs. 130 - 260 per tonne are incurred on collection, transportation and disposal of solid waste in Indian cities. It does not include the cost of land used for this purpose. Based on the paying capacity of urban residents, the methods of solid waste disposal vary from no garbage collection at all to landfills, composting and recycling. It has generally been noted that solid waste management much like wastewater treatment and disposal, receives low priority than other municipal services. In many of the urban areas solid waste is disposed of in low-lying areas without any specific plan for filling the site or any arrangement for leachate and gas control. Proper solid waste disposal is also hampered by the non-availability of suitable landfill sites, partly due to high land costs and partly due to rapid urban growth.

Urban Transport

Urban transport is one of the most crucial sectors of infrastructure development. While urban centers are considered as engines of growth, urban transport is supposed to be the wheels of that engine. With high rate of growth of urban centers there has also been an exponential rate of increase in urban travel demand. In view of the poor public transport system in many of the large cities and metropolitan centers private modes of various types have increased tremendously. With the result streams of heterogeneous traffic could be seen moving on an inadequate and obsolete road network system. Congestion, delays, accidents, high level of energy consumption and increasing level of pollution are some of the manifestations of the poor urban transport system in India. The congestion on the roads is increasing continuously. In central areas of majority of the metropolitan cities in our country the speed is as low as 5-10 kmph. India has the dubious distinction of having one of the highest incidences of road accidents. In 2016 about 6 lakh road accidents and about 1.45 lakh deaths were reported the high level of pollution caused by traffic in cities is assuming alarming proportions. Nearly 15-20% of urban developed land is under transport use but situation of urban transport is not satisfactory. Large urban areas, particularly the peripheral and fringe areas have very poor transport services.

Number of motorised vehicle is increasing at a fast rate in urban areas. Delhi alone has about 10% of motor vehicle population of the country. Traffic volume in metropolitan cities is of high intensity and is increasing continuously. The urban road network is low in capacity, obsolete in pattern and poor in surface quality. The road density varies greatly from as low as 1.59 lane km/sq km in Vijayawada to 12.44 lane km/sq km in Ahmedabad. The encroachment along road is high in most of the urban areas. The encroachment of carriage way in urban areas ranges between 10-39%. Non-destined and through traffic on urban roads is also very high ranging from 11-35 %. Expenditure on urban transport is also low as compared to other municipal services. Role and potential of intermediate public transport system have not been fully exploited.

Power

Among various infrastructural facilities, power is most important for sustained growth and development. The installed generating capacity increased nearly thousand folds from 1362 MW in 1947, 1433.4 KWH in 2016. The per capita consumption of electricity, which was less than 15 units in 1951, increased to 1222 KWH in 2016. Despite these achievements, there are power cuts, low voltage, low frequency and high incidences of breakdowns.

Water Supply

The objective of a public protected water supply system is to supply safe and clean water in adequate quantity, conveniently and as economically as possible. Rising demand of water due to rapid urbanisation is putting enormous stress. While planning the water supply system for an area, it is evident to consider water conservation aspects, which may be possible through optimal use of available water resources, prevention and control of wastage of water and effective demand management.

Table 8.1: Water Supply Standards

Sr. No.	Classification of town/cities	Recommended maximum water supply levels (lpcd)
1.	Towns provided with piped water supply but without sewerage system	70
2.	Cities provided with piped water supply where sewerage system is existing/contemplated.	135
3.	Metropolitan and Mega cities provided with piped water supply where sewerage system is existing/contemplated	150

Source: CPHEEO Manual, 1999.

Notes:

(i) In urban areas, where water is provided through public stand posts, 40 lpcd should be considered

(ii) Unaccounted flow of Water (UFW) is the difference between the quantity of water supplied to a city's network and the metered quantity of water used by the customers. UFW has two components: (a) physical losses due to leakage from pipes, and (b) administrative losses due to illegal connections and under registration of water meters. The above figures exclude UFW, which should be limited to 15% for new proposed systems.

(iii) Water requirement for the town/city will be 135 to 150 lpcd. The water needs of the town will be partially met by making provision of Rain Harvesting Structures in all the buildings.

(iv) Figures include requirements of water for commercial, institutional and minor industries. However, the bulk supply to each establishment should be assessed separately with proper justification.

(v) Piped water supplies should be designed on continuous 24 hours basis to distribute water to consumers at adequate pressure at all points (using grid supply system).

(vi) For towns where one storeyed buildings are common and for supply to the ground level storage tanks in multi-storeyed buildings, the minimum residual pressure at ferrule point should be 7m for direct supply. Where two storeyed buildings are common, it may be 12m and where three storeyed buildings are prevalent 17m or as stipulated by local byelaws.

(vii) The consumption of water when supply is metred is less compared to that when the water charges on flat rate basis. Hence in order to achieve optimal utilisation of water, metering is recommended.

(viii) CPHEEO manual specifies design period for various components, broadly 30 years for civil works and 15 years for electro–mechanical works. In fixing a design period, the useful life of structures and equipment employed, taking into account obsolescence as well as wear and tear, design constraints, rate of population growth, etc. should be incorporated and integrated with overall planning of the city.

(ix) PPP could be introduced in phases, either on Build, Operate and Own (BOO) or Build, Operate, Own and Transfer (BOOT) basis. Primarily, it is possible in two ways i.e. privatization of the existing water supply systems and secondly, privatization of systems in townships, housing colonies, business and commercial complexes, etc.

Fire Hydrants and Fire Fighting

The fire hydrants are located at suitable points and they can be operated either manually or automatically. In manual operation, a pump has to be started manually after opening the hydrant valve. In automatic operation, the pump will start automatically when the hydrant valve is opened manually.

The hydrant valve should be designed for the prescribed discharge under pressure such that a jet throw of water is obtained from the nozzle of hose pipe. This system has wide applications and in one sense, it is the backbone of all fire protection systems. It can be installed for multi-storeyed buildings, power plants, textile mills, hospitals, paper mills, airports, warehouses, printing presses, etc.

Water spray is used to extinguish fire and depending on the type of spray, the system can be grouped into the following two categories:

(i) Multi-fire system: In this system, it is designed to have a coarse water spray discharged at high velocity. Such an arrangement gives the water spray to reach upto the base of flame zone.

(ii) Protect spray system: In this system, it is designed to have a fine water spray discharged at low velocity. Such an arrangement cools the burning surface and creates invert vapour in the combustion zone.

The following table shows the different types of fire extinguishers and their use on different classes of fires.

Table 8.2: Various Types of Fire Extinguishers

Sl. No.	Type of Fire Extinguisher	Classes of Fire	Description
1.	Water/Soda Acid type	A	General paper, wood, cloth and other carbonaceous materials.
2.	Dry Chemical Powder	B	Inflammable liquid,oil, gasoline chemicals, paints and solvents.
		C	Electrical installations, motors, switchgears and compressed gases.
		D	Metals i.e. Magnesium, Sodium, Potassium.
3.	Carbon dioxide	B and C	As above in B and C
4.	Halon	B and C	As above in B and C
5.	Chemical Foam	B	As above in B and C

The CPHEEO Manual recommends fire fighting water demand as a function of population, i.e. water demand for fire fighting purpose = 100 P, where P stands for forecasted population may be adopted for communities larger than 50,000. It is desirable that one third of fire fighting requirements form part of the service storage. The balance requirement may be distributed in several static tanks at strategic points. These static tanks may be filled from nearby ponds, streams or canals by water tankers wherever feasible. The pressure required for fire fighting would have to be boosted by fire engines.

Water Requirements for Institutional Buildings

Table 8.3: Water requirements for Institutional Buildings

Sr. No.	Institutions	Litres per head per day
1.	Hospital (including laundry) (a) no. of beds exceeding 100 (b) no. of beds not exceeding 100	(a) 450 (per bed) (b) 340 (per bed)
2.	Hotels	180 (per bed)
3.	Hostels	135
4.	Nurses homes and medical quarters	135
5.	Boarding schools/colleges	135
6.	Restaurants	70 (per seat)
7.	Airport and seaports	70

8.	Junction stations and intermediate station where express stoppage (both railway and bus stations) is provided	70
9.	Terminal stations	45
10.	Intermediate stations (excluding mail and express stops)	45 (could be reduced to 25 where bathing facilities are not provided)
11.	Day Schools/colleges	45
12.	Offices	45
13.	Factories	45 (could be reduced to 30 where no bath rooms are provided)
14.	Cinema, concert halls and theatres	15

Source: CPHEEO Manual, 1999.

Water Required for Industrial Units

Table 8.4: Water requirement for Industrial Units

Industry	Unit of Production	Water Requirement in Kilolitres per unit
Automobile	Vehicle	40
Distillery	Kilolitre (proof alcohol)	122-170
Fertilisers	Tonne	80-200
Leather	100 kg (tanned)	4
Paper	Tonne	200-400
Special Quality paper	Tonne	400-1000
Straw board	Tonne	75-100
Petroleum refinery	Tonne (crude)	1-2
Steel	Tonne	200-250
Sugar	Tonne	1-2
Textile	100 kg (goods)	8-14

Source: CPHEEO Manual, 1999.

Railway Station water requirements

Water requirement for a Railway Station for various uses (per day) is given below:

- 15 litres per passenger (Metcalf Eddy)
- 455 litres per employee (CPHEEO Manual)

- Apron washing – 10 litres per sq meter as per Indian Railways Work Manual (IRWM)
- Cleaning/mopping of platform and floor – 5 litres per sqm.
- Visitors - 5 litres per visitor
- Catering – 45 litres per passenger
- Gardening/Horticulture – 22500 litres per hectare (IRWM)
- Cleaning of trains on platform – 500 litres per coach (IRWM)
- Cleaning of trains in washing lanes – 3600 litres per coach (IRWM)
- Watering of trains – 1800 litres/ coach (IRWM)
- Fire fighting as per CPHEEO Norms
- Commercial – 45000 litres per hectare per day (IRWM)
- UFW – 15% of total demand for new system (CPHEEO)
- 75% of total capacity shall be filled at the station for long haul trains (passing trains)

Water requirement for metro station may be calculated based on the type of station (underground or elevated). In absence of any specific norms to calculate water demand for metro station, the water estimation can be calculated from the above mentioned information for stations. Parameters such as staff requirement, HVAC requirement if station is underground, toilet requirement and passenger requirement to be considered based on the facilities provided at metro stations.

District Meter Area Planning (Bulk metering)

The term 'district metering' is used to describe the method whereby flow meters are installed on all major supply lines and strategic points within the distribution system. The meters should be used to monitor the overall performance of the system establishing average daily flows into various districts. District meter areas ideally consist of 2000 to 5000 properties.

Size of the district meter should be such that it is capable of recording night flow without loss of accuracy and also must be capable of supplying peak flow without introducing serious head loss. The District Meters should be read at weekly intervals at the same time of day as previous readings of the meter.

Billing and Collection

Revenue management system is an important aspect of any Water Supply System as it governs the financial aspect. Besides fixing a tariff structure, billing and collection of revenue play an important part. The water charges to be fixed taking into account the ability of the system to meet the expenditure on the following heads:

- Operating Cost (excluding establishment cost),
- Establishment Cost,
- Depreciation,
- Debt Services and Doubtful Charges,
- Asset replacement fund.

Tariff structure should be fixed and revised periodically. Automatic increase of tariff periodically on index basis can also be adopted. Where the same authority also provides sewerage system, charges for this can also be included as a percentage of the water charges.

There are various methods by which Water Billing can be done. The user is advised to refer 'Manual on Operation and Maintenance of Water Supply Systems' of CPHEEO while fixing the tariff, billing and collection system.

Leakage Control

The overall objective of leakage control is to diagnose how water loss is caused and to formulate and implement action to reduce it, to technically and economically acceptable minimal. The water losses can be termed into two categories, i.e. Physical losses and Non-Physical. The Physical Loss is mainly due to leakage of water in the network and losses from pipes, joints and fittings, reservoirs and overflow of reservoirs and sumps. The Non-Physical Loss is due to theft of water through illegal, already disconnected connections, under-billing either deliberately or through defective meters, water wasted by consumer through open or leaky taps, errors in estimating flat rate consumption, public stand posts and hydrants. The major activities which should be taken up for efficient monitoring and leakage control are:

- **Preliminary data collection and planning—**The water distribution drawings are to be studied and updated. The number of service connections is to be obtained and in the drawings of the roads the exact locations of service connections marked. The district and sub-district boundaries are suitably fixed taking into consideration the number of service connections, length of mains, and pressure points in the main. The exact locations of valves, hydrants with their sizes should be noted on the drawings.
- **Pipe location and survey—**Electronic pipe locators can be used during survey. These instruments work on the principle of Electromagnetic signal propagation. It consists of a battery operated transmitter and a cordless receiver unit to pick up the signals of pre-set frequency. There are various models to choose from.
- **Assessment of pressure and flows—**Data loggers are used to record the pressure and flows. It is an instrument which stores the raw data electronically so as to be able to transfer it to the computer with a data cable link. Two types of portable data loggers are used either with a single channel or dual channel. In the absence of electronic equipment, the pressures can be ascertained by tapping and providing a pressure gauge. Flows can be assessed by using meters on a bypass line.
- **Locating the leaks—**Walking and sounding are the two general methods or their combination can be used to detect possible location of leakages. Leakage can be detected by walking over the main looking for tell-tale signs of presence of water. Whereas sounding is the cheapest and an effective method of detecting leaks in a medium.

- **Assessment of leakage—**To conduct tests for assessment of leak the following equipment are needed:
  - — Road measurer
  - — Pipe locator
  - — Valve locator
  - — Listening sticks or sounding rods
  - — Electronic sounding rods

Water Quality Standards

The water quality standards as prescribed by the Bureau of Indian Standards are tabulated below:

Table 8.5: Organoleptic and Physical Parameters of Drinking Water Characteristics

Sr. No.	Characteristics	Requirement (Acceptable limit)	Permissible limit in the absence of alternate source	Method of Test, ref. part of IS 3025	Remarks
1.	Colour, Hazen units, Max	5	15	Part 4	Extended to 15 only, if toxic substances are not suspected in absence of alternate source.
2.	Odour	Agreeable	Agreeable	Part 5	Test cold and when heated Test at several dilutions
3.	pH Value	6.5-8.5	No relaxation	Part II	-
4.	Taste	Agreeable	Agreeable	Parts 7 and 8	Test to be conducted only after safety has been established
5.	Turbidity, NTU, Max	1	5	Part 10	-
6.	Total dissolved solids, mg/L Max	500	2000	Part 16	-

Source: IS 10500: 2012.

Note: It is recommended that the acceptable limit be implemented. Values in excess of those mentioned under acceptable render the water not suitable, but still may be tolerated in the absence of an alternative sources but up to the limits indicated under permissible limit in the absence of alternate source.

Table 8.6: General parameters concerning substances undesirable in drinking water

S. No.	Characteristics	Requirement (Acceptable limit)	Permissible limit in the absence of alternate source	Method of test, Ref. No.	Remarks
1.	Aluminium (as A1) mg/I, max	0.03	0.2	IS 3025 (Part 55)	-
2.	Ammonia (as total ammonia-N), mg/l, max	0.5	No relaxation	IS 3025 (Part 34)	-
3.	Anionic, detergents (as MBAS) mg/l, max.	0.2	1.0	Annex K of IS 13428	-
4.	Barium (as Ba), mg/I, max	0.7	No relaxation	Annex F of IS 13428 or IS 15302	-
5.	Boron (as B), mg/L max	0.5	1.0	IS 3025 (Part 57)	-
6.	Calcium (as Ca), mg/l, max	75	200	IS 3025 (Part 40)	-
7.	Chloramines (as CIZ), mg/l, max.	4.0	No relaxation	IS 3025 (Part 26) or APHA 4500-CLG	-
8.	Chloride as (CI)/mg/1, max	250	1000	IS 3025 (Part 32)	-
9.	Copper (As CU), mg/l, Max	0.05	1.5	IS 3025 (Part 42)	-
10.	Fluoride (as F) mg/l, max	1.0	1.5	IS 3025 (Part 60)	-
11.	Free residual chlorine, mg/1, min	0.2	1	IS 3025 (Part 26)	To be applicable only when water is chlorinated. Tested at consumer end. When protection against viral infection is required it should be minimum 0.5 mg/l.

12.	Iron (as Fe), mg/L	0.3	No relaxation	IS 2025 (Paet 53)	Total concentration of manganese (as Mn) and iron (as Fe) shall not exceed 0.3 mg/l)
13.	Magnesium (as Mg.) mg/l, max	30	100	IS 3025 (Part 46)	-
14.	Manganese (as Mn), mg/l, max	0.1	0.3	IS 3025 (Part 59)	Total concentration of Manganese (as Mn) and iron (as Fe) shall not exceed 0.3 mg/l
15.	Mineral Oil, Mg/l, max	0.5	No relaxation	Clause 6 of IS 3025 (Part 39) Inframed partition method	-
16.	Nitrate (as NO_2), mg/l, max	45	No relaxation	IS 3025 (Part 34)	-
17.	Phenolic compounds	0.001	0.002	IS 3025 (Part 43)	-
18.	Selenium (as Se), mg/l, max	0.01	No relaxation	IS 3025 (Part 56) or IS 153303	-
19.	Silver (as Ag), mg/l, max.	0.1	No relaxation	Annex J of IS 13428	-
20.	Silphate (as SO_4), mg/l, max	200	400	Is 3025 (Part 24)	May be extended to 400 provided that Magnesium does not exceed 30
21.	Sulphide (as H2S), mg/l, max	0.05	No relaxation	IS 3025 (Part 29)	-
22.	Total alkalinity as Calcium, Carbonate, mg/l, max.	200	600	IS 3025 (Part 21)	-
23.	Total hardness (as $CaCO_3$), mg/l, max	200	600	IS 3025 (Part 21)	-
24.	Zinc (as Zn), mg/l	5	15	IS 3025 (Part 49)	-

Source: IS 10500: 2012.

Table 8.7: Permissible Limits of Toxic Substances

S. No.	Characteristics	Requirement (Acceptable limit)	Permissible limit in the absence of alternate source	Method of test, Ref. No.	Remarks
1.	Calcium (as Ca) mg/L	0.003	No relaxation	IS 3025 (Part 41)	-
2.	Cynide (as CN), mg/l,	0.05	No relaxation	IS 3025 (Part 27)	-
3.	Lead (as Pb), mg/l, Max	0.01	No relaxation	IS 3025 (Part 47)	-
4.	Mercury (as Hg), mg/l, Max.	0.001	No relaxation	IS 3025 (Part 47)	-
5.	Molybdenum (as Mo), mg/l, Max	0.02	No relaxation	IS 3025 (Part 2)	-
6.	Nickel (as Ni), mg/l, max	0.07	No relaxation	IS 3025 (Part 54)	-
7.	Pesticides, mg/l, Max.	As given above	No relaxation	As given above	-
8.	Polychlorinated biphenyls, mg/l, Max	0.0005	No relaxation	ASTM 5175	-
9.	Polynuclear aromatic hydro-carbons (as PAH), mg/l, Max	0.0001	No relaxation	APHA 6440	-
10.	Total arsenic (as As mg/l, Max)	0.01	0.05	IS 3025 (Part 37)	-
11. (a)	Tribalomethane Bromoform, mg/l Max	0.1	No relaxation	ASTM D 3973.85 or APHA 6232	-
(b)	Dihromochloromethane, mg/1 Max				
(c)	Bromodichloron ethane, mg/L, Max	0.06	No relaxation	ASTM D 3973085 or APHA 6232	-
(d)	Chloroform, mg/l, Max.	0.2	No relaxation	ASTM D 3973-85 or APHA 6232	-

Source: IS 10500: 2012.

Table 8.8: Pesticide Limits of Radioactive Substance

S. No.	Characteristics	Requirement (Acceptable limit)	Permissible limit in the absence of alternate source	Method of test, Ref. No.	Remarks
1.	Alpha emitters Bq/l, Max	0.1	No relaxation	Part 2	-
2.	Beta emittersBq/l, Max	1.0	No relaxation	Part 1	-

Source: IS 10500: 2012.

Table 8.9: Pesticide Residues Limits of Drinking Water

S. No.	Pesticide	Limit mg/l	USEPA	AOAC/ISO
1.	Alachlor	20	525.2.507	-
2.	Atrazine	2	525.1.8141 A	-
3.	Aldrin/Dieldrin	0.03	508	-
4.	Alpha HCH	0.01	508	-
5.	Beta HCH	0.04	508	-
6.	Butachlor	125	525.1.8141 A	-
7.	Chlorpyriphos	30	525.2.8141 A	-
8.	Delta HCH	0.04	508	-
9.	24-Dichlorophenoxyacetic acid	30	515.1	-
10.	DDT (cp and pp – Isomers of DDT, DDE and DDD)	1	508	AOAC 990.06
11.	Didosulfan (alpha, beta and sulphate)	0.4	508	AOAC 990.06
12.	Ethion	3	1657 A	-
13.	Gamma – HCH (Landane)	2	508	AOAC 900.06
14.	Isoproturon	2	508	-
15.	Malathion	190	532	-
16.	Methyl parathion	0.3	8141 A	-
17.	Monocrotophos	1	8141 A	-
18.	Phorate	2		-

Source: IS 10500: 2012.

Table 8.10: Bacteriological Quality of Drinking Water

S. No.	Organisms	Requirement
1. All water intended for drinking:		
(a)	E-coli thermotolerant coliform bacteria	Shall not be detectable in any 100 ml. Sample
2. Treated water entering the distribution system		
(a)	E-Coli or thermotolerant coliform bacteria	Shall not be detectable in any 100 ml. Sample
(b)	Total coliform bacteria	Shall not be detectable in any 100 ml sample
3. Treated water in the distribution system		
(a)	E-Coli or thermotolerant coliform bacteria	Shall not be detectable in any 100 ml sample
(b)	Total coliform bacteria	Shall not be detectable in any 100 ml sample

Source: IS 10500: 2012.

Land requirement for Water Supply System

Identification of land for water infrastructure is an essential parameter. It is necessary to earmark land for Water Treatment Plant (WTP) in Development Plans. Also land for overhead reservoirs, pumping stations should be marked at the zonal level or local area plan level. However, land requirement may vary based on the capacity of WTPs and upgradation of technology. Below is the table, which recommends land requirement based on different capacities:

Table 8.11: Recommended Land Requirement based on Capacities

S. No.	Capacity	Land Requirement (Hectares)
1.	5 MLD	0.10
2.	10 MLD	0.19
3.	50 MLD	0.93
4.	100 MLD	1.87
5.	200 MLD	3.73
6.	500 MLD	9.34

Source: CPHEEO.

Note: Additional 0.63 ha of land can also be considered for staff quarters

Design Period for Water Supply Components

Table 8.12: Design Period for Water Supply Components

S. No.	Components	Design period (in years)
1.	Storage Dams	50
2.	Infiltration works	30
3.	Pumping (i) Pump house (civil works) (ii) Electric motors and pumps	 30 15
4.	Water treatment units	15
5.	Pipe connection to several treatment units and other small appurtenances	30
6.	Raw water and clear water conveying mains	30
7.	Clear water reservoirs at the head works, balancing tanks and service reservoirs (overhead or ground level)	15
8.	Distribution system	30

Source: Manual on Water Supply and Treatment, 1999, CPHEEO.

National Water Policy, 2012 by Ministry of Water Resources was formulated to govern the water resources planning and development along with its optimum utilisation. The Policy provides following recommendations regarding urban settlements:

- Urban water supply and sewage treatment must be integrated along with its billing,
- Least water intensive sanitation and sewerage systems with decentralized sewage treatment plants should be incentivized.
- Water reuse must be encouraged in urban settlements,
- Urban domestic water systems need to collect and publish water accounts and water audit reports indicating leakages and pilferages, which should be reduced.
- In urban and industrial areas, rain water harvesting and desalinisation where techno-economically feasible, should be encouraged to increase availability of utilizable water.State Governments shall draft State Water Policy for decentralised or micro level water management to yield better results.

Rain Water Harvesting

The term water harvesting refers to collection and storage of natural precipitation and also other activities, aimed at harvesting surface and groundwater, prevention of losses through evaporation and seepage, and all other hydrological studies and engineering interventions, aimed at conservation and efficient utilization of the limited water endowment of a physiographic unit, such as a watershed.

The various options, which can be covered under water harvesting are the following:

- Construction of storage structures for "in-situ" collection of rain water.
- Farm ponds for collection of runoff, either for supplemental irrigation or for-augmentation of groundwater.
- Check dams for storing runoff in first order (small) streams.
- Percolation tanks at appropriate sites for augmentation of groundwater.
- Construction of ponds and reclamation/revitalization of traditional water arresting structures.

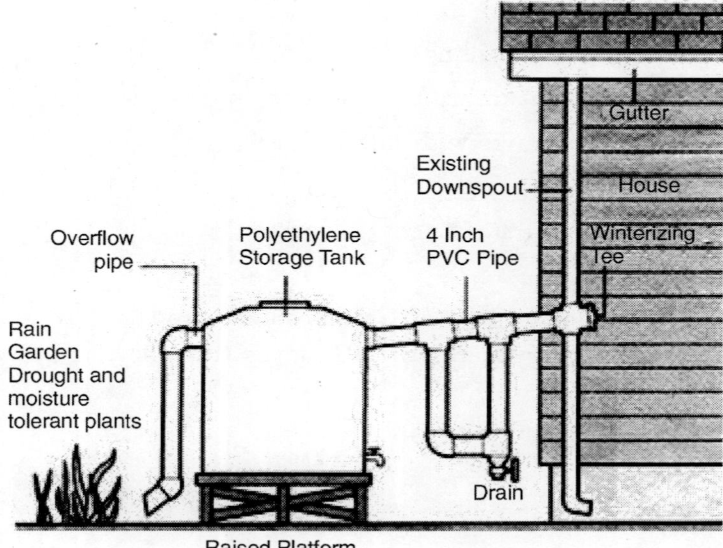

Fig. 8.1. Rainwater Storage Tank Detail

- Artificial recharge through wells.
- Reduction of evaporation from surface water bodies and soils.
- Prevention of seepage losses in appropriate situations.
- Enhancement of runoff through mechanical arid chemical treatment in catchment areas.
- Sub-surface dams to arrest base flow of groundwater.
- Soil and water conservation practices comprising contour and terrace bunding.
- Control of seawater incursion in coastal aquifers/prevention of sub-surface discharge of groundwater to sea.
- Control of transpiration without affecting normal plant growth.

Artificial Recharge Techniques

A variety of methods have been developed to recharge ground water. Common artificial recharge techniques are briefly described below:

1. Direct surface techniques by:
   - Flooding
   - Basins or percolation tanks

- Stream augmentation
- Ditch and furrow system
- Over irrigation

2. Direct sub-surface techniques:
   - Injection wells or recharge wells
   - Recharge pits and shafts
   - Dug-well recharge
   - Bore-hole flooding
   - Natural openings, cavity fillings.
3. Combination surface - sub-surface techniques by:
   - Basin or percolation tanks with pit shaft or wells.
4. Indirect Techniques by:
   - Induced recharge from surface water source.
   - Aquifer modification

The 'Manual on Artificial Recharge of Groundwater', prepared by Ministry of Water Resources, Central Ground Water Board (CGWB), gives the following options for artificial groundwater recharge:

1. Ditch and Furrow Method
2. Lateral Ditch Pattern
3. Dendritic Pattern
4. Contour Pattern
5. Spreading Basin or Percolation Tanks
6. Gully Plug / Check Dam / Nala Bund / Gabbion Structures
7. Dug Well Recharge
8. Recharge Shafts / Pits / Trenches
9. Artificial Recharge through Injection Well
10. Induced Recharge from Surface Water Sources
11. Subsurface Dykes / Underground Bandharas

Source: www.cgwb.gov.in

While the various options given above differ in terms of their connotations, the common conceptual thread is that they describe water management on a small or micro-scale, which is different from construction of major dams or river diversions and canal networks for irrigation of command area.

1. Secondary Treatment of Rain Water
2. W.C.
3. Washing machine
4. Garden Water outlet/tap
6. Rain water tank
7. Rain water storage after Primary Treatment
8. Municipal Water Inlet
9. Bath tub inlet
10. Kitchen Sink

Fig. 8.2. Rainwater Harvesting and grey water recycling: In most of the regions in India, water is a critical problem. By rainwater harvesting, wastewater recycling, primary treatment and checking of leakages, the problem can be mitigated to a great extent.

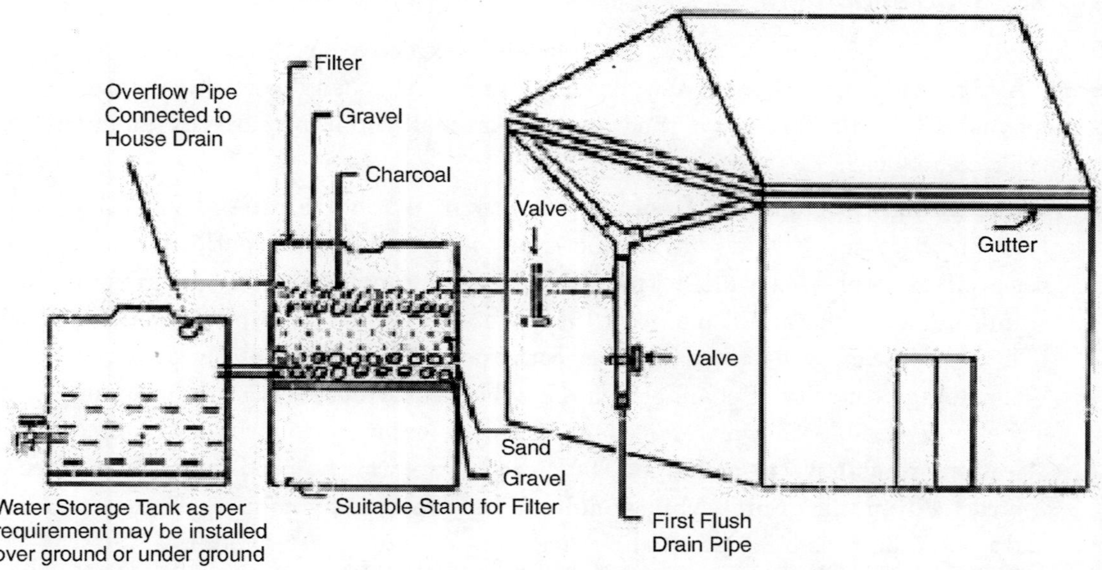

Fig. 8.3: Rainwater can be stored in tanks for drinking and cooking after primary treatment

When untreated effluents are discharged into the ground, these contaminated waters are absorbed by the soil and thus the ground water is polluted. Large-scale exploitation of water lowers the water level and dries the soil. This makes the maximum absorption of the domestic sewage and industrial effluents including presticides causing the groundwater pollution.

No other method will be efficient to decrease the solid content except the membrane separation technique. The groundwater may be recharged with the rainwater with the help of percolation wells.

The high-level contents of the parameters observed may be minimised if the groundwater is recharged with the available storm water in the rainy season. This not only dilutes the constituents of the groundwater but also raises the groundwater level that depletes due to large-scale exploitation.

Consider a building with flat terrace area of 125 sqm. The average annual rain fall is say 750 mm. Suppose there is no loss of water from terrace floor, then in one year, there will be rainwater on the terrace floor to a height of 750 mm.

Area of Terrace = 125 sq.m

Height of Rainfall = 750 mm (0.75 m)

Volume of Rainfall = 125 × 0.75

= 93.75 Cum or 93,750 litres.

Assuming that only 60% of the total rainfall is effectively harvested, Volume of Water harvested = 93,750 × 0.60 = 56,250 litres.

A family of six needs about 21,900 litres of water per year.

Thus harvested water of 56,250 litres is more than the double required by a family of six.

Watershed Development

The term watershed refers to a topographically distinctive area which is drained by a stream. A watershed can be of a few hundred to few thousand hectares in size. If the topography is undulating, the area of the watershed is small and it increases as the undulation in a terrain is reduced.

(a) **On-channel Storage and Recharge of Storm Water Channels:** Several seasonal streams become activated during the monsoons providing the outlet to flood waters as well as local area runoff. The channels may run through urban areas or their hinterlands. With careful planning these waters can be stored on the channel itself. The waters can be detained through construction of appropriate located regulators. The storage capacity of channels can be enhanced by deepening and widening them, wherever possible. Storm water channels can be enlarged to form on-channel lake at locations conductive to recharge. The stored water can be used from the surface or extracted from the ground while simultaneously recharging aquifers. These reservoirs also offer the possibility of creating rich urban bio-diversity habitats.

(b) **Off-channel Storage for Flood waters:** As all storm water cannot be stored on channel, possibilities exist for the creation of off-channel reservoirs linked to the main channel. The creation of off-channel reservoirs, especially wherever a suitable recharge area exists in the neighbourhood of a channel, is a useful device for storing water for the lean season. These reservoirs also offer the possibility of creating rich urban bio-diversity habitats.

(c) Storage in Lakes and Depressions: In urban areas, lakes have often been misused for dumping of solid waste and sewage disposal. The storage capacity of these can be increased by desilting and widening. The water quality would need to be improved by replicating the principles of wetlands by systematic induction of aquatic plants and fish. This is a very low cost treatment and subsequently only clean water would enter the underlying aquifer. The groundwater table is the most economical form of storage, without any expense in construction of reservoirs. Water can thereafter be extracted from the aquifer by battery of shallow tubewells for a long duration extending into the lean season. The wetland habitats comprising oxbow lakes, marshes, low lying lands on the floodplains, lakes, estuarine lands, abandoned quarries, artificial lakes over good recharge zones can help in the sustenance of the ecology, and also for other activities such as recreation, flood prevention, water storage, water extraction and natural water treatment.

(d) Floodplain Reservoirs for Conjunctive Extraction: Very often the most copious fresh water aquifers underline the floodplains. In urban areas, there is no place to store the monsoon discharge of the river due to lack of topographical relief. To overcome this difficulty simple reservoirs on the floodplain can be created by scooping out earth at appropriate locations and letting these reservoirs to be filled up by the expanded monsoon season flow of the river.

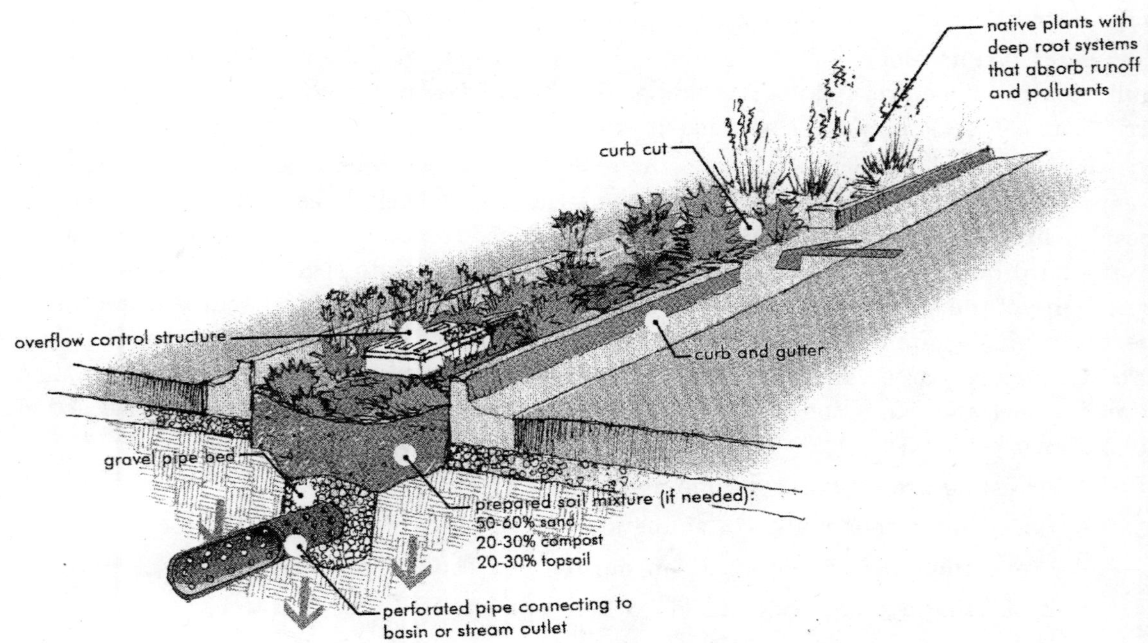

Fig. 8.4: Curbside Rain Garden for Sustainable Drainage

Source: www.environment-agency.gov.uk/suds/

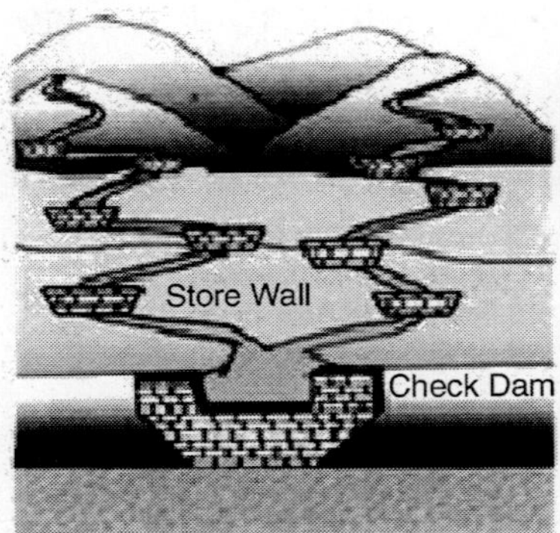

Fig. 8.5: Rainwater harvesting by small check dams

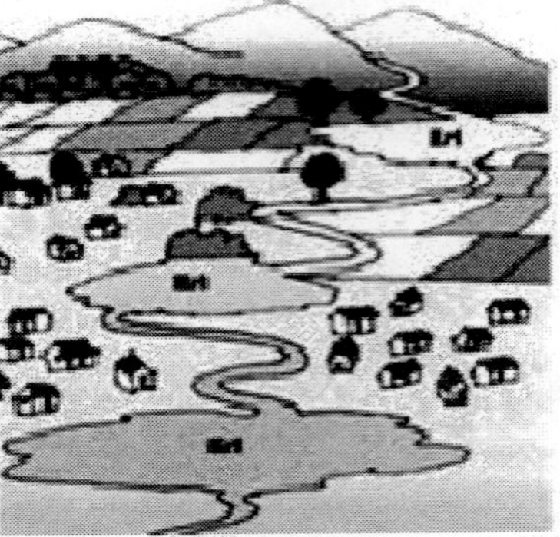

Fig. 8.6: Traditional water harvesting through eris (lakes)

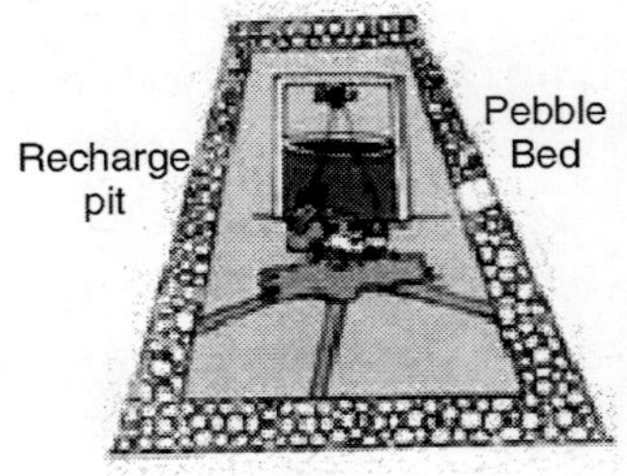

Fig. 8.7: Recharge ground water by pebble bed

Fig. 8.8: Check dam and gully control structure

Fig. 8.9: Contour bunding

Fig. 8.10: Ridge sand furrows and trenching

Watershed development, bio-drainage, conservation/revival of ponds, check dams, swales, gully control structures, contour bunding, ridges and furrows, rainwater harvesting micro-irrigation, etc. are essential for sustainable water and drainage management.

In order to adopt appropriate measures for augmenting ground recharge, it is necessary to spread water harvesting techniques by construction of check dams arid percolation tanks, besides direct injection methods utilising the abandoned structures available in large numbers in the hard rock region. Before undertaking direct recharge into such abandoned structures, suitability of the structure for receiving recharge and also the quality of source water should be thoroughly examined to confirm the technical feasibility. Rain water harvesting and groundwater recharge can be suitably dovetailed with watershed development programmes aimed at soil and water conservation by arresting the run-off. This involves several actions as outlined below:

- Arresting groundwater decline and improving its accessibility
- Benefiting water quality in aquifers
- Preventing surface water run-off during monsoons
- Enhancing availability of surface water at a specific place and time
- Reducing power consumption
- Conserving and recycling urban waste water.

Key Action Areas

- Organising mass awareness campaigns through hand-outs, posters and community level involvement.
- Practising and implementing rain water harvesting and ground recharging through local bye laws.
- Motivating communities to participate in *shramdan* camps for cleaning ponds, tanks,wells and borewells; and reutilising them for groundwater storage.
- Financial support for construction of check dams and creation of catchment ponds.
- Recycling waste water subject to quality and dual piping system.
- Recharging industrial effluents after treatment.

Guidelines for Water Conservation

- Redesigning cisterns/tanks/reservoirs for conservation of water, e.g. traditional 3.5 gallon toilet cistern can be replaced by a 5 to 7 litres.
- Using urban waste water effluents after suitable treatment for horticulture, etc.
- Recycling of waste water.
- Ground water recharge by bio-swales, rainwater harvesting, porous paving and artificial recharge techniques
- Conserving monsoon water in Johads, check dams, percolation tanks, village ponds, etc. and their regular desilting.
- Using existing or defunct wells and tube wells for purpose of recharging and rainwater harvesting.

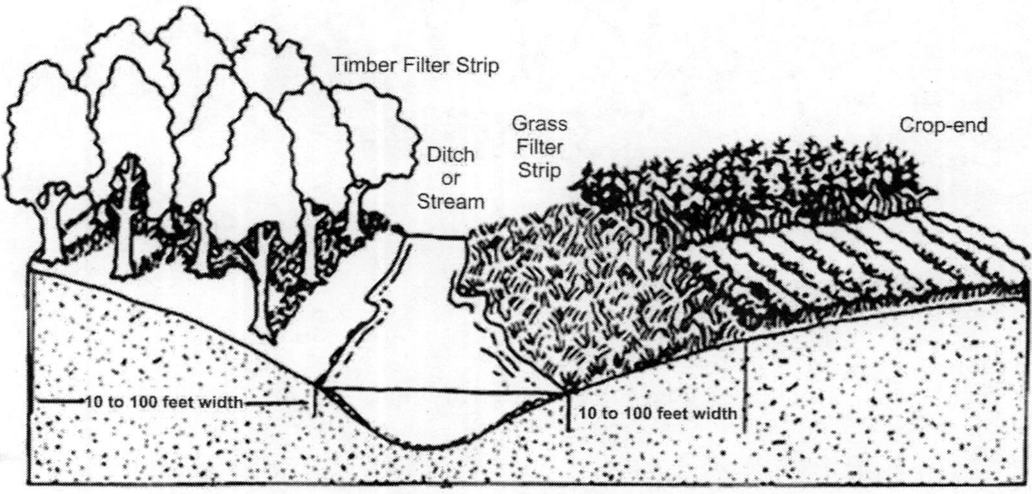

Fig. 8.11 Vegetative filter strip.

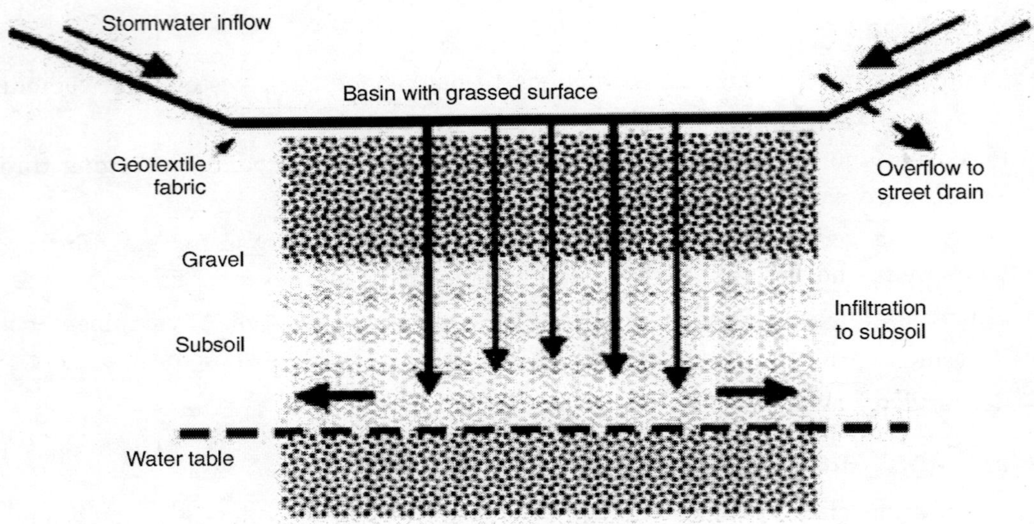

Fig. 8.12: Detail-Filter Strip.

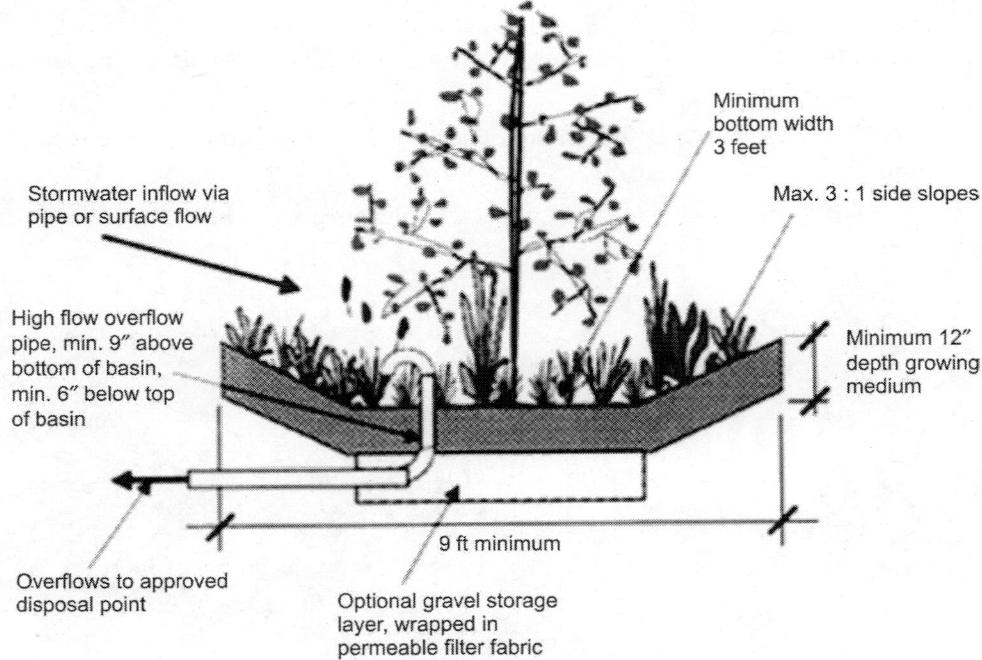

Fig. 8.13: Infiltration basin.

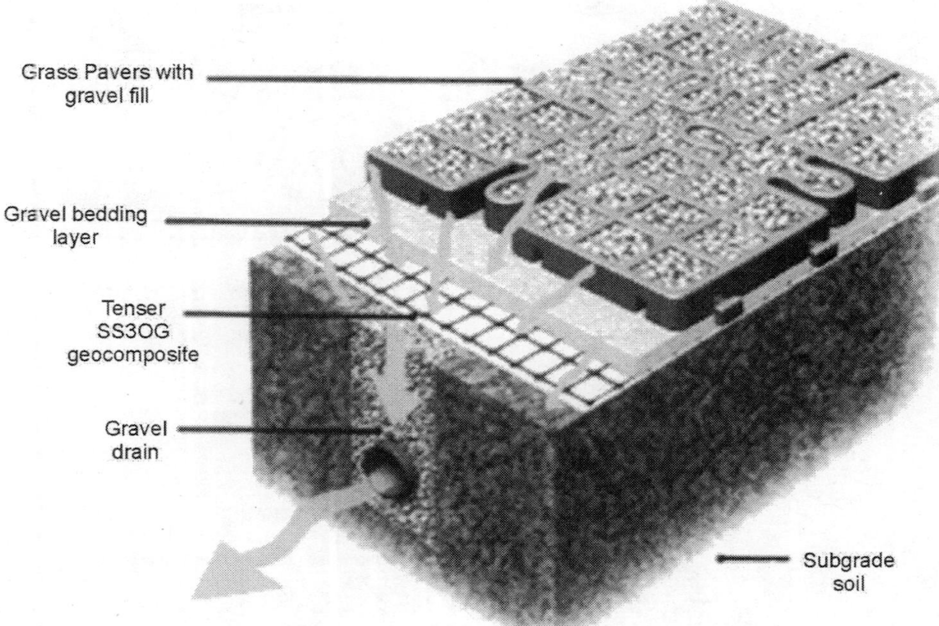

Fig. 8.14: On-site water retention (porous paving)

Fig. 8.15: Rainwater Harvesting by an Infiltration Trench

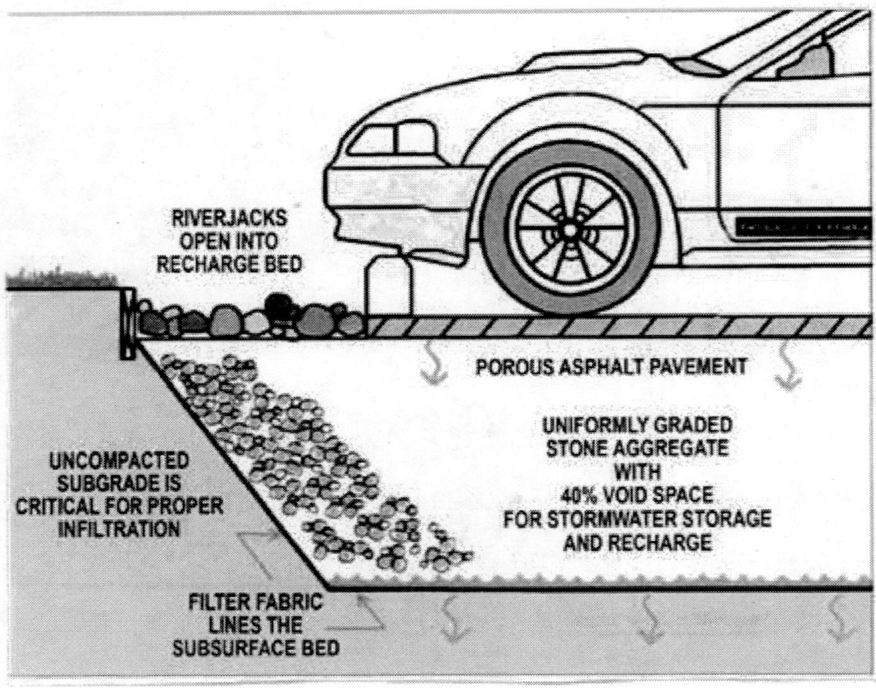

Fig. 8.16: Roadside Recharge Bed

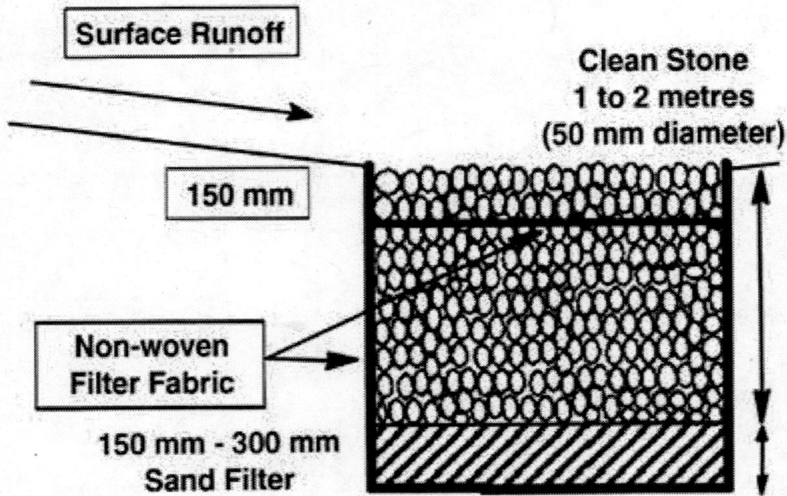

Fig. 8.17: Section of infiltration trench

In view of the rapid urbanisation, coupled with diminishing water resources, it is necessary to conserve available water, and harvest rain water to the maximum extent possible through various measures as given below:

- Leak detection and water supply network maintenance and rectification.
- Rain water harvesting through in-situ tanks, check dams, etc.

- Controlling indiscriminate extraction of groundwater
- Recharging of aquifers.
- Meters to be installed along trunk mains and for bulk consumers and tariff review.
- Percolation structures, wherever suited, be encouraged in open grounds and roadside will help recharge bore-wells and provide water for gardening, car washing, etc.
- Mandatory system of roof-top rain water harvesting.
- Recycling and reuse of treated waste water
- Soft parking, landscape and pavements filled with pebbles and coarse sand to allow percolation.

Rain water falling on roof is collected and injected into groundwater reservoir through abandoned dug well, hand pump or in a water storage tank.

Filtration and Water Treatment

Surface and sub-soil water is generally impure which needs primary and secondary treatment to make it useful or potable. Drinking water must meet the highest quality, purity and hygiene requirements. Thus, the development of filtration technology has always been important. The filter design constitutes an optimum solution for both single and multi-player filters:

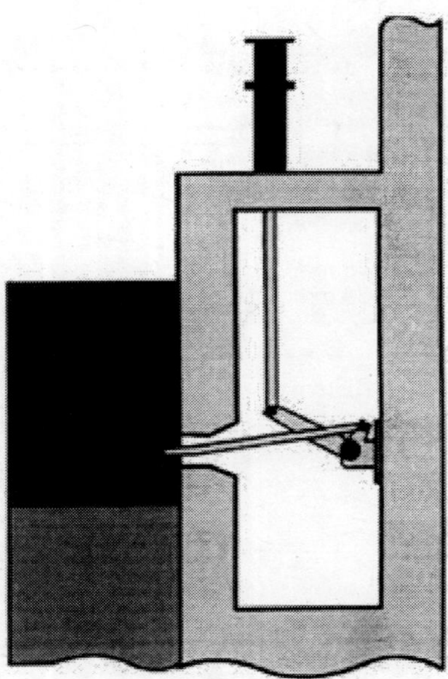

Fig. 8.18: Schematic Diagram of Flap Valve.

- Outlet regulation: best conditions for direct filtration.
- Compact assembly of the back washing connections.
- Highly flexible filter media combinations.
- No filter media losses.
- Low backwash water consumption.

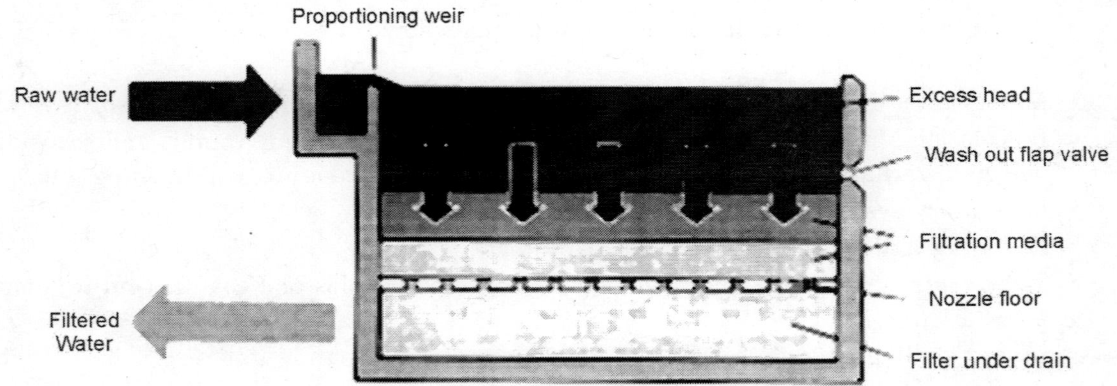

Fig. 8.19: Schematic Diagram of the Filter Cell

One essential feature of the filter is the internal flap valve. The flap valve is situated at the front of the filter cell, just above the top level of the filter medium. The pneumatic or electric actuation is equipped with a positioner for the phased opening of the flap valve. Backwashing is based on the excess head principle, which means that the rising process can be precisely matched to individual operating conditions.

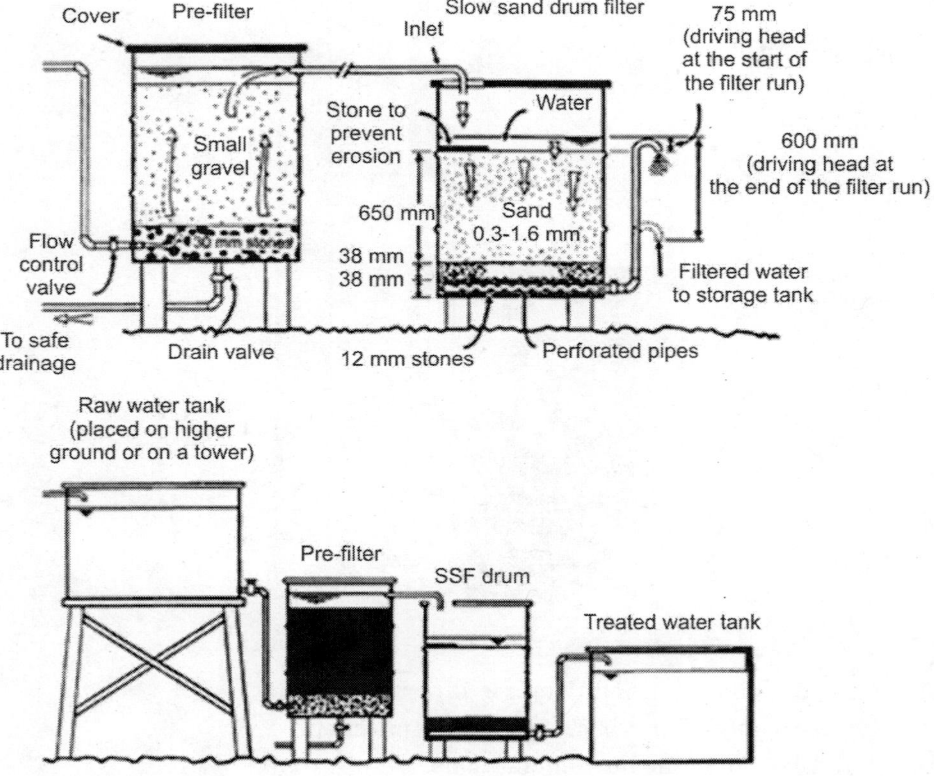

Fig. 8.20: Slow Sand Drum Filter and Pre-filter.

There are several packaged systems such as small, high rate and pressurized sand filter with backwash. A carbon filter may also be incorporated.

Table 8.13: A Comparison of Slow Sand Filters and Rapid Filters

	Slow sand filter (SSF)	**Rapid filter**
Filter medium	Fine	Coarse
Filtration rate	Low: 0.1-0.3 m/h	High: 5-15 m/h
Mechanisms	Sedimentation, adsorption, straining for the removal of impurities, chemicals and microbiological proceses	Sedimentation, adsorption, straining chemical and microbiological processes
Main mechanism for removal of impurities	Microbiological	Physical mechanisms, especially adsorption
Principal application	Treatment of low turbidity water (<20 NTU) for distribution as potable water post-chlorination may still be carried out	Treatment of low turbidity water-chlorination is required before distribution. Treatment of high turbidity raw water, following flocculation and sedimentation.
Principal advantages	Substantially reduces pathogenic bacteria, viruses and cysts to produce potable water without further treatment. No machinery required	Relatively small and compact
Principal disadvantages	Can only effectively treat low turbidity water	Cannot produce potable water without further treatment. Backwashing water required to clean filter, which usually involves pumps.

Table 8.14: Advantages and Disadvantages of Chlorine Use as a Disinfectant

Advantages	**Disadvantages**
It comes in several forms: powder, granules, liquid, gas	It is powerful oxidizing agent which must be handled carefully so that it does not breathe chlorine fumes
It is usually readily available and relatively cheap in one form or another	It does not effectively penetrate particulate matter
It dissolves easily. residual chlorine remaining in treated water provides some protection against further contamination	It can give an unpleasant taste when slightly overdosed, which could dissuade people from drinking safe water.
It is effective against a wide range of pathogens	Its effectiveness against some pathogens-cysts, ova, viruses requires higher chlorine concentrations and a longer contact time

Sewerage and Sanitation-National Urban Sanitation Policy

The aim of the National Urban Sanitation Policy (NUSP, 2008) is to transform Urban India into community driven, totally sanitized, healthy, and liveable cities and towns. Basic features laid down in NUSP given below should be adhered for planning of the cities:

- Cities must be open defecation free
- Must eliminate the practice of manual scavenging and provide adequate personnel protection equipment that addresses the safety of sanitation workers
- Municipal sewage and storm water drainage must be safely managed
- Recycle and of treated sewage for non-potable applications should be implemented, wherever possible
- Solid waste collected and disposed of fully and safely
- Services to the poor for sustaining results
- Improved public health outcomes and environmental standards.

The objective of public waste water collection and disposal system is to ensure that sewage or excreta and sullage discharged from community is properly discharged, collected, transported, treated to the required level of degree and finally disposed of without causing any health or environmental problems.

As per CPHEEO manual, 80% of water supply may be expected to reach the sewers, however, it recommends designing the system by considering minimum wastewater flow of 100 litres per capita per day. Further details are available in National Mission on Sustainable Habitat, Adaptation and Mitigation Measures in the field of Water Supply and Sanitation, CPHEEO, MOUD.

Table 8.15: Recommended Design Period for Sewerage Systems

S. No.	Components	Recommended Design Period (Years)	Clarification
1.	Collection system (Sewer Network)	30	The system should be designed for the prospective population of 30 years, as its replacement is not possible during its use.
2.	Pumping stations (Civil Works)	30	Duplicating machinery within pumping station would be easier and cost of civil works will be economical for full design period.
3.	Pumping Machinery	15	Life of pumping machinery generally 15 years.
4.	Sewage Treatment Plant	30	The construction may be in a phased manner as initially the flows may not reach the designed levels and it will be uneconomical to build the full capacity plant initially.
5.	Effluent Disposal and Utilisation	30	Provision of design capacities in the initial stages itself is economical.

Source: Manual on Sewerage and Sewage Treatment, CPHEEO, 2013.

Decentralised Wastewater Management System (DWMS)

DWMS has emerged as a pragmatic alternative, which reduces the load of centralised wastewater treatment unit. As per MoUD, Decentralized Waste-water Management may be defined as "the collection, treatment, and disposal/reuse of wastewater from individual homes, clusters of homes, isolated communities, industries, or institutional facilities, as well as from portions of existing communities at or near the point of waste generation". In case of decentralized systems, both solid and liquid fractions of the wastewater are utilized near the point of its origin, except in some cases when a portion of liquid and residual solids may be transported to a centralized point for further treatment and reuse.

MoUD (Guidelines for Decentralised Waste Water Management, MoUD, 2012) in association with Indian Institute of Technology (IIT), Madras has developed guidelines on DWMS, which recommends 15 years of design period for DWMS, if possible. Another way to design a DWMS is to estimate the present day capacity and plan the system for an additional 20% capacity. Further, the detailed guidelines as mentioned in Manual on Sewerage and Sewage Treatment of CPHEEO (2013) can be referred while developing DWMS units in a city which elaborates siting criteria, components and other design consideration including wastewater characteristics and waste water treatment.

While the conventional sewerage may be a comprehensive system for sewage collection and transport, it also remains as a highly resource intensive technology. Consequently, high capital cost, and significant O&M cost of this system inhibits its widespread adoption in all sizes of urban areas. The implementation of Centralized Wastewater Management System (CWMS) should not be considered as the only option available for collection, transportation and treatment of sewage. There are certain factors, which govern the selection of options between CWMS and DWMS.

Recognizing the many applications and benefits of sewage reuse, some important points may be kept in view, such as;

(i) Review the impact of the population growth rate
(ii) Review of potential water reuse applications and water quality requirements
(iii) Review of appropriate technologies for sewage treatment and reuse
(iv) Considering the type of management structure that will be required in the future, and,
(v) Identification of issues that must be solved to bring about water reuse for sustainable development on a broad scale.

It has been emphasized that if sewage from the urban and semi-urban areas are reused for a variety of non-potable uses, the demand on the potable water supply would be reduced.

The choice of appropriate technology also depends on several factors such as composition of sewage, availability of land, funds and expertise. Different operation and maintenance options have to be considered with respect to sustainable plant operation, the use of local resources, knowledge and manpower.

Effluent Standards

As per MoEF, the general effluent standards for discharging the waste-water are given in table below:

Table 8.16: General Effluent Standards for Waste Water Discharge

S. No.	Components	Standards			
		Inland surface water	**Public Sewers**	**Land for Irrigation**	**Marine Coastal Areas**
1.	Colour and Odour	All efforts should be made to remove colour and unpleasant odour as far as practicable			
2.	Suspended Solids	100	600	200	For process waste water 100 For cooling water effluent 10 percent above total suspended matter of influent.
3.	Particulate size of suspended solids	Shall pass GSO micron IS Sieve	-	-	(a) Floatable solids, max. 3 mm (b) Settle-ablesolids, max. 850 microns
4.	pH Value	5.5 to 9.0	5.5 to 9.0	5.5 to 9.0	5.5 to 9.0
5.	Temperature	Shall not exceed 50°C above the receiving water temperature	-	-	Shall not exceed 50°C above the receiving water temperature
6.	Oil and grease mg/l, Max.	10	20	10	20
7.	Total residual chlorine mg/m Max	1.0	-	-	1.0
8.	Ammonical nitrogen (as N), mg/l Max.	50	50	-	50
9.	Total Kjeldahl Nitrogen (as NH_3), mg/l Max	100	-	-	100
10.	Free Ammonia (as NHS), mg/l Max.	5.0	-	-	5.0
11.	Biochemical Oxygen demand (3 days at 27°C), mg/l, Max.	30	350	100	100
12.	Chemical Oxygen Damand, mg/l, Max.	250	-	-	250
13.	Arsenic (as As), mg/l, Max.	0.2	0.2	0.2	0.2

14.	Mercury (as Hg), mg/l, Max.	0.01	0.01	-	0.01
15.	Lead (as Pb), mg/l, Max	0.1	1.0	-	2.0
16.	Cadmium (as Cd), mg/l, Max	2.0	10	-	2.0
17.	Hexavalent Chromium (as Cr+6), mg/l, Max.	0.1	2.0	-	1.0
18.	Total Chromium (as Cr.), mg/l, Max.	2.0	2.0	-	2.0
19.	Copper (as Cu), mg/l, Max.	3.0	3.0	-	3.0
20.	Zinc (as Zn.), mg/l, max	5.0	15	-	15
21.	Selenium (as Se) mg/l, Max	0.05	0.05	-	0.05
22.	Fluoride (as F), mg/l, Max	2.0	15	-	15
23.	Dissolved Phosphates (as P), mg/l Max	5.0	-	-	-
24.	Sulphide (as S), mg/l, Max	2.0	-	-	5.0
25.	Phenolic compounds (as CSHS OH, mg/l, Max	1.0	5.0	-	5.0
26.	Radioactive materials:				
(a)	Alpha emitter micro curie/ml	10.7	10.7	10.8	10.7
(b)	Beta emitter micro curie/ml	10.6	10.6	10.7	10.6
27.	Bio-assay test	90% survival of fish after 96 hours in 100% effluent	90% survival of fish after 96 hours in 100% effluent	90% survival of fish after 96 hours in 100% effluent	90% survival of fish after 96 hours in 100% effluent
28.	Manganese (as Mn)	2 mg/l	2 mg/l	-	2 mg/l
29.	Iron (as Fe)	3mg/l	3 mg/l	-	3 mg/l
30.	Vanadium (as V)	0.2 mg/l	0.2 mg/l	-	0.2 mg/l
31.	Nitrate Nitrogen	10 mg/l	-	-	20 mg/l

Source: Manual on Sewerage and Sewage Treatment Systems, CPHEEO, 2013.

Recommended norms for Sewage and its uses

The recommended treated sewage quality, proposed to be used, is given in the table below:

Table 8.17: Recommended upper limits of treated Sewage quality for specified activities at point of use

S. No.	Parameter	Toilet flushing	Fire Protection	Vehicle Exterior washing	Non-contact impoundments	Landscaping, Horticulture and Agriculture Crops which are eaten			
						Horticulture/Golf course	Non edible crops	Raw	Cooked
1.	Turbidity (NTU)	<2	<2	<2	<2	<2	AA	<2	AA
2.	SS	Nil	Nil	Nil	Nil	Nil	Nil	Nil	Nil
3.	TDS	2100							
4.	pH	6.5 to 8.3							
5.	Temperature °C	Ambient							
6.	Oil and Grease	10	Nil	Nil	Nil	10	10	Nil	Nil
7.	Minimum Residual Chlorine	1	1	1	0.5	1	Nil	Nil	Nil
8.	Total Kjeldahl Nitrogen as N	10	10	10	10	10	10	10	10
9.	BOD	10	10	10	10	10	20	10	20
10.	COD	AA	AA	AA	AA	AA	AA	AA	30
11.	Dissolved Phosphorous as P	1	1	1	1	2	5	2	5
12.	Nitrate Nitrogen as N	10	10	10	5	10	10	10	10
13.	Faecal Coliform in 100 ml	Nil	Nil	Nil	Nil	Nil	230	Nil	230
14.	Helminthic Eggs/litre	AA	AA	AA	AA	AA	<1	<1	<1
15.	Colour	Colourless	Colourless	Colourless	Colourless	Colourless	AA	Colourless	Colourless
16.	Odour	Aseptic which means not septic and no foul odour							

Source: Manual on Sewerage and Sewage Treatment Systems, CPHEEO 2013.

In order to achieve desired water quality, standards of chlorination, granular activated carbon adsorption/Ozonation and/or various kinds of filtration, including membrane, are recommended. For recreational impoundments for non-human contact, residual chlorine is not required so as to protect aquatic species of flora and fauna.As per the Manual of Sewerage and Sewage Treatment, the following provisions are to be followed for usage of treated sewage, sludge and biogas utilization:

(a) Reuse of treated sewage should be taken up after discussions between ULB, water boards, PHEDs/Jal Nigams and the public, as the case may be. Various possible reuse methods such as farm forestry, greenbelt development and lawns in road medians.

(b) Utilization of sludge in public areas is not possible due to issues of public acceptance and hence it is best to focus on farm forestry.

(c) Utilization of alternative energy, like energy harnessed from bio-methanation and to evaluate the ambient temperature suitability of sludge vs economics.

(d) Reuse of treated sewage to a minimum extent of 20% by volume shall be mandatorily explored and the proposed use for achieving this 20% target shall mandatorily form part of the CSP.

(e) Utilization of sludge as a construction material (as porous pavement, bricks, etc.)

Recycling of Waste Water

Various sewage treatment technologies, given below, are adopted in sewerage system to treat wastewater up to secondary level, as per the effluent standards in India as well as in other parts of the world. These technologies are:

1. Activated Sludge Process (ASP)
2. Waste Stabilisation Pond Systems (WSPS)
3. Upflow Anaerobic Sludge Blanket Process (UASB)
4. Duckweed Pond System (DPS)
5. Facultative Aerate Lagoon (FAL)
6. Trickling Filter (TF)
7. Biological Filtration and Oxygenated reactor (BIOFOR) Technology
8. High Rate Activated Sludge Biofor-F Technology
9. Fluidized Aerated Bed (FAB)
10. Submerged Aeration Fixed Film (SAFF) Technology
11. Cyclic Activated Sludge Process (CASP)

The salient features and comparison of these technologies in terms of their applicability, land requirement, capital cost and operation and maintenance (O&M) costs are given in the table below.

Table 8.18: Fact Sheet for Various Treatment Process

S. No.	Recycling Technique	Applicability	Land Requirement (Per MLD in Hectares)	Capital Cost (Rs. per MLD	O & M cost (Rs. Million/ Year/MLD)
1.	Activated Sludge Process (ASP)	• The most widely used option for treatment of domestic waste water for medium to large towns where land is scarce.	0.15-0.25	2-4	0.3-0.5
2.	Waste Stabilisation Pond System (WSPS)	• In warm conditions • Easy land availability • Where power supply is expensive or unreliable. • Where social preference for aquaculture	0.8-2.3	1.5-4.5	0.06-0.1
3.	Upflow Anaerobic Sludge Blanket Process (UASB)	• The suitability of this technology may be doubtful as a stand alone secondary treatment option	0.2-0.3	2.5-3.6	0.08-0.11
4.	Duckweed Pond System (DPS)	• Low strength domestic waste water after sedimentation with influent BOD < 80 mg/L • In combination with existing WSP • Easy land availability • As a polishing pond for an existing activated sludge plant or other technology based STPs.	2-6	1.5-4.5	0.18
5.	Facultive Aerate Lagoon (FAL)	• Standalone system • As a pre-treatment unit for WSP • As an upgradation option for overloaded WSPs	0.27-0.4	2.2-2.9	0.15-0.2

6.	Trickling Filter (TF)	• Stand alone system if operated at slow rates • As a high rate roughing filter for high BOD waste water • In combination with ASP	0.25-0.65	Not available but slightly lower than ASP	
7.	Biological Filtration and Oxygenated reactor (Biofor-F Technology)	• Decentralised approach	0.04	6.5-8.1	0.86
8.	High rate Activated Sludge (Biofor-F Technology)	• Decentralised approach	0.08	5.2	0.18
9.	Fluidized Aerated Bed (FAB)	• Small to medium flows in congested locations • Sensitive locations • Decentralised approach • Relieving existing overloaded STPs.	0.06	3-5	0.6.0.75
10.	Submerged Aeraction Fixed Film (SAFF) Technology	• Small to medium flows in congested locations • Sensitive locations • Decentralised approach • Relieving existing overloaded trickling filters.	0.05	7	1.14
11.	Cyclic Activated Sludge Process (CASP)	• Small to medium flows in congested locations • Sensitive locations • Decentralised approach • Relieving existing overloaded trickling filters	0.1-0.15	Not availa-ble	Expected to be higher than ASP

Source: Compendium of Sewage Treatment Technologies, National River Conservation Directorate, MOEF, 2009.

Land availability plays an important role in providing such facilities. Land requirement may vary based on the technology adopted for sewage treatment. However, it is evident to mark the required land on development plan. It is recommended to decide the most suitable technology in advance based on the various parameters as given above.

Septage Management

For effective septage management plan, robust data on septage arrangements, their quantity and locations of its generation etc. are required. The ULBs would need to make arrangements to collect baseline data, like type of latrine disposal, effluent disposal arrangement, size, age, when it was last cleaned, access to the on-site system, arrangement for disposal of effluent, if any of existing installations, to plan for workable desludging schedules. It is advisable to divide the city into different sanitary zones (if not already done) and carry out the baseline survey in one or a fewof these zones, pilot desludging area-wise schedules to learn operational issues and devise solutions, before upscaling the entire system. The selection of zone could be based on availability of septage disposal sites – existing STPs could be potential septage disposal/application sites or trenches provided in solid waste land fill sites or suitable urban forestry sites where the septage trenches would serve to fertilize the plants. In order to be economical and financially competitive, it is suggested that households in demarcated septage management zone should be within 20 to 30 km travel distance from the identified treatment and disposal sites.Further a two step process is to be followed for selection of the treatment system:

1. To determine the appropriate treatment option on the basis of size of town, land availability, proximity/availability of sewage treatment plants and proximity to residential areas; and
2. To conduct a techno-economic feasibility to choose the most appropriate technology on the basis of capital, operations and maintenance costs.

The steps in planning and implementing septage management are given below:

1. Collect data on the households and other properties with on site arrangements in the city.
2. List out the municipal, private and other septic tank/pit cleaning services active in the city
3. Identify catchment wise land for septage treatment facility such as use existing STP where available; or acquire land, if not available for construction of septage treatment facility
4. Formulate draft Regulations for septage management
5. Choose technology for septage treatment: prepare design of Septage Treatment and Disposal Facility (STDF) along with operations and maintenance costs
6. Conduct techno-economic feasibility of the STDF
7. Implement construction of septage management and disposal facility
8. Purchase vehicles and vacuum trucks, etc.
9. Launch awareness campaigns
10. Initiate training and capacity building
11. Provide cleaning services incrementally based on survey of tanks and pits.

Further, the guidelines for selection of Septage Disposal System are summarized below:

Table 8.19: Guidelines for the Selection of Septage Disposal System

Town/Category	Conditions	Recommended Technologies	Capital Cost	O & M Cost	Management
Unserved Class-III, IV and V towns and rural communities	Remote land area available with suitable site and soil condition.	Sludge drying beds and waste stabilization pond	Low	Low. User fees to recover O and M costs	Municipality or private (if implemented by private sector through a management contract)
	Land available but close to settlement	Lime stabilization sludge drying beds and waste stabilization pond.	Low to medium	Low to medium. User fees to recover O and M costs	Municipality or private (if implemented by private sector through a management contract).
	Inadequate land area with unsuitable site and soil condition, but available STP capacity within 20-30 km distance.	Disposal STP	Low to medium	Low to medium. User fees to recover O and M costs.	Municipality
Partially sewered medium size (Class-II Towns)	Land area available with suitable site and soil condition but close to settlements	Lime stabilization, sludge drying beds and waste stabilization pond.	Low to medium	Low to medium User fees to recover O and M costs	Municipality or private
	Inadequate land area, but available STP capacity	Disposal at STP	Medium	Medium User fees to recover O and M costs	Municipality or private
	Inadequate land area no available STP capacity.	Disposal at independent mechanical treatment facility	High	High User fees to recover O and M costs	Municipality or private

Class-I and metro cities	Available STP capacity	Disposal at STP	Medium	Medium, User fees to recover O and M costs	Municipality or private

Source: Advisory Note - Septage Management in Urban India, MoUD, 2013.

Recommended Norms for Public Toilets

The general standard guidelines for public toilets in public area and modified norms for public toilets recommended in the CPHEEO manual are given below.

Table 8.20: Norms for Public Toilets in Public Area

Type	Norms
Public Toilet	On roads and for open areas @ every 1 km., including in parks, plaza, open air theatre, swimming area, car parks, and fuel stations. Toilets shall be disabled-friendly and in 50-50 ratio (M/F).
Signage	Signboards on main streets shall give directions and mention the distance to reach the nearest public convenience of visitors. Helpline number shall be pasted on all toilets for complaints/queries.
Modes	Pay and use or free. In pay and use toilets entry is allowed on payment to the attendant or by inserting coin and user gets 15-20 minutes.
Maintenance/Cleaning	The toilet should have both men and women attendants. Alternatively automatic cleaning cycle covering flush, toilet bowl, seat, hand wash basin, disinfecting of floor and complete drying after each use can be adopted, which takes 40 seconds. Public toilets shall be open 24 hours.

Source: Manual on Sewerage and Sewage Treatment Systems, CPHEEO, 2013.

Drainage and Storm Water Management

Urban drainage system includes a network of sewers, drainage channels (minor system) and flood runoff paths (major system}. The minor system includes streets, sewers, and open channels, either natural or constructed. The minor system is planned to safely convey runoff from a storm with a specified recurrence interval, usually 5-10 years. The major system is utilised when the capacity of the minor system is exceeded. It is composed of whatever paths have been provided for runoff to flow to a receiving stream. Hence the problem of how much drainage and how much to confine and move in normal circumstances is solved by this classification.

Separated sewers consist of storm water networks that carry mainly surface runoff from streets, roofs, parking lots, and other surfaces towards the nearest receiving water body and separate sanitary sewers. Sanitary sewers carry household and commercial sewage and industrial waste waters towards a treatment plant. Combined sewers are used for collection and conveyance of both surface runoff and sanitary sewers in one conduit. Combined sewer invariably suffers from the disadvantages of sluggish flow during most part of the year leading to the depositing of sewage solids and creating foul and offensive conditions. Further, it is costly. In view of these reasons combined system is not usually recommended for Indian conditions.

Urban Drainage Planning

Planning of urban drainage is based on the following performance requirements:

(a) Hydraulic
(b) Environmental
(c) Structural
(d) Operational

Accordingly a drainage master plan combines a number of options, both structural and non-structural, keeping in view various factors such as rainfall, catchment area, levels/ contours, land configuration, environmental parameters, traffic impact, utilities and services, etc. It incorporates stormwater quality enhancement and pollution reduction by various methods-sedimentation, filtering, infiltration, biological uptake and straining. Thus appropriate options-grass buffer/swale, porous pavement, extended detention basin, wetland basin, retention pond, sand filter, wetland channel and tunnel are integrated with the proposed drainage system.

The main disposal line should, as far as possible, follow the line of natural drainage. Drains should be in straight lines, or in long easy curves. Sub-mains should also follow the line of natural drainage. Laterals should be laid in the line of greatest slope. Intercepting drains are an exception generally being placed across the slope. Three principal types of lateral sub-drainage systems are the herring bone, gridiron and parallel systems. The parallel system is the most economical type because it involves the least duplication of drainage by laterals and mains. The preferable arrangement is short mains and low laterals rather than the reverse.

The spacing of laterals depends on the physical composition and texture of the soils. A minimum slope of 1 per cent (1 ft. in 100 ft.) is recommended. Steeper slopes are better.

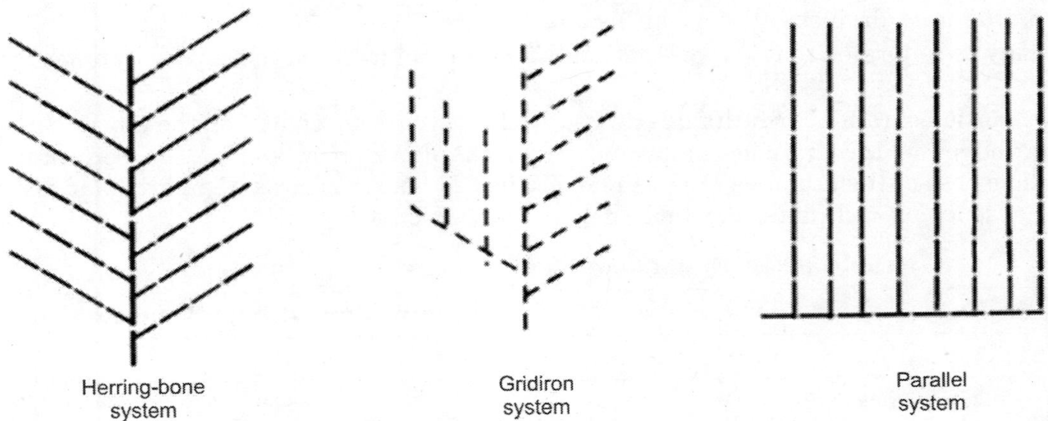

Fig. 8.21: Sewerage System Layout Options

Source: Handbook of Drainage and Construction Products. ARMCO Drainage and Metal Products, Inc., Middletown, Ohio.

Calculation of Volume of Flow for Drainage System

During rainfall periods there can be a considerable amount of storm water that does not infiltrate into the ground surface and most of this becomes the excess overland flow or direct surface runoff. There are many contributing factors for analysing the quantity and temporal variations of this flow; these include geology of the land, topography, geography, rainfall intensity and pattern and the land use type.

Estimation of such runoff reaching the storm sewers, is dependent on the intensity and duration of precipitation, characteristics of the tributary area and the time required for such flow to reach the sewer. There are various methods available to calculate the runoff, the two of the below mentioned methods can be adopted to calculate runoff:

(a) Rational Method

(b) Kirpich Equation Method

Rational Method

It is based on the assumption that the entire precipitation over the drainage district does not reach the sewer. The characteristics of the drainage district, such as, imperviousness, topography including depressions and water pockets, shape of the drainage basin and duration of the precipitation determine the fraction of the total precipitation which will reach the sewer. This fraction known as the coefficient of runoff needs to be determined for each drainage district.

The National Disaster Management Authority (NDMA) has prescribed that "all future storm water drainage systems for peak flow for any city should be designed after taking into consideration a runoff Coefficient of up to 0.95164 using the rational method". The runoff reaching the sewer is given by the expression,

$$Q = 10 \, C \, i \, A$$

Where Q is the runoff in m^3/hr;

C is the coefficient of runoff,

i is the intensity of in mm/hr, and

A is the area drainage district in hectares.

It may be reiterated that Q represents only the maximum discharge caused by a particular storm.

The portion of rainfall, which finds its way to the sewer is dependent on the imperviousness and the shape of the drainage area apart from the duration of storm. The percentage of imperviousness of the drainage area can be obtained from the records of a particular district. In the absence of such data, the table below may serve as a guide.

Table 8.21.: Runoff coefficients for various surfaces

S. No.	Type of Area	Percentage of Imperviousness
1	Commercial and Industrial Area	70-90
2.	Residential Area – High Density – Low Density	 61-75 35-60
3.	Parks and undeveloped areas	10-20

Source: National Disaster Management Guidelines—Urban Flood Management, 2010.

When several different surface types or land use which comprise the drainage area, a composite or weighted average value of the imperviousness runoff coefficient can be computed, such as:

$$I = 1/A \times (A_1 \times 11 + A_2 \times 12 + A_3 \times I3 + \ldots\ldots\ldots + An \times In)$$

Where, the subscripts refer to respective sub-drainage area types, and 'A' is the total drainage area.

Kirpich Equation Method

The time of concentration is defined as the time it takes for a drop of water in the remotest point in a drainage basin to travel to the outlet. As calculation methods go, the Kirpich formula is one of the most widely used methods.

$$Tc = 0.01947 \times L0.77\ S\text{-}0.385$$

Where:

Tc = Time of concentration (hours)

L = Maximum length of water travel (m)

S = surface slope, given by H/L (m/m)

H = difference in elevation between the remotest point in the drainage basin and the outlet (m)

The Kirpich equation is normally used for natural basins with well defined channels. If there are many undefined channels that are grassed or vegetated throughout, the Kirpich formula will likely under-estimate the time of concentration, and so a factor of 1.3 - 1.5 should be added. If most of the drainage basins are non-natural (in urban system) with concrete or other smooth channels, the result should be decreased by about 40 - 60%.

Drainage system may carry sewage flow and storm water flow separately or in combination. When conduit carry only sanitary sewage without rainfall inputs, computation is simple. It starts with the projection of population and then go to the water supply level. Per capita sewage production is a function of standard of living and water use. Climate is yet another factor. In arid area 40% water used reaches the sewer. In intensively developed area it is 90% and generally 80%. Industries and commercial establishment may have their own source of water supply, but discharge their used flow into the public sewer. Often industrial waste may damage the sewer because of acidity. Tolerance limits of industrial effluent need to be checked before it is allowed to discharge in to the public sewer. The provision should be allowed for infiltration of ground water to the sewer. Based on materials of sewer, type of joints, position of ground water level; infiltration may range from 500 to 5000 litres a day per km of sewer per cm diameter of sewer and 250-500 litres/ day per manhole. The above guidelines will help to determine the total daily-flow in the sewers.

For planning purpose it may be more convenient to express sewage flow per unit area than per capita. If, for example, average sewage flow is 300 litres/capita per day, the population density of 100 persons/ha and 100% increase for infiltration, the peak flow rate is 1/14 of average flow, then allowing infiltration; the unit flow rate is 2*300 (litres/cap day) *100 (persons/ha)/14*60*60-1.2 litre/(s-ha).

Table 8.22: Urban Population-Density Profiles

Town Population	Density persons/ha
Up to 5,000	75-150
5,001 to 20,000	150-250
20,001 to 50,000	250-300
50,001 to 100,000	300-350
100,000 plus	350-1000

Table 8.23: Peak Flow Factor for Urban Population

Population	Peak Flow Factor
Upto 20,000	3.50
20,001 to 50,000	2.50
50,001 to 7,50,000	2.25
Above 7,50,000	3.00

Table 8.24: Runoff Coeficient for Rational Formula

Description of Area	Runoff Coefficient
Business/Downtown	0.7 to 0.95
Neighbourhood	0.5 to 0.7
Residential	
Single family	0.3 to 0.5
Multi-units detached	0.4 to 0.6
Multi-units attached	0.6 to 0.75

Description of Area	Runoff Coefficient
Residential	0.6 to 0.75
Suburban	0.25 to 0.4
Apartments	0.5 to 0.7
Industrial Light	0.5 to 0.8
Heavy	0.6 to 0.9
Parks, Cemetries	0.1 to 0.25
Playground	0.2 to 0.35
Unimproved Open Space	0.1 to 0.3
Parks and garden	0.0 to 0.1

Table 8.25: Runoff Coefficient Related to Types of Surface

Surface Character	Runoff Coefficient
Pavement Asphalt and concrete	0.70 to 0.85
Brick	0.75 to 0.85
Roof	0.75 to 0.95
Lawns-Sandy Soil Flat 2% or less	0.05 to 0.10
Average 2-7% slope	0.10 to 0.15
Steep (greater than 7%)	0.15 to 0.20
Lawns-Tight Soils Flat 2% or less	0.13 to 0.17
Average 2 to 7% slope	0.18 to 0.22
Steep (greater than 7%)	0.25 to 0.35

Storm Water Flows

Storm water runoff is the portion of precipitation which drains over the ground surface. Estimate of such runoff reaching the storm sewer depends upon intensity and duration of precipitation, characteristics of the tributary area and the time required for such flow to reach the sewer. This may be estimated by rational method. hydrograph method, rainfall-runoff correlation studies and digital computer models, inlet method or empirical formula.

The typology of floods, which are a common occurrence in Indian cities, comprises the following categories:

- Water originating from rural and sub-urban areas flowing through the urban zones;
- Water originating from the adjacent urban areas;
- Surface water from rivers and the other streams flowing under extremely high levels near the areas considered. Water can enter the city either through streets and open areas or through the underground sewer network;
- Water from over-topping or breaking of dykes and flow;
- Water from rising ground water levels;
- Water from the rainfall over the area considered.

Table 8.26: Typology of Flood Types, Characteristics and Impacts

Flood type	Characteristics of flooding and impacts
Type A	Localized flooding caused by inadequate drainage of stormwater runoff, which can happen virtually every time it rains where the provision of drainage infrastructure is very poor. The main impacts of these events are related to a deterioration in environmental health conditions - notably those related to water-related diseases.
Type B	Flood events of this type occur less frequently than type A floods, but affect larger areas. The impacts may include temporary disruption to transportation systems and inconveniences to city life. These events contribute to the propagation of water-related diseases and can cause structural damage, but not as severe as those related to type C events.
Type C	Large-scale inundation causing widespread disruption and damage affecting communities and businesses throughout cities.These events are infrequent and often reach the headlines due to the dramatic scale of the impacts and structural damage.

There is considerable empirical evidence to indicate that flooding and poor drainage have a significant impact on the prevalence of illness and that large-scale flooding may disrupt water supply and sanitation systems and result in disease epidemics. In poorly drained areas with inadequate sanitation, urban runoff mixes with excreta spreading pathogens around communities and increasing risks to health from various waterborne diseases. Infiltration of polluted water into low-pressure water supply systems can contaminate drinking water and is frequently a source of gastro-intestinal disorders. Wet soils in poorly drained areas, which become faecal contaminated due to poor sanitation, also provide ideal conditions for the eggs of parasitic worms, such as roundworm and hookworm, which can cause debilitating intestinal infections.

Open drainage channels are potential sources of infection and disease, especially to children who play in polluted water from drains. Flooded septic tanks and leach pits and blocked drains provide breeding sites for Culex mosquitoes, which transmit filariasis, a condition that can lead to elephantiasis and its painful swelling of the legs.

Non-Structural Storm Water Management Strategies

Non-structural storm water management strategies for mitigation of flood impacts focus upon preventive action and rely predominantly on behavioural changes in order to be effective. These are particularly relevant in low-income communities in tropical climates, where flooding is inevitable and resources for infrastructure are scarce. A well-coordinated and balanced combination of both structural and non-structural measures is required as part of the long-term flood mitigation strategies. Examples of different types of non-structural storm water management strategies, Environmental Health Problems and Drainage Options are summarized in the table below:

Table 8.27: Non-structural Strategies for Flood Control and Mitigation of Environmental Health Problems

Flooding problems	**Action/Response**
Flood avoidance	Preventive responses which aim to ensure that flood problems are avoided.
Flood mitigation	Immediate response to flood warning before a flood, and the course of action to take during a flood to reduce risks.
Flood recovery	Action to be taken after a flood event to enable communities to recover from the impacts of a flood event.
Environmental health problems	
Solid waste management	Control of solid waste to avoid blockages and reduction in hydraulic capacity of the drainage system.
Pollution mitigation	Reduction in the discharge of pollutants into the stormwater drainage system.
Vector control	Improved practices to reduce vector transmission of diseases related to urban drainage and flooding.

Table 8.28: Drainage Options

Drainage Option	Physical Form
(a) Natural catchments	Natural channels, Streams, water courses
(b) Partly Sewered	Man-made ditches, open channels, sewers
(c) Combined Sewer Systems	Open channels, combined sewers, overflow treatment facilities
(d) Fully Separated Sewer System	Sewers, Treatment facilities, outfalls
(e) Advanced Drainage Systems with Real Time Control	Separate sewer, Trunk sewer, Infiltration ponds and source control storage basins, etc.

The frequency of storm for which the sewers are to be designed depends upon the importance of the drainage area. Commercial and industrial land use should be subjected to least flooding than residential area. The suggested frequency of flooding is as follows:

(a) Residential Area

— peripheral areas — twice a year

— central high priced area — once a year

(b) Commercial/High Priced Area — once in two years

For each length of storm sewer, the drainage area should be indicated clearly on a map. The boundaries of each tributary are dependent on topography (ridge line), and land use, nature of development and shape of the drainage basins are considered.

Drainage System Layout

Data requirement for the layout of urban drainage system include road map, location of building and other utilities, floor elevation of buildings, soil, topography (contour map), undeveloped area and future expansion. Since gravity flow is used in drainage system a detailed map of site level may be highly useful. Having collected all data, plot on a base map, tentative location of sub-mains, interceptors and trunk mains. Interceptor and trunk mains shall pass through the lowest point in the drainage area and extend through the entire area of the drainage divide. Lateral and collecting sewers are connected to the interceptor sewer and proceed along slope. Collecting sewers should be located in all streets and right of way.

Manholes shall be provided at all changes in grade, pipe size, direction of flow and quantity of flow. Maximum manhole spacing in a straight stretch cannot be more than 200 m for pipes more than 600 mm and for 200 to 300 mm dia pipes it is 133 m (400 ft). For larger pipes no maximum is prescribed. If part of the area is yet to be developed provide terminal manhole which can be later connected.

Hydraulic Design of Sanitary Sewer

1. First draw a line to represent the proposed sewer in each street. It can pass through a side of the street or to the centre, but shall be away from water supply main and preferably at a lower elevation.
2. The arrow is drawn near the line to indicate the direction of flow of sewage based onthe slope of the ground.
3. Locate manhole and number it.
4. Then sketch the limits of the service area for each lateral.
5. Measure the several service areas.

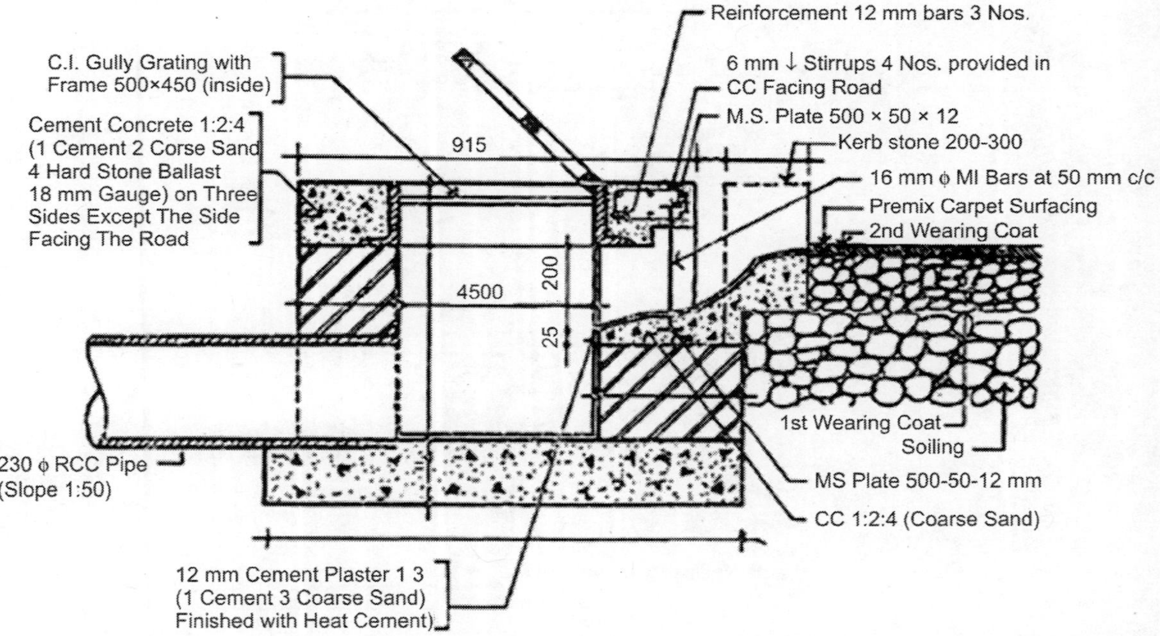

Fig. 8.22: Typical Section showing Position of Gully Chamber, at 15 m c/c both sides of the road in a staggered position connected to the roadside drain with 230 mm φ RCC pipe.

Natural Drainage Channels

A large number of drainage channels wind their way across settlements on their way to the river channels. A few are in good shape whereas many are carriers of polluted water with certain stretches having become open lavatories. While the sewage water can be piped in the centre of channel, other undesirable activities would be prevented with the provision of alternatives such as Sulabh Shauchalayas and fencing barriers.

Existing water channels as nallas is urban areas can be used for continuous on-channel recharge of ground water, transfer water from these channels to various storages and also store water from the channels with the help of sluice gates. Continuous recharge would take place through deep holes on the channel floor. This would be a complex exercise which would require computer modelling of channel capacities, transfer mechanisms, storage capacities, flood prevention and systems operation.

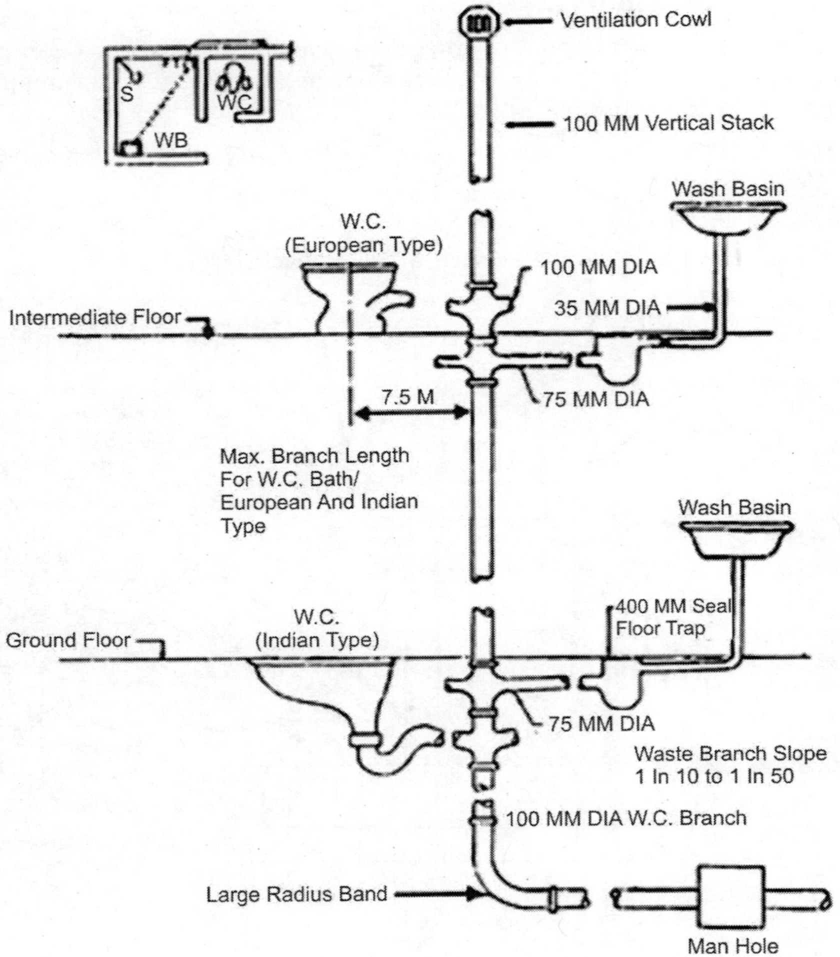

Fig. 8.23: Single Stack System of Building Drainage.

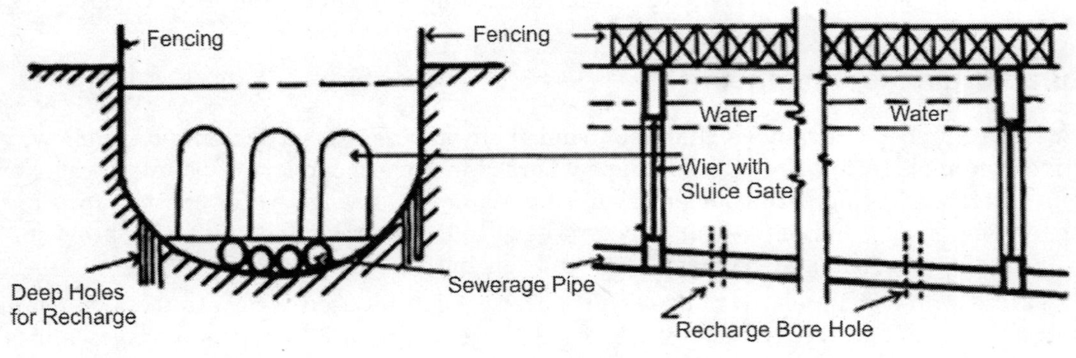

Fig. 8.24 Suggested Treatment of Natural Drainage Channels in Urban Areas

The channel once filled with water thus could constitute urban waterway. Its cleanliness would be maintained with the use of root zone system, mosquito weed, guppy fishes to consume mosquito larvae, and aeration. The channel would be shaped, landscaped, deepened to increase the water storing capacity wherever possible. Their banks would be the green lungs of city. While serving the primary function of on-channel groundwater recharge they would also modify the micro-climate. The conjunctive use of groundwater along with on-channel recharge would also be possible. Their use for urban watersports, recreation, hotels, floating offices, waterborne transport (with sluice gate barriers) would be examined and integrated in the system as revenue generating components.

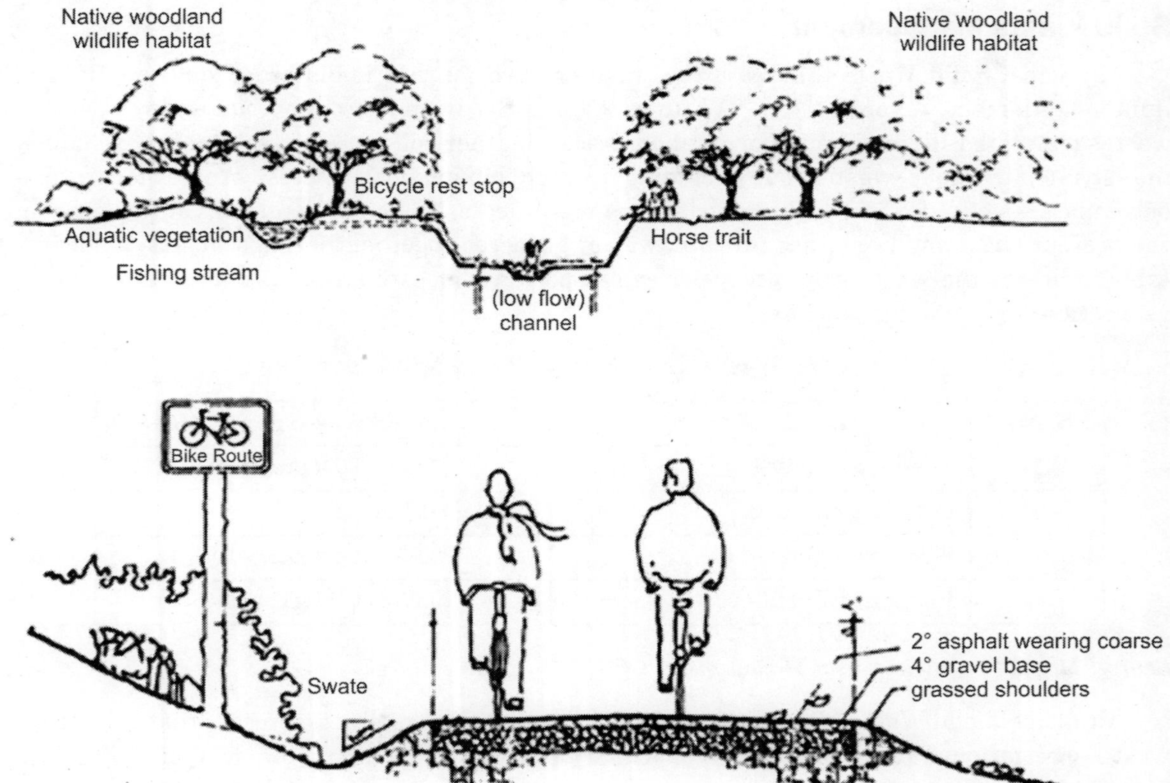

Fig. 8.25 Urban Drain as Green Corridor.

Electricity

Based on the estimated requirements of power supply as per the National Electricity Policy published in 2005, the recommended consumption is 1000 units per capita per year or 2.74 kWh per capita per day, which includes domestic, commercial, industrial and other requirements.

The actual estimation of power can be made based on the industrial development(type and extent), commercial development, domestic and other requirements. The provision of one electric substation of 11KV for a population of 15,000 can be considered as general standard for electricity distribution.

Ministry of New and Renewable Energy has come out with strategic plan for new and renewable energy sector for the period 2011-17. Ministry has identified local bodies as one of the main users who can be encouraged to utilise energy from biomass and urban waste, etc. A National Rating System (GRIHA) has been developed to promote green buildings in different climatic zones of the country. A green building designed through solar passive concepts, including active renewable energy systems, can save substantial conventional energy apart from generating energy for meeting various requirements in different seasons.

Solid Waste Management

Municipal Solid Waste (MSW) is the trash or garbage that is discarded day to day in a human settlement. According to MSW Rules 2000, MSW includes commercial and residential wastes generated in a municipal or notified areas in either solid or semi-solid form excluding industrial hazardous wastes but including treated bio-medical wastes. Waste generation encompasses activities in which materials are identified as no longer being of value (being in the present form) and are either thrown away or gathered together for disposal. The following table indicates the waste generation per capita per day for estimation and forecast of waste generation for planning purposes:

Table 8.28: Waste Generation Per Capita per Day

S. No.	Land use type	Estimated waste generation
1	Residential refuse	0.3 to 0.6 kg/cap/day
2.	Commercial refuse	0.1 to 0.2 kg/cap/day
3.	Street sweepings	0.05 to 0.2 kg/cap/day
4.	Institutional refuse	0.05 to 0.2 kg/cap/day

Source: Manual on Solid Waste Management, CPHEEO - 2000

Municipal Solid Waste Management (MSWM) refers to a systematic process that comprises waste segregation and storage at source, primary collection, secondarystorage, transportation, secondary segregation, resource recovery, processing, treatment, and final disposal. For effective MSWM following steps should be followed, hence appropriate considerations should be made at planning stage. A systematic process could be followed to reduce waste disposal at landfill site or no disposal at all. GIS/GPS/ICT techniques for Solid Waste Management need to be used for landfill site selection, site assessment of illegal dump-sites, routing efficiency for solid waste collection and monitoring waste collection performance.

Storage of waste at source is the first essential step of Solid Waste Management. Every household, shop and establishment generates solid waste on day-to-day basis.The waste should normally be stored at the source of waste generation till collected for its disposal. Bio-degradable waste and non-bio-degradable waste should be collected in separate bins at the source.

- Green coloured bins - Waste bins for bio-degradable waste
- White coloured bins - storage of recyclable wastes
- Black coloured bins - storage of other wastes

Primary collection of waste is the second essential step of Solid Waste Management activity. Primary collection system is necessary to ensure that waste stored at source is collected regularly and it is not disposed of on the streets, drains, water bodies,etc.

Local bodies should arrange for the primary collection of waste stored at various sources of waste generation by any of the following methods or combination of more than one method:

- Doorstep collection of waste through non-motorised and motorised vehicles with active community participation.
- Collection through community bins
- Door step or lanewise collection of waste from or collection from planned and unplanned areas or collection from the community bins to be provided by local bodies

All the waste collected through Primary Collection System from the households, shops and establishments has to be taken to the processing or disposal site either directly necessitating a large fleet of vehicles and manpower or through cost effective systems which are designed to ensure that all the waste collected from the sources of waste generation is temporarily stored at a common place called "Waste Storage Depots" and then transported in bulk to the processing or disposal sites. Such temporary arrangement for storage of waste is popularly known as dust bin, dhalaos, etc. This facility has to be so designed that the system synchronizes with the system of primary collection as well as transportation of waste. Locations for bins/ depots of appropriate size should be identified at planning stage.

Transportation of the waste

Transportation of the waste stored at waste storage depots at regular intervals is essential to ensure that no garbage bins/containers overflow and waste does not litter on the streets. Hygienic conditions can be maintained in cities/towns only if regular clearance of waste from temporary waste storage depots (bins) is ensured. Transportation system has to be so designed that it is efficient, yet cost effective. It should synchronize with the system of waste storage depot and should be easily maintainable.

Solid Waste Treatment Technologies

There are various technologies available for treatment and processing of waste in an environmentally sound manner. However, a technology suitable for one may not be appropriate for others. The comparison of these technologies is shown in table below:

Table 8.29: Comparison of Different Solid Waste Treatment Technologies

Element	Composting	Refuse derived fuel	Biomethanation	Gasification / Pyrolysis	Incineration
Technically and economically feasible size of operation per day fresh waste	50 TPD and above	100 TPD and above	1 TPD at small scale and above 50 TPD at larger scales of pure organic waste	500 TPD and above. Due to high moisture in our waste, suitable only for segregated dry waste.	500 TPD and above due to high moisture in our waste. Suitable only for segregated waste. However, sizes as small as 10-50 TPD of waste are available for commercial sale but not advisable due to high running costs.
Adopted Capacity for study	500 TPD	500 TPD	500 TPD	500 TPD Plant	500 TPD
Land required for adopted capacities	6 Ha	3 Ha	4 Ha	10 Ha	4 Ha
Waste Characteristics	Moisture Content >50% Organic Matter >40% C/N Ratio between 25-30	Moisture Content <45% Volatile Matter >40%	Moisture Content >50% Organic Matter >40% C/N Ratio between 25-30	Moisture content <45% Net Calorific Value >1200 Kcal/Kg	Moisture Content <45% Net Calorific Value >1200 Kcal/kg
Waste Suitability	Suitable for MSW Characteristics of India	Not suitable for MSW characteristics in India but workable with use of Auxiliary Fuel	Suitable for MSW characteristics of organic waste in India	Not suitable for MSW characteristic in India but workable with use of Auxiliary Fuel	Not suitable, due to high moisture in our waste.
Typical investment for assumed capacities (excluding cost of land)	INR 17-20 Cr. For a 500 TPD Plant	INR 17-20 Cr. For a 500 TPD Plant	Approximately INR 75-80 Cr for a 500 TPD Plant	INR 80-90 Cr. For 500 TPD Plant	NA
Recurring cost	INR 300 per ton of input waste	INR 290 per ton of input waste	INR 100 per ton input waste	NA	-
Recoverable	250 Kgs of compost per ton of waste	200 Kgs pellets per ton of waste	80 cum of bio gas / ton of waste plus 200 Kgs of manure / ton	NA	-

Volume reduction	45-55%	55-65%	55-65%	>80%	>80%
Environmental issue	Impurities in compose due to mixed waste, traces of heavy metals, leachate runoff	Problems in burning exhaust	Problems if mixed feed stock	Ash handling and Air Pollution	Ash handling and Air Pollution (emission of particular matter, chlorinated compounds dioxins / furans)
Technology Reliability	Running successfully in India	Running successfully in integrated facilities	Small scale organic treatment plant operational but mixed waste large scale plants failed in India	Insufficient operational experience for MSW	Only Plant in India failed due to mismatch in waste quality. MSW 2000 has recommended for incineration of waste only after doing a waste suitability analysis and providing adequate flue gas management methods.
Limitation	Large Land Requirement, Non acceptance of compost as soil enrichener in some areas of the Country Process depends highly on factors such as waste quality & climatic conditions	Fluff / Pellets can be used a fuel in large industries, e.g. In cement kilns with necessary permissions from the PCBs and required pollution control measures.	The technology requires pre-segregated homogenous biodegradable waste as mixed waste retards efficiency of the process. Hence applicability is limited to highly organic and homogenous waste streams like market wastes.	Requires waste with high calorific value. Expensive flue gas remediation methods to attain achievable outputs.	Expensive technology, waste criteria must have low moisture content and high calorific value, which is not found in Indian Waste. Costly flue gas remediation methods to attain achievable outputs.

Source: Toolkit for Solid Waste Management, Jawaharlal Nehru National Urban Renewal Mission, MoUD.

Disposal of Waste

Waste after treatment must be disposed in a manner that does not create any instance of environmental pollution and public nuisance. The MSW Rules 2000 define waste disposal as an activity which involves "final disposal of municipal solid wastes in terms of the specified measures to prevent contamination of groundwater, surface water and ambient air quality".

The landfill design shall aim to minimize the following:

- The ingress of water into the landfill,
- The production of leachate, its subsequent outflow and uncontrolled dispersions into surrounding aquatic environment,
- The accumulation, migration and uncontrolled release of landfill gas into the atmosphere.

Landfill Gas Extraction (LFG)

The waste deposited in a landfill gets subjected, over a period of time, to anaerobic conditions. This leads to landfill gas production containing about 45 to 55% methane. This methane can be recovered through a network of pipes and utilised as a source of energy. Landfill gas extraction systems add to efforts to reduce climate change initiatives as it helps reduce Green House Gas emissions through avoidance of landfill gas (mainly comprising methane) into the atmosphere.

Waste composition is the most important factor in assessing the LFG generation potential and total yield at a site. Inorganic and inert wastes will produce little or no LFG; more organic wastes will produce greater amounts of LFG on a per unit basis. Similarly, moisture content in waste also impacts the LFG generation from waste. For example highly organic wastes such as food wastes are able to produce LFG, but comprises large water, which inherently does not produce LFG but will aid the rate of LFG evolution.

While planning for LFG, pH and nutrient content of the waste should also be considered. The generation of methane in landfills is greatest when neutral pH conditions exist. Numerous toxic materials, such as heavy metals, can retard bacterial growth in portions of a site and consequently slow gas generation. Another parameter that influences the LFG generation rate is the particle size and density, which may affect the transport of nutrients and moisture throughout the landfill.

Construction and Demolition (C&D) Waste

As per the (draft) Construction and Demolition Waste Rules, large waste generators of 500 MT are to process (recycle and reuse) construction and demolition waste at the site-minimum 20% of process waste at the site for reconstruction purposes meeting structural requirements. Recent initiatives of MoUD, such as Redevelopment of East Kidwai Nagar (New Delhi) Government Residential Complex, have shown that it is possible to provide for 100 per cent recycling and reuse of C&D Waste at the construction/ demolition site itself in a decentralised mode. Such models obviate the need for transporting the C&D waste to a centralised unit and also for transporting the reuse material such as bricks, to the construction sites. This would be cost effective, besides environment friendly and would also avoid movement of the waste related transport vehicles through the city.

Municipal Solid Waste (Household)

While regional and centralised waste processing has been tried out over the years, the availability of landfill sites is becoming a growing problem, as residents do not like a landfill site in their vicinity. Many cities had set up landfill sites and plants on the outskirts, but such outskirts have gradually become part of the city, owing to natural outgrowth, and the residents have started agitating for removal of the landfill. A viable solution has been tried out in the New Moti Bagh Government Residential Complex in New Delhi, wherein a small plant of 3 to 5 tonnes capacity set up in less than a quarter of land and recycles the household and green waste into fuel cake and manure.Small plants make sorting easy and avoid the need for any collection point. Carefully planned, the recycling process can do away with the need for land fill altogether. The financial viability of any waste recycling system would depend on (a) reuse of the recycled material and (b) levy of some user fee on those who generate the waste.

Nuclear or Radioactive Waste

Nuclear or radioactive waste means any waste material containing radio nuclides in quantities or concentrations. The disposal of such waste include the release of radioactive material to the environment in a manner leading to loss of control over the future disposition of the radio nuclides contained therein and includes emplacement of waste materials in a repository beings or animals or in research activities in these fields or in the production or testing of biological waste. Such waste must be managed through "Atomic Energy (Safe Disposal of Radioactive Wastes) Rules, 1987".

E-Waste

E-waste or electronic waste means waste generated from Electrical and Electronic Equipment (EEE), whole or in part or rejects from their manufacturing and repair process, which are intended to be discarded. "The E-waste (Management and Handling) Rules, 2011" should be followed for disposal of E-Waste.

Bio-Medical Waste

Hospital waste/Bio-medical waste is generated during the diagnosis, treatment or immunization of human beings or animals or in research activities in these fields or in the production or testing of biological waste. Hospital/Bio-medical waste must be handled and disposed of as per guidelines laid in "Bio-Medical Waste (Management and Handling) Rules, 1998".

Domestic Gas Supply

A technically feasible area/locality/ society / building shall have provision to lay Medium Density Polythylene (MDPE) pipelines and its lanes shall have free accessibility for fire tender in case of any emergency. The under developed slum areas, water-logging areas, places with soak pits, narrow lanes that do not have room for excavation and/or the narrow and/ or crowded lanes which prevent accessing the area in case of emergency and structurally unstable buildings shall be considered technically not feasible.

A technically feasible domestic PNG connection shall have provision for connecting the customer's premises with the service MDPE pipeline with the riser for the customers building. The connectivity service pipeline to customers building from the mainline should be possible without posing any hindrance or safety hazard.

The provision of the domestic and trans-country pipelines shall be as per the PNGRB Technical and Quality Standards and specifications, which ensures overall safety,quality, and convenience. The last updated PNGRB rules and regulations shall be followed for:

- Design, Layout, Construction and Maintenance of City Gas Distribution Infrastructure
- Pressure Standards and Maintenance
- Materials of Construction
- Selection of Location for City Gate Stations (CGS)

The municipalities and development authorities to make provisions for:

- Right of Usage (RoU) to be pre-defined in the Right of Way (RoW) of the city roads, as per the norms of PNGRB to be compatible with the other utilities,
- The safety norms prescribed by PNGRB to be included in the Development Control Regulations by the development authorities,
- Land for city gas stations to be provisioned in the urban extensions, avoiding congested areas. Land requirement for the CGS may be minimum 2000 sq. mtrs.

Telecom Services

Utility corridor: The telecom services, including broadband, are to be integrated withthe utility corridor and Right of Way (RoW) permission should be made available to telecom services, similar to tower installation with buffers and distances prescribed by the State Governments.

Building regulations: Modifications in the building regulation of the dense cities may be allowed for accessing telecom and broadband services to the end users.

Large facility installation: Municipalities and local authorities to provide large facility installation of telecom and broadband services in the peri-urban areas.

Service Level Benchmarking for Infrastructure Services

The MoUD has initiated an exercise to define Service Level Benchmark (SLBs). Measuring service levels of civic agencies implies measuring outcomes, and indirectly reflects on institutional capacity, financial performance and other parameters. The Handbook of Service Level Benchmarking prepared by MoUD can be referred while providing basic infrastructure facility such as water supply, sewerage, drainage and solid waste management for efficient functioning.

Considering the importance of SLBs to measure the performance of above mentioned infrastructure facilities it is suggested that SLB should be considered as benchmarks for measuring, reporting and monitoring the performance and comparing inter and intra-city level infrastructure. The MoUD (Advisory note on Improving Urban Water Supply and Sanitation Services, MoUD, 2012) has suggested SLBs for different utility services in an urban area, which are mentioned in table below:

Table 8.30: Service Level Benchmarks

Sr. No.	Indicators	Benchmark Levels
	Water Supply	
1	Coverage of WS connections (Population)	100%
2	Per capita availability of WS at consumer end	135 Lpcd
3	Extent of metering of WS connections	100%
4	Extent of Non-Revenue Water	20%
5	Continuity of Water Supply	24x7
6	Efficiency of redress of Customer Complaints	80%
7	Quality of Water Supplied	100%
8	Cost recovery of in Water Supply Service	100%
9	Efficiency in collection of Water Supply Charge	90%
	Sewerage	
1	Coverage of Wastewater network service	100%
2	Collection efficiency of Wastewater network	100%
3	Adequacy of Wastewater treatment capacity	100%
4	Quality of Wastewater treatment	100%
5	Extent of reuse & recycling of treated Wastewater	20%
6	Extent of cost recovery in Wastewater management	100%
7	Efficiency of redress of Customer Complaints	80%
8	Efficiency in collection of sewerage charges	90%
9	Coverage of toilets	100%
	Storm Water Drainage	
1	Coverage of storm Water Drainage network	100%
2	Incidence of water logging / flooding	0
	Solid Waste Management	
1	Household level Coverage of Solid Waste Management service	100%
2	Efficiency of Collection of Municipal Solid Waste	100%
3	Extent of segregation of Municipal Solid Waste	100%
4	Extent of Municipal Solid Waste recovered / recycled	80%
5	Extent of scientific disposal of Municipal Solid Waste	100%
6	Extent of cost recovery in Solid Waste management service	100%
7	Efficiency of redress of Customer Complaints	80%
8	Efficiency in collection of user charges	90%

Source:Advisory Note on Improving Urban Water Supply and Sanitation Services, MoUD, 2012

Public Private Partnerships (PPP) for Infrastructure

Public private partnerships (PPP) are arrangements between government and private sector for the purpose of providing public infrastructure, community facilities and related services. Such partnerships are characterized by the sharing of investments risk, responsibility and reward between the partners. The reasons for establishing such partnerships vary but generally involve the financing design, construction, operation and maintenance of responsibilities of the private and public sector partners may differ on individual servicing initiatives, the overall role and responsibilities of government do not change. Public private partnership is one of a number of ways of delivering public infrastructure and related services. It is not a substitute for strong and effective governance and decision making by government. In all cases, government remains responsible and accountable for delivering services and projects in a manner that protects and serves the public interest.

Various market factors need to be considered, including existing and future demand for the service (price, future market conditions and the scale of the project). The basis of the analysis should be life-cycle costs.

Benefits of Public Private Partnerships

- **Savings:** With public private partnership, local government may be able to realize cost savings for both, the construction of capital projects as well as the operation and maintenance of services.
- **Risk Sharing:** Local government can share the risks with a private partner. Risks could include cost overruns, inability to meet schedules for service delivery, difficulty in complying with environmental and other regulations, or the risk that revenues may not be sufficient to pay operating and capital costs.
- **Improved Level of Service or Maintaining Existing Level of Service:** Introduction of new technology that often reduces the cost or improves the quality and level of service.
- **Enhancement of Revenues:** Public private partnerships also offer the opportunity to introduce innovative revenue sources that would not be possible under conventional methods of service delivery.
- **More Efficient Implementation:** Efficiencies may be realized through combining various activities such as design and construction, and through more flexible contracting and procurement, quicker approvals for capital financing and a more efficient decision-making process.
- **Economic Benefits:** Increased involvement of local government in public-private partnerships can help to stimulate the private sector and contribute to increased employment and economic growth. Public-private partnerships are not the solution for the delivery of all services. There are risks in proceeding with public private partnerships.

Types of Public-Private Partnerships

1. **Operations and Maintenance:** The local government contracts with a private partner to operate and maintain a publicly owned facility.
2. **Design-Build:** The local government contracts with a private partner to design and build a facility that conforms to the standards and performance requirements of the local government. Once the facility has been built, the local government takes ownership and is responsible for the operation of the facility.
3. **Turnkey Operations:** The local government provides the financing for the project but engages a private partner to design, construct and operate the facility for a specified period of time. Performance objectives are established by the public sector and the public partner maintains ownership of the facility. This form of public private partnership is applicable where the public sector maintains a strong interest in ownership but seeks to benefit from private construction and operation of a facility.
4. **Wrap-around Addition:** A private partner finances and constructs an addition to an existing public facility. The private partner may then operate the addition to the facility for a specified period of time or until the partner recovers the investment plus a reasonable return on the investment.
5. **Lease-Purchase:** The local government contracts with the private partner to design finance and build a facility to provide a public service. The private partner then leases the facility to the local government for a specified period after which ownership vests with the local government.
6. **Temporary Privatization:** Ownership of an existing public facility is transferred to a private partner who improves and/or expands the facility. The facility is then owned and operated by the private partner for a period specified in a contract or until the partner has recovered the investment plus a reasonable return.
7. **Lease-Develop-Operate or Buy-Develop-Operate:** The private partner leases or buys a facility from the local government, expands or modernizes it, then operates the facility under a contract with the local government. The private partner is expected to invest in facility expansion or improvement and is given a specified period of time in which to recover the investment and realize a return.
8. **Build-Transfer-Operate:** The local government contracts with a private partner to finance and build a facility. Once completed, the private partner transfers ownership of the facility to the local government. The local government then leases the facility back to the private partner under a long-term lease during which the private partner has an opportunity to recover its investment and a reasonable rate of return.
9. **Build-Own-Operate-Transfer or Build-Operate-Transfer:** The private developer obtains exclusive franchise to finance, build, operate, maintain, manage and collect user fees for a fixed period to amortize investment, At the end of the franchise, title reverts to a public authority.
10. **Build-Own-Operate:** The local government either transfers ownership and responsibility for an existing facility or contracts with a private partner to build, own

and operate a new facility in perpetuity. The private partner generally provides the financing.

Some of the key issues that need to be addressed for attracting private participation across different areas in urban sector include:

- **Institutional Reform and Framework:** The procedure for invitation of private sector should be preceded by introducing reforms in the municipalities and other local bodies.
- **Cost Recovery and Pricing:** As of now, there is quite an amount of subsidization,so the present pricing structure for these facilities does not make them too attractive to private bidders.
- **Project Planning Process:** The capability of an urban infrastructure project to attract private investment depends on how the project is planned. Inadequate understanding on the part of ULBs is one of the key concerns of private entrepreneurs planning to invest in infrastructure projects.
- **Multiplicity of Organizations:** Multiple agencies at the central, state and local levels have led to various clearances required at various levels. These have led to delays in project execution and are a major hurdle for private participation.
- **Lack of Information Database:** As has been noticed with all type of infrastructure projects, lack of authentic data on urban infrastructure acts as one of the main problems for private promoters planning to set up projects in this area.
- **Large Investment Backlog:** A huge investment backlog is present in the different segments of the urban infrastructure area. So investment requirements of private investors or operators are pushed up in a major way if they plan to provide reasonable quality of service.
- **Bulky Size of Projects:** Another major reason for lack of private initiative in investing in new infrastructure projects is the bulky size of the project. So risk profiles of these projects are also huge. If projects are broken up into smaller ones, private participation is likely to be better.

There are the common issues that come up for private entrepreneurs planning to set up or take over operations of existing projects in all segments of the urban sector. Addressing these issues will, hence lead to an increase in private initiative in these projects. Other than providing sops to the private promoters to investment in infrastructure projects, the government is also taking some steps to improve the investment environment. Regulators for various sectors are being set up. This will increase the accountability and better the performance of the existing infrastructure facility providers. It is also being seen that the government is trying to move to a free market pricing regime and not sticking to subsidised pricing of infrastructure facilities.

Cost Recovery and Financial Viability

It is generally seen that in most of the projects the default rate is quite high. The defaults could be due to a variety of factors ranging from low cost recovery from the beneficiaries, non-payment by implementing agency to the lending institution (e.g. HUDCO) for various reasons including inadvertent diversion of income from one project to another project or inability of the State Government to make budgetary allocation for the loan as promised, etc. It is generally felt that efficient cost recovery depends upon four factors: those relating to beneficiaries; those relating to the collection of machinery; those relating to the financier; and those relating to certain externalities. The cost recovery from the beneficiaries could be poor due to:

1. Delays in completion of project which could in turn be explained by delays in completing documentation/releases, etc.
2. Low affordability of the beneficiaries;
3. Poor quality of the infrastructural facilities provided;
4. Low beneficiary participation in such infrastructural projects.

Even when the cost recovery from the beneficiaries is not a cause of concern, the agency may be unable to pay back for a variety of reasons:

1. The repayments from beneficiaries may not be enough to cover the scheduled repayment to the lender. This would be so if the agency subsidises the users over and above what is available from the lender to the agency.
2. Weaknesses in the administration and management of collection mechanisms are directly related to poor collection performances. An essential pre-requisite to secure efficient cost recovery is the articulation of efficient collection mechanisms.
3. Finance required for establishment expenses and/or for new projects and for repayments to be made to other agencies.
4. Non-receipt of expected funds from Government or other agencies.

The link between cost recovery from the project and repayment to the financier for the project may be quiet weak in most cases. Most agencies do not keep accounts project-wise but only agency-wise. Further, each project might be financed by resources from more than one agency. Absence of a proper system of double entry accounting can create problems.

The defaults could also be due to practices at the financier level. Inadequate attention to expected cash flows and unrealistic projections at the time of project appraisal; delays in releases could lead to cost over-runs. These may force the agency either to pass on the extra cost to the beneficiaries (which might have had negative impact on demand or cost recovery) or to raise funds from other sources at higher cost.

One can not underestimate the impact of certain externalities. Such externalities could be macro economic variables like general state of the economy, inflation, etc. which may impact both through demand and supply factors; lack of political will to administer effective measures for securing full recovery; natural recovery; natural calamities, etc. The sectoral policies and programmes may also influence the outcome.

Public-Private Partnership Strategy

Public-private and inter-governmental partnerships are increasingly becoming common. Several Local bodies in India have initiated contracting out municipal services to the private sector. The centrally sponsored schemes of infrastructure development are generally based on a partnership approach in which the Central and state governments share the project cost. An important suggestion in this regard could be to constitute 'Corporate Divisions' of urban bodies/infrastructure agencies, which should be manned by professional managers and financial experts which may take up mega-projects and city level services/ transport projects as commercial ventures.

Leveraging strategy can be applied to mobilise private sector and institutional resources, and get multiplier effect from budgetary allocations. Budgetary finance and low interest loans can effectively help to attract private and institutional funds. For this purpose special fund may have to be created by the Government for infrastructure projects to help financially weak urban bodies. Such an infrastructure fund based on the principle of 'leveraging strategy' had been provided in the Five Year Plans of Gujarat. Leveraging Strategy should take into account the specific potential of development and market demand, which could be channelised and redirected by public investments and trigger larger private sector investments.

It is utmost importance that the local government finances are strengthened and urban development is reoriented as self-financing. The emphasis should be on developing new partnerships, optimisation of land based resources and adoption of innovative management options.

PPPs can be undertaken through a range of alterntives such as BOT, BOOT, etc. They enable governments to transfer construction and commercial risks to the private sector which is best suited to manage them. However, considerable work is needed to create an enabling environment which should not only attract private investment but must also be seen to be in the public interest and this is best assured if the process is seen to provide services at reasonable cost and in a transparent manner. If we adopt best practices, it will be possible to create credible PPP projects that evoke a positive public response and do not require re-negotiation or payment of unforeseen liabilities by the government or the users.

PPPs are best implemented through standardized arrangements that constitute a stable policy and regulatory regime where private capital derives greater comfort and seeks the least possible risk premium. Model Concession Agreements (MCAs) would be used for providing a stable regulatory and policy framework. The MCA for PPP in highways has already been approved and published. Similar work is in progress in other sectors.

PPPs involve dealing with the private sector. Sometimes this gives rise to the suspicion that the corporate investors are getting a favoured treatment. Transparent processes and consultations with stakeholders combined with effective competitive bidding for PPP projects help in improving perceptions and enhance the acceptability of PPP projects. The presence of effective regulatory bodies can also enhance public confidence though the development of a credible regulatory institution will inevitably take time. This approach also provides the requisite comfort to public servants who are responsible for awarding projects to private entities. The key to making PPPs acceptable is to create an environment where PPPs are seen to be a way of attracting private money into public projects, not putting public resources into private projects.

Source: Government of India, Planning Commission (2006), An Approach to the llth Five Year Plan (2007-12).

The Government of India Guidelines

The Ministry of Finance has introduced a scheme to support public-private partnerships. Certain guidelines in this scheme are as follows:

Eligibility

1. In order to be eligible for funding under this Scheme, a PPP project shall meet the following criteria:
   (a) The project shall be implemented, i.e. developed, financed, constructed, maintained and operated for the Project Term by a Private Sector Company to be selected by the Government or a statutory entity through a process of open competitive bidding;
   (b) The PPP Project should be from one of the following sectors:
      (i) Roads and bridges, railways, seaports, airports, waterways;
      (ii) Power;
      (iii) Urban transport, water supply, sewerage, solid waste management and other physical infrastructure in urban areas;
      (iv) Infrastructure projects in Special Economic Zones; and
      (v) International convention centres and other tourism infrastructure projects;

Provided that the Empowered Committee may, with approval of the Finance Minister, add or delete sectors/sub-sectors from the aforesaid list,

   (c) The project should provide a service against payment of a predetermined tariff or user charge.
   (d) The concerned Government / statutory entity should certify, with reasons; that the tariff/user charge cannot be increased to eliminate or reduce the viability gap of the PPP; that the Project Term cannot be increased for reducing the viability gap; and that the capital costs are reasonable and based on the standards and specifications normally applicable to such projects and that the capital costs cannot be further restricted for reducing the viability gap.

Government Support

(i) The total Viability Gap Funding under this scheme shall not exceed twenty percent of the Total Project Cost; provided that the Government or statutory entity that owns the project may, if it so decides provides additional grants out of its budget, but not exceeding a further twenty percent of the Total Project Cost.

(ii) Viability Gap Funding under this scheme will normally be in the form of a capital grant at the stage of project construction. Proposals for any other form of assistance may be considered by the Empowered Committee and sanctioned with the approval of Finance Minister on a case-by-case basis.

(iii) Viability Gap Funding up to ₹ 100 crore (₹ One hundred crore) for each project may be sanctioned by the Empowered Institution subject to the budgetary ceilings indicated by the Finance Ministry. Proposals up to ₹ 200 crore (₹ Two hundred crore) may be sanctioned by the Empowered Committee, and amounts exceeding ₹ 200 crore may be sanctioned by the Empowered Committee with the approval of Finance Minister.

(iv) Unless otherwise directed by the Ministry of Finance, the Empowered Institutions may approve project proposals with a cumulative capital outlay equivalent to ten times the budget provisions in the respective Annual Plan.

(v) In the first two years of operation of the Scheme, projects meeting the eligibility criteria will be funded on a first-come, first served basis. In later years, if need arises, funding may be provided based on an appropriate formula, to be determined by the Empowered Committee, that balances needs across sectors in a manner that would make broad base the sectoral coverage and avoid preempting of funds by a few large projects.

Procurement Process for PPP Projects

(i) The Private Sector Company shall be selected through a transparent and open competitive bidding process. The criterion for bidding shall be the amount of Viability Gap Funding required by a Private Sector Company for implementing the project where all other parameters are comparable.

(ii) The Government or statutory entity proposing the project shall certify that the bidding process conforms to the provisions of this Scheme and convey the same to the Empowered Institution prior to disbursement of the Grant.

An example of the successful engagement of private sector in the real estate is Bengal Ambuja Housing Development Ltd., a joint venture between Gujarat Ambuja Cements Ltd (49.99 per cent) and the West Bengal Housing Board (49.99 per cent). Bengal Ambuja has completed several large and medium sized housing projects that constitute homes in the LIG, MIG and HIG segments. Bengal Ambuja has also developed projects in partnership with other agencies, apart from the state housing board. For example, Urvashi, a project spread over 94 acres located in Durgapur in the distant suburbs, was developed in partnership with the Asansol Durgapur Development Authority. Another example of a successful PPP initiative is the township in Rajarhat, developed in a JV with SP Real Estate. This township comprises 20,000 housing units, out of which 12,000 units are LIG flats and 8,000 units are MIG flats. These units are allocated by means of a draw of lots, and only accept application up to a certain income level.

While the partnership approach can help to improve the image and mobilize private resources, such projects are invariably those which have market demand. Market led development based on short term partnership may not be viable in the long run, and could adversely effect the labour welfare policies, social security, social services and equity.

The concept of public-private partnership aims at 'rolling back the frontiers of state' and revitalizing the enterprise. A basic purpose of the partnership is to reduce the burden of state's investment and to attract private sector resources. However, it is yet to be seen whether direct private sector investments can be mopped up for basic infrastructure projects, like solid waste management, trunk sewer, water supply, roads and bridges and social housing without adversely affecting the nature of 'social service' which such projects provide.

Compulsory and Competitive Tendering for Public Services

In India, there is a crisis of delivery of public services. The country is facing a resource crunch and there is all-round dissaatisfaction with the performance of the local governments with mounting establishment expenditure. There is a serious concern to refurbish the sagging image of the local government and public bodies. We have to find alternatives.

For this, the experiences of the UK in the field of compulsory and competitive tendering system and public-private partnership provide relevant and reliable examples.In pursuit of "value for money", the UK government evolved the concept of "compulsory and competitive tendering" for delivery of public services. Under this programme, the private sector is seen as an agent of change. The local authorities have no more the monopoly as the sole providers of public services like electricity, public transport, housing or sanitation but they have to compete int he market with private sector. The concept has been introduced in the UK in the form of consequential legislation and by adoption of a working strategy and a new structure. The strategy involved:

- Denationalisation of public corporations.
- Sale of public corporations/government asets.
- Liberalisation or removing restrictions on competition for public services.
- Contracting out of public services by competitive tendering.

The following premises and objectives are advanced for this strategy:

- To provide a high level of public service.
- To save money and to obtain better value for public money.
- Surival of the fittest.
- To save management time.
- To obtain expertise not available in-house.
- To retain flexibility.
- To re-establish management control.

Competitive tendering has opened up new avenues to monopolised services. These have provided an opportunity to test the effectiveness of existing services against avilable alternatives. Competition helps to reduce the burden of the state and results in an improvement of public services. The concept of CCT has been institutionalised as a legal provision within the Local Government Act of the UK.The local and public service authorities in the UK are obliged to follow the prescribed system for tendering of its services. This has resulted in a drastic change in the government strcuture, security of employment and the overall attitude of the officials towards the public. In case the bid is not in the favour of the existing local body or public sector, the employees have to find an alternate job.

There is a considerable slimming down of government bodies and corporations. Many of the local authorities have geared up for the competition, whereas some local bodies which were too big, unproductive or unable to change their working have been wound up. These included London County Council and smaller bodies with specific tasks and jurisdiction, like the Docklands Authority were created.

Debriefing and Review

1. What are the definitions of intrastructure with reference to urban development?
2. How water supply is planned in terms of quantity and quality for a town? Mention the mandatory standards required to be followed.
3. How sewerage and sanitation help to develop a sanitized, healthy and liveable city? What are the basic approaches?
4. What options are available for rainwater harvesting and recharge of groundwater?
5. Write short notes on the following:
   (i) Watershed management
   (ii) Swales
   (iii) Dual piping
   (iv) Filter strips
6. Explain the concepts and approaches of Urban Drainage Planning.
7. Write short notes on the following:
   (a) Zero run off drainage
   (b) Retention ponds
   (c) Service Level Benchmarks
   (d) Non-revenue water
   (e) Electric grid sub-stations
   (f) Renewable energy
8. Explain the various approaches for solid waste management differentiated on the basis of character of wastes?
9. Write short notes:
   (i) Construction and demolition waste
   (ii) Bio-medical waste
   (iii) Toxic waste
   (iv) Bio-degradable waste
   (v) e-waste
10. Explain the concepts of PPP for urban services and its advantages and disadvantages.

CHAPTER

9

URBAN TRANSPORT

Rapid motorization in India is visible by frequent traffic congestion, parking problems, air pollution, traffic accidents and increasing time spent on commuting. Its impact on the natural and the built environment (noise, pollution, traffic accidents, community severance) are discernable all over. The fast-growth of private vehicles is seen as a most intractable source of carbon emissions. Environmental footprints of urban transport include the amount of resources (including embedded energy) used in their production, amount of waste produced by their disposal, and continued use of fossil fuels. In Delhi 72 per cent of emissions (suspended particulate matter) are from motorized vehicles. Of these the private vehicles, which are 90 per cent of total motorized transport, carry 31 per cent of vehicular trips and are responsible for 90 per cent of emissions. Violent traffic and transport impacts the health and safety of the people. With less than 1 per cent of the world's vehicle population, India accounts for 6 per cent of world's road accidents and 10 per cent of world's road fatalities. More than 1.41 lakh people die in road accidents and more than 1 million fatal road accidents happen every year. The victims are mostly pedestrians or cyclists for whom there is hardly any dedicated space on the roads, though 30 to 40 per cent of citizens walk or cycle to work.Urban transport services are hardly accessible to all, especially the elderly, children, women and disabled.

Studies show that road transportation needs 4 to 5 times the energy that is needed by a train. The energy used by a car to carry a passenger over one kilometer is 3 to 4 times that of a bus. Greenhouse gas emission per passenger of public transport (bus, rail and trams) is about one-twelfth that of a car. Although NMTs (including walking) are ideal from the point of view of emissions, in terms of kilometers travelled, these cover only 1 to 2 per cent of the total kilometers travelled, even if the proportion of trips are as high as 40 to 50 per cent, as in Delhi and other megacities.It implies that rail based public transport, bus, cycle and walking provide a greener transportation, which help in reduction in use of fossil fuels and conservation of natural resources. A compact and smart city with mixed land use, cleaner, fast and low energy public transport provides sustainable mobility.

Table 9.1: Environmental Sustainability of Different Modes of Transport

	Air Pollution	Noise	Ugliness	Unsafe
Walking	5	5	5	3
Cycling	5	5	4	2
Car	1	2	2	2
Tram	5	3	3	3
Light Rail (L.R), Surface	5	3	3	4
Rapid Rail (RR), Surface	5	2	2	4
Rapid Rail (RR), Elevated	5	1-2	2	5
Rapid Rail, Tube	5	5	5	5
Bus, Mixed Traffic	1-2	3	4	3
Bus, Reserved Lane	3	3	4	3

Legend: 1 = very bad, 2 = bad, 3 = average, 4 = good, 5 = very good

Source: Vuchic, R.V (1981) "Urban Public Transportation Systems and Technology", Prentice Hall, Englewood Cliffs, New Jersey, cited by Raman Parti and Surjit S Katoch, Efficient Transportation Planning and System Integration for Healthy Environment of Large Cities, Proceedings of International Conference on Energy and Environment March 19-21, 2009

The urban structure plays a vital role in making public transport viable and reducing the need to travel. The World Development Report (2009) of the World Bank cites the example of Atlanta and Barcelona. Atlanta has a metro network of 74 km while Barcelona has 99 km. These may seem comparable but per capita CO_2 emission for Atlanta is 10 times that of Barcelona. The difference is mostly explained by Barcelona being more compact while its American rival is spread out. As a result, less than 4% of Atlanta's population lives within reasonable walking distances of a metro station compared to 60% for Barcelona. If Atlanta now tries to give its citizen the same accessibility, it would have to build 2800 new metro stations and 3400 km of new tracks. The lesson learnt is that public transport, land use and walkability are interlinked and need to be planned together. The study by Newman and Kenworthy (1999) indicates that energy consumption in the transportation increased with reduction in urban densities. Sprawling developments are mainly responsible for traffic jams, congestion, accidents and air pollution.

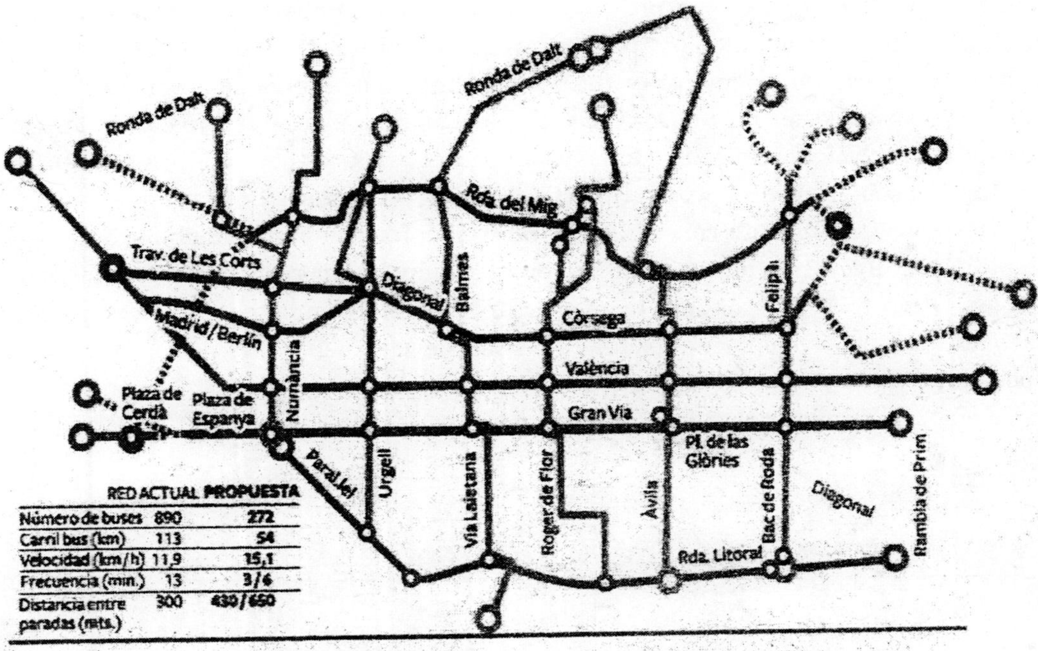

Fig. 9.1: Barcelona: Public Transport Oriented Urban Form

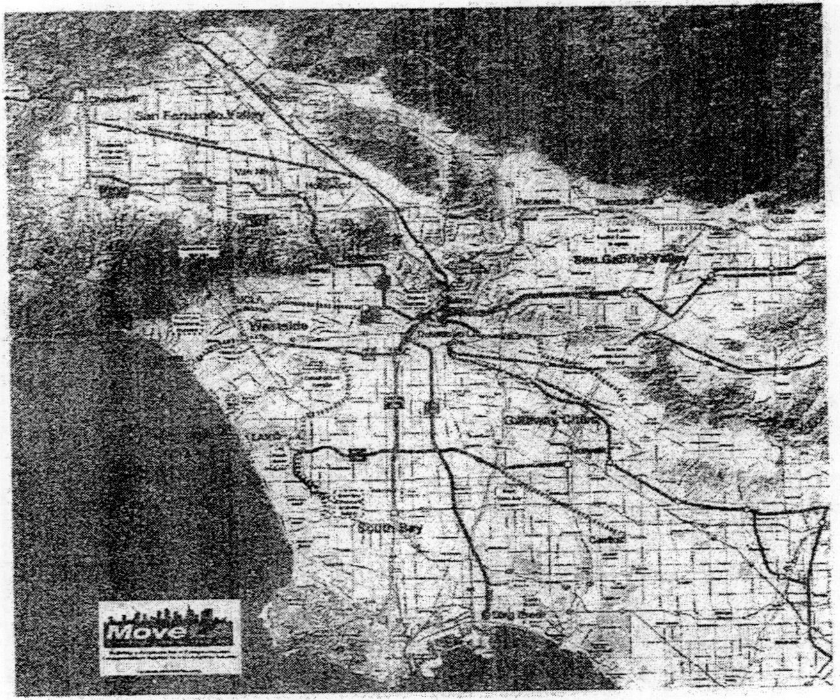

Fig. 9.2: Los Angeles: Poor Ridership of Public Transport

Charles Correa developed the plan of New Bombay (Mumbai) along the MRT corridor, which he called the string, along with a series of new cities, the beads, in the region. The junction of transport nodes constitutes the regional transport and business node. The Master Plan of Delhi is based on poly-nodal, poly-nuclear concept in the organisation of Districts, Communities and Neighbourhoods. However, in actual practice there had been a centrifugal, centripetal transport network with gridlocks all over. The growth of large cities had been usually concentric, leading to congestion in the central areas and numerous inter-sections. The building of flyovers/grade separators provide only temporary relief to the perennial congestion. Often it is not possible to restructure the city completely, but mixed land use, compact and smart development, transit oriented development, car, pools, efficient public transport and taxies, improving road capacity and using Intelligent Transport Systems Management can provide solutions to the problem.

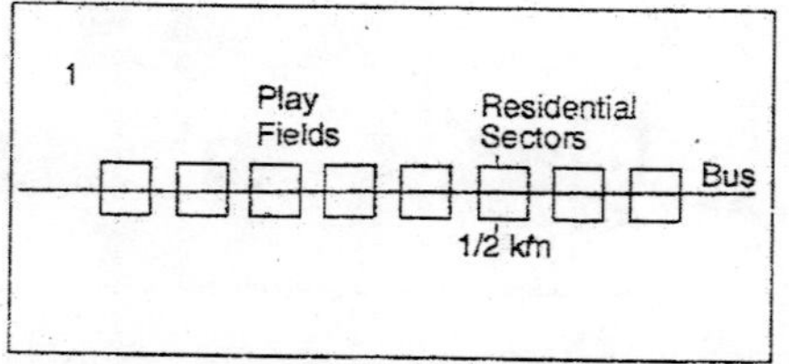

1. A series of sectors (some exclusively residential, others mixed residential-employment ares, depending on need) growing along a bus line (secondary MRT). The fact that the system is linear—as opposed to a grid—makes for a corridor of medium density demand and thus for an efficient bus system

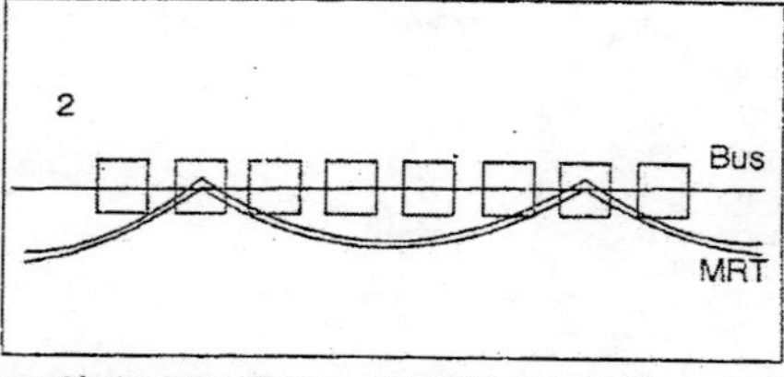

2. However, with the intensification of densities, the traffic grows and a primary MRT becomes necessary by acquiring developed load, knocking down buildings, etc. or reserving this land from the beginning. This is difficult because of squatters, and secondly, because it would leave no-man's land in the middle of the town.

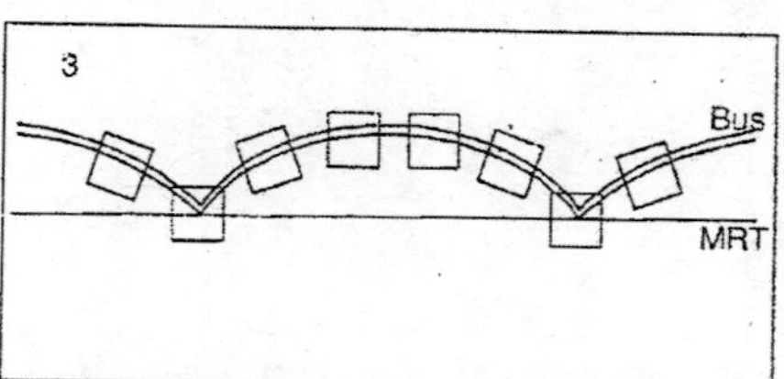

3. Why not reverse the pattern, *i.e.* start with a bus line which meanders; later on, when the train is installed, its alignment is direct. This pattern more clearly reflects the alignment constaints of the system

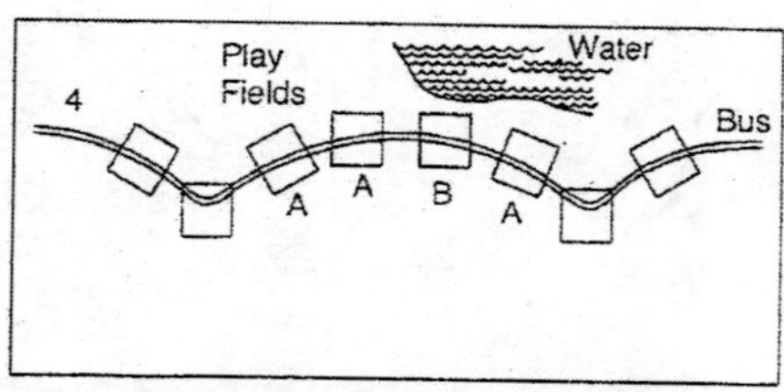

4. How the system grows. We start with a bus line (secondary MRT) generating a series of sectors of approximately equai importance. Let's call it type B.

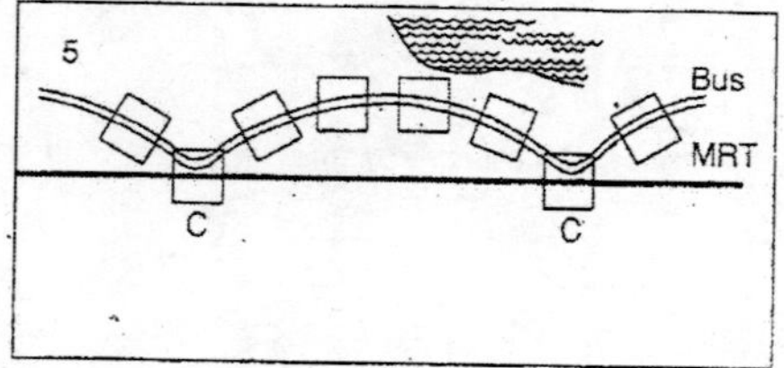

5. As the traffic grows and the primary MRT is installed, the interchanges generate additional activity, upgrading these particular sectors

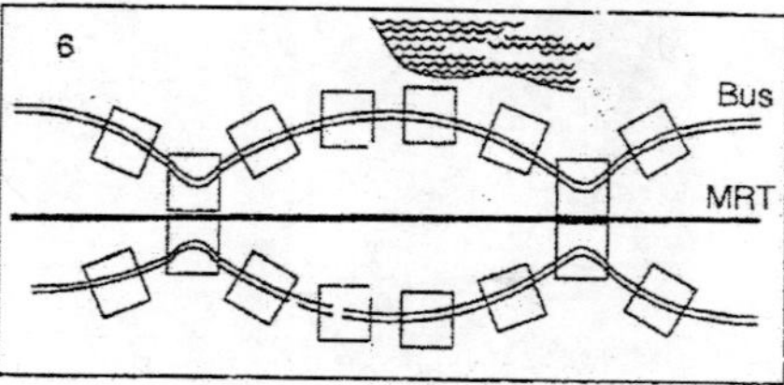

6. With time, a second bus line can be installed opening up a whole new section of the hinterland.

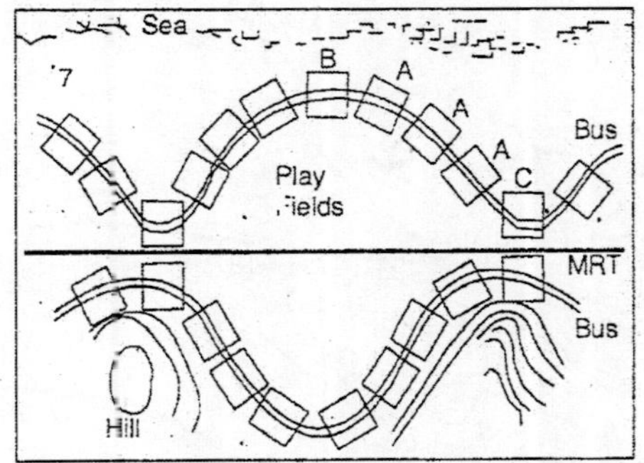

7. The system shown diagramatically on the new Bombay site (which runs between hills and water).

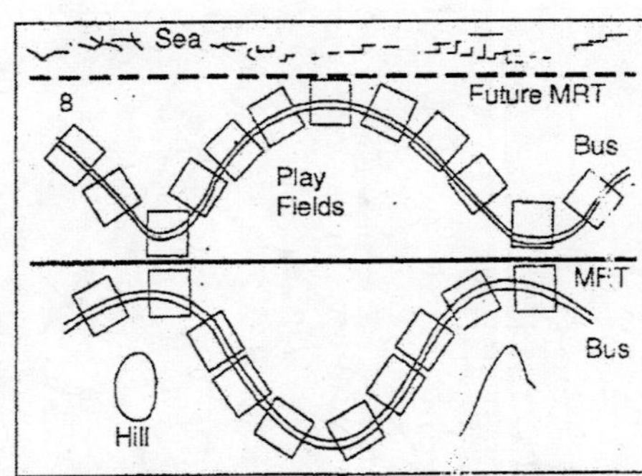

8. In future, in case densities and traffic grow beyond expectation, an additional primary MRT can be installed. This upgrades the importance of some type 'A' sectors (which now provide an opportunity for locating new social infrastructure and other facilities for additional population).

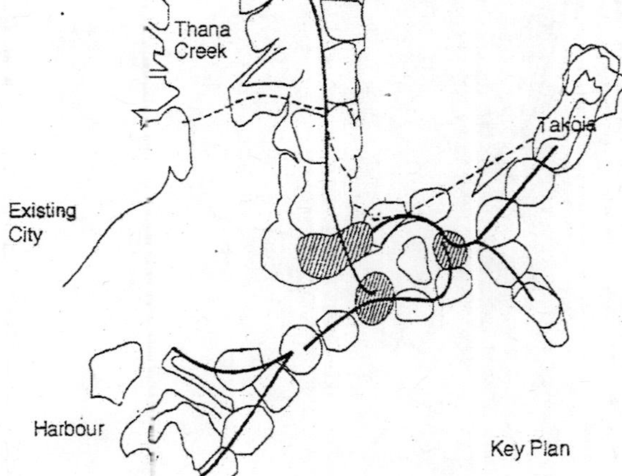

9. The basic structural plan for new Bomaby: three such linar spines arranged in a pin-wheel around the CBD. Each spine is hooked into the CBD at one end and into the regional transport network at the other, thus relating out CBD to the region around.

Transport Node cum-CBD

Fig. 9.3: The concept of New Bombay (Mumbai) developed by Charles Correa is based on 'beads in a string' pattern, the string being the MRT corridor tying up the nodes, that is, new cities in the region

Source: Frampton, Kenneth (1996), Charles Correa, Perennial Press, Mumbai

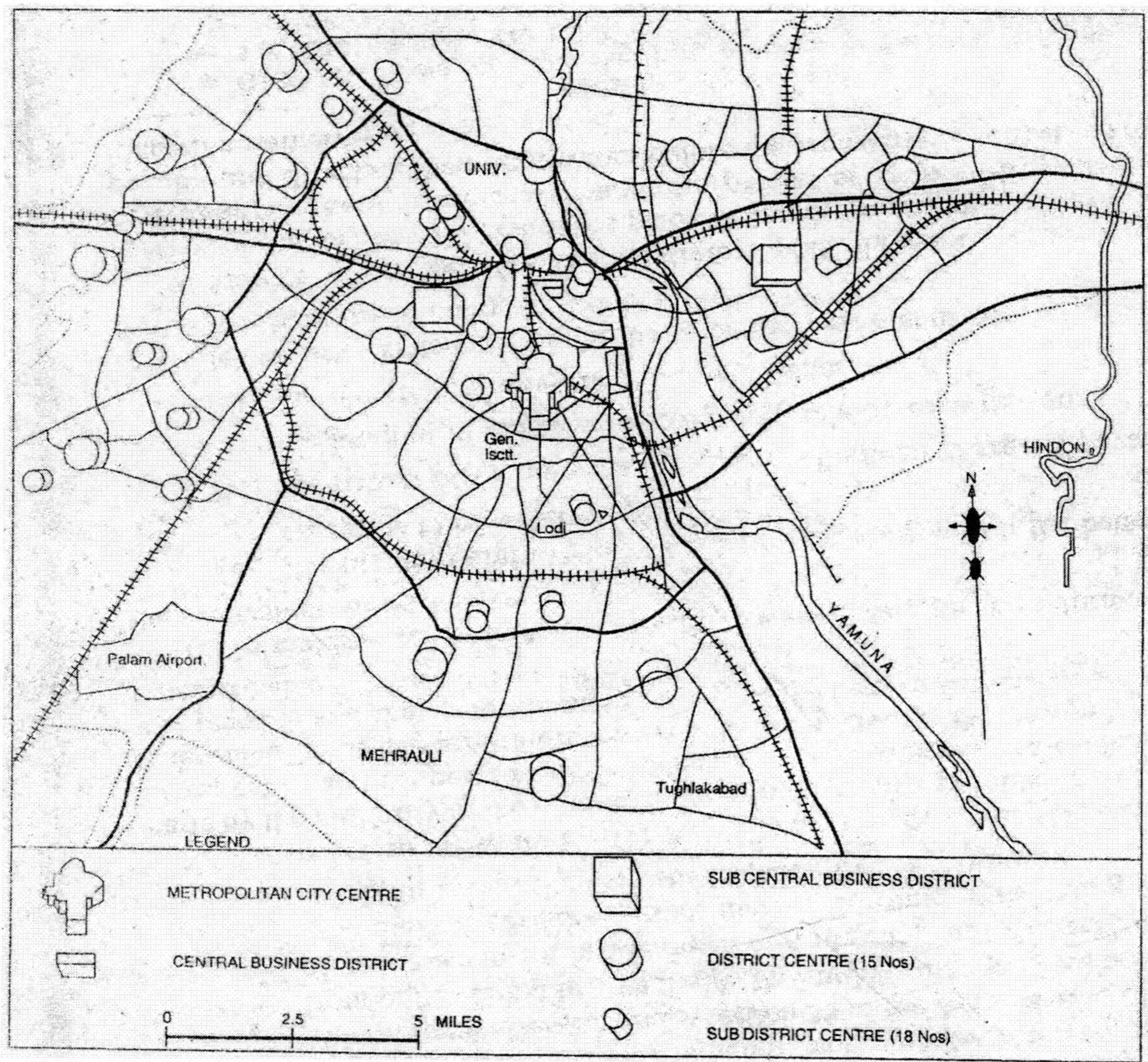

Fig. 9.4: The five tier commercial centres in the Master Plan of Delhi were based on the concept of poly-nodal, poly-nuclear hierarchy of Districts, Communities and Neighbourhoods. However, there had been a centrifugal, centripetal transport pattern and gridlocks.

Source: Jain, A.K., 2012, Sustainable Urban Transport and Systems, Khanna Publishers, New Delhi

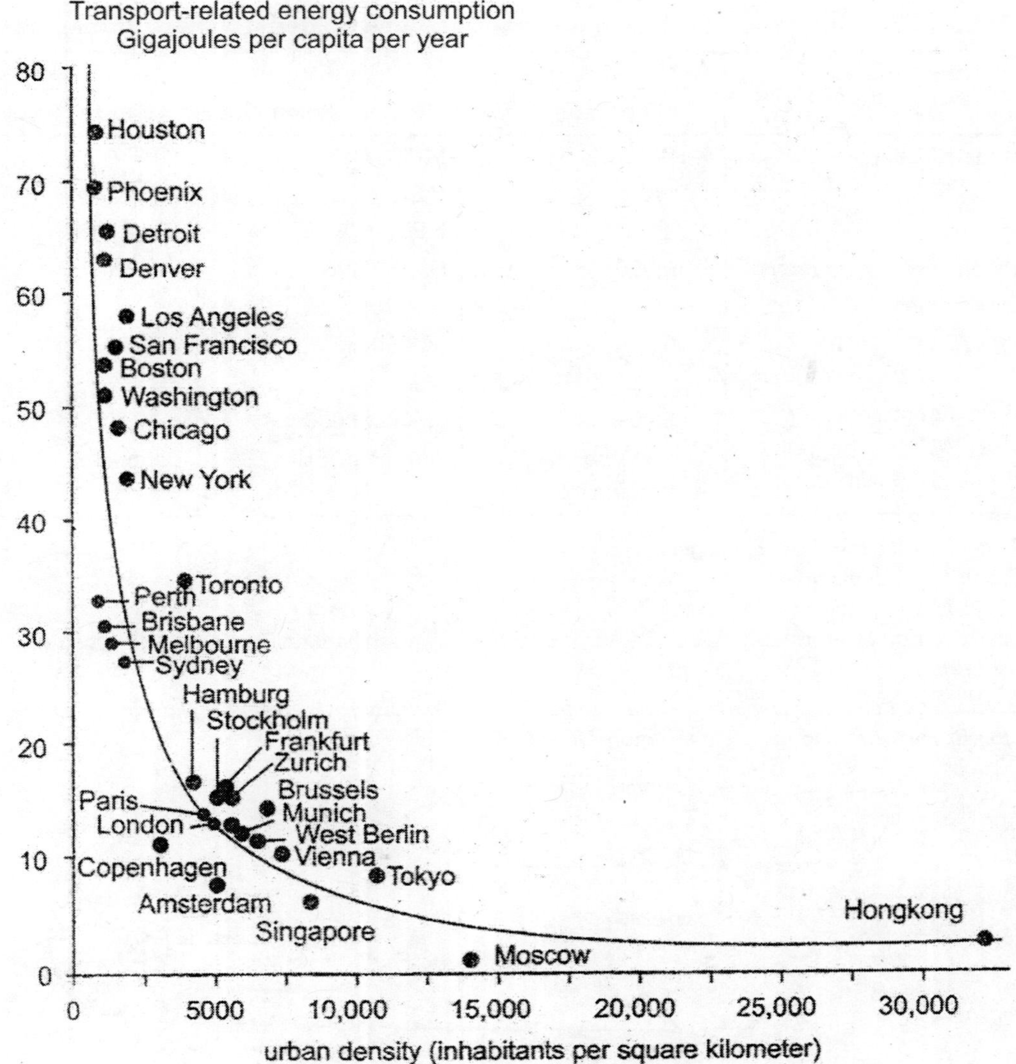

Fig. 9.5: Newman and Kenworthy's hyperbola "Urban density and transport-related energy consumption" shows a high correlation between urban density and intra-urban transport-related energy consumption per capita.

Source: Newman, Peter, R Kenworthy, 1999, Sustainability and Cities: Overcoming Automobile Dependence, The Centre for Resource Economics, Washington DC, USA.

Dense and compact urban planning can effectively reduce the vehicle kilometer travelled and trip length which result in lesser accidents, pollution and noise. Density is highly correlated with modal distribution and the intensity of automobile use, as shown in Table 9.2 given below:

Table 9.2: City typology based on average urban density and transport

Urban density	Low >25 persons/ha	Medium 50-100 persons/ha	High < 250 persons/ha
Modal distribution	MPT: 80% PT: 10% NPT: 10%	MPT: 50% PT: 25% NPT: 25%	MPT: 25% PT: 50% NPT: 25%
Automobile use (km/pers/yr)	> 10,000	5000-10,000	< 5,000
Public transport use (trips/person/yr)	< 50	50-250	> 250
Petrol consumption for transport (MJ/persons/year)	> 55,000	3,500-20,000	< 15,000
Representative positions	North American and Australian cities	European cities	Asian cities

MPT: Motorised Public Transport,
PT : Public Transport,
NMT : Non-motorised Transport,
Density: Number of inhabitants and jobs per hectare of net urban surface (omitting green and water surfaces)

Source: Newman, Peter, R Kenworthy, 1999, Sustainability and Cities: Overcoming Automobile Dependence, Centre for Resource Economics, Washington DC, USA.

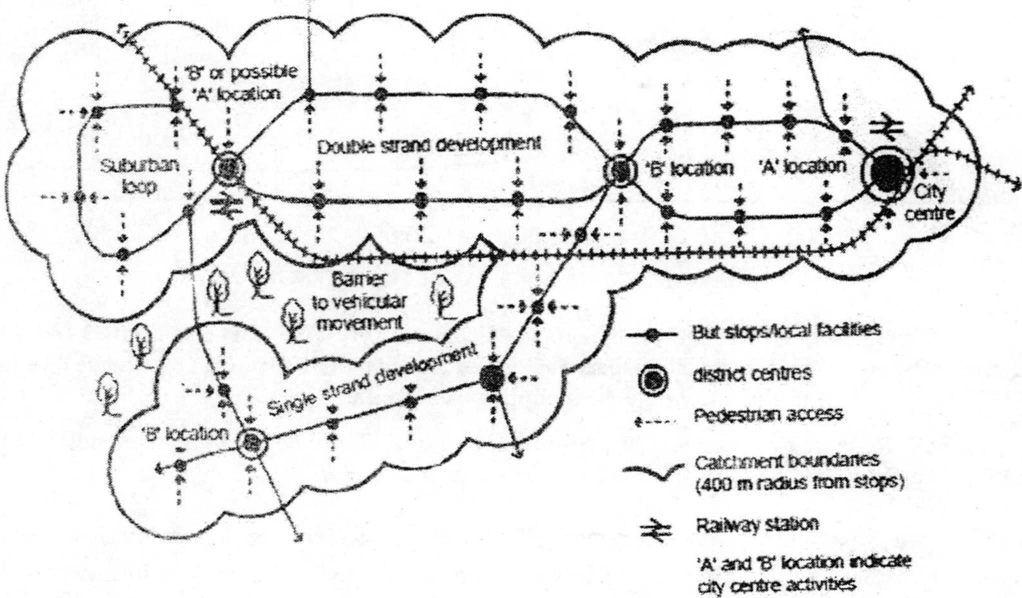

Fig. 9.6: Principles of walk to work and public transport planning comprise linear catchment zones, magnets, loops, limited lateral movement and fast, stopping services.

Source: Barton H. et. al. (2003) Shaping Neighbourhoods, Spon Press, London.

This needs a review of current planning regulations and development practices. For example, zoning codes often require more parking and wider streets than considered appropriate. Zoning codes also discourage commercial activities and secondary living units in residential areas, and require large setbacks for homes and businesses that reduce densities and land use mix. Another barrier is that the real estate industry is highly segmented by land use category (such as single-family housing, multi-family housing, retail, office and warehouse). Each category has its own practices, markets, trade associations and financing sources, which require a more integrated approach to development.

Residents in a well-designed neighbourhood with good walkability, mixed land use, connected streets, and local services tend to drive 20-30% less than residents in automobile dependent areas vehicle travel reduction may be even greater, if urbanism is coordinated with TDM strategies, such as transit improvements, car sharing, road pricing, parking, management and commuter trip reduction programs. This can provide a variety of economic, social and environment benefits, such as reduced traffic congestion, parking costs, accident risk, pollution and urban sprawl. It can significantly improve liveability, interaction and cohesion, with increased traffic safety due to narrower streets and slower traffic (traffic calming).

Transit Oriented Development

The concepts of Transit Oriented Development (TOD), Travel Demand Management (TDM) and Corridor Development form the basis of walk to work, compact and smart urban planning, seek to establish a close relationship among the residential, employment and service locations. For integration of land-use and transport planning, mixed land use helps in minimising the need to travel. A walkable community provides a fundamental building block in creating a sustainable urban form. As such, a city comprises a network of overlapping communities, each focused on a local centre, within which people can access on foot most of the facilities and services for day-to-day living. Each of these communities is defined by the walking catchment or "ped-shed", which is generally around 300 to 500 m, or a 5 to 8 minutes walk. Walkability is about making it possible for the average citizen to be able to lead his/her life by relying largely on walking for day to day activities. This needs an urban design consideration, such as density, mixed use, street life, pedestrian crossings, tree shade, public places and so on. All these parameters are important in their own right but walkability is a simple way to encapsulate this philosophy of integrated transport and urban planning.

Organisation of land use, circulation pattern and decisions regarding density, Floor Area Ratio and other controls should be around the public transport system, so as to which reduce the need of personal vehicles. The spatial model based upon the principle of "less travel, more energy saving", promotes a compact development. This can also significantly help in saving fossil fuel consumption, climate change and environment. Critical instruments for this option include land use synergy with public transport, infrastructure development, mixed land use and e-governance. Communications, such as telecommunications, electronic mail, video-conferencing, radio-paging, mobile-phones, computer networking, e-mail, etc. provide the alternatives to physical movement.

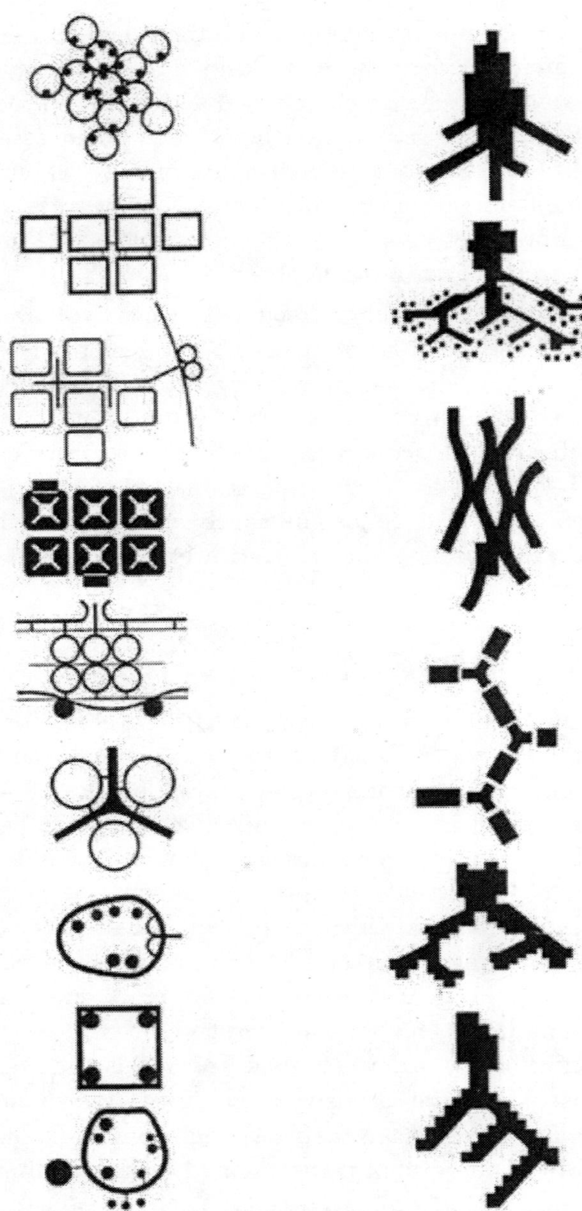

Fig. 9.7: Various forms of city structure can be developed for walkability, efficient public transport, as well as for organisation of community module, greens and social infrastructure. The basic principle for city structure for sustainable transport are i) creating a walkable city, ii) a smart and compact city, iii) controlling urban sprawl, iv) promoting mixed land use, v) promoting public transport by travel demand management/transit oriented development and corridor planning. Usually arterial roads (60 m and above) should be spaced at 500 m, collector sub-arterial roads (30 to 60 m) at 300 m and local streets (up to 40 m) at 150 m. Accordingly a module/sector can be designed, for example 800 mx1200 m in Chandigarh. The industry, warehousing and transport terminals should be located outside the urban periphery

Planning of transport in synergy with land use can effectively address the issues of urban mobility. It aims to reduce the need to travel and encourages walkablity together with maximizing the efficiency of the public transport system and non-motorised transport, in the following ways:

- Walk to work (W2W), "local hubs" within 10 minutes walking and cycling distance
- Integrated planning of urban transport corridors
- Mixed land use, rationalisation of land use and density
- Multi-modal integration of buses, trams, metro rail, rail corridors and LRT
- Potential of using subterranean space
- Communication as a viable substitute to physical movement, thus reducing need to travel.
- Encouraging cycles and NMV
- Safety of the movement for children, pedestrians, women, disabled and elderly
- Low noise and traffic calming

Safe and accessible cities are compact, walkable and sustainable, which are designed to enhance local identity, provide diverse housing options, land use efficiency, generate local employment and provide comfortable, safe, affordable, reliable and non-polluting public travel modes. Most of the local facilities are reachable by a convenient 5-minute (400 to 500 meter) walking, with dedicated paths for walking and cycling. Neighbourhood facilities, shops, schools, parks, clubs and city centres are located along the pedestrian, cycle and public transport corridors. The urban form plays an important role in the safe urban mobility by accommodating all modes to travel, including walking, wheelchair, cycling, public transit and people by a safe, efficient and attractive road network, with generous footpaths and trees. Buildings are located directly onto street fronts to ensure passive surveillance of public spaces that increases personal safety. Streets are provided with service roads and pooled parking area at every kilometre that keeps the footpaths and building front free from on-street parking.

Transit Oriented Development Principles

TOD is generally characterized by compact, high-density, mixed use development near new or existing high quality public transportation infrastructure that provides housing, employment, entertainment and civic functions within walking distance of the transit system. Pedestrian-oriented design features of TOD encourage residents and workers to use their cars less and ride public transit modes.

The primary goals of TOD are to:

1. Reduce/discourage private vehicle dependency and induce public transport use - through policy measures, design interventions & enforcement.
2. Provide public transit access to the maximum number of people through densification and enhanced connectivity.

A dynamic city-level integrated transport-land use model needs to be prepared to assess transportation and landuse planning needs of the city. Integrated redevelopment schemes of the influence area of MRTS stations be prepared based on the following TOD principles:

1. Pedestrian and Non-Motorized Transport (NMT) friendly environment

- Design for pedestrian safety, comfort and convenience.
- Create street-level activity and vibrant urban spaces.
- All impediments/encroachments shall be removed from footpaths all over the city to create safe walking environment in all colonies, office /shopping areas, terminal areas, etc.
- At least five safe street-level crossing opportunities per kilometre of road with approximately 250 m being maximum spacing between two crossings should be provided. Depending on context, these crossings may be signalized and/or traffic calmed to reduce vehicular speed and increase safety.
- Pedestrian Signals should be synchronized with the nearest full-traffic signals, for smooth movement of traffic along with safe pedestrian/NMT crossing.
- Pedestrian oriented vehicle-free spaces need to be created in all institutional, regional and work centres.
- New areas should plan for pedestrian zones, plazas and activity spaces based on locations of public transport nodes/stations, employment centres, residential communities and local/city level destinations.
- Street-level activity and well-watched streets need to be created through mixed-use, avoiding opaque boundary walls, creation of hawking/vending zones and round-the-clock activities, to ensure a safe environment for pedestrians.
- Planning, design, implementation and maintenance of pedestrian routes and facilities needs to be prioritized.
- As per National Mission on Sustainable Habitat (NMSH) parameters, to create active streets for pedestrians, (i) Primary pedestrian access for buildings should be from the main street, with location as per shortest walking distance from nearest bus-stop; (ii) The main building facade should face the street, located on the property line without setback or with active use within set back and transparent edge that contribute to street safety. (iii) Commercial frontages should have facades with minimum 50% transparency (untinted) to facilitate visual surveillance of streets, Compound walls, if present, should be transparent above a height of 100cm. High security government buildings may apply for exemption. (iv) Vending spaces should be marked in addition and adjacent to the walking path, especially along high pedestrian volume areas to activate the street and make it safe. (v) Space to be planned for utilities including drinking water kiosks and toilets, so that the walking space is enhanced but not compromised.

2. Design for cyclists and NMT Users

- All streets and public spaces shall be universally accessible.
- Prepare a cycling master plan for the city that creates a network of routes integrating all arterial roads, eco-mobility corridors along nallahs, heritage routes, school precincts as well as other recreational routes.
- On all arterial roads fully segregated cycle/NMT tracks should be provided with provision for safe parking in park and ride lots. Wherever full ROW is not available, the cycles/NMT may be allowed to flow in mixed-traffic condition.
- In new areas, cycle tracks should be provided at the sub-arterial and local level roads and streets.
- In all areas of the city, the use of cycles/rickshaw as a non-motorised mode of transport should be consciously planned along with pedestrianisation.
- Plan and implement city wide, affordable and accessible cycle sharing/rental schemes to encourage public transit users in particular and public in general to use cycle as a mode to perform their first and last mile journey as well as to make regular short trips without using private vehicles.
- A cycle sharing/rental system could be planned/implemented by any public/private agency comprising of an owner and an operator, with the government. playing the role of facilitator. The extant guidelines in this regard may be followed.
- In case new pedestrian/NMT networks need to be added in built-up/developed areas, appropriate incentives may be given.

3. Connectivity and Network Density

- Disperse high traffic volumes of traffic over a network of streets rather than concentrating traffic on few major streets and junctions.
- Provide the shortest direct route to pedestrians and non-motorized modes to station as well as between individual buildings/complexes.
- Integration of infrastructure development and travel demand management (TDM) strategies e.g. bus lanes, station plazas, intersection improvements, etc.

4. Multi-Modal Interchange

- Minimize travel time and cost for majority of commuters. Provide multiple mode options for all sections of society with safety and affordability. Ensure reliable, frequent and affordable public transport systems/networks across the city. Minimize the number and time required for mode transfers for maximum number of commuters.
- Prioritize pedestrians, public transport, IPT and NMT modes over private modes in design and management of urban spaces.

5. Inducing Modal Shift

- As far as possible, locate public transport stations, homes, jobs and civic facilities within easy access of each other, to incentivize walking and cycling/NMT use, especially for short distances.

- Dis-incentivize private motor vehicle use. Limit supply and appropriately price private parking spaces to discourage private vehicle use in TOD Zones.

6. Placemaking and Ensuring Safety

- Create a safe, vibrant, comfortable urban "place", by providing round-the-clock active streets and incidental spaces to relax. Introduce mixed land use and other informal street activities like vendors, etc. to promote round-the-clock activity and also promote informal surveillance.
- Minimize boundary walls and setbacks of compounds, and build to the edge of the street R/W. Street walls with transparency, built-to-edge buildings, minimum setbacks and non-opaque fences help provide natural surveillance of public spaces.

7. High Density, Mixed-use, Mixed-Income Development near stations

- Maximize densities within TOD in order to facilitate maximum number of people walking or cycling, or use NMT or feeder services easily to access public transit facility.
- In greenfield development, higher the density, lower the per kilometre infrastructure cost.
- Enable a balanced mix of jobs and housing along MRTS corridors coupled with caps on parking supply, higher housing affordability through design and technology options, and improved efficiency and equity in the resulting developments.

Development Control Norms for Transit Oriented Development (TOD)

The Influence Zone of MRTS Corridors shall be designated as Transit Oriented Development (TOD) Zone where the following development control norms shall apply:

FAR and Density:

(i) TOD norms of FAR and density may be availed through the preparation and approval of comprehensive integrated scheme of minimum 1 Ha, with maximum ground coverage of 40%. In case of MRTS/Government Agencies, the minimum plot size for development shall be 3000 sq.m., but all other development norms shall apply.

(ii) Cluster Block approval may be given for a minimum area of 3000 sq.m. only, if an approved influence zone plan or integrated scheme for the area exists.

(iii) For any integrated scheme, a max. FAR of 400 and a maximum density of 2000 persons per hectare (PPH) are permissible. The entire amalgamated plot will be considered for calculating the FAR and density. FAR utilization shall not be less than 400. Mandatory EWS FAR of 15% over and above the maximum permissible FAR shall be applicable. Additional FAR may be availed through TDR only for schemes larger than 1 Ha.

(iv) All residents residing in that scheme area shall have to be accommodated within the same scheme, with no induced displacement of existing residential population.

Mix of Uses

In all integrated schemes, a minimum of 30% of overall FAR shall be mandatory for Residential use, a minimum 10% of FAR for commercial use and minimum 10% of FAR for community facilities. Mix of uses and FAR utilization for the remaining 50% FAR shall be as per the land use category designated in the Zonal Plan.

Table 9.3: Indicative FAR utilization and mix of uses within various land use categories falling within TOD Zone (except Recreational)

Landuse as per ZDP (At Least 50% of total FAR to be as per ZDP Use)	Indicative Mix of Uses within FAR Utilization			
	Minimum Residential*	Minimum Commercial	Minimum Facilities**	Indicative Mix of Uses within remaining 50% FAR, as per ZDP landuse
Residential	30%		10%	Of the remaining FAR, at least 20% or more (upto 70% of total) is for Residential use. Other uses are permitted upto 30%.
Commercial	30%		10%	Of the remaining FAR, at least 40% or more is to be for commercial use. Other uses are permitted upto 10%.
Industrial	30%		10%	Remaining 50% of FAR to be for Industrial use.
Government	30%		10%	Remaining 50% of FAR may be for any Government use.
Transportation	30%		10%	Remaining 50% of FAR may be for any use after meeting all operational requirements for transportation facilities.
Public and Semi-public Facilites (PSP)	30%		10%	Of the remaining FAR, at least 40% or more is to be for PSP use. Other uses are permitted upto 10%.
Mixed-Use	30%		10%	Remaining 50% of FAR may be for any use.

Notes:

*1. The mandatory residential component shall comprise 50% units of size ranging between 32-40 sq.m. and the balance 50% comprising homes of average size of 65 sq.m. For EWS having FAR of 15% over and above the permissible FAR will be applicable.

**2. The mandatory facilities and commercial component shall include the requirements of the residential population in that land parcel.

3. DMRC/RRTS/Railways (MRTS) to be exempted from providing the minimum 30% Residential component which is part of the TOD norms. In case residential is provided in MRTS projects, the mix of dwelling unit sizes (for middle income group) may not be made applicable to DMRC/RRTS/Railways. Minimum scheme area for development to be relaxed to 3000 sq.m. for DMRC/RRTS/Railways (MRTS) agencies.

Source: DDA (2015) Amendment to Master Plan for Delhi -2021, Gazette of India Notification dated 14th July 2015

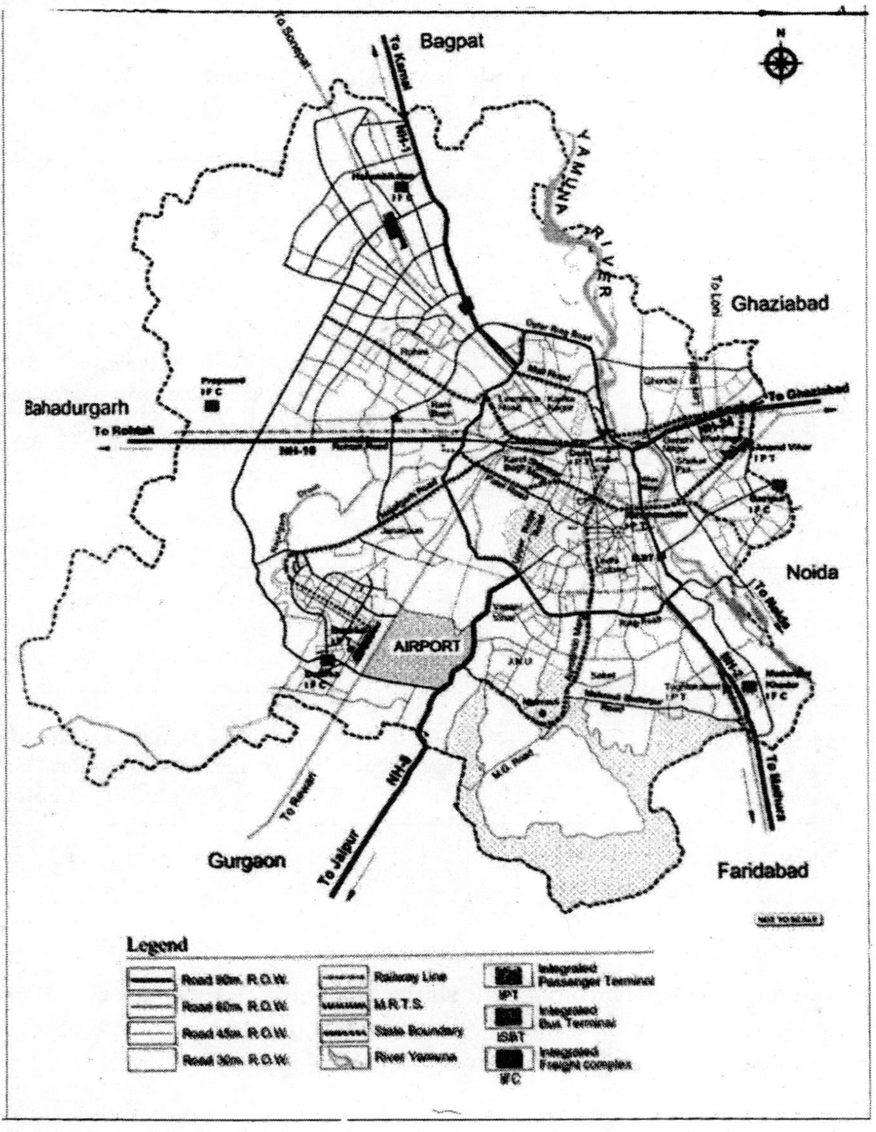

Fig. 9.8: Multi Modal Transit System of Delhi provides a network of Roads, Ring Railway, Metro, BRT, private vehicles and non-motorised, informal transport.

Roads

(i) Of the area taken up for development as integrated scheme, at least 20% of land shall be handed over as constructed roads/circulation areas to the local body/road owning agency for public use. However, FAR can be availed on the entire amalgamated land parcel.

(ii) Land to be surrendered as built roads/public spaces to the extent of at least 10% shall be along one side, to be consolidated with the adjacent plot, wherever applicable.

(iii) The roads handed over to government will be designed, developed, maintained and kept encroachment free by the developer and will remain open for general public at all times. Appropriate property tax rebates may be given to developer entities for keeping the roads/public spaces encroachment free and making them available to general public.

(iv) Road Networks to be planned with a vehicular route network of approximately 250m c/c and pedestrian network of approximately 100m c/c. Additional thoroughfares should be provided as required.

(v) The Authority will prepare/approve plans for TOD Zones indicating the ROWs, public spaces, build-to lines and connectivity links to Metro Stations and probable areas where amalgamation can take place with land parcels of 1Ha or more. The regulations/ guidelines for creating arcades, boulevards, paseos, woonerfs and other active streets shall be tentatively indicated in the influence zone plans prepared and approved by the Authority.

Green Public Open Space Provision

(i) 20% of the area of the amalgamated plot shall be designated as green Public Open Space which shall be designed, developed and maintained by the developer and will remain un-gated and open for general public at all times, failing which it will be taken over by public agency.

(ii) The location and design guidelines for such spaces shall be tentatively indicated in the influence zone plans by the Authority.

(iii) In addition to the above, at least 10% of plot area shall be in the form of Green/ Recreational area for the exclusive use, including circulation and common areas. In plots less than 1 Ha, this may be provided in the form of accommodation reservation i.e. as part of common terraces, rooftops, podiums, etc.

(iv) Areas indicated as Master Plan/Zonal Level Recreational will remain unchanged.

Social Infrastructure

(i) Social Infrastructure may be allocated the required built-up area within planned re/ development schemes in the form of Accommodation Reservation, instead of individual plots.

(ii) Open area requirement of the social infrastructure uses shall be accommodated/ integrated into the multi-use Public Open spaces provided in the area. For example, school playgrounds may be provided within the Neighbourhood Play Area.

(iii) After approval of the integrated scheme and demarcation of civic/PSP sites and recreational open space, change of use shall not be permitted.

Green Buildings

(i) The entire development has to be with minimum 3 star or gold rating as per approved rating agencies and appropriate rebate in the property tax may be applicable.

(ii) As the TOD development will take place through redevelopment and reconstruction, no levy on additional FAR is applicable except additional services charges.

Impact Assessment

Once the Influence Zone plans for TOD areas are prepared indicating the street networks, indicative amalgamation areas, location of public spaces, active edges, etc. a complete assessment of traffic generation and its dispersal, requirement of services, mitigation measures for environment impact will be done and got approved from bodies concerned so that the redevelopment process through TOD can be effective and beneficial for general public. Challenges arising during implementation need to be addressed progressively.

Source: DDA (2015) Amendment to Master Plan for Delhi -2021, Gazette of India Notification dated 14th July 2015

Non-Structural and Non-Invasive Transport Planning

The planners can significantly affect the safety and viability of public transport by arranging roads, footpaths and land uses. The quality of bus and train services can be higher where the maximum number of people can reach their destination by the minimum number of routes. Linearity is therefore a key feature. The points where routes cross (nodes) then become the prime locations for local jobs and services and the focus for pedestrian and cycling routes. Public transport accessibility has to be considered not as an after-thought, but as the starting-point for neighbourhood planning, with land uses attached to the public transport network.

Popular solutions like widening of roads, construction of flyovers/grade separators and mega transport terminals are pursued by transport organizations and political leadership, who consider these as a matter of prestige and professional achievement. However, these often prove to be short term and sometimes even worsen the situation.Planning interventions and non-invasive, non-structural solutions such as promoting public transport and land use integrity need to be adopted.

It is being increasingly realized that the structural solutions, like flyovers built at enormous cost, provide only a temporary relief and fail to keep pace with the growth of traffic. For a synergy between land use and public transport system, it is necessary to restructure the city by Transit Oriented Development, higher density, FAR and mixed land use for a compact and smart growth with an integrated multi-modal public transit system. Simultaneously transport infrastructure, roads, dedicated two wheelers, cycle and pedestrian tracks are to be improved.

As urban transport in Indian cities contributes up to two-third of the emission and pollution, it is crucial that the concepts of walk to work, inter-modal public transit, mixed land use, e-governance, transit oriented development and travel demand management are adopted, rather than just end of the pipe, pollution under check certification. Low carbon, green mobility is crucial for an efficient, sustainable and healthy society.

Fig. 9.9: East Delhi TOD Hub, Architects DOM and CP Kukreja Associates

Fig. 9.10: Skeleton Parking Cluster at every km to avoid parking on footpaths and building fronts

Source: Unified Traffic & Transportation Infrastructure Planning and Engineering Centre (UTTIPEC)

Integrated land use planning considers Travel Demand Management (TDM) solutions, such as ride share program, mobility management programs, shared parking and user charges. These aim to encourage people to reduce car trips by incentives and support to reduce peak-period driving, including better cycling facilities and flexible working hours. The core of integrated planning is to improve public transit and increase its service efficiency by dedicated corridors (e.g. BRT) better vehicles and stations, more frequent services, reduced crowding, improved walking conditions of transit stations, and priority to high occupant vehicles (buses and carpools).

Location Efficient and Transit Oriented Development is a set of planning practices to create more attractive, efficient and safe communities. These can significantly improve accessibility and reduce per-capita automobile travel, by various design features. The land use reforms can be implemented at various local level, site and block level, and city level. These reforms do not exclude automobile travel, but aim to increase transportation options and give priority to walking, cycling and public transit, which provide more direct travel between destinations. Increased connectivity has shown a reduced per capita vehicle travel and reduced traffic volumes as the people can conveniently go to work and shopping by walking and cycling and children can walk to school, parks, recreation centre and gym. These concepts can be incorporated into existing urban communities. Existing urban areas can implement traffic calming and pedestrian improvements, reallocate road space, use parking management and encourage location efficient development.

Transportation Planning Norms and Standards

Classification of Urban Roads

1. **Urban Expressway:** Expressways are divided highways for through traffic with full or partial control of access and generally with grade separations at major crossroads.
2. **Arterial road:** They are the primary roads for ensuring mobility function. They carry the largest volumes of traffic and longest trips in a city. These roads are characterized by mobility and cater to through traffic with restricted access from carriageway to the side. In such cases, special provisions should be introduced to reduce conflict with the through traffic.
3. **Sub-Arterial Road:** This category of road follows all the functions of an Arterial Urban road and is characterized by mobility, and caters to through traffic with restricted access from carriageway to the side. It carries same traffic volumes as the arterial roads. Due to its overlapping nature, Sub arterial roads can act as arterials. This is context specific and is based on the function and the land use development it passes through.
4. **Distributor/Collector Roads:** As the name suggests, these are connector roads, which distribute the traffic from access streets to arterial and sub-arterial roads. They are characterized by mobility and access equally. It carries moderate traffic volumes compared to the arterial roads. Due to its overlapping nature, distributor roads can act as sub-arterial and as access streets, depending upon the function and the land use of the surroundings.

5. **Local Street:** These are intended for neighbourhood (or local) use on which through traffic is to be discouraged. These roads should be made pedestrian and bicycle friendly by using modern traffic calming designs to keep the speeds within limits as per design.
6. **Access Street:** These are used for access functions to adjoining properties and areas. A majority of trips in urban areas usually originate or terminate on these streets.

Table 9.4: Design Speed and Space Standard for Urban Roads

S. No.	Road Types	Design Speed (kmph)	Space Standard (Row in m)
1.	Urban Expresssway	80	50-60
2.	Arterial Road	50	50-80
3.	Sub Arterial Road	50	30-50
4.	Distributor/Collector Roads	30	12-30
5.	Local Street	10-20	12-20
6.	Access Street	15	6-15

Source: Urban Road, Code of Practice Part 1, MoUD.

Urban Street Design Guidelines

Urban Street Design Guidelines, developed by the Ministry of Urban Development along with the IRC and Delhi Development Authority (UTTIPEC) are given below:

Table 9.5: Carriageway Width for each type of road

S. No.	Types of Roads	Characteristics	Width of each car lane (m)	Width of each Bus lane (m)
1.	Urban Expresssway	Minimum 6 lanes divided (using a median)	3.0 to 3.5 m width each	3.5 m (segregated)
2.	Arterial Road	Minimum 6 lanes divided (using a median)	3.0 to 3.5 m width each	3.5 m (segregated)
3.	Sub-Arterial Road	Minimum 4 lanes divided (using a median)	3.0 to 3.5 m width each	3.5 m (segregated) or Painted lane
4.	Distributor/Collect or Roads	Maximum 4 lanes of 3.0 m width each (excluding marking) or 2 lanes of 3.0 to 3.3 m width each (excluding marking) with or without an intermittent median	2 lanes of 3.0 to 3.5 m width each	Mixed traffic
5.	Local Street	1 to 2 lanes, (undivided); traffic calming is required	2.75 to 3.0 m width each	Not required
6.	Access Street	1 to 21 lanes, (undivided) of 2.75 to 3.0 m width each	2.75 to 3.0 m width each	Not required

Source: Code of Practice Part 1, MoUD.

Notes:

1. Footpath, NMT provisions and Right of Use (RoU) of various infrastructure shall also be assigned in the RoW at the stage of finalisation of road network and hierarchy.
2. RoW shall also include a well planned utility corridor.
3. Road levels to be defined at the Local Area Plan level to ensure integrated road levels with drainage system and slope.
4. No roads to have two different road levels without a proper median or a separator.

Footpath

Footpath should be normally designed for a Standard Level of Service (LOS), thereby providing wide pedestrian facilities for pleasant and comfortable walking. Under resource constraint LOS can be adopted for deciding the width of footpath as mentioned in Table given below. The width of footpaths depends upon the expected pedestrian traffic and may be fixed with the help of the following norms subject to not being less than 1.8m:

Table 9.6: Capacity of Footpath & its Design

Width of sidewalk (m)	Design Flow in Number of Persons per hour			
	In Both Directions		Only in one direction	
	LOS B	LOS C	LOS B	LOS C
1.8	1350	1890	2025	2835
2	1800	2520	2700	3780
2.5	2250	3150	3375	4725
3	2700	3780	4050	5670
3.5	3150	4410	4725	6615

Source: IRC 103-2012.

Passenger Car Units (PCU)

The PCU standards as per the vehicle type for planning the area requirements are given in Table below:

Table 9.7: PCU Standards

S. No.	Vehicle Type	Equivalency factor
1.	Passenger car, tempo, auto, jeep, vans, tractor	1.0
2.	Truck, bus, agricultural tractor-trailer	3.0
3.	Motor-cycle, scooter and cycle	0.5
4.	Cycle-rickshaw	1.5
5.	Horse drawn vehicle	4.0
6.	Bullock cart	5.0
7.	Hand-cart	6.0

Source: JNNURM Rapid Training Programme, Preparation of DPRs, UDPFI guidelines and IRC 106 (1990)..

Design Service Volume

The Design Service Volume standards as given in IRC Code 106-1990 for designing road capacity, are given in table below:

Table 9.8: Design Service Volume Standards

S. No.	Type of Carriageway	Total Design Service Volume for different road categories		
		Arterial	Sub-Arterial	Collector
1.	2-Lane (one way)	2400	1900	1400
2.	2-Lane (two way)	1500	1200	900
3.	3-Lane (one way)	3600	2900	2200
4.	4-Lane undivided (two way)	3000	2400	1800
5.	4-Lane divided (two way)	3600	2900	—
6.	6-Lane undivided (two way)	4800	3800	—
7.	6-Lane divided (two way)	5400	4300	—
8.	8-Lane divided (two way)	7200	—	—

Source: IRC Code 106-1990.

Parking

Equivalent Car Space (ECS) for different vehicles is given below:

Table 9.9: Recommended ECS for various types of vehicles

S. No.	Vehicles Type	ECS
1.	Car/taxi	1.00
2.	Two Wheeler	0.25
3.	Auto Rickshaw	0.50
4.	Bicycle	0.10
5.	Trucks/Buses	2.5
6.	Emergency Vehicles	2.5
7.	Rickshaw	0.8

Source: DPR for Multi-level Parking Facility at Ghaziabad, Main Report, NCRPB and ADB, 2010.

Recommended Parking Standards (ECS) Based on Land use Type

Table 9.10: Parking Standards

S. No.	Land use Type	ECS	Notes
1.	**Residential**		
	Residential Plot-Plotted Housing	2 Equivalent Car Space (ECS) in plots of size 250-300 sqm and 1 ECS for every 100 sqm, built up area in plots exceeding 300 sqm.	--
	Residential Plot-Group Housing	2.0 ECS/100 sqm built up area	--
	Cluster Court Housing	2.0 ECS/100 sqm built up area	--
	Guest House/Lodging and Boarding House/Dharmshala	2 ECS per 100 sqm. of built up area	--
2.	**Commercial Centres**		
	Convenience Shopping Centre/Local Shopping	2 ECS per 100 sqm of floor area	--
	Service Market	2 ECS/100 sqm of floor area	--
	Community Centre/Non-hierarchical Commercial Centre	3 ECS/100 sqm of floor area	--
	District Centre/Sub-Central Business District Sub-city Level Commercial areas	3 ECS/100 sqm of floor area	--
	Commercial Plot: Retail and Commerce, Metropolitan City Centre	3 ECS/100 sqm of floor area	--
	Hotel	3 ECS/100 sqm of floor area	For population between 2-10 lakh – 1 car parking space for every 4 guest room. For population between 10-50 lakh- 1 car parking space for every 3 guest rooms. For population more than 50 lakh – 1 car parking space for every 2 guest rooms.
	Service Apartments	3 ECS/100 sqm of floor area	--

	Any other commercial centre including commercial component along with Railway/MRTS and ISBT	3 ECS/100 sqm of floor area	--
	Integrated Freight Complex/Wholesale Market	3 ECS/100 sqm of floor area	In case of plots up to 300 sqm Common parking is to be provided.
3.	**Socio-Cultural Facilities**		
	Community Hall	3.0 ECS/100 sqm	--
	Recreational Club	2 ECS/100 sqm of floor area	--
	Socio-cultural activities such as auditorium, music, dance and drama centre/meditation, spiritual centre, etc.	2 ECS/100 sqm of floor area	--
	Science Centre	2 ECS/100 sqm of floor area	--
	International Convention Centre	3 ECS/100 sqm of floor area	--
	Old Age Home/Care Centre for Physically/Mentally challenged/Working women/men hostel/Adult Education Centre/Orphanage/Children's Centre/Night Shelter	1.8 ECS/100 sqm of floor area	--
	Sports facility for international sports event	2 ECS/100 sqm of floor area	--
4.	**Public-Semi Public**		
	Integrated Office Complex	1.8 ECS/100 sq m of floor area	The norms for Government offices/Public Sector Undertakings shall be as per integrated office complex
	District Court	1.8 ECS/100 sqm of floor area	--
	Head Post Office with Administrative office and with/without delivery office	1.33 ECS/100 sqm of floor area	--

	Amusement Park	3 ECS/100 sqm of floor area	--
	ISBT/Metro	2 ECS per 100 sqm of floor area	--
	Hospitals	2 ECS per 100 sqm of floor area	--
	Veterinary Hospital	1.33 ECS per 100 sqm of floor area	--
	Veterinary Dispensary	1.33 ECS per 100 sqm of floor area	--
	Nursing and Paramedic institute	2 ECS per 100 sqm of floor area	--
	Medical College	As per norms of Medical Council of India/Regulatory Body	--
5.	**Industry**		
	Industrial Plot up to 50 sqm area	2 ECS/100 sqm of floor area	--
	Industrial Plot 51 sqm – 400 sqm area	2 ECS/100 sqm of floor area	--
	Industrial Plot 401 sqm and above	2 ECS/100 sqm of floor area	--
	Flatted Group Industry (Min Plot size 400 sqm)	2 ECS/100 sqm of floor area	--

Source: Master Plan for Delhi (MPD) 2021.

Parking standards are prescribed in above table, however, where it is not prescribed; it could be followed as given in the following Table.

Table 9.11: Permissible ECS for different land uses

S. No.	Use Premises	Permissible Equivalent Car Spaces (ECS) Per 100 sqm of floor area
1.	Residential	2.0
2.	Commercial	3.0
3.	Manufacturing	2.0
4.	Government	1.8
5.	Public and Semi-Public Facilities	2.0

Source: MPD 2021.

Space Standards for Parking

For the provision of car parking space, the space standards shall be as per the following Table.

Table 9.12: Space standards for Parking

S. No.	Type of Parking	Area in sqm per ECS
1.	Open	23
2.	Ground Floor (covered)	28
3.	Basement	32
4.	Multi-Level with Ramps	30
5.	Automated Multilevel with lifts	16

Source: MPD 2021.

Bus Terminals

The functions of bus terminal primarily include movement of vehicles, passengers, etc. with provision of necessary facilities for their smooth flow. The terminal serves as a point where necessary information to user is made available. To create seamless multimodal connectivity, the bus terminal should be integrated with other modes of transport (train, metro, bicycle, pedestrian, private car)

A bus terminal also functions as the centre of a neighbourhood with high density mixed use activities in its vicinity. To provide a safe and attractive place at all times, the presence of residential housing, shopping complexes, offices and other commercial activities are to be encouraged around the terminal. A passenger bus terminal broadly needs to perform the following functions:

(a) Passengers and Vehicles Movement, parking and safety.

(b) Areas for Passengers

(c) Areas for Vehicles

(d) Crew Facilities

(e) Management Facilities

The functions related to both passengers and vehicles include:

- Concentration
- Loading
- Dispersal
- Unloading

Passengers oriented facilities include provision of:

- Passenger platforms to board and alight (with ramps for disabled & elderly)
- Ticketing facilities
- Waiting lounges

- Rest houses/rooms
- Baggage Storage Facilities
- Commercial: Shopping and retail facilities
- Utilities, Services and Amenities (including public toilets, ATM, drinking water, etc.)
- Information System
- Shelter from weather
- Communication and postal facilities
- Eating places

The components related to buses include provision of:

- Bays for loading and unloading
- Idle bus parking spaces
- Facilities related to maintenance
- Information system for movement with terminal

The components to meet the needs of crew are:

- Rest rooms
- Information system
- Communication facilities
- Eating places

The facilities for the management in terms of:

- Demand management on account of concentration
- Incurring minimum expenditure
- Development of centralised information
- Ensuring better control

Design Criteria

The design of terminal needs studies to determine the size of terminal and various factors to be taken into consideration in planning the facilities and activities include the following:

- Traffic Demand
- Traffic Characteristics
- Function of Terminal
- Type and Sophistication of Facilities

The other factors to be considered in terminal design so as to establish activity and facility inter-relationship are:

(a) Segregation of terminal and non-terminal traffic

(b) Segregation of vehicular and pedestrian traffic and movement

(c) Segregation of traffic by type, function and direction

(d) Coordination of different activities in terms of functional and spatial inter-relationship

(e) Provision of a clear signage and information for the drivers.

(f) Provision of necessary and identified facilities to meet requirement of all user groups achieving minimum passenger and vehicular processing time

(g) Achieving overall functional and spatial efficiency

(h) Achieving smooth flow of all types of traffic to and from terminal.

Planning Norms and Space Standards

(a) Capacity of an intracity bus terminal: 1.5 lakh passengers/day

(b) One bus bay for 5000 passengers per day: Loading

(c) One bus bay for 10,000 passengers per day: Unloading

(d) Peak hour load: 10% of daily passenger load

(e) Occupancy/bus: 50 ideal

(f) Time taken for loading: 6 to 12 min

(g) Time taken for unloading: 3 to 6 min

Space standards for Parking Facilities

Table 9.13: Bus Bays - Parking Standards

Type of Parking	Area/vehicle
Idle Parking	146 sqm
Angular	76 sqm
Parallel	104 sqm

Source: UDPFI Guidelines, 1996.

Integrated Freight Complex

The basic functions of an integrated freight complex are:

(a) To provide facilities for regional and intra-urban freight movement.

(b) To provide facilities for freight in transit as well as inter-change of mode.

(c) To provide warehousing and storage facilities and link these sites with specialised markets.

(d) To provide servicing, loading and boarding, idle parking, restaurants and other related functions in the complex.

The functional objectives of wholesale complex-cum-truck terminal should be:

(a) To provide adequate facilities for wholesale trade activities, which include:

(i) Auction areas

(ii) Wholesale shops and subsidiary storage capacity

(iii) Parking facilities

(iv) Wholesales godowns, cold storage, etc. together with handling facilities and equipment

(b) To provide adequate parking space and facilities for trucks expected to utilise the terminal. These facilities include:
   (i) Service/Repair and fuel filling facilities
   (ii) Rest/recreation for drivers
   (iii) Weighing of trucks, etc.

(c) To provide adequate facilities for office/storage activities of trucks operating at terminal. These include:
   (i) Godown space
   (ii) Office space
   (iii) Loading/unloading facilities
   (iv) Weighing of goods vehicle, etc.

Apart from the above mentioned facilities, the complex must provide for a number of associated/ancillary facilities and services, some of which are:

(d) Provision, for goods movement within the complex in terms of truck movement and loading, unloading / stacking of goods.

(e) Building and amenities for administration and security measures necessary for complex.
   (i) Facilities like banking, postal truckers, etc. required for business transactions
   (ii) Amenities for wholesales, truckers and their employees
   (iii) Areas for shops, eating houses and other service establishment
   (iv) Provision of lighting, water supply and garbage, sewerage disposal.

Space Norms

The Space norms in terms of quantum handled (kilograms) per square meter area for selected commodities as per Central Warehousing Corporation (CWC) are given below:

Table 9.14: Space Norms

Commodity	Wt./Area (Kg/Sqm)
Food grains	1054
Fruit and Vegetables	721
Hardware and Building Material	1054
Iron and Steel	904
Timber	968
Machinery	968
Auto Parts	968
Textile	968
Chemicals and fertilisers	968

Source: Central Warehousing Corporation.

The broad land use break-up of an integrated freight complex recommended by the UDPFI Guidelines 1996 continues to be relevant, which is as follows:

Table 9.15: Broad Land Use Break Up for Integrated Freight Complex

Use Type	Percentage of Area
1. Wholesale Market	35.0
2. Warehousing	8.0
3. Booking Agencies	2.0
4. Commercial and Public/Semi-Public	5.0
5. Utilities and Services	3.0
6. Service Industry	4.0
7. Parking	12.0
8. Circulation	25.0
9. Others	6.0
Total	100.0

Source: UDPFI Guidelines, 1996.

As a general guideline, the area required for a truck terminal (Transport Nagar) should be reserved at the rate of one hectare per 300 tonnes of daily goods inflow into the complex. In case of integrated freight complex, the area necessary would be one hectare per 400 tonnes of daily goods inflow into the complex.

Travel Modelling for Public Transit Choice

A travel model is a simplified representation of travel behaviour through use of mathematical equations and data analysis. Models are based on the theory that an individual's travel choices are a function of his or her socio-economic characteristics (household size, income, and vehicle ownership), geographic location (distance to work, shops, etc.) and modal choices (road, rail, bus, NMT) available to them. Modelling is an attempt to replicate this behaviour using statistical analysis. The process is complex and requires large amount of data.

The accuracy of a travel model depends on many factors: land use and demographic data, quality of travel survey data, technical expertise of the developer, and assumptions used. Therefore, a model should be evaluated as whole and never as a function of the forecasts produced. A model should always be calibrated well so that it can replicate current year conditions within reason before using it to produce forecasts. Model calibration and validation should be done at every step of the process to ensure quality of forecasts.

Models are a simplified simulation of travel behaviour producing rational travel choices based on the controlled variables within a model. In the real world, variables are constantly changing and individuals don't always make the most rational decisions. Therefore model forecasts should only be used as one element in transport planning.

The most commonly used method of forecasting is 4 step Aggregate Model; this model includes trip generation, distribution, modal split and assignment.

An individual decides whether to make a trip, where and when to go, which mode to select, and which route to take based on his needs, income, occupation, vehicle ownership, etc. and the choices available to them. The choices could be different modes of transportation (car, 2 wheelers, public transport, bicycle, etc.) different times of day travel (peak, off peak) or competing destinations (shopping mall, downtown).

The recommended share of public transport modes based on city size, which is mentioned in Table below:

Table 9.16: Recommended derived Modal Split

City Size	Recommended Modal Spilt-Public Transit
Below 1 Million	30%
Arount 1 Million	35%
1.5 Million	40% plus
3.0 Million	50% plus
6.0 Million	70% plus
9.0 Million	75% plus (85% with a mass transit system)

Source: UDPFI Guidelines, 1996.MRT Options for the City

Every city is different and requires its own study of the potentially realistic options. The guidelines shown in Tables 9.17 and Table 9.18 are to assist decision makers in narrowing down the options. As can be seen in the table, population density is an important criterion. City shape/form (linear or circular) also influences the concentration of demand; therefore, this factor may be incorporated when selecting appropriate MRT options.

Table 9.17: MRT options for the City

S. No.	MRTS Options	City Requirements
1.	Bus Rapid Transit (BRT)	• When more than about 100 buses per hour per direction (bphpd) use the busway
		• Cities with a medium to high-density urban area
		• BRT should be one of the first considerations in MRT system development.
		• BRT system can be developed as trunk systems as well as feeders to an existing (or planned) MRT system.
		• Suitable for cities where an MRT system needs to be developed quickly and incrementally as conditions and funding allow.
		• A well-developed traffic planning/management capability should be available (this may be brought in initially)
		• Existing bus and paratransit operations can be regulated/ restructured Road space is available for BRT development (2-4 lanes from existing roads)

		• Bus Only Lane (BOL) can be recommended in the following two cases: (a) One lane busway (4 meters for a single lane) is available and the passenger demand is below 6,000 bphpds (b) Multiple lane busways (7 meters for two lanes, or 10.5 meters for three lanes) are available and the passenger demand exceeds 6,000, but is below 12,500 bphpd.
2.	Light Rail Transport (LRT) including monorail, transways	• Cities with a medium-to high-density urban area
		• Cities where environmental issues are critical and there is a need to attract car users to use public transport systems; however, if the core requirements are operational effectiveness.
		• LRT system should be developed that is more flexible and costs less.
		• Appropriate for cities with an existing tram operation, which may be cost-effectively enhanced.
		• A well-developed traffic planning/management capability should be available.
		• Existing bus and para-transit operations can be regulated/restructured.
		• Road space is available for LRT development (2-3 lanes from existing road) or existing tram track can be converted to an LRT route.
3.	Metro Rail	• Existing public transport flows on the main corridor of the order of 10,000-15,000 passengers per hour per direction with more than 15 km trip length.
		• City incomes that are not low
		• Prospects for sustained economic growth and an expanding centre (in case of metropolitan regions)
		• Existence of a low-cost metro alignment.
		• Fares policy–a fares policy on metro and bus systems to encourage ridership yet limit the need for financial support.
		• A well-developed traffic planning/management capability should be available.
		• Existing bus and para-transit operations can be regulated/restructured.
		• Strong and largely autonomous management of metropolitan region, with clear objectives.

Source: Guidelines and Toolkits for Urban Transport Development Module 1 Comprehensive Mobility Plan.

Table 9.18: Technical Parameters of Public Transport Options

	Metro	LRT	Tram	High Capacity	BRT	Bus Primary Lane	City Bus
Line Capacity (PAX/hr/dir.)	40,000-75,000	15,000-45,000	5,000-15,000	20,000-35,000	7,500-15,000	5,000-7,500	Below 1,000
Cost per km (Infrastructure, vehicles, OCC, Maintenance)	Very high	High	Medium/high	Medium/high	Medium	Low	Very Low, only bus stops and maintenance stop required
Alignment	Double-track railway	Double-track railway, elevated, at grade or in tunnels	Double-track tramway, at-grade	4 Bus Lanes (2 per direction)	2 to 3 Bus Lanes	2 Bus Lanes	Use public roads
Segregation	100% segregated in tunnels, elevated or at-grade	High degree of segregation preferred, but sections with shared right of way possible	Uses public roads, but may have reserved right of way on sections with higher demand	All Bus Lanes must be segregated to achieve high capacity	Bus Lanes must be in general segregated, exceptions possible, reduce capacity and speed	Bus Priority Lanes must be exclusively for buses	None
Road space required	None	None in case of elevated and tunnel alignment, 2 lanes at-grade, additional space required for stations and terminals	2 Lanes, additional space may be required for stations and terminals, tracks can be shared with public roads or pedestrian roads	4 Lanes; more linear space for Interchanges and Terminals	2 Lanes, possibly 3 or 4 at Stations and Interchanges, space for major Interchanges and Terminals	2 to 3 Lanes (3 to 4 Lanes at Bus Stops)	Shared with cars and pedestrian
Vehicles	High capacity EMU	Medium to high capacity EMU's (upgraded trams as an option)	Trams, articulated and/or with wagons as an option	Special articulated bus with at-floor boarding and wide doors	Articulated buses; pre-paid boarding required	Standard City Bus, articulated as option	Standard City Bus
Passengers per Vehicle/Train	1,200-2,500	250-1,500	Depends on length	180-240	150-180	75-100	75
Traction	Electric	Electric	Electric	Diesel	Diesel (Electric as an option)	Diesel	Diesel
Feeder System	Necessary	Necessary	Not necessary	Necessary	Desired	Not necessary	Not necessary
Flexibility of route changes	Very low	Low	Low	Very low	Medium	Medium	Very high
Ticketing System	Closed	Closed	Open	Closed	Closed or open	Open	Open

Source: Guidelines and Toolkits for Urban Transport Development Module 1, Comprehensive Mobility Plan, MOUD, New Delhi.

Personal rapid transit system is emerging as an alternative mode of transportation in many nations. This system is capital intensive and has long payback period, besides, the system is feasible where passenger flow in the main corridor is higher than the demand for the metro rail and the paying capacity is higher.

Traffic Calming and Noise Control

The need for traffic calming has become urgent in India, which involves reducing speeds, noise and volumes by various measures such as no horn zoning, traffic circles at intersections, raised crosswalks, and partial street closures to discourage short-cut traffic through residential neighbourhoods. Traffic calming may be necessary on certain streets, such as high security zones, areas fronting university, colleges, schools, hospitals, etc. Traffic Calming/Noise Control measures involve notifying No Horn Zones, constitution of area-wise Noise Control Circles, preparation of Noise Monitoring and Control Plan (NMCP), hybrid electric vehicles, speed breaker/hump, landscape noise buffers and rubberised road surface.

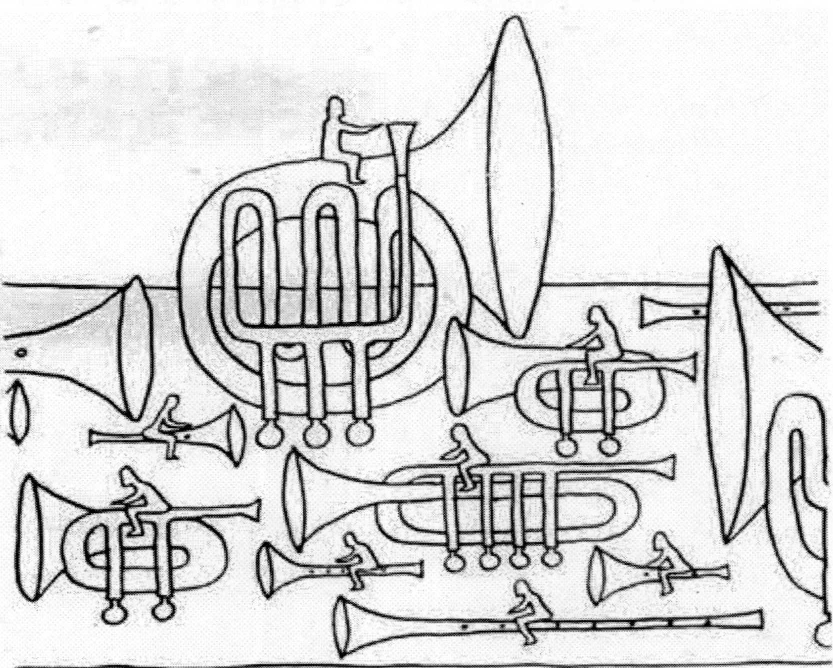

Fig. 9.11: Indian drivers are so fond of blowing horn that amused the architect Patrick Crooke to sketch the above cartoon.

Barrier Free Access

All housing and mixed use developments should be within easy walking distance of good public transport services that give access to the main centres of urban activity. Access is also influenced by gradients (especially for older people) and psychological barriers such as Foot Over bridges (FOB), subways or intimidation by road traffic. Foot-over Bridges (FOB) and subways are hardly used as they cause inconvenience and insecurity to the users. As a result, the pedestrians risk their lives crossing the high intensity, high speed roads. It is necessary to provide wide and safer pedestrian corridors at grade while the motorised vehicles move up and down. The walkways also need to cater to wheelchair users that require avoidance of steps and provision of curb ramps. This may be possible by raising the carriageway of the road by about 2 to 3 meters, so that pedestrians keep moving freely at the ground level without mingling with vehicular traffic. Such facility should be provided on all major roads, national and state highways, in front of village abadi, transport nodes (Railway Stations, Metro Stations, Bus Terminals, etc.), and also forests and wildlife areas. The walking zone should be barrier free and designed as per the specifications.

Public transport has to be disabled and wheelchair friendly with tactile flooring low floor buses with footboard at level with the platform and proper street lighting for the safety and security of pedestrians. A dedicated bicycle lane has to be built along every road. The fixed signs, maps, variable message signs, pedestrian crossings, integrated fare collection systems, protection systems and communication are important elements of safe mobility.

In order to deliver an inclusive, safe and barrier free mobility for all, it is necessary to synergise supply and demand side measures. Various options are available, which can be considered in combination or separately depending upon the context, traffic volume, sustainability (social, economic and environmental), costs and feasibility. Public transport is to be planned keeping in view the operational characteristics of different modes and their optimum efficiency/ridership.

Fig. 9.12: Highways, Ring Roads and Arterial Roads should be signal free, grade separated and provide dedicated space for Buses and Metro.

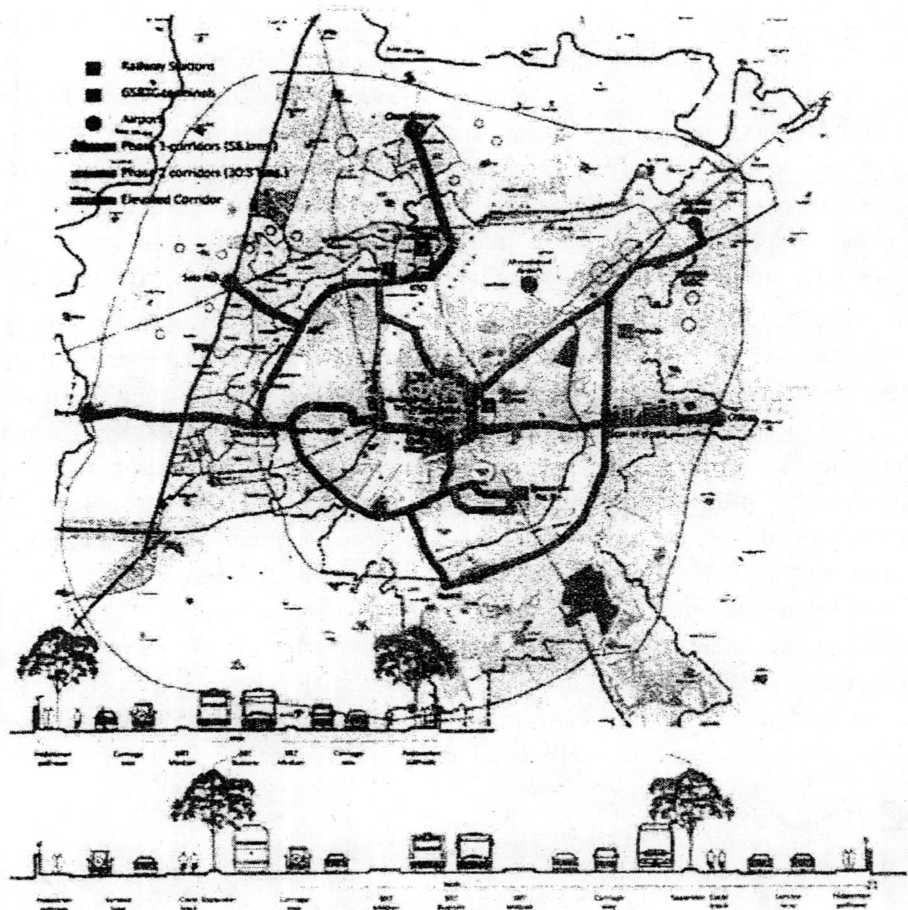

Fig 9.13: Janmarg Bus Rapid Transit System, Ahmedabad

Informal and Non-motorised Transport

Informal and intermediate modes of transport, which include 3 wheelers, vans, pickups, rickshaws, manual thelas and rehri, etc. cater to about 30 to 60% of passengers and goods movement in the cities like Delhi. As compared to small truck, the autos and rickshaws are substantially cheaper, which by multiple trips deliver as much as a 5-ton truck in a day. Courier services, perishables, such as milk, vegetables, fruits, groceries and other short-haul deliveries are increasingly being made by auto-rickshaw, van or tricycle, These reach in the narrow lanes and congested areas where public authorities do not allow trucks/public carriers during day time and also during frequent VVIP visits, processions, ceremonies, etc.

However, the intermediate and informal transport sector is riddled with numerous challenges, including lack of parking space and road right of way, harassment by traffic and transport officials, poor vehicle safety and fitness standards, lack of insurance, etc. Although competitive and affordable, low fares force the operator using substandard fuels, polluting engines and preclude service improvements.The predisposition among motoring class and transportation officials is to expedite automobile flows, and they usually fail to appreciate the importance of informal transport. This mindset together with the pressures from customers and automobile industry add to the marginalization of informal transport. There is absence of any kind of normative policy framework for informal motorized transport services, which is a part of overall city transport. Delhi had about 60,000 transport related shops and repair facility, of which one-third are illegal or informal. Keeping in view the service rendered by informal transport and workshops, there is a need to integrate them with land reservations.

There is ample scope and need to develop and plan for NMTs and intermediate public transport (IPT) to improve their safety, efficiency, speed, and comfort. By adopting standards, protocols and legal provisions, together with simple technical innovations, such as installing a two-speed gear system would enable the rickshaw-puller to pedal easily. Redesigning the handlebars in such a way that the rickshaw-puller does not have to strain his wrist and lungs, its efficiency can be substantially improved. The puncture proof or tubeless tyres, using lighter and more durable, sturdier metal, a better designed seat can provide a more comfortable ride to the commuter. To meet the requirements of school children a motor with a battery to run for small distances and a multi-speed gear system can be fixed for smooth and easy pulling. To rectify the imbalances, which often cause overturns in the conventional rickshaw, the geometry of the design can be improved, together with other aspects of safety. In Agra, state of the art designer rickshaws have made them prestigeous for the users, besides being more efficient, less polluting and more comfortable.

Fig. 9.14: Dedicated Right of Way for Pedestrians, Cyclists and Buses

Bicycle and Pedestrian Planning

Cycle Tracks

Cycle infrastructure and track width requirements are based on vehicle dimensions, volume and clearance requirements of moving vehicles (cycle rickshaw, freight rickshaw).These requirements vary for straight riding cyclists and those manoeuvering a bend at a cruising speed.

Exclusive lanes for slow moving vehicles-bicycles, rickshaws and pedestrians along with spaces for street vendors are also essential. Hawkers and roadside vendors provide services to bus commuters and pedestrians therefore designed spaces would discourage them from occupying the carriageway. This improves the capacity of the lanes designed for motorized vehicles and increases safety of bicyclists and pedestrians.

Table 9.19: Cycle/NMT track

S.No.	Arterial Roads	Sub-Arterial Roads	Distributary Roads	Access Roads
Non-Motorised Vehicle	Segregated Cycle Track	Segregated Cycle Track	Cycle Lane	Mixed/traffic
Location	Between Carrigeway or street parking and footpath on either edge of the carriageway	Between Carrigeway or street parking and footpath on either edge of the carriageway	On the edge of the carriageway, adjacent to the footpath or parking.	Not Applicable
Gradient	1:12–1:20	1:12–1:20	1:12–1:20	1:12–1:20
Lane width	2.2 to 5.0	2.2 to 5.0 m	1.5 to 2.5 m	Mixed with motorized vehicular traffic
Minimum Width	2.5 m for a two lane cycle track and 1.9 m for a common cycle track and footpath	2.0 m for a two lane cycle track and 1.7 m for a common cycle track and footpath	1.5 m	1 m (painted)

Source: Code of Practice Part 1, MoUD, 2012.

General Guidelines

1. Increase the proportion of public roads, and take up traffic calming with dedicated corridors for pedestrians and cyclists. The length of dedicated cycleway can be gradually increased by planned target each year. Likewise the length of pedestrian-friendly streets can be targeted each year.

2. Provide incentives to increase the proportion of institutions, businesses and dwellings with facilities for bicycles (e.g., daytime storage).
3. Increase on a priority-route basis the proportion of public transit vehicles capable of carrying bicycles.
4. Develop an active campaign to publicise the personal, community and eco-system, health benefits of cycling and walking.
5. Create and publicise targets to increase the annual share of work and shopping trips taken by bicycle or by walking.
6. Provide end of trip facilities , like bike racks, storage lockers and shower changing facilities at railway/metro/bus station, offices, shopping centres, etc.

Source: Adapted from Kenworthy and Laube (1999)

Fig. 9.15: Streetscaping

Source: DIMTS

Sustainable Urban Transport

For sustainable and safe urban mobility the corridor plans and strategy for safe and non-violent mobility should cover the following:

- Reduce need to travel by Transit Oriented Development and Travel Demand Management
- Improvement of public transport, sidewalks , cycle tracks, NMVs underpasses and overpasses
- Safety oriented planning and engineering specifications, norms and practice
- Upgrading of traffic control - multi-functional and sophisticated signal control and ITS
- Drivers' license regime
- Work Zone Safety

It is necessary to provide wide and safer pedestrian corridors at grade while the motorised vehicles move up and down. The walkways also need to cater to wheelchair users that require avoidance of steps and provision of curb ramps. Such facility should be provided on all major roads, national and state highways, in front of village abadi, cattle grazing fields, transport nodes (Railway Stations, Metro Stations, Bus Terminals, etc.), and also forests and wildlife areas.

Fig. 9.16: A Pedestrian Passage

Fig. 9.17: A 10 to 15 m wide pedestrian underpass is created by raising the vehicular carriageway by 2 to 3 m and dipping the pedestrian passage by 0.5 to 1.0 m. It shall be provided at regular intervals on all NH, SH, Arterial roads where there is sizable volume of pedestrians, NMTs/cycles, cattle/wildlife. Similar provision is required on the railway lines for safe passage of pedestrians and animals.

Planning for pedestrian zone and road safety

(i) Identifying accident prone points, pedestrian movement, volumes and areas

(ii) Prepare area-wise/corridor-wise pedestrian and road safety plans with dedicated footpaths, NMTs and cycle lanes

(iii) Underpasses at grade for pedestrians and cattle at regular intervals

Engineering and implementation

(i) Road management plan, repair, drainage and work zone management

(ii) Speed breakers

(iii) Maintenance to aim zero defect roads

(iv) Road markings, zebra lines

(v) Provide railings and crash barriers, signage, orientation points and guide maps

Traffic regulation/control and audit

(i) ITS, Intelligent signals, alarm and communication system, unified CCTV command platform be installed

(ii) Streamline drivers' licensing procedures, training and behavior

(iii) Check overloading of goods vehicles and joy rides

(iv) No free U turn, No blind corners, keep right of way and crossings free from parking, bus stops, kiosks, taxi stands, encroachments, etc.

(v) Online complaints and redressal system to be in place

(vi) Inter-state/city and inter-departmental coordination,

Help in emergency

(i) Helpline, surveillance, first aid, trauma centres, ambulance service

(ii) Integrated/common complaint centre

Institutional capacity building, public participation and support

(i) Organisational resources, financial strengthening and capacity building

(ii) Promote active safety campaigns by participation of public, road users/citizens

(iii) Accountability, monitoring framework

(iv) Revisiting Motor Vehicle Act and other legal framework

(v) Pedestrians right be deemed as a human right

Keeping in view the importance of road safety, it needs to taken up as a mission, with a well structured action plan. It should move beyond reactive actions to the incremental radical and transformative. These include regulatory, strategic, governance and performance aspects of road safety ladder. The 'National Road Safety Mission' under the PM and 'State Road Safety Missions' under the CMs of each State may be constituted in order to give serious attention to the issue, which it deserves.

Debriefing and Review

1. What do you understand by environmental sustainability in Urban Transport?
2. What is the relationship between urban structure and public transit efficiency?
3. Explain the principles of walk to work and public transport planning.
4. Explain the concept of Transit Oriented Development.
5. Write short notes on the following
   (i) Travel demand management and conservation of transport
   (ii) Parking, ECS, Parking Norms
   (iii) Classification of Urban Roads
   (iv) Multi-modal transit systems
   (v) Traffic noise control
   (vi) Cycle tracks
   (vii) Non-motorised transport
   (viii) Passenger car unit
   (ix) Bus terminals, transport nodes
   (x) Stack parking
   (xi) Integrated freight complex
   (xii) MRTS/LRT
   (xiv) Barrier free access
6. What are the approaches and tools of safety on roads?
7. Explain the smart/ITS tools for transport planning and management.

CHAPTER

10

Housing for All

Concentration of poor and their isolation have condemned generations of low income areas to entrenched poverty, fragmented environments and asymmetrical societies. Shelter is a direct manifestation of poverty and lack of it is a major cause of poverty. In order to meet the housing shortage of 18.78 million units, of which 96% pertains to Economically Weaker Sections (EWS) and Low Income Group (LIG), the Government of India has launched the Pradhan Mantri Awas Yojana (2015). This aims to provide housing to all by 15th August 2022. The mission seeks to build 20 million housing units (revised to 12 million) and make Indian cities slum free by taking up the slum rehabilitation projects. The mission defines an 'affordable housing project' as one where 35% of the houses are constructed for EWS category. Economically Weaker Section (EWS) households are defined as households having an annual income up to ₹ 300,000. An EWS house is a dwelling with a carpet area of up to 30 sqm with adequate basic civic services and infrastructure services like toilet, water, electricity, etc. Low Income Group (LIG) is defined as households having an annual income between ₹ 300,000 up to ₹ 600,000. An LIG house is a dwelling unit having carpet area up to 60 sqm. Slum is defined as a compact area of at least 300 persons or about 60-70 households of poorly built, congested tenements in unhygienic environment, usually with inadequate infrastructure and lacking proper sanitary and drinking water facilities.

The program provides an interest subsidy of 6.5 per cent on housing loans with tenure of up to 15 years for EWS and LIG. This equates to nearly Rs 100,000 to Rs 230,000 per unit. It mandates ownership of a house in the name of women, or joint ownership. The PMAY plans to make all 4041 Indian cities slum free. It requires the cities to prepare a Slum Free City Plan of Action (SFCPoA) for redevelopment of slums and by leveraging the locked potential of land under slums to provide houses to the eligible slum dwellers.

"In situ" Slum Redevelopment	Affordable Housing through Credit Linked Subsidy	Affordable Housing in Partnership	Subsidy for beneficiary-led individual house construction
- Using land as a resource. - With private participation - Extra FSI/TDR/FAR, if required to make projects financially viable.	- Interest subvention subsidy for EWS and LIG for new house or incremental housing. - EWS: Annual Household Income Up to Rs. 3 lakh and house size up to 30 sqm. - LIG: Annual Household Income between Rs. 3-6 lakhs and house size upto 60 sqm.	- With private sector or public sector including Parastatal agencies. - Central Assistance per EWS house in affordable housing projects where 35% of constructed houses are for EWS category.	- For individuals of EWS category requiring individual house. - State to prepare a separate project for such beneficiaries. - No isolated/splintered beneficiary to be covered.

Fig. 10.1: Pradhan Mantri Awas Yojana-Four Verticals envisage in-situ slum redevelopment, no eviction, PPP, land as a resource, incentive FAR, interest subvention, mandatory provision of 35% EWS units (30 sqm dwelling unit area) and cost ceiling. The Affordable Housing under PMAY now covers Middle Income Group ((MIG) with dwelling size from 80 sqm to upto 150 sqm.

Source: MOHUPA, 2015

Based on the needs of housing for the poor a comprehensive framework and city-wide strategy is to be worked out by each city and the State to provide housing to all and make the city slum free. The PMAY sees land as a resource, and recognizes the need for in-situ slum development, single window time bound clearance for layout and building plans, deemed sanctions of EWS/LIG housing schemes, higher Floor Area Ratio (FAR) and density norms, innovative technologies, capacity building and financial/accounting and administrative reforms.

Since Independence in 1947, the Government of India, State governments and the private sector have made various attempts to provide access to housing for all. These efforts have failed to reach the poor in spite of subsidies, discounted land costs, low cost construction and low interest rates. A major barrier has been an inadequate and vague definition of affordable housing. The way of defining the social housing, Low Income Group (LIG) and Economically Weaker Section (EWS) has left out the poorest of the poor, who even may not know what their income is or how to account for it. These people include the vegetable / fruit vendors, feriwala, tailor, salesman, rickshaw puller, cycle/auto-rickshaw drivers, bus cleaners/ driver, cobbler, domestic servant, rag pickers, sweeper, home guard, watchman, barber, porter, binder, casual labourer, plumber, painter, machine operator, blacksmith, etc.

India's total work force has 92% in the unorganized sector. Of this vast mass, the enterprises and micro-businesses comprise 98%. Of these, 98% have no social security cover. Many of these people are migrants and are women, children, aged and disabled. They have no bank account, no assets, no shelter and not even an identity or ration card. The world's largest democracy does not provide shelter for its majority population - the poor. This must change.

The poor are malnourished, lack minimum shelter, sanitation and drinking water; they are illiterate; and cannot afford to send their children to the school. They face the risks of unemployment, child labour, insecurity in old age, unhealthy living conditions, dangerous working conditions, etc. These are the people who live in slums - the backbone of the actual, day-to-day working economy. A study conducted by Participatory Research in Asia (PRIA) and Indicus Analytics on the Economic Contribution of the urban poor found that the slum population contributes 7.5 per cent of the country's urban gross domestic grass product (2013).

Most of the poor live in the unplanned areas (slums, old city, villages, etc.) which remain under-serviced. These settlements continue to face the threat of demolition and pressures from the officials. Yet the residents in these settlements provide essential services without asking much. They have the right to security of residence and urban services.

What Jane Jacobs said in 1961 about the USA is relevant for India today. '*There is a wishful myth that if only we had enough money to spend-the figure is usually put at a hundred billion dollars we could wipe out all our slums in ten years, reverse decay in the great, dull, gray belts that were yesterday's and day-before-yesterday's suburbs, anchor the wandering middle class and its wandering tax money, and perhaps even solve the traffic problem. But look what we have built with the first several billions. This is not the rebuilding of cities. This is the sacking of cities*'.

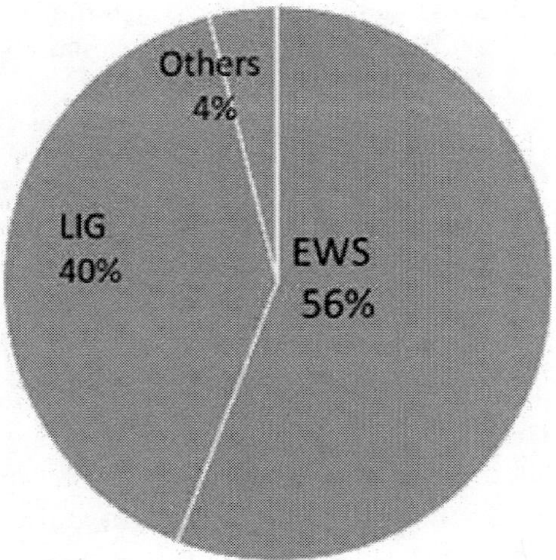

Fig. 10.2: 96% of housing shortage pertains to EWS and LIG.

Where the Poor Live

In general, the poor live in six types of housing areas:

1. Slum and jhuggi-jhompri clusters/basti
2. Unauthorised colonies
3. Old City /villages
4. Public Housing- Site and Services,
5. Public Housing -Built up Units
6. Private Housing.

About one-sixth of the population lives in the slums, bastis and Jhuggi jhompri clusters, which are mainly the settlements of the poor. The pavement dwellers/homeless comprise about 1 per cent of the total population. Traditional areas, villages and old city have about one-third of the population and unauthorised colonies have about one-sixth of the population. Public sector housing and site and services provide housing to about 32% of Delhi's population. The role of the private sector in EWS/LIG housing is almost negligible.

Fig. 10.3: The Homeless Mother India

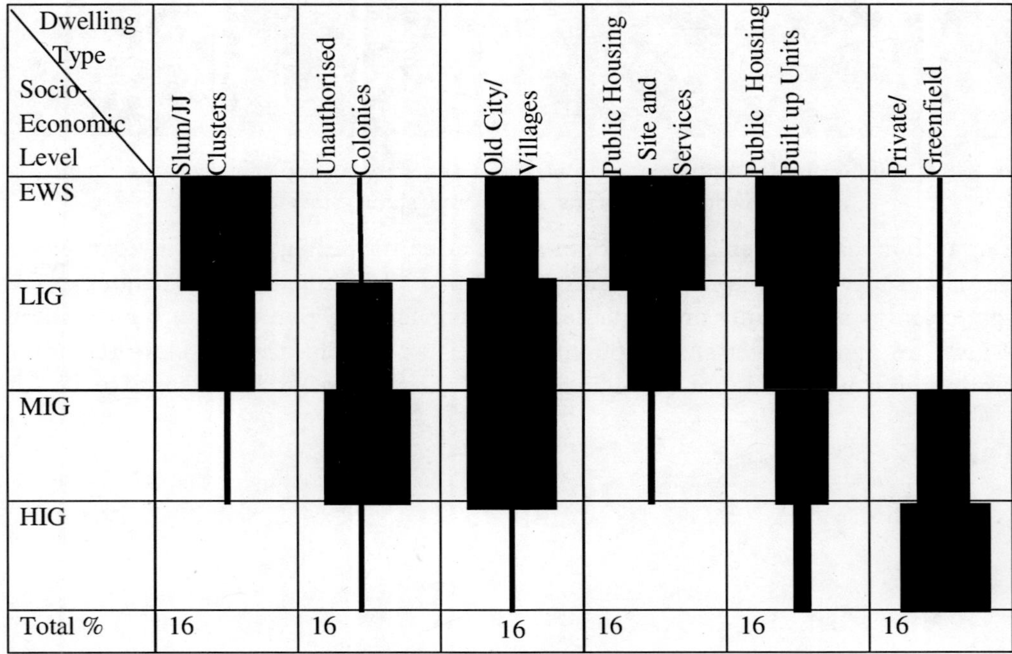

Fig. 10.4: Where the Poor Live

Notes:

(i) Figures have been rounded up for clarity

(ii) Government staff housing (3%), Homeless/pavement dwellers (1%) have not been shown.

(iii) As per MOHUPA (2015) EWS covers a family having income up to Rs 3 lakh per annum and the LIG from Rs 3 lakh up to Rs 6 lakh per annum

Sources: Census of India 2011, Delhi Development Authority, and A.K. Jain (2016). Building Twenty Milliion Homes and other sources

Fig. 10.5: In Mumbai half a million people sleep on the streets, and ten times as many live in crowded, dangerous slums and shanty towns

The unauthorised colonies in peri-urban areas often have illegally sub-divided plots, non-conforming land use and unapproved buildings. Slums and Jhuggi-Jhompri/squatter clusters and illegal colonies are mainly on public lands except for a few on private lands. The illegal colonies have an average plot size of 60-200 sqm. They largely accommodate the MIG. The EWS family living in a hutment (jhuggi) occupies an average land area of 8 to 12 sqm.

Fig. 10.6: Slum/JJ Clusters house about one-sixth of population, comprising 80 to 90% EWS/ LIG

Fig. 10.7: Forty Percent of Population in Slums Lack Access to Toilet

Fig. 10.8: Unplanned, Unauthorised Colonies usually manifest progressive land development, construction and sub-division of plots with narrow streets and without common space. These colonies come up by a nexus among coloniser/developer, political leaders and officials

Upgrading Existing Housing

Public housing schemes have failed to cater to the homeless, squatters and slum dwellers. People struggling to survive break planning law because it excludes the poor. The growth of slums is the growth of failure in the housing and planning system. There is a total housing shortage of 18.78 million dwelling units (MOHUPA, 2015). There are about 15 million dwelling units (80 per cent) which are old, dilapidated and congested. Thus, 20 million houses (revised to 12 million) need not be built on greenfield sites, but 15 million existing dwelling units can be upgraded and retrofitted.

Fig. 10.9: While multistory apartments provide housing to the rich and middle class, slums and hutments provide shelter to the poor.

Transforming Slums and Poverty

According to Christopher Benninger, 'Transforming slums and poverty is visualizing the city from the "other way around!". Put the last person first, the hutment dwellers, the informal sector hawker, the small scale repairman, the physically challenged, domestic servants, street vendors, rickshaw wallah and casual workers. Put yourself in the position of elders, women, children and a diverse array of city dwellers whose lives are affected intimately and almost moment by moment by distant professional decisions that shape the city. Seek paths and channels to facilitate and empower them into becoming stakeholders, harnessing their huge energies and amplifying their contributions'.

We need to look again at what we mean by shelter, land policy, infrastructure development, concepts of planning, land use, tenure and building regulations. Innovative approaches have to be worked out to provide shelter by community resources, which should be differentiated according to the specific issues and local context. Universal solutions may not work.

Many migrants, labourers, casual workers, beggars, etc. in the city do not have shelter and live on pavements near their jobs. For them a regular dwelling unit on the ownership basis is unthinkable. Thus, the definition of shelter should include rental units, dormitories, hostels dharmshalas, lodge, transit camps and night shelters. As a human right, the city should provide a network of dormitories, old age home, orphanages, women's hostels, dharmshalas, lodge, transit camps and night shelters. The night shelters should be located near the Railway Stations, Bus Terminals, major markets and work centres. The general policy should be to upgrade and adapt existing dwellings, facilities and municipal services.

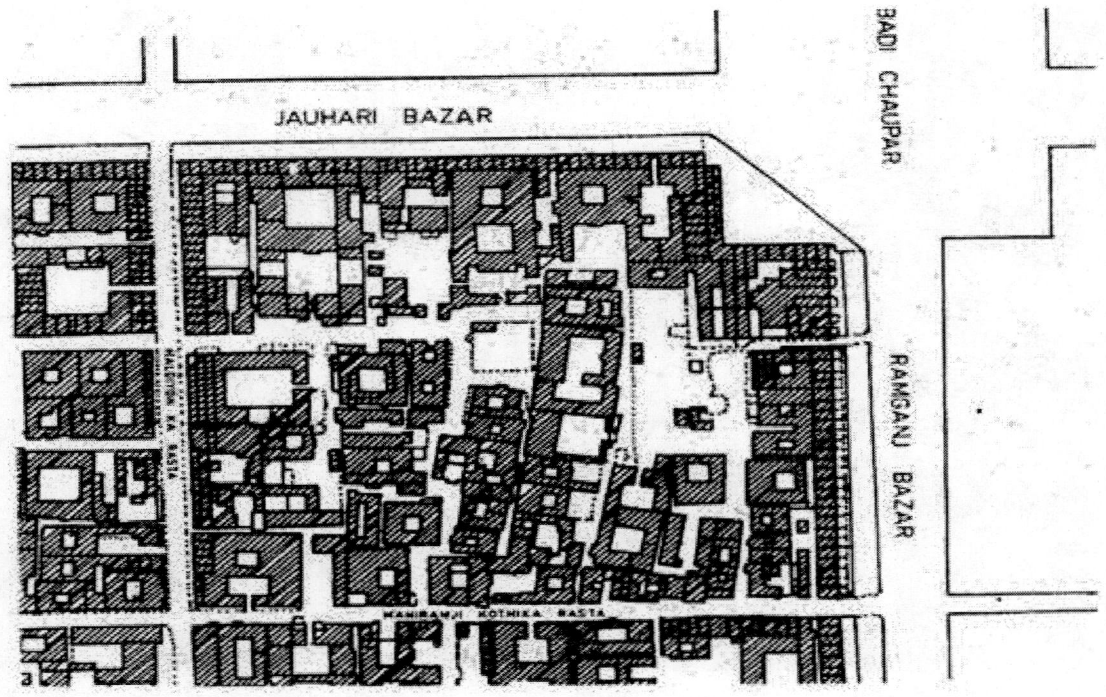

Fig 10.10: Plan of traditional city, Jaipur responds to local culture and climate. Communities are organised in Mohalla (housing clusters), based on occupations, with courtyard houses. At the junction of the roads is the chaupar (public square)

Source: Yatin Pandya, 2007

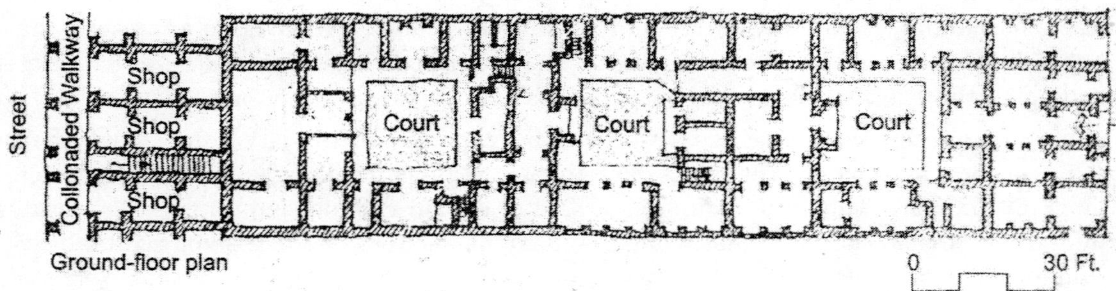

Fig. 10.11: A large Haveli with multiple couryards in Jaipur

Source: Kulbhushan Jain, 2000

For the poor, shelter and livelihood overlap. Their shelter intertwines with earning and micro-jobs; the rickshaw puller often sleeps in his rickshaw. Why should he have no other possibility? The concept of land use zoning has to include housing along with small shops, social space, facilities, utilities and work places. Every housing and slum rehabilitation project has to be based on the specific local issues and provide choices of in-situ upgrading, relocation, land sharing or re-blocking. All the slum settlements in a city need to be networked, planned together and improved.

Rental Housing

As many poor families cannot afford even to pay the subsidised down payment, it is necessary to lay thrust on rental housing, review the rental legislation, the tenure system and adopt rental housing strategies.

Social housing must be affordable. As a rule about half of the social housing units should be available on a rental basis, convertible to ownership after 10 years. This will give the occupier an incentive to improve his or her life. The funding pattern can be four layered. The Government of India can contribute 50 per cent. The State government and local bodies can contribute one-third. The families can contribute the remaining one-sixth. Transfer of Development Rights (TDR) and incentive Floor Space Index (FSI) can be useful tools. Smart cards should be issued to EWS/LIG and slum families so that benefits reach those who have genuine need.

Keeping in view the barriers in rental housing the Government of India has formulated Draft National Urban Rental Housing Policy (NURHP, 2015) which suggests various policies, administrative and legal measures, and financial incentives to promote rental housing,

Rental Housing Policy needs to be more closely integrated with the Pradhan Mantri Awas Yojana, which focuses on EWS/LIG, informal sector, workers, women and aged.

For a city-wide spread of EWS/ LIG housing, provision of one-third to one-half number of such units have to be rental. The developer shall hand over such housing units to the government against reimbursement of cost of construction. Non-profit associations or RWAs may manage such properties.

Bonus FSI, as done by MMRDA, can incentivize the development of rental housing. Models such as Rental Housing Vouchers given to homeless, destitute, aged, women, etc. and Low Income Housing Tax Credit (LIHTC) of the US, which gives rebate in income tax against investment in low income rental housing, can have multiplier effects in its creation.

Access to Land

The cost of the land for social housing and slum housing can be met by cross subsidy, compulsory reservation, land pooling and reconstitution, and by other similar instruments. To acquire greenfield sites has become very costly and difficult. It is necessary to use brownfield sites, through recycling existing urban areas, including the slum and squatter settlements and encroached land. Land cost should be excluded from social housing projects to make them affordable and viable. This implies mandatory reservation of land for social housing in all public and private housing projects. It is also necessary to optimise land use by higher density and FAR, and to reduce the cost and time in land development, construction and infrastructure provision.

Fig. 10.12: Slum Resettlement Under Mumbai Urban Transport Project with 225 sqft Dwelling Units

Source: World Bank.

Establishment of an electronic land register to show accurately who owns what. This may take time, but should not delay the other elements of the national process of achieving housing for all. It is necessary to identify many parcels of under-used or idle land, including government owned land that could support affordable housing development. Unused and underused sites can be dedicated to housing development through reforms in the planning regulations, land pooling and by mixed land use.

Shelter and Community Development

Housing for the poor supports their survival. It thus helps to change and empower them, and with them the whole nation. It requires a holistic approach in planning and design. Housing acts as a vehicle for poverty reduction, social empowerment, community interaction, and access to health, educational and recreational facilities. Thus, housing enriches society, proves the truth of beliefs and social values, and provides a better quality of environment. Everyone can gain. The five elements viz., the people, community, local activities, place and resources should be interfaced. Besides defining a minimum house (say 30 sqm minimum dwelling unit or 10 sqm per capita), a housing cluster should provide a minimum space of about 5 sqm per capita each of green area/open space/play area, social infrastructure and transport and utilities. These can integrate housing with health, livelihood, natural resources, climate and culture. Participatory planning is necessary to achieve the housing goals, establish the requirement of the resources and to accomplish the plans. No plan, however good, can be implemented unless it is supported by the people and stakeholders at all levels of decision making and implementation. Spatial, financial and institutional structures can be better coordinated.

Fig. 10.13: According to the Census 2011 over 65 million people in Urban India live in slums and 80% of housing shortage is due to dilapidation and congestion of existing areas, which need to be redeveloped with more space, better services, parks and common facilities.

The overall responsibility to devise ways of providing land and trunk services lies with the government. There should be collaboration with the community and private agencies, down to the level of the panchayat and the activist group. Activist groups arise when problems appear to be neglected. The communities should be involved in surveys of their housing problems, and the housing boards, municipal bodies and service agencies should jointly develop the programs which the communities can take up.

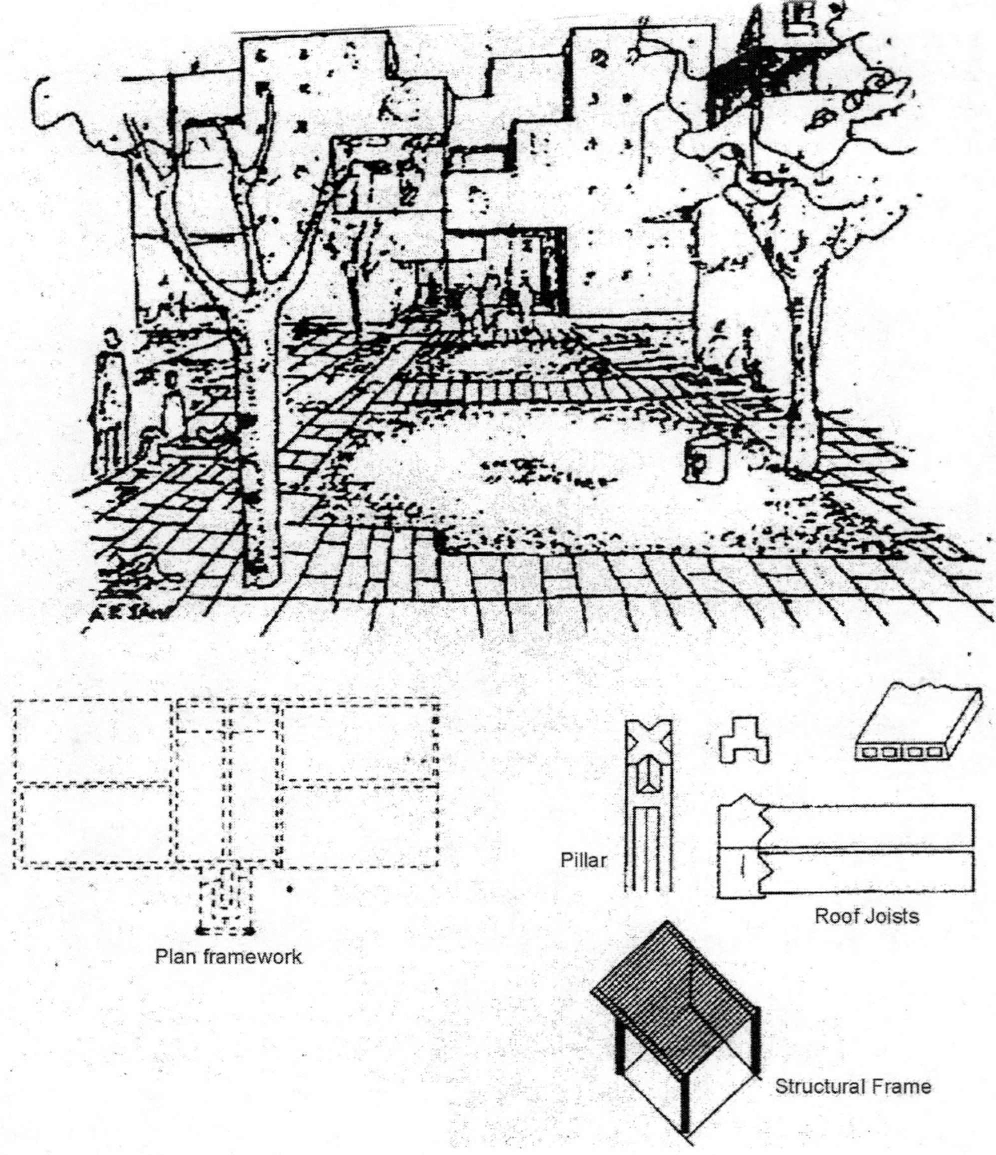

Fig. 10.14: Skeleton social housing provides platforms with wet core for expandable house of the poor (A.K. Jain)

The organization of urban space into the 'communities' is a key to a cross-sectoral spatial coalition of social, economic and environmental systems. Social housing projects need to focus on the following:

- Infrastructure improvement: roads, drains, water, sanitation, street lighting and community halls;
- Health: promotional and preventive via maternal and child health clinics, health awareness and facilities;

- Education: pre-school, non-formal education and literacy;
- Facilitating community based participatory planning;
- Community development: institution building, gender awareness, vocational training and economic support;
- Encouraging small home-based occupations;
- Promoting micro-credit facilities; and
- Networking among slum communities.

Housing development can drive economic growth and improve the quality of life of people by better services, governance and urban mobility. If this causes the transformation of existing housing areas, including slums, into communities which the inhabitants value, there is a general social enhancement of value, a general social and political gain. This would be possible by the preparation of Service Level Improvement Plan (SLIP), Action Plan and DPRs which focus upon water supply, sewerage, septage, storm water drains, urban transport, development of green areas and parks and other social amenities.

An Alternative to Public-Private Binary

Generally, the approach of Government towards low cost housing is supply driven with private sector partnership. This may endanger the access of housing to the EWS and LIG housing and may be bought over by the investors/ speculators. As a result, a large number of new dwelling units built by private developers and in PPP remain unoccupied. The Census 2011 pointed out the paradox that as many as 11.09 million houses are lying vacant, on the face of the total housing shortage of 18.78 million dwelling units.

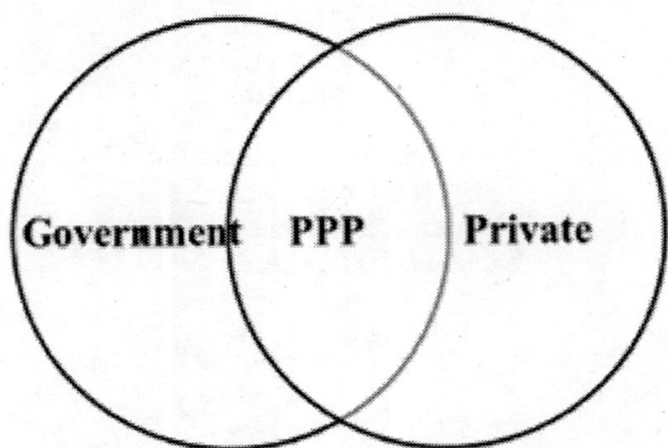

Fig. 10.15: Public-Private Binary

This poses a need to re-examine the supply driven approach towards housing, which is often without the participation of the dwellers. The public-private partnership model is largely focused on greenfield development and marginalises the poor. There are few exceptions where PPP model in social housing has succeeded. One such project is Sukhobrishti at Rajarhat, Kolkata.

There is need for developing a new paradigm, which is gender sensitive, community led, participatory and local and is based on the principle of equitable allocation of resources, space and land. Inclusive housing provides everyone with a house with linkages, livelihoods, water, electricity, toilets and security. This makes us to rethink about the model of public-private binary and evolve a third option, which is based on the following principles:

- Community as the core actor in the shelter process
- Demand -driven approach rather than supply-driven
- Local communities control the money and resources
- Promote a broader concept of upgrading and improvement of existing shelters
- Promote variations rather than standard solutions
- Synchronize shelter and poverty reduction
- Optimum utilization of urban land with focus on brownfields
- Capacity development, community empowerment and new partnerships.

The third option does not exclude private or private sectors. They participate in the collective model and energise the collective community sector.

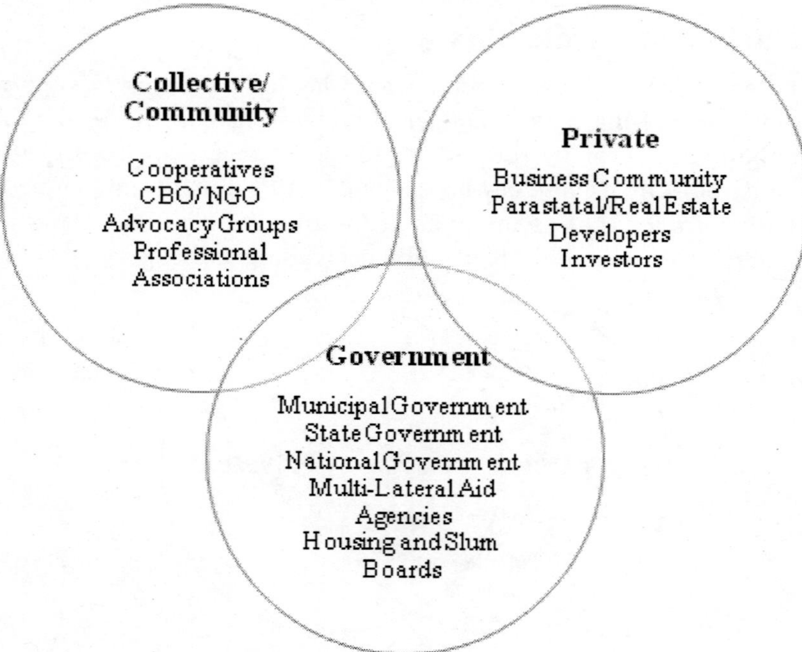

Fig. 10.16: Collective Community Sector as Third Option

Development Controls and Housing Form

Some have argued that to solve the housing shortage, it is necessary to liberalise the Floor Area Ratio (FAR) and have higher densities. There is no doubt that it is essential to optimise land use by rationalizing the FAR and residential density. It does not follow, however, that higher FAR can help to create more social housing. Sometimes an increased FAR has led to creation of vacant, speculative housing with no relation to the social needs and poverty. The Floor Area Ratio has to be seen in *combination with* plot coverage, density, housing form and the local urban context which could accomplish a dynamic urban environment. FAR, land use and densities involve a balanced trade-off between open and built-up spaces, and land and infrastructure development. It is necessary to reserve a proportionate amount of land for transport corridors, social facilities, social housing and public green spaces against the grant of higher FAR/FSI and land use conversion.

Housing density and Floor Area Ratio (FAR) need to be considered on the basis of certain principles in a given context, which include the following:

(a) Whether higher density and FAR are relevant to the needs and resources of the poor?

(b) Whether these facilitate self-built housing?

(c) Whether these promote livelihoods and income generation?

(d) Whether the social housing is a commodity?

(e) Whether these are equitable and enable access to housing for all?

(f) Whether these make housing more expensive, unsafe and involve higher levels of maintenance?

(g) Whether these facilitate incremental housing?

(h) Whether these make legal land development difficult for the poor?

(i) Whether these allow rental tenure or constrain access to shelter?

(j) What are the gender implications and whether women and children have safe and useful common/open space?

(k) How economical is the provision of basic services-toilets, sanitation, waste disposal and recycling, water, electricity, drainage and sewerage?

(l) What are the densities and FAR that can meet the target of housing for all in a city?

(m) Is the regulatory framework too complex and opaque for a common developer and community based development?

(n) Does the planning and regulatory frameworks provide the choices and options according to local culture, climate, geography, land values, housing demand and level of technology?

Various types of existing housing forms available to the EWS and LIG categories can be evaluated against these criteria. These include slum clusters, chawls, traditional/inner city, urban villages, unauthorized colonies, site and services, public sector built-up apartments, private sector housing, cooperative housing, etc. Although unplanned housing developments appear to meet most of the needs of the poor, the planned developments ignore most of the criteria. This means incorporating the positive aspects of unplanned developments, such as chawls in Mumbai which provide cluster/courtyard walk-ups, compact, high density and affordable rental housing. This is a sensible way to tolerate these adaptations, rather than outlawing them.

Densities of 600 dwelling units per hectare can be achieved in walk-ups (15 m height). For those at the base of the pyramid, (EWS and LIG), there can be walk-ups, low rise -high density development. Those at the centre, i.e. middle-income group can have mid-rise (up to 12 storeys). Those who are rich, at the peak, can have high rise development. The main principle is affordability, which includes cost of land, construction and services. The costs increase with the height. High rise building also restricts growth and expansion of individual units and mixed land use, which is one of the essential needs of the poor. The notion that high-rise housing leads to larger densities may not be true as it needs proportionately a higher amount of open space, community facilities and more distance between the buildings for light and ventilation.

Fig. 10.17: Housing design has to be community-led, which is evolutionary and synchronises with livelihoods, gender, equity and security

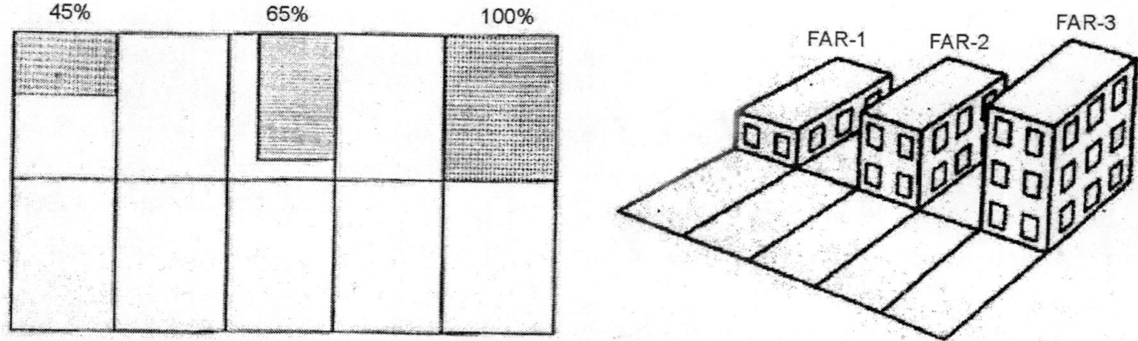

Fig 10.18: Different Plot Coverages-Horizontal Densification

Fig. 10.19: Different FARs-Vertical Densification

Source: Acioly, Claudio & Forbes Davidson, Density in Urban Development, Building Issues, Vol. 8, 1996, Lund Center for Habitat Studies, Sweden

While deciding the FAR a balance has to be struck between the cost of land per unit and construction cost. While higher density and FAR may reduce the cost of land, the cost of construction increases steeply beyond walk ups (15 m height). As a rule of thumb, cost increases by 20 per cent beyond walk up height owing to lifts, foundation, fire sprinkler system, services, generator, etc. and thereafter 5 per cent per floor. There are also implications with respect to safety of women, elderly and children, home based occupations, community interaction and communications. High rise living also is technology-intensive and has negative environmental consequences: heat island effect, air pollution, increased carbon footprint and danger from fire and earthquake. Much energy is spent on lifts, pumps and air-conditioning as well.

Yet, in view of wide differences in climate, geography, culture, housing demand and land costs, it is risky to prescribe general guidelines for housing form, densities and FARs. In the areas with paucity of land, horizontal development may not be feasible, but one may have to go vertical to meet the aim of housing for all. In such cases, it is necessary to incorporate flexibility of space by creating living platforms and terraces, where the residents get common open spaces and can furnish and finish their dwellings according to their needs and resources. A simple prefab system can provide economical and fast development. Ground floor, some portion of upper floors and terraces can be reserved as community space and for common facilities.

This requires meticulous planning and design which optimizes open space, greenery and play spaces, community spaces and puts limits to congestion, vandalism, crimes and other dangers. Accordingly, FAR and density standards should not depend on commercial pressures.

The dwelling units can be built on a self-build model or evolutionary design with built up floor, roof and service core on various floors. This approach recognizes the right of each family to develop its own dwelling according to its own priorities, needs and resources and allows for gradual development and changes. Evolutionary design defines the house-core relationship, i.e. the design of a built core, its location and the development alternatives for various stages of growth, both horizontal and vertical, around the core, i.e. the cell. Growth options indicate the direction as well as the feasible transformations offered by the initial core.

Inclusive and Adequate Housing

According to UN Habitat (Habitat III Issues Paper, 2015) adequate housing must provide more than four walls and a roof. A number of conditions must be met before particular forms of shelter can be considered to constitute "adequate housing." These elements are:

- Security of tenure: housing is not adequate if its occupants do not have a degree of tenure security which guarantees legal protection against forced evictions, harassment and other threats.
- Availability of services, materials, facilities and infrastructure: housing is not adequate if its occupants do not have safe drinking water, adequate sanitation, energy for cooking, heating, lighting, food storage or refuse disposal.
- Affordability: housing is not adequate if its cost threatens or compromises the occupants' enjoyment of other human rights.
- Habitability: housing is not adequate if it does not guarantee physical safety or provide adequate space, as well as protection against the cold, damp, heat, rain, wind, other threats to health and structural hazards.
- Accessibility: housing is not adequate if the specific needs of disadvantaged and marginalized groups are not taken into account.
- Location: housing is not adequate if it is cut off from employment opportunities, health-care services, schools, childcare centres and other social facilities, or if located in polluted or dangerous areas.

- Cultural adequacy: housing is not adequate if it does not respect and take into account the expression of cultural identity.

Each housing and slum re-development plan should address specific local issues and provide flexible choices of in-situ upgrading, relocation, land sharing or re-blocking. The local area plan should network all the settlements, where the local stakeholders plan together. Uniform standards that are set too high can price poor households out of formal housing. It may be better to provide basic shelter in appropriate locations, even with limited space as dormitories, hostels, etc. if it can house lowest-income households until their incomes rise. The existing housing stock and new units are complimentary parts of the solution. Existing housing, even in poor condition, may serve residents better by placing them where they have social connections and access to employment. Cities need to provide housing where residents can flourish, whether by building new units or upgrading and retrofitting of existing stock.

The critical concerns in redevelopment of slums and infill development are water supply and power, which are under severe stress. These require strategic interventions as follows:

(i) Preparation of services plan of redevelopment, slum rehabilitation, social housing and regularisation projects

(ii) Mandatory adoption of waste water recycling and renewable energy, water conservation, energy efficiency as per ECBC/Green Building Code, which can save 10 to 15 % of water and energy.

(iii) Checking of leakages, thefts and transmission losses which can save about 15 to 20 % of water and power

(iv) Enhancing organisational efficiency.

Optimizing housing development and construction

Housing development involves time-bound action planning and effective monitoring to overcome delays and cost overruns. To meet the huge urban housing targets there is no option but to optimize and harness the resources of both public and private sectors, that would synergise the advantage of both the government and the private sector towards gradual transition. It will also encourage new partnerships and a healthy competition in building 12 million houses in a time bound manner.

This needs optimizing the housing development and construction to achieve quality, productivity and flexibility, together with reducing time and costs. There is a need to innovate the construction to achieve efficiency, quality of service and sustained maintenance. This applies to standards and specifications, infrastructure, construction, maintenance, together with energy and environment concerns. According to McKinsey Global Institute, the critical housing cost reduction strategies at design and construction stage include the following:

- Pre-manufacturing: build components off-site using industrial processes, deliver parts as needed.
- Planning Optimization: apply critical path management techniques to optimize plan implementation by realistic scheduling.
- In-site lean execution: use lean techniques to standardize procedures that eliminate waste in individual activities and improve construction flow balancing.

- Process Step Productivity: eliminate low value added activities and wasted time to optimize process efficiency.
- De-specification of structural design: Avoid over-specification of non-value-added components.
- Standardization of micro-design: Identify substitutes and use design-to-cost to set specifications.
- Determine sourcing strategy for each category of construction activity, detail sub-contractor management
- Housing Optimization by volume increase through bundling, labour saving production, low-cost sourcing, and capacity optimisation of housing agencies, including the public, private and community sectors
- Technical Optimization: Standardize and identify substitutes with advanced costing tools.

Automated procedures can give precision to building construction and components and enable accuracy. Computer-Aided Manufacturing (CAM) and Computer Integrated Manufacturing (CIM) for pre-fabricated components, viz. ceilings, walls, roofs, etc. are integral to the process of industrialized construction. The simulation of construction process enables better control of time, machine, expenditure and the manpower, which could be reduced at least by half to one-third in comparison to the conventional construction. It is necessary to adopt industrialized building systems for efficient and economical housing delivery.

For an appropriate delivery of affordable housing project, the selection of developers and an operational model are critical. It involves the following:

(a) Developer qualification: Qualify the set of developers through structural criteria and build a competitive market.

(b) Land scoring: Score land parcels for potential development and qualification for appropriate incentives.

(c) Public-private-community partnership framework: develop operating model, tendering process and legal and contractual structure for public-private and community partnerships.

(d) Reverse tendering: for government lands with all approvals in place transferred to developers who return maximum number of affordable EWS/ LIG dwelling units.

Capacity Building and Regulatory System

It is essential to optimize the capacity of housing boards, banks and housing financial institutions, developers, and housing cooperatives. In addition, the capacities of communities and cooperatives should be strengthened.

In order to streamline the land market and regulate the transactions, as well as to discourage encroachments on public lands, it is necessary to make property registration, mutation and transfer simple, transparent and quick. To bring in accountability in the real estate sector, rating of developers and projects and licensing of real estate agents/brokers/ realtors need to be implemented, as mandated in the Real Estate (Regulation and Development) Act, 2016. To deal with the problem of land titles, it is necessary to introduce the Torrens

System of property title registration. This will curb litigation on the question of ownership and rights to land. It is also necessary to expedite procedures for project approval.

Financing

For financing of the social housing, besides the contribution of the Central Government, State Governments, Housing Agency and the individuals, rebate and exemptions in income tax, GST, rental income, excise duty, stamp duty and mortgage funding can help in macro and micro-financing. Building materials/ components banking can be another trigger of housing resources.

Delivery

There is a huge gap between policy planning and delivery. The PMAY envisages building about 2 to 3 million houses per year, while only 3.93 lakh houses were built and 30.73 lakh had been sanctioned upto November 2017. This requires removing various barriers, such as non-availability of land and finances, delays in approval of plans and primitive construction methods. Reforms in Development Control Regulations, Building Bye-laws and financing rules and regulations are other essential pre-requisites.

In order to accomplish the goal of building 12 million houses by the year 2022, it is necessary to change the strategy from mass housing to housing by the masses. This involves community partnerships, action planning, rigourous project monitoring and accountability.

The Way Forward

The Pradhan Mantri Awas Yojana (PMAY) for building houses for all by the year 2022 can be a game changer in the life of the poor, provided it focuses on the following:

- The classification of households based on income and categorisation of housing into EWS, LIG, MIG, etc. need to be reviewed as it leaves out the migrants, students, single /working women, etc. Definition of the housing has to be more inclusive, which covers hostels, dormitories, transit camps, night shelter, senior citizen homes, etc.
- The bulk of the poor cannot afford subsidised dwelling unit on ownership basis and to pay the loan instalments. As such, rental housing needs to be given a dedicated thrust.
- About 80% of housing shortage is due to congestion, dilapidation and over-crowding. This calls for redevelopment, rehabilitation and retrofitting strategies, rather than greenfield development. This would also help in retaining the livelihoods and social integrity of communities and also reduce the need of land acquisition.
- As social housing is a non-profit sector, it is necessary to think beyond the public-private binary and develop a third option, where the local community is the driver, and housing is not considered as a commodity. Public and private sectors have to pro-actively support and participate in community led housing programs which should synchronise with poverty reduction, livelihoods, facilities, gender equity and security.
- Differential and evolutionary planning norms for housing design can leverage housing supply.

- Adoption of innovative and disruptive technologies and optimising the building resources are necessary for the efficient use and economy of materials, time and money.
- Reforms in planning and building regulations, including mixed land use, Floor Area Ratio and densities are essential for effectively lowering the costs, saving of time and for optimum use of the land. Land being a critical resource needs to be assembled in alternative ways, such as land pooling and compulsory reservation.

Housing for All can be accomplished by developing new strategies of inclusionary housing, access to land, services, finances, employment and social facilities in the implementation dynamics.

Debriefing and Review

1. What is the assessment of urban housing shortage in India? What are the current programmes to meet the shortage?
2. Explain the salient features of PMAY.
3. Give details of approaches towards making a slum free city.
4. Write short notes on the following:
   (i) Rental housing
   (ii) Affordable housing
   (iii) Access land for EWS/LIG housing
   (iv) Community development
   (v) Urban renewal and in-situ rehabilitation
   (vi) Collective community sector in housing development.
5. How development control norms can enhance housing delivery for the poor. Discuss the pros and cons of high rise versus low rise housing.
6. Write short notes:
   (i) Night shelter
   (ii) Emergency shelter
   (iii) Housing standards
7. How construction sector can help in cost reduction in social housing?
8. How finances can be arranged to meet the need of social housing?
9. What are the new ways of housing management, action planning, project monitoring and accountability in housing delivery?

CHAPTER 11

Towards a New Land Policy

Land is the basis of all human activities, shelter and development of infrastructure services. Traditional planning entailed large scale appropriation of rural lands for urban development, i.e. housing, commercial centres, industries, roads and highways, parks, recreational, educational and health facilities, etc. The recent agitations and court cases, e.g. at Rewari (proposed development hub under DMIC project), Bhatta Parsaul, Greater NOIDA and

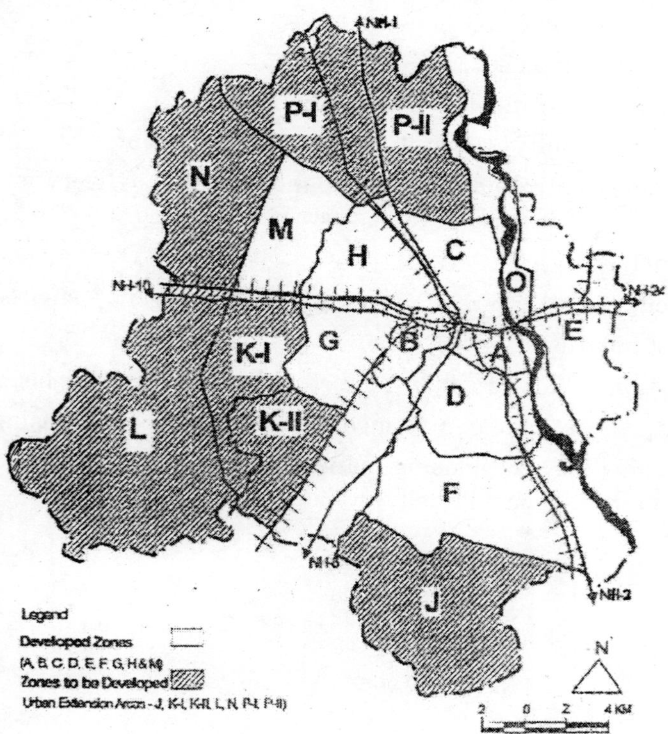

Fig. 11.1: As per the Master Plan for Delhi 2021 Delhi would add five sub-cities in the greenfields, that would expand its urban area to 92,000 Ha for a population of 23 million in 2021

Singur SEZ (WB) highlight the widespread discontentment against coercive land acquisition. The Government in 2013 enacted the Right to Fair Compensation and Transparency in Land Acquisition, Rehabilitation and Resettlement Act, which has replaced the Land Acquisition Act of 1894. It obliges the government and others to give rehabilitation package to displaced people, if they buy over 50 acres of land in urban areas and 100 acres in rural areas. Under the new Act land can be acquired by the government for its own use, or for the public purposes. Farmers will get four times the market price in the rural areas, while in the urban areas it will be double the market price. As such, new models of land pooling, Private Sector Participation (PSP) and Public-Private Partnership (PPP) in land assembly and development are being increasingly adopted in India in view of a) difficulty in land acquisition, b) to generate private sector resources by a market led approach, c) land monetization so as to improve the finances for investments in housing, infrastructure services, public transport, etc., and d) to meet the growing demands of urbanization.

Urbanisation and Land Policy

During the initial years after the Independence, the policies for compulsory land acquisition were adopted. Land Acquisition Act of 1894 had been applied for acquisition of land for planned development with government centric planning, land management and development, including infrastructure services, housing and construction.

The liberalization of the Indian economy (1992) gave a new thrust to urban and infrastructure development and private sector entered in a big way in real estate, housing and infrastructure projects, including ports and airports, rail freight corridors and Special Economic Zones (SEZs). The emergence of transport corridors with a substantial increase in industrial investment, services, flow of goods and people along them has been a significant feature of spatial change in recent years. The "Golden Quadrilateral" network of National Highways linking Delhi, Mumbai, Chennai and Kolkata as well as North-South and East-West Corridors, promote this type of growth. One of the recent initiatives is 1483 km long Delhi-Mumbai (Western) Industrial Corridor (DMIC) and 1,279 km long) Delhi-Kolkata (Eastern) Rail Freight Corridor. A separate corridor for freight trains would enable the Railways to achieve higher speed, facilitate guaranteed transit time to the customer, reduce unit cost of transportation and provide a competitive edge over the other modes of transport.

At present public-private partnerships in urban development are being promoted by the government by an enabling policy framework. The centrally sponsored urban development schemes are based on a partnership approach in which the Central and state governments share the project cost. To mobilise private sector and institutional resources and get multiplier effect from budgetary allocations, a facilitating approach is being adopted by the government.

In view of difficulties in acquisition of land, several State Governments have enacted Land Pooling Acts/Legislations, e.g. Andhra Pradesh (especially for Amravati, new Capital), Delhi, Gujarat and Maharashtra (modified Town Planning Acts), etc.

Urban Land Policy in Various States in India

Land is a State subject and various State Governments in India have adopted their own land policies for urban development. Realising the potential of urban sector in economic development, the privatisation of urban development is being increasingly adopted by the state governments in order to:

- Gain revenue from value addition of erstwhile agricultural land for planned development;
- Reduce the call on government funds;
- Overcome capital shortages and making urban development self-financing;
- Obtain the gains of private sector efficiency in land development, transport corridors, housing, commercial development, educational and health facilities and infrastructure services,
- Introduce competition in the supply of housing and other developments;
- Open up new areas of business for the private sector and create jobs,
- Better use of underutilised, idle, waste lands in improving the overall economy of the State/city.

Partnership Models in Delhi

The Tehkhand scheme covering an area of 14.3 Ha of land, is planned for construction of 3,500 houses for resettlement of slum dwellers with 750 high category houses (for market sale) along with development of sites for various facilities. The bids were invited and India bulls/DLF consortium won the bid. The DDA's main contribution was land, whereas private developers would bear expenses for construction, site development, etc. besides paying the bid amount to the DDA. This mode is being extended to several encroached sites of the DDA, Delhi Government, MCD, NDMC, etc. for in-situ slum rehabilitation. The Development Control norms of MPD-2021 allow a density of 600 to 900 EWS/LIG dwelling units per hectare and an FAR of 400. Commercial component up to 10% of floor area provides self-employment opportunities to Slum & JJ dwellers and make the scheme financially viable. Broadly 60% of land can be used for slum rehabilitation, community facilities/greens and remaining 40 % for market sale housing. Part of land/FAR can be used for mixed land use and facilities. The sites of facilities such as schools, religious place, community halls, shopping centres, etc. shall revert back to the DDA.

Another partnership project floated by the DDA in 2006 was for the Commonwealth Games Village on NH 24 covering 11 Ha. Construction of 1168 flats was offered by the DDA to the bidder against upfront payment and constructing the entire Commonwealth Games Village flats together with site development, parking and services. The DDA and developer were to share one-third/two-third flats. The bid was won by MG Emaar. However, due to financial difficulties of the developer, the share of DDA subsequently increased to 768 flats. This approach minimized the investment of the DDA in construction and development and can be extended for redensification and redevelopment of old areas/housing. With incentive/ additional FAR, several PPP schemes are being worked out by the CPWD, NBCC and L&DO such as redevelopment of Kidwai Nagar, Sarojni Nagar, R.K. Puram, Nauroji Nagar, etc. The government land can also be bundled for infrastructure development, major roads, metro corridors, facility corridors in urban extensions, transport terminals, depots and stations with hotels, property development services, etc. through partnership with private sector. However, land bank is a pre-requisite for this kind of PPP.

Land Pooling Model of Delhi Development Authority

The Delhi Development Authority constituted under the Delhi Development Act, 1957 for Planning and Development of the Capital, is vested with the responsibility of preparing and enforcing a master plan. The master plan provides planning policy, and it is the planning law for Delhi having various stipulations like development controls, (land use, FAR, density, setbacks, height, parking, road width, subdivision regulations, etc.), standards of physical and social infrastructure, redevelopment guidelines.

Since 1961 the DDA has followed the policy of large scale acquisition of land for planned development. However, the Master Plan of Delhi-2021 (MPD-2021), has envisaged a paradigm shift in land assembly and development, and stipulates land pooling policy. The land pooling policy would be the basis of development of the proposed five new sub-cities.

These sub-cities would accommodate a total population of 95 lakhs, which includes about 33 lakh existing population. The total area under five sub-cities is 66,657 ha, which includes regional park/ forests/ water bodies, mandatory agricultural green belt (54 border villages measuring about 11,000 ha), existing built-up areas/villages/unauthorised colonies, etc. (about 7681 ha) and land reservations for power plants, services, utilities, solid waste, sewerage, etc. Out of total urbanisable area of 42,334 ha, an area of about 27,628 ha is estimated to be available for new developments. Of this about 50 per cent (say 14000 ha) will be available for new residential development, 15-20 per cent for greens, 10-12 per cent for transportation and seven to nine per cent for commercial and industrial uses. About one-fourth of the proposed urban area comprises facility corridors, mainly having integrated transit corridors, commercial, public and semi-public facilities, government and institutional uses.The zonal plans of all five zones in urban extensions of Delhi have been approved and notified. As notified in the Gazzette of India dated 5th September 2013, the Land Pooling Model for land assembly & development is based on the following parameters:

(i) The two categories of land pooling are Category I for 20 Ha and above and Category II for 2 Ha above but less than 20 Ha.

(ii) The land returned to Developer Entity (DE) in Category I (20 Ha and above) will be 60% and land retained by DDA 40%.

(iii) The Land returned to Developer Entity (DE) in Category II (2 Ha to less than 20 Ha) will be 48% and land retained by DDA 52%.

(iv) The distribution of land returned to DE (60%) in terms of land use in Category I will be 53% residential, 2% City level Public/Semi Public and 5% city level commercial. The distribution of land returned to DE (48%) in terms of land use in Category II will be 43% as Gross residential, 2% City Level Public/ Semi-Public and 3% City Level Commercial.

(v) DE shall be returned land within 5 km radius of pooled land subject to other planning requirements.

This policy has been under revision and a draft has been notified in January 2018, which proposes the following:

(a) Minimum area for Group Housing shall be 2 Ha.

(b) The developer shall retain 60% of land and remaining 40% shall be surrendered for services, receational and PSP Facilities to DDA.

(c) FAR for group housing and City Level Commercial and PSP shall be as per MPD norms.

(d) 15% of FAR for EWS housing shall be given over and above the permissible FAR. EWS housing unit size to rang between 32-40 sqm.

(e) Parking is to be provided as per norm of 2 ECS/100 sqm of built up area under Residential development. However, in case of the housing for EWS, parking @ 0.5 ECS/100 sqm of BUA to be provided.

(f) Incentive for Green Building norms as per MPD-2021 to be applicable for Group Housing.

(g) Sub-division of residential areas and provision of facilities shall be as per MPD 2021.

(h) Form Based Codes (FBCs) will regulate building and development controls.

(i) Tradable FAR is allowed as per the norms.

Pre-requisites for Implementation of the Land Pooling Model

The existing urban areas and urban extensions in Delhi, covering about 750 sq.km of area, witness various typologies of development. MPD-2021 gives detailed guidelines for various kinds of developments in existing urban areas and the urban extension zones. These areas include village abadis, unauthorized colonies, squatter and slum areas, agricultural areas, green/ ridge, farm houses, and proposed major roads/transportation networks, facility corridors (PSP facilities, recreational, industrial, commercial and utilities), residential/housing, etc. For a comprehensive and integrated development in the proposed urban extension, it is necessary to start with and ensure availability of transport corridors and basic services, without causing displacement. This needs a hybrid land policy that would be a combination of compulsory land pooling or acquisition, preferably through land return or Transferable Development Rights and Accommodation Reservation. In contiguous large tracts of lands, land pooling on voluntary basis, together with compulsory land pooling/ and return may work, but in isolated developments (such as built up areas, regularized unauthorised colonies, etc.) Town Planning Scheme, Transferable Development Rights (TDR), reservations by easement and urban design controls (especially for composite redevelopment of TOD zones) may be more suited. The basis of grant of development right, including incentive FAR can be balanced with the recovery of External Development Charges (EDC), conversion charges, FAR charges, betterment levy, etc. which would vary as per land use, location and FAR.

As far as possible land pooling and return transactions should be on the spot. This will save the land owners and developers from anxiety and need for personal contacts. This will also reduce huge administrative work, court cases, land transfer hassles, land security and vigilance. It will be necessary for the DDA to create its zonal land banks and acquire the lands (by compulsory land pooling) required for Master Plan Roads (30 m and above) and facility corridors. This will enable the service agencies to pre-plan and extend essential public utilities, infrastructure services such as roads, utilities, ESS, water works, main sewers and drains. These are developed by different agencies/departments, which normally take 4 to 5 years. Without these services, land pooling policy may not work and create a bad image of the developers as well as the DDA/government.

Lack of proper Land Information System and widespread practices of power of attorney can be other major hurdles in implementation of the Land Pooling Model in a transparent, efficient manner. Land Information System is the basis of its administration, which needs following reforms:

- Institutional, policy and legal reforms;
- Application of information communications technologies (ICT) including computerised, digitised data management, geographic information system (GIS), electronic data capture, web-based applications, satellite position systems, national spatial data infrastructure (NSDI) and e-governance;
- Digital Planning, financing, valuation and taxation;
- Capacity development

UP Model

In UP the Ghaziabad Development Authority (GDA) has adopted a joint venture model of urban development in which a consortium/joint venture between the builders/developers/ GDA take up the development. Ghaziabad Development Authority acts as a facilitator. The land is purchased by the developers by negotiations with the land owner failing which the GDA acquires the land under the Land Acquisition Act (LAA). For funding the acquisition, the JVP is selected on the basis of the bids. The private developer earns revenue from the sale of property/flats on 60% of land in the free market. Apart from the lesser investments, it provides free of cost facilities, plots to the GDA, who also earns annual revenue of 1% from the developer. 20% of the plots/flats are reserved for the EWS/LIG at predetermined rates. The model is applicable in selected residential areas with a minimum size of 50 acres.

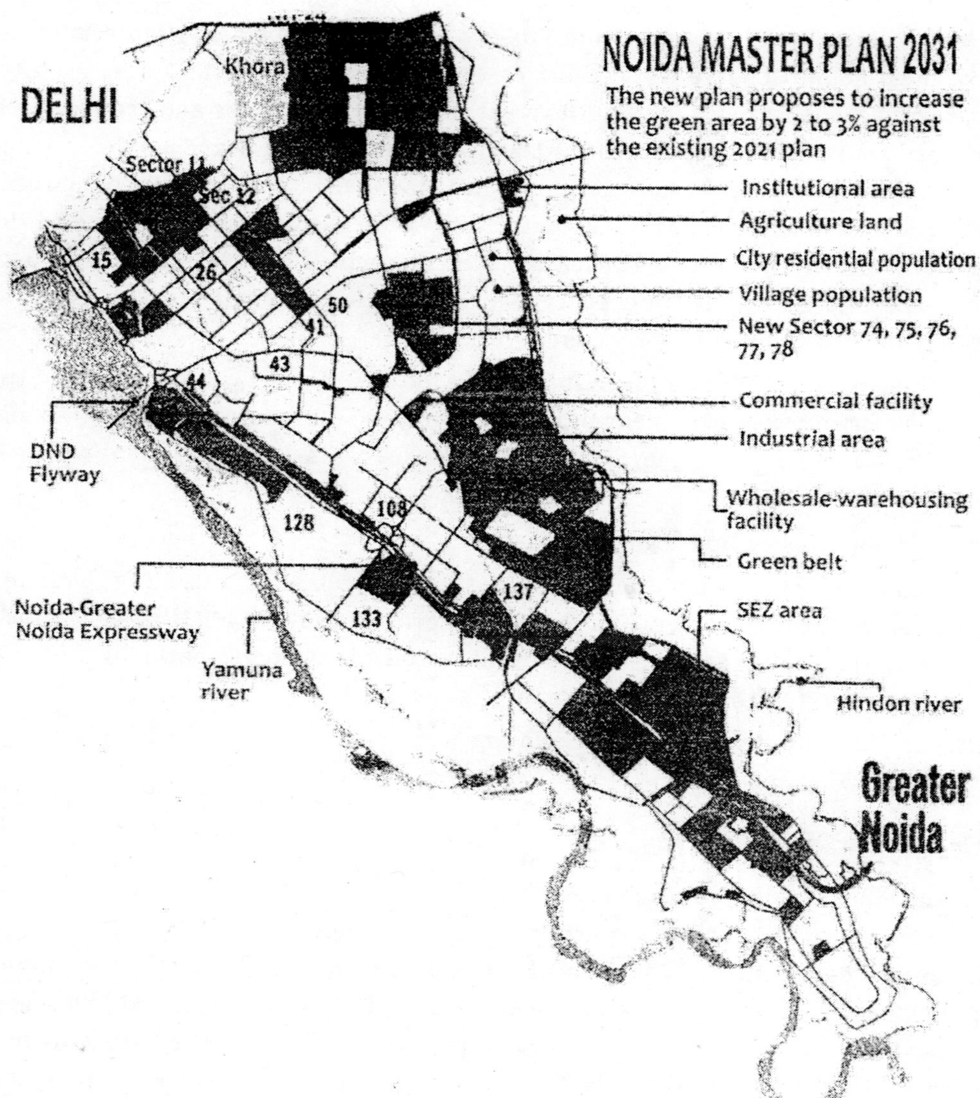

Fig. 11.2: Noida Master Plan-2031

The UP Government during recent years has adopted the policy of land- infrastructure bundling for coordinated development of infrastructure and real estate. In NOIDA/Greater NOIDA land is being used as a resource for infrastructure development. The private sector has been invited to develop the major roads, public facilities and utilities against allotment of land for residential, commercial and industrial development. The Formula-one Racing Track and Yamuna Expressway in the Greater NOIDA have been developed in this manner with the entire investments of the private sector except land which was acquired by the NOIDA/Government of UP.

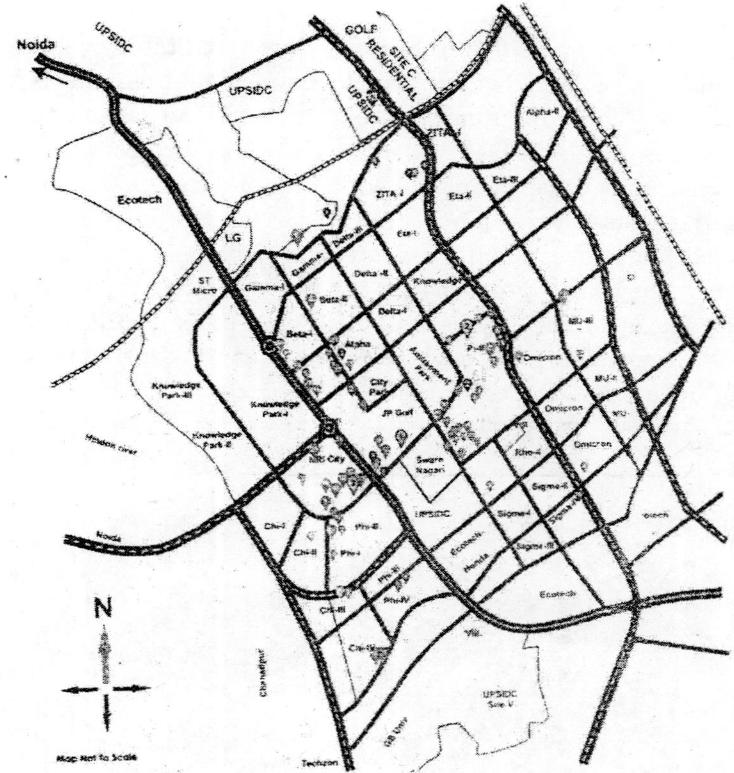

Fig. 11.3: Greater Noida Master Plan

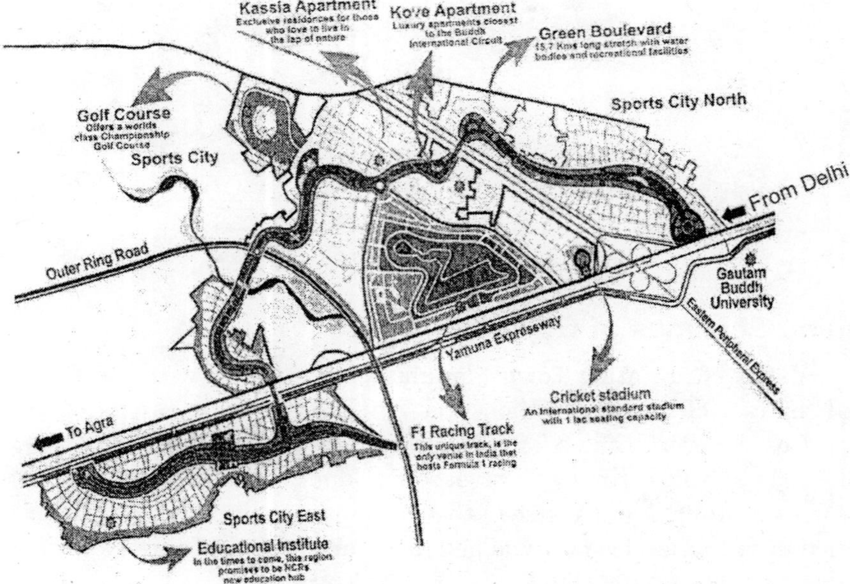

Fig. 11.4: Jaypee Green Sports City, Greater Noida. The Formula one racing track and Yamuna Expressway Developed by Private Investment through Land-Infrastructure Bundling

Haryana Model

The Haryana Urban Development Authority acts as a facilitator by issuing licenses after permitting the acquisition of land by the private developers from the farmers directly at negotiated market prices. The minimum applicable size for the scheme is 40 hectares. The model takes care of the layout level facilities only. The entire process of negotiating the land purchase and development is to be completed within three years. It requires the colonizer to provide for 20% of the plots/flats to EWS/LIG categories at predetermined rates. Haryana Government attracted huge investments, industries and multi-nationals in the State by its private sector urban policy. The provision of the basic services and major roads is often deficient which depends upon the payment of EDC and other charges to the HUDA/Local Bodies and Haryana Government. Although the conditions of license impose a ceiling of 15% profit, it is more of an academic prescription.

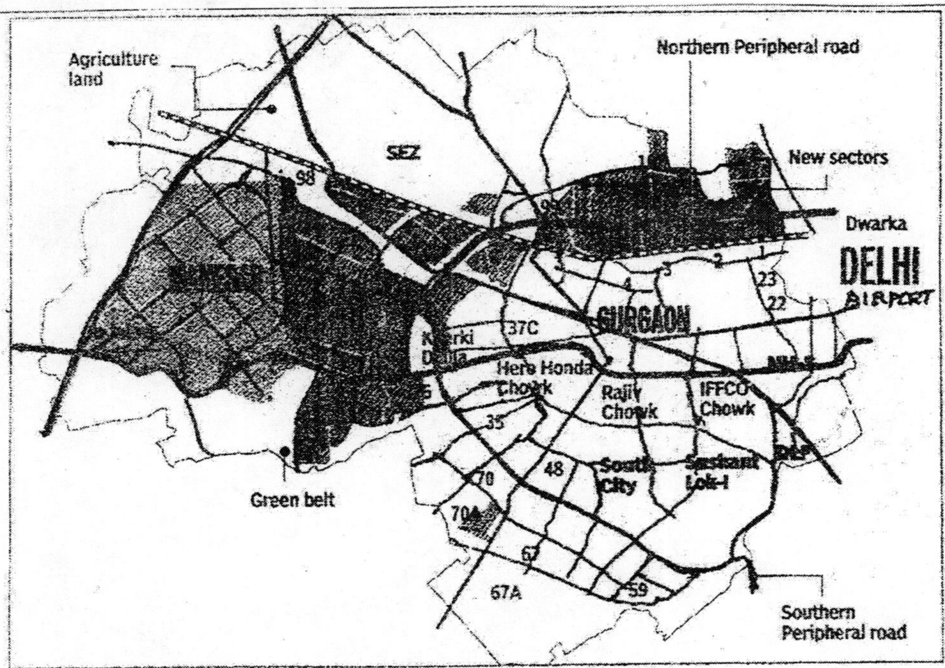

Fig. 11.5: Gurgaon Master Plan 2025

Town Planning Schemes of Gujarat

The responsibility of initiating Town Planning Scheme rests with the Development/Local Authority and the cost of implementation of a TP scheme is met through the budget of the local authority. Cost recovery from a TP scheme project is in the form of owner's contribution, which is upto half of the estimated increase in land value. The model is applicable in residential pockets with an average size of the scheme varying between 10 Ha to 400 Ha. The model is attractive to the landowner who gets back about 70% of the land. To cater to EWS/ LIG housing, reservation of 10% land is made, which is inadequate.

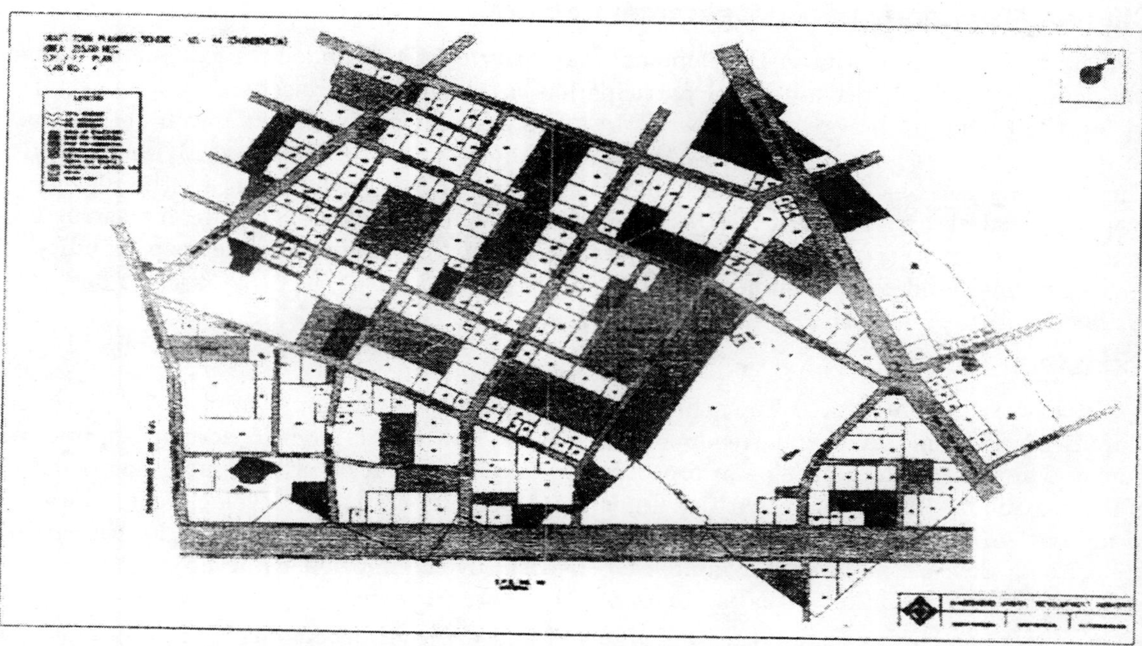

Fig. 11.6: Town Planning Schemes, Gujarat, TP Scheme no. 44 at Chandkheda (215 ha)

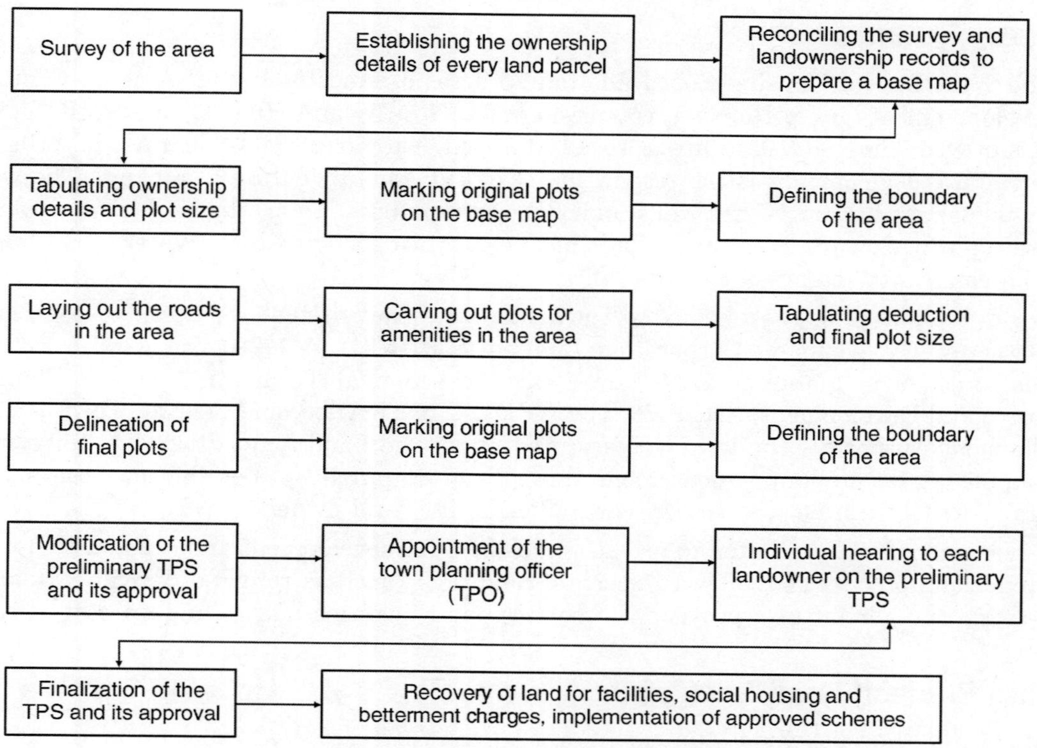

Fig. 11.7: Town Planning Scheme Process

Chennai–Guided Urban Development Model

The Chennai Metropolitan Development Authority (CMDA) guidelines for Guided Urban Development envisage private sector participation on a minimum project size of four hectares within the Chennai Metropolitan Area (CMA). The guidelines stipulate minimum of 60 plots per gross hectare of land of which 75 percent are to be reserved for EWS and LIG households. These can be purchased by the government at a fixed price or disposed of by the developer at price fixed the government/CMDA. The land assembly, provision of site infrastructure (roads, drainage, water supply, power, sewerage, street lights, etc.) are the responsibility of developer. The land under community facilities, roads and parks, etc. (30%) is handed over to the CMDA free of cost.

Rajasthan Model

In Rajasthan, Integrated Township Scheme stipulates a minimum area of 100 acres in Jaipur, 50 acres in Divisional Headquarters (except Bharatpur) and 25 acres in Municipal Towns. The local authority helps in procurement and consolidation of land including transfer of lands available with local authorities/Rajasthan Housing Board. The developer is encouraged to take up Township development, even if the developer owns at least 2/3rd of the prescribed area. About 65% of the land is available for disposal by the developer and 35% of total area under facilities/circulation/parks is surrendered to local authority.

Conversion charges for land use for internal and external development are deposited by the developer for the development of roads, drainage, water supply and power, etc. As an option IDC and EDC can be paid by way of 15% and 5% of land respectively.

West Bengal Model

The West Bengal Housing Board allotted 25 acres of land to Gujarat Ambuja Company for development of Group Housing, comprising of LIG, MIG and HIG. The LIG/MIG houses are 4 storeyed and HIG flats are 8 to 14 storeyed, with a permissible FAR of 250. The infrastructure development is the responsibility of JVC (Joint Venture Company). The water supply is managed through tube wells/underground tank/boosting arrangement. For sewerage disposal, a Mini Sewage Treatment Plant has been provided. The Storm Water is discharged into the canal after treatment of the effluent.

For development of Rajarhat New Town the State Government set up the West Bengal Infrastructure Development Corporation Limited (WBIDCO) in 1999. The New Town area was declared as a 'Planning Area' under the West Bengal Town and Country Planning (Planning and Development) Act, 1979. The WBIDCO has now become the New Town Kolkata Development Authority. The land was acquired under the Land Acquisition Act, 1894 which was supplemented by land procurement through direct purchase. For this purpose a Land Procurement Committee was set up with officials and land owners.

Government land is allotted to private developers for development and construction based on a tendering process and subject to certain conditions, such as return of EWS/LIG housing units, part commercial use, provision of services and facilities and ceiling on cost of social housing.

Andhra Pradesh-Land Pooling in Vijaywada for BSUP Housing Scheme

In 2007-08 the Vijaywada Municipal Corporation (VMC) acquired 226 acres of agricultural land for urban development. A new system of land sharing was adopted, under which land was shared between farmers and VMC in the ratio of 60:40 without cash compensation to the farmers. Several rounds of negotiation resulted in this partnership, wherein the farmers would part with their 40% land for development by Vijaywada Municipal Corporation (mainly for the construction of houses under BSUP Scheme) and related infrastructure and the rest 60% of serviced land is returned to the farmers for urban uses.

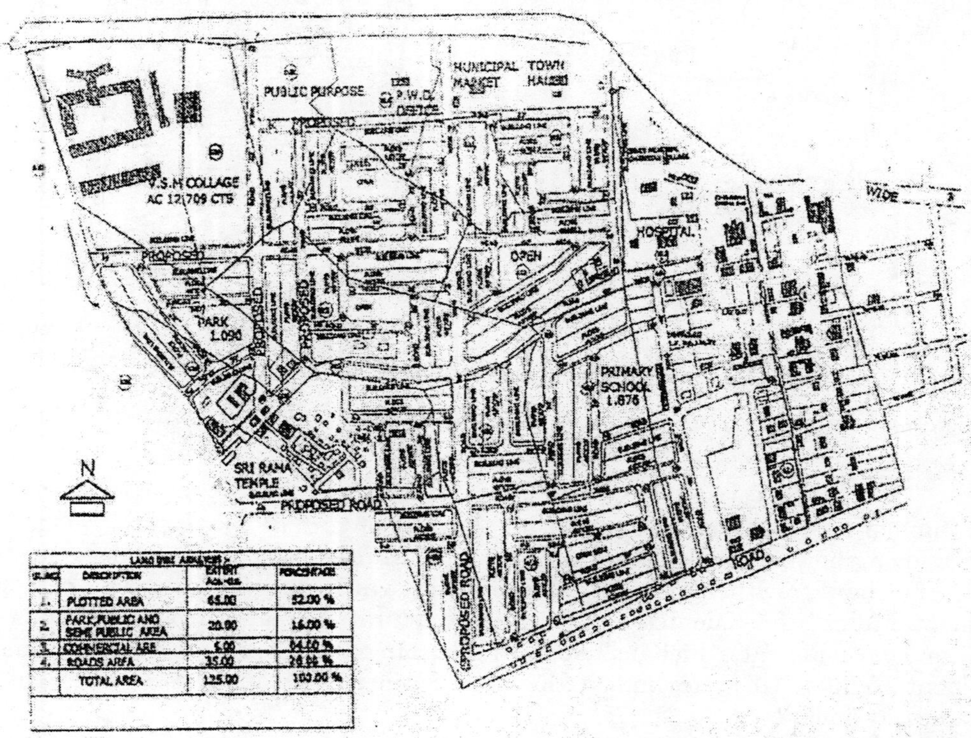

Fig 11.8: Ratnampeta Area Development Plan, Vijaywada, Andhra Pradesh

Source: Special Development Authority, Visakhapatnam.

Kerala Plot Reconstitution

Trichur Urban Development Authority (TUDA) carried out an innovative Plot Reconstitution (PR) Scheme (1982-86) covering an area of 7.5 Ha. Earlier a proposal was framed for development of a central bus stand, market/shopping, hotel, etc. which involved the acquisition of land through Kerala LA Act, 1961. There were strong objections against the land acquisition. The TUDA decided to resort to the technique of plot reconstitution inviting the land owners for negotiations. As a result Plot Reconstitution Scheme was worked out where by the TUDA received more than 2 Ha of land free of cost and without lengthy land acquisition procedure. The nine land owners got developed land (about two-third of original land) with roads, services and enhanced value (about 7.7 times). The scheme was completed in six years from the date of agreement. Another land mark in Kerala is the adoption of Integrated District Development Planning (IDDP) dovetailed with participatory Local Development Planning (LDP). This ensures integrated urban and rural development with public participation.

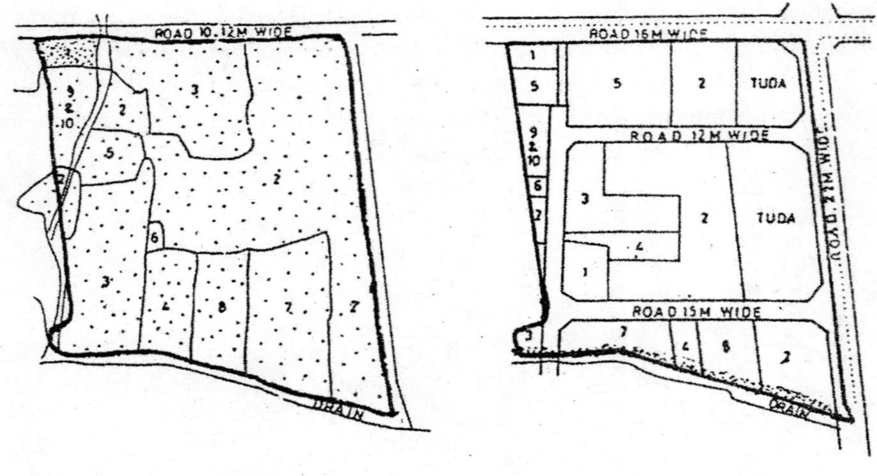

Original Land Holdings　　　　Final Land Holdings

Fig. 11.9: Land Reconstitution Scheme in Trichur, Kerala

Source: Banashree Banerjee, Urban and Rural Planning Thought, (1984) SPA, New Delhi

Mumbai Experience

The Mumbai experience stands out for its plurality of land development strategies and is gradually moving beyond Town Planning Scheme which causes sprawl and does not cater to fast pace of urban growth and high value of land which demand compact, high density development. Mumbai has adopted a differentiated, plural approach for various kinds of land assembly and development, which include Town Planning Scheme, Land Pooling, Transferable Development Right (TDR), Accommodation Reservation (AR) and use of air rights (over railway lines/stations, etc.)

The various land management approaches in Mumbai are as follows:

Table 11.1: Plural Land Management Strategies in Mumbai

Predominant Consideration		Land Policy
1.	Planning/regularisation of existing/new development on private lands	Town Planning Scheme
2.	Obtaining land for public purpose or conservation of heritage buildings in already developed areas	Transfer of Development Right and Accommodation Reservation (TDR &AR)
3.	Mobilising financial resources	Development of Government land at vantage locations, use of air right at railway stations, etc.
4.	Planned development in fringe areas including redevelopment/renewal of old areas.	Incentive based guided land development.

5.	New Town Development in green-field sites	Land acquisition under LA Act, Land policy with option of one eighth land return (60% in Naina New City).
6.	In-situ slum rehabilitation	Incentive based slum redevelopment and cooperatisation, cross subsidised by market sale component and bonus FSI

Learning from Other Countries

The political and cultural ideologies of a country are reflected in its land policy. In China, land is viewed as a public resource, with use rights subject to government approval. In Thailand and Philippines, land is a subject of private ownership and market transactions. The approach in Indonesia is an intermediate stage between two extremes. These approaches have significant impacts on the government's land policies, which are integral to urban system and its cross-sectoral linkages.

How efficiently the land market works can be seen from the perspective of the city administration, real estate developers, business and households, in particular the urban poor. From the viewpoint of the city government, a good example is the system in the Tokyo region, by designating "preferred and deferred" areas as part of land development strategy. From the view point of real estate developers, one of the best examples is that of Bangkok, where there are minimal planning and building regulations. From the urban poors' viewpoint, good examples are mandatory loans and land sharing, and cross-subsidy system in Manila where lower interests are charged for smaller loans.

Planning and regulatory systems play an important role in land management by guiding and controlling the spatial impacts or externalities of the multitude of short term decisions by the private sector. These are linked to the issues of governance, sectoral investments, fiscal policies and other aspects of urban management. There are several examples of efficient integrated planning and regulatory systems. In Seoul, fiscal policies are used to encourage the faster use of vacant land and to discourage speculation. In Jakarta, Manila and Dhaka, effective strategic planning/structural planning approaches are adopted rather than static, costly and urban centric master plans. In Manila, more effective forms of public participation in the development process have been introduced.

There are variety of techniques to improve the urban poor's access to land, involving direct subsidies through public housing, sites and services projects, housing credit schemes and slum upgrading programs. A number of innovative in-situ slum rehabilitation policies have been tried such as land sharing in Bangkok and its variations in Kuala Lumpur. A good example is Myanmar's hut-to-apartment scheme, where government sells land to private developers provided that they give a percentage of the houses constructed to its low income households on the site. The Community Mortgage Programs in Bangkok and Manila are also helping the urban poor.

The Capital Investment Folio (CIF) for the Metro Manila Commission in coordinating the spatial plans with infrastructure investment strategies and allocating responsibilities. A similar process was developed for the Jabotabek Metropolitan Development Plan. The Kuala Lumpur Structure Plan is an example of effective delineation of functions, including coordination of planning and financing systems for urban development at national, metropolitan and local levels.

Several cities in Bangladesh, Philippines and Australia have taken the initiatives to streamline land transaction procedures and integrate land information management. Such improvements include cadastral mapping, land registration and titling, institutional streamlining and reduction in number of approvals for real estate projects.

Singapore has a comprehensive land information system which meets the needs of all government departments with particular interests in land as well as providing a 'one stop shop' for the public. Malaysia has developed a computer-assisted mapping system, originally intended for managing land registration information, but has now become a multi-purpose GIS.

In the Tokyo region, effective coordination of urban expansion is facilitated by meticulous planning of physical, financial and regulatory mechanisms, including Spatial Data Infrastructure. In the National Capital Region (Philippines) urban expansion is coordinated by a comprehensive land information for growth centres (e.g. Subic, Clark, Mailaque), which support a decentralised urban structure.

To ensure planned development, while safeguarding the rights of land owners,land pooling and readjustment model envisages that an equal portion of land is deducted from every agricultural plot as contribution of land for physical and social infrastructure and to raise resources. Land remaining with land owner is reconstituted so that he gets regular shaped plots and frontage on public road. Land owners contribute fund in proportion to land holding to finance infrastructure development cost. This method has been adapted in Town Planning Schemes in India and had its roots in "land pooling" in Germany, which is also being followed in Australia, Japan, Thailand, Taiwan and South Korea.

Land Readjustment Scheme (LRS) in Korea is used as a major tool to secure the land for the construction of large complexes. Under the programme, once a certain area is declared as the development site, some portion (one-fourth) of land is set aside for public use such as roads, recreation area and other facilities (5%) and another portion of land is retained by the government/developer (9 to 10 %) to cover the cost of development. By the increase in land value after the development, the owner realises substantial profit on his remaining land (60 to 65%). In order to prevent the speculation, the government introduced Public Development Scheme (PDS) under the Land Development Promotion Act. Under the Act land can be purchased compulsorily by the public authority. The LPR Scheme involves:

(i) Land Pooling and Return without compensation

(ii) Relaying of pooled land

(iii) Carrying out infrastructure work and subdivision of land

(iv) Re-allotted part of developed land back to the owners, and

(v) Selling surplus developed land to meet the cost of development.

The method minimises public expenditure in the conversion of raw rural land to developed urban land. At the same time, original owners end up with reasonable compensation, with the value added plots. The public agency obtains land for circulation, open spaces, etc. free of cost, besides getting residential, commercial and industrial plots through which the amount incurred towards provision of infrastructural facilities is ploughed back . However, many original land owners feel deprived due to loss of occupation and agricultural income and the cost of moving/displacement. The process of LPR brings public investments in infrastructure and obviates the need for financial transactions which both parties typically find difficult. The public authority does not have to find the cash for acquisition and the land owners do not have to pay a Betterment tax/EDC.

An Overview

The following table gives an overview of the models of private sector participation in urban development in Haryana, Uttar Pradesh, Gujarat and Maharashtra. It also summarizes the major issues involved.

Table 11.2: An Overview of Private Sector Participation in Urban Land and Development

Particular	Haryana	Uttar Pradesh	Gujarat	Maharashtra
Legal Framework	HUDA Act 1975 Haryana Ceiling on Land Holding Acts, 1972 Haryana SEZ Act 2005 NCRPB Act, 1985 E (PC) Act, 1985	• UP Land Ceiling Act 1973 • UP Urban Planning and Development Act, 1973 • UPSEZ Development Authority Act, 2002 • NCRPB Act, 1985 • E (PC) Act, 1985	Gujarat T P and Urban Development Act, 1976	• Mumbai MC Act, 1888 • MRTP Act, 1966 • MMRD Act, 1974 • MHAD Act, 1976 • Development Control Regulations for MMR, 1999
Regulatory Framework	PPP HUDA : Rules, Regulations, Building Bye-laws Master Plan/Regional Plan/Zonal Plan Haryana Urban Land Policy (2011), SEZ Policy License pd. 2 Yrs(+3yrs) Bank Guarantee 25% of IDC and EDC	• Joint Venture Equity Sharing (10% private & 90% government) • LDA/GDA/Noida/Greater Noida, etc. : Rules, Regulations, Building Bye-laws • Master Plan/Regional Plan/Zonal Plan • Integrated City Development Policy 2005 • Hi-tech Township Policy, 2003, SEZ Policy • UP State Housing Policy	• Town Planning Scheme • Transferable Development Rights • Slum Redevelopment • Incentivized Guided Development • Development Plans, Rules and Regulations • Development Control Regulations • Building Bye-laws, • Government/Executive Orders	

Land Assembly	Negotiated market land purchase Government- under Land Acquisition Act :	• Negotiated market land purchase • Govt. land purchase at market value linked/ to Consumer Price Index/ or against 20% developed land/ 5% of plots reserved for land owners, + 15% uprooting allowance + 15 sqm shop • Allotment of govt. land under Land Infrastructure Bundling	Land Acquisition by Government: • TDR/ AR (Additional FSI) • Cash/one eighth developed land at market price (Navi Mumbai) , 60% in Naina	
Minimum Area	100 Acres (10 acres for group housing projects)	Minimum Area : 50 Acres (20 Ha)	Not specified (10 Ha as per practice for TPS) Land return average 50-70%	Not specified, TPS 50 to 70 % land return
Reservation for EWS/LIG	20% EWS/LIG (50-125 sq.m plot/flat) 25% plot/flats (on no profit no loss)	20% EWS/LIG plot/flat) 40% units (on no profit no loss)	10 to 15% of residential land for EWS/LIG mainly serves middle and upper income	10 to 15% of residential land for EWS/LIG
Scope and Coverage	Mainly Greenfield	Mainly Greenfield	New TP Schemes, Old Area Redevelopment, Slums/ Unauthorized Colonies Incentive Based Guided Land Development	
Time Frame	3 to 7 years	3 to 7 years	5 to 10 years upto plan sanction, 3 to 5 years for development	5 to 15 years
Major Innovations	Project cost mobilized from developer equity, users installments and commercial financing. Equitable FAR for lands required for public roads/ corridors, etc. Lesser restrictions and interference in private sector development.	Land Infrastructure Bundling One window approval Purchasable FAR	Land sharing for public roads, greens and facilities without need for acquisition 50-50 cost sharing for ED/ Internal Dev.	Plural PPP Policy covering TPS, infrastructure services, /chawls/old city /slums TDR, Accommodation Reservation, Slum re-development, , mixed use development, etc Land monetization and efficiency Incentivized guided development

Major Issues	Resistance from farmers against acquisition, inadequate compensation, litigations/court cases, encroachment on govt. lands/roads Piecemeal development due to withholding of land by the owners/farmers/speculators Delay in obtaining approvals Huge profits despite ceiling Scattered location of projects and urban sprawl Redevelopment of existing urban areas not covered Lack of external services and public transport Lack of inter-departmental coordination Development of services delayed being linked to EDC/ Cost Recovery Illegal subdivision of rural lands Lack of social housing Poor recovery of Betterment Charges Poor maintenance of colony/project/roads	• Compromise with planned development • Fragmented land holdings and sprawl • Long time in finalization and approval of T P Schemes • Poor land bank of government/ULB • TPS popular in Gujarat but not suitable for large scale development • Perceived bias in favour of land owners, ULB subsidizing TPS development by 50 to 80% • Inefficient resource use, poor cost recovery (TPS) • Poor infrastructure standards • Poor environmental quality • Poor Regulatory standards/ administrative/political interference • Subdivision of plots without services, in anticipation of regularization • Lack of social housing • Delay in external & internal development and poor maintenance.

Cross-Cutting Issues

There are various cross-cutting issues in land assembly and development policies which should be addressed for planned development:

- Integrated Planning is a major challenge which needs to be balanced with spot zoning, minimum size of land holding, facilities and transport networks, etc. Integrated development addresses the issues of environmental sustainability, city expansion, restructuring, development controls and land use.
- Major transport corridors and external/peripheral infrastructure services need to be in place prior to real estate disposal to consumers/buyers.
- Inclusive Development- The city belongs to all and the poor, informal sectors have a claim on equitable access to land resource, housing, services, jobs, etc.
- Spatial- Financial - Infrastructure Interactions - Various aspects of land development have to be viewed in a regional context which integrates spatial, financial and infrastructure services, such as water, power, drainage and transportation.
- Institutional Coordination- land management involves many public and private institutions and requires horizontal and vertical coordination. There is a need to clearly define the roles and functions of the organizations involved in land management.
- Redevelopment of old, unplanned areas, unauthorized colonies and slum rehabilitation to be ensured by incentivized development rights. This needs innovative options of land assembly and planning.
- Legal frame and regulatory process reforms are the cornerstones of the land policy which include one window/online approval, simplified procedures, protecting consumers interests, licensing and enforcement.

Emerging Concepts and Principles

Innovative concepts can be adopted to address the critical issues in land management as given below:

Integrated and Sustainable Development: A compact city form has significant implications on urban land, housing and sustainability. Critical instruments for this policy option include coordination with public transport, infrastructure development, mixed land use, and coordination of different levels of government. Data from international cities, indicate correlation of urban density with transport, energy use and carbon emissions. The "compact and smart growth" and transit oriented development, create more accessible land use patterns and reduce the amount of travel. This also supports a high transit share, and makes walking and cycling attractive. The examples of successful compact, smart city planning includes Singapore's integration with radial and circumferential mass rapid transit, Curitiba's integration with bus rapid transit on the linear main roads, Freibourg's integration with light rail transit and environmental commuter pass, and Holland's land use policy based on the categorisation of locations according to the accessibility to public and road transport.

Shanghai provides an interesting case study of urban turnaround. It has achieved densification together with manifold increase in its green area, transport infrastructure, social facilities and urban services. Shanghai in 1990 had average road area per capita of 2.28 sq.m. and 1.02 sq.m of public green area per capita. By 2003, it increased average road area per capita more than five folds to 12.3 sq.m. and public green area per capita more than nine folds to 9.16sq.m. This was possible by the planned densification and redevelopment. The planning strategy envisages that that the areas (disaggregated in a city/zone/sector/local hierarchy) under circulation/roads, green spaces and social infrastructure are around 10sq.m./ per capita each. This should be the basic factor to determine the 'carrying capacity' of urban land and to compute the density and Floor Area Ratio (FAR) The focus of sustainable development is not the buildings but the greens, common social facilities/utilities, and roads/ parking which determine the quality of urban development. With increasing demand for space, a balance is to be maintained between redevelopment and urban expansion.

The Land Pooling Legislation: In Indian cities, it is becoming extremely difficult to acquire lands on large scale for planned development. The process of land pooling is being adopted an alternative which involves the preparation of a development plan/land pooling scheme that indicates the areas required for public uses such as streets, parks and schools, etc. The cost of providing the infrastructure for the entire area is calculated, and also the estimated market value of the improved land. A portion of the land, the estimated market value of which equals the cost of development, is then transferred to the local government in return for carrying out the improvement. Alternatively, EDC, Conversion Charges, Betterment Levy, etc. are recovered against grant of development rights with compulsory surrender of land for common greens, transport infrastructure, social housing and facilities required at local level. The scheme does not envisage in-situ development of land but is returned in the nearest vicinity as per approved layout plan so as to ensure planned development. An advantage of land pooling is that layout and reblocking are affected without the need of acquiring individual pieces of land for the facilities and infrastructure. At the same time, it provides an early return on the public investments through the sale of the land ceded to the local government. Its implementation involves land pooling legislation and detailed regulations.

The Concept of "Excess Condemnation" is another method which can be employed to serve the twin objectives of providing a public road, highway or such facility and generate revenue by the acquisition of additional lands which are directly affected by such provision. The adjacent area is developed by the local body, the land value of which increases as a result of facility/road, and it accrues to the local body, rather than to individuals. The concept of property development along major public transport corridors/MRTS has been adopted in Delhi with grant of 50% additional FAR. This helps building up of a land bank of the local body.

Inclusive Development: A hazard of the market driven approach of urban development can be marginalization of the poor. The National Urban Housing and Habitat Policy (2007) suggests that the governments make mandatory provisions for the EWS, construction workers and informal sector, for which about 10 to 15% of residential land and 20 to 25% of FAR may be reserved in all housing developments, both by the private and public sectors. The developer is expected to hand over such housing/ land to the government after providing basic community infrastructure (access paths, water hydrants/hand pumps, toilet blocks, drains, sanitary provisions and street lights). The cost of land and development of basic infrastructure could be borne by government. The Master Plan for Delhi 2021 (MPD-2021) provides a mandatory component of social housing for which an incentive Floor Area Ratio of 15% of permissible FAR is given to the developer. This helps in citywide provision of EWS/LIG housing without need of extra land. Social housing thus generated could be given on rent, lease or license to slum dwellers, EWS/LIG families or their cooperatives.

Spatial, Financial and Infrastructure Integration: Land management involves coordination among the local, state and central governments with horizontal and vertical linkages among planning, engineering, finance, legal, housing and management departments. Coordinated spatial, financial and infrastructure planning can be achieved by Capital Investment Folio (CIF), similar to what was developed for the Metro Manila Commission. This helps in coordinating the spatial plans with infrastructure investment strategies and allocating responsibilities. This also considers sustainability factors, such as form of urban expansion, which minimizes energy use, minimize development on high value agricultural land, avoid vulnerable groundwater resources and optimize use of land (e.g. mixed use areas, redevelopment and redensification, multiple use of buildings, etc.). The preparation of integrated District Plan that covers urban, peri-urban and rural areas along with the local plans based on a participatory, financial planning and decentralized decision making process provide a strategic and effective mechanism that links spatial planning to financial, economic and infrastructure development.

Infrastructure Bundling: Urban projects such as slum redevelopment, roads, and airports are being financed through award of land for market to partly compensate the cost of development. Slum Rehabilitation at Kathputli Colony, New Delhi, IGI Airport, New Delhi, redevelopment of the New Delhi Railway Station, Sports City/F-1 Racing Track, Yamuna

Expressway (UP) and Ganga Expressway in Uttar Pradesh are some of the examples of such projects where the cost of project and infrastructure development is part-funded by the award of land rights.

Special Purpose Vehicle (SPV) mechanism is being adopted for integrated city level major infrastructure projects that can be financially viable, but faces difficulties in raising resources. Such projects can be funded through financial SPV having ₹ 10,000 crore for core project like Integrated Transit Corridor, Delhi Mumbai Industrial Corridors (DMIC), roads, highways, water supply, sanitation, public transport, land development, power generation, etc. The government provides support in the form of land, equity contribution, package of concessions, dedicated levies to repay loans and a transparent regulatory framework.

The Concept of White Zoning: As adopted in Singapore, white zoning allows flexibility in land use. Depending upon the feasibility of land use and floor area permissibility, the developer pays the land use and FAR charges. This strengthens the financial base of urban local body to provide services and amenities. The Old City, unplanned areas and major corridors can be taken up for special or white zoning. This way the old, dilapidated areas are renewed and upgraded with a wider participation of the owners and without need for acquisition of virgin, unserviced lands.

The Concept of Transit Oriented Development: Relatively low and uniform Floor Area Ratio (FAR) have distorted urban land market by promoting sprawl, increasing transportation and infrastructure overheads. It is necessary that the FARs are rationalised to permit higher density development in the areas with adequate infrastructure and public transportation capacities, both existing and future. Gains in property values can be recouped for infrastructure development.

Betterment Levy: For the sake of equity and fair distribution of public resources, the concept of betterment levy obliges the land owners to return a part of land value addition or profit that results from public investments. Betterment levies help to finance urban development and public services by the ULB and service agencies.

Transferable Development Right: Transferable Development Right enables the land acquisition for public purpose without monetary compensation, but by way of grant of additional FAR /FSI. This helps in obtaining lands for road widening, new roads, development of parks, playgrounds, civic amenities, etc.

Accommodation Reservation: The Accommodation Reservation is a form of in-situ TDR which allows the land owners to develop the sites reserved for road widening or an amenity in the development plan using full permissible FSI/FAR on the plot. This way the reservations for social housing, parks, utilities, retail markets, dispensaries, etc. are implemented on private lands without the need to acquire the land by payment of compensation (MMRDA, 1996 and BDA, 2007).

Evolving a New Land Policy

Cities witness heterogeneous typologies of land and development for which a uniform approach does not work. The approach should ensure availability of basic transport corridors and services, cause minimum displacement with equity towards small land holders, slums/

squatters and poor. This needs a hybrid land policy that would be a combination of compulsory land acquisition through cash/ alternative land allotment, development rights, FAR/FSI, and Land Pooling & Readjustment. While in contiguous large tracts of lands, land pooling and return may work, for isolated developments and built up areas, in-situ redevelopment can be promoted by grant of development rights, including incentive FAR. The infrastructure development can be financed through the recovery of EDC, conversion charges, FAR charges, Betterment levy, etc. However, to ensure the availability of infrastructure and corridors prior to real estate disposal it is necessary to separate the surrender/ return of land and payment of EDC, Betterment levy, Conversion Charges, FAR Charges, etc. vis-à-vis grant of development right and change of land use. The local authority may have to acquire lands for major services/corridors and amenities by offering return of developed land, development rights (TDR/AR), along with cash compensation and other incentives like jobs. The land owners can be given a choice or a combination of cash compensation, land barter and development right. Flexibility in planning and land management will facilitate innovative solutions, affordability and state of art services and facilities. Better information base, including GIS, computerization of land records and inventory of land, property and other assets are the pre-requisites for implementation of new non-coercive land policy and partnership of land owners in urban process.

Land Pooling and return should go hand in hand which requires creating a land bank. This will enable the service agencies to pre-plan and extend infrastructure services and will facilitate on the spot land return/adjustment.

The proposed hybrid land policy should be based on the following basic premises:

(a) A differentiated approach covering new urban extension areas, built up areas, villages, unauthorized colonies, agricultural green belt, etc.

(b) Legal back up for surrender and return of private lands against FAR and TDR

(c) Separating the surrender/ return of land and payment of EDC, Betterment Levy, Conversion Charges, FAR charges, etc. vis-à-vis grant of development right and change of land use.

(d) Equitable development rights which include village, old city, Special Area, slums, squatters and unauthorized colonies

(e) To ensure availability of roads and basic services with a futuristic perspective while opening up urban extension areas for PPP/real estate sector.

(f) Ensuring planned development by joint approach through rebates as per size of lands.

The justification of additional FAR has to be based up on the principles of TDR/ AR or by surrender of land. Against acquisition of facility corridors, the land owners can have a choice among cash compensation, land barter, development right, etc. Flexibility in planning and land management will facilitate innovative solutions, affordability and state of art services and facilities. Better information base, including GIS, computerization of land records, inventory of land, property and other assets are the pre-requisites for implementation of land policy.

Planning norms, density, FAR, /TDR and AR can open up new avenues for using the land as a resource for urban turnaround through the public private partnership. It is essential to optimise utilization of urban land vis-a-vis Floor Area Ratio and residential density and enhance the land potential. A sustainable urban form depends upon mixed land use, reduction of automobile dependence, efficient supply of open spaces, social and physical infrastructure and revitalization of dilapidated, old areas. The tools of Land Pooling and Readjustment, Transferable Development Rights and land monetisation can be effectively used for state of art, sustainable infrastructure services while promoting private sector participation. A gradual transition is necessary by a hybrid approach integrating government and private sector resources.

The infrastructure services and transportation play a major role in guiding PPP and local planning. A public land bank and planning with a futuristic vision are the pre-requisites to facilitate the provision of infrastructure, transportation corridors and public utilities/ amenities that promote private sector participation. This needs a closer spatial, institutional, financial interaction for planned development of physical and social infrastructure, social housing, public greens and transport networks.

The Betterment levy could be an effective instrument for financing of urban development, particularly for infrastructure services and low income housing.

This needs simultaneous process reforms and management, bridging gap between demand and supply, overcoming delays and cost overruns, time-bound action planning and effective monitoring. Technological interface is necessary with respect to standards and specifications, infrastructure, construction and maintenance vis-a-vis energy and environment concerns. There is a need to adopt new contracting procedures for efficiency, quality of service, delivery and transparency.

To meet the huge urban targets there is no option, but to optimize and synergize the resources of both public and private sectors. Various models of land assembly and public-private partnerships are being implemented in India and other countries which provide important lessons. These experiences make explicit the need to evolve a plural approach and a hybrid land policy that responds to urban variety and ensures development of infrastructure and transport networks prior to real estate disposal. In order to harness the advantages of both the government and private sectors a gradual transition by a hybrid approach can integrate best of the two worlds.

Implementation and Regulatory Process

The private sector participation in land assembly and its development involves various regulatory functions, such as given below:

- Working out the rules, regulations, procedures and guidelines, grant of licenses for land pooling in real estate, infrastructure development, redevelopment, housing, etc.
- Spatial Data Infrastructure (SDI) /computerization of land records, on-line, one window approval of plans.
- Compulsory acquisition of land which effect the composite and land assembly, planning and infrastructure development
- Procedures for grant/revoke of licenses, approvals and planning permissions.
- Model agreement and MOU with land owners for land pooling, preparation and approval of the plans of land pooling/assembly and land return.

- Issue of Transfer of Development Right and Accommodation Reservation Certificates.
- Enforcement and monitoring of regulation for private /PPP developer, housing and service agencies, etc. including progress of work and financial transactions.
- Regulations/procedures to oversee the compliance of the legal, administrative and financial commitments.
- Financing and accounting procedures for private sector developer/partner.
- Procedures to deal with appeals, grievances and complaints.

The land policy needs simultaneous process reforms for better control over resources, bridging the gap between demand and supply, overcoming delays and cost overruns, time-bound planning and effective monitoring. Technological interface vis-a-vis energy, water and environment with reference to standards and specifications, infrastructure, construction, maintenance is a major consideration. There is a need to adopt new contracting procedures for efficiency, quality of service, delivery and transparency. The following chart gives a list of the actionable tasks.

Table 11.3: Land Management Tasks

Tasks	Specific Actions
a) Advanced and coordinated development of transport networks, main roads, infrastructure services, etc.	• Availability of land for transport and service networks/corridors. • Service agencies should prepare plans of land requirement and its acquisition and allotment. • Preparation of detailed plans. • Preparation of Service Plans with service agencies • Preparation of DPR for PPP projects, • Work programming of agencies responsible for land management, maintenance engineering, planning, and utilities. • Preparation of a land information system, digitise land data/ ownership details land management program, land regulation and transfer, etc • Working out External and Internal development cost/estimates and. financing structure/sources. • Action Plan combining plan funds, EDC, betterment levy, etc.
b) Acquisition of land for development of public, social and government uses/ facilities.	• Availability of land under utility/grid/road/services corridors • Funding-development charges, EDC, Betterment levy. • Planning and development of Facilities Corridors and public open spaces. • Launching land pooling/ adjustment/return projects.
c) Immediate transfer/ return of land holdings to the land pool participants and its registration	• Publication of areawise plans and program for land pooling and development. • Government land bank for spot exchange/adjustment of land with land poolers • Notification for compulsory acquisition of all land under facility corridors/ Master Plan Roads and of those not participating in land pooling • Promotion, persuasion and information sharing on web (planning, land, infrastructure, finances, etc.). • Land management/acquisition option under TDR and Reservations. • Launch Land Pooling/Return projects.

a) Timely and orderly planning of land into roads, facilities, open space and building plots (with title documents) and grant of planning permission	• Monitoring of demand, and supply of housing areas/units. • Subdivision regulations linked to the land use zoning. • Efficient administration of development regulations, planning permission, TDR/AR, and Land Banking • SDI/digitised land/property information. • Online/one window planning permission.
b) Increased supply of low-cost housing and redevelopment & redensification of existing urban zones	• Implementing Redevelopment Guidelines, promoting TOD, taking up pilot projects. • Grant of ownership to eligible /repolarised households in slums, unauthorised colonies, etc. on the basis of clusters of 2000 to 4000 sq.m which can be voluntarily taken up for redevelopment into a composite group housing with enhanced FAR of 400 with one-third of area as a soft parking/common greens, schools, etc. and 10% of FAR for commercial activities • Encouraging private lands to redevelop and infill development • Allocating share of land from land pooling projects for social housing. • In-situ upgrading slum and squatter settlements
c) Coordinated and speedy development	• Time lines, Action programmes, quality control and monitoring. • Streamlining approval procedures • Financing Plan and management • Building Materials, Codes and Specifications. • Category-wise pre-selection of the experts/ consultants/ contractors for award of work on pre-determined approved rates, without the need of time consuming tendering, EOI, etc for each project. • Timely recovery of development, conversion, FAR, Betterment Levy, Service charges, etc. • To assist PPP/ RWA/ Community to take up social housing, Redevelopment, Regularization of illegal settlements, conferring land titles/registration/ licenses.

Source: Jain A.K., 2014, Revisiting Land Acquisition and Urban Process, Readworthy Publishers, New Delhi

The partnership strategy may not succeed without complimentary organisational innovation and reforms. Reforms have to be viewed in context of promoting planned development by way of partnerships and privatisation while ensuring sustainable and inclusive urban development. This needs a hybrid, regulatory framework and an urban planning system that integrates the physical, economic, and social development. There is a need to revisit the existing procedures, development control norms and space standards keeping in view the growing economy, land crunch, and changing needs of the people. To fit in the new land policy and PPP framework, it is necessary to streamline and simplify the regulatory framework as a single window system. In order to respond effectively and efficiently to the demands of PPP regime in land, housing, redevelopment and infrastructure development, it may be necessary to constitute a 'Special Purpose Vehicle' in the ULBs/ Development Authorities and infrastructure agencies.

How effectively, speedily and judiciously, the matters of licensing, approvals, regulation and enforcement can be handled is a critical issue in the new scenario. Real Estate (Regulation of Development) Act enables the setting up of an Urban Regulatory and Appellate Authority to regulate the process of land and property development, infrastructure development, redevelopment, housing, etc. and to oversee the compliance of the legal, administrative and financial commitments.

Debriefing and Review

1. Explain the links between urban land policy and urban development.
2. Write a note on the Right to Fair Compensation and Transparency in Land Acquisition, Rehabilitation and Resettlement Act, 2013. How it compares with the Land Acquisition Act of 1894?
3. Explain the process of Town Planning Scheme for land consolidation and planned development.
4. What are the basic parameters and salient features of land pooling scheme?
5. What are the models of private sector participation in urban land assembly and development in India. Highlight the issues involved.
6. What regulatory systems are necessary for land pooling and private sector participation in land assembly and development?

CHAPTER 12

Planning a Safer and Resilient City

Climate is a changing phenomenon of heat, temperature, radiation, sunlight, humidity, rain precipitation, wind, greenhouse gases, bio-geo-chemical cycles, etc., which are transferred over the land surface. Climate change has become an imminent reality with a rise in global temperature, changes in rainfall, floods, droughts and intense heat waves. These are witnessed in India since last few years. A drastic increase in atmospheric concentrations of water vapours, carbon-dioxide, methane and nitro-oxide, and other greenhouse gases help trap heat near the earth's surface.

With increasing vehicular and industrial emissions, fossil fuel usage and urban growth, coupled with growing air conditioning demand, it is projected that the urban heat can increase by 4°C. The population's health and productivity will be affected by high ambient summer temperatures. In such circumstances, action to reduce the climate change effect must become a priority.

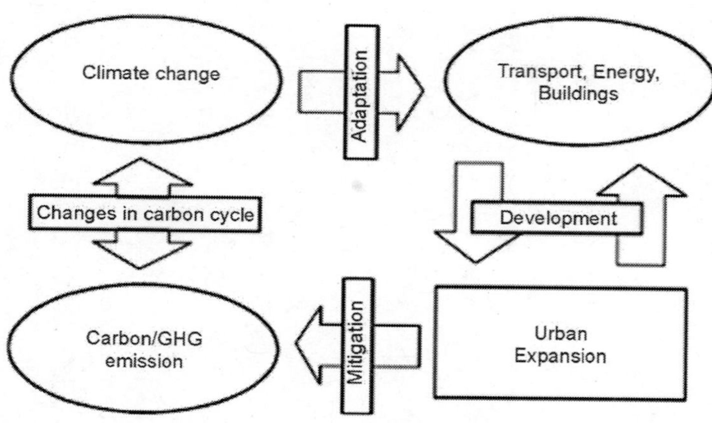

Fig. 12.1: Vicious Cycle of Climate Change

Source: UN Habitat

The SDG 11 aims to make human settlements inclusive, safe, resilient and sustainable. Also, the SDG 13 aims to take urgent action to combat climate change and its impact.

Inclusive and sustainable habitat implies decoupling natural resource use and environmental impacts from economic growth. Low carbon habitat can mitigate GHG emission and also adapt to the impact of climate change. Mitigation of and adaptation to climate change imply new ways of habitat planning and applications of new technologies and systems for energy, construction, infrastructure development and transport.

Urbanisation and Climate Change

India's urbanisation and economic development are changing the lifestyles of its people. Increasing production, mobility, consumption and living in comfort are enhancing the carbon emissions and climate change. Models predict an average increase in temperature of 2.3 to 4.8°C in India for the benchmark doubling of carbon dioxide scenario. Although per capita carbon emissions in India at 1.2 metric tons (mt) per year is one of the lowest in the world, which is predicted to become double within next 10 years. Already in the urban areas the people with cars and air conditioners emit 4.5 mt of carbon dioxide/greenhouse gases per year, while the low income people without car and air conditioners, emit an average of 1.1 mt of CO_2/GH gases. As per UN Climate Change Panel, a benchmark of 3.0 mt per capita per year should be the upper limit.

India with more than 1210 million people, 3.3 million sq. km of area, 29 States, 7 Union Territories having 671 districts, 7936 cities and towns, and 6,41,000 odd villages, is vulnerable to droughts, floods, cyclones and earthquakes. Landslides, avalanche and forest fires also occur frequently. Among the 36 States/Union Territories in the country, 22 are multi-disaster prone. As much as 40 million hectare of land in the country has been identified as flood prone, and on an average 18.6 million hectare of land is flooded annually. About 57% of area of the country is vulnerable to seismic activity. 18% of country's total area and about 68% of total sown area is drought prone, affecting approximately 50 million people. India has a long coastline of 8040 km, which is exposed to tropical cyclones and tsunami.

Devastating floods, typhoons and a series of hurricanes are being associated with climate change. According to the initial report of the United Nations Framework on the Convention on Climate Change, the predicted impacts of climate change in India include a surface air temperature rise up to 4° Celsius by 2100, up to 30% decline in agriculture yield in rain-fed areas and an increase in incidences of extreme events, such as droughts, floods, cyclones, urban heat islands, earthquakes and changes in microclimate due to shortwave radiant energy from the sun and long-wave radiant energy exchange between the surface and the atmosphere.

Urban Heat Island (UHI)

UHI is a phenomenon where certain urban area is significantly warmer than its surrounding areas. The temperature difference usually is larger at night than during the day, and is most apparent when winds are weak. The main cause of the urban heat island is modification of the land surface by urban development, using materials which effectively retain heat and waste heat generated by transport and energy usage. As a result, there is a corresponding increase in average temperature, which is hotter than the surrounding area.

There are several causes of an urban heat island (UHI), as given below:

- The principal reason for the night time warming is due to building's surface heat radiating into the relatively cold night sky.
- The rapid rate of urbanisation, increasing concrete surface area, less green patch, dark colour roof tops.
- The urban sprawl, road building, and high and medium-rise expansions.
- Surface radiative properties (albedo and emissivity) in the highly concrete core urban areas cause a change in the energy balance, leading to higher temperatures than surrounding rural areas.
- Lack of vegetation of urban areas, which inhibits cooling by evapo-transpiration.
- The tall buildings within urban areas provide multiple surfaces for the reflection and absorption of sunlight, increasing the heat and the "urban canyon effect".
- The blocking of wind by the buildings inhibits cooling by convection.
- Waste heat from automobiles, air conditioning, industry, and other sources, pollution in urban areas also increase the UHI.

UHIs can affect local meteorology, including the altering of local wind patterns, the development of clouds and fog, the humidity, and the rates of precipitation, shower and thunderstorms. Rainfall rates downwind of cities become irregular and increase as compared to upwind.

Some practical and simple measures that can be adopted are the following:

- Replace high radiation absorbing surfaces such as dark roofs, asphalt streets and parking lots with highly reflecting materials.
- Adopt passive design to minimise energy use, including space heating, cooling and cooking, utilize higher efficiency air conditioning systems, industrial processes, and transportation systems that produce less anthropogenic heat,
- Inclusion of green space, city forests, better spaced buildings and better public transportation, including non-motorised transport.
- Landscape development, green cover and green buildings. Landscape development includes plantation, trees, vegetation, maintaining drainage slopes and channels of wind flow, ensuring the soil conditions, especially porosity to permit absorption of water by avoiding unnecessary paving and roads.

These measures can bridge the gap between adaptation and mitigation that avoid urban heat island syndrome and making the habitat more comfortable.

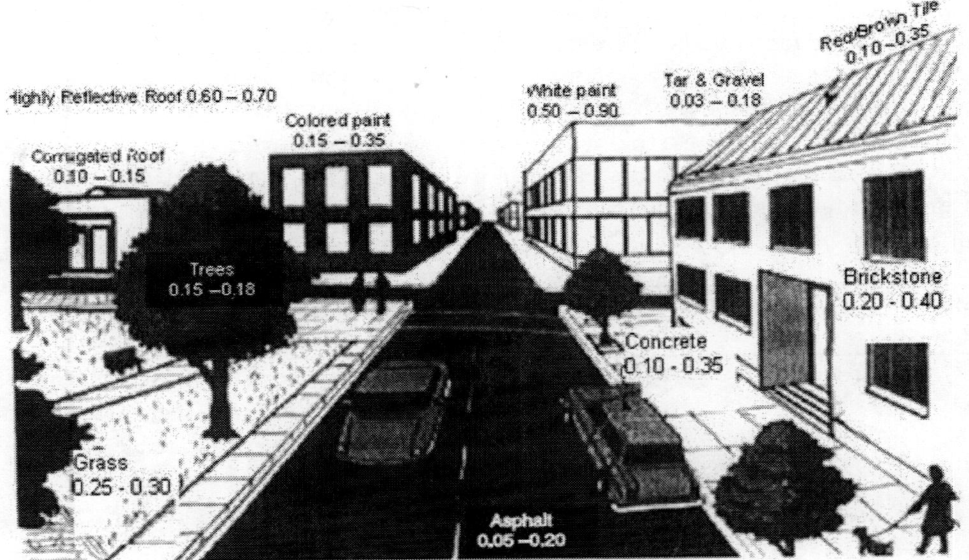

Fig. 12.2: Albedo and Heat Island Effect: As a city grows, new factors modify the local climate and have a complex character consisting of a mosaic of different surface materials. Each surface material has a different albedo, a measure of the amount of solar radiation reflected back into space. For a city as a whole the albedo can be as low as 10-15%, which means that a lot of the incoming solar radiation is absorbed by the city. Additionally, most of the building materials used in the construction are characterized by a high heat capacity and high heat conductivity. Increased heat enhances photochemical reactions, which increases the particles in the air and thus contributes to the formation of smog and clouds. Urban heat islands also impact local weather, altering local wind patterns, spurring the development of clouds and fog, increasing the number of lightning strikes, and influencing the rates of precipitation.

Source: http:yosemite.epa.gov.oar/globalwarming.nsf/co

According to the Indian Network for Climate Change Assessment (2010), 58 per cent of the total emissions in 2007 were caused by the energy sector, followed by the industrial sector at 22 per cent, agriculture at 17 per cent, waste at 3 per cent, land use change and forestry at 1 per cent. Of the total carbon dioxide (CO_2) emissions 85% were contributed by activities of the energy sector. Of the total methane CH_4 and nitrous oxide NO_2 emissions 78% were due to the agriculture sector.

Climate change can bring considerable changes in the hazard profile of the region by changing the type of hazards, changing the hazard intensities, magnitude and frequency. Many of these impacts may not be uniform across spatial and temporal scales. Deviating floods in Bangladesh, India, Nepal and Pakistan, typhoons in Philippines and a series of hurricanes in Florida are being associated with climate change.

Without the so-called greenhouse gases, including carbon dioxide, methane, nitrous oxide, and water vapour, earth would be too cold to inhabit. These gases in earth's atmosphere absorb and emit heat energy, creating the greenhouse effect that keeps our planet's temperature liveable.Water vapour is the most plentiful greenhouse gas on the planet, accounting for about 60 percent of the current greenhouse effect. Even ozone helps trap some of the heat that makes life on Earth possible, but the 'ozone hole' is a separate issue not directly related to global warming.Since the industrial revolution, people have burned vast amounts of coal, petroleum, and other fossil fuels to create heat and power. This releases carbon dioxide, the most plentiful human-produced greenhouse gas, into the atmosphere. As a result more heat is trapped in earth's atmosphere instead of radiating out into space.

The relationship between earth's water cycle and global warming creates a well-known feedback loop. Warmer temperatures cause more evaporation from land and oceans, which produces more water vapour, which in turn contributes to warmer temperatures.

Table 12.1: Climatic Change, Possible and Potential Impacts on Cities

Climate change	Impact	Urban Planning Consequences
Increased Temperatures	Depletion of Ground water Water Shortage Drought Degraded air Quality(smog)	Distress migration to cities/towns due to droughts in rural areas Interruption of food supply networks and higher food prices Potential energy price increases (e.g., from reduced hydro-electricity generation in places where it exists) Exaggerated urban heat island effect Increased energy demands for cooling Need for higher and/or additional wastewater treatment Population health impacts (e.g., increased mortality during heat waves, decreased access to food/nutrition)
Increased precipitation	Increased risk of land slides or mud slides on hazard slopes	Interruption of food supply networks Property damage (homes and businesses) Disruption of livelihoods and city/town economies Damage to infrastructure not designed to standards of occurrences being experienced in urban and rural areas Displacement and population movement from informal settlements built on steep slope, hazard lands, etc. More favorable breeding grounds for pathogens (e.g., mosquitoes and malaria) Population health impacts (increased incidences of water-borne diseases like cholera)
Sea-level rise.	Coastal flooding Salt water intrusion into groundwater supplies in coastal area increased storm surge hazard	Displacement and population movement from property damage (homes and businesses) Damage to infrastructure not designed to standards of occurrences being experienced Increased storm disruption of livelihoods and urban economies, population health impacts (injuries, increased mortality and illness)Property damage (homes and businesses) Damage to infrastructure not designed to standards of occurrences being experienced Population health impacts (injuries, increased mortality, distress) Interruption of food supply networks Increased risk of landslides or mudslides on hazard slopes

Source: Adapted from Developing Local Climate Change Plans, UN-HABITAT/International Institute for Environment & Development (2010).

Climate change has a variety of potential implications for urban areas. In terms of exposure, a key risk relates to changes in the frequency and intensity of heavy rain, storms, droughts, heat waves, wild fire and other hazard events. The urban centers more at risk are those where these events are already widespread.

Table 12.2: Projected impacts on urban areas of changes in extreme weather and climate events

Climate phenomena and their likelihood	Major projected impacts
Warmer and fewer cold days and nights Warmer and more frequent hot days and nights over most land areas Warmer temperatures	Reduced energy demand for heating Increased demand for cooling Declining air quality in cities Reduced disruption to transport due to snow, ice effects on winter tourism Changes in permafrost, damages to buildings and infrastructures
Warm spells/heat waves. Frequency increases over most land areas	Reduction in quality of life for people in warm areas without air conditioning; Impacts on elderly, very young and poor including significant loss of human life Increases in energy usage for air conditioning
Heavy precipitation events, frequency increases over most areas	Disruption of settlements, commerce, transport and societies due to flooding Pressures on infrastructures, potentials for use of rain in hydropower generation Significant loss of human life, injuries; loss of and damage to property
Areas affected by drought increases	Water shortages for households, industries and services Reduced hydropower generation potential Potential for population migration
Intense tropical cyclone activity increases	Disruption by flood and high winds; Disruption of public water supply Withdrawal of risk coverage in vulnerable areas by private insurer (at least in high income countries) Significant loss of human life, injuries; loss of and damage to property Potentials for population migration
Increased incidence of extreme high sea level (excludes tsunamis)	Costs of coastal protection *versus* costs of land-use relocation; Decreased freshwater availability due to salt –water intrusion Significant loss of human life, injuries; loss of and damage to property Potential for movement of population and infrastructure

Source: IPCC 2007 with modifications.

The Quest for Sustainable Habitat

The pursuit of sustainable development requires striking a balance between economic goals, human needs (social, cultural, livability and health) and environmental integrity. This involves a process of effective citizen participation in decision-making. An economic system that is self-reliant and securing ecological basis for development are the prerequisites of sustainable development. We need to relook at the fundamentals of human settlements and evolve a sustainable system whereby harmony and interrelationship between nature and life can be re-established.

Sustainable development is basically a concern of 'design with nature'. It means development and human interventions in natural system to the extent of carrying capacity of an area. The carrying capacity of an area is the population or level of activity that can be sustained for a given length of time without depletion of the resources or breakdown of the biological natural systems.

Sustainability is a subject which concerns everyone and cuts across various activities, disciplines and levels. It is thus an all embracing and complex agenda to plan for. Although disaggregated for analytical purpose, the ecology, landscape and cultural processes need to be tackled in an integrated manner by sustainable planning and development.

The challenge of urban planning is to identify the effects of environmental problems in terms of health effects, productivity amenity, ecological values, and other key indicators and develop policy directions and plan which address these issues.

Table 12.3: Policy Responses Integrating Ecosystem Services

	Policy directions	Examples of potential responses
1.	Renewable energy to reduce dependence on non-renewable sources	• Community energy systems in Freiburg (Germany) and travel management in Calgory (Canada)
2.	Carbon-neutral cities to cut and offset carbon emissions	• Zero–carbon housing in Denmark • Urban woodlands in Sacremento (USA)
3.	Small–scale, distributed power and water systems with more energy-efficient service provision	• Water sensitive design that uses the complete water cycle in Hanoi (Vietnam) • Waste water agro-systems in Kolkata (India) • Local power systems and cooperatives in Malmo (Sweden)
4.	Increasing photosynthetic spaces as part of green infrastructure development to expand renewable sources of energy and local food	• Local food provision in Devon (UK) • Biomass in Vaxjo (Sweden) • Green roofs and materials in Shanghai (China)
5.	Eco–efficiency to enable the use of waste products to satisfy urban energy and material resource needs	• Industries reduce waste and resource requirements by sharing waste and resources in Kalundborg (Denmark)

6.	Local strategies that increase 'pride in place' by enhancing the implementation and effectiveness of innovations.	• Ambitious recycling targets in Cairo (Egypt) • Maximising urban densities in Hammarby Sjostad (Sweden)
7.	Sustainable transport that reduces the adverse impacts of dependence on fossil fuels.	• Participatory systems that localize energy, food, materials and local production in Medeilin (Colombia) • Planning systems that capture the value of ecosystem services and creating a 'local sustainability currency' in Curitiba (Brazil) • Urban form and density in Vancouver (Canada) Transit systems in London (UK) • Street planning and mobility management in Tokyo (Japan)
8.	Development of 'cities without slums' to improve access to safe drinking water, sanitation and reduced environmental degradation.	• Respecting community structure in slum resettlement in Kampung (Indonesia) • Planning for the informal economy in Somalia (UN–Habitat initiative)

Source: Adapted from UN-HABITAT (2009)

Renewable Energy and Efficiency

The power demands in cities are growing exponentially, generation of which emits about one-fourth of carbon footprint. This needs action to reduce the power demand, and resorting to energy efficiency. Load management techniques should be adopted and schemes to minimise power losses should be enforced. Renewable energy sources like solar/wind energy needs mandatory incentives and instruments. Cooling, heating and lighting often account for bulk of the electrical consumption, which can be reduced by adopting energy efficiency practices, such as:

- Incorporating daylight design in all the buildings on a mandatory basis
- Adoption of energy efficient practices by regulation and energy labeling of lighting, air-conditioning, air-cooling products, building glass, and imposition of minimum efficiency of lighting and electrical installations.
- Utilisation of heat reflective insulation on the roofs
- Use of renewable sources of energy
- Use of technology which would consume minimum energy to maintain desired human comfort conditions. For example, replacement of bulbs by fluorescent lamps/CFLs may bring in substantial savings in electrical consumption.
- Adoption of alternative cooling and air-conditioning systems, such as passive evaporative cooling micronisers (PECM), passive downdraft evaporative cooling (PDEC), earth air tunnel, shafts and courtyards for natural cooling and ventilation.

India is endowed with abundance of sun. However, its potential in producing energy is still to be explored. In a cloudless region roof area of 100 sq. mt receives about 500 KW per day from eight hours of sunshine. In the hot-arid regions (the greatest solar radiation intensity occurs between latitudes 15 and 35 degree north or south) more than 3,000 hours of solar radiation could be obtained and even in the warm-humid region there are about 2300 hours of solar variation. Where there is a lack of conventional materials such as coal, oil, or gas, it is that use is made of the solar energy which is generally abundant in India. Solar water heating for domestic hot water or as part of a home heating scheme has become more widely used in some countries as a response to the energy and environment crisis. As solar energy is initially captured in the form of heat, it is therefore best use of a variety of heating purposes. Solar water heaters (e.g. for canteens, schools, homes and hotels), solar steam cookers and water distillation units provide examples of practical applications of solar energy. It is time that solar energy is made mandatory for cooking in the establishments (hotels, restaurants, railway stations, langars, religious centers, etc) wherever more than 3000 meals are cooked per day. This has already been successfully adopted in the Brahmkumaris headquarters at Mount Abu in Rajasthan, Auroville, Akshardham temple in New Delhi and Sai Baba Sansthan in Shirdi.

Photovoltaic power generating systems can be used in remote electric supplies for water pumps, electric fences, communications and navigation equipment; stand-alone power systems for consumer products like computers, radios, walkway lighting and auto-battery chargers. These are already in practical use, which need to be taken further as a movement.

Wind power, which is inexhaustible and non-polluting, is a promising way out of the energy crisis. The grouping of large windmills is capable of generating 10,000 or more kilowatts of electric power. Already new type of vertical-axis wind turbines have been designed and installed in various parts of the country, which are producing electrical energy, being utilised for grinding and to pump water. They are cheaper and far more efficient than the traditional horizontal-axis wind mills.

Emissions and City Form

Urban centres in low-income countries have lower levels of emissions per capita than cities in high-income countries. In fact carbon emissions per capita in cities from high-income countries are often much higher when compared to emissions in the cities of developing countries. Houston, Texas, and the District of Columbia, for instance, have carbon emissions that are 19-20 fold as high as those in Mumbai, Delhi and Kolkata. Yet, other wealthy cities such as Stockholm and Barcelona have lower levels of emissions per capita than some South African cities. Why is this so? Several inter-related factors shape or determine the patterns of energy use and emissions by different populations and sectors.

According to the studies, the size, growth, structure and density of population are key determinants of cities' carbon emissions and other environmental impacts. A negative correlation exists between population density and atmospheric emissions; for instance one percent increase in the density of urban areas would relate to approximately 0.7 percent decline in CO pollution at the city-level, with other factors held constant. Spatially compact and mixed-use urban developments have different benefits in terms of carbon emissions:

1. Reduced costs for heating and cooling resulting from smaller homes and shared walls in multi-unit dwellings. For instance, households in buildings with five or more units consume 38 per cent of the energy of households in single-family homes.
2. The use of energy systems covering a broader area (e.g. district) for cooling, heating and power generation as well as lesser line losses related to electricity transmission and distribution. The use of micro-grids to meet local requirements of electricity can create efficiencies in storage and distribution.
3. Reduced average daily vehicle-kilometres travelled (VKT) in freight deliveries and by private motor vehicles per capita. Population density increases accessibility to such destinations as stores, employment centres and theatres. It has been found that with all other variables constant except density, the household in a neighbourhood, with 1,000 fewer units per square mile drives almost 1,200 miles more and consumes 65 more gallons of fuel per year over a household in a higher density neighbourhood.

A basic need is to create a sustainable urban structure, comprising modules of local hub/ neighbourhood, community and district/zones, which allows a compact form with mixed land use with the following mandate:

- Integrated planning of land use and public transport
- Reorganisation of land use and rationalisation of density, urban restructuring for travel reduction.
- Integration of bus, MRTS, metro rail, rail corridor, cycles, walking, stations and terminals, integrated traffic and transit operation, control and management, and using subterranean space for transport and parking.
- Telecommunication, electronic mail, video conferencing, radio paging, mobile phones, computer networking, e-mail for participatory e-governance to save travel.

The spatial model impacts the sustainability (less travel time and thus energy saving). A compact city structure should be developed to achieve the following:

- Urban Form: (i) High dense settlements (ii) Less dependence on automobile (high density) (iii) Clear boundary from surrounding areas;
- Spatial Characteristics: (i) Social fairness (high dense settlements) (ii) Self-sufficiency of daily life (iii) Independence of government (clear boundary); and,
- Social Functions: There is close relationship between compact urban form and the sustainability by reduction of automobile dependence, efficient supply of social infrastructure and public services, active community relationship by high-dense habitation, and revitalization of inner city.

Compact cities can have significant implications to climate change and environment. Critical instruments for this policy option include coordination with public transport, infrastructure development, mixed land use, urban boundary and coordination of different levels of government. Data from international cities indicates correlation of urban density with less transport energy use and car use per capita. Smart growth land use practices aim to create more accessible land use patterns, which reduce the amount of travel needed to reach goods and services.

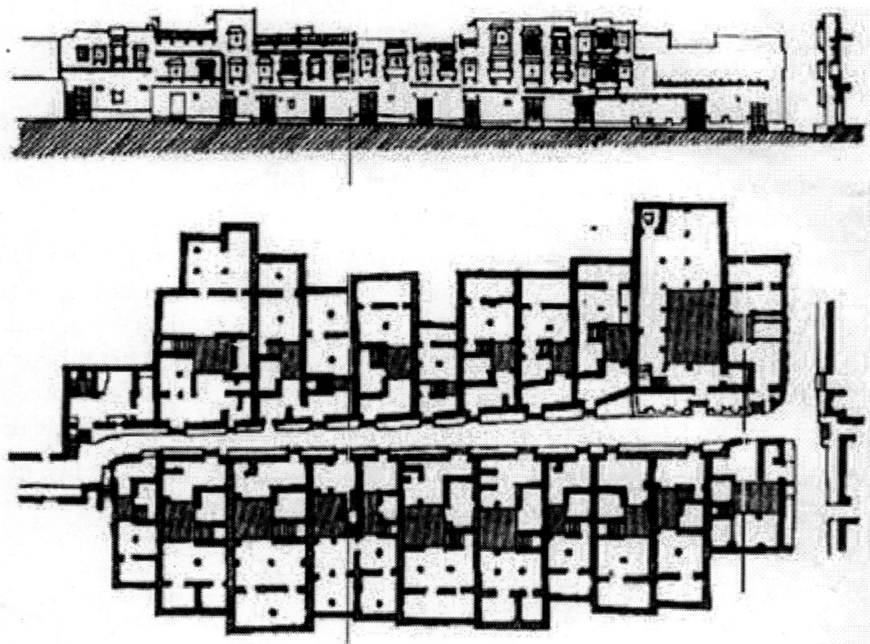

Fig. 12:3 Jaisalmer: Typical residential street-compact, walkable, high density and low energy urban form (after Kulbhushan Jain)

Travel and transport demand can be reduced by mixed land use and better synergy among public transport, walking, NMTs, urban structure (form, density and floor area ratio) and by transit oriented development. An important element of policy should aim to shift private vehicle users to public transport. Apart from aspects like frequency, inter-modal integration, a possible single ticketing systems, the quality of public transport, particularly buses, would need to be significantly upgraded, inter-alia, keeping in view the element of clean and green fuel and traffic calming. Organisation of land use, circulation pattern and decisions regarding density, Floor Area Ratio and other controls should be around the Public Transport System, which reduce toe need of personal vehicles and transport. The spatial model should be based upon the principle of "less travel, more energy savings." As such, a compact development can significantly help in saving fossil fuel consumption, climate change and environment. Critical instruments for more accessible urban pattern include synergy with public transport, infrastructure development, mixed land use and e-governance, which reduce the need to travel. A least-cost life cycle analysis of urban mobility options and transportation systems across arrange of carriageways and modes should establish an optimum long term mix. A mix of pedestrians, bicycles people movers, hyper- trams, hyper-buses and ferries provides safer, faster and cheaper mobility than the personal car. This call for replanning of urban form which promotes walkability and NMTs and curtail the need to travel. Transport policy and plans linked to pollution control, including noise, should be part of a City Plan. Providing a barrier free environment is a mandatory requirement for outdoor and indoor environment.

Although disaggregated for analytical purpose, the ecology, landscape and cultural processes need to be tackled in an integrated manner by sustainable planning and development.

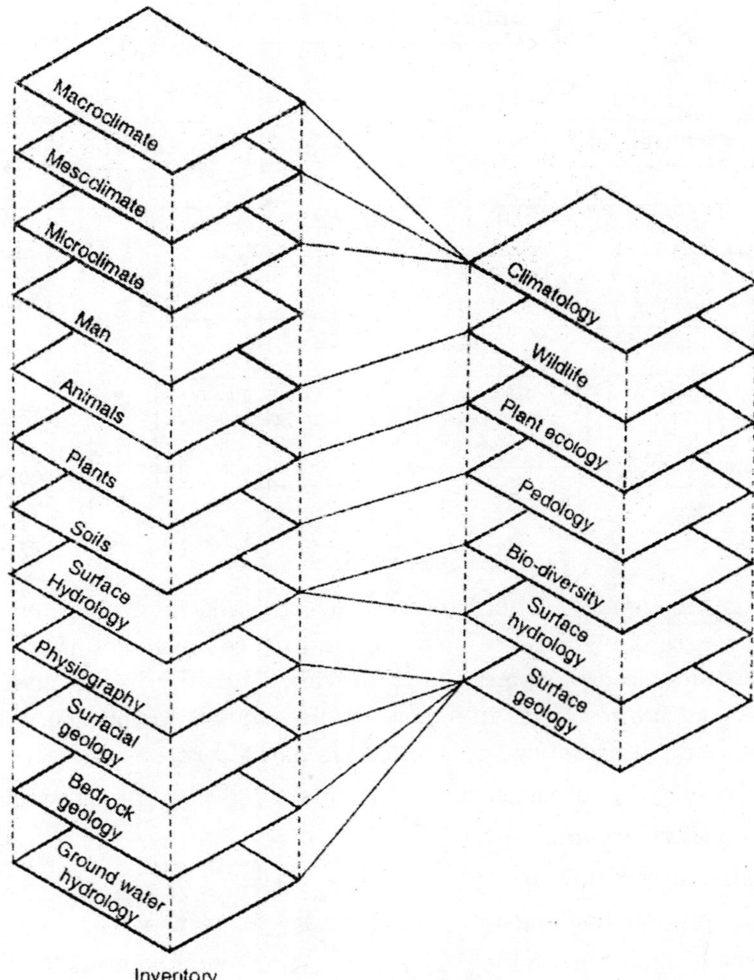

Fig 12.4: Layer cake representation of the phenomena of ecology, landscape and cultural processes

The physical context, i.e.geography, geology, hydrology, vegetation and climate form the foundation of land use and intensity of activity in a particular site. The urban process including consumption, food production, energy and waste management should embody the principle of circular metabolism and recycling, which ensures the integrity of the five elements of the nature.

The cities of India have a rich and diverse environment, derived from their natural and historic character. The environment is a product of past and the present, which is impacted by the urban demographic changes, consumption and emissions. Urban environment components can be categorized as shown below:

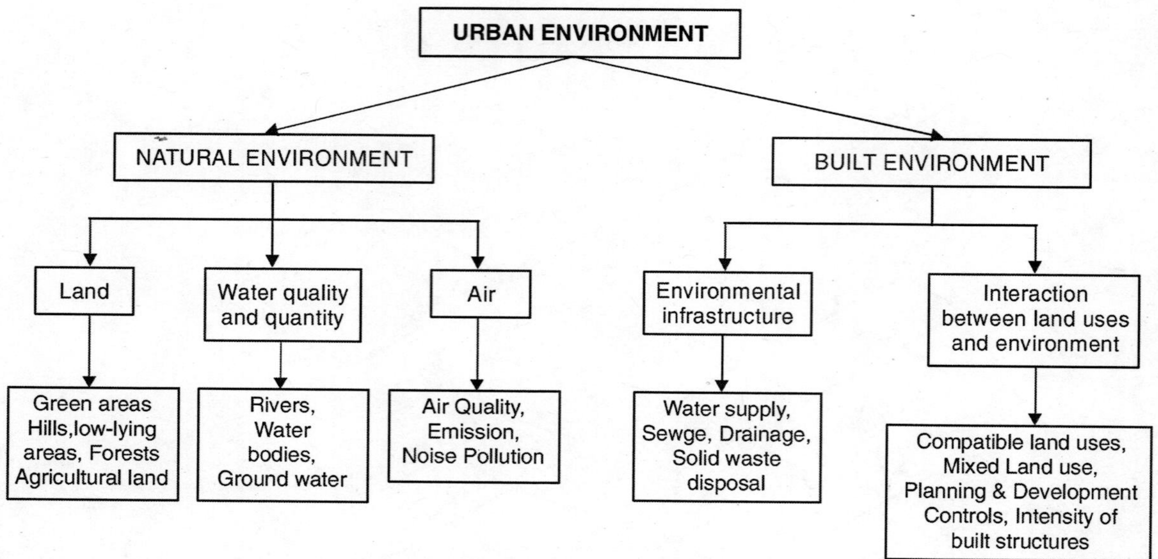

Fig. 12.5: Urban Environment

Urban population in India continues to grow, which leads to pressure on environmental resources, cause resource depletion and pollution and hence adversely affect human health. The objective of sustainable development is to provide a healthy living environment to the citizens, and to manage the resources in a sustainable manner. Major issues that have to be tackled in the environmental management plan are as follows:

- Conservation of green areas, fertile land, forests, geology and hydrology
- Rejuvenation of rivers and water bodies
- Ground water augmentation
- Pollution prevention and control (water, air, noise, transport)
- Management of pollution sources (industries, transport, households)
- Provision of efficient environmental infrastructure (solid waste, water supply, energy, sewage, sanitation, etc.)
- Provision of compatible mixed land uses

As such, an environmental management plan covers the aspects of air, noise, surface water, ground water and green spaces. Each aspect needs an integrated, community action.

Attributes and Components of Disaster Resilience

The following six components have been identified the disaster resilience:

1. Robustness

- Continuity in designated functions besides a level of perturbation and disruption
- Clustering of services to avoid cascading failure
- Contingency terms and inclusion of community

- Safety parameters-accessibility, evacuation planning
- Compliance of Development Controls, regulations and building bye-laws
- Resources and team deployment operation of disaster management centres
- Training program for livelihood recovery, inclusion of marginalized groups
- Community leadership and incentives to adopt risk reduction measures

2. Redundancy

- Heterogeneity/diversity in resources for uncertain and unpredictable conditions
- Ability of horizontal restructuring to avoid delays
- Synchronization in distributed actions
- Back up in service provisions, transport and other infrastructural services
- Segmentation in communication technology
- Role of institutions in recognizing new agents.

3. Resourcefulness

- Reprioritization, generation and distribution of resources
- Availability and accessibility of resources
- Efficiency of safety nets for support during no income period
- Investments for structural reforms
- Sharing of technical information with the community
- Role of social capital and community partnership
- Efficiency of collective action from the community.

4. Reformability

- Horizontal and vertical integration for avoidance of time delays
- Single window clearance for continuity in operation of services
- Flexibility and adaptability to change usage, activity and location
- Role rotation in planning and operations are efficient
- Acceptance of new and emerging modes of recovery

5. Recoverability

- Distribution of roles and resources for efficient recovery
- Capacity to include diverse actors for recovery
- Capacity building program for self-organization and recovery
- Cities and Climate Change
- Efficiency of risk transfer mechanism/insurance/catastrophic bonds
- Accessibility and disbursement of funds to the affected communities
- Emergency operation centers and available logistics
- Adaptability and learning capacity of communities.

6. Rapidity

- Efficiency of immediate response on self-help basis
- Efficiency of emergency responses for collective action
- Readiness of institutional framework
- Emergency and evacuation warning system
- Efficiency of contingency funds.

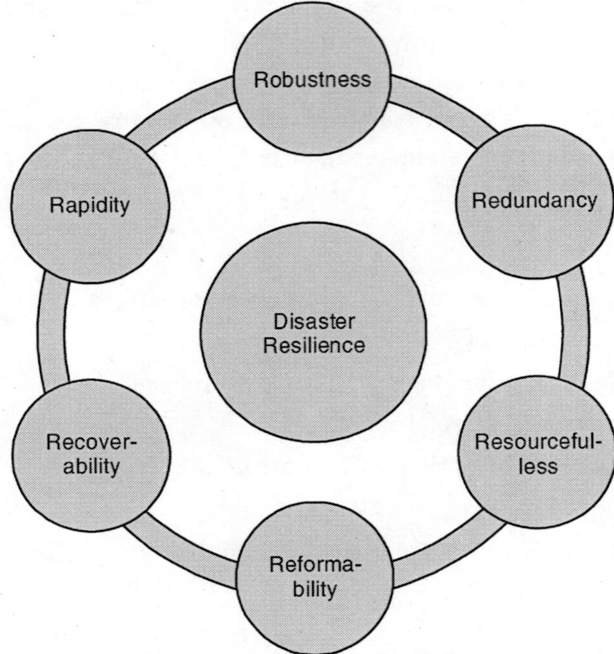

Fig. 12.6: 6 Rs of Disaster Resilience

Sources: James Smart, (2012), the Role of Post Disaster Institutions in Recovery and resilience-A Comparative Study of Three Disasters-Victorian Bushfire (2009), Queensland Floods (2010-11) and Canterbury Earthquake (2010-12),Institute of Governance and Policy Studies, Victoria University, Wellington and Malhotra, Nirmita, (2013), Disaster Resilience, Architecture-Time Space and People, Journal of Council of Architecture, New Delhi.

Habitat Design Code

Recognizing the fact that human life, the built form, climate and environment are inextricably inter-linked, a habitat design code, comprising the following can be evolved:

(a) Spatio-Gravitational Context

- City structure commensurate with the dynamics of growth, decentralization of activities, economy of scale and better quality of life.
- Higher level of mixed land use, density and compact urban form based on environmental performance criteria.

- A coherent urban form, place-making, controlled street-scape, enveloping of inner city land marks, nodes, pedestrian precincts, chowks and squares.
- Wider variety and inter-mixing of socio-cultural activities, relationship of commecial and public activities with public transportation.
- Prioritise brownfield redevelopment, services, traffic and housing improvements rather than the greenfield.
- Built form consistent with historical, socio-cultural context and particular potential of an area/region.
- Exclusion of environment endangering landuses.

(b) **Local Economic Promotion and Poverty Reduction:** In order to address the needs of the majority of the people, that is poor, a major focus area has to be local economic promotion and poverty reduction. Among young people there is a widespread perception that the future holds nothing for them. As a result, a large number of the unemployed are forced to take on informal, illegal or uncertain jobs, and entrepreneurial potential and development opportunities lie untapped. The economic development stagnates, while the vicious circle of poverty perpetuates. As such, there is an urgent need to focus on the local and regional economy of the city, facilitating micro and small business and attracting investments that provides jobs and reduces poverty. At least 10 per cent of commercial area/shops be reserved for the informal sector (street vendors, food, fruit and vegetable stalls, etc.).

(c) **Energy:** The concept of energy efficiency, renewable energy and Zero-fossil Energy Development (ZED) can reduce the level of energy demand and slow down the rate at which resources are depleted. Energy efficiency involves a synergy of the various levels of planning, design, construction and maintenance, leading to a sustainable and energy efficient regime. The renewable energy not only helps in energy generation, but also in a pollution-free environment.

(d) **Thermo-atmospheric and Climate:** Water, shade, channeling of cooling breeze as prime-elements for a comfortable micro-climate, minimum exterior surface to maximum internal volume, correct orientation; atriums and internal courtyard to reduce glare and dissipate heat, compact grouping and clustering of buildings to minimize expose of wall surface, use of open spaces, platforms, chowks, porch and squares for social intensity and public safety.

(e) **Sustainable transport:** Transport in cities may contribute nearly two- thirds of the total suspended particulate matter and 18 per cent of carbon emissions posing a serious threat to the environment and health of the people. The objective should be to provide access to people and places by 'green' modes of urban transport. These include walking, bicycling, intermediate public transport modes, bus ways, dedicated bike tracks, CNG powered vehicles, trains, etc. Inherent with this is the aim to curtail the need for commuting and to shorten the distances by various strategies, such as decentralisation of work centers, compact urban form, and by telecommunications, electronic mail, mixed land-use zoning, etc. The alternative modes of transport need not be high cost and high technology solutions, but there are several low cost options, which can be explored. Polluting and life endangering transport modes have to be discouraged, while environment friendly modes need to be given the center-stage. An important element of policy should aim to shift private vehicle user to public transport. A walkable community should provide a fundamental building block in creating a sustainable urban form. The concepts of walk to work, transit oriented development, travel demand management and smart growth, promoting NMTs, multi-modal integration, last mile connectivity and e-governance are pillars of sustainable urban mobility.

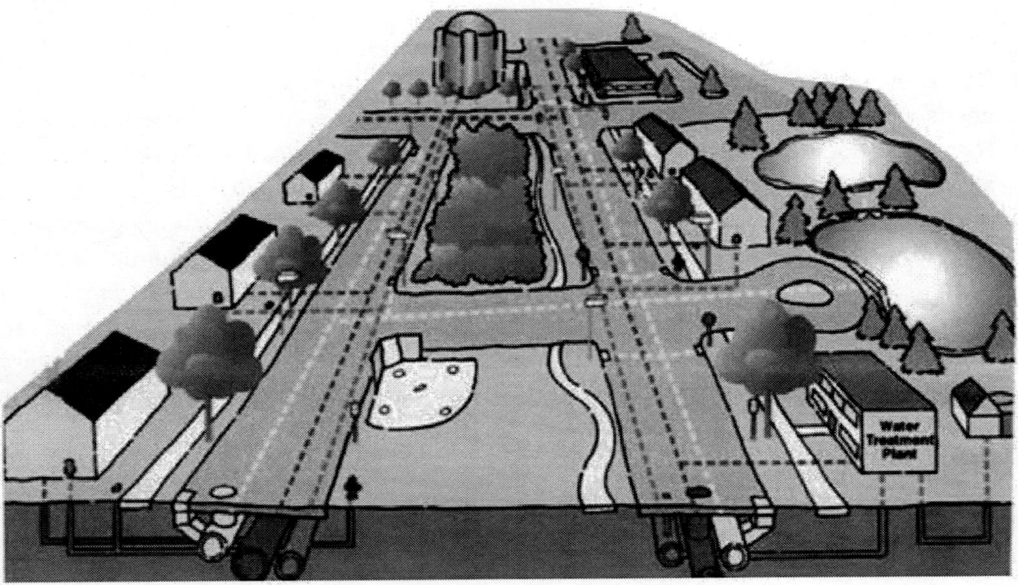

Fig. 12.7: Green and Smart Infrastructure comprises rainwater harvesting, bio-drainage, bio-remedied aquifer recharge, renewable energy, smart grids, carbon capture, tri-generation energy, broadband, wastewater recycling, pneumatic waste segregation and collection, micro-irrigation, enzyme based STP, earth air tunnel for cooling, etc.

(f) Decentralised and Smart Services and Recycling: In the context of emerging environmental awareness, the need to save air, water and land from pollution is a major concern. Drinking water, sanitation, solid waste treatment and drainage are important aspects of the human environment. The performance of present sanitation system needs to be reassessed with reference to environment, hygiene and their accessibility. Various alternative technologies, based on decentralized services, like Extended Aeration Technique, Bio-gas Production, Bubble Diffusion Process, Flotation, Anaerobic reactors, etc. which are already in vogue, should be explored for urban sanitation.

Widespread method of land filling for solid waste disposal is an environmental disaster. Decentralized systems based on recycling, energy generation and organic decomposing should be explored for solid and liquid waste treatment. Bio-reactor composting and vessel system, vermi-composting, etc. are new generation technologies for treatment of wastes.

(g) **Conservation of Surface Water Sources:** The rivers and water bodies in urban areas usually have a high level of pollution, which is mainly form the untreated sewer and waste form adjacent industrial/urban areas. Besides, the enforcement of Water Pollution Act, an environment based strategy as given below, is essential for their improvement:

- Linking of the natural water body and river with the population by access and landscape development.
- Control of pollution of water from industry, drainage, sewerage, flyash, garbage and waste dumping.
- A drainage and flood control strategy linked with water supply.
- Control of land uses which are incongruous with environment, such as polluting industry and coal based thermal power plants.

(h) **Watershed Planning:** The revival of the concept of watershed development, harvesting and conservation of rainwater and recharging of underground water can substantively resolve the urban water crisis. Several technologies, such as decentralized and compact water treatment units, solar/aerobic/oxidation and root zone cleaning systems can be employed to purify potable water form natural sources.

(i) **Vegetation and Organic Life:** For an urban area, about one-fourth of the total area should be available for recreational land use, which includes district/regional/ local parks, urban forests, sports and playgrounds, etc. Besides this, about 10 to 15% of the area should be planned for neighbourhood parks and playsgrounds within the residential areas. In a city about 10 sq. m of recreational area per capita should be reserved as open space. A system of landscaped linkages connecting various parts of the city, neighbourhoods and important monuments should be planned. The garden, both at community and dwelling scale, should provide a sense of oasis and shelter from oppressive climate. Peripheral green belts can be utilised as wind breakers, filters of dust-storms and as transition zones.

(j) **Green-ways for Drainage:** The development of greenways along natural drainage corridors and harvesting of rain water in balancing lakes and ponds has been a new frontier in water management. Instead of resorting to conventional drainage, the concept of "zero run-off" may be adopted by using a series of retention ponds. Such ponds, reservoirs and sediment traps can be located at the catchment zones on low-lying ground, which is ear marked for greenery. This system offers distinct advantages over conventional drainage system, such as replenishment and enrichment of underground water table and augmentation of water reserve, availability of rolling greens and improving the micro-climate.

Flowing greens and inter-connected park-ways bring the landscape in the midst of concrete jungle. There is no need for elaborate gardening of the green ways, but their wild, simple and natural stretch by itself would be ecologically important. Such trails could be one of the cheapest form of drainage and protect biotic diversity and preserve woodland habitat. These act as air filters and tie the neighbourhoods together.

(k) **Sonic:** Noise is emerging as a major pollutant and irritant in the Indian cities, and a cause of health hazard. Against permissible level of 50 to 60dB (a), the sound level invariably exceeds 80 dB(A). Faulty and leaking silencers, over-use of motor horns, screeching tyres, rattling bodies of vehicles plying on rough roads accentuate noise level from the traffic. Besides the noise from commercial and industrial activities in residential zones, unabated use of sound amplifiers, generator sets and fire crackers often disturb the peace in urban areas.

The urban form, land use planning, landscape and green buffers can help in reducing the noise levels. It is not desirable to locate residential areas along major arteries and non-residential activities inside the residential localities that would invite traffic. By proper land use planning, mixed land use, location of public/semi public and commercial activities along major transport arteries, a buffer can be created for residential zone. The green buffer with thin leave trees, land formations, mounds, embankments, etc. provide effective barriers to transmission of noise.

(l) **Climate and Disaster Resilience:** The planning for climate change involves the convergence of various sectors into a strategy and establish a link between climate change and GHG/CO_2 emissions. The spatial area can be delineated as natural conservation zone based on its vulnerability (coastal areas, cyclone, earthquake, landslide, droughts, etc.). Accordingly, a series of geographically linked and disaggregated regional-district-local-sectoral plans, all telescopically connected, can be developed. However, the focus is on the local action plan which is connected both ways-up and down in geographical scale and also on its sides with various sectoral plans. (land, water, air, infrastructure services, shelter, public health and hygiene, transport, energy, greenery/forest, tourism, etc.).

The strategy of climate and disaster resilience depends on the unique natural features of urban areas, population size and rate of growth, the level of income and economic development, the diverse spatial dimensions of environmental problems and the roles of local actors.

(m) **Gender Equity and Safety:** The cities in India have become insecure, crime and danger prone, particularly for the vulnerable sections of the society - the poor, women, elderly, children and disabled. A study finds that two out of three women have faced incidents of sexual harassment more than once during the year, mostly in public spaces, roadside and public transport. Various surveys bring out the 'gender service gap' in terms of inequitable access to basic services like water and toilets for women. The lack of clean and safe public toilets for women and girls may result into sexual harassment and even violence.

The safety of women is a central issue. Various initiatives include the setting of the rescue and rehabilitation centers, re-integration of victims of trafficking; the setting up of 'One Stop Crisis Centres' provision of shelters, police desks, legal, medical and counseling services, and 24x7 help lines. This also needs incremental actions, such as enhancement of street lighting, establishment of 'Multi-Utility Zones' (MUZs), pedestrian safety, safer roads, provision of public toilets for women, especially in the slums and streets and safer public transport with CCTV and alarm system.

The planning of a city can contribute in crime prevention by gender sensitive design of shared, lively and defensible spaces, mixed land use and adequate shelter/tenements for the poor, together with spaces for vending and informal trades that promote livelihood and community surveillance.

The habitat articulates the environment and vice versa. It is necessary to readdress the urban process taking a dynamic and holistic approach, where human element, physical environment and built-form synthesise into a workable equation. The old paradigm of development needs to be reformed with the larger goals of inclusion, equity, environmental sustainability, and climate and disaster resilience.

Debriefing and Review

1. What is undersood by climate change? What is its impacts on urban environment?
2. Explain the following:
   (i) Sustainable development goals (SDG-11)
   (ii) Cycle of Climate Change
   (iii) Paris Climate Agreement
   (iv) Gender Equity and Safety
3. Explain the phenomenon of urban heat island.
4. What can be the critical urban policy directions to address the climate change?
5. Explain the concept of urban climate resilience via-a-vis urban land use and disaster management.
6. What are the major components of Habitat Environment?
7. Explain the concept of green and smart infrastructure for sustainable development.

CHAPTER

13

VILLAGE PLANNING

Since Independence, India has struggled with its huge development backlog of rural areas. Since more than 68 % of its population is dependent on agriculture, rural development and agriculture have been the political imperatives. The 12th Five Year Plan of the Government of India (Planning Commission) revolves around the theme of 'Inclusive Growth'. The concept of Inclusive Growth believes that what is of greatest value often cannot be counted or appropriately valued in monetary terms-such as life itself. Economics is considered to be a tool used in the service of higher values. Inclusive growth postulates people centred development and recognise the role and stakes of the poor, informal sector, women, children and elderly. It also recognises the role of the social economies of households and local communities in creating real wealth. Greater local autonomy and self-reliance are important features of people-centric, inclusive development to enable the local communities to engage in local development by using local resources. Development needs to move beyond the program centric approach and embrace the vision and concept of inclusive planning which integrates several isolated programs into a composite whole.

Cropping pattern and off-farm activities in rural areas have been dependent on urban markets and productive inputs, thus narrowing the gap between the urban and rural. All settlements clearly fall into an interlinked economic system. The neglect of some components adversely effects the entire system and being pro-rural or pro-urban becomes an increasingly quaint bias in an integrated economy. The dual economy has proved a myth, as also, much of the urban-rural divide. The rural businesses are increasingly investing in commercial crops and agro-industries with emerging corporate management styles. The employment absorption potential for poor workers in rural areas is approaching a threshold and pushing them towards the urban pastures. Yet one finds the deepest levels of poverty and deprivation in 6,41,000 villages in India. In spite of various plans and programmes, the rural areas often suffer from unfulfilled basic needs.

The unfulfilled basic needs of rural poor lie in four areas: (i) Survival, health and hygiene, jobs, drinking water, energy, sanitation; (ii) Transformational: skills, education and knowledge; (iii) Supportive; shelter, transport and recreational and (iv) Empowerment: economic, social, human dignity, justice, equity, information, local governance, etc. However, the most visible day to day sufferings relate to job and shelter together with interlinked physical and social infrastructure/services. It also articulates the convenience and dignity of the women. The basic demand of shelter enables the family to better livelihood, health (particularly of women and children), living comfort and social status. It provides a kind of social net which the rural poor needs for survival. The government of India has initiated various schemes of rural development and since 1985 had been implementing the Indira Awas Yojana. The Pradhan Mantri Awas Yojana (Gramin) has been launched in 2016, which has replaced the IAY

Rural Development Plans and Programs

The 73rd Constitutional Amendment Act, 1992, is a watershed in rural development and self-governance. This has made it mandatory for State Governments to constitute District Planning Committees (DPCs) which have to to consolidate plans prepared by panchayats and municipalities. The preparation of development plans requires exploring the potential of the districts, priority of various plans and schemes, financial resource mobilisation, environmental sustainability and specific projects for achieving integrated planning and inclusive growth of rural areas.

The development of rural area depends on location of various economic and social activities, their integration and proper linkages within and outside the areas. Anticipated development activities and organizational framework at different level also affect the economy and form of existing settlements, and the emergence of new settlements.. As such the development plans of Districts, Taluka, Tehsil and Panchayats need to be prepared and merge together for balanced development.

The 73rd Constitutional Amendment Act, 1992 has empowered the panchayats and local bodies. Its Eleventh Schedule (Article 243-G) has listed 29 items for consideration in development plans. Panchayats have power to prepare the plans for economic and social development and implement various schemes in their respective areas, which cover following items as per Eleventh Schedule:

Item No. 1: Agricultural Productivity

Item No. 2: Land Improvement

Item No. 3: Minor Irrigation

Item No. 4: Animal Husbandry

Item No. 5: Fisheries

Item No. 7: Minor Forest Products, etc.

Item No. 10: Rural Housing

Item No. 11: Drinking Water

Item No. 14: Rural Electrification

Item No. 17: Education

Item No. 18: Technical and Vocational Education

Item No. 19: Adult and Non-formal Education

Item No. 24: Family Welfare

Item No. 25: Women and Child Development, etc.

Social development of the rural areas is a part of development plan, which should integrate various schemes, particularly the connectivity under PURA and Bharat Nirman.

Providing Urban Amenities in Rural Areas (PURA)

The formation of cluster of rural settlements, which acts as a viable planning unit, is linked to the nearest towns so as to receive a growth impulse and integrates it with the urban economy. It emphasizes the importance of urban infrastructure in rural areas, and envisages the following rural connectivities:

(i) Physical Connectivity (roads, transport facilities, etc.)

(ii) Economic Connectivity (Banks, Commercial organizations, etc.)

(iii) Knowledge Connectivity (School, colleges, vocational education, etc.)

(iv) Societal Connectivity (Hospital, recreational facilities, place of worship, etc), and

(v) Electronic Connectivity (Phone, internet, cable, etc.)

It is envisaged to prepare the Economic Plan, Structure Plan and Implementation Plans for the District/villages /Panchayat areas.

Bharat Nirman

Bharat Nirman for rural infrastructure covers the development of the following:

- Irrigation
- Rural Roads
- Rural Housing
- Rural Water Supply
- Rural Electrification
- Rural telecommunication, connectivity, etc.

Various targets that have to be achieved include the following:

(i) To connect all rural habitations with population over 1000 (over 500 in hill, tribal and desert areas) with all weather roads.

(ii) To construct 1,46,000 km of new rural roads

(iii) To upgrade and modernize 1,94,000 km of existing rural roads

Pradhan Mantri Gram Sadak Yojana

More than 6.41 lakh villages in India are located in different terrains, e.g. plains, hilly, desert, swamps, costal region, mountainous region, backwater areas, tribal pockets, etc. The climatic conditions also vary from place to place to a great extent. Due to improper planning, some villages are having multi-road connection while others are deprived of even single road connection. Under Pradhan Mantri Gram Sadak Yojna (PMGSY), it has been decided to give at least one road connection to each village. It is centrally sponsored programme with 100% financial assistance. All PMGSY roads are guaranteed defect free by the contractors for a period of 5 years and maintained by him. Funds for the maintenance contract are provided from the State Budget. After a period of 5 years, the roads are transferred to the District Panchayat for maintenance.

Rural electrification

The rural electrification programme has been included as a component of Pradhan Mantri Gramodaya Yojana(PMGY) and is being encouraged to pool resources from other schemes under Minimum Needs Programme (MNP) and Rural Infrastructure Development Fund (RIDF) to achieve 100 per cent electrification. A new scheme called Accelerated Rural Electrification Programme (AREP) has been launched, under which the participation of Decentralized Power Producers, PRIs, Rural Co-operatives, NGO, etc. is being encouraged. The Ministry of Power is pushing the concept of Rural Electricity Supply Companies (RESCOs) involving the private sector players by leasing out solar panel based light systems to village homes. In May 2018, the Government of India declared achieving 100 per cent eletrification of all the villages in India.

Indira Awaas Yojana (IAY)

The IAY targets rural families below poverty line who are either houseless or live in unserviceable kutcha houses. It aims to provide an identity and sense of security to rural poor households. Under the scheme, a maximum assistance of ₹ 35,000 per house in plain areas and ₹ 38,500 per house in hilly/difficult areas is given to BPL family. Assistance is also provided for upgradation of kutcha houses @ ₹ 15,000 per unit. 60% of the houses are reserved for SC/ST beneficiaries.

About 139 lakh houses had been constructed under IAY all over the country since its inception upto January 2006. There is a provision of free electricity connection for IAY houses under Rajiv Gandhi Gram Vidutikaran Yojana.

The funding of IAY is shared between the Centre and States in the ratio of 75:25. In the case of UTs, entire funds of IAY are provided by the Centre. However, in the case of NE States, the funding pattern has been changed and is in the ratio of 90:10. All nationalized banks have been instructed to include the IAY houses under the Differential Rate of Interest (DRI) scheme for lending upto ₹ 20,000/- per housing unit at interest rate of 4%. The criteria for allocation of IAY funds to the States and UTs envisages assigning 75% weightage to housing shortage and 25% to SC/ST component. Further, 60% of the IAY allocation is meant for benefiting SC/ST families, 3% for physically handicapped and 15% for minorities. Also the IAY houses are allotted in the name of women.

It needs to be revisited keeping in view traditional collective living pattern as well as the changing aspirations of the people. The scheme needs to be aligned with various other programmes of rural development (like MGNREGA, health, education, child development, water, sanitation, etc.). It needs to be more participatory and planned in a wider framework of inclusive growth. The Government of India has recently announced to build 10 million rural houses under Pradhan Mantri Awas Yojana (Rural).

Mahatma Gandhi National Rural Employment Guarantee Act

MGNREGA aims at rural employment through small works, like connecting a village by paved road, construction of culvert, construction of fishery ponds, construction of rainwater reservoir, construction of drain along a road, social forestry, horticulture, irrigation canals, etc.

A unique feature of the MG NREGA Scheme is that it is 'rights' centric, and is not a 'dole', or charity. The government has recognised the need for implementation of fundamental rights of the citizens-such as education, employment and information, which have empowered the poor people and is leading towards inclusive development. When people are given rights by legal instrument the role of cunning politician and officials diminishes who sometimes try to scuttle the good work.

A striking feature of MG NREGA projects has been 'value for money'. It is observed that small investments, such as a construction of a drain, retaining wall for flood protection, small culvert, retrofitting a bridge on a local stream/drains, construction of half kilometre road, where the expenditure is around ₹ 1 to 5 lakh, have given immense relief to the rural population in ameliorating day to day hardships. The ownership of the job card has given a sense of pride and self respect to the rural poor, apart from a better livelihood. There is no visible distress migration and about 40 to 45 % of the job card holders are women.

However, MGNREGA schemes face some challenges as given below:

- Lack of overall Development Plan and Block Plans, lack of staff, lack of convergence, too much paperwork and overlapping in monitoring, lack of autonomy and defined powers, non-banking villages, notified wage less than market wage resulting in difficulty in getting local labour.
- Low wages in view of inflation
- expenditure and day loss in wage collection
- Delay in payment of wages, expenditure and loss of 1 day in wage collection in non- banking areas.
- Corruption
- poor roads, shortages of power, sewage and sanitation
- Lack of dispensaries/healthcare facilities, doctors, veterinary hospitals, community marriage halls
- Frequent accidents and deaths of cattle on highways
- Lack of public transportLack of farmers' markets, warehousing, cold storage, fish market, milk chilling and marketing facilities, etc.
- Expensive fertilisers, obsolete irrigation facilities and agricultural tools, etc.

There are frequent complaints that the present wage is below market rate and there are delays in the payment. The delay in the payment of wages is mainly due to non-availability of local bank or post office. This point out towards a need to take the bank or post office to the doorstep of villages/NREGA site and proactivate the banks/post office officials to put up regular camps for making the wage payment, wherever necessary. Providing accommodation at R.G. Seva Kendra, VCDC/Block office will facilitate decentralised functioning of the banks and post offices. Lessons can be learn from success stories, such as Rae Bareli District where business correspondents provide banking facilities and NREGA payments are made at the doorstep of the villagers.

One of the issues is concerning the corruption and leakage of public funds. According to the officials most of such complaints are frivolous and stem from political/public rivalries which should not camouflage the 'success' and 'achievements'.

The issue of MGNREGA Scheme needs to be tackled at the 'systemic' levels, for which following actions are necessary:

- The order to reduce ad hoc decision making and unintended investments, or diversion of NREGA funds, the preparation of District Development Plan and Block Action Plans are essential.
- This should be complimented by prescribing Standard Operating Procedures and defining coordination roles.
- A system of checks and balances shall be put in place by defining powers to approve the scheme/finances, norms and standards, specifications, issuing regular public bulletins, notices, etc.
- By using computer, internet, website, press briefings, handouts, etc. information should be shared with the public, apart from the implementation of the RTI Act.
- Define the powers, responsibilities and accountability at various levels.
- Asset management and adoption of GIS based Computerised Land Record (CLR)

The schemes of Rural Empowerment and Development should harmonise with the aspirations and reforms such as transparency, self-governance, local autonomy and new technology (such as solar energy, bio-gas production, wastewater recycling, systems building, etc.).

Towards an Inclusive Approach

In spite of numerous laudable programmes and huge investments, the reality of rural development is rather dismal. There is a continuous distress migration to the cities and most of the villages lack the basic amenities and services, like pucca road, transport, communications, drinking water supply, power, sanitation, healthcare, irrigation facility and jobs for survival and sustenance. There are gross inequalities in access to rural finances, services and subsidies. The power is concentrated in the hands of few and the village administration is by and large urban-controlled. The concepts of citizen empowerment, participatory governance and decentralization are confined to the seminars and papers. The decision making is often piecemeal, disjointed, ad-hoc, motivated and lacks an overall perspective. A lion's share of subsidies is eaten up by the administration/ establishment structure and their salaries. The programmes are too many, so are the departments involved in each one of them. There is often overlapping and lack of clarity about the organizations and their accountability. The programmes often exceed the time and financial allocations and the facilities, including housing built up by the government bodies have many a times remain unoccupied.

The rural schemes often suffer from lack of linkages with livelihood, health, amenities and well-being needs, ecological orientation and poverty alleviation programmes. The spatial dimension of the program is usually missing. The projects and plans are prepared and implemented by the technical professionals and officials with urban mindset and do not belong to the people. The convergence among Central, State and annual, and among regional, district and local/village plans is often missing. Participatory learning with the target groups provides useful clues towards adopting a 'needs based approach'.

With a little external support the rural poor are often capable of meeting their survival needs. The organized sector has a vital role in helping the rural poor in meeting their needs. The experience indicates that the supportive needs really help the rural poor in climbing up the economic ladder. The provision of basic services and facilities in the rural context is a major concern. Accordingly the rural amenities and services and the priorities of planning, development and investments should be worked out. Based on participatory learning, a network of rural amenities and facilities can be provided keeping in mind the public transport facility, topography and characteristics of potential areas. A system of clustering of the facilities will lead to a conceptual hierarchy of rural settlements, such as 'cities in green field', PURA centres, growth centres, etc. The plans of rural development need to be based upon the critical aspects of community enablement, funding, administrative reality, equity principle, employment creation, integrated development, poverty alleviation and basic needs provisions. This would lead to the plans which are pro-poor, participatory and meaningful for the local rural population and are implementable.

Amartya Sen's seminal ideas on 'Development as Freedom' focus on the topic of how development policy can address cultural needs and values in the context of rural deprivation and social exclusion and oppressions. It provides a practical review of the range of multi-dimensional approaches to poverty reduction for rural development. He mentions that 5 freedoms, viz., Political, Economic, Social, Transparency and Security are simultaneously necessary for integrated development. A major reason for failure of economic development programs in rural India is that they did not take into account the traditional matrix of social operation. This is something very deeply integrated in the psyche of rural population and needs to dealt with as part of development program.

No plan or program can be successful unless it is tied up with community empowerment and addresses to the oppressive traditions, customs and practices. This means evolving a tactical strategy based on enablement of rural community, viz., economic enablement, spatial enablement, social enablement and technological enablement. The governance system needs to change towards an effective decentralization, devolution and deregulation. The plans and programs should enable the rural people towards transformation of the prevailing image of backwardness, inferiority, oppressions, depressions and poverty.

Along with provision of better irrigation, roads, services, connectivity, social facilities and housing, it becomes imperative to lay emphasis on sustainable livelihoods both on the farm and non-farm sector. The strategy for livelihood linked with shelter is contingent upon the issues like:

- Preparation of integrated District Development and Local Area (Village) Development Plans

- Community development through formation of local cooperatives and harnessing the spirit of self-help, self-rule and self-reliance.
- Family welfare, women and child development, education and healthcare
- Financial and social inclusion
- Adoption of ICT, communication and connectivity
- Models of public private partnership
- Incentives from the government
- Planning and construction parameters such as plot size, built up area and technical specifications, etc.
- Livelihood–macro and micro policy, together with District Planning and Development Cluster, etc.
- Specific roles for specific stakeholders

In view of the perennial problems of droughts, floods and other natural hazards in rural areas, housing and infrastructure should be safe and sustainable. Although, India has made progress in the development of codes, standards and guidelines on disaster resistant constructions, but the use of these technologies is still inadequate due to lack of awareness and absence of enforcement of codes and standards in the construction of buildings. Proper land use zoning, land sub-division and development and building controls for urban activities in disaster sensitive areas need to be worked out in detail. The major flood plains could be left as agricultural fields, natural parks, playgrounds, picnic areas, plant nurseries, orchards and gardens. Water and sewerage treatment plants should not be located in flood prone areas to avoid dislocation of these services during floods. Indiscriminate clustering of fire prone uses, industry, storage of hazardous chemicals, etc. should be avoided.

Rural Planning

The plans of rural development have to begin at the grassroots levels, keeping in view the need to provide a network of day to day facilities and amenities to the people. As much the plans are to be based upon the critical aspects of community development, funding, administrative reality, equity principle, employment creation, integrated development, poverty alleviation and basic needs provision. Based on accessibility a graph can be developed for the provision of rural facilities. The plans have to be participatory and meaningful for the local rural population.

Planning activity is the integration of time and resources is a spatial dimension. It is usually divided into 3 interconnected phases-Long Term, Short term and Annual plan. Long term plans are usually policy programe, short term are strategic plans (usually for 5 years) and project plans are operational, action plans.

Planning is a roadmap towards reaching the destination and shows the best way to get there in time. It is targeted towards achieving certain objectives, goals or results. Objective or goals are the ends towards which activity is aimed. Planning attempts to integrate various systems, which form a complex unity. As such it sets certain parameters, norms and benchmarks. Planning has four important goals:

(i) To off-set uncertainity and change

(ii) To focus attention on objectives, benchmarks, norms and systems

(iii) To make operations economical and time bound

(iv) To guide, control and implement.

Strategies indicate a progress of action and development of priority areas/sectors and resources to attain comprehensive objectives. The programme of objectives of an organization and their changes resources used to attain these objectives and policies governing the acquisition, use and disposition of these resources. The determination of the basic long term objectives and the adoption of action plans, and allocation of resources are necessary to achieve these goals.

Some success stories are available, which provide useful lessons for rural development. The rural-urban integration in Kerala by District Planning continuing of one of such examples. It reinforces the idea of interdependent rural-urban networks, rather than stand alone District Planning or rural settlements.

The State of Kerala launched a highly participatory planning process through formation of 14 DPCs which have undertaken the task of integration of the Panachayat Plan (rural areas) as well as those prepared by 55 municipalities and 3 municipal corporations (urban areas). This is a bold attempt to take the planning process to the grassroots level with maximum involvement of the masses. It is known as People's Plan Campaign. The common people are encouraged to actively participate in identifying local problems and finding solutions. The unique feature of Kerala experiment is the high level autonomy to the local bodies to determine their own priorities. The planning process of preparation of District Plan involves various stages, which include formation of strategic perspective for development, formulation and preparation of Annual Plan of gram panchayats/ municipalities. The preparation of district plan is taken up based on feedback from the people, especially the poor.

The planning of rural-urban integration at the district level is to be achieved through DPCs by preparing a plan for the whole district. All the departments of the District Administration are involved in District Planning which forms a comprehensive planning framework.

Kollam Model of Integrated District Planning (Kerala)

In an effort to institutionalize the decentralized planning process in Kerala, which was initiated in campaign mode, the 10th Five Year Plan gave emphasis to spatial planning by the Local Self Government Institutions. This helped in linking the spatial planning to the decentralized planning process of Local Self Government Institutions.

The District Planning Committee, Kollam initiated the Integrated District Plan for the District (IDDP) and a Local Development Plan (LDP) for each Local Self Government Institution in the district. The matter was taken up to State Planning Board and a Kerala Government Order was issued to prepare these plans as a pilot project in Kollam with Town and Country Planning Department as the nodal agency. Subsequently a Handbook for the Preparation of IDDP and LDP for Kollam was prepared by the State Planning Board.

The process of preparation of IDDP and LDP started in Kollam District in August 2003, with the training programmes for various stakeholders of the project and primary data collection at the Grama Panchayat and Municipality levels was carried out for the one and a half year. About 12000 stakeholders, ranging from DPC members to NGO's at the Gram Panchayat level were given training which created awareness about the project among stakeholders.

The process of preparation of the Plans starts with collection of data. Up to the analysis stage, the sequential steps of plan preparation are almost parallel for both the plans. Findings from the analyses are utilized for both the Plans as and when required. Based on the analyses, the district level development issues are identified and the development goals and objectives are set. Based on that, Draft IDDP is prepared for the district incorporating suggestions of LSGIs. The Draft IDDP thus prepared is an input for the identification of development issues and setting up of development goals and objectives of each LSGI is the frame within which the Draft LDPs are prepared. Based on suggestions and proposals of the Draft LDPs, the Draft IDDP is modified and finalized. Once the draft IDDP, approved by the DPC, is sanctioned by the State Government, the Draft LDPs are finalized.

Block and Jilla Panchayat Development Plans are prepared based on policies and strategies of sanctioned Integrated District Development Plan and sanctioned Local Plans within their administrative boundary. The projects and programmes are based on the policies and strategies

District and Local Level Plans are implemented by the Jilla and Block Panchayats. An important highlight of the planning is a focus on provision of facilities and infrastructure is the rural areas which provide a comparable quality of life in urban area.

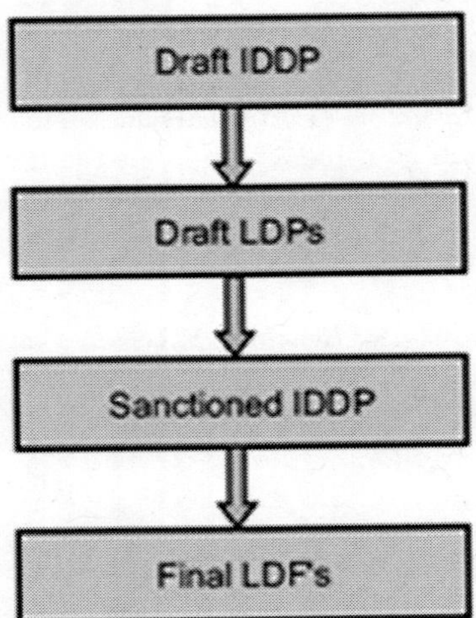

Fig. 13.1: Local Development Plans form part of Integrated District Development Plan

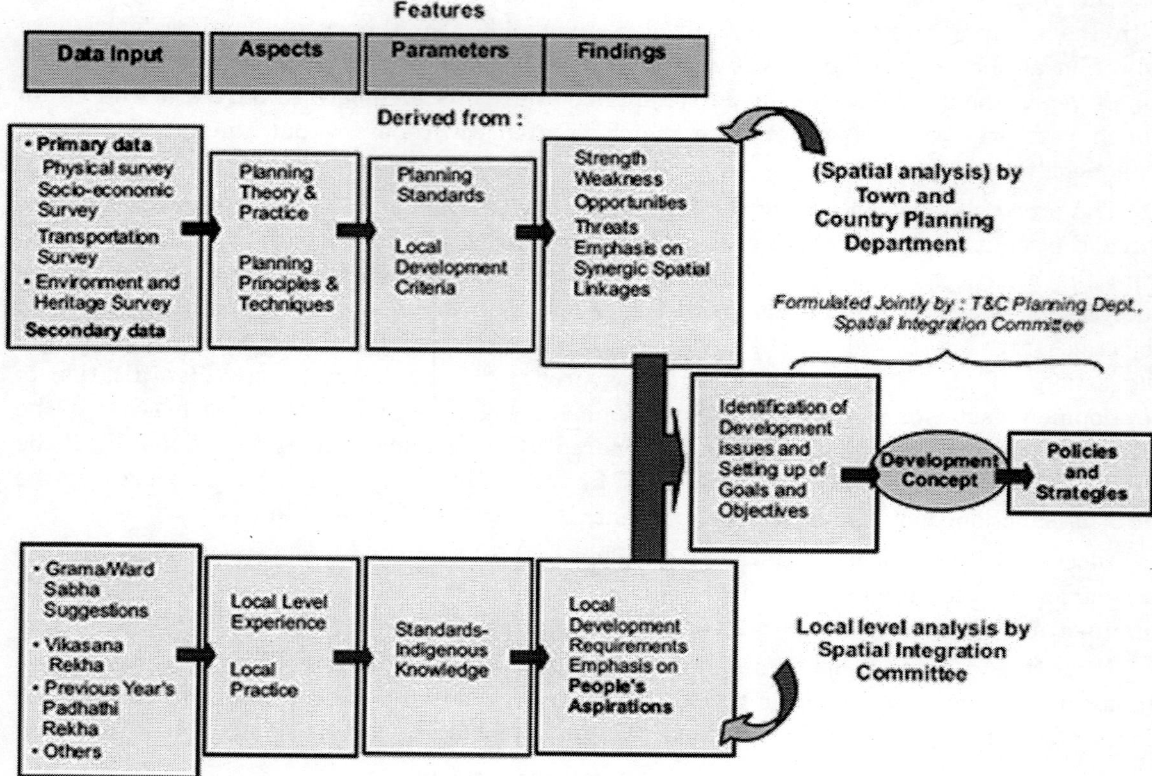

Fig. 13.2: IDDP and LDPs are prepared based on top down and grassroot up approach. The data collection, analysis and carving out of local level proposals are done at the grass root level which is later modified, based on the policies derived at a higher level, i.e. at the District level while preparing the IDDP. At the same time the policies at the higher level are formulated taking into account the proposal at the lower level (LSGI level). State of the art technology - GIS, GPS, satellite imagery are utilized in the preparation of LDP and IDDP.

Source: State Planning Board, Government of Kerala, 2003, Handbook for the Preparing IDDP and LDP.

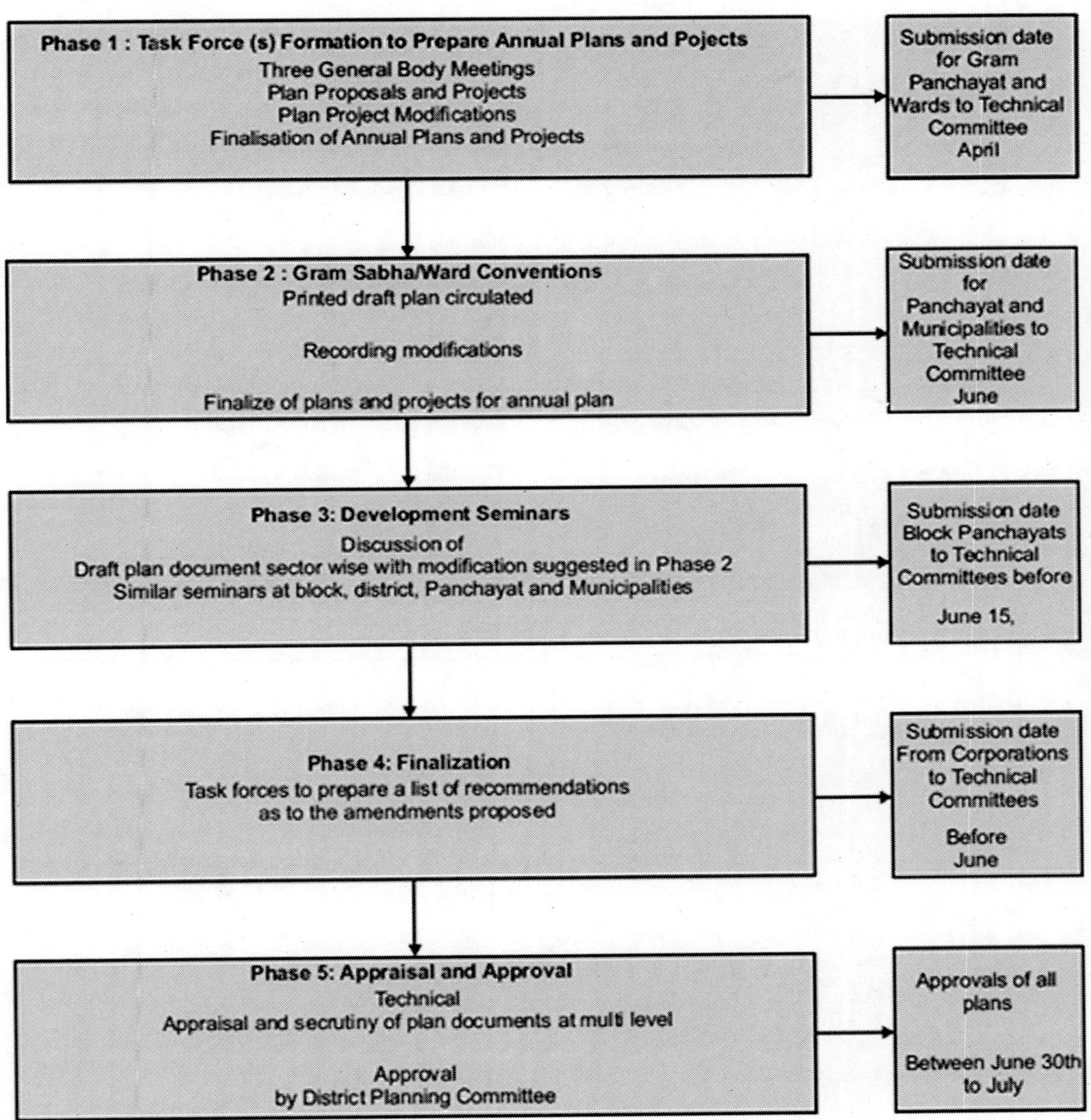

Fig. 13.3: District and Local Plan Formulation Procedure

Source: State Planning Board, Govt. of Kerala, 2003, Handbook for the Preparing IDDP and LDP.

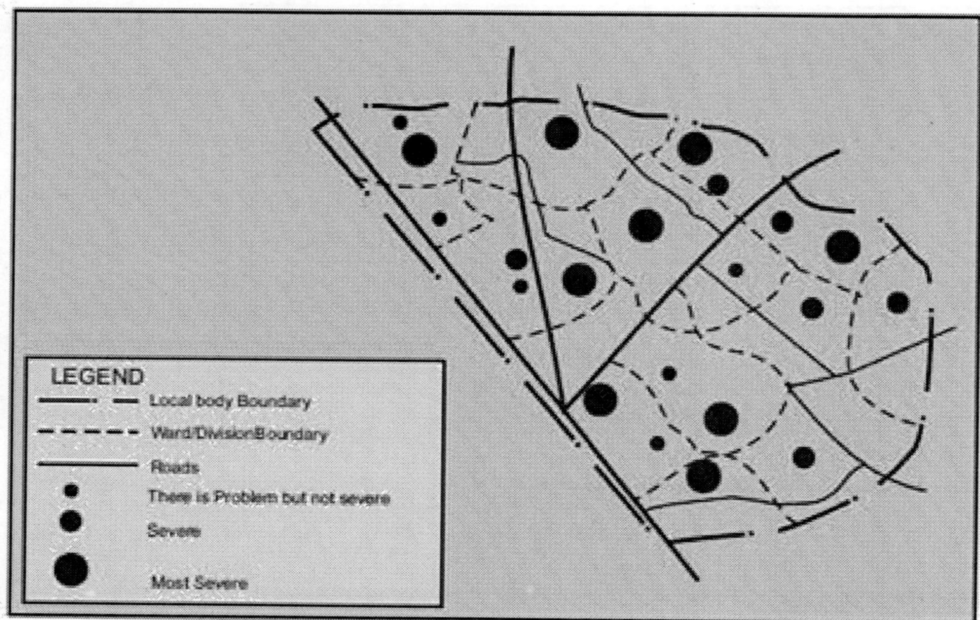

Fig. 13.4: Integrated District Development Plan: Problem Severity Map

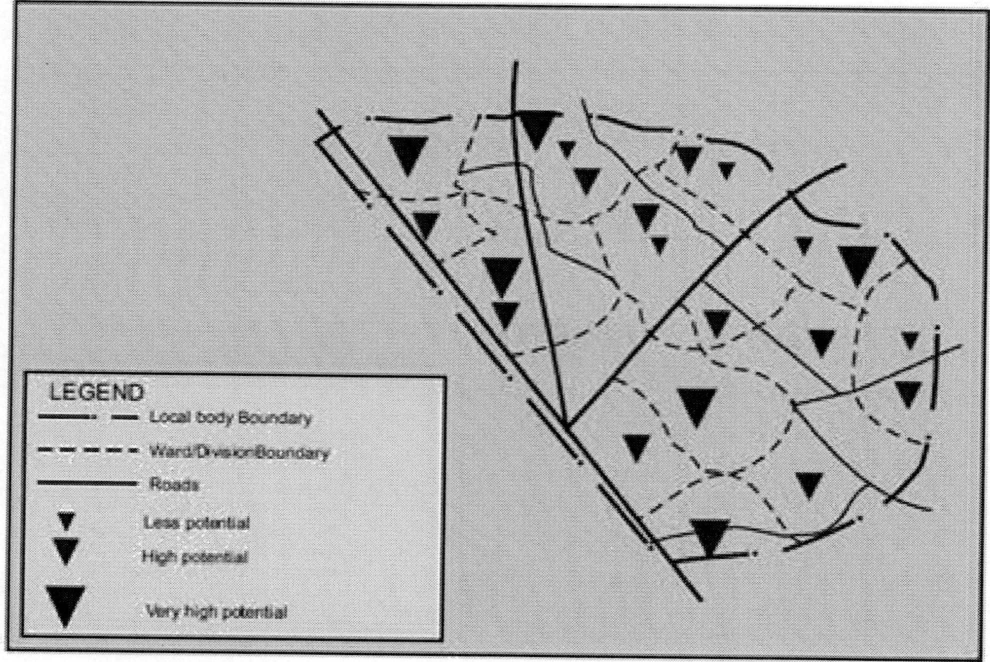

Fig. 13.5: Integrated District Development Plan: Potential Map

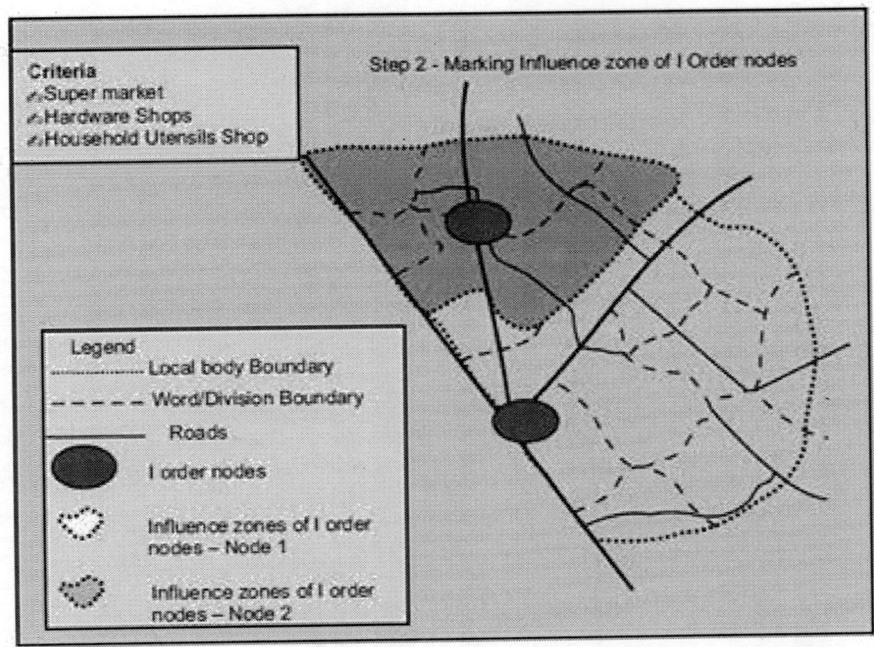

Fig. 13.6: Map showing Influence Zone of First Order Node

Source: State Planning Board, Govt. of Kerala, 2003, Handbook for Preparing the IDDP and LDP.

Fig. 13.7: Map showing Influence Zone of Second Order Node

Source: State Planning Board, Govt. of Kerala, 2003, Handbook for Preparing the IDDP and LDP.

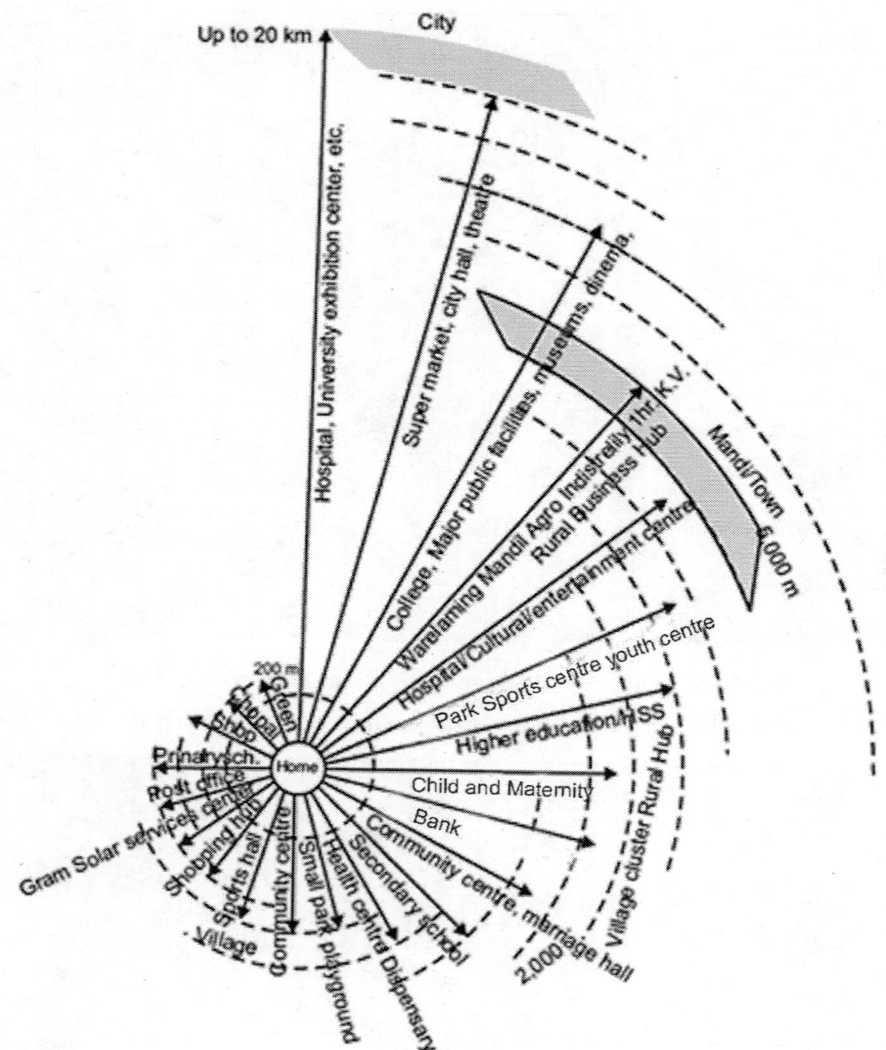

Fig. 13.8: Local Rural Hub and suggested Distances of Public Facilities within a District Development Plan

Table 13.1: Hierarchy of Facilities based on Easy Accessibility and Catchment Population			
8–12 km radius	City facilities	University, Higher Education, Shopping Mall/Centre Hospital	Transport Hub Infrastructure Centre
4–6 km radius	Mandi Town	Theatre/Multiplex, Sports Centre Library	Agro-industry Centre Workhouse, Bus Terminal, Rural Business Hub, Weekly Market/Panchayat Services, Marriage Hall

For rural planning following thumb rules may be adopted, which would vary according to the context, geography and economy:

- Supporting the concept of community formation to promote self-help, self-rule, self reliance. This needs help from the government/umbrella cooperative organizations and dedicated professionals (architects, engineers, NGOs, etc.) to work as catalyst.
- The village cluster development plan should be integrated with various schemes such as PMAY (Gramin), PURA, MGNREGA, Bharat Nirman, together with financial allocations.
- Identify the land for rural housing and various facilities. Housing cluster of minimum 8 houses as a unit in place of individual stand alone shelter. Minimum shelter area: 7.5 sqm/person. Minimum dwelling size 30 sqm with space for cattle, tools, etc. Cater to all income groups for inclusive development and social integration.
- Area for social facilities and services: 4 to 7.5 sqm per person.

  (Schools, utilities, administration, clinics, Community hall, anganwari, recreation center, women's workshop, bank, fuel and ration shop, etc.)
- Area for internal roads: 4 to 7.5 sqm per person
- Area for parks, playgrounds: 4 to 7.5 sqm per person
- Health post and clinic (1,000 sqm plot): 1 per 5,000 people

  Hospital cum Maternity center (6000 sqm): 1per 25,000 people
- Primary School (0.8Ha): 1 per 5,000 population

  Sr. Sec. School (1.6 Ha): 1 per 25,000 population

  Vocational Training Center (0.5Ha):1 per 25,000 population
- Police Post/ Station (0.5 Ha): 1 per 25,000 population
- Community Hall, Women Welfare Center, Anganwari, Literacy Centre (1 Ha): 1 per 25,000 Population
- Ration shop, fuel shop, bank, post office, convenience shopping (0.2 Ha per 5,000 population)
- Weekly market/Haat (1.0 Ha per 25,000 population)

Together with development of land, roads and shelter, parallel action needs to be taken for the development of the following:

- Drinking (treated) water supply.
- A pond in each cluster, so as to contain storm/flood overflow and also for cattle
- Decentralised sanitation and sewerage system
- Electricity/power/solar energy/phone and other networks
- Solid waste management and recycling
- Agro-industry, food processing, warehousing, logistics, bus terminal, farmer's market, etc.

Community spaces ranging from large public multi-purpose maidans/spaces to courtyards offer open space for markets, sports, cattle gathering and marriages festivals or just informal gatherings. Service slots provide play areas for the children in close proximity to their houses. Schools, dispensaries and markets are placed adjacent to gardens, play areas and other recreational facilities. The main green links form continuous pedestrian passages, widening occasionally to accommodate the parks. By making the green areas usable spaces as against being merely ornamental, these have better chances of being maintained. The basic facilities such as schools, healthcare, police post, post office, shopping, workshops, open spaces and the community hall in sufficient numbers and varied sizes will sustain a viable, self-sufficient neighbourhood. A good mixture of land uses and activities is promoted for a balanced growth. All the essential utilities, such as the water supply, sewerage, surfaced roads, storm-water drainage, electricity lines and street-lighting are to be provided, so that an acceptable quality of environment is achieved.

Community Development and Rural Housing

The concept of community development aims to capture the positive aspects of collective living and the village ambience. A variety of housing typologies can be developed through community and cooperative efforts where people of similar vocations/faith or lineage live together. The architects facilitate them to design and build their house as per their particular needs, resources and taste. Each cluster will have common space for the community, which can be used for common services, work area and venue for religious and cultural functions. The layout of housing will attempt recreating traditional values of community living:

- Housing cluster approach (comprising minimum of 8 houses) in place of individual shelter/structure.
- Integrated development together with employment generation, economic activities, and community facilities.
- Ample green areas, parks, tot-lots play/ sports fields and rain water harvesting ponds.
- Chowks and squares at cluster level to recreate traditional community living.
- An attractive and cohesive picture.
- Housing integrated with self-employment opportunities and artisan workshop,
- Modular system of housing development.
- Gradual augmentation of services, innovative decentralised systems of solar/wind energy, sewerage, solid waste disposal and drainage.
- Rural Building Center to evolve and apply traditional construction skills, interfaced with modern construction technology.

The new housing should be able to make a statement that the poor and rural people do not deserve third class shelter under the pretext of economy. Low cost housing need not be ugly. To make the housing schemes bankable and to minimise the need of subsidy, land bundling with food park, farmers market, agro-industrial estate and commercial/ mixed use can be adopted. Rental housing convertible into ownership after 10 years would help the poor in accessing shelter and also obviate illegal transfers and sale.

The design solutions should encourage the 'self-help' and symbiotic spirit of the community. Pre-cast systems combined with traditional methods can offer excellent economy and speed of construction. To encourage, refine and develop modern methods and inspire traditional skills, a network of Rural Building Centres need to be developed at the initial stage of development. This would also promote the potential of self-help, latent in the community. Rural Building Centres (RBCs) may be established in rural areas to harness the local skills and resources in building and infrastructure development. The traditional techniques, skills and building materials can be interjected with modern technology by dissemination of information on Cost Effective and Environment Friendly (CEEF) construction in rural areas. The RBC will help in skill up- gradation and creating a pool of trained rural construction work force for construction and building activities. Active support of the Government to the local cooperatives can implement rural housing and infrastructure projects in an efficient, cost effective manner.

To facilitate, incentivise and to adopt a business friendly approach, it would be worthwhile to consider creating a 'Rural Employment Generation and Infrastructure Corporation', a corporate entity on the lines of REC. To start with a Corporation could be established whereby about 50 per cent of the central government funds for rural development could be channelized for PPP project under MORD schemes while the remaining 50 per cent can be utilised through the state government /rural development department.

These measures will greatly help in reshaping the rural geography of India and will promote inclusive growth.

Debriefing and Review

1. What are the main programmes of rural development in India?
2. Under 73rd CAA (Article 243-G) the panchayats have the power to prepare the plans of economic and social development. What are the main subjects of plans of rural development?
3. Write short notes on the following:
   (i) PURA
   (ii) Bharat Nirman
   (iii) Indira Awas Yojana
   (iv) PMAY (Rural)
   (v) MGNREGA
4. Explain the Kollam model of District Planning and the lessons learnt for village development.
5. Explain the concepts of (a) Rural Hub and (b) Mandi Towns
6. Give a comparative chart highlighting major differences in approaches to urban and rural planning in India.

CHAPTER
14

Legal Framework for Town Planning

Town Planning involves planning, development and management of land, infrastructure services, facilities, housing, etc. which attract several legal provisions. These can be broadly categorised as given below:

- Land
- Land use, planning and building activity, regulation and enforcement
- Local authority, urban development authority, housing board Acts
- Property tenure, transfer and transaction
- Environment management
- Infrastructure services and transport
- Heritage management
- Slum rehabilitation
- Rent control
- Real estate regulation and management
- Apartment ownership
- Labour laws
- Company Acts
- Taxation Acts

A town planner may not be an expert in wide ranging legal frameworks and their nuances, however he/she should be aware of the need for complying with these laws. The legislation is usually categorised at 3 levels-Central (which may be applicable co-currently in the States), State and Local. Most of the Acts have Subordinate Legislation in the form of Rules, Regulations and Bye-laws. There are also quasi-legal administrative orders, gazzette notifications, etc. which operate at local levels.

The Land Acquisition Act, 1894: The Land Acquisition Act, 1894 enables the Government is notify the land required for public purpose for acquisition. After the award of the compensation/damages. The collector has the powers the acquire land. After agitations by farmers is West Bengal, UP and in other states, the law has been revised.

The Right to Fair Compensation and Transparency in Land Acquisition, Rehabilitation and Redevelopment: The Right to Fair Compensation and Transparency in Land Acquisition, Rehabilitation and Resettlement Act (2013) has replaced the Land Acquisition Act of 1894. It obliges the government and others to give rehabilitation package to displaced people, if they buy over 50 acres of land in urban areas and 100 acres in rural areas. Under the new Act land can be acquired by the government for its own use, or for the public purposes. Farmers will get four times the market price in the rural areas, while in the urban areas it will be double the market price.

The Land Pooling Legislation: In Indian cities, it is becoming extremely difficult to acquire lands on large scale for planned development. The process of land pooling is being adopted as an alternative which involves the preparation of a development plan /land pooling schemes which indicate the areas required for public uses such as streets, parks and schools, etc. The cost of providing the infrastructure for the entire area is calculated, and also the estimated market value of the improved land. A portion of the land, the estimated market value of which equals the cost of development is then transferred to the local government in return for carrying out the improvement. Alternatively, EDC, Conversion Charges, Betterment Levy, etc. are recovered against grant of development rights with compulsory surrender of land for common greens, transport infrastructure, social housing and facilities required at local level. The scheme does not envisage in-situ development of land but is returned in the nearest vicinity as per approved layout plan so as to ensure planned development. An advantage of land pooling is that layout and reblocking are affected without the need of acquiring individual pieces of land for the facilities and infrastructure. At the same time, it provides an early return on the public investments through the sale of the land ceded to the local government. Its implementation involves a back up of land pooling legislation and detailed regulations.

Development Authority, Town Planning Acts and Regional Development Acts

The concept of development authority for undertaking urban development was incorporated for the first time in India by the Delhi Development Act of 1957. The Act provides for the constitution and incorporation of a high-powered Development Authority for Delhi for securing the development of Delhi according to plan, for which purpose the authority is conferred with wide powers of acquisition, development and disposal of lands, the carrying out of building and other operations and the execution of works in connection with water supply and other services and amenities. The Authority is responsible for preparing, enforcing and implementing Master Plan and Zonal Development Plans in the National Capital Territory of Delhi. The Act repealed the UP Urban Improvement Act of 1919 which was in operation in Delhi and replaced the Delhi Improvement Trust by the Delhi Development Authority (DDA).

The enactment of the DD Act gave impetus to a number of other states to follow suit.

Table 14.1: Development Authority, Urban Development and Town Planning Act

Sl. No.		Name of the Act	State/Union Territory in which in force
1.	1957	The Delhi Development Act	Delhi
2.	1958	The Durgapur (Development and Control) Act	West Bengal
3.	1970	The Jammu and Kashmir Development Act	Jammu and Kashmir
4.	1971	The Faridabad Complex (Development and Regulation) Act	Haryana
5.	1972	The Calcutta Metropolitan Development Authority Act	West Bengal (Repealed)
6.	1973	The UP Urban Planning and Development Act	Uttar Pradesh
7.	1974	The Bombay Metropolitan Region Development Authority Act	Maharashtra
8.	1975	The A.P. Urban Areas (Development) Act	A.P.
9.	1975	The Bangalore Development Authority Act	Karnataka
10.	1976	The Gujarat Town Planning and Development Act	Gujarat
11.	1977	The Haryana Urban Development Authority Act	Haryana
12.	1979	The West Bengal Town and Country (Planning and Development) Act	West Bengal
13.	1981	The Bihar Development Authority Act	Bihar
14.	1982	The Jaipur Development Authority Act	Rajasthan
15.	1982	The Orissa Development Authority Act	Orissa
16.	1985	The Bangalore Metropolitan Region Development Authority Act	Karnataka
17.	1985	The Guwahati Metropolitan Development Authority Act	Assam
18.	1985	National Capital Region Planning Board Act	NCR/Delhi
18.	1986	The UP Special Areas (Development) Act	Uttar Pradesh
19.	1987	The Karnataka Urban Development Act	Karnataka
20.	1990	The Mizoram Urban and Regional Development Act	Mizoram
21.	1990	The Punjab Regional and Town Planning Act	Punjab

The Delhi Development Act, 1957

Delhi Development Act was enacted by Parliament on 27.12.1957. This Act provides for the development of Delhi according to the plan and for matters ancillary thereto. The main provisions of the Act are:

(i) To constitute an Authority to be called the Delhi Development Authority (DDA).

(ii) The DDA, as soon as may be, carry out a civic survey of land prepare a Master plan for Delhi. The Central Government may by Notification, declare any area in Delhi to be a development area for the purpose of this Act. The development of land shall be undertaken or carried out in this area after obtaining permission from the Authority in accordance with the provisions of this Act.

(iii) Any land required for the purpose of development, or for any other purposes, under this Act, the Central Government may acquire such land under the provisions of the Land Acquisition Act, 1894. The DDA may take action against a person who is developing/constructing land in contravention of the Master Plan or Zonal Development plan or without permission.

(iv) The Authority can demolish, stop development or seal the unauthorised development.

(v) The Authority shall be entitled to levy upon betterment charges in respect of the increasing value of the properly resulting from execution of the development.

For development and disposal of land, provisions have been made under the Nazul Rules, 1981 notified under the Delhi Development Act, 1957. There are number of other laws, rules, regulations and policies which relate to transfer of lands, formation and functioning of housing cooperative societies/associations and other matters of urban development in National Capital Territory of Delhi.

Under the Act, the Master Plan for Delhi provides a legal basis of development, planning controls and enforcement.

Delhi Development Act provides that simultaneously the zonal development plans shall be prepared within the frame of the Master Plan. These contain site plan(s) and uses for the development of a zone for various activities as per norms/standards prescribed in the Master Plan. Also, it contains land reservation for roads, open spaces and sites for creation of buildings, sites for amenities, etc. Specified densities will be shown for preparation of layout plans and provision of other matters which may be necessary for proper development of an area. Under the master Plan land use zones have been specified for entre Delhi, which have been classified in 9 categories, namely residential, commercial, manufacturing, transportation, utility, government, public and semi-public, agricultural and water body. These nine land use categories have been sub-divided into 37 use zones. Each use zone is further sub-divided into a number of use premises which are reflected in the layout plans when prepared. This three tier land use control system is envisaged for various urban functions with a view to promote quality of life of people of Delhi with most appropriate development of land. In each use zone, various use premises are permitted as a part of a layout plan/Local Area Plan. Within the master plan framework a 'Development Code' has been prescribed. The basic purpose is to promote quality of life of people by organising an appropriate development of land in accordance with the development policies and land use proposals. This code deals with 37 designated use zones and 136 use premises. It also deals with various controls which are to be exercised for designing of buildings on such use premises with regard to coverage, FAR, height, parking, setbacks, open spaces, etc. These controls and norms are also termed as zoning regulations.

Building Bye-Laws

Delhi Development Act, 1957 (Section 53 A) empowers Authority to make rules, regulations or bye-laws in respect of certain matters which include water supply, drainage and sewage disposal, erection and re-erection of buildings, including grant of building permission, license and imposition of restrictions on use and sub-division of buildings, sub-division of land into building sites, roads and lanes, recreational sites and sites for community facilities, and development of land, improvement schemes, and housing schemes. These shall not contravene any of the provisions of Master Plan or Zonal Development Plans. Building Bye-laws have been prepared to control the building activities in Delhi. All mandatory Master Plan/Zonal Plan Regulations specified under the Development Code are applicable.

Building byelaws are crucial for real estate and building development sector. These are usually municipal functions and involve obtaining various no-objection certificates, approvals and permissions from various statutory bodies (e.g., land ownership, land use, services agency, Fire Department, Urban Art Commission, Airports Authority, Archaeological Survey/ Department, Ministry/Department of Environment/Forests, etc.). It also involves interim inspections by the connected municipal agency/authority during the construction. Building bye-laws *mutatis-mutandis* incorporate development controls/codes. In view of undue delays and widespread corruption urban local bodies are resorting to on-line building approvals, simplification of bye laws and a common platform for coordination of approvals by various departments.

Punjab Municipal Act, 1911

Before the introduction of provincial autonomy in India, the only form of the Government was the Government of local bodies known as 'Local Government'. Prior to the enactment of Punjab Municipal Act, the Act XV of 1867 was the only legislation. Punjab Municipal Act is a code of law, governing Municipal Committees. The application of this Act was extended to Delhi and the New Delhi Municipal Council was established in 1926.

The Delhi Municipal Corporation Act, 1957

Under this act, Delhi Municipal Corporation was established with elected members and a full time Commissioner. The jurisdiction of MCD was over areas not covered by NDMC and Cantonment Board and it also covers rural areas within National Capital Territory of Delhi. The Corporation performs municipal functions like health, education, provision and maintenance of services, the registration of births and deaths, etc. Apart from the above obligatory functions, the Corporation also had some discretionary functions like-cultural and physical education, maintenance and aid to libraries and museums, etc. Vide DMC Amendment Act, 2011, the Delhi Municipal Corporation has been trifurcated.

The Slum Areas (Improvement and Clearance) Act, 1956

This Act provides for the improvement and clearance of slum areas in certain Union Territories and for the protection of tenants in such areas from eviction. This Act came into force from 29.12.1956. The major provisions of the Act are:

(i) Competent Authority can declare following areas to be a slum area:
   - area in any respect unfit for human habitation; or
   - area by reason of dilapidation, overcrowding, faulty arrangement and design of such buildings, narrowness or faulty arrangement of streets, lack of ventilation, light of sanitation facilities, or any combination of these factors, which are detrimental to safety, health or morals.

(ii) Empower the competent Authority to acquire or take up improvement of buildings unfit for human habitation and enforcement of notice requiring execution of works of improvement. The expenses of maintenance of works of improvement, etc. are recoverable from the occupiers of buildings. Competent Authority can order demolition of buildings unfit for human habitation.

(iii) Competent Authority has powers to declare any slum area to be a clearance area and order slum clearance and redevelop the area.

(iv) Central Government can acquire the land and make available to the competent authority for the purpose of redevelopment.

(v) The Competent Authority may, by general or special order, authorise any person with
   - power to enter land, adjoining area where work is in progress.
   - breaking into buildings
   - powers to remove offensive or dangerous trade from slum areas.
   - order for demolition of buildings in certain cases.

Legislation for Controlling Land Use and sub-division

These legislations have been enacted for controlling land use and are regulatory in nature and seek to impose controls with a view to prevent haphazard development in the areas in which they are in operation.

Table 14.2: Land Use Control Legislation

Sl. No.	Year	Name of the Act	State/Union Territory
1.	1905	The Andhra Pradesh Land Encroachment Act	Andhra Pradesh
2.	1905	The Tamil Nadu Land Encroachment Act	Tamil Nadu
3.	1945	The U.P. Roadsides Land Control Act	Uttar Pradesh
4.	1948	The Bihar Restriction of Uses of Land Act	Bihar

5.	1948	The M.P. Regulation of Uses of Land Act	Madhya Pradesh
6.	1948	The J&K Prevention of Ribbon Development Act	J&K
7.	1951	The Punjab Development of Damage Areas Act	Punjab
8.	1952	The Capital of Punjab (Development and Regulation) Act	Chandigarh
9.	1952	The Punjab New Capital (Periphery) Control Act	Chandigarh/Punjab and
10.	1953	The Punjab Peripheral Development Control Act	Haryana
11.	1954	The Natural Calamities and Destroyed Areas Improvement Act (J & K)	J & K
12.	1954	The Orissa Prevention of Land Encroachment Act	Orissa
13.	1954	The Rajasthan Colonization Act	Rajasthan
14.	1955	The U.P. (Regulation of Building Operations) Act	Uttar Pradesh
15.	1958	The J.K. Control of Building Operation Act	J & K
16.	1958	The Punjab Nangal Township (Periphery) Control Act	Punjab
17.	1960	The Gujarat New Capital (Periphery) Control Act	Gujarat
18.	1960	The M.P. Town (Periphery) Control Act	Madhya Pradesh
19.	1960	The Punjab New Mandies Township (Development and Regulation) Act	Haryana
20.	1961	The Punjab Talwara Township (Periphery) Control Act	Punjab
21.	1963	The Maharashtra Ownership Flats (Regulations of the Promotion Construction, Sale, Management and Transfer) Act	Maharashtra
22.	1963	The Punjab Scheduled Roads and Controlled Areas Restriction of Unregulated Development Act	Punjab and Haryana
23.	1964	The Karnataka Highways Act	Karnataka
24.	1968	The Himachal Pradesh Road Side Land Control Act	Himachal Pradesh
25.	1964	The Punjab Urban Estate (Development and Regulation) Act	Punjab
26.	1970	The Pondicherry Land Encroachment Act	Pondicherry (Puducherry)
27.	1972	The West Bengal Apartment (Regulation of Construction and Transfer) Act	West Bengal
28.	1973	The Himachal Pradesh Mandi Townships (Development and Regulation) Act	Himachal Pradesh
29.	1975	The Punjab Regulation of Colonies Act	Punjab
30.	1976	The Bihar Public Land Encroachment Act.	Bihar
31.	1976	The Himachal Pradesh New Towns Periphery Control Act	Bihar

32.	1976	The Urban Land (Ceiling and Regulation) Act (Central Act)	Most of the States and Union Territories have repealed this Act
33.	1978	The Himachal Pradesh Land Preservation Act	Himachal Pradesh
34.	1987	The Andhra Pradesh Apartments (Promotion of Construction and Ownership) Act	Andhra Pradesh
35.	1991	The Karnataka Regulation of Unauthorised Constructions in Urban Areas Act	Karnataka
36.	1995	The Punjab Apartments and Property Regulations Act	Punjab
37.	1976	Tamil Nadu Urban Land (Ceiling and Regulation) Act	Tamil Nadu

The Public Premises (Eviction of Unauthorised Occupants) Act, 1971

The powers under this Act are exercised by a Estate Officer appointed by the Central Government. The main provision of the Act is to seal public premises under unauthorised occupation by a process of law as given in the Act.

The Ancient Monuments Preservation Act, 1904

This Act provides for the preservation of ancient monuments and objects of archaeological and historical importance. The main provisions of the Act are:

(i) The Central Government, may by notification, declare an ancient monument to be a protected monument.

(ii) Ancient Monuments:
- Acquisition of rights and/or guardianship of a monument.
- Preservation of ancient monuments by agreement.

(iii) The Central Government to control mining, quarrying, excavating, blasting and other operations for the purpose of protecting or preserving any ancient monument.

(iv) The Central Government has also powers with respect to:
- maintenance of certain protected monuments
- protection of place of worship from misuse, pollution or descration.
- right of access to certain protected monuments.

The Cantonments Act, 1924

Under the Cantonments Act, the Central Government can declare any place or places which are required for the services of Indian Army or the Indian Air force to be a Cantonment and define the limits of the Cantonment. Under this Act, every cantonment was to have a Cantonment Board and an Executive Officer. The Cantonment Boards set up under this Act have to carry out municipal functions in the cantonment area, excluding those coming under the direct control of the forces. In 1938 under this Act, Delhi Cantonment Board was set up for the Cantonment Area of Delhi.

The Wakf Amendment Act, 1984

The Act, which came into force in 1984, provides the constitution of Wakf Boards with a view to manage, notify, protect control, administor and develop Muslim Wakf Properties, in accordance with the land use, Master Plan or any other law which may be in force locally.

Improvement Trust Acts

During the beginning of 20th century, most of the towns and cities had organic growth. The eariliest planning enactments were in the form of improvement Trust Acts. The first one was enacted in Bombay in 1898, under which an improvement trust was established in Bombay in 1898. This was followed by similar enactments in other states. Out of a total of 14 improvement Trust Acts enacted in the country before and after the independence, four have been repealed, two partly repealed, one repealed but was revived later and the rest are still continuing.

Table 14.3: Improvement Trust Acts in India

Sl. No.	Act	Year	Present Status
1.	Bombay Improvement Act	1898	Repealed
2.	Mysore Improvement Act	1903	Repealed
3.	The Calcutta Improvement Act	1911	Continues
4.	The U.P. Town Improvement Act	1919	Partly Repealed
5.	The Punjab Town Improvement Act	1922	Continues
6.	The Nagpur Improvement Trust Act	1935	Repealed but revived
7.	The City of Bangalore Improvement Act	1945	Repealed
8.	The Madras Improvement Trust Act	1948	Repealed
9.	The Bihar Town Planning and Improvement Trust Act	1951	Continues
10.	The Orissa Town Planning and Improvement Trust Act	1956	Continues
11.	The Howrah Improvement Act	1956	Continues
12.	The Rajasthan Urban improvement Act	1959	Continues
13.	The M.P. Town Improvement Trust Act	1960	Partly Repealed
14.	The Karnataka Improvement Board Act	1976	Continues

The National Capital Region Planning Board Act, 1985

The objective of this Act is to keep Delhi within manageable size and to ensure the development of the surrounding regions in the States of Rajasthan, U.P. and Haryana in a coordinated manner. The Act provides for the constitution of a statutory Planning Board for preparation, coordination and monitoring of the National Capital Region Plan. The Board under the Act also controls the land uses and development of infrastructure in the National Capital Region. The Act provides for preparation of a regional plan, functional plans, sub-regional plans and project plans.

The Delhi Urban Art Commission Act, 1973

This Act provides for the establishment of Delhi Urban Art Commission with a view to preserving, developing and maintaining the aesthetic quality of urban and environmental design within Delhi. This Act came into force from 1.1.1974.

The Commission advises the Central Government and local bodies in the matter of preserving, developing and maintaining the aesthetic quality of urban and environmental design within Delhi in respect of any project of building operations or engineering operations or any development proposal which affects or is likely to affect the skyline or the aesthetic quality of surroundings or any public amenity provided therein.

Every Local Body before according approval in respect of any building operations, engineering operations or development proposals for the following matters shall refer the same to the Commission for scrutiny of the Commission and its advise shall be binding on the Local Body:

- District Centres, Civic Centres, Residential Complexes, Public Gardens, Parks, etc.
- Redevelopment of area within NDMC area.
- Redevelopment of areas in the vicinity of Jama Masjid, Red Fort, etc. and other places of historical importance.
- Conservation, preservation and beautification of monumental buildings.
- Under-passes, over-passes and regulations of street furniture and hoardings;
- Location and plans of power houses, water towers, television and other communication towers and other allied structures.
- Any other project which is calculated to beautify Delhi or to add to its cultural activity or to enhance the quality of the surroundings.

Architects Act, 1972

This Act, enacted by the Parliament on 31st May 1972, provides for the registration and regulation of Architects and for matters connected therewith.

State Housing Board Acts

Various States have enacted Housing Board Acts for the setting up of Housing Boards for preparing and execution of housing schemes for the public.

Table 14.4: Housing Board Acts

Sl. No.	Year	Name of the Act	State/Union Territory
1.	1956	The A.P. Housing Board Act	Andhra Pradesh
2.	1961	The T.N. State Housing Board Act	Tamil Nadu
3.	1961	The Gujarat Housing Board Act	Gujarat
4.	1962	The Karnataka Housing Board Act	Karanataka
5.	1965	The UP Avas Evam Vikas Parishad Adhiniyam	Uttar Pradesh
6.	1968	The Orissa Housing Board Act	Orissa
7.	1970	The Rajasthan Housing Board Act	Rajasthan
8.	1971	The Kerala State Housing Board Act	Kerala
9.	1971	The Haryana State Housing Board Act	Haryana
10.	1971	The Bihar State Housing Board Act	Bihar
11.	1972	The H.P. Housing Board Act	Himachal Pradesh
12.	1972	The West Bengal Housing Board Act	West Bengal
13.	1972	The Punjab Housing Development Act	Punjab
14.	1972	The Assam State Housing Act	Assam
15.	1973	The M.P. Grih Nirman Mandal Adhiniyam	Madhya Pradesh
16.	1973	The Pondicherry Housing Board Act	Pondicherry
17.	1976	The Maharashtra Housing Board Act	Maharashtra
18.	1976	The J & K Housing Board Act	J & K
19.	2010	Delhi Urban Shelter Improvement Board	Delhi

Delhi Rent Control Act, 1958

The Act provides for the control of rent and eviction, rates of Hotels, Lodging Houses etc. and for the lease of vacant premises to Government in certain areas in the Delhi. The major provisions of the Act are:

(i) This Act extends to the areas within the limits of NDMC, Delhi Cantonment Board and to such urban areas within the limits of MCD. The Government premises are excluded from this.

(ii) Fixation of standard rent and protection of tenants against eviction.

(iii) Right to recover immediate possession of premises to accrue to certain persons.

(iv) Recovery of possession for:

- occupation and re-entry
- for repairs and rebuilding and re-entry - in case of tenancies for limited period.

(v) Permission to construct additional structures and special provision regarding vacant building sites.

The Delhi Land Holding (Ceiling) Act, 1960

This Act provides for the imposition of the ceiling in the National Capital Territory of the Delhi and for matters connected therewith. The main provisions of the Act are:

(i) Ceiling on Holdings
(ii) Submission of Returns
(iii) Procedure for determination of excess land
(iv) Excess land to vest in Government
(v) Compensation.

The Delhi Lands (Restrictions on Transfer) Act, 1972

This is an Act to impose certain restriction on transfer of lands which have been acquired by the Central Government or in respect of which acquisition proceedings have been initiated by the Government, with a view to preventing large scale transactions of purported transfers of such lands in the market.

The Delhi Road Transport Laws (Amendment) Act, 1971

This is an Act which provides for the establishment of the Road Transport System for the National Capital Territory of Delhi and further to amend the Road Transport Corporation Act, 1950 and the Delhi Municipal Corporation Act, 1957. Under this Act, the Delhi Transport Corporation which looks after these functions was established. Earlier, these functions were performed by MCD and was known as Delhi Transport Service and later as Delhi Transport Corporation.

Water Prevention and Control of Pollution Act, 1974 (Amended in 1988)

The powers under this Act are exercised by the Central Board or the Joint Board with the main function to promote cleanliness of streams and wells in different areas of the State/ Union Territories.

Air (Prevention and Control of Pollution) Act, 1981

To counter the problems associated with air pollution, ambient air quality standards were established under the 1981 Act. The Act provides means for the control and abatement of air pollution. The Act seeks to combat air pollution by prohibiting the use of polluting fuels and substances, as well as by regulating appliances that give rise to air pollution. Under the Act establishing or operating of any industrial plant in the pollution control area requires consent from state boards. The boards are also expected to test the air in air pollution control areas, inspect pollution control equipment, and manufacturing processes.

The Forests (Conservation) Act, 1980

This Act was adopted to protect and conserve forests. The Act restricts the powers of the State in respect of de-reservation of forests and use of forest land for non-forest purposes (the term non-forest purpose includes clearing any forest land for cultivation of cash crops, plantation crops, horticulture or any purpose other than re-afforestation).

Environment (Protection) Act, 1986 (EPA): This Act is an umbrella legislation designed to provide a framework for the co-ordination of central and state authorities established under the Water (Prevention and Control) Act, 1974 and Air (Prevention and Control) Act, 1981. Under this Act, the central government is empowered to take measures necessary to protect and improve the quality of the environment by setting standards for emissions and discharges; regulating the location of industries; management of hazardous wastes, and protection of public health and welfare.

From time to time the central government issues notifications under the EPA for the protection of ecologically-sensitive areas or issues Rules and Regulations, and guidelines for matters under the EPA.

The projects requiring an Environmental Impact Assessment report are termed as Category 'Bl' and remaining projects termed Category 'B2', do not require an Environment Impact Assessment report. For categorization of projects into Bl or B2 except item 8 (b), the Ministry of Environment and Forests have issued the guidelines. All projects and activities listed as Category 'B' in Item 8 of the Schedule (Construction / Township / Commercial Complexes / Housing) shall not require scoping and will be appraised on the basis of Form I/ Form 1A and the conceptual plan.

Table 14.5: Mandatory EIA for Building/Construction Projects/Area Development Projects and Townships (2006)

8(a) Building and Construction projects	<20,000 sq. metres and <1,50,000 sq. metres of built-up area#	Any project or activity specified in Category 'B' will be treated as Category 'A' if located in whole or in part within 10 Km from the boundary of: (i) Protected areas notified under the Wildlife. (Protection) Act, 1972; (ii) Critically polluted areas as identified by the Central Pollution Control Board from time to time; (iii) Eco-sensitive areas as notified under section 3 of the Environment (Protection) Act, 1986, such as, Mahabaleswar Panchangi, Matheran, Pachmarhi, Dahanu, Doon Valley and (iv) interstate boundaries and international boundaries.
8(b) Townships and Area Development	Covering an area 50 ha and or built up area $\geq$ 1,50,000 sq. mtrs. ++	Provided that the requirement regarding distance of 10 km of the inter-state boundaries can be reduced or completely done away with by an agreement between the respective states or U.Ts having the common boundary in the case the activity does not fall within 10 kilometers of the areas mentioned at item (i), (ii) and (iii) above

(built up area for covered construction; in the case of facilities open to the sky, it will be the activity area) ++All projects under Item 8(b) shall be appraised as Category B1

National Green Tribunal (NGT) Act, 2010

The National Green Tribunal was established on 18.10.2010 under the National Green Tribunal Act, 2010 for effective and expeditious disposal of cases relating to environmental protection and conservation of forests and other natural resources including enforcement of any legal right relating to environment and giving relief and compensation for damages to persons and property and for matters connected therewith or incidental thereto. It is a specialized body equipped with the necessary expertise to handle environmental disputes involving multi-disciplinary issues. The Tribunal shall not be bound by the procedure laid down under the Code of Civil Procedure, 1908, but shall be guided by principles of natural justice.

The Tribunal shall provide speedy environmental justice and help reduce the burden of litigation in the higher courts. The Tribunal is mandated to make and endeavour for disposal of applications or appeals finally within 6 months of filing of the same. New Delhi is the principal Place of sitting of the Tribunal and Bhopal, Pune, Kolkata and Chennai shall be the other 4 places of sitting of the Tribunal.

Real Estate (Regulation and Development) Act, 2016

The Real Estate (Regulation of Development) Act has been notified and States are expected to legislate in keeping with the provisions of the proposed law. They will also set up regulators to give effect to the bill which recommends a three-year jail term or penalty which may amount to a percentage of project cost for failure to register.The law obliges the developers and the builders to provide details of the number and size of plots, layout plan, carpet area and plinth area of flats, apartments of their housing complexes.

Importantly, it will prevent builders from changing the plans or inserting charges as the sale agreement will be considered binding. The will also post a list of authorised brokers and dealers.The legislation seeks to prevent advance payments being extracted from buyers without a written sale agreement containing project time line, payment details and possession date. The promoter will not be able to cancel the sale deed unilaterally. If there is sufficient reason to do so, a notice will have to be given and the money will have to be given and the money paid will be returned with interest fixed to bank rate. The promoters would furnish a bank guarantee equal to 5% of estimated cost of project.

Provisions in the Real Estate Regulation Act

1. Project of be registered with the regulator before any development on the land (launch of project).
2. Promoter should have all approvals and sanctions from respective authorities in order to register the project.
3. Promoter can't accept a deposit or advance before entering into agreement of sale with the buyer.

4. Promoter will have to disclose all material details, including schedule of the project and the basic services being provided.
5. Regulatory authority to ensure a framework of standard procedures and norms for speedy processing and grant of planning permissions and building approvals across states.
6. Penalty, if builder fails to meet the provisions, including imprisonment of up to three years.

The Act seeks to ensure that the promoter, developer and builders are able to deliver apartments in time. The Act provides protection to the allottees against any fraud. It provides for speedy construction and as per structural and building bylaws.

Transfer of Property Act, 1882

The Act came into being to define and amend, certain parts of law relating to the transfer of property by act of parties. It does not deal with the transfer of property by operation of law or with the passing of property, after death. Therefore, it may be said to be complementary to the law of testamentary and intestate succession.

The Act does not define "immovable property" exhaustively but only excludes from the definition "standing timber, growing crops or grass". Even the definition in the General Clauses Act is not exhaustive; which says "immovable property shall include land, benefits arising out of land and thing attached to the earth".

Attached to the earth means:

(a) rooted in the earth as in the case of trees;

(b) embedded in the earth as in the case of walls or buildings; or

(c) attached to what is so embedded for the permanent beneficial enjoyment of that to which it is attached.

Property of any kind may be transferred, except as otherwise provided by this Act or by any other law for the time being in force:

(a) The chance of an heir-apparent succeeding to an estate, the chance of a relation obtaining a legacy on the death of a kinsman, or any other mere possibility of a such nature, cannot be transferred.

(b) A mere right of re-entry for breach of a condition subsequent cannot be transferred to anyone except the owner of the property affected thereby.

(c) An easement cannot be transferred apart from the dominant heritage.

(d) All interest in property restricted in its enjoyment to the owner personally cannot be transferred by him.

(e) A right to future maintenance, in whatsoever manner arising, secured or determined, cannot be transferred.

(f) A mere right to sue cannot be transferred.

(g) A public office cannot be transferred, nor can the salary of a public officer, whether before or after it has become payable.

(h) Stipends allowed to military, naval, air force and civil pensioners of the Government and political pensions cannot be transferred.

(i) No transfer can be made (1) in so far as it is opposed to the nature of the interest affected thereby, or (2) for an unlawful object or consideration within the meaning of section 23 of the Indian Contract Act, 1872 (9 of 1872), or (3) to a person legally disqualified to be transferee,

(j) Nothing in this section shall be deemed to authorise a tenant having a non-transferable right of occupancy, the farmer of an estate in respect of which default has been made in paying revenue, or the lessee of an estate, under the management of a Court of wards, to assign his interest as such tenant, farmer or lessee.

The Act deals with Transfer of Property by act of parties including sale, mortgage and charge, lease, exchange, gift and actionable claims.

The Registration Act, 1908

With the increase in land and housing disputes and unauthorised occupation of immovable property the doctrine of notice is constantly being tested. The main object of the Registration Act, 1908 is to provide for, inter alia, notice to general public as to the transactions in immovable property by execution of certain documents. The Act deals with the various authorities with whom the documents can be registered; the registrable documents; the time within which the documents can be presented for registration; the place where the documents can be registered; the power of certain Authorities to enforce appearance of executants and witnesses, the duties and powers of registering officer and the power to impose penalties, etc.

The Inspector General of Registration is the head of establishment. Registrars and Sub-Registrars may be appointed for the districts as may be formed by the State Government for this purpose. The State Government may also appoint an Inspector General.

The following documents are compulsorily registrable:

(a) instruments of gift of immovable property;

(b) other non-testamentary instruments which purport or operate to create, declare, assign, limit or extinguish, whether in present or in future, any right, title or interest, whether vested or contingent, of the value of one hundred rupees and upward of immovable property;

(c) non-testamentary instruments which acknowledge the receipt or payment of any consideration on account of the creation, declaration, assignment, limitation or extinction of any such right, title or interest;

(d) leases of immovable property from year to year, or for any term exceeding one year, or reserving a yearly rent;

(e) non-testamentary instruments transferring or assigning any decree or order of a court or any award, when such decree or order or award purports or operates to create, declare, assign, limit or extinguish; whether in present or in future, any right, title or interest, whether vested or contingent, of the value of one hundred rupees and upward, or an immovable property;

Any of the following documents may be registered under this Act, namely:

(a) instruments (other than instruments of gift and wills) which purport or operate to create, declare, assign, limit or extinguish, whether in present or in future, any right, title or interest, whether vested or contingent, or a value less than one hundred rupees, to or in immovable property;

(b) instruments acknowledge the receipt or payment of any consideration on account of the creation, declaration, assignment, limitation or extinction of any such right, title or interest;

(c) lease of immovable property for any term not exceeding one year, and lease exempted under section 17;

(d) instruments transferring or assigning any decree or order of a Court or any award when such decree or order or award purports or operates to create, declare, assign, limit or extinguish, whether in present or in future, any right, title or interest whether vested or contingent, of a value less than one hundred rupees of an immovable property;

(e) instruments (other than wills) which purport or operate to create, declare, assign, limit or extinguish any right, title or interest to or in immovable property;

(e) wills; and

(f) all other documents not required by section 17 to be registered.

No document, required to be registered, shall affect any immovable property comprised in the document unless it is registered. Similarly, it will not be received as an evidence of any transaction affecting such property.

Need to Review Town Planning Acts

The first town planning legislation came in the year in 1915 when the Bombay Town Planning Act was passed. This was only applicable to the areas under Bombay Province and even the city of Bombay was excluded in the original Act, unless special permission from government was obtained. It was first made applicable to Bombay city in 1944 after explosion of a ship in Bombay Harbour with heavy damages to buildings in Mandvi area.

The Act was inspired by the British Town Planning Act, 1909, with several similarities and differences. Both Acts provide for making Town Planning Schemes for areas under process of development and the local authorities desiring to develop an area under the provision of T.P. Act becomes statutory. Against the elaborately described social objectives in the Town Planning Act in UK, the objective of Bombay Act was more physical, orderly development, provision of amenities and services, including roads, sewer and drains. The British T.P. Act provides for zoning of areas for housing, shopping, etc and not detailed planning of each and every plot. There is a provision for recovery of betterment charges but hardly any such charges are recovered from owners of lands falling in the T.P. Scheme.

The main drawback of T.P. Schemes in Bombay had been the inordinate delays involved in the laid down procedures under the Act. Subsequently, Punjab Town Improvement Trust (1920), UP Improvement Trust (1919), Madras Town Planning Act, 1920 and other States also enacted similar Acts. Many States in India modelled or modified their Town Planning legislation on the basis of Town and Country Planning Act, (1947) of United Kingdom, Model Town and Regional planning and Development Act (1962) drafted by the Town and Country Planning Organisation (TCPO) and Urban Development Plan Formulation and Implementation Guidelines (1996) prepared by the Institute of Town Planners, India for the Ministry of Urban Development, Government of India. The UDPFI Guidelines have been revised as the Urban and Regional Development Plans Formulation and Implementation Guidelines (URDPFI) in 2015. In view of 74th CAA, Right to Fair Compensation in Land Acquisition, Resettlement and Rehabilitation Act 2013, a revised Model Town and Country Planning and Development Law has been drafted as a part of URDPFI guidelines.

The current planning and its legal frameworks in India have not kept pace with the socio-economic, environmental and technological changes. This involves radical changes in legal and institutional frameworks, which are in pace with the new strategies of land management, planning, infrastructure development, pollution prevention and urban resilience. The new approach has to be inclusive for integration of poor in the wider urban system and should address the local issues of planning and development. The performance of the urban local bodies involves a reformed legal, institutional and regulatory framework, together with their capacity building in planning, land management, infrastructure development, housing and financial management. Bringing together multiple agencies on a common, unified platform is a major area of public policy and legal framework that can direct the cities on a sustainable and inclusive path. This requires an umbrella legislation which facilitates the local, district, regional and State to plan and work in unison, while also safeguarding their autonomy. For example, NCRPB, DDA, DUAC and Heritage Conservation Committee in New Delhi can be merged on a common platform with a close relationship with urban planning.

This demands radical changes in the conventional planning approach based on information, intelligence, systems and structures, but on the criteria of inclusion, intuition, innovation, charisma, culture, emotions, disruption, values, aspirations and endurance. This means that the legal framework has to be flexible having the attributes of subtraction, unification, multiplication and division. It should be able to adjust and align with the socio-economic, ecological and technological changes. To illustrate, the computer, telephone, personal diary, calculator, camera, bank and post office are combined in a mobile phone, which is an apt example of substraction, unification, multiplication and division. This analogy can be applied while reviewing the legal and institutional frameworks of planning and urban development.

Debriefing and Review

1. List major Acts related to town planning and urban development.
2. Briefly explain the following:
   (i) Town Planning Acts
   (ii) Improvement Trust Acts
   (iii) Development Authority Acts
   (iv) 73rd and 74th Constitutional Amendment Acts
3. Give a comparative chart of Land Acquisition Act, 1894 and Right to Fair Compensation and Transparency in Land Acquisition, Rehabilitation and Resettlement Act, 2013.
4. Explain the legal provisions for environmental protection.
5. What is the role of urban regulations and Building Bye Laws vis-a-vis Town Planning?
6. Explain the legal status of development control regulations and Building Bye–Laws.
7. Taking an example of an Urban Local Body Act or Town Planning Act, what are the important sections which should be changed, keeping in view the changing urban scenario?

BIBLIOGRAPHY

Acioly, Claudio & Forbes Davidson (1996) Density in Urban Development, Building Issues, Vol. 8, Lund Center for Habitat Studies, Sweden.

Action Enterprise (2014) India Exclusion Report, BFC, Bangalore.

ADB, (2011) Inclusive Cities, ADB, Manila.

Adrian and Gordon Gill (2011) Toward Zero Carbon, Image Pub., Australia.

Aga Khan Trust for Culture (2011) Historic City Program, Prestel, New York.

Ahluwalia, M. S. (2011) Prospects and Policy Challenges in the Twelfth Plan, Economic and Political Weekly, Vol. 46, 21, p. 88-105.

Aijaz, Rumi (2015) India's Urbanisation Experiences, Operations Research Foundation, New Delhi.

AMDA (2009) Land Policy for NCTD-2021, Association of Municipal and Development Authorities, New Delhi.

Anurag, R. (2007) Green is not just a colour: architecture towards a sustainable development. Architecture + Design 24(10) 92-100.

Archaeological Survey of India, Legislations http://asi.nic.in/asi_legislations. asp 2007.

Archer, R W. (1993) Urban redevelopment with landowner participation using the land pooling/ readjustment technique. Bangkok: Asian Institute of Technology.

Arvind, K., Baker, N., Yannas, S. & Szokolay, S. V. (ed), (2001). Climatic Responsive Architecture, Tata McGraw Hill, New Delhi.

Baker, Lee and David Sims (1991) India Public/Private Partnerships in Land Development.
Commonwealth Secretariat, London.

Bandhopadhya, Dr. Bibek (1998) Solar Water Heating, IREDA News, Jan.-March, 1998.

Bangalore Development. Authority (BDA) (2007) Report on Comprehensive Development Plan (Revised) Bangalore.

Bansal, A. and A.K. Jain (1986) Acquisition, Development and Colonisation of Land in Gurgaon: The Impact of Strategies and Programmes, Research Study for Indian Human Settlement Program, New Delhi.

Bansal, N. K. & Minke, G. (eds) (1995) Climatic Zones and Rural Housing in India.

Banashree, Mitra (1987) Land Supply for Low Income Housing in Delhi, Seminar IHS Rotterdam.

Barbara Harris-White, (ed) (2016), Middle India and Urban-Rural Development, Four Decades of Change, Springer, New Delhi/London.

Barton, H., Davis, G. and Guise, R. (1995) Sustainable Settlements: A Guide for Planners, Devgners and Developers, Research and Consultancy Unit, University of West of England, UK.

Barton H. (2003) Shaping Neighbourhoods, Spon Press, London.

BEE, (2007) Energy Conservation Building Code, Bureau of Energy Efficiency, New Delhi

BEE, (2009) Energy Conservation Building Code User Guide, Bureau of Energy Efficiency, New Delhi

Bell, Keith Cliford, World Bank (2011) Land Governance, in Coordinates, December, pp. 18-20, New Delhi.

Benninger, Christopher (2011) Letter to a Young Architect, CCBA Pvt. Ltd., Pune

Benninger, Christopher (2016) Architecture for Modern India, CCBA, Pune/Skira, Milano.

Bertaud, Alain (2014) Converting land into affordable housing floor space, Policy Research Working Paper Series 6870, The World Bank.

Bhatia, Gautam (2014) For the New Prime Minister, Times of India, 25th May 2014, New Delhi.

Billand, Charles J. (1990) Delhi Case Study: Formal Serviced Land Delivery, Washington D.C Prepared for A.I.D. PADCO.

BIS, (2005 and 2016), National Building Code of India, Bureau of Indian Standards, New Delhi.

Boesiger, W (Ed.) (1999) Le Corbusier-Complete Works, Birkhauser Publishers, Bese.

Brown, A. (2015) Planning for Sustainable and Inclusive Cities in the Global South, GIZ/DFID.

Bunyard Peter (1978) Sewage Treatment in a Swedish Sculpture Garden, Ecologist, No.1, Jan-Feb.

Calvita, Nico and Alan Mallach (2010) Inclusionary Housing in International Perspective: Affordable Housing, Social Inclusion and Land Value Recapture, Cambridge, MA, Lincoln Institute of Land Policy.

Census of India (2011) Primary Census Abstract - Data Highlights, India, Series 1, New Delhi: Office of the Registrar General and Census Commissioner, India.

Census of India (2012) H-Series Tables on Census Houses, Household Amenities and Assets, 2011, Registrar General and Census Commissioner, India, Ministry of Home Affairs, New Delhi.

Census of India, (2011) Census Report, Government of India, New Delhi.

CPCB (2000), Status of water supply and wastewater generation, collection, treatment and disposal *in class I cities*, Central Pollution Control Board, Delhi.

CPCB (2000) Status of water supply and wastewater generation, collection, treatment and disposal *in class II towns*, Central Pollution Control Board, Delhi.

Central Public Health Engineering and Environment Organisation (CPHEEO) 1999, Manual on water supply, New Delhi.

CPHEEO (2013) Manual on Sewerge and Sewage Treatment, New Delhi.

CPHEEO (2000) Manual on Solid Waste Management, New Delhi.

Centre for Policy Research (2012) Governing Indian Mega-Cities, New Delhi.

Centre for Science and Environment (2012) Excreta Matters, 71 Cities Survey, CSE, New Delhi.

Chen, M Skinner, C (2014) The Urban Informal Economy: Enhanced Knowledge, Appropriate Policies and Effective Organisation, Routledge, New York.

Chennai Metropolitan Development Authority, Master Plan for Chennai, CMDA, Chennai.

Christ, Emanual and Christoph Ganenbein (2015) Typology, Review No. III, ETH, Zurich.

Cities on Water (1991) Impact of Sea Level Rise on Cities and Regions, Proceedings of the Commonwealth Science Council, London.

Courtney, J. (1978) Urban Land-Use Regulation, in Urban Land Policy: Issues and Opportunities, edited by H. Dunkerly and C.M Whitehead, World Bank, Washington.

Crowe, Timothy D. (2000) Crime Prevention through Environmental Design, 2nd Edition, Stoneham, MA Butterworth, Heinemann.

CRY (2012) Annual Survey report 2012-13, New Delhi.

Davis, John Emmeus (ed) (2010) The Community Land Trust Reader, Lincoln Institute of Land Policy. May.

DDA (1981) Disposal and Development of Nazul Land Rules, New Delhi.

DDA (2007) Master Plan for Delhi : 2021, Delhi Development Authority, New Delhi.

De Soto, H. (2000) The Mystery of Capital: Why Capitalism Triumphs in the West and Fails Everywhere Else, Basic Books, New York.

Delhi Development Authority (DDA) Guidelines on Land Management. New Delhi, Unpublished reports, 1992 and 2014.

Deshpande, Subhash (2006) Vacuum Sewerage System, *IPT Journal,* Jan-Feb 2006.

Doxiadis, C. (1965) 'Islamabad, the Creation of a New Capital' Town Planning Review, 36(1).

DPU & HIC (2015) Habitat III National Reporting Processes: Locating Right to the City and the Role of Civil Society, University College, London.

Drakatis Smith (2001) Handbook of Urban Studies, Sage Publication, London.

Dreze, Jean, and Amartya Sen (1996) India, Economic Development and Social Opportunity, New Delhi: Oxford University Press.

DUAC/Divya Kush (2014) New Ashok Nagar, DUAC, New Delhi.

DUAC/M.N. Ashish Ganju (2014) Aya Nagar Urban Development, DUAC, New Delhi.

DUAC/Sameer Mathur and R.B. Singh (2014) Delhi Greenways, DUAC, New Delhi.

DUAC/Aruna R. Grover & Satish Khanna (2016) Patparganj Slum Redevelopment Scheme, DUAC, New Delhi.

DUAC/Amit Ghosal (2016) Adarsh Nagar, Ward No. 14, DUAC, New Delhi.

DUAC/Ashok B.Lall (2016) Malviya Nagar, Hauz Rani and Khirki Extn. Ward Nos. 161, 162, 189, 191, DUAC, New Delhi.

DUAC/Amit Ghosh (2016) Punjabi Bagh, Ward No. 103, DUAC, New Delhi.

DUAC/Rahoul B. Singh (2016) Rajuvenation of Najafgarh Waterway, DUAC, New Delhi.

DUAC/MN Ashish Ganju (2016) Lado Sarai, Ward No. 169, DUAC New Delhi.

DUEIIP (2001) Status Report of Delhi 21, Delhi Urban Environment and Infrastructure Improvement Project, Government of India, Ministry of Environment and Forests and Government of NCT of Delhi, Planning Department, New Delhi.

Dupont, V. (2008) Slum Demolition in Delhi Since the 1990s: An Appraisal, Economic and Political Weekly, Vol. 43, 28, (2008), Mumbai.

Erpenstein, Annette (2012) Back to the Future: The Rebirth of Public Place in Seoul, Trialog.

Faetanini, M et al, (2011) Urban Policies and the Right to the City in India, CSH and UNESCO, New Delhi.

Fonesca, Rory (1979) The Walled City of Old Delhi in Shelter and Society (ed. Paul Oliver), Praeger, New York.

Frampton, Kenneth (1996) Charles Correa, Perennial Press, Mumbai.

Agarwal, Anil & Sunita Narain (1997) Dying Wisdom (India's Traditional Water Harvesting System), Centre for Science & Environment, New Delhi.

GEAG (2009) Vulnerability Analysis, Gorakhpur City, GEAG, Gorakhpur.

Gehl Jan (2010) Cities for People, Island Press, Washington/London.

Ghertner, D Asher (2015) Rule by Aesthetics - World Class City in Making in Delhi, Oxford University Press, New Delhi.

Girardet, Herbert (1997) Sustainable Cities - A Contradiction in Terms, Architectural Design, London.

GOI (1956) Slum Areas (Improvement and Clearance) Act, Government of India.

GOI (2006) Integrated Energy Policy, Expert Committee Report, Planning Commission, Government of India. http://planningcommission.nic.in/reports/genrep/rep_intengy.pdf.

GOI, Ministry of Urban Development (website), JNNURM Toolkit, Guidelines and Progress (2006-13), New Delhi.

GOI, Tendulkar Committee Report (2009) Planning Commission, Government of India, New Delhi.

Goodall, Christ (2007) How to Live a Low Carbon Life, Earthscan, London.

Gotsch Peter (2012) IDEAN Principles-Ingredients of Sustainable and Resilient Neighbourhoods.

Government of India (2007) Urban National Housing and Habitat Policy, Ministry of Urban Affairs and Employment, New Delhi.

Government of India (2008) PM's council on climate change, National Action Plan for Climate Change, New Delhi.

Government of India (2009) National Mission on Sustainable Habitat, MOUD, New Delhi.

Government of India (2012) Task Force Report on Urban Housing, Ministry of Housing and Urban Poverty Alleviation New Delhi.

Government of India (2013) Twelfth Five Year Plan, Planning Commission, New Delhi.

Government of NCT Delhi (2013) Delhi Human Development Report, Oxford, New Delhi.

Government of India (2011) Report of the High Powered Committee on Urban Infrastructure, (Isher Ahluwalia Report), Ministry of Urban Development, New Delhi.

GTZ (2006) *Capacity Building for Ecological Sanitation,* Paris: UNESCO.

Guerrleri, Pilar Maria (2018) Negotiating Cultures, Oxford University Press, New Delhi.

Harody, I. E., Mitlin, D., Satterthwaite, D. (1992) Environmental Problems in Third World Cities. Earthscan Publications Ltd., London.

Hough, Michael (1995) Cities & Natural Process, Routeledge, London.

IBM Institute for Business Value Analysis, How City System can be Made Smarter with Instrumentation, Interconnection and Intelligence.

ICLEI (2007) Preparing for Climate Change: A Guidebook for Local, Regional and State Government, Washington.

ICLEI, (1997), Local Agenda 21 Survey, UN Department for Policy Coordination and Sustainable Development, Washington.

IEA (2008) India Energy Efficiency Policies and Measures: Energy Conservation Building Code, http:// www.iea.org/textbase/pm?mode=pm&id=4162&action=detail.

IEA (2007) Energy balances of Non-OECD countries, International Energy Agency.

IGBC (2007) LEED - India, Green Building Rating System, abridged reference guide for new construction and major renovations (LEED-India NC), version 1.0, Indian Green Building Council, Hyderabad. http://www.igbc.in/site/mmbase/attachments/48344/LEED.Abrid_Ver.pdf

INTACH (1999) *Delhi: The Built Heritage* (2 vols), New Delhi.

INTACH (1994) Special Issue on Heritage, Architecture + Design, May-June 1994.

IPCC (2007) Climate Change, Impacts Adaptation and Vulnerability, IPCC, Cambridge and New York.

Jacobs, Jane (1961) The Death and Life of American Cities, Random House, USA.

Jacobus, Ricks (2015) Inclusionary Housing Creating and Maintaining Equitable Communities, Cambridge MA Lincoln Institute of Land Policy.

Jain A. K. (2009) Urban Land Policy and Public Private Partnership for Real Estate and Infrastructure Projects, Readworthy Publications, New Delhi.

Jain A.K (2013) Dillinama, Synergy books New Delhi.

Jain A.K (2013) Sustainable Urban Transport and System, Khanna Publishers, New Delhi.

Jain A.K (2014) Revisiting Land Acquisition and Urban Process, Readworthy Publications, New Delhi.

Jain A.K (2014) Right to Toilet, Readworthy Publication New Delhi.

Jain A.K. (2010) Urban Planning and Governance, Bookwell, New Delhi.

Jain A.K. (2009) Planning for Inclusive Social Infrastructure, Readworthy Publications, New Delhi.

Jain A.K. (2015) Transforming Delhi, Bookwell, New Delhi.

Jain A.K. (2016) Building Twenty Million Homes, Discovery Publishing House, New Delhi.

Jain A.K. (2016) Landscape Architecture- Planning, Engineering and Horticulture, Discovery Publishing House, New Delhi.

Jain AK (2017) Urban Transformation, Discovery Publishing House, New Delhi.

Jain AK (2018) City Planning for a Changing India, Bookwell, New Delhi.

Jain, A K. (2010) Urban Housing and Slums, Readworthy Publications, New Delhi.

Jain, A. K. (2011) Making Infrastructure Work, Discovery Publishers, New Delhi.

Jain, A. K. (2015) Conservation of Cultural Heritage, Discovery Publishers, New Delhi.

Jain, A. K. (2015) Regeneration of Rivers and Water Resources, Discovery Publishers, New Delhi.

Jain, A. K. (2015) Smart Cities: Vision and Action, Discovery Publishers, New Delhi,

Jain, A. K. (2015) Towards Cleaner and Hygienic Cities and Villages, Discovery Publishers, New Delhi.

Jain, A. K. (2011) The Informal City, Readworthy Publishers, New Delhi.

Jain, A.K. (2007) Water - A Manual for Architects, Engineers, and Managers, Daya Publishers, New Delhi.

Jain, A.K. (2001) Ecology and Natural Resource Management, Management Publishing Co. Dehradun.

Jain, A.K. (2007) A Practical Guide to Disaster Management, Pragun, Delhi.

Jain, A.K. (2009) Low Carbon Cities-Policies, Planning and Practice, Discovery Publishers, New Delhi.

Jain, A.K. (2015) The Idea of Green Building, Khanna Publishers, New Delhi.

Jain, Kulbhushan and Meenakshi Jain (2000) Architecture of the Indian Desert, AADI Centre, Ahmedabad and the University of Virginia, US.

Jain, Shikha (2004) DRONAH, Presentation on "Heritage Legislation in India", an overview, IHCN, second biennialconference, Hyderabad, AP, 18-20 Dec. 2008.

Jain, Shikha Havelis: A Living Tradition of Rajasthan, Shubi Pub, Gurgaon.

Jodidio, Phillip (2015) Heritage of the Mughal World, Aga Khan Historic City Programme, Prestel, Munich

Kabre, C. (2010) A new thermal performance index for dwelling roofs in the warm humid tropics, Building and Environment, 45: 727-738.

Kachru, Upendra (1994) A Novel Method of Cooling and Heating of Buildings-Envelope Conditioning, Proceedings on Conference - Excellence in Housing, Feb-24th and 25th, Dallas, Texas, Energy Efficient Building Association, USA.

Kenworthy and F.B. Laube (1999) An International Sourcebook of Automobile Dependence in Cities, University Press of Colorado, Boulder.

Kenworthy, J. (2013) 'An International Comparative Perspective on Fast Rising Motorization and Automobile Dependence' in Urban Transport in the Developing World: A Handbook of Policy and Practice, edited by Harry T. Dimitriou and Ralph Gakenheimer, Edward Elgar Publishing Ltd., Cheltenham, UK.

Klaus, Daniels (1994) The Technology of Ecological Building, Birkhauser, Verlag, Berlin.

Koenigsberger, Ingersoll, Mayhew, Szokilay (1975) Manual of Tropical Housing and Building; Orient Longman Private Limited.

Kundu, Amitabh (2006) Trend and Patterns of Urbanisation and their Economic Implications in India, Infrastructure Report (2006) Infrastructure Development Finance Company, Oxford University Press, New Delhi.

Landsberg, H. E. (1981) The Urban Climate. Academic Press, New York.

Laul, Anil (2014) Green is Red, ASHRAY, Anangpur, Haryana.

Lowry, W. P. (1988) Atmospheric Ecology for Designers ana Planners. Peavine Press, McMinnville, Oregon.

Manda, Vikas (2014) Land Acquisition Law in India: A Historical Perspective, International Journal of Innovative Research and Studies (May).

Martin Khor and Lim Li Lin, eds (2001) Provision of Public Housing in Singapore in Good Practices and innovative Experiences in the South, Vol. 2, Social Policies, Indigenous knowledge and appropriate technology.

McHarg, Ian (1969) Design with Nature, New York, Natural History Press .

McKinsey Global Institute (2014) A Blueprint for addressing the global affordable housing challenge, New York.

McKinsey Global Institute (2010) India's Urban Awakening: Building Inclusive Cities, New York.

Mehrotra, Nirmita (2013) Disaster Resilience, Architecture-Time Space and People, Council of Architecture, New Delhi.

Mehta, Dinesh and Mira Mehta (1995) Land for Shelter Delivery of Serviced Land in Metropolitan India. Ahmedabad, India: Prepared for USAID Centre for Environmental Planning, Ahmedabad.

Mehta, Dinesh and Pushpa Pathak (1996) in Brockman, Royston. A.C., and Allen Williams (ed.) *Urban Infrastructure Finance.* Asian Development Bank, Philippines.

Mehta, Meera (1999) A Review of Public-Private Partnerships in Water and Environmental Sanitation in India. Report prepared for the Department for International Development, New Delhi, May 1999.

Ministry of Housing and Poverty Alleviation (2015) Pradhan Mantri Awas Yojana Guidelines, Government of India, New Delhi.

Ministry of Rural Development, (1999) *Total Sanitation Guidelines,* Government of India, New Delhi.

Ministry of Urban Development (2001) The Constitutional (Seventy-Fourth) Amendment Act, 1992, Power to the People: The Nagarpalika Act, Government of India, New Delhi.

Ministry of Urban Development (2011) Report of the High Power Committee on Urban Infrastructure, New Delhi.

Ministry of Urban Development (2014) Swachh Bharat (Clean India) Campaign, Government of India, New Delhi.

Ministry of Urban Development (2015) AMRUT, (Atal Mission for Rejuvenation and Urban Transformation) Government of India, New Delhi.

Ministry of Urban Development (2015) HRIDAY (Heritage and Redevelopment for Integrated Development), Government of India, New Delhi.

MOUD (2009) Toolkit for Solid Waste Management, JNUURM, New Delhi.

MOUD/ITPI (1996) UDPFI Guidelines, New Delhi.

MOHUPA, (NBO) (2012) Urban Housing Shortage, 2012-17, New Delhi.

Ministry of Urban Development (2015) Smart City Mission Guidelines, Government of India, New Delhi.

Misra, B. (1990) A Comparative Study of Urban Land Management (ULM) in Selected Developing Asian Countries and Japan in Economic Region Planning Research, No 93, Economic Research Center Nagoya University, Nagoya, Japan.

MNRE (2010) Green Rating for Integrated Habitat Assessment, Ministry of New and Renewable Energy, Government of India, New Delhi, http://www.grihaindia.org/index.php.

MNRE (2014) Report on New and Renewable Energy, Ministry of New and Renewable Energy, Government of India, New Delhi, http://www.grihaindia.org/index.php.

Modi, Narendra (2010) Convenient Action, Mcmillan, New Delhi.

MoEF (2006) Environmental Clearances, Ministry of Environment, Forests and Climate Change, Government of India, New Delhi, http://moef.nic.in/modules/project-clearances/ehvironment-clearances.

MOHUPA (Ministry of Housing and Urban Poverty Alleviation) (2013), Inclusive Urban Planning, for Poor Report, Government of India, New Delhi.

MOHUPA (Ministry of Housing and Urban Poverty Alleviation) (2015) Model Tenancy Act, Government of India, New Delhi.

MOHUPA (Ministry of Housing and Urban Poverty Alleviation) (2015) National Urban Rental Housing Policy (Draft), Government of India, New Delhi.

MOHUPA (2016) Habitat III National Report Government of India, New Delhi.

MOHUPA, (NBO) (2013) State of Housing in India: A Statistical Compendium, New Delhi.

MOHUPA, (NBO) (2013) State of Slums in India, A Statistical Compendium, New Delhi.

MoUD (2012) "Improving Urban Water Supply & Sanitation Services, Advisory Note", Ministry of Urban Development, Government of India, April 2012.

MOUD/Wilbur Smith Associates, (2008) Traffic and Transport Policies and Strategies in Urban Areas in India, Ministry of Urban Development, New Delhi.

Narain, Sunita. (2002) The Flush Toilet is Ecologically Mindless, *Down To Earth,* New Delhi, Feb.

National Commission on Urbanisation (1988) Report of the National Commission on Urbanisation, MOUAE, New Delhi.

National Council of Applied Economic Research (1995) India Infrastructure Report, New Delhi.

National Council of Applied Economic Research (2013) Land Pooling Policy for Delhi, New Delhi (unpublished).

National Sample Survey Office (2010) Migration in India, NSS 64th Round (July 2007 to June 2008), Ministry of Statistics and Programme Implementation, New Delhi.

Newman, Peter, R Kenworthy, (1999) Sustainability and Cities: Overcoming Automobile Dependence, The Centre for Resource Economics, Washington DC, USA.

OECD (2010) Organising Local Economic Development, The Role of Development Agencies and Companies, OECD.

Pandya, Y. (2007) Towards symbiosis of nature and architecture, Architecture + Design.

Parry, M., N. Arnell, P. Berry, D. Dodman, S. Fankhauser, C. Hope, S. Kovats, R. Nicholls, D Satterthwaite, R. Tiffin and T. Wheeler (2009) *Assessing the costs of adaptation to climate change: a review of the UNFCCC and other recent estimates,* International Institute for Environment and Development / Grantham Institute for Climate Change, London.

Plummer Jenelle (2012) Focusing Partnerships, Earthscan, London

Punjab Government (1988) A Gazetteer of Delhi 1883-4, Reprint Vipin Jain, Gurgaon.

Rai, Markandey (2012) Creating Safe and Secure Metropolitan City: the UN Perspective, UN Habitat, Nairobi.

Rao P.K. (1991) Safeguards for Sound Concrete, Indian Architect and Builder, October 1991.

Rees, William E. (1997) Ecological Footprints and Urban Transportation, Velocity, Barcelona.

Replogle, M. (1993) Bicycle and cycle rickshaws in Asian cities, 6th conference on urban transport in developing countries, CODATU-VI, Tunis.

Ribeiro, E.F.N. (1985) Improved Sanitation and Environmental Health Condition with Evaluation of Sulabh International Low Cost Sanitation in Bihar, Patna: Sulabh International.

RICS (2010) Making Affordable Housing Work in India, RICS, CBRE and LEVVEL, London.

RTPI, (2014) Fostering Growth-Understanding and Strengthening the Economic Benefit of Planning, RTPI, London.

Sampat, Preeti (2013) Limits to Absolute Power: Eminent Domain and the Right to Land in India, EP Weekly, May 11, pp.40-52.

Sanjay, P. (1992) Energy conscious architecture: an endless quest, Architecture + Design.

Satterthwaite, D. (2007) *The Transition to a Predominantly Urban World and its Underpinnings,* Human Settlements Discussion Paper, IIED, London.

Satterthwaite, D. (2008) Cities contribution to global warming: Notes on the allocation of greenhouse gas emissions. Environment and Urbanization, 20 (2).

Satterthwaite, D., S. Huq, H. Reid, M. Pelling and P. Romero Lankao (2007) *Adapting to climate change in urban areas: the possibilities and constraints in low- and middle-income nations,* IIED Human Settlements Discussion Paper Series, Climate Change and Cities, London.

Saxena, K. B. (2011) Rehabilitation and resettlement of displaced persons. Chapter three in Development-Induced Displacement, Rehabilitation and Resettlement in India, Routledge Contemporary South Asia.

Scriver Peter and Amit Srivastava (2015) India- Modern Architecture in History, Reaktion Books, London.

Shiva, Vandana. S. Javi, S.M. Fontana (2011) The Great Indian Land Grab, Navdanya, New Delhi.

Shivaramakrishnan K.C. (2015) Planning for Metropolitan Region, Oxford University Press, New Delhi.

Smart, James (2012) the Role of Post Disaster Institutions in Recovery and resilience -a comparative Study of Three Disasters-Victorian Bushfire (2009), Queensland Floods (2010-11) and Cantebury Earthquake (2010-12), Institute of Governance and Policy Studies, Victoria University, Wellington.

Sorensen, Andre (2000) Conflict, Consensus or Consent: Implications of Japanese Land Readjustment Practice for Developing Countries, Habitat International Vol. 24 pp. 51-73.

Steinberg, Florian (1996) Conservation and Rehabilitation of Urban Heritage in Developing Countries, Habitat International, June.

Subrahmanyum G.V. (2009) Revised Environment Clearance Process, Prescription to the Ministry of Environment and Forests, New Delhi.

Synder, Michael (2015) The Wealth of Nation, The Caravan, New Delhi (December).

TCPO (2011) Status of Town and Country Planning Departments and Acts in different States and UTs in India. Spatio-Economic Development Record, Vol 18, No. 5, New Delhi.

Tewari, S. (2013) ICLEI ACCCRN Process, Presented at the International Conference on Resilient Cities, Experiences from ACCCRN in Asia and Beyond, New Delhi.

Thurow, C. (1983) Improving Street Climate through Urban Design Planning. Advisory.

Uchida, Hirotsugu and Andrew Nelson (2008) Agglomeration Index - Towards a New Measure of Urban Concentration, Background Paper Prepared for World Development Report.

UN Global Compact and Oxfam (2015) Poverty Footprint: Overview, New York/London.

UN Habitat (2003) The Challenge of Slums - Global Report on Human Settlements, London.

UN Habitat (2007) Enhancing Urban Safety and Security, Nairobi.

UN Habitat (2013) States of the World's Cities 2012/2013: Prosperity of Cities, Nairobi.

UN Habitat (2014) A Practical Guide to Designing, Planning and Executing City-wide Slum Upgrading Programmes, Nairobi.

UN Habitat (2015) Habitat III Issues Paper, Nairobi.

UN, (2013) A New Global Partnership: Eradicate Poverty and Transform Economies through Sustainable Development, New York.

UNDP and UN Solution Exchange (2012) Social Inclusion of Manual Scavengers. A Report of National Round Table Discussion Organised by United Nations Development Programme and

UNEP (2015) District Energy in Cities: Unlocking the Potential of Energy Efficiency and Renewable Energy, New York.

UNESCO (2010) Historic Districts for All, New Delhi, UNESCO.

UN-Habitat (2011) Cities and Climate Change, Global Report on Human Settlements, Earthscan, UK/USA/Nairobi.

UN-Habitat (2013) Planning and Design for Sustainable Urban Mobility, Global Report on Human Settlements, Earthscan, UK/USA/Nairobi.

UN-Habitat (2010) The State of the World's Cities: Bridging the Urban Divide, London, Washington D.C., Earthscan.

UN-Habitat/International Institute for Environment & Development (2010) Developing Local Climate Change Plans, UK/USA/Nairobi.

Unified Traffic and Transport Infrastructure Planning and Engineering Centre (UTTIPEC)/ MOUD/DDA (2015) Transit Oriented Development Guidelines, notified in Gazette of India dated 14 July 2015, New Delhi.

UNISDR (2015) United Nations Global Assessment Report on Disaster Risks, UN Office for Disaster Risk Reduction, Geneva.

USAID (1991) Constraints Affecting the Efficiency of Urban Land Markets in India, New Delhi

Volwahsen, Andreas (2002) Imperial Delhi, Prestel Verlag, Munich.

Vuchie, R.V. (1981), Urban Public Transport System and Technology, Prentice Hall, Eaglewood Cliffs, New Jersey.

Watson, V. (2009) The Planned City Sweeps Away the Poor: Urban Planning and 21st Century Urbanisation, Elsevier, Progress in Planning 72 (2009) p. 151-193.

William E. Soper (1979) Surface Application of Sewage Effluent and Sludge, Madison, Wiscosin, USA.

World Bank (2013) Voices of the Poor, Washington, USA.

World Bank (2015) Leveraging Urbanisation in South Asia, Washington, USA.

World Bank (2002) India's Transport Sector, the Challenges Ahead, Washington, D.C.

World Bank (2009) Reshaping Economic Geography: The World Development Report Washington DC.

World Health Organisation (2004) World Report on Road Traffic Injury Prevention, Geneva.

Yeang Kenneth (1999) The Green Skyscraper, the Basis for Designing Sustainable Intensive Buildings, Prestel, New York.

Zerah, Marie-Helene (2000) Water: Unreliable Supply in Delhi, Manohar, New Delhi.

Zerah, Marie-Helene, Soel Ruet and Saravanan (2002) The Water and Sanitation Scenario in Metropolitan Cities - Delhi, Kolkata, Chennai & Mumbai, French Institute in India, New Delhi.

www.healthplaces.org.in

www.igbc.in

www.marimatic.fi

www.planetaction.org

www.windowfarms.org